Lecture Notes in Computer Science 6862

Commenced Publication in 1973
Founding and Former Series Editors:
Gerhard Goos, Juris Hartmanis, and Jan van Leeuwen

Alfredo Cuzzocrea   Umeshwar Dayal (Eds.)

Data Warehousing and Knowledge Discovery

13th International Conference, DaWaK 2011
Toulouse, France, August/September 2011
Proceedings

 Springer

Volume Editors

Alfredo Cuzzocrea
ICAR-CNR
University of Calabria
via P. Bucci 41 C
87036 Rende (CS), Italy
E-mail: cuzzocrea@si.deis.unical.it

Umeshwar Dayal
Hewlett-Packard Labs
1501 Page Mill Road, MS 1142
Palo Alto, CA 94304, USA
E-mail: umeshwar.dayal@hp.com

ISSN 0302-9743   e-ISSN 1611-3349
ISBN 978-3-642-23543-6   e-ISBN 978-3-642-23544-3
DOI 10.1007/978-3-642-23544-3
Springer Heidelberg Dordrecht London New York

Library of Congress Control Number: 2011934786

CR Subject Classification (1998): H.2, H.2.8, H.3, H.4, J.1, H.5

LNCS Sublibrary: SL 3 – Information Systems and Application, incl. Internet/Web
and HCI

Typesetting: Camera-ready by author, data conversion by Scientific Publishing Services, Chennai, India

Printed on acid-free paper

Springer is part of Springer Science+Business Media (www.springer.com)

Preface

Data warehousing and knowledge discovery is an extremely active research area where a number of methodologies and paradigms converge, with coverage on both theoretical issues and practical solutions. From a broad viewpoint, data warehousing and knowledge discovery has been widely accepted as a key technology for enterprises and organizations, as it allows them to improve their abilities in data analysis, decision support, and the automatic extraction of knowledge from data. With the exponentially growing amount of information to be included in the decision-making process, data to be considered become more and more complex in both structure and semantics. As a consequence, novel developments are necessary, both at the methodological level, e.g., complex analytics over data, and at the infrastructural level, e.g., cloud computing architectures. Orthogonal to the latter aspects, the knowledge discovery and retrieval process from huge amounts of heterogeneous complex data represents a significant challenge for this research area.

Data Warehousing and Knowledge Discovery (DaWaK) has become one of the most important international scientific events that brings together researchers, developers, and practitioners to discuss the latest research issues and experiences in developing and deploying data warehousing and knowledge discovery systems, applications, and solutions.

The 13th International Conference on Data Warehousing and Knowledge Discovery (DaWaK 2011), continued the tradition by discussing and disseminating innovative principles, methods, algorithms, and solutions to challenging problems faced in the development of data warehousing and knowledge discovery, and applications within these areas. In order to better reflect novel trends and the diversity of topics, like the previous edition, DaWaK 2011 was organized into four tracks: Cloud Intelligence, Data Warehousing, Knowledge Discovery, and Industry and Applications.

Papers presented at DaWaK 2011 covered a wide range of topics within cloud intelligence, data warehousing, knowledge discovery, and applications. The topics included data warehouse modeling, spatial data warehouses, mining social networks and graphs, physical data warehouse design, dependency mining, business intelligence and analytics, outlier and image mining, pattern mining, and data cleaning and variable selection.

It was encouraging to see that many papers covered emerging important issues such as social network data, spatio-temporal data, streaming data, non-standard pattern types, complex analytical functionality, multimedia data, as well as real-world applications. The wide range of topics bears witness to the fact that the data warehousing and knowledge discovery field is dynamically responding to the new challenges posed by novel types of data and applications.

From 119 submitted abstracts, we received 109 papers from Europe, North and South America, Asia, Africa, and Oceania, further confirming to us the wide interest in the topics covered by DaWaK within the research community. The Program Committee finally selected 37 papers, yielding an acceptance rate of 31%.

We would like to express our most sincere gratitude to the members of the Program Committee and the external reviewers, who made a huge effort to review the papers in a timely and thorough manner. Due to the tight timing constraints and the high number of submissions, the reviewing and discussion process was a very challenging task, but the commitment of the reviewers ensured a successful result. We would also like to thank all authors who submitted papers to DaWaK 2011, for their contribution to the excellent technical program.

Finally, we send our warmest thanks to Gabriela Wagner for delivering an outstanding level of support on all aspects of the practical organization of DaWaK 2011. We also thank Amin Anjomshoaa for his support of the conference management software.

August 2011   Alfredo Cuzzocrea
                                                  Umeshwar Dayal

Organization

Program Chair

Alfredo Cuzzocrea   ICAR-CNR and University of Calabria, Italy
Umeshwar Dayal   Hewlett-Packard Laboratories, Palo Alto, CA,
      USA

Program Committee

Alberto Abello	Universitat Politecnica de Catalunya, Spain
Reda Alhajj	University of Calgary, Canada
Elena Baralis	Politecnico di Torino, Italy
Ladjel Bellatreche	LISI/ENSMA, France
Bettina Berendt	Humboldt University Berlin, Germany
Petr Berka	University of Economics Prague, Czech Republic
Jorge Bernardino	SEC, Polytechnic Institute of Coimbra, Portugal
Elisa Bertino	Purdue University, USA
Stephane Bressan	National University of Singapore, Singapore
Longbing Cao	University of Technology Sydney, Australia
Frans Coenen	The University of Liverpool, UK
Bruno Cremilleux	Université de Caen, France
Judith Cushing	The Evergreen State College, USA
Alfredo Cuzzocrea	University of Calabria, Italy
Karen Davis	University of Cincinnati, USA
Frank Dehne	Carleton University, Canada
Antonios Deligiannakis	Technical University of Crete, Greece
Alin Dobra	University of Florida, USA
Josep Domingo-Ferrer	Universitat Rovira i Virgili, Spain
Dejing Dou	University of Oregon, USA
Curtis Dyreson	Utah State University, USA
Todd Eavis	Concordia University, USA
Johann Eder	University of Klagenfurt, Austria
Floriana Esposito	University of Calabria, Italy
Vladimir Estivill-Castro	Griffith University, Australia
Christie Ezeife	University of Windsor, Canada
Ling Feng	Tsinghua University, China
Eduardo Fernandez-Medina	University of Castilla-La Mancha, Spain
Sergio Greco	University of Calabria, Italy
Se June Hong	RSM emeritus, IBM T.J. Watson Research Center, USA
Frank Hoppner	University of Applied Sciences Braunschweig/Wolfenbuettel, Germany

Andreas Hotho	University of Kassel, Germany
Jimmy Huang	York University, Canada
Yong Hwan-Seung	Ewha Womans University, Korea
Hasan Jamil	Wayne State University, USA
Chris Jermaine	Rice University, USA
Murat Kantarcioglu	University of Texas at Dallas, USA
Panagiotis Karras	National University of Singapore, Singapore
Martin Kersten	CWI, The Netherlands
Jens Lechtenbörger	Universität Münster, Germany
Wolfgang Lehner	Dresden University of Technology, Germany
Carson K. Leung	The University of Manitoba, Canada
Jinyan Li	National University of Singapore, Singapore
Xuemin Lin	UNSW, Australia
Patrick Martin	Queen's University, Canada
Michael May	Fraunhofer Institut für Autonome Intelligente Systeme, Germany
Carlos Ordonez	University of Houston, USA
Apostolos Papadopoulos	Aristotle University, Greece
Jeffrey Parsons	Memorial University of Newfoundland, Canada
Torben Bach Pedersen	Aalborg University, Denmark
Adriana Prado	INSA-Lyon, LIRIS, France
Lu Qin	The Chinese University of Hong Kong, China
Zbigniew W. Ras	University of North Carolina, USA
Mirek Riedewald	Cornell University, USA
Stefano Rizzi	University of Bologna, Italy
Domenico Saccà	University of Calabria and ICAR-CNR, Italy
Maria Luisa Sapino	Università degli Studi di Torino, Italy
Kai-Uwe Sattler	Ilmenau University of Technology, Germany
Timos Sellis	Institute for the Management of Information Systems and NTUA, Greece
Neeraj Sharma	India IBM Labs, India
Alkis Simitsis	Stanford University, USA
Domenico Talia	University of Calabria, Italy
David Taniar	Monash University, Australia
Yufei Tao	Chinese University of Hong Kong, China
Dimitri Theodoratos	New Jersey's Science and Technology University, USA
A Min Tjoa	IFS, Vienna University of Technology, Austria
Juan Trujilo	University of Alicante, Spain
Panos Vassiliadis	University of Ioannina, Greece
Gottfried Vossen	University of Münster, Germany
Wei Wang	UNSW, Australia
Ranga Vatsavai	Oak Ridge National Laboratory, USA
Marcos Vaz Salles	Cornell University, USA
Wolfram Wöß	University of Linz, Austria
Robert Wrembel	Poznan University of Technology, Poland

Carlo Zaniolo   University of California, Los Angeles, USA
Bin Zhou   Simon Fraser University, Canada
Esteban Zimanyi   Université Libre de Bruxelles, Belgium

External Reviewers

Cem Aksoy   New Jersey Institute of Technology (NJIT),
                         USA
Kamel Boukhalfa   USTHB, Algiers, Algeria
Nicola Di Mauro   Università degli Studi "Aldo Moro", Bari, Italy
Claudia d'Amato   Università degli Studi "Aldo Moro", Bari, Italy
David Gil   University of Alicante, Spain
Úrsula González-Nicolás Universitat Rovira i Virgili, Spain
Fernando Gutierrez   University of Oregon, USA
Sara Hajian   Universitat Rovira i Virgili, Spain
Shangpu Jiang   University of Oregon, USA
Shrikant Kashyap   National University of Singapore
Elli Katsiri   Research Center ATHENA, Greece
Christian Koncilia   Alpen Adria Universität Klagenfurt, Austria
Selma Khouri   ESI, Algiers, Algeria
Jens Lechtenbörger   University of Münster, Germany
Haishan Liu   University of Oregon, USA
Sadegh Nobari   National University of Singapore
Kostas Patroumpas   National Technical University of Athens,
                         Greece
Deolinda Rasteiro   ISEC - Institute Polytechnic of Coimbra,
                         Portugal
Domenico Redavid   Università degli Studi "Aldo Moro", Bari, Italy
Oscar Romero   Universitat Politècnica de Catalunya, Spain
Zhitao Shen   University of New South Wales, Australia
Jordi Soria   Universitat Rovira i Virgili, Spain
Jichao Sun   New Jersey Institute of Technology (NJIT),
                         USA
Manolis Terrovitis   Research Center ATHENA, Greece
Rolando Trujillo   Universitat Rovira i Virgili, Spain
Paolo Trunfio   University of Calabria, Italy
Elisa Turricchia   University of Bologna, Italy
Xiaoying Wu   New Jersey Institute of Technology (NJIT),
                         USA
Vincent Yip   University of Oregon, USA
Weiren Yu   University of New South Wales, Australia
Xiaodong Yue   University of Technology Sydney, Australia
Yiling Zeng   University of Technology Sydney, Australia
Liming Zhan   University of New South Wales, Australia
Zhigang Zheng   University of Technology Sydney, Australia
Lin Zhu   University of Technology Sydney, Australia

Table of Contents

Data Warehouse Performance and Optimization

Data Warehouse Partitioning Techniques

Analytics over Large Multidimensional Datasets

Pattern Mining

Matrix-Based Mining Techniques

Data Mining and Knowledge Discovery Techniques

Data Mining and Knowledge Discovery Applications

Stream, Sensor and Time-Series Mining

ONE: A Predictable and Scalable DW Model

João Pedro Costa[1], José Cecílio[2], Pedro Martins[2], and Pedro Furtado[2]

[1] ISEC-Institute Polytechnic of Coimbra
jcosta@isec.pt
[2] University of Coimbra
{jcecilio,pmom,pnf}@dei.uc.pt

Abstract. The star schema model has been widely used as the facto DW storage organization on relational database management systems (RDBMS). The physical division in normalized fact tables (with metrics) and denormalized dimension tables allows a trade-off between performance and storage space while, at the same time offering a simple business understanding of the overall model as a set of metrics (facts) and attributes for business analysis (dimensions). However, the underlying premises of such trade-off between performance and storage have changed. Nowadays, storage capacity increased significantly at affordable prices (below 50$/terabyte) with improved transfer rates, and faster random access times particularly with modern SSD disks. In this paper we evaluate if the underlying premises of the star schema model storage organization still upholds. We propose an alternative storage organization (called ONE) that physically stores the whole star schema into a single relation, providing a predictable and scalable alternative to the star schema model. We use the TPC-H benchmark to evaluate ONE and the star schema model, assessing both the required storage size and query execution time.

Keywords: DW, DSM.

1   Introduction

Data warehouses are stored in relation DBMS systems as a set of tables organized in a star schema, with a central fact table and surrounded by dimension tables. The fact table is highly normalized, containing a set of foreign keys referencing the surrounding dimension tables, and stores the measure facts. Usually, these fact tables represent a huge percentage of the overall storage space required by the data warehouse (DW). That's one reason why the central fact table is highly normalized, in order to minimize data redundancy and thus reducing the table storage space. On the other hand, dimension tables are highly denormalized and represent only a small amount of the overall DW storage space. The potential gains in terms of storage space that could be achieved by normalizing dimensions does not pay-off the decline in query execution performance, requiring more complex query execution plans and extra memory and processing requirements for processing the additional joins.

Since DWs store historical measures of the business data, their size is continuously growing, particularly the central fact table which has to store the new data measures

A. Cuzzocrea and U. Dayal (Eds.): DaWaK 2011, LNCS 6862, pp. 1–13, 2011.
© Springer-Verlag Berlin Heidelberg 2011

that are being produced by the operational systems. Due to their nature, fact tables usually are only subject to insert operations, while the same doesn't necessary happen to dimension tables. Along with insert operations, at lower rates when compared with the fact table, some update operations are also made to dimension tables.

This continuous increase in size, present some problems to the hardware infrastructure capability to process such increased volume of data. DBMS engines generate complex query execution plans, considering different data access methods and joining algorithms which are sensitive to the hardware characteristics such as the available memory and processing capabilities. Distributed and parallel infrastructures also have to take into account the available network bandwidth required for exchanging temporary results between nodes. There's no simple method to determine the minimal requirements of the supporting hardware infrastructure in order to scale up with the data volume increase. IT departments that have to manage and fine tune DW systems, when recognizing that the hardware infrastructure is unable to satisfactorily process such data volumes, usually try to solve this problem by acquiring more processing power and replacing existing infrastructure with newer expensive machinery, or by adding additional processing nodes. This decision is made with the assumption that the newer infrastructure, with more memory and faster CPUs, will be sufficient of handle such volume increase, without a real knowledge of its data volume processing capacity.

In this paper, we evaluate whether the premises that lead to the definition of star schema model for storing DWs in relational DBMS still upholds in current hardware systems, where storage space and becoming increasingly faster at affordable prices, and the availability and affordable distributed data processing infrastructures composed of Common-off-the-Shelf (COTS) hardware. We propose to extend the denormalization applied to dimension tables to the overall star schema model, reducing the fact tab and the dimension tables to a single table containing all the data. We called this single relation storage organization "ONE". We evaluate the impact of such organization in both storage and processing requirements.

In section 2 we discuss some related work on DW storage and processing organization. Section 3 presents the denormalization process and illustrates the storage requirements with the TPC-H schema. Section 4 discusses how the processing costs of ONE compare with the base TCP-H schema. Section 5 uses the TPC-H benchmark to experimentally evaluate the query execution times of ONE storage organization. Finally, we conclude with section 6.

2   Related Works

Both academia and the industry have been investigating methods, algorithms and strategies for speedup the execution time of queries that need to join several relations. Some had investigated the different join algorithms, such as, sort-merge, hash join, grace-hash join and hybrid-hash join [1][2][3][4]. Other investigated access methods, such as btree and bitmap indexes [5]. Materialized views [6] use extra storage space to physically stored aggregates for well known and planned queries. Sampling [7] trades-off precision for performance by employing the power of offered by statistical methods to reduce the volume of data that need to be processed for computing an acceptable result. Vertical partitioning and column-wise store engines [8], [9] as proved to be effective in reducing the disk IO and thus boosting query performance.

Works on denormalization includes [10,11,12][but fall short on demonstrating the performance gains of obtained by denormalization the whole star schema model, and doesn't offer a clear insight of the query performance predictability and scalability.

3 ONE Storage Model

In this section, we present ONE as an alternative storage organization for the star schema model, and discuss the major advantages and disadvantages of the proposed model. We use the TPC-H schema model to illustrate the storage trade-off.

A normalized central fact table reduces the overall DW storage size, since it only stores a set of measures (m), which are mainly numerical attributes (facts) with a fixed width, and a set of foreign keys (n) that are also numerical identifiers. The size of fact tables increases as a function of the number of tuples.

$$factTable_{size}(N_{tuples}) = N_{tuples} \times (n_{foreign\ keys} + m_{measures})$$

For joining the relations, the star schema model has to include a set of extra primary and foreign keys which usually are artificially generated (surrogate keys) and do not have operational meaning. These keys increase the DW storage requirements. In some star schema models, the number of foreign keys represents a large percentage of the number of fact table attributes. This is particularly relevant for some special types of fact tables (factless fact tables), which do not have measures and only store foreign keys, where each tuple represents an event without measures.

For instance, in TPC-H benchmark, which is not a typical star schema model, but is well known by the data warehouse community, we observe (in table 1) that 1 of the 61 columns of the benchmark schema are keys, which represents a 30% increase in the number of attributes and 8% increase in storage size.

Table 1. Increase in the number of attributes

	#Attributes (non keys)	#Key Attributes	#Attribute %increase	Space %increase
REGION	2	1	50%	4%
NATION	2	2	100%	9%
SUPPLIER	5	2	33%	6%
CUSTOMER	6	2	33%	5%
PART	8	1	13%	3%
PARTSUPP	3	2	67%	6%
ORDERS	7	2	29%	8%
LINEITEM	13	3	25%	10%
Total	46	15		

In the TPC-H schema, the additional surrogate keys and foreign keys added to LINEITEM table represent a 25% increase in the number of the table attributes. It only represents a 10% increase in storage size though, due to the fact that this schema is not a typical star schema, as discussed in [13], and does not follow the principles of muldimensional modeling explained in [14]. In the SSB schema [13], the overhead created by including keys corresponds to a 70% increase in both the number of attributes and the space required by the foreign keys attributes on table LINEITEM.

Foreign keys are justified by the need to join fact tables with the surrounding dimension tables. However, this requires more complex query execution, since join algorithms are usually the heaviest of operations on a data warehouse. Access methods and join algorithms were thoroughly investigated and evaluated by both the academia and the DBMS industry. The query optimizer has to choose the most appropriate execution plan and to fine-tune the alternative execution plans with hardware characteristics, taking into account aspects such the available memory for hashing and sorting.

The ONE Storage Model

In ONE storage organization, the whole star schema model is physically stored in a single relation without primary and foreign keys. This single relation, named ONE in figure 1, contains all the attributes from both the fact table and dimension tables. The cardinality of ONE is the same as the greatest cardinality of the star schema relations. Usually it is set as the cardinality of the fact table. This denormalization increases the overall space necessary for storing all the data, since data from dimension tables are redundantly sorted in ONE relation. For instance, each tuple of table SUPPLIERS is, on average, inserted (repeated) 60 times. This redundancy requires extra storage space for storing all the denormalized data, and consequently may cause performance issues, since it now is more IO dependent.

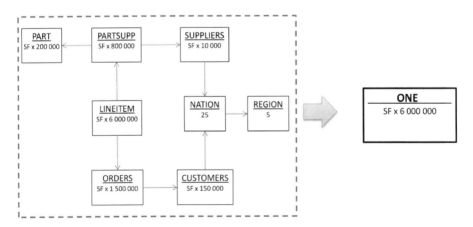

Fig. 1. The TPC-H and ONE schema

However, in a single relation no primary keys and foreign keys are required, which, as discussed above and shown in table1, represents about 25% of the number of attributes. Moreover, most RDMS engines create an index structure for each table primary key, which represents additional space. These index structures, and related storage requirements, are also not necessary on the denormalized schema.

Considering *ss* as storage space by a schema model, the total storage space occupied by a DW is

$$ss_{DW} = ss_{tables} + ss_{pk_{indexes}} + ss_{fk_{indexes}}$$

The storage space required by ONE is determined as

$$ss_{ONE} = ss_{table\ ONE} + 0 + 0$$

We define φ_{ss} as the storage space increase ratio in comparison with the base DW star schema model

$$\varphi_{ss} = \frac{ss_{ONE} - ss_{dw}}{ss_{dw}}$$

Without considering the block (or page) overheads, and the number of tuples that can fit within each page block, since they are engine dependent, and considering the maximum space required for each variable length attribute (VAL), we conclude that the denormalized schema requires at most a 5,3x increase in the storage size.

VAL attributes with an average size below the maximum size will have a greater impact in the overall size of ONE, since it affects all tuples in the relation, whereas in the base schema it only affects the size of the related relation. For instance, if the size of a VAL attribute from table CUSTOMER is reduced by half, it represents almost negligible impact in overall schema size, since CUSTOMER only represents 3% of the overall schema, whereas in ONE the storage size is reduced proportionally to the percentage of the attribute size in the overall tuple size. Size variability of VAL attributes from LINEITEM or ORDERS will have greater impact in the overall size, since they (in conjunction) represent 80% of the total space.

Table 2. Disk space required by each relation

SF = 1	Nº Rows	Space	%
REGION	5	1 KB	0%
NATION	25	5 KB	0%
SUPPLIER	10 000	1,9 MB	0%
CUSTOMER	150 000	31,3 MB	3%
PART	200 000	30,5 MB	3%
PARTSUPP	800 000	164,0 MB	14%
ORDERS	1 500 000	190,3 MB	17%
LINEITEM	6 000 000	726,7 MB	63%
Total		**1 144,7 MB**	**100%**

The overall storage space required by ONE to store the data increases by a factor of 5,3x , as show in table 3, which shows the storage space required by each storage organization and the corresponding space ratio, for a scale factor of 1. The storage space ratio is reduced to less than 4x when we also take into account in the equation the space occupied by indexes.

Table 3. Storage space required by each schema organization

Schema (SF1)	Size (MB)	φ_{ss}
base TPC-H	1.144,7 MB	5,323
base TPC-H + Indexes	1.448,4 MB	3,998
ONE	7.238,4 MB	

With a scale factor of 1 (SF=1), we observe that the required space increase to about 7GB. For quite some time, this increase in storage was unacceptable since storage space was expensive, disks had limited capacity and with slow transfer rates. However, currents disks are acceptably fast, providing sequential transfer rates of hundreds of MB per second, at affordable prices (with prices below 0.05€/GB).

Looking to the relation sizes, we may observe that queries that solely require data from table LINEITEM will become slower, since they need to read and process almost 10x more data (not tuples) in comparison with the base star schema. However this is not a typical query. The usual DW query pattern involves selecting (or filtering) some attributes from dimension tables and then joining with the central fact table, before performing some aggregated computations to the data from the central fact tables.

4 Query Processing

In this section, we discuss and compare the query processing costs and requirements for processing queries against ONE, without joins, and the hybrid hash join, which, as discussed and evaluated in [3], is a join algorithm that delivers enhanced performance execution time for large relations.

Queries submitted to the DW require that the central fact tables be joined with one or several surrounding dimension tables. In what concerns query execution costs, the storage space isn't an issue, the real issue that we have to be concerned is the required IO operations, and particularly the random reads which are expensive and the available memory. If it is possible to process joins and sorts in memory, this will be important, since it saves expensive disk write operations.

Query optimizers have to evaluate and assess which combination and orchestration of access methods, joining algorithms and joining order in order to determine the query execution plan with minimum costs that fits to the hardware characteristics. For this, they resort to several supplementary structures containing statistical information and data distribution histograms of the data that resides in each relation. This is fundamental to better estimate the query selectivity over each relation and thus determine which access method to use, and the joining order and algorithm.

Predictable Execution Time

ONE does not require any join algorithm, since data is already joined, thus the query optimizer complexity is reduced, and it has reduced memory requirements, in contrast with the memory requirements of the joining algorithms. Since ONE only requires memory for sorting and grouping, it has minimal memory requirements to process queries.

The bottleneck of ONE is IO dependent, since it requires more IO operations to process the denormalized data. However, this characteristic offers a predictable and simpler method to determine the query execution time. Since, no joins are required, and query execution presents minimal memory requirements, the query execution time can be determined as a function of the employed access method and the number and complexity of filtering conditions and the selected computations. The relational star schema model is more unpredictable since the query time and the number of IO operations are widely amplified as the volume data surpasses the available memory.

A Comparative Analysis with Hybrid Hash Join

Hash Join algorithms use a hash function to partition two relations R and S into hash partitions and are particularly efficient for joining large data sets. The optimizer selects the smaller relation as the inner relation, used as the lookup driver relation, to probe each tuple of the outer relation. The optimizer selects the smaller of two tables or data sources to build a hash table in memory on the join key. It then scans the larger table, probing the hash table to find the joined rows. This method is best used when the smaller table fits entirely in memory. The optimizer uses a hash join to join two tables if they are joined using an equijoin and a large amount of data need to be joined together. When the available memory is insufficient to store the entire inner relation, it uses a Hybrid Hash Join algorithm which partitions both relations into partitions such as a hash table for the inner relation to fit into memory. Corresponding partitions of the two input relations are then joined by probing the hash table with the tuples from the corresponding partition of the larger input relation. Partitions that cannot fit into memory have to temporally be written to disk before being joined together.

Consider relation R and S, where R is the smaller relation. For a relation R, consider that t_R is the number of tuples of R, b_R is the number of blocks (or pages) of R, ts_R is the tuple size of R and tpb_R is the number of tuples of R that can fit in a block (or page) with size $block_{size}$. The cost of joining relations R with S, using a Hybrid Hash Join algorithm [3][2] can be computed as

$$
\begin{aligned}
HHJ(R, S) = {} & (t_R + t_S) \times I_{hash} \\
& + (t_R \times ts_R + t_S \times ts_S) \times (1 - q) \times I_{copy} \\
& + 2 \times (b_R + b_S) \times (1 - q) \times IO \\
& + (t_R + t_S) \times (1 - q) \times I_{hash} \\
& + t_R \times ts_R \times I_{copy} \\
& + t_S \times I_{probe} \times F_{hash}
\end{aligned}
\tag{1}
$$

Considering that $q = b_{R_0}/b_R$, and b_{R_0} is the size of the first partition that can reside in memory, and that does not need to be written to disk. To process a query Q that require that two relation R and S, be joined together, we can determined the overall cost, without considering other costs such as filtering, grouping and aggregating, for executing the query as

$$Exectime_{tpch} = (b_R + b_S) \times IO + HHJ(R,S) \qquad (2)$$

With ONE storage organization, the cost for executing the same query, without considering filters and computations, can be determined as

$$Exectime_{one} = \frac{t_S}{tpb(ts_S + ts_R)} \times IO \qquad (3)$$

with $tpb(ts_R) = \left| \dfrac{block\ size}{ts_R} \right|$

Assuming that $\left\lfloor \dfrac{block_{size}}{ts_R} \right\rfloor \cong \dfrac{block_{size}}{ts_R}$

$$Exectime_{one} = \frac{t_S \times (ts_S + ts_R)}{block_{size}} \times IO \qquad (4)$$

For the query execution cost with ONE storage organization to be smaller than the base TPC-H storage schema using hybrid hash joins for joining relations R and S, the following inequality must be satisfied.

$$\frac{t_S \times (ts_S + ts_R)}{block_{size}} \times IO \le (b_R + b_S) \times IO + HHJ(R,S) \Leftrightarrow$$

$$HHJ(R,S) \ge IO \times \frac{ts_R}{block_{size}} \times (t_S - t_R) \Leftrightarrow$$

$$HHJ\ (R,S) \ge IO \times b_R \times \left(\frac{t_S}{t_R} - 1 \right) \qquad (5)$$

For ONE to outperform the base TPC-H schema, the Hybrid Hash Join cost must be greater than the IO cost for reading the b_R blocks of relation R multiplied by the a ratio of number of tuples between relations S and R. Figure 2 depicts graphically the results of the inequality of the equation 4, with a IO sequential read costs of 15ms, 10ms and 5ms respectively. The t_S/t_R ratio is represented as the x axis, b_R is the z axis and y axis depicts the function result. This result was obtained with a 30% value for q.

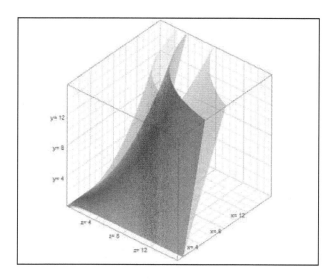

Fig. 2. HHJ graph using equation 5

5   Evaluation

We evaluated the ONE storage organization using a default installation of the PostgreSQL[15] 8.4 DBMS engine in a Dual Core Pentium D, at 3.4Ghz, with 2GB Ram, a 150GB SATA disc drive, and running a default installation of Ubuntu Maverick Linux distribution.

We have created two different schemas, the base TPC-H schema as defined in the benchmark, and the ONE schema comprised by a single relation containing all the attributes of the relations with the exception of the surrogate keys (primary and foreign keys). The former was populated with the DBGEN data generator [16] and the later with a modified version that generate the denormalized data as single file.

For each setup, we measured the elapsed time for generating and loading the dataset, indexing and analyzing the schema, and the time taken to execute the TPC-H queries. The loading costs, time taken to load the data, create the required indexes and finally analyzing the schema, were almost the same for both setups: the base TPC-H star schema, named TPC-H and the denormalized star schema model, named ONE.

Queries ran on denormalized schema (ONE), were rewritten in order to use the denormalized relation instead of the star schema relations, and the joining conditions were removed. No specific tuning or tweaking was made to queries or relations.

We have evaluated and populated both setups using scale factors {0.1, 0.3, 0.5, 1, 3, 5, 10}. For each setup, we run each query 30 times and obtained the query execution time. For each query, we excluded the two smaller and greater results.

Fig. 3 shows the average and stddev execution time obtained for all queries for different scale factors, ranging from 0.1 to 10. As discussed above, the average execution time of ONE scales linearly with the data volume, depicting a perfect line. This is due to the simpler query execution cost, which doesn't require joins and is fairly independent of the available memory.

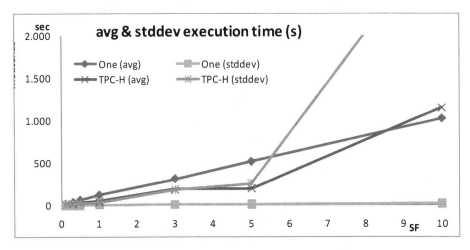

Fig. 3. Execution time (avg and stddev) for varying SF

Furthermore, the standard deviation of ONE is impressive. While TPC-H performs better, at small scale factors, since a large amount of the inner relations resides in memory, requiring less IO operations, the query execution time is highly unpredictable. One, with a scale factor of 10 (SF=10), presents an average query execution time faster than TPCH.

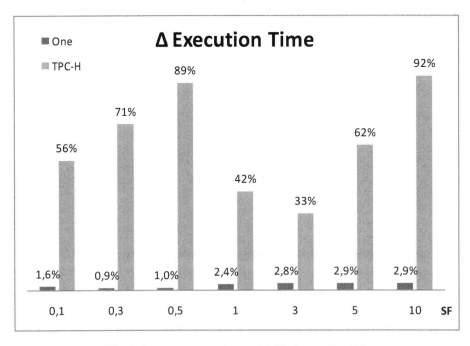

Fig. 4. Query execution time variability for varying SF

Because ONE doesn't have to perform join operations, only filters, grouping and aggregation operations, it provides a very predictable execution time. We observe that, in Fig. 4, which depicts the execution time variability considering all the queries, ONE presents a low variability (below 3% to the average execution time). This means that ONE for a given scale factor (SF) can execute queries with a predictable response time.

Fig. 5 depicts the average execution time for queries 1 to 9. From the figure, one thing that stands out is that ONE presents an execution time with minimal variability across the queries with the same scale factor, while the base TPC-H schema presents a large variability across queries. Another interesting aspect is that, as expected, the query execution times of ONE are greater than those obtained with TPC-H. However the execution time ratio is smaller than the storage space ratio as discussed in previous sections.

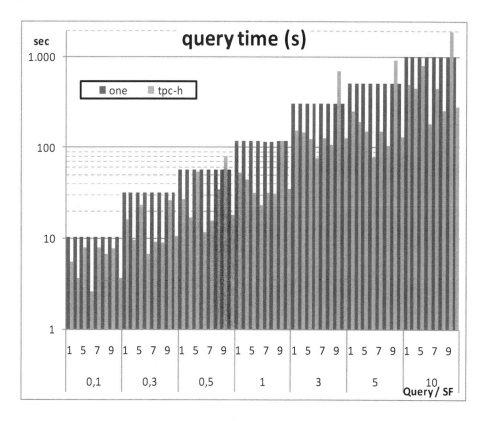

Fig. 5. Average execution time for varying SF for queries 1-9

Query execution time obtained by ONE may appear unimpressive, since some queries present worse times when compared with the base star schema model, however the execution time are almost constant, as expected from the results from figure 4 (query time variation below 3%).

Moreover, as the data volume increases (ex. SF10) and hash joins are not solely done in memory the query execution time of the base star schema are getting closer to those obtained for ONE, since hash joins need to perform IO writes and reads.

ONE storage model offers a reliable and predictable execution time, which can be estimated as a function of the data volume and the underlying hardware storage system. As ONE scales linearly with the volume of data, the DBA knows, with an appreciable confidence, how the infrastructure that supports the DW will behave with the data increase. Moreover, since a large amount of the query execution cost is from the IO operations, particularly the sustained transfer read rate, we can, with high confidence, estimate how current hardware systems behave and estimate the performance gains obtained by hardware upgrades even without testing it.

6 Conclusions

In this paper we discussed the issues and limitations currently presented by the star schema model, and we proposed and evaluated ONE as an alternative storage organization which stores the denormalized star schema model, and thus eliminating the processing costs associated with the joining algorithms and the additional IO operations (random and sequential) when the available memory is insufficient to process in-memory joins, resulting in a simpler and more predictable model.

We also demonstrate that ONE offers optimal scale-up scalability with minimal intra-query IO operations and network data exchange operations. One also allow DBA and IT managers better estimate and determine the current limitations of existing hardware infrastructure and determine the requirements of the new infrastructure to handle a given data volume without even testing it.

References

1. Pavlo, A., et al.: A comparison of approaches to large-scale data analysis. In: Proceedings of the 35th SIGMOD International Conference on Management of Data, pp. 165–178 (2009)
2. Patel, J.M., Carey, M.J., Vernon, M.K.: Accurate modeling of the hybrid hash join algorithm. In: ACM SIGMETRICS Performance Evaluation Review, NY, USA (1994)
3. DeWitt, D.J., Katz, R.H., Olken, F., Shapiro, L.D., Stonebraker, M.R., Wood, D.A.: Implementation techniques for main memory database systems. In: ACM SIGMOD Record, New York, NY, USA, pp. 1–8 (1984)
4. Harris, E.P., Ramamohanarao, K.: Join algorithm costs revisited. The VLDB Journal — The International Journal on Very Large Data Bases 5, 064–084 (1996)
5. Johnson, T.: Performance Measurements of Compressed Bitmap Indices. In: Proceedings of the 25th International Conference on Very Large Data Bases, pp. 278–289 (1999)
6. Zhou, J., Larson, P.-A., Goldstein, J., Ding, L.: Dynamic Materialized Views. In: International Conference on Data Engineering, Los Alamitos, CA, USA, pp. 526–535 (2007)
7. Costa, J.P., Furtado, P.: Time-Stratified Sampling for Approximate Answers to Aggregate Queries. In: International Conference on Database Systems for Advanced Applications, Los Alamitos, CA, USA, p. 215 (2003)

8. Stonebraker, M., et al.: C-store: a column-oriented DBMS. In: Proceedings of the 31st International Conference on Very Large Data Bases, pp. 553–564 (2005)
9. Zhang, Y., Hu, W., Wang, S.: MOSS-DB: a hardware-aware OLAP database. In: Proc. 11th International Conference on Web-Age Information Management, pp. 582–594 (2010)
10. Yma, P.: A Framework for Systematic Database Denormalization. Global Journal of Computer Science and Technology 9(4) (August 2009)
11. Sanders, G.L.: Denormalization Effects on Performance of RDBMS. In: Proceedings of the 34th Hawaii International Conference on System Sciences (2001)
12. Zaker, M., Phon-Amnuaisuk, S., Haw, S.-C.: Optimizing the data warehouse design by hierarchical denormalizing. In: Proc. 8th Conference on Applied Computer Science (2008)
13. O'Neil, P., O'Neil, E., Chen, X., Revilak, S.: The Star Schema Benchmark and Augmented Fact Table Indexing. In: Nambiar, R., Poess, M. (eds.) TPCTC 2009. LNCS, vol. 5895, pp. 237–252. Springer, Heidelberg (2009)
14. Kimball, R., Ross, M., Thornthwaite, W., Mundy, J., Becker, B.: The Data Warehouse Lifecycle Toolkit, 2nd edn. Wiley Publishing, Chichester (2008)
15. "PostgreSQL", http://www.postgresql.org/
16. "TPC-H Benchmark", http://www.tpc.org/tpch/

The Planning OLAP Model - A Multidimensional Model with Planning Support

Bernhard Jaecksch and Wolfgang Lehner

TU Dresden, Institute for System Architecture,
Database Technology Group, 01062 Dresden, Germany
bernhard.jaecksch@mailbox.tu-dresden.de,
wolfgang.lehner@tu-dresden.de

Abstract. A wealth of multidimensional OLAP models has been suggested in the past, tackling various problems of modeling multidimensional data. However, all of these models focus on navigational and query operators for grouping, selection and aggregation. We argue that planning functionality is, next to reporting and analysis, an important part of OLAP in many businesses and as such should be represented as part of a multidimensional model. Navigational operators are not enough for planning, instead new factual data is created or existing data is changed. To our knowledge we are the first to suggest a multidimensional model with support for planning. Because the main data entities of a typical multidimensional model are used both by planning and reporting, we concentrate on the extension of an existing model, where we add a set of novel operators that support an extensive set of typical planning functions.

1 Introduction

With the rise of decision-support-systems and the use of data-warehouses in many modern companies, the research community devised various models to support multidimensional analysis in the process of On-Line Analytical Processing (OLAP) [4]. The common data entities to model such multidimensional data are so called cubes consisting of a set of orthogonal dimensions and mostly numerical fact-data characterized by the values of the different dimensions. The main aspect of OLAP is the navigation through and aggregation of multidimensional data. The models provide an algebra of operators that often contains typical operators of relational algebra transferred to the multidimensional scenario and extended by navigational operators to group, select and aggregate data, also termed as slice/dice and roll-up/drill-down operations.

Business planning is an important task in many companies where business targets are defined for future periods to provide specific guidelines for current operations and a comparison whether goals have been reached or not. As such, planning is an important part of many practically used decision-support-systems. However, to our knowledge, none of the existing multidimensional models supports planning functionality. We strive to overcome the limitation of existing

A. Cuzzocrea and U. Dayal (Eds.): DaWaK 2011, LNCS 6862, pp. 14–25, 2011.

models to support planning functionality as part of OLAP. As the basic data entities are the same for planning and reporting, we build on an existing OLAP model an extend its set of operations with novel operators to support a list of typical planning functions.

The paper is structured as follows: in the next section we describe related work in the field of OLAP models as well as the multidimensional model that serves as foundation for our OLAP model with planning support. Section 3 introduces a list of typical planning functions by example. Our novel operators to support planning are introduced in Section 4 where we show how to express the planning functions with the set of extended operators. We finish with a conclusion in Section 5 providing an outlook for an implementation of our model.

2   Foundation and Related Work

Starting with the Data Cube operation by Gray et al. [6] as an extension of SQL, a wealth of multidimensional models have been proposed. Similar to the Data Cube, the first models by Li et al. [9] and Gysses et al. [7] were extensions to the relational model. The field of statistical databases also dealt with the quantitative analysis of large amounts of scientific data and, faced with similar problems, suggested different models. Prominent candidates are the Summary Tables model by Ozsoyoglu et al. [10] and the graphical model for Statistical Object Representation (STORM) by Rafanelli et al. [12]. While all these models, divide the data into *qualifying* and *quantifying* information, most modern models are base on the concept that the qualifying information defines a multidimensional space represented by a cube where each axis is called a dimension. The quantifying information at the intersection points, called measures or facts, is characterized by the dimensions. Typical and often cited representatives are the Multidimensional Database Model by Agrawal et al. [1], the F-Table Calculus by Cabibbo et al. [3], the Cube Operations model by Vassiliadis et al. [13], the Multidimensional Object model by Lehner [8] and the Cube Data model by Datta et al. [5]. Vassiliadis provides a good classification and survey of these models in [14]. The suitability of the models to implement a practical and complex data-warehouse scenario was evaluated by Pedersen et al. [11] according to an extensive set of typical requirements such as explicit hierarchies, multiple and flexible hierarchies per dimension, symmetric treatment of dimensions and measures and explicit aggregation semantics. Since none of the previous models fulfilled all requirements they suggested their own model, the Extended Multidimensional Data model (EMDM). As this model satisfies all of the above requirements we considered it a suitable foundation for our planning extensions.

The basic EMDM model entity is a multidimensional object $MO = (S, F, Dim, R)$, which is a four-tuple consisting of an *n-dimensional fact schema* S, a set of facts F, a set of *dimensions Dim* and a set of corresponding *fact-dimension relations* R that map the facts to elements of the dimensions. A key aspect of the model is that everything that characterizes a fact is regarded dimensional. That includes measures and as such dimensions and measures are treated symmetrically. An n-dimensional fact schema S is a two-tuple (FS, D) with FS describing a fact type and D being a set of dimension types $D = \{T_i, i = 1..n\}$. Each dimension type T itself is a four-tuple $(C, \prec_T, \top_T, \bot_T)$, where C is a set of category types $\{C_j, j = 1..k\}$ of T that form a partial ordering $\prec_T$ with $\top_T$ and $\bot_T$ as the top and bottom elements of the ordering. There is always a single top element that contains all other elements. For certain category types it often makes sense to aggregate them. To support the different aggregation types in the model, three different classes of aggregation functions exist: constant c, average functions ϕ and sum functions Σ. For these classes an ordering exists such that $c \subset \phi \subset \Sigma$. For each dimension type T the model provides a function that determines the aggregation type for a category type. A dimension Dim_i has a dimension type T that is defined in the fact schema of an MO as explained in the previous section. $Dim_i = (Ca, \prec)$ is a two-tuple with Ca being a set of categories $\{Ca_j\}$ and $\prec$ a partial ordering on all dimension values e in each category Ca_j with $Type(e) = C_j$. Furthermore, all values e in the dimension Dim_i are smaller than value $\top$ and the most granular values are contained in category $\bot_T$. To establish a connection between facts and dimensions, fact-dimension relations are introduced. A fact-dimension relation R is a set of two-tuples $\{(f, e)\}$ where f is a fact and e is a dimension value. Therefore, the fact is characterized by the dimension value e. Values from different dimension categories can determine the same fact. Also it must be ensured in the model that each fact in R is characterized by at least one dimension value. Thus, if there is no suitable dimension value to characterize a fact, the value $\top$ is used. Based on these entities an algebra with a list of operators is part of the model. As basic operators, all operations from relational algebra like *selection, projection, rename, union, difference* and *join* are adopted to operate on MOs. In addition, the *aggregate formation* operator allows to built aggregates and group facts. Typical OLAP operators like roll-up, *drill-down, SQL-like aggregation* and *star-joins* are expressed in terms of the basic operators.

3   Common Planning Functions by Example

The example used throughout the paper has the schema shown in Figure 1, consisting of 5 dimensions with dimension types *Article, Location, SellDate, Price* and *Quantity*. They characterize the *Sale* of a product. Usually, *Price* and *Quantity* would be considered as measures, so we call them the measure dimensions. Each dimension consists of different categories that form one or more hierarchies per dimension. For the two dimensions *Article* and *Location* Figures 2 and 3 show dimension values and their partial ordering.

The measure dimensions contain numerical values, where quantities are integral numbers and prices are values taken from real numbers. In Table 1 we list the facts for our example in column 1 and each entry represents a fact. The other columns represent the dimensions that characterize the fact and the value(s) in each row represent the dimension value(s) forming, together with the fact, (an) element(s) of the fact-dimension relations.

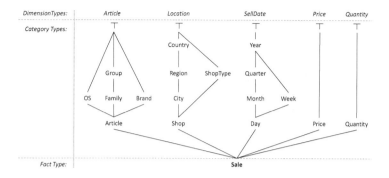

Fig. 1. An example schema

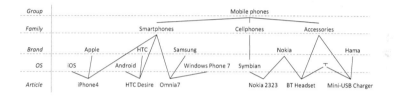

Fig. 2. Dimension values and partial ordering for dimension *Article*

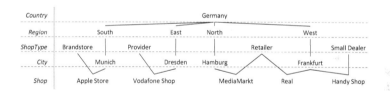

Fig. 3. Dimension values and partial ordering for dimension *Shop*

The following example introduces a list of common planning functions in a typical business planning scenario. Our model should be able to express each of these functions. Assume a company that sells phones and accessories to shops and retailers. Our example schema shows a multidimensional object with a list of facts that capture sales for year 2010. It is the task of a controller to plan sales quantities and prices for year 2011.

Step 1. As a first step he wants to base his plan on the values of the previous year and therefore he needs a planning function that **copies** data from 2010 into year 2011. The new MO would now contain twice as much facts as before.

Step 2. Because of recent market trends the company decides to sell only smartphones in 2011 and therefore a **delete** planning function deletes all standard cellphone sales from 2011.

Table 1. Lists of facts in the example schema

Fact	$R_{Article}$	$R_{Location}$	$R_{SellDate}$	R_{Price}	$R_{Quantity}$
f_1	iPhone4,iOS, Apple,Smartphones	AppleStore,Munich, BrandStore	2010-05-06, 05, Q2, 2010	699.00	50
f_2	Desire,Android, HTC,Smartphones	Vodafone Shop, Dresden,Provider	2010-04-23, 04, Q2, 2010	479.00	35
f_3	Omnia 7,Windows Phone 7,Samsung, Smartphones	Media Markt, Hamburg,Retailer	2010-12-14, 12, Q4, 2010	389.00	10
f_4	2323,Symbian, Nokia, Cellphones	Real,Frankfurt, Retailer	2010-01-11, 01, Q1, 2010	79.95	110
f_5	BT Headset,Nokia, Accessories	HandyShop,Dresden, Smalldealer	2010-03-27, 03, Q1, 2010	24.55	70
f_6	USB Charger,Hama, Accessories	Real,Frankfurt, Retailer	2010-08-13, 08, Q3, 2010	12.99	45

Step 3. For the year 2011 the prices are lowered by 5% compared to the previous year. Therefore the planner calls a **revalue** planning function to apply these changes. Furthermore, he wants to know the planned revenue that is based on sales quantities and price.

Step 4. For a each retailer the planner requests the estimated quantity of sold items from the sales person that is responsible for this customer. These quantities are now entered to the plan at aggregated customer level and must be distributed to individual facts using a **disaggregation** planning function.

Step 5. Finally, the controller wants to use the current data of 2010 and the planned data of 2011 to predict a sales quantity trend for 2012. He requires a planning function that calculates a **forecast** and generates a set of forecasted facts.

After all these steps, the complete plan data is created and can be used for reports and comparisons with the actual data of 2011. The list of planning functions that was involved includes copy, delete, calculate expressions to revalue quantitative values, disaggregation of new values from an aggregated level to the most granular fact level and forecasting new values.

4   An OLAP Model for Planning

In the following section we extend the EMDM and develop our novel model algebra to support planning. One major aspect of planning is that it changes fact data. All the models existing so far make the assumption that fact data is a read only set of values and all operators have navigational, i.e. read only semantic. With planning new facts will be created or existing facts are manipulated. Therefore, the novel operators for planning must support this. From the list of basic planning functions shown in Section 3 not all require a separate operator. Similar to the original model, where typical OLAP operators like roll-up and drill down are expressed in terms of the basic aggregation formation operator, we only need a few basic operators to keep the extended algebra simple and minimal.

4.1   Basic Planning Operators

Value Mapping. An important basic operation, e.g. for the copy function, is *value mapping*. When new plan data has to be generated one can copy facts from a previous year. As a result, for a set of facts, one or more dimension values change. For example, to copy along the time dimension the values must change from one year to another. The mapping operator takes as input a set of mapping functions, which map a combination of source dimension values to corresponding target values. As fact-dimension relations are the glue between facts and dimensions, the mapping operator modifies these relations. We formally denote the mapping operator as:

Definition 1. *Value mapping* $\gamma\left[\{m_r, r = 1..s\}\right](MO) = (S', F', Dim', R')$ *takes a set of mapping functions* m_r, *which have the form* $m_r(e_1, .., e_i, .., e_n) \mapsto e'_i$, *with*

- $S' = S$, $F' = F$, $Dim' = Dim$
- $R' = \{R'_i, i = 1..n\}$
- $R'_i = \{(f', e'_i)|f' \in F' \wedge e'_i = m_r(e_1, .., e_i, .., e_n) \wedge e_1 \rightarrow_1 f, .., e_i \rightarrow_i f, .., e_n \rightarrow_n f \wedge e'_i \rightarrow_i f'\}$

Intuitively a mapping function m_r is applied to a fact-dimension relation R_i and maps the input value to itself or, for matching values, to a different dimension value. It is important that the mapping function is aware of dimension hierarchies and provides a complete mapping from one part of the hierarchy lattice structure to another. If we consider the *SellDate* hierarchy of our example schema and want to map from the year 2010 to the year 2011, a mapping function $f_{2010 \mapsto 2011}$ must provide a mapping for all dimension values that are in the partial ordering below 2010 to the respective values in the hierarchy below 2011. Thus *Q1-2010* would be mapped to *Q1-2011* and so on.

Duplication. The value mapping operator from the previous section modifies fact-dimension relations, but the set of facts is not changed. To introduce new facts, as it is necessary for a copy function, we add the duplication operator to the model, which duplicates the facts of an MO. The resulting MO' has identical dimension structure and fact-dimension relations with the exception that for each fact in MO there is a new fact in MO' that is characterized by the same dimension attributes and values.

Definition 2. *Duplication* $\tau(MO) = (S', F', Dim', R')$ *with*

- $S' = S$
- $F' = \{f'|\exists f \in F \wedge e_1 \rightarrow_1 f, .., e_n \rightarrow_n f \wedge f' \neq f \wedge e'_1 \rightarrow_1 f'_1, .., e'_n \rightarrow_n f'_n \wedge e_1 = e'_1 \wedge \ldots \wedge e_n = e'_n\}$
- $R' = \{R'_i, i = 1..n\}$
- $R'_i = \{(f', e'_i)|\forall (f, e_i) \in R_i \wedge f' \in F' \wedge e'_i \in Dim'_i\}$

Disaggregation. A typical planning function is to enter an aggregated value for a group of facts and then calculate how it distributes to the individual fact values that contribute to the aggregated value. The disaggregation can be viewed as the reverse operation to the aggregation. In contrast to the drill-down operation, the disaggregation operation defines a new sum value and *changes* all contributing values accordingly. We define the disaggregation operator similar to the aggregation formation operator as the inverse operator α^{-1}. As input it takes a set of dimension values, that define the aggregation level where the new sum value is entered. Additional parameters are a distribution function g^{-1} and an aggregate function g that determines how the values are aggregated. Finally, a new dimension value e_{new} is given as well as the index t of the target dimension and the index r of a reference dimension. It is allowed that $t = r$, in which case the new value is distributed according to the original fractions dimension Dim_t.

Definition 3. *Disaggregation is* $\alpha^{-1}\left[e_1, .., e_n, g^{-1}, g, e_{new}, t, r\right](MO) = (S', F', Dim', R')$, *where*

- $S' = S,\ F' = F,\ Dim' = \{Dim_i, i = 1..n \wedge i \neq t\} \cup \{Dim'_t\}$
- $Dim'_t = (Ca'_t, \prec'_t),\ \prec'_t = \prec_{t|Dim'}$
- $Ca'_t = \{Ca'_{tj} \in Dim_t | Type(Ca'_{tj}) = \top_{Dim_t} \vee (Type(Ca'_{tj}) = \bot_{Dim_t} \wedge e'_{tj} = g^{-1}(e_{rj}, e_{new}, e_{old}) \wedge e_{rj} \in Ca_{rj} \wedge Type(Ca_{rj}) = \bot_{Dim_r} \wedge SUM(Group(e'_1, .., e'_n)) = e_{new} \wedge e_{old} = g(Group(e_1, .., e_n)) \wedge (e'_1, .., e'_n) \in Ca'_1 \times \cdots \times Ca'_n \wedge (e_1, .., e_n) \in Ca_1 \times \cdots \times Ca_n)\}$
- $R' = \{R'_i, i = 1..n \wedge i \neq t\} \cup \{R'_t\},\ R'_i = \{(f', e')|f' \in F' \wedge e' \in Dim'_i\}$
- $R'_t = \{(f', e'_i)|\exists (e_1, .., e_n) \in Ca_1 \times \cdots \times Ca_n \wedge f' \in F' \wedge e'_i \in Dim'_t \wedge e'_i = g^{-1}(e_{ri}, e_{new}, e_{old}) \wedge \forall e_i \in Dim_t \exists e_{ri} \in Dim_r\}$

The fact-schema S' of MO' is the same as that of the original MO since only values are changed and no dimensions are added or removed. The set of facts is the same, too, because the disaggregation operator does not introduce new facts. It only maps the facts for the target dimension to new values. The set of dimensions is again taken from the original MO, but the target dimension Dim'_t changes in the sense that intuitively the new dimension values are calculated based on the new sum and the fractions of the given reference dimension Dim_r. The category attributes Ca'_{tj} of the target dimension are either the top attribute, or they are in the class of the most granular attribute and their new dimension values are calculated using the distribution function g^{-1}. The distribution function calculates the new dimension values e'_{tj} using the new sum e_{new} as input, the old reference aggregate value e_{old} and the respective dimension value e_{rj} of the reference dimension. The aggregate value e_{old} is obtained by applying the reference aggregate function g to the grouping of $Group(e_1, .., e_n)$ at the level of the given input dimension values. Finally, the fact-dimension mapping R'_t is adapted such that the facts are now mapped to the new dimension values calculated by the distribution function. This includes, the requirement that for each fact-dimension mapping in the target dimension there exists a fact-dimension mapping in the reference dimension.

By allowing arbitrary functions for the distribution function g^{-1} and the reference aggregate function g, different types of distribution can be achieved. For example, a typical distribution function that calculates the new fraction based on the percentile of the reference value from the old sum value is $g^{-1}(e_r, e_{new}, e_{old}) = e_r * e_{new}/e_{old}$ together with $g = SUM$. The reference dimension can be the same as the target dimension. For a uniform distribution, the reference aggregate function should be $g = COUNT$ and for a constant distribution $g^{-1}(e_r, e_{new}, e_{old}) = e_{new}$. The following example illustrates how disaggregation works: we distribute a new article quantity of 384 to all sales facts in *Germany* for the year *2010*. The input MO contains all 5 dimensions *Article, Location, SellDate, Price* and *Quantity* and is not restricted. The parameters for the disaggregation are:

$$\alpha^{-1} \left[\top_{Article}, Germany, 2010, \top_{Price}, \top_{Quantity}, g^{-1}, g, \right.$$
$$\left. e_{new} = 384, t = 5, r = 5 \right] (MO) = MO'$$

The distribution function g^{-1} is the standard function explained in the previous section and the reference aggregate function g is SUM. The target dimension *Quantity* now contains the new dimension values that would result in the new sum 384 when the reverse operation, i.e. the aggregate formation, would be applied to MO'. The disaggregation affects all facts $f_1, .., f_6$ in the example and the fact-dimension mapping $R_{Quantity}$ would change from

$$\{(f_1, 50), (f_2, 35), (f_3, 10), (f_4, 110), (f_5, 70), (f_6, 45)\}$$

to

$$R'_{Quantity} = \{(f_1, 60), (f_2, 42), (f_3, 12), (f_4, 132), (f_5, 84), (f_6, 54)\}$$

Calculated Dimensions. Another cornerstone of planning is to calculate various expressions on multidimensional data. We therefore allow expressions on multidimensional objects. Since everything is a dimension in the model and the facts are objects that are described by dimension values, such an expression is an operation on dimension values. We realize this within our model by defining a *calculated dimension* $\overline{Dim}$ of type $T = (C_j, \prec_T, \top_T, \bot_T)$ similar to basic dimensions as a two-tuple $\overline{Dim} = (Ca, \prec)$. The set Ca contains the categories of the dimension and $\prec$ is the partial ordering on all dimension values. The difference is, that a category attribute $Ca_i \in \overline{Dim}_{n+1}$ is now defined in terms of an expression where the operands are category attributes of other dimensions $Ca_i = \otimes(Ca_j, Ca_k)$ with $Ca_j \in Dim_r$, $Ca_k \in Dim_s$ and $\otimes$ being an arbitrary binary operator from the following list $\{+, -, *, /, \wedge, \vee\}$. In the same manner expressions can contain arbitrary scalar functions and operators by extending the definition of a calculated category type to the general form $Ca_i = \otimes(\{Ca_j\})$ where $Ca_j \in Dim_r, j = 1..m, r = 1..n + 1, i \neq j$ and $\otimes$ is an arbitrary unary, binary or n-nary operator or scalar function applied to a number of category attributes. It is possible that the expression references other category attributes of the calculated dimension. This is useful for example to add constant to the expression by defining a category attribute that only has one dimension value and reference it in other expressions. To calculate such an expression we add a calculated dimension to a multidimensional object using the following operator:

Definition 4. *The add dimension operator* $+\left[\overline{Dim_{n+1}}\right](MO)$ $=$ (S', F', Dim', R') *takes as input a multidimensional object MO and a calculated dimension* $\overline{Dim_{n+1}}$ *where*

- $S' = (FS', D')$, $D' = \{T'_i, i = 1..n\} \cup \{T_{n+1}\}$, $T'_i = T_i$, $F' = F$
- $Dim' = \{Dim'_i, i = 1..n\} \cup \{Dim_{n+1}\}$, $Dim'_i = Dim_i$
- $\overline{Dim_{n+1}} = (Ca_{n+1}, \prec)$
- $Ca_{n+1} = \{Ca_{n+1,i} = \otimes(\{Ca_{rj}|Ca_{rj} \in Dim_r, j = 1..m, r = 1..n\})\}$
- $R' = \{R'_i, i = 1..n\} \cup \{R'_{n+1}\}$, $R'_i = R_i$
- $R'_{n+1} = \{(f', e'_{n+1,i})|f' \in F' \wedge e'_r i \to f' \wedge e'_{n+1,i} = \otimes(e'_{ri}) \wedge$
  $e'_{ri} \in Ca_r\}$

To calculate an expression between values of two different MOs, first a join operator should be applied to create a combined MO and then a calculated dimension containing the expression is added.

As an example we will calculate the *revenue* for our mobile phone data. Therefore we add a dimension $Dim_{revenue} = (Ca, \prec)$ with $Ca = (Revenue, \top)$, $Revenue = Qty * Price$ and add this dimension to our multidimensional object $+[Dim_{Revenue}](MO)$. The resulting MO' now has an additional Revenue dimension where the dimension values of the *Revenue* category attribute are calculated for each fact as the product of the *Quantity* and *Price* dimension values.

Forecast. The need for a *forecast* operator is directly motivated by the respective forecast planning function. Besides copying values or enter plan values manually, it is often useful to use a forecasting function fc to project trends of historical data into the future. For the forecast operator this means creating a set of new fact values for a category attribute Ca_t (most often from a time dimension). An ordering $O[Ca_t]$ is required for all dimension values e_{ti} of type Ca_t. Let $O[Ca_t] = 1..m$ with $O[Ca_t](e_{ti}) < O[Ca_t](e_{tj}), i \neq j, i = 1..m, j = 1..m$ if e_{ti} is smaller than e_{tj} in terms of ordering O. The forecast function $f(F, O[Ca_t], tgt, k)$ can be an arbitrary forecasting algorithm like exponential smoothing or ARMA models [2]. It takes as input a set of facts F, an ordering $O[Ca_t]$ for these facts based on a given dimension Dim_i with $Ca_t \in Dim_t$, an integral number tgt which specifies the number of new facts it should produce and an index $k = 1..tgt$ that specifies which of the forecasted values it should return. We can now write the following definition for the forecast operator:

Definition 5. $\phi[f, O, Ca_t, Ca_v, tgt](MO) = MO' = (S', F', Dim', R')$ *with the fact schema staying the same* $S' = S$, *the set of facts is extended by* tgt *new facts and*

- $F' = F \cup \{f''_j | j = 1..tgt \wedge T_1 \to_1 f''_j \wedge ... \wedge T_i \to_i f''_j \wedge ... \wedge T_n \to_n f''_j \wedge e'_t \to_t$
  $f''_j \wedge e'_v \to_v f''_j \wedge i \neq t \wedge i \neq v\}$
- $Dim' = Dim$, $R' = \{R'_i | i = 1..n \wedge i \neq t \wedge i \neq v\} \cup \{R'_t, R'_v\}$
- $R'_i = R_i \cup \{(f''_j, T_i)|j = 1..tgt \wedge f''_j \in F'\}$
- $R'_t = R_t \cup \{(f''_j, e'_t)|j = 1..tgt \wedge f''_j \in F' \wedge O[Ca'_t](e'_t) = max(O[Ca'_t](e_k)) +$
  $j \wedge k = 1..n\}$
- $R'_v = R_v \cup \{(f''_j, e'_v)|j = 1..tgt \wedge f''_j \in F' \wedge e'_v = f(F, O[Ca_t], tgt, j)\}$

In essence the forecast operator produces l new facts, which are mapped to an ordered set of dimension values such that the new facts are mapped to the l successors of the last dimension value from the existing facts. Furthermore, for a given (measure) dimension each new fact is mapped to its projected new value according to the prediction of the forecasting algorithm.

4.2   Expressing Typical Planning Functions

The following section lists typical planning functions that are necessary to support planning applications. For each of these functions we describe it in terms of operators of our novel Planing-OLAP model.

Delete. The delete operator deletes fact values from a multidimensional object. We make no distinction here between an MO' where facts have only been filtered and actual deletion. Therefore, the planning operator delete can be expressed with the selection operator. Let $MO = (S, F, Dim, R)$ and p an arbitrary predicate, that selects the values for deletion, then $\sigma[\neg p](MO) = MO' = (S', F', Dim', R')$ results in MO' that only contains the *not*-deleted values.

Copy. When we introduced the *value mapping* operator, we already emphasized that copying is an important part of planning to set a starting point for subsequent planning operations with data based on historic values. The copy operator can be expressed in terms of the value mapping basic planning operation combined with the duplication. The new MO' is created by applying a mapping to an MO^{Copy} that contains duplicates of the original facts. Let $M = \{m_r, r = 1..s\}$ be a set of mapping functions, then copying is defined as: $\cup(\gamma[M](\tau(MO)), MO) = MO' = (S', F', Dim', R')$.

Disaggregation. The disaggregation planning function can be directly mapped to the disaggregation operator of the model.

Revalue. The revalue planning function is used to change a set of values according to a formula. To execute such calculations within our Planning-OLAP model, we use calculated dimensions.

Forecasting. Similar to the disaggregation planning function, the *forecasting* planning functions has a direct representation as an operator in our Planning-OLAP model and can therefore expressed with a call to this operator.

5   Impact and Conclusion

When comparing the Planning-OLAP model with traditional OLAP models then the distinction is, that the latter is based purely on read operations whereas the planning operators write or generate data. As planning has a simulation character, it is often the case that generated data is continuously adjusted until a

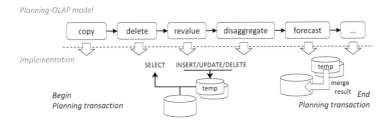

Fig. 4. Implementation scheme for the Planning-OLAP model

final result is obtained. As such it can be viewed as a long running transaction containing a mixture of read (*roll-up, drill-down, slice and dice*) and write (*disaggregate, copy, revalue, forecast and delete*) operations. While the transaction bracket is not necessary for the read-only traditional OLAP, it makes sense for the Planning-OLAP model where only the final result of a planning transaction should become visible and persistent. The scheme in Figure 4 outlines how this usage paradigm of the Planning-OLAP model can be mapped to a relational system using SQL. At the begin of a planning transaction one or more temporary tables are created that will contain the modifications of the current transaction and final results are merged into the original tables at the end of the transaction. Each operator is mapped to a combination of SELECT and INSERT/UPDATE/DELETE statements that modify the temporary tables. For example the disaggregation operator has to update every measure value that contributes to the overall sum. However, as the disaggregation operator contains possibly complex distribution logic, the orchestration of these statements to yield the correct result must either be done by the application or may be encapsulated in a stored procedure. Clearly, a direct integration of this functionality into the database system as a native operator would facilitate standardized and application independent behavior and allow for optimizations. This is similar for other operations such as value-mapping and forecasting. Therefore, we argue that in the future, these operations should be first-class citizens in a database system, equal to many navigational OLAP operators that are already supported natively by major database systems today.

Although, there exists a wealth of OLAP models in the literature, none of the existing models incorporated planning functionality. Many requirements have been formulated for OLAP modeling to support real-world scenarios. While many requirements are already met by some of the models, none of it explicitly supported planning, which is a vital part of OLAP today. We proposed a novel Planning-OLAP model that uses the Extended Multidimensional Data Model (EMDM) as a foundation. By introducing a set of novel planning operators our model is capable of supporting an extensive list of standard planning functions, which we illustrated by examples. Since the Planning-OLAP model contains operators that change data according to complex semantics, the challenge on the implementation level is to have planning operators as first-class citizens within a database system.

References

1. Agrawal, R., Gupta, A., Sarawagi, S.: Modeling Multidimensional Databases. In: Proc. of 13th. Int. Conf. on Data Engineering ICDE, vol. 7, p. 11 (1997), http://eprints.kfupm.edu.sa/51421/
2. Box, G., Jenkins, G.: Time Series Analysis: Forecasting and Control (1970)
3. Cabibbo, L., Torlone, R.: Querying Multidimensional Databases. In: Database Programming Languages, pp. 319–335. Springer, Heidelberg (1998), http://www.springerlink.com/index/f76731r05m5u662j.pdf
4. Codd, E., Codd, S., Salley, C.: Providing OLAP (On-Line Analytical Processing) to User-Analysis: An IT Mandate (1993), http://www.citeulike.org/user/MoritzStefaner/article/4937436
5. Datta, A.: The Cube Data Model: a Conceptual Model and Algebra for On-line Analytical Processing in Data Warehouses. Decision Support Systems 27(3), 289–301 (1999), http://linkinghub.elsevier.com/retrieve/pii/S0167923699000524
6. Gray, J., Bosworth, A., Layman, A., Pirahesh, H.: Data Cube: A Relational Aggregation Operator Generalizing Group-By, Cross-Tab, and Sub-Total. In: ICDE, pp. 152–159 (1996)
7. Gyssens, M., Lakshmanan, L.V.S.: A Foundation for Multi-Dimensional Databases. In: Proceedings of the International Conference on Very Large Data Bases, pp. 106–115. Citeseer (1997), http://citeseerx.ist.psu.edu/viewdoc/download?doi=10.1.1.46.7255&rep=rep1&type=pdf
8. Lehner, W.: Modeling Large Scale OLAP Scenarios. In: Advances in Database TechnologyâĂŤEDBT 1998, p. 153 (1998), http://www.springerlink.com/index/1VR766FUCVW7NY4T.pdf
9. Li, C., Wang, X.S.: A Data Model for Supporting On-Line Analytical Processing. In: Proceedings of the Fifth International Conference on Information and Knowledge Management - CIKM 1996, vol. 199, pp. 81–88 (1996), http://portal.acm.org/citation.cfm?doid=238355.238444
10. Ozsoyoglu, G., Ozsoyoglu, Z., Mata, F.: A Language and a Physical Organization Technique for Summary Tables. In: Proceedings of the 1985 ACM SIGMOD International Conference on Management of Data, pp. 3–16. ACM, New York (1985), http://portal.acm.org/citation.cfm?id=318899
11. Pedersen, T., Jensen, C., Dyreson, C.: A Foundation for Capturing and Querying Complex Multidimensional Data. Information Systems 26(5), 383–423 (2001), http://citeseerx.ist.psu.edu/viewdoc/download?doi=10.1.1.22.6209&rep=rep1&type=pdf
12. Rafanelli, M.: A Functional Model for Macro-Databases. ACM SIGMOD Record 20(1), 3–8 (1991), http://portal.acm.org/citation.cfm?id=122050.122051&coll=GUIDE &dl=ACM&idx=J689&part=periodical& WantType=periodical&title=ACMSIGMODRecord
13. Vassiliadis, P.: Modeling Multidimensional Databases, Cubes and Cube Operations. In: Proceedings of Tenth International Conference on Scientific and Statistical Database Management (Cat. No.98TB100243), pp. 53–62 (1998), http://ieeexplore.ieee.org/lpdocs/epic03/wrapper.htm?arnumber=688111
14. Vassiliadis, P., Sellis, T.: A Survey on Logical Models for OLAP Databases. SIGMOD Record 28, 64–69 (1999)

Extending the Dimensional Templates Approach to Integrate Complex Multidimensional Design Concepts

Rui Oliveira[1], Fátima Rodrigues[2], Paulo Martins[3], and João Paulo Moura[3]

[1] Informatics Department, School of Technology and Management
Polytechnic Institute of Leiria, Portugal
rui.oliveira@estg.ipleiria.pt
[2] GECAD-Knowledge Engineering and Decision Support Research Center
Informatics Engineering Dept., School of Engineering,
Polytechnic Inst. of Porto, Portugal
mfc@isep.ipp.pt
[3] GECAD-Knowledge Engineering and Decision Support Research Center
Informatics Engineering Dept., University of Trás-os-Montes e Alto Douro, Portugal
{pmartins,jpmoura}@utad.pt

Abstract. In the past, several approaches have been devised to semi-automate the multidimensional design (MDD) of Data Warehouse (DW) projects. Such approaches highly contribute to more expertise-independent and deterministic MDD results. Among them, only the Dimensional Templates Approach (DTA) focuses on solving the critical resource containment problems of DW prototypes.

Originally, the DTA allows solely the generation of basic MDDs. In this paper, we depict an extension to address complex MDD issues. These include (i) date/time hierarchies, (ii) many-to-many relationships, (iii) hierarchically structured data and (iv) coverage facts. The proposed enhancements, including a rebuilt generation algorithm, allow more accurate and broadening results than the original DTA. Throughout the paper, references are made to a real case study to which the improved DTA has been applied using two developed prototype tools.

Keywords: Dimensional Templates, Multidimensional Design, DW.

1 Introduction

The multidimensional design (MDD) stage is known to be one of the most resource consuming stages in the development of Data Warehouse (DW) projects [1, 2]. The accuracy requirements it imposes are not easy to balance with the time and human resources they rely on. Business requirements must be gathered, data sources must be deeply analysed, DW expertise must be acquired, and performance plus storage sustainability must be assured.

Aiming to accelerate the MDD stage of DWs, several semi-automated methods have been devised. Some of these are exclusively oriented towards available

A. Cuzzocrea and U. Dayal (Eds.): DaWaK 2011, LNCS 6862, pp. 26–38, 2011.

data information, *data-driven* [3–5], others primarily guided by end-users requirements (EURs), *user-driven* [6–8], and others still a mixture of both, *mixed-driven* [9–11]. Among the major handicaps of these methods (not simultaneously found in all of them) are the need for a deep understanding of data sources by DW designers, multidimensional experts manual intervening and, specially, specifically formatted and validated data source documentation. Most importantly, these methods produce results which are not reusable between scenarios, despite their hypothetical similarities.

Recently [12] presented the Dimensional Templates Approach (DTA), a mixed-driven semi-automated MDD approach. It proposes the semi-automation of MDDs specifically for DW prototypes. As explained there, the DTA has the potential to better comply with cost and time constraints of DW prototypes comparing to other approaches. However, the original work allows solely the generation of basic dimensions and fact tables, which presents as insufficient for the DTA to be considered a strong alternative. Extra developments towards greater accuracy and application range are, thus, required. In this paper we present such developments to deal with date/time hierarchies, many-to-many data relationships, hierarchically structured data and coverage facts. To accomplish this, the DTA notation syntax was extended and its basic generation algorithm was deeply enhanced, now presented with high detail.

The improved DTA has been successfully applied to a real-world DW prototype case study, the SAD-IES (Decision Support System for Higher Education Institutions) project. References to it are made throughout the paper to illustrate the developments made (oppositely, the original DTA work had been solely applied to an academic case study). The SAD-IES project, currently undergoing on the Polytechnic Institute of Leiria (IPL), consists primarily in the development of a DW prototype. In the future, the DW should support the institutes's management board into better plans of action concerning its students' motivation and performance. Currently, the project deals with the business processes of *students evaluation* and *students assistance to classes*.

The paper is structured as follows. Section 2 presents relevant background on the DTA. Section 3 describes the DTA's non-addressed issues and the required enhancements to handle them. Section 4 details the rebuild generation algorithm considering the enhancements proposed. Section 5 concludes the paper.

2   Related Work

In the past, valuable approaches have been devised to semi-automate the MDD of DWs, with focus on diminishing the time consumed and reducing MDD subjectivity while maintaining high quality standards. In chapter 1 we have referenced the most recent and relevant. Their further presentation and discussion was considered beyond the scope of this paper. Besides, [13] provides an extensive comparison of these approaches in terms of MDD flexibility.

Among these approaches, the DTA is still the only one to specifically target DW prototype resource problems. Considering the potential denoted in [12], it thus makes sense to support new developments on it.

2.1   The Dimensional Templates Approach

The DTA detaches from other approaches in a core aspect: it stands on the conviction that a pre-built generic and configurable solution better handles resource containment during DW prototype MDD than specific tailored solutions. It proposes the use of the *template* concept, largely adopted in other Informatica areas. The approach focus on three main goals: refinement resilience, human interaction avoidance and design effort optimisation.

Succinctly, a DTA template (named *dimensional template*) consists of a generic configurable MDD solution for a specific business process. Each dimensional template is composed by a set of *rationale diagrams*: tree-oriented charts that map pre-defined EURs (named *goals*) to the types of source data required to satisfy them (named *markers*). Each goal can be progressively decomposed into child-goals using AND/OR tree-branches. Figure 1 depicts a much simplified rationale diagram taken from the SAD-IES project. From this diagram, cropped from the template addressing the *students evaluation* business process, the following statements can be retrieved:

- The goal "AVG/MAX/MIN grad. grade" can be satisfied at two different grain levels (named *reasonable grains*): *UnitSeasonEval* (in which facts must represent a student's grade in a specific evaluation season) and *UnitExam* (in which facts must represent a student's grade in a specific exam).
- The parent-most goal "Students grades" can be satisfied if *at least one* of its child goals ("AVG/MAX/MIN grad. grade", "Curricular unit precedences" and "AVG #students switching scholar year") is satisfied. This is true considering that an *OR-decomposition* is being used to decompose the goal.
- The child goal "AVG #students switching scholar year" can be satisfied at the grain level *UnitSeasonEval* if its child goals ("#students switching scholar year","Registered students in scholar year") are *simultaneously* satisfied (now, and *AND-decomposition* has been used).
- The child goal "Registered students in scholar year" can be satisfied at the level *UnitSeasonEval* if source data simultaneously addresses three contexts: *who* is the student involved (marker *student_id*); *which* curricular unit is involved (marker *unit_id*); *when* did the register occur (marker *scholar_year*).

Once a dimensional template is built and made available (DTA's first stage, *construction* stage), it can be requested (DTA's second stage, *acquisition* stage) and then configured according to the needs of a specific DW prototype scenario (DTA's third and final stage, *generation* stage). During the third stage, MDD operations are automated by means of a *generation algorithm*. The same available dimensional template can be reused indefinitely throughout different scenarios.

3   Extending the Dimensional Templates Approach

The original DTA provides basic notation for designing simplistic rationale diagrams, along with a subjective generation algorithm. Therefore, it can only target the simplest scenarios. Following subsections present the DTA's handicaps and propose related enhancements.

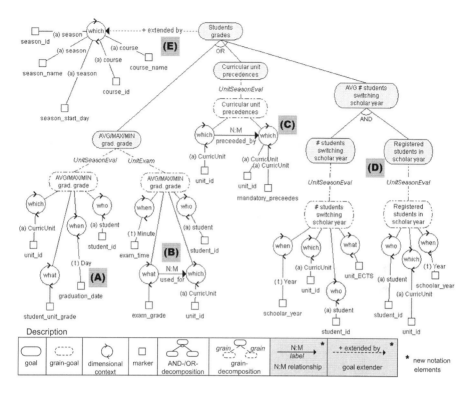

Fig. 1. One of the rationale diagrams used in the SAD-IES project, simplified for reading simplicity. It depicts date/time hierarchy handling *(A)*, many-to-many relationship *(B)*, HSD data *(C)*, coverage facts handling *(D)* and perspective usage *(E)*.

3.1 Time-Related Data

A crucial step in the MDD stage of any DW project is to define time-related data's granularity [1]: too much/less detailed data in date/time dimensions is equally harmful to the process of decision support.

Although *time granularity* differs from *facts granularity*, both concepts are related. For instance, assuming the case study's fact granularity as *a student's grade in a curricular unit exam*, relevant information would be lost if time related data was set at the *day* level instead of *hour* level (e.g.: "Do students perform better in the morning or in the afternoon?", "Which is the minimum advisable time gap between exams taken in the same day by a student?"). However, if facts granularity represented less detail, like *a student's grade in a curricular unit evaluation season, day* level would suffice. Hence, date/time grain depends on facts' detail level.

Secondly, source data's detail also limits the choice of the date/time grain. It would be incoherent and predictably harmful to set date/time dimensions to a deeper detail level than the one retrievable from source data. Consider again the case study in which source systems store students' exam pre-register with a *year-month-day* detail: *day* is bound to be the bottommost acceptable detail level to associate with register-related facts; if more detail was forced into the DW (like *hour*), erroneous data would have to be associated to each student's register (e.g., a fake hour).

Time-related data issues were not handled on the DTA original work. Here, they are dealt by adapting the DTA's *tagging method* (each marker receives a tag depending on the dimensional context that marker connects to). Now, each marker linked to a *when* dimensional context must be tagged with the *(t)* tag, followed by the name of the minimum adequate date/time grain for that marker. Figure 1 depicts the application of a (t)-tag to the marker *graduation date* using *day* detail level (labelled as **(A)**). In the illustrated situation the template designer is stating "It is required to retrieve graduation date from data sources with (at least) day information so that the 'AVG/MAX/MIN grad. grade' goal can be fulfilled.".

(t)-tagging benefits from the fact that Time's structure is universal, known in advance and naturally hierarchic: one *century* contains *years*, each of which contains *months*, each of which contains *weeks* and so on. Thus, when a marker is (t)-tagged, no uncertainty exists whatsoever about the date/time hierarchy level that tag refers to.

3.2   Many-to-Many Relationships

Most commonly, dimension table records relate to facts in one-to-many relationships [1], while many-to-many relationships' only occasionally occur. As an exercise, let it be assumed that a fact in the case study represents *a student's grade in a curricular unit exam*: a common one-to-many relationship relates each student's exam grade (a fact) to *one* curricular unit, which in return can be related to *many* exam grades; a many-to-many relationship, however, would determine that a student's exam grade can be used at *many* curricular units instead of one.

Originally, the DTA reckons only one-to-many relationships, which limits the accuracy of the generated MDD results. Therefore, the *N:M* notation element (*N:M* stands for *many-to-many*) has been created, as shown in Figure 1. The *N:M* element can be applied to pairs of dimensional contexts ⟨what,c⟩, with *c* IN {how,when,which,who,where}. When used in this context, the *N:M* element *indicates* (without *imposing*) the reasonable expectancy that data can relate in a many-to-many fashion. The *N:M* element "used_for" shown in Figure 1, labelled as **(B)**, states "Each student's grade in a taken exam can relate to several curricular units." (a common practice nowadays).

3.3   Hierarchically Structured Data

We refer to hierarchically structured data (HSD) not as one-to-many data relations inside dimensions and crucial to data roll-up and drill operations (like the classic recurrent example of date/time dimensions' hierarchy). Rather, we refer to HSD as data resuming into hierarchies due to source's organisational constraints. An example taken from the case study is *curricular unit precedences*, by which a curricular unit's student success is known/supposed to depend on a previous graduation at other curricular units (for instance, to obtain a graduation in the X unit a prior graduation is advised in the Y unit; furthermore, Y unit's success depends on graduating at the Z unit).

The original DTA work disregards HSD. In fact, it provides no mechanisms in rationale diagrams structure to address this special type of data relationships. To fill this void, the *N:M* element was again chosen since HSD is commonly of a many-to-many nature. In the just given example, the X curricular unit can require Y and Z as its precedents (*many*); these, in return, can be required as precedents not only by X but also by *many* others. This discussion resembles the *parts explosion* problem [1].

Since the N:M element is used for many-to-many relationships as well as to address HSD, a distinction is required. This is made at the dimensional context level: HSD uses the N:M element to perform a connection of a dimensional context to itself; also, no *what* dimensional context coexist in the same grain-goal. Figure 1 depicts the use of the N:M element "preceeded_by" in the "Curricular unit precedences" grain-goal (labelled as (**C**)). It states that each curricular unit may have a precedence towards other curricular unit(s) and that such precedence can be of a mandatory nature.

3.4   Dealing with Coverage Facts

A varying amount of the facts found in source systems are not strictly business process facts. Called *coverage facts* [1], these reflect *second tier* source occurrences required to answer a restrict set of EURs. Consider the case study's main facts' granularity to be "students' grades in a curricular unit's evaluation season". Second tier events like "students registering in curricular units" are only required to punctually complement main facts. In Figure 1, the goal "AVG # number of students switching scholar year" is satisfiable by simultaneously analysing the ratio *number of students switching scholar year/registered students in scholar year* (labelled as (**D**)): while this ratio's numerator is answered by main facts, the denominator is answered by coverage facts.

Dealing with coverage facts requires no additional notation elements in rationale diagrams. Rather, their detection is made by the generation algorithm (step 3) solely by interpreting the combination of elements used in rationale diagrams. Section 4.2 explains how this is achieved.

3.5   Handling Perspective Analysis

The quality of a DW depends on its capacity to allow data analysis under different perspectives. The EUR taken from the case study "How did students' grades evolve in a course basis per evaluation season?" answers the simpler

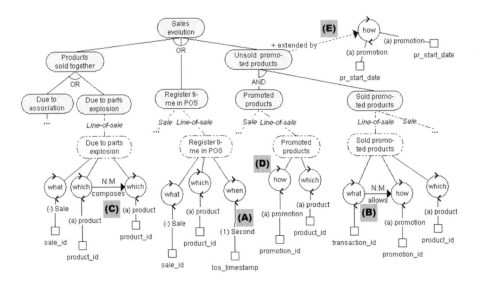

Fig. 2. A rationale diagram illustrating the DTA enhancements used on Figure 1 now applied under the context of retail sales [1]. Labels *(A)* to *(E)* equally apply.

question "How did students' grades evolve?". In fact, the more detailed first question is a biased version of the second using the *course* and *evaluation season* perspectives. Therefore, *perspectives* are additional analysis extensions one can perform on a goal. *Perspectives* are not explicitly handled in the DTA.

In the current work, we handle perspectives as goal refinements. To do so, the enhanced DTA adds the *goal-extender* notation element, representing a specific perspective analysis for a goal. Figure 1 depicts the use of a goal-extender, labelled as **(E)**. Through that association it is stated the high value of *optionally* analysing students' grades based on *course* information, particularly its *id* (marker *course_id*) and *name* (marker *course_name*).

Markers linked to goal-extenders represent the same as when attached to grain-goals: required data. The difference resides in the mandatory profiles of the relations: (i) *all* of a grain-goal's markers have to be mapped for it to be a *satisfied* grain-goal and therefore used by the generation algorithm (section 4.1); (ii) only *one* of a goal-extender's markers requires mapping for the corresponding perspective to be considered by the algorithm.

3.6   Enhanced DTA's Broadening Scope

Figure 2 intends to demonstrate the broadening scope of the enhanced DTA by using a scenario (*retail sales*, [1]), much different from this paper's primary SAD-IES case study. Using the same notation elements to model MDD concepts in such disparate scenarios shows the flexibility and straightforwardness of the approach. Numerous other examples could be used to illustrate the broadening applicability of the enhanced DTA: it was considered as an exercise of redundancy. From Figure 2 the following aspects are relevant:

- Grain levels *sale* and *line-of-sale* are available (in increasing order of detail);
- Sold products can be components of other products [1] (C);
- A selling product can be under several promotions simultaneously (B).

4   Improving the DTA Generation Algorithm

The current section details the rebuilt algorithm's *step 5*, responsible for delivering MDDs. It necessarily incorporates the enhancements discussed on the previous section.

4.1   The Generation Algorithm Basics

The DTA algorithm consists of five steps, each triggered by the successful ending of its previous. Succinctly, these are as follows ((Dn) represent DTA's original definitions, helpful for referencing):

Step 1. From the available goals in a template, its user chooses those which adapt to the particular DW scenario (D1: chosen goal). From these, the corresponding list of markers can be retrieved (D2: mappable marker).

Step 2. *Mappable markers* (D2) are mapped to real data (either manually or in an automated fashion, depending on source's metadata), now becoming *mapped markers* (D3: mapped marker);

Step 3. Each grain-goal related to a chosen goal (D1) having all of its markers mapped (D3) will become *satisfied* (D5: satisfied grain-goal);

Step 4. Once all satisfied grain-goals (D5) are found, the corresponding rationale AND/OR decomposition-trees are read to deliver *satisfied goals* (D6: satisfied goal) from the set of chosen goals (D1).

Step 5. MDDs are generated considering only the set of satisfied goals (D6) and their related mapped markers (D3).

4.2   Further on Satisfied Grain-Goals: Step 3

It was found that a further categorisation of satisfied grain-goals (D5) was sufficient to identify coverage facts from rationale diagrams without requiring additional notation elements (as discussed in section 3.4). This categorisation divides grain-goals into *status* grain-goals (D5.1: status grain-goal) and *basic* grain-goals (D5.2: basic grain-goal).

Status grain-goals are the subset of satisfied grain-goals which contain no *what* dimensional context (exemplified in Figure 1 by the grain-goal "Registered students in scholar year", labelled as **(D)**). The absence of the *what* dimensional context in a grain-goal indicates that a coverage fact is present. *Basic* grain-goals are the ones in the remaining subset of satisfied grain-goals (D6). This extra division is of high value in the generation process since *status* grain-goals allow the generation of coverage fact tables (Table 1).

Table 1. Comparing the DTA and the enhanced DTA (*e*-DTA) MDD abilities

MDD achievement	DTA	*e*-DTA	How achieved
Dimension (with basic attributes)	x	x	*DTA original work*
Fact table	x	x	*DTA original work*
Coverage fact		x	Status grain-goals (label D)
Bridge table		x	N:M element (labels B,C)
Fixed time dimension	x		*DTA original work*
Adjusted time dimension		x	(t)-tagging (label A)
Adjusted dimension's attributes		x	Goal-extender element (label E)

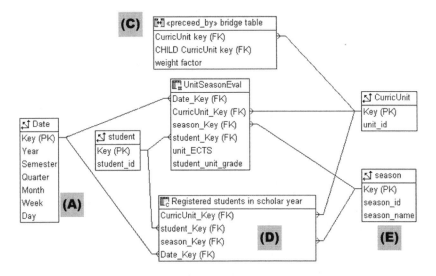

Fig. 3. Generated MDD considering that all goals of Figure 1 are satisfied. The labels of Figure 1 are reused to relate the rationale diagram with the corresponding results.

4.3   The Generation Algorithm: Step 5

Figures 4 and 5 present the restructured generation algorithm (optimised for reading simplicity) with reasonably high detail. Like in the DTA, for each distinct reasonable grain referred in the satisfied goals (D6), a corresponding algorithm execution is required (D7: algorithm iteration).

Figure 3 depicts the generated MDD considering that all of the goals of Figure 1 are satisfied at the *UnitSeasonEval* detail level (like in the SAD-IES project). Labels (A), (C), (D) and (E) match the labels in Figure 1. Table 1 resumes the relation between the proposed enhancements and new MDD achievements with the ones in original DTA.

```
0. SET min_time_grain = -1, triads_extend = {}
1. SET satisf_grain_goals = set of basic grain-goals (D5.2) having same
                            grain as the iteration's grain (D7)
2. IF satisf_grain_goals is not empty THEN
 2.1 CREATE iteration's fact table f_c
 2.2 SET usable_markers = set of usable markers (D4) belonging to
                          satisf_grain_goals
 2.3 SET usable_markers_what = subset of usable_markers linked to a what
                              dimensional context
 2.4 SET pairs = set of distinct pairs <marker,marker.grain> retrieved
                 using usable_markers_what
 2.5 FOR EACH pairs_i, 1<i<pairs.count, DO
         IF pairs_i.marker.grain = iteration.grain THEN
            CREATE measure in table f, using pairs_i.marker.name
         ELSE
            IF pairs_i.marker.grain < iteration.grain AND
               dimension d_grain not exists, grain=pairs_i.marker.grain, THEN
                  CREATE degenerated dimension d_grain in fact table f}
 2.6 SET usable_markers_when = subset of usable_markers linked to a when
                              dimensional context
 2.7 SET triads=distinct triads <marker,marker.grain,marker.time_grain>
                retrieved using usable_markers_when
 2.8 FOR EACH triads_i, 1<i<triads.count, DO
         IF triads_i.marker.grain = iteration.grain THEN
            IF dimension d_date not exists THEN CREATE dimension d_date
            CREATE FK (d_date->table f)
            IF triads_i.marker.time_grain > 'day' THEN
               IF dimension d_time not exists THEN CREATE dimension d_time
               CREATE FK (d_time->table f)
            SET min_time_grain = MIN(min_time_grain,
                                     triads_i.marker.time_grain)
```

Fig. 4. Pseudocode for the algorithm's *MDD generation* step (part 1)

2.8 *(continued)*

as on part 1 $\Big\{$

```
      IF triadsⱼ.marker.grain = iteration.grain THEN
         (...)
      ELSE
         IF triadsⱼ.marker.grain < iteration.grain THEN
            IF dimension d_grain not exists, grain=triadsⱼ.marker.grain, THEN
               CREATE dimension d_grain with FK (d_grain->table f)
            ELSE
               IF d_grain exists AND d_grain is degenerated THEN
                  CREATE FK (d_grain->table f)
                  UNSET d_grain as degenerated dimension
            CREATE column in d_grain named as triadsⱼ.marker.name
2.9 FOR EACH dimensional context ctx {how,where,which,who} DO
      SET usable_markers_ctx = subset of usable_markers linked to ctx
      SET pairs=set of distinct pairs <marker,marker.agent> retrieved
               using usable_markers_ctx
   FOR EACH pairsᵢ, 1<i<pairs.count, DO
      IF dimension named pairsᵢ.marker.agent not exists THEN
         CREATE dimension d_agent with FK (d_agent->table f)
      ELSE
         IF d_agent has no FK to f THEN CREATE FK (d_agent->table f)
      CREATE column in d_agent named as pairsᵢ.marker.name
2.10 SET triadsNM=set of distinct triads <context_to,agent_to,NMlabel>
               retrieved using satisf_grain_goals plus
               N:M-relationships starting in what dim. context
2.11 FOR EACH triadsNMᵢ, 1<i<triadsNM.count, DO
      SET dimension d_agent=get dimension for agent triadsNMᵢ.agent_to
      CREATE bridge table bt with FK(bt->d_agent) and FK(bt->d_agent)
2.12 SET triadsNM=set of distinct triads <context_to,agent_to,NMlabel>
               retrieved using satisf_grain_goals and
               N:M-elements starting in a dimensional context
               other than what
2.13 FOR EACH triadsNMᵢ, 1<i<triadsNM.count, DO
      SET dimension d_agent=get dimension for agent triadsNMᵢ.agent_to
      CREATE bridge table bt with FK(bt->d_agent) and FK(bt->d_agent)
      CREATE column weight_factor in bt
2.14 SET goal_ext=set of goal extenders linked to satisf_grain_goals
2.15 FOR EACH goal_extᵢ, 1<i<goal_ext.count, DO
      SET triads_ext=distinct <marker,marker.agent,goal_extᵢ.dim_context>
               triads retrieved from goal_extᵢ's mapped markers
2.16 FOR EACH triads_extᵢ DO, 1<i<triads_ext.count
      IF d_agent not exists, agent=triads_extᵢ.marker.agent THEN
         CREATE dimension d_agent with FK (d_agent->table f)
      CREATE column in d_agent named as triads_extᵢ.marker.name
3. SET satisf_grain_goals = set of status grain-goals (D5.1) with the
               same grain as the iteration's grain (D7)
4. IF satisf_grain_goals not empty THEN
   4.1 CREATE iteration's coverage fact table f
   4.2 REPEAT steps 2.2 TO 2.16
5. IF min_time_grain = -1 THEN
      IF d_date exists THEN
         CREATE columns in d_date considering min_time_grain value
         IF d_time exists THEN
            CREATE columns d_time considering min_time_grain value
```

Fig. 5. Pseudocode for the algorithm's *MDD generation* step (part 2)

5   Conclusions

This paper presents an extension to the DTA work [12]. In it, dimensional templates were proposed for semi-automating the MDD stage of DW prototypes. Despite its advantages, the original DTA allows solely the generation of basic MDDs. The here proposed enhancements enable the creation of more complex MDDs by dealing with date/time hierarchies, many-to-many relationships, HSD, coverage facts and perspective analysis. To achieve that purpose, notation elements were introduced and the step 5 of the generation algorithm was rebuilt, now particularly objective and detailed in contrast with the original one.

The enhanced DTA has been applied to a real world case study, the SAD-IES project. Throughout this paper several references are made to it to better contextualise the proposed improvements. The prototype tool referred in the original DTA paper was updated accordingly to the here proposed enhancements, both in terms of rationale diagrams' design support as well as algorithm's execution. Figures 1 and 3 were generated using that same prototype tool.

Regarding future work, additional improvements to the approach are being considered towards the relevant deliverance of mini-dimensions. Also, optimising the rationale diagrams design notation is possible and advisable to reduce particular redundancy occurrences.

References

1. Kimball, R., Ross, M.: The Data Warehouse Toolkit: The Complete Guide to Dimensional Modeling. John Wiley & Sons, Inc., New York (2002)
2. Adelman, S., Dennis, S.: Capitalising the DW. White Paper, DMReview (2005)
3. Jensen, M.R., Holmgren, T., Pedersen, T.B.: Discovering Multidimensional Structure in Relational Data. In: Kambayashi, Y., Mohania, M., Wöß, W. (eds.) DaWaK 2004. LNCS, vol. 3181, pp. 138–148. Springer, Heidelberg (2004)
4. Song, I.Y., Khare, R., Dai, B.: SAMSTAR: a semi-automated lexical method for generating star schemas from an entity-relationship diagram. In: ACM 10th Intern. Workshop on Data Warehousing and OLAP, pp. 9–16. ACM, New York (2007)
5. Romero, O., Abelló, A.: Automating Multidimensional Design from Ontologies. In: ACM 10th Intern. Workshop on Data Warehousing and OLAP, pp. 1–8. ACM, New York (2007)
6. Phipps, C., Davis, K.C.: Automating Data Warehouse Conceptual Schema Design and Evaluation. In: 4th International Workshop on Design and Management of Data Warehouses, DMDW 2002, pp. 23–32. CEUR (2002)
7. Winter, R., Strauch, B.: A Method for Demand-Driven Information Requirements Analysis in Data Warehousing Projects. In: 36th Hawaii International Conference on System Sciences, HICSS 2003, pp. 1359–1365. IEEE Computer Society, Los Alamitos (2002)
8. Prat, N., Akoka, J., Comyn-Wattiau, I.: A UML-based Data Warehouse Design Method. Journal of Decision Support Systems 42(3), 1449–1473 (2006)
9. Vrdoljak, B., Banek, M., Rizzi, S.: Designing Web Warehouses from XML Schemas. In: Kambayashi, Y., Mohania, M., Wöß, W. (eds.) DaWaK 2003. LNCS, vol. 2737, pp. 89–98. Springer, Heidelberg (2003)

10. Giorgini, P., Rizzi, S., Garzetti, M.: GRAnD: A Goal-Oriented Approach to Requirement Analysis in Data Warehouses. Decision Support Systems 45, 18 (2008)
11. Mazón, J.-N., Trujillo, J.: A Model Driven Modernization Approach for Automatically Deriving Multidimensional Models in Data Warehouses. In: Parent, C., Schewe, K.-D., Storey, V.C., Thalheim, B. (eds.) ER 2007. LNCS, vol. 4801, pp. 56–71. Springer, Heidelberg (2007)
12. Oliveira, R., Rodrigues, F., Martins, P., Moura, J.P.: Dimensional Templates in Data Warehouses: Automating the Multidimensional Design of Data Warehouse Prototypes. In: Filipe, J., Cordeiro, J. (eds.) Enterprise Information Systems. LNBIP, vol. 24, pp. 184–195. Springer, Heidelberg (2009)
13. Romero, O., Abelló, A.: A Survey of Multidimensional Modeling Methodologies. International Journal of Data Warehousing & Mining 5, 1–23 (2009)

OLAP Formulations for Supporting Complex Spatial Objects in Data Warehouses

Ganesh Viswanathan and Markus Schneider

Department of Computer & Information Science & Engineering
University of Florida
Gainesville, FL 32611, USA
{gv1,mschneid}@cise.ufl.edu

Abstract. In recent years, there has been a large increase in the amount of spatial data obtained from remote sensing, GPS receivers, communication terminals and other domains. Data warehouses help in modeling and mining large amounts of data from heterogeneous sources over an extended period of time. However incorporating spatial data into data warehouses leads to several challenges in data modeling, management and the mining of spatial information. New multidimensional data types for spatial application objects require new OLAP formulations to support query and analysis operations on them. In this paper, we introduce a set of constructs called C^3 for defining data cubes. These include *categorization*, *containment* and *cubing* operations, which present a fundamentally new, user-centric strategy for the conceptual modeling of data cubes. We also present a novel *region-hierarchy* concept that builds spatially ordered sets of polygon objects and employs them as first class citizens in the data cube. Further, new OLAP constructs to help define, manipulate, query and analyze spatial data have also been presented. Overall, the aim of this paper is to leverage support for spatial data in OLAP cubes and pave the way for the development of a user-centric SOLAP system.

Keywords: spatial data cube, user-centric OLAP, region hierarchy.

1 Introduction

Data warehouses and OLAP systems help to analyze complex multidimensional data and provide decision support. With the availability of large amounts of spatial data in recent years, several new models have been proposed to enable the integration of spatial data in data warehouses and to help analyze such data. This is often achieved by a combination of GIS and spatial analysis tools with OLAP and database systems, with the primary goal of supporting *spatial analysis dimensions*, *spatial measures* and *spatial aggregation operations*. However, this poses several new challenges related to spatial data modeling in a multidimensional context, such as the need for new spatial aggregation operations and ensuring consistent and valid results. Moreover, existing commercial geographic data management systems force database designers to use logical data structures

A. Cuzzocrea and U. Dayal (Eds.): DaWaK 2011, LNCS 6862, pp. 39–50, 2011.

heavily influenced by implementation concerns. This paper takes an unique approach to alter this implementation dependent view for modeling OLAP systems, by using a lattice theoretic approach based on the (hyper)cube metaphor to model multidimensional data. We present a user-centric conceptual modeling strategy that incorporates spatial data as first class citizens in data hierarchies. The modeling and querying of complex hierarchical structured multidimensional data in a large scale presents interesting challenges through the entire spectrum of spatial data warehouse development from designing conceptual data models accommodating complex aggregations on hierarchical, multidimensional spatial data, to developing the logical schema and finally, storage and the physical implementation. In this paper, we focus on the conceptual data model design that would allow the user to easily yet effectively create spatial data cubes, and navigate and analyze them. The model we present here is an extension of the $\mathcal{B}ig\mathcal{C}ube$ approach [1] that presents a strict type structured hierarchy of classes to model the hierarchical data dimensions in data cubes. We start by introducing a new region-hierarchy or *regH* representation for complex structured region objects into a partially ordered lattice structure. Then, we introduce the C^3 constructs, which stand for the three primary constructs required for data-cube creation and maintenance, namely, *Categorization, Containment* and *Cubing* or *Combination*. Categorization helps to organize base data values into meaningful categories, containment helps to assign a hierarchy of ordering over the categories, and finally cubing forms an association between categories of different hierarchies in order to signify a new subject of analysis (measure value). Further, we also introduce new OLAP formulations to support the spatial data in cubes, such as the *geo_ construct* operator which allows the creation of new spatial regions from complex region hierarchies to facilitate analysis.

The rest of this paper is organized as follows. Section 2 reviews existing work in spatial data warehousing and provides a case study in the form of a Product Sales data cube that is used in the rest of the paper. Section 3 presents the *regH* concept, which is a *region-hierarchy* specification to help incorporate complex structured spatial objects in data warehouses for performing analysis. Section 4 presents the C^3 constructs for spatial data cube definition and construction. Section 5 presents new OLAP formulations such as geo_ construct, slice and dice, and discusses spatial topological relations among complex regions using the poset structures. Finally, Section 6 concludes the paper and mentions topics for further research.

2   Related Work

Spatial data warehousing (SDW) has become a topic of growing interest in recent years. This is primarily due to the explosion in the amount of spatial information available from various sources such as GPS receivers, communication media, online social networks and other geo-spatial applications. Consequently several spatial OLAP tools are now available to help model and analyze such data.

An early approach to spatial online analytical processing (SOLAP) is [2], which mentions essential SOLAP features classified into three areas of requirements. The first is to enable *data visualization* via cartographic (maps) and non-cartographic displays (e.g., 2D tables), numeric data representation and the visualization of context data. Second, *data exploration* requires multidimensional navigation on both cartographic and non-cartographic displays, filtering on data dimensions (members) and support for calculated measures. The third area discussed involves the *structure of the data*, for example, the support for spatial and mixed data dimensions, support for storage of geometric data over an extended time period, etc. The conceptual design models for spatial data warehouses are extensions of ER and UML diagrams or ad-hoc design approaches. Among extensions of ER models, [3] presents a clear integration of spatial data for OLAP by extending the MultiDimER and MADS approaches. Among other ad-hoc design approaches, [4] presents a formal framework to integrate spatial and multidimensional databases by using a *full containment* relationship between the hierarchy levels. In [5], the formal model from [6] is extended to support spatially overlapping hierarchies by exploiting the partial containment relations among data levels, thus leading to a more flexible modeling strategy. For a comprehensive review of spatial data warehouse design models the reader is referred to [7,8].

For modeling spatial data there are now several established approaches in the database community. [9,10] provide a robust discussion of spatial data types by introducing types such as *point*, *line* and *region* for simple and complex spatial objects and describe the associated spatial algebra. Composite spatial objects (collections of points, lines and regions) are presented as *spatial partitions* or *map* objects. Similarly, the Open GIS Consortium also provides a Reference Model [11] as a standard for a representing geo-spatial information. Qualitative spatial operations include topological relations [12] such as *disjoint, meet, overlap, equal, inside, contains, covers* and *coveredBy*, and cardinal direction relations. Quantitative relations on spatial objects include metric operations based on the size, shape and metric distances between objects or their components. All these operations can be used to query and analyze spatial data in the data warehouse.

3   Modeling Data Cubes with Complex Spatial Data

In this section, we describe a new approach to design and model cubes for complex, hierarchical, multi-structured data. Spatial data such as points, lines and polygons or regions often display such semantics. Consider for example, Figure 1 that illustrates a *complex region* object which consists of three regions with one of them inside the *hole* of another. The figure also displays a single *face* of a region object (which can also be regarded as a *simple region*) with multiple holes. To facilitate the handling of such complex data in multidimensional data cubes, we introduce the *regH* or *region-hierarchy* concept that aims to provide a clear hierarchical representation of a complex region that can be incorporated as first class citizens into spatial data cubes.

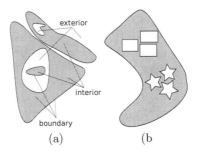

Fig. 1. Illustration of (a) a complex region object with three faces and its interior, boundary and exterior point sets, and (b) a single face, also denoted as a simple region with holes

The first step to accommodate complex spatial data in OLAP cubes is to explore and extract the common properties of all structured objects. Unsurprisingly, the hierarchy of a structured object can always be represented as a directed acyclic graph (DAG) or more strictly, as a tree.

Figure 2a provides a more detailed visualization of a complex region object with three faces labeled as F1, F2 and F3. The interior, exterior and boundary point sets of the region are also displayed. After performing a plain-sweep operation the cyclic order of the region's boundary is stored to represent a each face uniquely. Figure 2b shows such as tree structure of a *region* object. In the figure, *face*[ ], *holeCycle*[ ], and *segment*[ ] represent a list of faces, a list of hole cycles and a list of segments respectively. In the tree representation, the root node represents the structured object itself, and each child node represents a component named *sub-object*. A sub-object can further have a structure, which is represented in a sub-tree rooted with that sub-object node. For example, the region object in Figure 2a consists of a label component and a list of face components. Each face in the face list is also a structured object that contains a face label, an outer cycle, and a list of hole cycles, where both the outer cycle and the hole cycles are formed by segments lists.

Further, we observe that two types of sub-objects can be distinguished called *structured objects* (SO) and *base objects* (BO) [13]. Structured objects consist of sub-objects, and base objects are the smallest units that have no further inner structure. In a tree representation, each leaf node is a base object while internal nodes represent structured objects. A tree representation is a useful tool to describe hierarchical information at a conceptual level. However, to give a more precise description and to make it understandable to computers, a formal specification would be more appropriate. Therefore, we propose a generic *region-hierarchy* as an alternative of the tree representation for describing the hierarchical structure of region (or multi-polygon) objects. Thus, we can define the structure of a region object from Figure 2b with the following structure expression: $\langle region : SO \rangle := \langle regionLabel : BO \rangle \langle face : SO \rangle [\ ]$. In the expression, the left side of := gives the tag declaration of a region object and the right side of := gives the tag declarations of its components, in this case, the

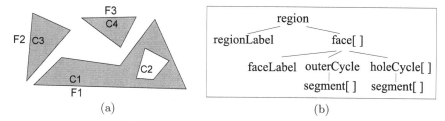

Fig. 2. Illustration of a complex structured region showing faces F1 (containing cycles C1 and C2), F2 (cycle C3) and F3 (cycle C4), and a hierarchical representation for the *region* (or multi-polygon) object

region label and the face list. Thus, we say the region object is *defined* by this structure expression. Using this representation, we can now recursively define the structure of structured sub-objects until no structured sub-objects are left undefined. A algebraic list of structure expressions then forms a specification. We call such a region specification that consists of structure expressions and is organized following some rules a *region-hierarchy* or *regH*.

It can be observed that the conversion from a tree representation to the regH is simple. The root node in a tree maps to the first structure expression in the region-hierarchy. Since all internal nodes are structured sub-objects and leaf nodes are base sub-objects, each internal node has exactly one corresponding expression in the regH, and leaf nodes require no structure expressions. The regH for a *region* object corresponding to the tree structure as in Figure 2a is thus defined as follows:

$$
\begin{aligned}
\langle region : SO\rangle &:= \langle regionLabel : BO\rangle\langle face : SO\rangle[\,]; \\
\langle face : SO\rangle &:= \langle faceLabel : BO\rangle\langle outerCycle : SO\rangle\langle holeCycle : SO\rangle[\,]; \\
\langle outerCycle : SO\rangle &:= \langle segment : BO\rangle[\,]; \\
\langle holeCycle : SO\rangle &:= \langle segment : BO\rangle[\,];
\end{aligned}
$$

The region-hierarchy provides a unique representation for complex multi-structured regions. This can be incorporated into data hierarchies in OLAP cubes by using the *extract* and *union* operators specified in section 5.

4 Data Model and C^3 Constructs

In this section, we present our data model for multidimensional data cubes supporting complex hierarchical spatial objects. These are extensions to the $\mathcal{B}ig\mathcal{C}ube$ approach [1], which is a conceptual metamodel for OLAP data defined over several levels of multidimensional data types.

To support complex objects in data warehouses we need new constructs that can handle data with complicated structures. However to keep the data warehouse modeling user-friendly, the approach taken for conceptual modeling and for applying aggregations must be simple. The C^3 constructs presented here satisfy both these requirements by providing the analyst with three simple and logical operations to construct data cubes, namely *categorization, containment* and *cubing*. Later by using classical OLAP operations such as slice, dice, rollup, drilldown and pivot, users can navigate and query the data cubes.

Categorization helps to create groupings of base data values based on their logical and physical relationships. Containment helps to organize the data categories into levels and place them in atleast a partial ordering in order to construct hierarchies. Cubing or Combination takes different categories of data from the various hierarchies an helps to create a data cube from them by specifying meaningful semantics. This is done by *associating* a set of members defining the cube to a set of measures placed inside the cube. Further, each of the C^3 constructs have a set of analysis functions associated with them, called the $\mathcal{A}$-*set*. An $\mathcal{A}$-*set* can include aggregation functions, query functions such as selections, and user-defined functions (UDFs). Since aggregations are fundamental to OLAP cubes, we first introduce the definition of an $\mathcal{A}$-*set* in Definition 1.

Definition 1. Analysis set or $\mathcal{A}$-*set*. *An analysis set or $\mathcal{A}$-set is a set of functions defined on the components of a data cube that are available for aggregation, querying and other user-defined operations. An $\mathcal{A}$-set has the following algebraic structure:*

$$\mathcal{A} = < \{a_1, ..., a_n\}, \{q1, ..., q_n\}, \{u1, ..., u_n\} >$$

where, a_i represents the ith aggregation function available, q_i the ith query function available and u_i the ith user-defined function (UDF) available in that particular cube component.

The $\mathcal{A}$-*set* is available as part of every category, hierarchy, perspective (data dimension) and subject of analysis (fact) in the data cube. The operations on the constituent elements of these cube components are specified by its corresponding $\mathcal{A}$-*set* .

Next, to facilitate the development of the C^3 constructs and additional OLAP formulations, we present some necessary terminology and definitions based on lattice theory [14] and OLAP formalisms [15,1].

Definition 2. Poset and its Top and Bottom Elements. *A partially ordered set or poset P is a set with an associated binary relation $\preceq$ that for any x, y and z, satisfies the following conditions:*

$$
\begin{aligned}
&Reflexivity: &&x \leq x \\
&Transitivity: &&\forall x \leq y \ and \ y \leq z \Rightarrow x \leq z \\
&Anti\text{-}Symmetry: &&\forall x \leq y \ and \ y \leq x \Rightarrow x = y
\end{aligned}
$$

For any $S \subseteq P$, $m \in P$ is a maximum or greatest element of S if $\forall x \in S : (m \geq x)$, and is represented as maxP. The minimum or least element of P is defined dually and represented as minP. A poset $(P, \preceq)$ is a totally or linearly ordered set (also called *chain*) if $\forall x, y \in P \Rightarrow x \leq y \text{ or } y \leq x$ With an induced order, any subset of a chain is also a chain.

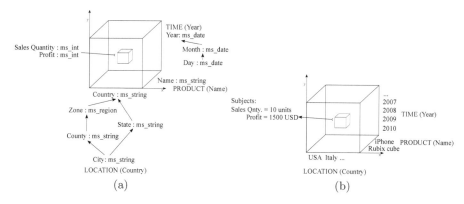

Fig. 3. *Product-Sales BigCube* (a) structure shows three *perspectives*: Time, Product and Location that define two *subjects* of interest: Sales-Quantity and Sales-Profit, and a (b) sample instance

The greatest element of P is called the top element of P and is represented as ⊤, and its dual, the least element of P is called the bottom element of P and represented as ⊥.

A non-empty finite set P always has a ⊤ element (by Zorn's Lemma). OLAP cubes often contain sparse data. To ensure that a bottom element exists and to make the OLAP operations generically applicable to all multidimensional cube elements, we perform a *lifting* procedure where given a poset P (with or without ⊥), take an element $0 \notin P$ and define $\preceq$ on $P_\perp = P \cup \{0\}$ as: $x \leq y$ iff $x = 0$ or $x \leq y$ in P.

Definition 3. Lattice. *Let P be a poset and let $S \subseteq P$. An element $u \in P$ called an upper bound of S if $\forall s \in S : (s \leq u)$. Dually, an element l in P is called the lower bound of S if $\forall s \in S : (s \geq l)$. The set of all upper bounds and lower bounds is represented as S^u and S^l respectively.*

$$S^u = \{u \in P \mid (\forall s \in S) : s \leq u\}$$
$$S^l = \{l \in P \mid (\forall s \in S) : s \geq l\}$$

An element x is called the supremum or the least upper bound of S if: $x \in S^u$ and $\forall x, y \in S^u : x \leq y$. This is represented as $supS$ or $\vee S$. The infimum or the greatest lower bound of S is defined dually and represented as $infS$ or $\wedge S$. A non-empty ordered set P is called a lattice if $\forall x, y \in P: x \vee y$ and $x \wedge y$.

Example: Consider the classical *product-sales* multidimensional dataset as shown in Figure 3a. The data cube has product, location and time perspectives (or data dimensions), and sales quantity and profit, for example, as the subjects of analysis (or facts). There are several hierarchies on location perspective such as {city,county,zone,country} and {city,state,country}. An instance of the data cube is shown in Figure 3b.

The basic data that needs to be stored (and later analyzed) in the data warehouse are values such as *1500* (of type *int*) for the profit in USD and *"Gainesville"* (of type *string*) for the City name. These are called the *base data values* of the dataset. The *base data type* for each value is indicated within parenthesis. According to their functionality, base data values can be either *members* when used for analysis along data dimensions, or *measures* when used to quantify factual data. Now we introduce the C^3 constructs and supporting OLAP formulations.

Real-world data always has some form of symmetric and asymmetric nature associated with its base data values. For e.g., all persons working in a University can be employees (symmetric relationship). Employees could be students, faculty or administrators (asymmetric relationship).

Definition 4. The first C in C^3: Categorization. *A categorization construct defines groupings of base data values based on the similarity of data as:* $\langle C, \mathcal{A}_c \rangle$ *where C is a category (collection of base values) and $\mathcal{A}$ is a set of analysis functions that can be applied on the elements of C. The base data values can be members or measures of the data warehouse.*

The exact semantics of *categorization relationships* are defined in one of three ways: *arbitrary* (for e.g., split 100 base values into 10 categories equally according to some criteria), *user-defined* (for e.g., *Gainesville, Chapel Hill* and *Madison* can be categorized as *College Towns*), or *according to real-world behavior* (such as spatial grouping, for e.g., *New Delhi, Berlin* and *Miami* can be categorized as *Cities*). Examples of $\mathcal{A}$-*set* functions on such categories include string concatenation, grouping (nesting) and the multiset constructor.

Example: In our case study, two examples of categories are City={("Gainesville", "Orlando", "Miami")} and Profit={ ("1500, "10000, "45000")} for the profit in USD. These are of types *string* and *int* respectively.

Definition 5. Category, Category Type and CATEGORY. *A category of elements $c \in S, S \subseteq BASE$, is a grouping of base data values such that a valid categorization relationship exists among the set of elements. A category type, provides the multiset data types for each category. The set of all available category types is defined as a kind CATEGORY.*

Categories help us to construct higher levels of $\mathcal{B}ig\mathcal{C}ube$ types, namely hierarchy, perspective and subject. Hierarchies are constructed using the containment construct over the categories, and perspectives are defined as a combination of hierarchies.

Definition 6. The second C in C^3: Containment. *The Containment construct helps to define hierarchies in the data. These data hierarchies are modeled as partially ordered sets (or posets) to use an extensible paradigm that supports different kinds of ragged and unbalanced hierarchies. The containment construct* *takes one or more data categories and builds a new partial ordering (data hierar-chy) from it. These data hierarchies are part of the generalized lattice structure that is established by the partial ordering of the constituent categories.*

The containment construct *is defined as a set inclusion from one level to another as* $< P, Q, \preceq, A >$*, where P and Q represent the categories of data on which* $\preceq$ *holds. The containment construct is analogous to a single path between two levels in a poset. The set of analysis functions that are applicable on a particular containment are available in* $\mathcal{A}$*. These functions can be applied which moving from the elements of one category to another. This helps to uniquely define operations on specific hierarchical paths in the perspectives of the cube.*

The semantics of the containment construct is defined by: (i) any arbitrary con-tainment, for e.g., fifteen base data values can be ordered into a four- level hier-archy using the structure of a balanced binary tree, (ii) user-defined containment : for e.g., products can be ordered into a hierarchy based on their selling price, (iii) according to real-world behavior: these reflect the fact that a higher level element *is a context of* the elements of the lower level, it *offers constraint to* the lower level values, it *evolves at a lower frequency than* the lower level elements, or that *it contains the* lower level elements. To define the multidimensional cube space we now need to third C in C^3 which is the cubing or combination con-struct. Before arriving at this, we first need to define the direct product of two lattices.

Definition 7. Direct Product. *The direct product* $P \times Q$ *of two posets P and Q is the set of all pairs* $(x, y), x \in P$ *and* $y \in Q$ *such that* $(x_1, y_1) \le (x_2, y_2)$*, iff* $x_1 \le x_2$ *in P and* $y_1 \le y_2$ *in Q.*

The direct product generates new ordered sets from existing posets. The direct product $L_1 \times L_2$ of two lattices L_1 and L_2 is a lattice with $\top := (x_1, y_1) \wedge (x_2, y_2) = (x_1 \wedge x_2, y_1 \wedge y_2)$ and $\bot := (x_1, y_1) \vee (x_2, y_2) = (x_1 \vee x_2, y_1 \vee y_2)$ for all $x_1, y_1 \in L_1$, $x_2, y_2 \in L_2$ and $(x_1, y_1), (x_2, y_2) \in L_1 \times L_2$. The use of direct product enables the creation of perspectives and subjects of analysis from a combination of member and measure value lattices.

Definition 8. The third C **in** C^3**: Cubing or Combination.** *The Combi-nation construct helps to map two semantically unique categories of data val-ues by a set of analysis functions. Given two ordered sets of categories P and Q, we define a order-preserving (monotone) mapping* $\varphi : P \to Q$ *such that if* $x \le y$ *in* $P \Rightarrow \varphi(x) \le \varphi(y)$ *in Q. Now, the combination construct is defined as* $\langle P, Q, \varphi, \mathcal{A} \rangle$*, where* $\mathcal{A}$ *is the set of analysis functions that can be applied on the combination relationship.*

A collection of lattices are together taken as *perspectives combine* to determine the cells of the $\mathcal{B}ig\mathcal{C}ube$, each containing one or more subjects of analysis. Se-mantically, subjects of analysis are thus unique, in that they are functionally determined by a set of perspectives, however, they are structurally similar to perspectives in being a collection of lattices.

Definition 9. $\mathcal{B}ig\mathcal{C}ube$. *Given a multidimensional dataset, the $\mathcal{B}ig\mathcal{C}ube$ cell structure is defined as an injective function from the n-dimensional space defined by the Cartesian product of n functionally independent perspectives P (identified by its members) to a set of r subjects (identified by its measures) S and quantifying the data for analysis as:*

$$f_\mathcal{B}\colon (P_1 \otimes P_2 \otimes \ldots \otimes P_n) \longrightarrow S_i$$
$$where\ i \in \{1, \ldots r\} \wedge (S_i, P) \in BASE$$

The complete $\mathcal{B}ig\mathcal{C}ube$ structure is now defined as a union of all its cells, given as:

$$\mathcal{B}ig\mathcal{C}ube\,(\mathcal{B}) = \bigcup_{i \in \{1, \ldots r\},\, f_\mathcal{B}} S_i$$

5   Spatial OLAP Formulations with the C^3 Constructs

In this section, we present OLAP formulations that help to apply analysis operations on data cubes with complex spatial data by using the C^3 constructs on the $\mathcal{B}ig\mathcal{C}ube$ model.

   First, we analyze how data cubes can be easily designed and modeled using the C^3 constructs as follows. The basic, low-level data types are available in the kind BASE. These include alphanumeric, time and geo-spatial data types. Elements of these types are the base data values which are first organized into Categories by using the *categorization* construct. This means that for e.g., "GNV", "LA", "MN" can be a category of cities. Analysis functions can be associated to the domain of the categories. For e.g., we can define a *union* function that takes the elements of cities and performs a union operation to yield a new polygon (country). The *geo_ construct* operation allows to extract any face of the complex region from the *regH* and construct a new region from it, for example, a city (Gainesville) from the country (USA). This is done using three topological operations *interior, boundary* and *closure* that remove possible anomalies such as dangling points or lines in the structure of the region. The interior $A°$ of a region A is given by the set of points contained inside the region object. The boundary ∂A gives the set of points covering the object. Thus, $A° \cup \partial A$ gives the closure $\overline{A}$ of A and this is used to construct the *regH* for the new spatial object from the base segment lists.

   The next step is to use the *containment* construct to define the hierarchical nature of the elements within the categories. This allows for the creation of explicit hierarchical paths between categories and the specification of analysis operations on each of them on uniquely or as a whole. An e.g., of analysis being using the containment construct is the often-used SUM aggregation operator on Sales quantity defined from City to State level.

   The final step is the creation of interacting lattice galaxies which is achieved by using the *combination* construct. The combination construct maps the categories in different hierarchies to others in the galaxy to create the data cube schema (cells). Elements of the data cube (objects within the cells) are identified by their defining cube perspectives.

We now provide examples of OLAP formulations that can applied on the $\mathcal{B}ig\mathcal{C}ube$ types and their instances thus defined.

Consider a $\mathcal{B}ig\mathcal{C}ube$ $\mathcal{B}$with n perspectives and i subjects of analysis. Let $m_1, \ldots, m_n$ be members from each of the n perspectives defining the set of measures $b_1, \ldots, b_i$. Then, the *restrict* operator returns the cell value by following the cubing from upto n perspectives of the $\mathcal{B}ig\mathcal{C}ube$ as $\langle\langle m_1, \ldots, m_n\rangle, b_1, \ldots, b_i\rangle$. For example, the sales quantity of iphones in Gainesville region in March 2011 is given by $\langle\langle$ *"iPhone"*, *"Gainesville"*, *"March2011"*$\rangle, 50\rangle$. The *slice* operation removes one perspective and returns the resulting $\mathcal{B}ig\mathcal{C}ube$ and *dice* performs slice across two or more perspectives. The resulting cells have the structure $\langle\langle m_1, \ldots, m_k\rangle, b_1, \ldots, b_i, \mathcal{A}\rangle$, where $1 \leq k \leq n$ and $\mathcal{A}$ provides the set of aggregation functions applicable on the measures of this subcube. These operations change the *state* of the $\mathcal{B}ig\mathcal{C}ube$, because any change in perspectives redefines the cells (measures) in it. *Pivot* rotates the perspectives for analysis across axes and returns a $\mathcal{B}ig\mathcal{C}ube$ with a different ordering of subjects. *Roll-up* performs specialization transformation over one or more constituent hierarchical levels, and *drill-down* applies the generalization transformation over one or more hierarchical levels. Given members $m_1 j, \ldots, m_k j$, $1 \leq j \leq n$ denoting k levels of ordering in each of the n perspectives, roll-up and drill-down operations yield a different aggregated state of the cube, as, $\langle\langle m_1 j, \ldots, m_k j\rangle, s_1, \ldots, s_i, \mathcal{A}_i\rangle$, where $s_i = f_i(b_1, \ldots, b_i), f \in \mathcal{A}$. *Drill-through* obtains the base data values with highest granularity. *Drill-across* combines several $\mathcal{B}ig\mathcal{C}ube$s in order to obtain aggregated data across the common perspectives.

For spatial measures, spatial relationships can be given directly by checking with the C^3 constructs and ordering in the poset. For example, to check for containment of a region X in region Y, we check the containment construct on X and Y. If $\langle X, Y, \preceq, A\rangle$ exists with $X \preceq Y$, then X is contained in Y. Similarly, the largest area contained contained in one or more given areas X_i is given by $\bot_X$. Dually, the smallest area containing one or more given areas Y_j is given by $\top_Y$. In this manner, lattice ordering along with the categorization, containment and cubing constructs provide a minimal set of formulations to create, manipulate and query spatial data cubes in a user-friendly manner.

6   Conclusions and Future Work

In this paper, we present a novel modeling strategy to incorporate support for complex spatial data in OLAP data cubes. First, we introduce a *region-hierarchy* that helps to represent a complex region object (with several faces and multiple holes) in a uniquely distinguishable manner. Then we present three new constructs called C^3, involving *categorization*, *containment* and *cubing* or *combination* that together help to easily build data cubes in a multidimensional environment. This provides a framework consisting of a user-friendly conceptual cube model that abstracts over logical design details such as star or snowflake schema and other implementation details. Later, new OLAP formulations are specified for manipulating spatial data hierarchies (*geo_construct*), and for querying. Overall, this *region-hierarchy* provides a unique approach to include spatial regions as first class citizens of data hierarchies in multidimensional data cubes. In the future, we plan to provide the complete set of OLAP operations for manipulating and querying spatial data cubes, and to provide translations from the hypercube to logical design (relational and multidimensional) to facilitate implementation of the SOLAP system.

References

1. Viswanathan, G., Schneider, M.: BigCube: A MetaModel for Managing Multidimensional Data. In: Proceedings of the 19th Int. Conf. on Software Engineering and Data Engineering (SEDE), pp. 237–242 (2010)
2. Rivest, S., Bedard, Y., Marchand, P.: Toward Better Support for Spatial Decision Making: Defining the Characteristics of Spatial On-line Analytical Processing (SOLAP). Geomatica-Ottawa 55(4), 539–555 (2001)
3. Malinowski, E., Zimányi, E.: Representing Spatiality in a Conceptual Multidimensional Model. In: 12th ACM Int. workshop on Geographic Information Systems, pp. 12–22. ACM, New York (2004)
4. Ferri, F., Pourabbas, E., Rafanelli, M., Ricci, F.: Extending Geographic Databases for a Query Language to Support Queries Involving Statistical Data. In: Int. Conf. on Scientific and Statistical Database Management, pp. 220–230. IEEE, Los Alamitos (2002)
5. Jensen, C., Kligys, A., Pedersen, T., Timko, I.: Multidimensional Data Modeling for Location-based Services. The VLDB Journal 13(1), 1–21 (2004)
6. Pedersen, T., Jensen, C., Dyreson, C.: A Foundation for Capturing and Querying Complex Multidimensional Data. Information Systems 26(5), 383–423 (2001)
7. Viswanathan, G., Schneider, M.: On the Requirements for User-Centric Spatial Data Warehousing and SOLAP. Database Systems for Advanced Applications, 144–155 (2011)
8. Malinowski, E., Zimányi, E.: Advanced Data Warehouse Design: From Conventional to Spatial and Temporal Applications. Springer, Heidelberg (2008)
9. Shekhar, S., Chawla, S.: Spatial Databases: A Tour. Prentice Hall, Englewood Cliffs (2003)
10. Guting, R., Schneider, M.: Realm-based Spatial Data Types: The ROSE algebra. The VLDB Journal 4(2), 243–286 (1995)
11. Open GIS Consortium: Reference Model, http://openlayers.org (accessed: April 11, 2010)
12. Schneider, M., Behr, T.: Topological Relationships between Complex Spatial Objects. ACM Transactions on Database Systems (TODS) 31(1), 39–81 (2006)
13. Chen, T., Khan, A., Schneider, M., Viswanathan, G.: iBLOB: Complex object management in databases through intelligent binary large objects. In: Dearle, A., Zicari, R.V. (eds.) ICOODB 2010. LNCS, vol. 6348, pp. 85–99. Springer, Heidelberg (2010)
14. Davey, B., Priestley, H.: Introduction to Lattices and Order. Cambridge University Press, Cambridge (2002)
15. Gray, J., Chaudhuri, S., Bosworth, A., Layman, A., Reichart, D., Venkatrao, M., Pellow, F., Pirahesh, H.: Data cube: A Relational Aggregation Operator Generalizing Group-by, Cross-tab, and Sub-totals. Data Mining and Knowledge Discovery 1(1), 29–53 (1997)

Multidimensional Database Design from Document-Centric XML Documents

Geneviève Pujolle[1], Franck Ravat[1], Olivier Teste[2],
Ronan Tournier[1], and Gilles Zurfluh[1]

[1] Université de Toulouse, Toulouse 1 Capitole
[2] Toulouse 3 Paul Sabatier
IRIT (UMR5505), Team SIG, 118 route de Narbonne, F-31062 Toulouse Cedex 9, France
{genevieve.pujolle,ravat,teste,tournier,zurfluh}@irit.fr

Abstract. Despite a decade of research in OLAP systems, very few works attempt to tackle the problem of analysing data extracted from XML text-rich documents. These documents are loosely structured XML documents mainly composed of text. This paper details conceptual design steps of multidimensional databases from such documents. With the use of an adapted multidimensional conceptual model, the design process allows the integration of data extracted from text-rich XML documents within an adapted OLAP system.

1 Introduction

OLAP (On-Line Analytical Processing) systems allow decision-makers to improve their management by consulting and analysing aggregated historical data with the use of multidimensional databases [15]. These systems are based on a well-mastered technique of numeric-centric data warehouses [30]. However, recent studies show that only 20% of corporate information system data is compatible with this numeric-centric approach [32]. The remaining 80%, namely "digital paperwork," mainly composed of text, stays out of reach of OLAP due to the lack of tools and adapted processing. Nowadays, analysts require integrating these data along with numerical business data.

This type of data does not have much structure. Recently, XML[1] technology has increased the availability of documents (notably textual documents) within corporate networks and provides a framework to structure textual data. However, despite numerous research works on numerical XML data integration [26], current OLAP systems do not cope with this data type. Due to the increasing amount of XML documents, integrating them into OLAP systems a new exciting challenge. In order to cope with textual data type, new design processes have to be developed.

1.1 Related Works: Design Processes

To our knowledge, design processes have only been specified for decisional information systems based on numerical data and not on textual data. These systems use

---

[1] XML, Extended Markup Language, from http://www.w3.org/XML/

A. Cuzzocrea and U. Dayal (Eds.): DaWaK 2011, LNCS 6862, pp. 51–65, 2011.

conceptual models to represent the multidimensional data. These conceptual multidimensional models describe schemas that represent analysis subjects as Facts (e.g. sale quantities) and analysis axes as Dimensions (e.g. where the sales were done). Three types of design processes have been considered.

Bottom-up approaches, are data-driven, i.e. multidimensional schemas are built from the analysis the available data sources [4,10,14,18,29]. Data sources are taken into account while analysis requirements are ignored. Notably in [4,10], the authors build a multidimensional schema from the E/R schemas of the data sources. This approach takes advantage of the data sources' semantics but, as the data source domain may be broad, this may require a great deal of resources and time.

Top-down approaches are requirement-driven, i.e. multidimensional schemas are derived from user requirements analysis [8,12,15,23,35]. For example, in [15] a general methodology is presented whereas in [23], the authors present a design process resting on UML notations. In these approaches, data sources are not taken into account, thus it is possible to design inconsistent schemas, due to unavailable data.

Finally *mixed approaches* combine the advantages of both previous processes [3,5,6,16,21,27]. User-requirements are translated into one (possibly more) "ideal" multidimensional schema and the analysis of data sources produces "candidate" multidimensional schemas. A confrontation phase ensures compatibility between the different schemas and allows designers to come up with a final schema.

However, all these processes have been conceived for models that rely on numerical analysis data. Moreover, identifying analysis indicators is hard in the context of textual documents. Despite several works on XML data integration [7,26] and numerous research on information extraction (see surveys such as [28,19]), these do not solve issues linked to identifying indicators. Thus, there is a need for:

- adapted multidimensional models running analyses on textual data extracted from XML documents;
- a design process taking into account user requirements as well as data sources.

Our objective is to offer a complete design process, taking into account textual content of XML documents in order to implement OLAP multidimensional databases.

1.2 Objectives and Contributions

Two types of XML documents exist [20]: *data-centric documents* are highly structured (e.g. the list of orders of an online sales Web service) and the order of the XML elements is not important (e.g. whether the sales order 1 is before or after the number 2 has no consequence); *document-centric documents* are more loosely structured and contain more text (e.g. press or scientific articles) and the order of the elements is very important (e.g. whether the first paragraph of the document is after or before the second paragraph has consequences). Using document-centric XML documents (particularly text-rich ones) in OLAP environments requires a specific model [24] that has no pre-defined analysis subjects (facts) as well as an adapted integration process [25].

The major objective of this paper is to detail the major steps of our design process [25] to build OLAP systems from document-centric XML documents. More specifically, the paper focuses on the mixed design process taking into account the user requirements as well as the available data sources.

The rest of this paper is organised as follows: section 2 presents the whole design process; section 3 is centred on the analysis of the user requirements in order to generate the multidimensional conceptual schema; section 4 deals with the confrontation phase between the obtained conceptual schema and the data sources; finally, section 5 details the implementation steps.

2 Overview of the Design Process

The design process is based on an interactive and incremental process in order to take into account user-requirements evolution and data sources' modifications. Each iteration is based on a mixed approach: first user-requirements are translated into a multidimensional database schema; second, the data sources are analysed in order to be integrated within the multidimensional database according to a bottom-up approach.

The design process starts by a concurrent analysis of the user requirements expressed through a conceptual schema (see stage 1 in **Fig. 1**) and the data sources, i.e. XML text-rich documents (see stage 2). A confrontation stage follows, ensuring compatibility between the data sources and the future multidimensional database–described by the conceptual schema (stage 3). A synonym dictionary is used in order to ease the process. Incompatibilities may then arise. They represent the missing or incompatible data in the sources to allow loading the multidimensional database. In case of incompatibility, either user requirements are revised (stage 4a) or data sources are enriched (stage 4b). This process is iterated until no more incompatibilities arise. Then, the structures of the multidimensional database are created (stage 5a) and loaded with data extracted from the data sources (stage 5b).

The different stages of our design process have been identified in [25]. In this paper, compared to our previous publication [25], we describe formally two of these stages: **the formal specification of the conceptual multidimensional schema from user/analysis requirements (1) and its semi-automatic validation during the confrontation phase (3).** A word is given on final implementation stages (5a,5b). We mainly focused our attention on stages 1 and 3 for two main reasons: 1) the fact that not only numerical data but also textual data may be used as analysis indicators requires new means for specifying user-requirements. And 2) XML data structures require an adapted confrontation process. Note that due to lack of space, the source analysis (2) will not be detailed.

The synonym dictionary is built from stages 1 and 2 of the design process. Its goal is to associate a system identifier (id) to each entry of the dictionary (either a lone term or a set of synonym terms). This id is used by the system during the automatic stages. The dictionary content is filled with element names used in the user-requirement analysis, in the multidimensional schema and by extracting available element names in the XML document sources. Associated user entries help in solving conflicts, e.g. by differentiating synonyms from homonyms.

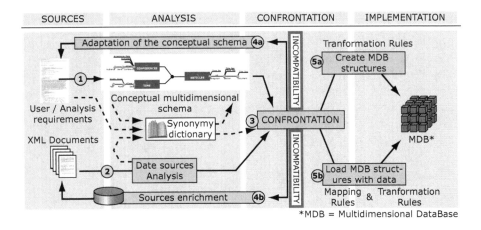

Fig. 1. General overview of the design process composed of 5 different stages

3   From User Requirement analysis to a Multidimensional Schema

The analysis of user-requirements allows the specification of a multidimensional database with a conceptual schema that models the available structures for specifying analyses (stage 1 in **Fig. 1**). Two steps compose this process: collecting user-requirements and specifying the conceptual schema from these requirements.

3.1   Collecting Requirements and Building a Requirement Matrix

The objective of this step is to obtain the list of the attributes used for analyses and to generate a conceptual multidimensional schema of the multidimensional database. This phase is divided into: 1) collect user-requirements; 2) translate requirements into typical analytical queries; 3) build the attribute list and, from that list, create a requirement matrix in order to 4) identify attributes that will interact together.

User requirements are collected from: *interviews* that provide a first description of typical analytical queries [33] (OLAP queries); the *analysis of documents* that are used by the decision-makers; and *questionnaires* that provide valuable complementary information on the domain of expertise.

Interviews and analysis of decision makers' documents provide the information necessary to write typical analytical queries expressed in a pseudo-query language. In some complex cases user-requirements are translated into dimensional pivot tables (left upper part of **Fig. 2**) for requirement validation [1,33]. Then, these tables are also translated into the pseudo-language. A query q is of the form: "*Analyse* what analysis subject (s) *according to* which analysis axes $(a_1...a_n)$ *for* what data restrictions $(r_1...r_m)$" (see examples in **Fig. 2**). The s is the analysis subject indicator, the a_i are attributes of analysis indicators and r_i are SQL-like restrictions on an attribute (called r_i for simplicity). This phase aims at identifying the attributes.

q_1: **Analyse** the number of references **according to** the author names of the article and their institute **and according to** the name of conferences where the articles was published **for** authors of the institute inst1.

q_2: **Analyse** the content of articles **according to** the author (name, team and institute or status) **and according to** the year of publication of the article **for** article contents limited to section of the type introduction.

q_3: **Analyse** the number of articles **according to** the name of the author **and according to** the years of publication **for** publications in a conference of international audience.

q_4: **Analyse** the number of project reports **according to** the authors **and according to** the month and year of publication of the report **for** reports of scientific type.

COUNT (Articles)	Institute	Inst1		
	Author	Au1	Au2	Au3
Conferences				
DaWaK		3	2	1
DEXA		2	-	-
CAiSE		1	1	2
Institute="Inst1"				

q_1 expressed through a pivot table

q_1=(s=Reference, a_1=name_author, a_2=institute, a_3=name_conference, r_1=institute)

q_1 expressed formally

Fig. 2. Example of typical queries (note that q_2 is based on textual data analysis)

In each query q, each s, a_i and r_i is an attributes. An attribute list A is constructed from all $q \in Q$ (the set of user-queries). The attributes are placed in a requirement matrix.

> **Definition.** The *requirement matrix* $M=A \times A$ is a square binary matrix, with the list of attributes in lines (future analysis subjects) and in columns (future analysis axes).

The matrix is built in three steps: 1) construction; 2) simplification; and 3) reordering. For *construction*, for i (respectively j) an attribute in line i (resp. in column j), M is defined such that:

- $M(i,j)=1$ ($i \neq j$) if $\exists\ q=(s,a_1...a_n,r_1...r_m) \in Q$ / ($s=i$ and $\exists\ a_k \in (a_1...a_n)$ and $a_k=j$). An attribute in line i (an analysis subject indicator), is analysed according to an attribute in column j (an analysis axis);
- $M(i,j)=1$ ($i=j$) if $\exists\ q=(s,a_1...a_n,r_1...r_m) \in Q$ / ($\exists\ r_k \in (r_1...r_m)$ and $r_k=i$). An attribute is used as a restriction;
- $M(i,j)=0$ ($\forall i, \forall j$) in all other cases

M represents the interactions between attributes: more precisely, subjects (lines) and analysis axes (columns) (see left part of **Fig. 3**). However, these attributes do not all interact with one another, thus it is necessary to isolate attribute *interaction groups*. This starts with a *simplification*: empty lines—attribute that are not used as subjects— or empty columns—attributes that are not used as analysis axes— are removed. The process is: For each line l, if $\forall j \neq l$, $M(l,j)=0$, l is removed; For each column c, if $\forall i \neq c$, $M(i,c)=0$ c is removed; In the removed lines, if $M(l,c)=1$ and $l=c$, then l (or c) was only a restriction r_i in Q. The information that l was associated with some s in some q is kept and l is added to a set R.

This is followed by a line and column *reordering* for grouping the cells with "1" around the diagonal of the matrix. The goal is to get the matrix as close as possible to a *block diagonal matrix*: a diagonal matrix in which all diagonal elements are square matrices of any size (even 1×1) and off-diagonal elements are 0. The solution is a reorganised matrix (*RM*) composed of pseudo-blocks that are diagonal matrix blocks that may partially overlap.

Finding a solution to this problem is similar to solving the travelling salesman problem. In order to offer an automatic solution, we used a genetic algorithm [9] (a good technique for the salesman problem [22]). The algorithm uses **chromosomes** to express the solution (the order of the lines and columns) and a fitness function that **maximises** the number of pseudo-blocks while **minimising** the overlap between these blocks. The algorithm runs with a population of a few thousands individuals over approximately 500 generations. For the moment, only **crossover** (of 80%) without **mutations** is performed. In the end, the pseudo-blocks represent attributes that interact together during analyses with an eventual share of attributes with another interaction group. In the right part of **Fig. 3**, two groups have been identified: the analysis of scientific publications (light gray/yellow) and the analysis of reports (dark grey/green). The shared part is the grey/red column headers. This part indicates that some information is shared between the two groups (here authors and dates).

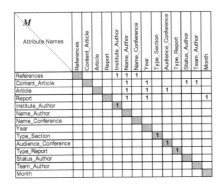
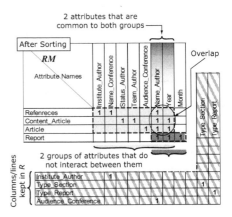

Fig. 3. Left: the requirement matrix (*M*); right: the same matrix reorganised (*RM*) with two groups identified and in grey the columns and the lines ignored during the reorganisation. Also, associated to R, (r=type_section, s=content), from q_2 and (r=type_report, s=report) from q_4.

Note that, although in our simple example, there is a complete disjunction between analysis subjects and analysis axes; it is not always the case in real-life examples.

The output of the algorithm is the set R and the reorganised matrix RM. This information will allow the design of a galaxy schema described hereafter.

3.2 Multidimensional Model for Documents: A Galaxy

For specifying analyses on text-rich XML documents (document-centric XML documents), there is a need for a model that: 1) represents text-rich document specificities; and 2) eases conceptual representation of the multidimensional structures while avoiding to provide limitations of predefined solutions to the user. To answer these requirements we have previously defined a specific model named Galaxy [24].

The galaxy is based on: 1) a unique dimension concept that represents an analysis axis, but also a possible analysis subject; and 2) groupings of these dimensions to show their compatibility for analysis specification. The model also allows linking attributes together (e.g. references of an article are articles themselves thus authors of cited articles may be used combined with authors of citing articles). Due to lack of space, this will not be detailed (consult [24,25] for more details).This model has the advantage of generalising all traditional models based on facts and dimensions (see [31] for a survey). In the galaxy model, the fact (subject of analysis) is not predefined but will be specified when querying as it will be one of the dimensions.

Definition: A *Galaxy* $G = (D^G, Star^G, Lk^G)$ where
- $D^G = \{D_1, \ldots, D_n\}$ is a set of *dimensions*,
- $Star^G : D_i \rightarrow 2^{D_i}$ is a function that associates each dimension D_i to its linked dimensions $D_j \in D^G$ $(D_j \neq D_i)$. This expression models nodes c_z (or cliques[2]) that may be expressed through: $\{D_{c1}, \ldots, D_{cn}\} \subseteq D^G \mid \forall i,j \in [c_1..c_n], i \neq j, \exists D_i \rightarrow 2^{Dj} \in Star^G$. This represents dimensions compatible within a same analysis.[3]
- $Lk^G = \{g_1, g_2, \ldots\}$ is a set of functions associating some attribute instances together (see [24] for more details).

A dimension is composed *attributes*, representing graduations of an analysis axis.

Definition: A *dimension* $D=(A^D, H^D, I^D, IStar^D)$ where:
- $A^D = \{a^D_1, \ldots, a^D_r\}$ is a set of *attributes*,
- $H^D = \{H^D_1, \ldots, H^D_s\}$ is a set of *hierarchies*,
- $I^D = \{i^D_1, \ldots, i^D_t\}$ is a set of *dimension instances*. Each attribute has a value for each instance $a^D_u(i^D_x)$, called an *attribute instance*.
- $IStar^D = \{IStar_1^D, IStar_2^D \ldots\}$ is set of functions $IStar_i^D : I^D \rightarrow \left(I^{D_1}\right)^* \times \ldots \times \left(I^{D_n}\right)^*$, each associating the instances of the D dimension to the instances of other linked dimensions through $Star^G$ $(\forall k \in [1..n], D_k \in D^G, D_k \neq D$ and $D_k \in Star^G(D)$, i.e. D_k is associated/linked to D).[2]

The attributes are hierarchically organised in the dimensions. Two types of attributes exist: *parameters* (a graduation of the analysis axis) and *weak attributes* (complementary data to the graduation—the parameter).

Definition: A *hierarchy* noted H^D_i or $H=(Param^H, Weak^H)$ where:
- $Param^H = <p^H_1, \ldots, p^H_{np}>$ is an ordered set of attributes, called *parameters*, which represent the levels of granularity of the dimension, $\forall k \in [1..n_p], p^H_k \in A^D$ and $p^H_1 = a^D_1$;
- $Weak^H : Param^H \rightarrow 2^{A^D - Param^H}$ is an application possibly associating *weak attributes* to parameters, completing the parameter semantic.

To ease the understanding of this model, we provide an associated graphic formalism [24] (inspired by [10]).

Example. In **Fig.** 4 a decision maker wishes to analyse the performance of research institutes. Two dimension groups (cliques) represent those which are compatible

---

[2] The notation $(I)^*$ represents a finite set of elements of I.

during a same analysis. The decision maker analyses scientific articles published at a certain date, in a certain conference (or journal) by authors; but he also analyses project reports published by authors at a certain date. In this example, each analysis axis and each potential analysis subject is represented with dimensions. For example: $D^{AUTHORS} = (A^{AUTHORS}=\{Author, Team, Institute, Status\}, H^{AUTHORS}=\{HA,HSt\}...)$

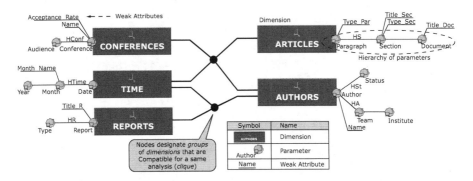

Fig. 4. The analysis of scientific articles and research reports modeled with a galaxy schema

3.3 Translating Requirements into a Multidimensional Schema

The galaxy schema will be designed from the matrix. Recall that user-requirements, specified by decision makers, are available through a cleaned and reorganised matrix (**Fig. 3**). From this matrix, the following process defines the elements of the galaxy schema: D^G, $Star^G$, for each $D \in D^G$: A^D, H^D and for each $H \in H^D$: $Param^H$ and $Weak^H$.

The design process of a galaxy schema from a requirement matrix follows 7 steps. Each step will be illustrated through an example given from **Fig. 3**; our objective being the construction of the galaxy in **Fig. 4**.

Step 1: determine useful attributes. List the line and column attributes. Add to the column attributes the set R.
Example. In our example:

– Line attributes: *References, Content_Article, Article, Report*;
– Column Attributes: *Institute_Author, Name_Conference, Status_Author, Team_Author, Audience_Conference, Name_Author, Year, Month, Type_Section, Type_Report*.

Step 2: Determining dimensions from column attributes. A dimension is specified as a grouping of column attributes. The dimension name is chosen to be fully representative of the concept described by its attributes. Attributes are manually grouped based on domain concept knowledge. Attributes in R are grouped with the help of the s associated attribute.
Example. Attribute grouping generates the A^D sets of each $D \in D^G$:

– A^{TIME}: *Month, Year*;
– $A^{AUTHORS}$: *Institute_Author, Status_Author, Name_Author, Team_Author*;
– $A^{CONFERENCES}$: *Name_Conferences, Audience_Conference*;

– $A^{ARTICLES}$: *Type_Section*;
– $A^{REPORTS}$: *Type_Report*.

Step 3: Determining dimensions from line attributes. Each line attribute that is not already associated to a dimension is added either to an existing dimension of a new dimension. The following constraint is applied: a line attribute that has a 1 with a column attribute **cannot** be grouped in the same dimension as the latter. Indeed, the 1 means that the line attribute is an analysis subject for the analysis axis (the dimension) represented by the column attribute. They both cannot describe the same dimension. Formally: a_i in line i is added to D provided that: $\nexists a_j \in A^D$ ($j{\neq}i$) / $M(i,j) = 1$. This constraint can be processed automatically.

Example. In our example, the following additions to dimensions are done:

– $A^{ARTICLES}$: *Content_Article, Article, References*;
– $A^{REPORTS}$: *Report*.

Step 4: Determining dimension hierarchies. The specification of dimension hierarchies is manually done, based on domain knowledge and source analysis. *Functional dependencies* such as one-to-many relationships in the data sources, i.e. cardinalities $[1..*]{\rightarrow}[1..1]$ between attributes a_1 and a_2, provide valuable information on how to hierarchically organise data, in this case, $Param^H = <a_1, a_2>$. Moreover, the tree-like structure of source XML documents can also be used to put in light hierarchies. Missing values are systematically handled by a generic "undefined" value. Any attribute used for grouping (in the a_i statements in Q) is placed in $Param^H$ sets, all others are placed in the $Weak^H$ sets and associated to the corresponding p_i in the $Param^H$ set (e.g. in $HTime$, $Month{\rightarrow}2^{Month\_Name}$).

Example. In our example:

– Domain knowledge allows the definition of: $Param^{HTime} = <Date,Month,Year>$;
– The tree-like DTD structure of the XML documents (scientific articles) shows the following hierarchy: $Param^{ARTICLES} = <Section,Document>$ (the new parameter *Document* will probably replace *Content_Article* and *Article* attributes, see step 7)

Step 5: Enrich dimensions. The designer, depending on his/her domain knowledge expertise and of the source analysis, can complement the schema by adding other attributes. The source analysis may provide new attributes previously unthought-of. The new attributes are either inserted in existing hierarchies or in new ones.

Example. In our example, a Paragraph attribute will be added to the ARTICLES Dimension: $Param^{ARTICLES} = <Paragraph,Section,Document>$; In the CONFERENCES dimension will be enriched by the Accept_Rate attribute (that appears in the DTD of the articles in the document sources). The corresponding level is the "conference" level, $Weak^{HConf}$: $Conference{\rightarrow}2^{Accept\_Rate}$.

Step 6: Determining the interactions between the dimensions. The requirement matrix shows blocks and pseudo-blocks of attributes. Each block determines a clique: c_i (i.e. the possible interaction between the attributes). Each attribute being associated to a dimension, interactions between the dimensions may be automatically determined and thus the functions $Star^G$ may be specified.

Example. In our example, 2 attribute blocks determine 2 dimension interaction groups

- Scientific article analysis: $D^{AUTHORS}$, $D^{ARTICLES}$, $D^{CONFERENCES}$ and D^{TIME};
- Reports analysis: $D^{REPORTS}$, $D^{AUTHORS}$ and D^{TIME}.

Step 7: Merging common parts and final adjustments. In this step, redundant attributes are removed or replaced, dimensions are eventually shared between cliques and the final schema is obtained. These adjustments are incorporated into the synonym dictionary, thus enriching the synonym sets.

Example. In our example:

- Report authors and article authors happen to have the same available information in the sources, thus both $D^{AUTHORS}$ dimensions will be fused;
- For similar reasons, the D^{TIME} dimensions will be fused;
- The attributes of $D^{ARTICLES}$: *Content_Article* and *Article* will be replaced by the more detailed ones found in phase 4: *Paragraph*, *Section* and *Document*.

Finally, the galaxy schema is obtained (see **Fig. 4**).

4   Confrontation

The galaxy schema represents only user-requirements. Thus the galaxy has to be validated with the data sources (stage 3 of our design process, see **Fig. 1**). The goal of this stage is to ensure that the multidimensional structures represented by the galaxy schema will be loaded with compatible data from the data sources. As this is a tedious and critical task we offer a semi-automatic process.

This process converts the galaxy schema into XML document structure (DTD). This structure eases the comparison with the source documents. These latter are supposed to be uniform and are also represented by a DTD. The DTD comparison generates a set of mapping rules that will transform the XML elements of the document source DTD into elements of the Galaxy DTD (see **Fig. 5**). A mapping rule is a link between a source element and a galaxy attribute: an XPath expression [34] designates the elements in the data sources and a database column name designates the galaxy attribute.

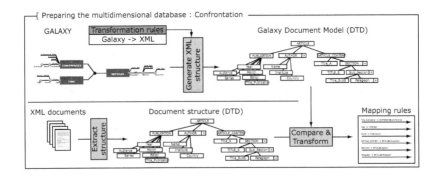

Fig. 5. Details of the confrontation phase

In a first step, the galaxy schema is converted into a DTD. Formally, for a galaxy G there exists a set (named C^G) composed of i cliques (noted c_i). All dimensions of a clique c_i are represented by D^{ci}, $D^{ci} \subseteq D^G$. The following algorithm is used to generate a DTD for each clique of the galaxy:

```
For each c_i in C^G Do
  Create new DTD_Galaxy_G_ci;
  Create new Element_Galaxy_G_root_ci;
  Append Element_Galaxy_G_root_ci to DTD_Galaxy_G;
  For each Di in Dci Do
    Create new Element_Dim_Di;
    Append Element_Dim_Di to Element_Galaxy_G_root_ci;
    For each H_i in H^Di Do
      Element_attribute_previous = Element_Dim_Di;
      For each p_i in Param^Hi Do
        Create new Element_Attribute_pi;
        Append Element_Attribute_pi to Element_Attribute_previous;
        Element_Attribute_previous := Element_Attribute_pi;
        For each wa_i in Weak^Hi and wa_i associated to p_i Do
          Create new Element_Attribute_wai;
          Append Element_Attribute_wai to Element_Attribute_previous;
        End_For;
      End_For;
    End_For;
  End_For;
End_For;
```

In this algorithm, the functions *"Create new element..."* create an XML element that represent one of the four corresponding conceptual element of the galaxy: a clique (the root of the generated DTD), a dimension, a parameter or a weak attribute. This XML element is composed of an XML attribute *Id* (the system identifier taken from the dictionary) and possibly other sub elements inserted by the algorithm. More specifically, an XML element that represents an attribute of the galaxy ("Element_Attribute_...") is composed of an identifier and a Content element (that contains the attribute data (PCDATA in XML DTD terminology) as well as child elements that represent other elements of the galaxy.

The confrontation step proceeds by associating elements of the *source DTD*, the DTD of the XML document sources and the *destination DTD*, the DTD that represents the galaxy. This process is semi-automatic and done by comparing the XML element names and with the help of the system identifiers from the dictionary. In ambiguous cases, the designer takes the final decision in associating source and destination elements (i.e. the XML tags) using suggestions made by the system.

Although the data source analysis is out of the scope of this paper, a few relevant features should be mentioned. To limit conflicts a pre-processing step is done on each XML document source. This step enriches the dictionary. For example, the INEX scientific journal collection [13] uses the tags <sec> for sections and <p> for paragraphs whereas the galaxy uses <section> and <paragraph>. Only XML elements are considered: attributes are either dropped or converted into sub-elements if source structure transformation can be considered. XML REF links are either ignored to avoid cycles or, if source modification is possible, replaced by the XML elements the REF points to. Elements need not necessarily be hierarchically organized in the sources: elements laid out flat can also be handled if cardinalities implied by the galaxy hierarchies are respected—e.g. elements author and institute can be laid out flat but there should only be one institute for each group of authors.

During the confrontation, other more complex incompatibilities may arise. The designer, either 1) modifies the user-requirements (the analysis objectives) implying a change in the galaxy schema; or 2) enriches the data sources with complementary data or documents (see stages 4a and 4b in **Fig. 1**). More details are provided in [25].

The entire process is iterated until no more errors arise and all the destination elements are linked, i.e. all elements of the galaxy—structures of the multidimensional database—have a data source element linked. Thus the implementation of the multidimensional database can be considered.

5   Multidimensional Database Implementation

Implementing the multidimensional database is possible once the galaxy schema is compatible with the data sources (stages 5a and 5b of **Fig. 1**). This is done with an automatic process according to two steps. This process is based on two sets of conversion rules. First, multidimensional database structures are generated from the galaxy schema (step 1 in **Fig. 6**). Second, data extracted from XML document sources is loaded within the structures of the multidimensional database (step 2 in **Fig. 6**).

During the first step, the galaxy schema is implemented with the use of conversion rules within an R–OLAP architecture (Relational-OLAP [15]), the most used OLAP implementation. Every dimension is converted into a relation (a table) and cliques are implemented through foreign keys. In the second step, correspondence rules, generated during the confrontation, are used to extract and transform the source XML document data. The conversion rules allow XML data to be compatible with the ROLAP structures previously created: character strings that hold numerical values are converted into numerical types before being inserted into the database tables. This may be done with a Model Driven Architecture (MDA) based process such as the one presented in [2].

Data loading is done with XQuery queries [34]. The queries assemble the XPath expressions of the mapping rules generated in the confrontation stage. The expressions are assembled in `for` and `let` expressions depending on the data source structure and cardinalities in the galaxy structure. Note that incompatible cases have been processed in the previous phase. Loading into the R-OLAP tables is done with SQL/XML instructions that use the generated XQuery expressions [17].

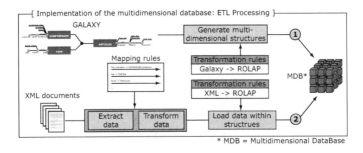

Fig. 6. Implementation of the structure (1) and the content (2) of the multidimensional database

6 Conclusion and Future Works

In order to get closer to the integration of a 100% of decisional data into OLAP systems we have specified a design process to implement OLAP systems loaded with text-rich XML document data. The method associates a galaxy model [24] to an adapted design process. Compared to existing multidimensional models, the galaxy model is used for the following advantages: 1) it is based on the unique dimension concept; 2) it takes into account document specificities (structure described with XML tags and textual content); 3) it provides document analysis perspectives that are not limited to predefined indicators; and 4) it generalises actual multidimensional models.

The design process has the advantage of taking into account simultaneously user requirements and the available data sources: 1) user requirements are expressed through typical analysis queries that are then translated into a galaxy schema; while 2) the data sources (documents) are analysed. Our mixed approach has the advantage to ease the implementation by using a semi-automatic confrontation stage: the elements of the galaxy schema are associated to elements in the XML document sources, using a pivot model (XML DTDs). Conflicts that may arise are solved through an iterative process. The third stage generates mapping rules that are used to during a fourth step to implement the multidimensional database schema, whose structure is directly derived from the galaxy schema. A CASE tool [25] (not detailed in this paper) completes the design process by assisting the user during the different design steps. The tool is a java graphical client linked to an Oracle 11g database running XMLDB. The process is done using Oracle SQL/XML structures and queries [17].

Among future works, we consider associating the design process to a formal specification of data source analysis for the integration of XML document sources that have several heterogeneous structures and reuse research from the data integration community [28,19]. I.e. XML documents with missing elements or elements described in several different formats. Moreover, a module is being currently implemented to allow the system to suggest to the user the possible associations between elements of the DTD that represents the XML document sources and the elements of the galaxy schema. This module uses the synonym dictionary.

References

1. Annoni, E., Ravat, F., Teste, O., Zurfluh, G.: Towards Multidimensional Requirement Design. In: Tjoa, A.M., Trujillo, J. (eds.) DaWaK 2006. LNCS, vol. 4081, pp. 75–84. Springer, Heidelberg (2006)
2. Atigui, F., Ravat, F., Tournier, R., Zurfluh, G.: A Unified Model Driven Methodology for Data Warehouses and ETL design. In: 13th Intl. Conf. on Enterprise Information Systems, ICEIS (to appear, 2011)
3. Bonifati, A., Cattaneo, F., Ceri, S., Fuggetta, A., Paraboschi, S.: Designing data marts for data Warehouses. ACM Trans. Softw. Eng. Methodol. 10(4), 452–483 (2001)
4. Cabibbo, L., Torlone, R.: A Logical Approach to Multidimensional Databases. In: Schek, H.-J., Saltor, F., Ramos, I., Alonso, G. (eds.) EDBT 1998. LNCS, vol. 1377, pp. 183–197. Springer, Heidelberg (1998)

5. Carneiro, L., Brayner, A.: X-META: A methodology for data warehouse design with metadata management. In: 4th Intl. Workshop Design and Management of Data Warehouses (DMDW). CEUR Workshop Proceedings (CEUR-WS.org), vol. 58, pp. 13–22 (2002)
6. Cavero, J.M., Piattini, M., Marcos, E.: MIDEA: A Multidimensional Data Warehouse Methodology. In: 3rd Intl. Conf. on Enterprise Information Systems (ICEIS 2001), vol. 1, pp. 138–144. INSTICC Press (2001)
7. Draper, D., Halevy, A.Y., Weld, D.S.: The Nimble XML Data Integration System. In: Proc. of the 17th Intl. Conf. on Data Engineering (ICDE), pp. 155–160. IEEE Comp. Society, Los Alamitos (2001)
8. Giorgini, P., Rizzi, S., Garzetti, M.: Goal-oriented requirement analysis for datawarehouse design. In: Proc. of 8th Int. Workshop on Data Warehousing and OLAP (DOLAP), pp. 47–56. ACM Press, New York (2005)
9. Goldberg, D.E.: Genetic Algorithms in Search, Optimization and Machine Learning. Addison-Wesley Longman Publishing Co., Amsterdam (1989)
10. Golfarelli, M., Rizzi, S.: Methodological Framework for Data Warehouse Design. In: ACM 1st Intl. Workshop on Data Warehousing and OLAP (DOLAP), pp. 3–9. ACM Press, New York (1998)
11. Gyssens, M., Lakshmanan, L.V.S.: A Foundation for Multi-dimensional Databases. In: 23rd Intl. Conf. on Very Large Data Bases (VLDB), pp. 106–115. Morgan Kaufmann, San Francisco (1997)
12. Hüsemann, B., Lechtenbörger, J., Vossen, G.: Conceptual data warehouse modeling. In: Proc. of 2nd Int. Workshop on Design and Management of Data Warehouses (DMDW). CEUR Workshop Proceedings (CEUR-WS.org), vol. 28, p. 6 (2000)
13. INEX, INitiative for the Evaluation of XML Retrieval (INEX), XML document collection used until 2005 (2005), http://inex.is.informatik.uni-duisburg.de/
14. Jensen, M.R., Holmgren, T., Pedersen, T.B.: Discovering Multidimensional Structure in Relational Data. In: Kambayashi, Y., Mohania, M., Wöß, W. (eds.) DaWaK 2004. LNCS, vol. 3181, pp. 138–148. Springer, Heidelberg (2004)
15. Kimball, R.: The data warehouse toolkit. John Wiley and Sons, Chichester (1996); 2nd edn. (2003)
16. Luján-Mora, S., Trujillo, J.: A Comprehensive Method for Data Warehouse Design. In: 5th Intl. Workshop on Design and Management of Data Warehouses (DMDW 2003). CEUR Workshop Proceedings (CEUR-WS.org), vol. 77 (2003)
17. Melton, J., Buxton, S.: Querying XML, XQuery, XPath and SQL/XML in context. Elsevier, Morgan Kaufman (2006)
18. Moody, D., Kortink, M.: From enterprise models to dimensional models: a methodology for data warehouse and data mart design. In: Proc. of 2nd Int. Workshop on Design and Management of Data Warehouses (DMDW). CEUR Workshop Proceedings (CEUR-WS.org), vol. 28, p. 5 (2000)
19. Noy, N.F.: Semantic integration: a survey of ontology-based approaches. SIGMOD Record 33(4), 65–70 (2004)
20. Pérez, J.M., Berlanga, R., Aramburu, M.J., Pedersen, T.B.: Integrating Data Warehouses with Web Data: A Survey. IEEE Trans. on Knowledge and Data Engineering (TKDE) 20(7), 940–955 (2008)
21. Phipps, C., Davis, K.C.: Automating data warehouse conceptual schema design and evaluation. In: 4th Intl. Workshop on Design and Management of Data Warehouses (DMDW). CEUR Workshop Proceedings (CEUR-WS., vol. 58, pp. 23–32 (2002)

22. Potvin, J.-Y.: Genetic algorithms for the traveling salesman problem. Annals of Operations Research 63(3), 337–370 (1996)

23. Prat, N., Akoka, J., Comyn-Wattiau, I.: A UML-based data warehouse design method. Decision Support System 42(3), 1449–1473 (2006)

24. Ravat, F., Teste, O., Tournier, R., Zurlfluh, G.: A Conceptual Model for Multidimensional Analysis of Documents. In: Parent, C., Schewe, K.-D., Storey, V.C., Thalheim, B. (eds.) ER 2007. LNCS, vol. 4801, pp. 550–565. Springer, Heidelberg (2007)

25. Ravat, F., Teste, O., Tournier, R., Zurfluh, G.: Designing and Implementing OLAP Systems from XML Documents. In: Submitted to Annals of Information Systems (AoIS), Special Issue on New Trends in Data Warehousing and Data Analysis. Springer, Heidelberg

26. Ravat, F., Teste, O., Tournier, R., Zurfluh, G.: Finding an Application-Appropriate Model for XML Data Warehouses. Information Systems (IS) 36(6), 662–687 (2010)

27. Romero, O., Abello, A.: A framework for multidimensional design of data warehouses from ontologies. J. Data & Knowledge Engineering 69(11), 1138–1157 (2010)

28. Sarawagi, S.: Information Extraction. Foundations and Trends in Databases 1(3), 261–377 (2008)

29. Song, I.-Y., Khare, R., Dai, B.: SAMSTAR: a semi-automated lexical method for generating STAR schemas from an ER diagram. In: Proc. of the 10th Int. Workshop on Data Warehousing and OLAP (DOLAP), pp. 9–16. ACM Press, New York (2007)

30. Sullivan, D.: Document Warehousing and Text Mining. Wiley John & Sons, West Sussex (2001)

31. Torlone, R.: « Conceptual Multidimensional Models ». In: Rafanelli, M. (ed.) Multidimensional Databases: Problems and Solutions, ch. 3, pp. 69–90. Idea Publishing Group, IGP (2003)

32. Tseng, F.S.C., Chou, A.Y.H.: The concept of document warehousing for multidimensional modeling of textual-based business intelligence. J. of Decision Support Systems (DSS) 42(2), 727–744 (2006)

33. Tsois, A., Karayannidis, N., Sellis, T.: MAC: Conceptual Data Modelling for OLAP. In: 3rd Intl. Workshop on Design and Management of Data Warehouses (DMDW). CEUR Worshop Proceedings, WS-CEUR.org, vol. 39, p. 5 (2001)

34. W3C XQuery, « XQuery 1.0 and XPath 2.0 Formal Semantics », recommandation du W3C (January 23, 2007), http://www.w3.org/TR/xquery-semantics/

35. Winter, R., Strauch, B.: A method for demand-driven information requirements analysis in DW projects. In: Proc. of 36th Annual Hawaii Int. Conf. on System Sciences, pp. 231–239. IEEE Comp. Society, Los Alamitos (2003)

Modern Software Engineering Methodologies Meet Data Warehouse Design: 4WD

Matteo Golfarelli, Stefano Rizzi, and Elisa Turricchia

DEIS, University of Bologna, Italy

Abstract. Data warehouse systems are characterized by a long and expensive development process that hardly meets the ambitious requirements of today's market. This suggests that some further investigation on the methodological issues related to data warehouse design is necessary, aimed at improving the development process from different points of view. In this paper we analyze the potential advantages arising from the application of modern software engineering methodologies to a data warehouse project and we propose 4WD, a design methodology that couples the main principles emerging from these methodologies to the peculiarities of data warehouse projects. The principles underlying 4WD are risk-based iteration, evolutionary and incremental prototyping, user involvement, component reuse, formal and light documentation, and automated schema transformation.

Keywords: Data warehouse; Design methodologies; Agile development.

1 Introduction

The continuous market evolution and the increasing competition among companies solicit organizations to improve their ability to foresee customer demand and create new business opportunities. In this direction, over the last decade, data warehouses have become an essential element for strategic analyses. However, data warehouse systems are characterized by a long and expensive development process that hardly meets the ambitious requirements of today's market. This is one of the main causes behind the low penetration of data warehouse systems in small-medium firms, and even behind the failure of whole projects [20].

As a matter of fact, data warehouse projects often leave both customers and developers dissatisfied. The main reasons for low customers' satisfaction are the long delay in delivering a working system and the large number of missing or inadequate (functional and non-functional) requirements. As to developers, they complain that —mainly due to uncertain requirements— it is overly difficult to accurately predict the resources to be allocated to data warehouse projects, which leads to gross errors in estimating design times and costs. In the light of the above, we believe that the methodological issues related to data warehouse design deserve some further investigation aimed at improving the development process from different points of view, such as efficiency and predictability.

A. Cuzzocrea and U. Dayal (Eds.): DaWaK 2011, LNCS 6862, pp. 66–79, 2011.

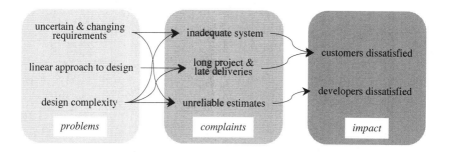

Fig. 1. Cause-effect relationships in customer and developer dissatisfaction

The available literature on data warehouse design mainly focuses on traditional, linear approaches such as the *waterfall approach*, and it appears to be only loosely related to the sophisticated design methodologies that have been emerging in the software engineering community. Though some works about agile data warehousing have appeared [12], there are also evidences that applying an agile approach *tout court* to data warehouse design has several risks, such as that of inappropriately narrowing the data warehouse scope [2]. In this paper we analyze the potential advantages arising from the application of modern software engineering methodologies to a data warehouse project and we propose *Four-Wheel-Drive* (4WD), a design methodology that aims at coupling the main principles emerging from these methodologies to the peculiarities of data warehouse projects.

Our *modus operandi* for this work is the following. First we identify the main problems behind data warehouse projects based on traditional methodologies, and we define our goals accordingly in terms of desired qualities of the software development process (Section 2). Then, from an analysis of the main software engineering methodologies we derive a set of design principles to be adopted in order to achieve the quality goals (Section 3). Then we apply these principles to build up our methodological proposal, inspired by practical evidences emerged during real data warehouse projects (Section 4). Section 5 completes the paper by discussing our proposal in the light of the related works.

2 From Problems to Goals

Our experience with real projects led us to attempt a classification of the main reasons why customers (meant as both sponsors and users) and developers often end up with being dissatisfied. Figure 1 summarizes the results of this investigation, distinguishing between problems, complaints, and their human impact, and emphasizing the existing cause-effect relationships between them. A closer glance at the *problems* column reveals that:

- Requirements for data analyses are often unclear and uncertain, mainly because decision processes are flexibly structured and poorly shared across large organizations, but also because of a difficult communication between users and analysts. Besides, the fast evolution of the business conditions may cause requirements to drastically change even in the short-term [5]. Failing to address these problems dramatically contributes to making users perceive the system as inadequate from the functional point of view and leads to inflating the overall project duration and cost by introducing unexpected delays in the development process.

- Data warehouses are normally built one data mart at a time; each data mart is developed following a linear approach, which means that the different phases are organized into a rigid sequence. Releasing a data mart requires 4-6 months, and it is very difficult to provide intermediate deliveries to be discussed and validated with users, who may easily feel not sufficiently involved and understood, and loose interest in the project.
- The intrinsic complexity of data warehouse design depends on several issues. Among the most influential ones, we mention a couple: data warehouse design leans on data integration, that in most cases is a hard problem; the huge data volume and the workload unpredictability make performance optimization hard. Problems related to data quality and performances have a particularly negative impact on the perceived system inadequacy.

We argue that these problems can be solved by working on four qualities of the software development process [4], as explained below.

1. The *reliability* of a development process is the probability that the delivered system completely and accurately meets user requirements. In our context, increasing the reliability of the design process can contribute to addressing the "inadequate system" complaint, i.e., to ensuring a high-quality and satisfactory final system.
2. By *robustness* we mean the process flexibility, i.e., its capability of quickly and smoothly reacting to unanticipated changes in the environment. A robust process can more effectively accommodate both uncertain and changing requirements.
3. The process *productivity* measures how efficiently it uses the resources assigned to the project to speed up system delivery. Increasing productivity leads to shorter and cheaper projects.
4. The *timeliness* of a process is related to how accurately the times and costs for development can be predicted and respected. A timely process makes resource estimates more reliable.

3   From Goals to Principles

To understand how the main software engineering methodologies devised in the last thirty years can help designers achieve our four quality goals, we analyzed the objectives and underlying principles of seven methodologies, namely *Waterfall* [21], *Rapid Application Development* [15], *Prototyping-Oriented Software Development* [18], *Spiral Software Development* [3], *Model-Driven Architecture*

[13], *Component-Based Software Engineering* [11], and *Agile Software Development* [1]. Overall, the emerging methodological principles can be condensed as follows:

- *Incrementality and risk-based iteration.* Developing and releasing the system in increments leads to a better management of the project risks, thanks to a proper prioritization of activities aimed at letting the most critical requirement features drive the design of the skeleton architecture. A stepwise refinement based on short iterations increases the quality of projects by supporting rapid feedback and quick deliveries [3,15].
- *Prototyping.* Complex projects are conveniently split into smaller units or increments corresponding to sub-problems that can be more easily solved and released to users. To facilitate requirement validation and obtain better results, system development is achieved by refining and expanding an evolutionary prototype that progressively integrates the implementation of each increment [18].
- *User involvement.* Project specifications are difficult to be understood during the preliminary life-cycle phases. A user-centered design increases customer satisfaction and promotes a high level of trust between the parties. Indeed, this feature focuses on constant communication and user participation at every stage of software development.
- *Component reuse.* The reuse of predefined and tested components speeds up product releases and promotes cost reduction as well as software reliability [11].
- *Formal and light documentation.* A well-defined documentation is a key feature to comply with user requirements. Moreover, formal analysis leads to clear and non-ambiguous specifications, and user involvement enables light and up-to-date documentation [1,13,21].
- *Automated schema transformation.* This feature involves the use of formal and automated transformations between schemata representing different software perspectives (e.g., between conceptual and logical schemata). This accelerates software development and promotes standard processes [13].

Table 1 summarizes the relationship between these methodological principles and the four quality goals introduced in Section 2, i.e., it gives an idea of how each principle can help increase each quality factor with specific reference to a data warehouse project. More details are given in the following section.

4   From Principles to Methodology: 4WD

In this section we propose an innovative design methodology, called *Four-Wheel-Drive* (4WD), leaning on the principles discussed in the previous section. These principles are applied in such a way as to effectively balance their pros and their cons, as resulting from practical evidences emerged during the real data warehouse projects 4WD was applied to. Besides the projects we were directly involved in, our findings are based on an elaboration of the experiences collected during the last five years by some practitioners we collaborate with.

Table 1. Expected impact of methodological principles on process quality goals

	Reliability	*Robustness*	*Productivity*	*Timeliness*
Incrementality and risk-based iteration	continuous feedback, clearer requirements	better management of change	better management of project resources, rapid feedback	early detection of errors
Prototyping	frequent tests, easier error detection		early deliveries	
User involvement	better requir. validation, better data quality			early error detection
Component reuse	error-free components		faster design	predictable development
Formal & light documentation	clearer requirements	easier evolution	faster design	
Autom. schema transformation	optimized performances	easier evolution	faster design	predictable design

As sketched in Figure 2, 4WD is based on nested iteration cycles. The external one is called *data mart cycle*; it defines and maintains the global plan for the development of the whole data warehouse and, at each iteration, it incrementally designs and releases one data mart. Data mart design is achieved by the *fact cycle*, that refines the data mart plan and incrementally designs and releases its facts[1]. Finally, fact design is based on two cycles (*modeling* and *implementation* cycles, respectively), that include the core of analysis, design, and implementation activities for delivering reports and applications concerning a single fact. The documents produced can be distinguished into releases (that correspond to project milestones) and deliveries (used for testing and validation). Remarkably, cycles are nested in a way that enables a reassessment of the decisions made during an outer iteration based on the evidences emerging from an inner iteration.

The main activities carried out in the data mart cycle are:

- *Architectural sketch*, during which the overall functional and physical architecture of the data warehouse is progressively drawn based on a macro-analysis of user requirements and an exploration of data sources as well as on budget, technological, and organizational constraints.
- *Conformity analysis*, aimed at determining which dimension of analysis will be conformed across different facts and data marts. Conforming hierarchies in terms of schema and data is a key element to allow cross-fact analysis and obtain consistent results.
- *Data mart prioritization*, based on a trade-off between user priorities and technical constraints.

---

[1] A fact is a concept relevant to decision-making processes, and it typically models a set of events taking place within a company (such as sales, shipments, and purchases).

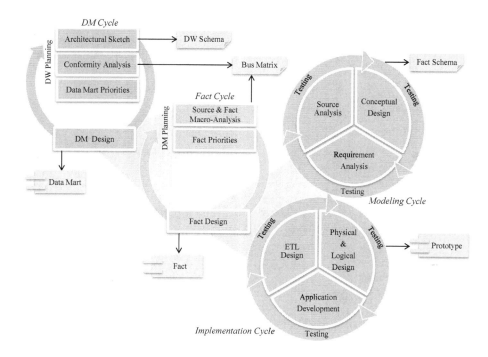

Fig. 2. A sketch of the 4WD methodology

- *Data mart design*, which builds and releases the top-priority data mart. After each data mart has been built, the three phases above are iterated to allow the data warehouse plan to be refined and updated.

The activities carried out within a fact cycle are:

- *Source and fact macro-analysis*, aimed at checking the availability, quality, and completeness of the data sources and determining the main business facts to be analyzed by users.
- *Fact prioritization* that, like for data marts, is the result of a trade-off between user requirements and technical priorities.
- *Fact design*, which develops and releases the top-priority fact. After that, the two phases above are iterated to allow the data mart plan to be refined and updated.

Finally, the activities necessary to release a single fact (or even a small set of strictly related facts) are grouped into two separate sub-cycles to emphasize that releasing a conceptual schema of a fact marks a clear separation between a modeling and an implementation phase for the fact itself. Validating the conceptual schema of a fact before implementation leads to reducing the number of implementation cycles, i.e., to faster fact cycles. While modeling should come before implementation, the activities included in each sub-cycle are not strictly sequential and can be differently prioritized by each project team. Each sub-cycle can be iterated a number of times before its results (the conceptual schema in the first case, the analysis applications in the second) are validated and released.

In the following subsections we will discuss how 4WD meets the principles introduced in Section 3. Then, we briefly present the main outcomes of the application of 4WD to a real project in the area of pay-tvs.

4.1   Incrementality and Risk-Based Iteration

As suggested by the RAD approach, iteration is at the core of 4WD and is coupled with incremental development, that aims at slicing the system functionality into increments; in each increment, a portion of the system is designed, built, and released. Developing a system through repeated cycles leads to lower risk of misunderstood requirements (higher reliability and timeliness), to faster software deliveries (higher productivity), and to more flexible management of evolving requirements and emerging critical issues (higher robustness) [15].

Though these advantages are largely acknowledged in all modern methodologies, the type of iterations and their frequencies vary from one another depending on the type of software to be developed. For example, agile methodologies pushes segmentation to the limit by centering iteration on the so-called *user stories*, meant as high-level functional requirements —concisely expressed by users in their business language— that can be released in a few days. Since functional requirements in data warehouse projects are mainly expressed in terms of analysis capabilities, agile data warehouse design often focuses each iteration on a small set of reporting or OLAP functionalities. While this may sound natural to business users, it can lead to dramatically increasing the overall design effort, because it gives little or no relevance to the multidimensional schemata adopted to store information. Indeed, as reported by designers who adopt functionality-centered iterations in data warehouse projects, a common problem is that they fail in recognizing that apparently different analyses, designed during separate iterations, are actually supported by the very same multidimensional schema.

In 4WD, the shortest iterations that release a tangible result to users are those for modeling and implementing a single fact, that are normally completed in 2-4 weeks overall. This release rate could seem to be not very high, but it is backed by quite more frequent deliveries. Indeed, the modeling and implementation cycles have a daily to weekly frequency; the deliveries they produce enable a progressive refinement of the fact conceptual schema and implementation through a massive test based on active involvement of users.

Incremental techniques require a driver to define an order for developing increments. In 4WD this is done when deciding data mart and fact priorities, and in both cases risk is the driver —as suggested by the Spiral Software Development approach [3]. The project team should balance the risk of early releasing data marts/facts that are not highly valuable to users —which would lead users to lose interest in the project— against the risk of ordering design activities in a non-optimal way —which would determine higher costs and a longer overall project duration. Some guidelines for reducing the risk in data mart prioritization are: (a) Give priority to data marts that include widely shared hierarchies, which makes the overall schema more robust and ensures that dimensions are fully conformed; (b) Give priority to data marts that are fed from stable and well-understood data sources; and (c) Postpone data marts based on unclear requirements, assuming that these requirement will be better understood as the user's involvement in the project increases. As to facts: (a) Give priority to facts that include the main business hierarchies and require the most complex ETL procedures; (b) Adopt a data-driven approach to design rather than a requirement-driven one whenever users do not appear to have a deep knowledge of the business domain; and (c) Plan the length of an iteration in proportion to the complexity of the fact, since failing a release in the early stage of a project will undermine the team credibility.

4.2   Prototyping

Prototyping has a crucial role in most modern software projects. In a data warehouse project, an *evolutionary* (where a robust prototype is continuously refined) and *incremental* (where the prototype is gradually enlarged by adding new subsystems) approach to prototyping is generally preferable to a *throw-away* approach (where the prototype is used to demonstrate a small set of functions and then is abandoned). In fact, the effectiveness of prototyping is maximized when the prototype is tested together with users, and in a data warehouse project this requires the whole data flow —from operational sources to the front-end through ETL— to be prototyped: a large effort, that should not be wasted. The main advantages of prototyping, with particular reference to a data warehouse project, can be summarized as follows:

- Prototypes help designers to validate requirements, because they allow users to evaluate designers' proposals by trying them out, rather than interpreting design documents. This is particularly crucial to enable a better understanding of hierarchies by users [24].
- Prototypes are especially valuable to improve the design of reports and analysis applications, due to their interactive nature. In general, prototype-based user-interfaces have higher usability [10].
- Prototypes can be used to advance testing to the early phases of design, thus reducing the impact of error corrections. For instance, an early loading test can be effectively coupled with a preliminary functional test of front-end applications to check for correct data balancing [8].
- Prototypes can be used to evaluate the feasibility of alternative solutions during logical design of multidimensional schemata and during ETL design. This typically leads to improved performance and maintainability, and to reduced development costs [24].

The above points are basically associated with an increase in reliability and productivity. More specifically, the impact on reliability is related to both data schemata, data quality, and performances. First of all, having a working prototype available during the early project phases enables the designer to keep a strict and constant control over the data schema to ensure that it fully supports user requirements. Then, data quality can be improved by closely involving users in testing the prototype using both real and ad-hoc generated data. Finally, an incremental approach can also be used to take better care of performance issues by following the modularity principle to separate correctness from efficiency. This means that a working prototype can be delivered first; then, performances can be improved during the following iteration to deliver an increment in the form of a working *and efficient* prototype.

4.3   User Involvement

Recent years have been characterized by a growing awareness that human resources are one of the keys to a project success. In this direction, some modern software design methodologies tend to emphasize organizational factors rather than technical aspects. For instance, agile approaches pursue the idea of creating responsible and self-organizing teams to maximize participation of developers and their productivity. They also focus on user involvement as a means to reduce the risk of expressing ambiguous requirements and make software validation easier and more effective [1].

4WD pays a large attention to user involvement because it has a substantial influence on process reliability and timeliness. User involvement can be promoted in different ways:

- All users should preliminary receive a comprehensive training to clarify the project goals, explain the multidimensional model, and introduce a shared language for conceptual design.
- Prototyping is the most effective way to have users participate in the design process and keep them aware of the project status.
- Due to the complex data transformation that is inherent to data warehouse systems, only users —who have insight of business data— can easily detect problems and errors. So, most testing activities should be based on user feedback. User involvement is specifically crucial for usability tests of reporting and OLAP front-ends, and for functional tests of ETL procedures.

4.4   Component Reuse

Applying a component-based methodology means using predefined elements to support the software development process [11]. This is often done by data warehouse designers, though mostly in an unstructured way. The components that can most effectively be reused in a data warehouse project are:

- Conformed hierarchies, that are reused in different facts and data marts. Using conformed hierarchies not only accelerates conceptual design, but is also the key for achieving an enterprise view of business in a data warehouse.
- Library hierarchies, that model common hierarchy structures for a given business domain. For instance, a customer hierarchy in a sales analysis has some basic features that can be easily reused in different data warehouse projects to reduce the effort in designing facts.

- Library facts, that define common measure and dimension structures as emerging from design best practices for a given business domain. Of course, library facts must be tailored to specific user needs; nevertheless, they may be very useful in requirement-driven approaches to give designers and users a starting point for conceptual design.
- ETL building blocks, meant as predefined extraction, transformation, cleaning, and loading routines (e.g., a routine for cleaning a geographical attribute against the list of ISO 3166-2 codes for administrative divisions, or one for loading a type-3 slowly-changing dimension from an operational data store). Reusing such routines reduces the ETL design effort and makes ETL more reliable due to the use of largely-tested algorithms.
- Analysis templates, that define a reference structure for reports and applications. In particular, sharing an analysis template across a data warehouse project is warmly suggested to standardize the interface presented to users.

4WD takes advantage of component reuse to accelerate development and increase robustness. While ETL tools already include some building blocks that can be easily reused through parameterization, identifying hierarchies and facts to be reused deserves more attention. 4WD devotes an ad-hoc phase (*conformity analysis*) to identifying hierarchies to be conformed using a bus matrix. Besides, conceptual schemata are a very effective tool to formalize the structure of facts and hierarchies and support their matching against the available libraries.

4.5   Formal and Light Documentation

In waterfall approaches, documentation is extensively used during the whole life-cycle to support the design process and represent and validate requirements. Other approaches, like RAD and agile methodologies, tend to discourage the use of documentation (other than the one automatically produced by tools) because it may lead to prematurely freezing requirements and slowing down iterations, and suggest to replace it with continuous communication with users [1,15].

While we agree that textual documentation should be reduced to the minimum, we firmly believe that formal documentation is a key factor to promote precise formalization of requirements, clear communication between designers and users, accurate design, and maintainability. In 4WD, the main role to this end is played by conceptual schemata. In particular:

- At the data warehouse level, we mostly use a simple but effective schema that summarizes the data marts, their data sources, and the profiles of the users who access them [9]. This high-level schema is first drawn during the architectural sketch phase, and refined after each data mart cycle. It is essentially used to share the basic functional architecture with users and to support the discussion of data mart priorities.
- At the data mart level, an important role is played by a *bus matrix* that associates each fact with its dimensions, thus pointing out the existence of

conformed hierarchies. This schema is built and progressively refined during the *conformity analysis* and *fact macro-analysys* phases, and is used to test that the designers has properly captured the existing similarities between different facts and different data marts, thus ensuring their integrability [9].

– At the fact level, we force designers to complete and release the conceptual schema of a fact *before* proceeding with implementation. Indeed, having users and designers clearly agree on the fact granularity and measures, as well as on the hierarchy structures and semantics, is the most effective way to avoid misunderstandings and omissions. Finding this agreement informally, or leaning on the logical/physical schema of the fact, is obviously hard and error-prone, while a (graphical) conceptual schema is clearly understood even by non-technical users. In particular, we adopted the Dimensional Fact Model [9] in a number of projects for public administrations (such as local health authorities, the Ministry of Justice, the State Accounting Department) and we verified that fact schemata are also understood by non-IT people such as physicians and jurists.

A major role in this context is also played by metadata, that multidimensional engines store to describe the structure of a data mart. Metadata can typically be exported to generate a documentation based on standard languages (such as XML) and models (such as the CWM); this also encourages interoperability, that is normally seen as a crucial issue in data warehouse projects.

4.6   Automated Schema Transformation

To reduce design complexity, the MDA approach proposes to use formal models for separately specifying a *Platform Independent Model* (PIM, it represents system functionalities at a conceptual level) and a *Platform Specific Model* (PSM, it gives a logical and platform-dependent representation of system functionalities), and to use automated transformations to derive a PSM from a PIM. In a data warehouse project, this can be applied to design both ETL procedures and multidimensional schemata, as shown in [23,16].

In 4WD, automated schema transformations are encouraged, mainly to speed up design and simplify evolution, as long as they need a reasonable effort from users to understand formal models and they do not require to invest too many resources in activities that are not directly valuable to users. We propose two metadata-based activities for automation, possibly supported by CASE tools:

– Supply-driven conceptual design. In supply-driven approaches, a basic conceptual schema for a fact can be automatically derived starting from the logical schema of operational data sources [17]. When applicable, this is a very effective way to cut design costs.
– Logical design. A logical schema can be automatically obtained from a conceptual schema by applying a set of transformations that express common design rules and best practices, possibly based on the expected workload [9].

4.7   Practical Evidences

4WD was applied to a project in the area of pay-tvs. The project had an over-all duration of 6 months and was carried out by an Italian system integrator specialized in BI applications.

During data warehouse planning two data marts were identified, namely administration and management control, that were prioritized according to their importance for users: the administration data mart was given higher priority because its size is definitely larger (9 vs. 3 facts). During data mart planning we organized the overall project in 7 releases (5 for the first data mart, 2 for the second one), each centered on at most 3 facts and taking from 10 to 26 days. Facts were grouped into a single release when they either shared several dimensions or had similar ETL processes (e.g., because measures were extracted from the same data sources and tables), as emerging from conformity analysis and source and facts macro-analysis. Each release was then assigned a value from the users point of view, an estimated nominal complexity, and a risk expressed as a percentage complexity overhead (ranging from 19 to 35%) to determine a worst-case complexity. The criteria used for establishing release priorities were: (1) advance the most valuable facts to early releases; (2) uniformly distribute the worst-case complexity; and (3) respect the dependencies in fact implementation. Besides, some fact were delayed because the development of specific extraction interfaces by external consultants was required for some of their source data; other facts were postponed due to some uncertainty on the requirements. After each release, its actual duration was compared to the estimated complexity. In 2 cases it turned out that the estimation was inaccurate; this was fixed right away by revising the remaining estimates and by changing the team composition.

One of the benefits of adopting 4WD in this project was the speed-up due to large user involvement and extensive prototyping. Users were enabled to access a web portal to signal the errors, and monitor the team's answers and the project state. This was particularly effective for improving the structure of reports and the business rules for detecting source data errors. Noticeably, all errors signaled by users were related to wrong data: user mainly own empirical knowledge, so it may be hard for them to reason from an abstract point of view (e.g., to evaluate an ETL flow or a report structure with no data loaded). The implementation effort was reduced by partially reusing existing reports and dimension tables, because those required by administration and management control users are quite standard. This was not the case for ETL, that required a strong personalization, so reuse was limited to some basic routines made available by the adopted ETL suite. Finally, adopting the DFM as a conceptual model enabled designers to produce a concise but exhaustive documentation, and to use a CASE tool to automate logical design [7].

5   Related Literature and Discussion

In this paper we started by identifying the main problems behind data ware-house projects, and we ended up with proposing an original methodology, 4WD, inspired by six basic principles of modern software engineering. In this section we critically compare 4WD with the existing data warehouse design methodologies.

Data warehouse design has been investigated by the research community since the late nineties. A classic waterfall approach was first proposed in [6]; a distinguishing feature was the inclusion of a conceptual design phase aimed at better formalizing the data schema. A sequential approach to design is also followed in [14], where an object-oriented method based on UML is proposed to cover analysis, design, implementation, and testing. Another UML-based method is presented in [19]; here, the use of the *Common Warehouse Metamodel* (CWM) is suggested to promote a more standard approach to conceptual design. All these methodologies follow a linear approach that hardly adapts to changes and is unsuitable when requirements are uncertain. In 4WD these problems are overcome thanks to iteration and prototyping.

Iterative solutions are typically adopted by methodologies like RAD and Agile. The work in [12] breaks with strictly sequential approaches by applying two Agile development techniques, namely *scrum* and *eXtreme Programming*, to the specific challenges of data warehouse projects. To better meet user needs, the work suggests to adopt a *user stories decomposition* step based on a set of architectural categories for the back-end and front-end portions of a data warehouse. However, it does not deeply discuss how this decomposition impacts on modeling and design. In this direction, 4WD emphasizes the key role of the multidimensional model as a driver for the development process and promotes fact-based iterations to increase its productivity while preserving reliability.

A different approach to tackle the data warehouse design complexity is the MDA methodology proposed in [16] to better separate the system functionality from its implementation. Strong relevance is given to the development of the data warehouse repository; the three main perspectives of MDA (CIM, PIM, and PSM) are defined using extensions of UML and CWM, and the inter-model transformations are described using the *Query/View/Transformation* (QVT) language. In practice, strictly applying this methodology may be hard due to the poor aptitude of users for reading formal models and investing resources in low-values activities. To overcome these issues, in 4WD automation is specifically targeted on supply-driven conceptual design and logical design. This reasserts the key role played by conceptual schemata of facts in 4WD.

A pragmatic comparison between data warehouse design methodologies is offered in [22], where 15 different solutions proposed by Business Intelligence software vendors are examined. The authors emphasize the lack of software-independent approaches, and point out that all the proposed solutions hardly can deal with changes and market evolution, which creates a robustness problem. To improve robustness, 4WD specifically relies on three key factors: (a) iteration breaks the linear development process by offering frequent deliveries and reviewing points; (b) a formal and light documentation provides a clear picture of the current specifications, facilitating the identification of the units to be evolved; (c) automating schema transformations reduces the time needed to propagate changes to the different levels.

References

1. Agile Manifesto: Manifesto for agile software development (2010), http://agilemanifesto.org/
2. Beyer, M., Richardson, J.: Agile techniques augment but do not replace business intelligence and data warehouse best practice. Tech. Rep. G00201031, Gartner Research (2010)
3. Boehm, B.W.: A spiral model of software development and enhancement. IEEE Computer 21(5), 61–72 (1988)
4. Ghezzi, C., Jazayeri, M., Mandrioli, D.: Fundamentals of software engineering. Prentice Hall, Englewood Cliffs (2002)
5. Giorgini, P., Rizzi, S., Garzetti, M.: GRAnD: A goal-oriented approach to requirement analysis in data warehouses. Decision Support Systems 45(1), 4–21 (2008)
6. Golfarelli, M., Rizzi, S.: A methodological framework for data warehouse design. In: Proc. DOLAP, pp. 3–9 (1998)
7. Golfarelli, M., Rizzi, S.: WAND: A CASE tool for data warehouse design. In: Proc. ICDE, pp. 7–9 (2001)
8. Golfarelli, M., Rizzi, S.: A comprehensive approach to data warehouse testing. In: Proc. DOLAP, pp. 17–24 (2009)
9. Golfarelli, M., Rizzi, S.: Data warehouse design: Modern principles and methodologies. McGraw-Hill, New York (2009)
10. Gordon, V.S., Bieman, J.M.: Rapid prototyping: Lessons learned. IEEE Software 12(1), 85–95 (1995)
11. Heineman, G.T., Councill, W.T.: Component-based software engineering: Putting the pieces together. Addison-Wesley, Reading (2001)
12. Hughes, R.: Agile Data Warehousing: Delivering world-class business intelligence systems using Scrum and XP. IUniverse (2008)
13. Kruchten, P.: The 4+1 view model of architecture. IEEE Software 12(6), 42–50 (1995)
14. Luján-Mora, S., Trujillo, J.: A comprehensive method for data warehouse design. In: Proc. DMDW (2003)
15. Martin, J.: Rapid application development. MacMillan, Basingstoke (1991)
16. Mazón, J.N., Trujillo, J.: An MDA approach for the development of data warehouses. In: Proc. JISBD, pp. 208–208 (2009)
17. Moody, D., Kortink, M.: From enterprise models to dimensional models: A methodology for data warehouse and data mart design. In: Proc. DMDW (2000)
18. Pomberger, G., Bischofberger, W.R., Kolb, D., Pree, W., Schlemm, H.: Prototyping-oriented software development — concepts and tools. Structured Programming 12(1), 43–60 (1991)
19. Prat, N., Akoka, J., Comyn-Wattiau, I.: A UML-based data warehouse design method. Decision Support Systems 42(3), 1449–1473 (2006)
20. Ramamurthy, K., Sen, A., Sinha, A.P.: An empirical investigation of the key determinants of data warehouse adoption. Decision Support Systems 44(4), 817–841 (2008)
21. Royce, W.W.: Managing the development of large software systems: Concepts and techniques. In: Proc. ICSE, Monterey, California, USA, pp. 328–339 (1987)
22. Sen, A., Sinha, A.P.: A comparison of data warehousing methodologies. Commun. ACM 48(3), 79–84 (2005)
23. Simitsis, A., Vassiliadis, P.: A method for the mapping of conceptual designs to logical blueprints for ETL processes. Decision Support Systems 45(1), 22–40 (2008)
24. Sommerville, I.: Software Engineering. Pearson Education, London (2004)

GEM: Requirement-Driven Generation of ETL and Multidimensional Conceptual Designs

Oscar Romero[1], Alkis Simitsis[2], and Alberto Abelló[1]

[1] Universitat Politècnica de Catalunya, BarcelonaTech
Barcelona, Spain
{oromero,aabello}@essi.upc.edu
[2] HP Labs, Palo Alto, CA, USA
alkis@hp.com

Abstract. At the early stages of a data warehouse design project, the main objective is to collect the business requirements and needs, and translate them into an appropriate conceptual, multidimensional design. Typically, this task is performed manually, through a series of interviews involving two different parties: the business analysts and technical designers. Producing an appropriate conceptual design is an error-prone task that undergoes several rounds of reconciliation and redesigning, until the business needs are satisfied. It is of great importance for the business of an enterprise to facilitate and automate such a process. The goal of our research is to provide designers with a semi-automatic means for producing conceptual multidimensional designs and also, conceptual representation of the extract-transform-load (ETL) processes that orchestrate the data flow from the operational sources to the data warehouse constructs. In particular, we describe a method that combines information about the data sources along with the business requirements, for validating and completing –if necessary– these requirements, producing a multidimensional design, and identifying the ETL operations needed. We present our method in terms of the TPC-DS benchmark and show its applicability and usefulness.

1 Introduction

"A gemstone or gem is a piece of attractive mineral, which –when cut and polished– is used to make jewelry or other adornments. Most gems are hard, but some soft minerals are used in jewelry because of their lustre or other physical properties that have aesthetic value." (Wikipedia)

As most of the raw materials and resources, gems are out there in large varieties and quantities, but we need to dig and work hard in order to get them and make profit out of them.

Data are the gems of the enterprise. They are available at large quantities, but we need to "dig" for recognizing the relevant and useful ones, and to adjust and polish them for making our valued assets, our "jewelry". The jewelry for an enterprise is any tool or means that facilitates strategic decision making and helps in satisfying business needs. Such a tool is a data warehouse (DW) that

A. Cuzzocrea and U. Dayal (Eds.): DaWaK 2011, LNCS 6862, pp. 80–95, 2011.

organizes the raw, source data in a way that enables decision support. Building a DW requires two essential constructs: the multidimensional (MD) design of the target data stores and the extract-transform-load (ETL) process that populates the target data stores from the source ones.

Nowadays, the construction of conceptual MD and ETL designs is an error-prone, manual process that undergoes several rounds of reconciliation and re-designing, until the business needs are satisfied. It is essential for the business of an enterprise to facilitate, speed up, and automate these design processes.

This paper presents a system called *GEM* (*G*enerating *E*tl and *M*ultidimensional designs). *GEM* starts with a set of source data stores and business requirements –e.g., business queries, service level agreements (SLAs)– and based on these, it produces a MD design for the target data stores, along with a set of ETL operations required for the population of the target DW.

The semantics, characteristics, and constraints of data sources are represented by means of an OWL ontology. The business requirements are expressed in a structured form. We consider functional requirements that drive the generation of the MD design constructs and also, soft or non-functional requirements –e.g., freshness, recoverability, availability– that can be used for giving "lustre" and adding value to our designs. For example, based on a freshness requirement we may decide which data source to use and according to a recoverability requirement we may choose to enrich the ETL process with recovering techniques.

For each business requirement, we identify the relevant part of the data sources (e.g., concepts, attributes, properties) needed to answer it. If we identify conflicts, we either suggest corrections or ask for user feedback. The output of these tasks is an annotated subset of the source ontology that corresponds to a business requirement. Next, we classify the relevant concepts as dimensional or factual and validate the result. We also explore schema information for identifying the respective ETL operations. Finally, we consolidate the individual designs, one for each business requirement, and get the conceptual MD and ETL designs.

Contributions. In particular, our main contributions are as follows.

- We present *GEM*, a system that facilitates the production of ETL and MD designs, starting from a set of business requirements and source data stores. To the best of our knowledge, *GEM* is the first approach towards the semi-automatic generation of both the ETL and MD conceptual designs, since we automatically generate mappings from sources to cubes.
- We propose novel algorithms finding and validating an ontology subset as a MD schema, and identifying ETL operators at the same time.
- We are able to deal with incomplete requirements and validate them.
- We evaluate our method using the schema and constructs of the TPC-DS benchmark and show the quality of the *GEM* designs.

Outline. The rest of the paper is structured as follows. Section 2 formulates the problem at hand and presents the *GEM* architecture. Sections 3 and 4 discuss the validation and completion of business requirements, respectively. Then,

Section 5 describes the validation of the MD design and Section 6 the identification of ETL operations. Section 7 evaluates *GEM* using the TPC-DS benchmark and Section 8 presents the related work.

2   *GEM* in a Nutshell

This section gives an overview of our system, *GEM*. Given two inputs, namely information about the operational sources and a set of user requirements, *GEM* produces two designs: the MD design of the target DW constructs and the conceptual ETL flow that interconnects the target constructs to the operational sources.

2.1   Inputs

Source Data Stores. We capture the semantics of the data sources in terms of an OWL ontology. In previous work, we have shown that a variety of structured and unstructured data stores can be elegantly represented as graphs, and we have also described how we can construct an appropriate ontology for such data stores by integrating a domain vocabulary with the data sources' vocabulary [17]. Here, due to space consideration, we assume that we do have an OWL ontology annotated with the *mappings* of those concepts and properties available in the operational data sources. For further details on how we get this ontology from the sources, we refer the interested reader to our past work [17]. Figure 3 (page 92) depicts an example ontology based on the TPC-DS schema [19].

Business Requirements. In typical DW and ETL engagements, the design starts from a set of functional and non-functional requirements (respectively f-req and nf-req, from here on) expressing business needs. Example requirements could be *"examine stocks provided by suppliers"* or *"a report on total revenue per branch should be updated every 10 minutes"*. Such requirements often come as service level agreements (SLAs) or business queries and are expressed in various forms, either structured or unstructured. Much work has been done in capturing and representing business needs. For example, SLAs expressed as free-form text, require natural language processing (NLP) techniques for being interpreted in a machine processable way. How to capture such requirements are out of the scope of this work. Here, without loss of generality, we consider requirements expressed in a structured way (e.g., by means of i* profiles [22]). Such requirements are represented in an XML file that contains two main parts.

The first part involves functional or information requirements that are captured by identifying the measures and dimensions of interest. In the previous example, *stocks* would be the measure and *suppliers* the dimensional concept.

$$< measures >< concept\ id =\ "stocks" / >< /measures >$$
$$< dimensions >< concept\ id =\ "suppliers" / >< /dimensions >$$

The second part, involves the non-functional requirements of interest for each concept indicated by the functional requirements. For example, the measures used by the *revenue report* (i.e., the respective view) should conform to a non-functional requirement for *freshness* that requires that the corresponding data should be updated at least every *10 minutes*.

> $<$*concept id* $=$ *"v_revenue"* $><$*nf_req* $>$
> $<$*freshness format* $=$ *"HH24:MI:SS"* $>$ < 00:10:00 $</freshness>$
> $</nf\_req><$*/concept* $>$

Due to space restrictions, we omit a detailed description of the XML structure for representing such requirements. Briefly, it contains:

- Levels of detail, which represent data granularity. The user may provide a discretization process for continuous (or with high cardinality) data types.
- Descriptors, which carry out selections over them (i.e., *slicers*). Type of comparison carried out; e.g., "in a given year YYYY".
- Measures, which should be analyzed. Aggregation function and a partial order between them; the latter is needed when we perform different aggregations (one order per dimension). In doing so, we would be able to distinguish between, for example, 'average of sums' and 'sum of averages'.

Note that although our XML structure captures multidimensional requirements over a domain (i.e., non-multidimensional) ontology, the expressivity we support is equivalent to that of the *dimensional expressions* introduced in [4].

In addition, we may have nf-reqs either for each one of the above three elements or for the whole design.

As a remark, different requirements affect different design levels. For example, a freshness requirement indicates how often an ETL flow should run in order to meet the required latency in updating the DW. However, such decision affects the execution level and should be taken under consideration at the physical model. Nevertheless, we may need to use this requirement during the conceptual design as well. For example, assume two source data stores containing the same data but placed in different locations for business reasons (e.g., two snapshots placed in two different branches of the organization). Assume also that the first data store is updated every hour and the second every 5 minutes or that the congestion of the network coming from the first data store is significantly greater than the one coming from the second source. If we have such information, then based on the freshness requirement we need to honor for our target data stores, we should decide to pull data from the second data store. Clearly, such decision is to be taken at the conceptual level.

However, we are interested in capturing all requirements. Those that cannot be used at the conceptual level (which is the focus of this paper) should be transferred to the subsequent, more detailed design levels, along with the outcome of this process; i.e., the conceptual ETL and MD designs. Hence, the designer of the logical and physical models does not need to revisit and reinterpret the original set of business requirements.

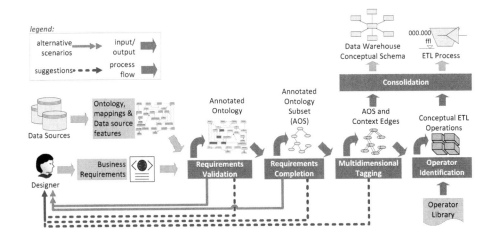

Fig. 1. System architecture

2.2   System Architecture

The process of producing the ETL and MD designs is a semi-automatic process comprising five main stages (see Figure 1). Here, we briefly describe these stages. The next sections provide more details for each stage.

Stage 1: Requirement Validation. First, the system checks if there is a mismatch among the business requirements (either functional or non-functional) in the XML and the data sources, by looking for the corresponding concepts in the ontology and checking whether they are mapped to the sources or not. In case of mismatch, it identifies the possible problems or it may suggest relaxation of the requirements. Otherwise, concepts in the ontology are selected and tagged as either Level, Descriptor or Measure. These concepts are also annotated with nf-reqs and composition of extraction mappings, if necessary.

Stage 2: Requirement Completion. After considering the business requirements, the system complements them with additional information gathered from the sources. This stage identifies intermediate concepts that are not explicitly stated in the business requirements, but are needed in order to answer the f-reqs. User feedback is welcomed for ensuring correctness and compliance to the end-user needs.

Stage 3: Multidimensional Tagging. Next, we tag the new concepts identified by the previous stage, as either factual or dimensional and validate the correctness of these completed f-reqs tagging according to MD design principles. Hence, we check two issues: i) first, whether the factual data is arranged in a MD space (i.e., if each instance of factual data is identified by a point in each of its analysis dimensions) and second, ii) whether the data summarization is correct by examining whether the following conditions hold [8]: (1) *disjointness* (the sets of objects to be aggregated must be disjoint); (2) *completeness* (the union of subsets must constitute the entire set); and (3) *compatibility* of the dimension, the type of measure being aggregated and the aggregation function.

Stage 4: Operator Identification. The ETL operations are identified in three phases. First, we use the annotations generated by the previous steps (i.e., mappings in Stage 1, intermediate concepts in Stage 2, and their taggings in Stage 3) for extracting schema modification operations. Then, we complement the design with additional information that might be found in the sources and with typical ETL operations regarding surrogate key and slowly changing dimensions.

Stage 5: Conciliation. The previous stages run once for each f-req. Eventually, the individual results obtained per f-req are conciliated in a single conceptual MD schema and a single ETL flow.

2.3   Output

At the end, we produce a conceptual, MD schema composed by facts and dimensions. In addition, we identify the ETL operations needed in order to interconnect the source data stores to the MD constructs.

3   Requirement Validation

Starting from the inputs discussed in Section 2.1, we validate the business requirements w.r.t. the available data sources, as follows: (a) we analyze the input XML file and *tag* the ontology concepts corresponding to the f-req, identifying possible mapping conflicts, and (b) we include and then validate assertions regarding nf-reqs and data sources features. The input XML file contains three kinds of concepts: measures, levels, and descriptors (see Section 2.1). So, first, we tag the corresponding concepts in the input ontology with these labels. Then, we check whether the tagged concepts can be mapped to the sources (either directly or by means of ETL operators). When an error occurs, user feedback is required. The validation method is as follows:

1. **if** the tagged concept is mapped to the sources **then** no further action is needed
2. **else if** the tagged concept is involved in a concept taxonomy **then**
   (a) **if** any of its subclass(es) has (have) a mapping **then** we annotate the tagged concept with the ETL operations 'renaming' and 'union'
   (b) **else if** any superclass has a mapping **then** we use the general concept mapped and annotate the required concept with ETL operations 'renaming' and 'selection'
      i. **if** *discriminant function* has not been specified in the input XML file **then** user feedback is required
      i. **if** the tagged node has several superclasses **then** 'minus' or 'intersection' are also considered (see Section 6 for details)
3. **else if** exists a (transitive) one-to-one association to a mapped concept **then** suggest it as a potential synonym
   (a) **if** the suggestion is accepted **then** the f-req is updated with the synonym concept
4. **else** the concept is not available in the data sources

4   Requirement Completion

This stage takes as input the annotated ontology produced in the previous stage and it *completes* the requirements regarding the sources. First, it identifies *intermediate concepts* that are not explicitly stated in the f-req, but needed to retrieve the required information. If an f-req cannot be met, it suggests alternative solutions. Finally, it produces the ontology subset needed to answer the business query at hand and additional annotations regarding ETL operations.

This stage starts with a pruning process. We identify how tagged concepts are related in the ontology and then, (a) we disregard concepts/relationships not mapped nor tagged (if a concept taxonomy is affected, we replace the concept pruned with the first superclass mapped/tagged); and next, (b) we prune all the mapped many-to-many (i.e., *-*) associations. Note that such associations violate the three summarization necessary conditions [8] and thus, they cannot be exploited for MD design. The outcome of this pruning is a *subset* of the input *annotated* ontology, which we call AOS. Since an arbitrary ontology can be represented as a graph, we will talk about *paths* between concepts and thus, we will also refer to concepts as *nodes* and to associations as *edges*.

Looking for Paths Between Tagged Concepts. For identifying how tagged concepts are related in the sources, we use the following algorithm that computes paths between tagged concepts.

1. **foreach** edge e **in** O **do**
   (a) **if** $right\_left\_concepts(e)$ **are** tagged **then** paths_between_tagged_concepts $\cup = e$;
   (b) **else if** $right\_concept(e)$ **is** tagged **then** max_length_paths $\cup = e$; //*Seed edges*
2. **while** size(max_length_paths) != ∅ **do**
   (a) paths := ∅;
   (b) **foreach** path p **in** max_length_paths **do**
      i. extended_paths := explore_new_edges(p, O); //*only considering edges not in p*
      ii. **foreach** path $p1$ **in** extended_paths **do**
         A. **if** $left\_concept(p1)$ **is** tagged **then** paths_between_tagged_concepts $\cup = p1$;
         B. **else** paths $\cup = p1$;
   (c) max_length_paths := paths;
3. **return** paths_between_tagged_concepts;

We start by identifying edges directly relating tagged concepts (step 1a) and edges reaching tagged concepts (from now on, *seed* edges; step 1b). For the sake of understandability, although the AOS has no directed edges, we say that the tagged node is in the seed edge right-end, and its counterpart to be in the the left-end. Then, the algorithm applies the transitive property starting from tagged concepts. At the first iteration, we explore new edges such that their right-end matches the left-end of a seed edge, and similarly for the forthcoming iterations (step 2(b)i). Intuitively, we explore paths starting from tagged concepts by exploring a new edge per iteration. This guided exploration has two main restrictions: we cannot explore any edge already explored in a given path (step 2(b)i) and if we reach another tagged concept we finish exploring that path (i.e., we have found a path between tagged concepts; step 2(b)iiA). Note that in a given iteration i, we only explore the longest paths computed in the previous iteration (steps 1b and 2c). Eventually, we explore all the paths and the algorithm finishes (step 2). Observe that step 1 can be computed by means of generic ontological reasoning.

This algorithm is *sound* since it computes direct relationships and propagates them according to the transitivity rule and *complete*, because it converges; note that each path is explored *only* once. This algorithm has a theoretical exponential upper bound regarding the size of the longest path between tagged concepts.

However, this theoretical upper bound is hardly achievable in real-world ontologies as they have neither all classes with maximum connectivity nor all paths are of maximum length. Moreover, note that *-* relationships were previously pruned. (See also our evaluation in Section 7).

Producing the Output Subset. Based on the paths between tagged concepts that the previous algorithm found, the following algorithm determines the ontology subset needed to answer the f-req.

1. **if** between two tagged concepts there are more than one path **then** we ask the user for disambiguation (i.e., which is the path fulfilling the semantics needed for the f-req at hand)
2. **foreach** pair of related tagged concepts not involving a descriptor **do**
   (a) Edges forming that path are annotated as aggregation edges, because these relationships determine the data granularity of the output

The AOS is compound by the paths selected in step 1. Note that these paths include the intermediate concepts (i.e., those not tagged but involved in the paths) and that the user may not select any path between a given pair of concepts. At this point, taxonomies are also disregarded.

Annotating the Ontology AOS. Having an AOS containing the new concepts needed to answer the f-req (besides those in the input XML file), we check whether the whole graph makes MD sense.

First, we check the semantics of each edge according to the tag -if any- of the related concepts and its multiplicity. According to these semantics, we tag each edge with MD relationships that it could represent; i.e., related MD concepts. Next, we consider *factual nodes* (those tagged as measures) and *dimensional nodes* (those either tagged as levels or descriptors). For guaranteeing the MD design principles (see Section 2.2), factual and dimensional nodes must be related properly. For example, factual data cannot be related to dimensional data by means of a one-to-many (i.e., 1-*) association, as by definition, each instance of factual data is identified by a point in each of its analysis dimensions. Dimensional data can only appear in the *-end of an edge when the other end is also tagged as dimensional data. Furthermore, non-complete associations –i.e., accepting zeros– in the dimensional end are not allowed either, as they do not preserve completeness.

Hence, we analyze the graph looking for not correct edges and try to fix them. For example, if the node in the *-end of a *-1 association is tagged as dimensional then, its counterpart should also be dimensional. If by doing so we have been able to infer an unequivocal label, this knowledge is propagated to the rest of the AOS. However, if we identify a meaningless conceptual relationship –i.e., when both ends are tagged in a forbidden way– the algorithm stops and alternative analysis scenarios are proposed. For this task, we use previously proposed techniques, as those described in [14].

5   Multidimensional Validation

This stage validates the AOS and checks whether its concepts and associations collectively produce a data cube. If the validation fails (according to the constraints discussed in Section 2.2), *GEM* proposes alternative analysis solutions. Otherwise, the resulting MD schema is directly derived from the AOS.

The previous stage might have propagated some tags when tagging the AOS associations (i.e., inferring unequivocal knowledge), but it does not guarantee that all the concepts have a MD tag at this point. Thus, we start this stage with a pre-process aimed at deriving new MD knowledge from non-tagged concepts, and each non-tagged concept is considered to play a dimensional role or a factual role. Furthermore, it would be possible to retag a dimensional node as dimensional/factual node. Next, we validate if any of these tags, eventually, are sound in a MD sense. Thus, in this step, we determine every potential MD tagging that would make sense for the input f-req and we also determine how these alternatives would affect the output schema, deriving (in some cases) interesting analytical options that may have been overlooked by the designer.

For each possible combination of new tags, an *alternative annotation* is created if the tags do not contradict the edge semantics already depicted in the AOS. Subsequently, each of these AOS will be validated and only those that make MD sense will be finally considered. Therefore, an f-req can produce several valid MD taggings for the same AOS and thus, multiple MD schemas.

The validation process introduced in this stage guarantees the *multidimensional normal forms* presented in [6,7] for validating the output MD schema, and the summarizability constraints discussed in [10]. The following algorithm is called once for each alternative tagging generated.

1. **If** $!factualdata(AOS)$ **then** return $notifyFail$("The requirement does not include any fact.");
2. **If** $!connected(AOS)$ **then** return $notifyFail$("Cartesian product is not allowed.");
3. **For each** $subgraphOfLevels \subset AOS$ **do**
   (a) **If** $cycles(subgraphOfLevels)$ **and** $contradictoryMultiplicities(subgraphOfLevels)$ **then**
       i. **return** $notifyFail$("Cycles cannot be used to select data");
   (b) **If** $existsTwoLevelsRelatedSameFactualData(subgraphOfLevels)$ **then**
       i. **return** $notifyFail$("Non-orthogonal Analysis Levels");
   (c) **For each** $(c_1, c_2) \in getToManyEdges(subgraphOfLevels)$ **do**
       i. **If** $relatedToNodesWithMeasures(AOS, c_2)$ **then**
          A. **return** $notifyFail$("Aggregation Problems");
4. **For each** $cycle \subset AOS$ **do**
   (a) **If** $contradictoryMultiplicities(cycle)$ **then**
       i. **return** $notifyFail$("Cycles cannot be used to select data");
   (b) **else**
       i. $askUserForSemanticValidation()$;
       ii. $add(AOS, newContextEdge(bottom(cycle), top(cycle), cycle))$;
5. **For each** $(c_1, c_2) \in getToManyEdges(AOS)$ **do**
   (a) **If** $relatedToNodesWithMeasures(AOS, c_2)$ **then**
       i. **return** $notifyFail$("Aggregation problems between Measures");

Step 1 ensures that the AOS contains factual data. Note that in our pre-process we could have tagged nodes as factual data that do not contain measures. From here on, we distinguish between *factual nodes* and *factual nodes with measures*. So this function returns false if all the nodes are tagged as dimensional data. Step 2 ensures that the AOS is *connected* to avoid "Cartesian Product".

The intuition behind steps 3 to 5 is shown in Figure 2. Step 3 validates levels subgraphs (i.e., subgraphs only containing level concepts) with regard to where factual nodes are placed. First, every subgraph must represent a valid dimension

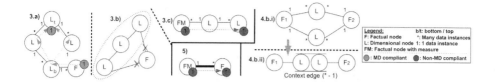

Fig. 2. Graphical representation of the multidimensional validation steps

hierarchy. We must be able to identify two nodes in the level subgraph which represent the *top* and *bottom* levels of the hierarchy (Step 3a). Two different levels in a subgraph cannot be related to the same factual node (Step 3b). Moreover, level - level edges raising aggregation problems in factual nodes with measures must be forbidden (Step 3c). Note that by convention we assume that in every *-1 edge (c_1, c_2), c_1 corresponds to the * end of the association. Hence, Step 3 validates the correspondences between dimensional nodes, whereas Step 4 generates the path of factual nodes (MD data retrieved); i.e., it validates cycles in the path of factual nodes to ensure that they are not used to select data, similarly to the validation of levels cycles in 3a. Once the cycle has been validated, the edges involved are clustered in a *context edge* (since cycles are checked to correspond a correct multi-path aggregation hierarchy, i.e., a one-to-many or one-to-one lattice) tagged with the lattice multiplicity, as shown in Figure 2. Finally, Step 5 looks for aggregation problems induced by factual nodes with measures at the 1-end of a 1-* edge –either context edge or not.

6   Operation Identification

For each graph validated as a data cube in the previous stage, we launch an ETL operation identification process, which is a semi-automatic process that comprises three phases.

Phase I. This phase identifies operations that are needed for mapping the source to target data stores, using the target schema produced in the previous stage. For example, for aggregating over states, we need a location dimension at the target site and to map it with source information about zip code, street address, and so on.

During this phase, we identify mainly schema modification operations as follows. *Selection* is generated from concepts having attached a selection condition: from slicers recorded in AOS; or when a required concept does not have any mapped source (neither it nor its subclasses), while some of its superclasses do have such mapping. *Union* appears when a required concept is not directly mapped to the sources, but some of its subclasses are. Similarly, *Intersection* and *Minus* are generated when a concept is not mapped but some of its superclasses are. *Join* is generated for every association in the ontology; if one or both of the association ends is not mandatory, we state it as outer. *Aggregation* is generated when a *-1 association is found so that there is a measure at its *-end.

Renaming is generated for each attribute in the data sources and gives to it the name of the corresponding ontological concept. *Projection* is generated for each concept and association in the ontology. *Function* expresses operations stated in the requirements, like a discretization process for an attribute to be used in a dimension or a transformation for an attribute to facilitate its interpretation as a measure.

Starting from the AOS, we iteratively synthesize several of its nodes into one single operation, as shown in the algorithm placed in the next page.

The *ETL* variable is a *directed acyclic graph* that tracks the ETL flow generated, whereas the $findOper(\text{ETL } g, \text{concept } c)$ function looks for a node in g, with no successors, such that it contains c. Step 1 considers extraction operations like a single table access, a union, an intersection or a minus operation, along with the corresponding selection, projection, renaming mechanisms, and functions. Step 2 fuses all data that do not involve any aggregation. Hence, for those AOS nodes related by means of 1-1 associations (i.e., identity), we join their corresponding operations in the ETL. We also join nodes connected with edges that do not involve aggregation (i.e., stemming from slicing requirements and identified in Section 4).

1. **For each** $c \in AOS$ **do**
    (a) $add(ETL, newExtraction(c))$;
2. **For each** $(c_1, c_2) \in edges(AOS)$ **do**
    (a) **If** $multiplicity((c_1, c_2)) = "1 - 1"$ **or not** $aggregationEdge((c_1, c_2))$ **then**
        i. $o_1 := findOper(ETL, c_1)$; $o_2 := findOper(ETL, c_2)$;
        ii. **If** $o_1 <> o_2$ **then** $add(ETL, newJoin(o_1, o_2, getGroupingAttrs(o_1)))$;
3. **For each** $o \in ETL$ **and** $successors(ETL, o) = \emptyset$ **and** $| outputEdges(AOS, o) | > 1$ **do**
    (a) $setGroupingAttrs(o, \emptyset)$; $e := outputEdges(AOS, o)$;
    (b) **For each** $(c_1, c_2) \in (e)$ **do**
        i. $o_2 := findOper(ETL, c_2)$;
        ii. $o := newJoin(o, o_2, getGroupingAttrs(o) \cup getGroupingAttrs(o_2))$;
        iii. $add(ETL, o)$;
    (c) $add(ETL, newAggr(o, getGroupingAttrs(o)))$;
4. **While not** connected(ETL) **do**
    (a) $(c_1, c_2) := first(\bigcup_{o=containsMeasure(ETL)} outputEdges(o))$;
    (b) $o_1 := findOper(ETL, c_1)$; $o_2 := findOper(ETL, c_2)$;
    (c) $o_3 := newJoin(o_1, o_2, (getGroupingAttrs(o_1) \setminus getAttr(c_1)) \cup getGroupingAttrs(o_2))$;
    (d) $add(ETL, o_3)$; $add(ETL, newAggr(o_3, getGroupingAttrs(o_3)))$;

Step 3 creates the basic cubes. First, we check the already generated operations that have no successors, and whose AOS nodes have more than one edge with the 1-end related to a concept in another ETL node without successors (observe that after step 2 only *-1 associations remain). Next, we successively join these operations. The grouping attributes of the final operation is the union of the grouping attributes of each joined operation. Note that a grouping operation is generated to guarantee that data is at the appropriate granularity.

Finally, step 4 connects all cubes produced, starting from those with measures, by following the order specified by the requirements. Since each AOS edge not used yet corresponds to an aggregation, we join the output of the operations (following the AOS aggregation edges), substitute the grouping attributes of c_1 by those of the new aggregation level c_2, and generate the grouping operation taking into account the new attributes. The choice of the aggregation function depends on the requirements (there, it should be associated to a corresponding measure and c_2) or a default one is used; e.g., SUM.

Phase II. During this phase, the designer might want to refine the design produced by checking for additional information at the sources that might be useful. (Part of this phase can be done before Phase I too.) For example, the domain ontology might relate *state* with *zip code* and *street address*. If there is a source containing information about "location" and contains both the street address and zip code in the same field, then such information is definitely useful, but the domain ontology cannot help. We can correct this by enriching the result with such a mapping and producing the appropriate function(s).

Nf-reqs can be exploited in a similar way. For example, a strict requirement regarding *recoverability* may suggest to consider adding recovery points at points of the flow that are generally known for being expensive (e.g., after the extraction phase or after an expensive blocking operator [16]). Of course the final decision on which are the good places to add recovery points is to be taken by an optimizer at the logical level [16].

The same holds when we work with f-reqs that involve the data itself. For example, a requirement like "make sure that each customer is considered once" can add a "de-duplicate customer info" operation to the design.

Phase III. The last phase complements the design with operations needed to satisfy standard business and design needs. This task is mainly automatic and involves typical DW operations that can be identified and added to the design *after* the consolidation phase.

For example, common practices suggest replacing production keys with surrogate keys. For that, the system identifies the respective production keys and enriches the design with appropriate 'surrogate key assignment' operations. Similarly, the system adds operations that take care of slowly changing dimensions (SCDs). There are standard dimensions that are not updated very often (e.g., dimensions that keep structural information about the organization such as geographical location, customer information or product information). Hence, the design can be enriched with operations that handle the update of such dimensions. Possible update operations for SCDs can be: do nothing (do not propagate changes), keep no history (overwrite old values with new data), keep history by creating multiple records in the dimensional tables with separate keys, keep history using separate columns, keep history by storing new data to an active table and keep (all or some of the) old values to 'history tables', or use a hybrid approach. Of course, here we list just a few frequently used operations. The list can go long and our method is extensible to adapt such a list.

7   Evaluation

We evaluated *GEM* using the TPC-DS benchmark [19]. TPC-DS provides a set of DW tables –both facts and dimensions– along with a set of data sources. ETL operations (or data maintenance functions according to TPC-DS) are also provided, for maintaining fact tables and dimensions. Finally, a set of business

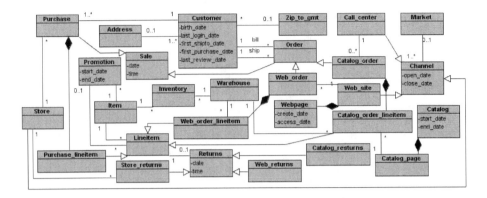

Fig. 3. Ontology for TPC-DS data sources

queries (i.e., business requirements) exists. Having all these constructs allows us to evaluate our method as follows. Starting only from the business queries and the data source, we use *GEM* for producing the DW schema and ETL operations. Then, we compare our solutions to the design constructs provided by the benchmark. Here, due to limited space, we show results concerning the store_sales cube (the results generalize throughout the whole benchmark though).

We worked as follows. We constructed an ontology containing all source tables, specializations, and added some additional concepts that do not map to data sources (see Figure 3). Thus, we intentionally make the ontology more complex by adding more classes to stress *GEM*; note, that adding more associations does not affect *GEM*, since these would be pruned during AOS creation.

First, we examine the search space produced for AOS creation. Figure 4 presents the number of algorithm iterations needed to converge, the total number of paths computed, the number of paths between tagged concepts (i.e., the output), and the maximum length of the output, per business query. The results show that the search space is not exponential regarding the length of the longest path. Indeed, although the average length of the longest path is 8, in the worst case, our algorithm computes no more than 178 paths (24 between tagged concepts). These findings verify the feasibility and efficiency of our approach in real-world cases. In fact, the worst total time did not exceed 900ms. Constructing AOS is the most expensive part of our method; the rest tasks are processed fairly fast, in much less time.

Next, we evaluated the quality of our solutions (see Figure 5). Every business query reveals a part of the final design (tables and attributes). Frequently, business queries reveal overlapping information. However, after a few iterations over these queries (in fact, after the fifth query) we identified correctly *all* target tables. Since numerous attributes are involved overall, identifying them requires digging into more requirements. After processing 11 business queries, we identified almost 40% of the total attributes. However, attributes are added throughout the whole process. For example, surrogate keys are identified after Phase III of the ETL operation identification task.

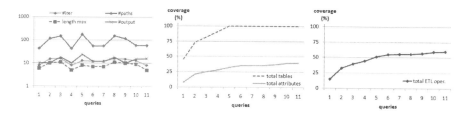

Fig. 4. Space   **Fig. 5.** MD coverage   **Fig. 6.** ETL coverage

Two observations can be made at this point. One may find tempting the fact that the target tables are identified really fast. Thus, after a certain point of her choice, the designer might want to stop this automatic process and start refining the design by herself. As an aside issue, many business queries involve the same target design constructs. This means that these constructs (e.g., tables) should be quite popular and this information can help us in the physical design; e.g., for choosing appropriate indices or partitioning schemes.

Similar are the findings for the identification of ETL operations (see Figure 6). *GEM* returned almost 60% of ETL operations after the completion of Phase I. The remaining operations (not shown in the figure) are mostly surrogate key assignments and a few SCDs, which are identified after Phase III. Therefore, *GEM* identifies the complete set of ETL operations for the TPC-DS case.

8   Related Work

Various efforts have been proposed for the conceptual ETL modeling. These include approaches based on ad hoc formalisms [20], on standard languages like UML (e.g., [9]), MDA (e.g., [11,12]), BPMN [1], and on semantic Web technology and graph transformations [17]. Most of these works do not specifically consider business requirements and do not describe how such requirements drive ETL design. Recent research on optimization of information integration flows proposed techniques for incorporating such objectives into ETL design [2,15,16,21]. However, none of the abovementioned research efforts considers synchronous creation of MD design. In addition, commercial, off-the-shelf ETL products do not offer functionality similar to the one described in this paper.

Many works have dealt with designing DW models; e.g., [3,5,11,13,18], to mention a few, but the list is long. However, in most works, it seems that the more the process gets automated, the more the integration of requirements is overlooked on the way. Recently, the use of ontologies was considered for facilitating this task [13]. However, that work aims at identifying the MD knowledge contained in the sources and overlooks business requirements. Another approach to MD design considers business requirements too [14], but the f-req are considered in the form of SQL queries, so a major design task is done manually. *GEM* automates this part and automatically creates such queries from f-req. In addition, *GEM* is different from all previous approaches in that it identifies the ETL operation at the same time.

9   Conclusions

We have presented *GEM*. A system that facilitates the (semi-)automatic generation of ETL and MD conceptual designs, starting from a set of business requirements and data sources. In particular, we have described how the requirements can be validated and enriched, in order to produce an annotated ontology containing correct information for both the sources and the requirements. Then, we have shown how to use this ontology for producing the MD and ETL conceptual designs. Finally, we have reported on our experimental findings working on the TPC-DS benchmark. Our future plans involve extending our techniques to the logical and physical levels, for facilitating their (semi-)automatic production.

Acknowledgements. This work has been partly supported by the Ministerio de Ciencia e Innovación under project TIN2008-03863.

References

1. Akkaoui, Z.E., Zimányi, E.: Defining ETL worfklows using BPMN and BPEL. In: DOLAP, pp. 41–48 (2009)
2. Dayal, U., Castellanos, M., Simitsis, A., Wilkinson, K.: Data Integration Flows for Business Intelligence. In: EDBT, pp. 1–11 (2009)
3. Golfarelli, M., Maio, D., Rizzi, S.: The Dimensional Fact Model: A Conceptual Model for Data Warehouses. IJCIS, 215–247 (1998)
4. Golfarelli, M., Rizzi, S.: Data Warehouse Design. Modern Principles and Methodologies. McGraw-Hill, New York (2009)
5. Hüsemann, B., Lechtenbörger, J., Vossen, G.: Conceptual Data Warehouse Modeling. In: DMDW, pp. 1–11 (2000)
6. Lechtenbörger, J., Vossen, G.: Multidimensional Normal Forms for Data Warehouse Design. Information Systems, 415–434 (2003)
7. Lehner, W., Albrecht, J., Wedekind, H.: Normal Forms for Multidimensional Databases. In: SSDBM, pp. 63–72 (1998)
8. Lenz, H., Shoshani, A.: Summarizability in OLAP and Statistical Data Bases. In: SSDBM, pp. 132–143 (1997)
9. Luján-Mora, S., Vassiliadis, P., Trujillo, J.: Data mapping diagrams for data warehouse design with UML. In: Atzeni, P., Chu, W., Lu, H., Zhou, S., Ling, T.-W. (eds.) ER 2004. LNCS, vol. 3288, pp. 191–204. Springer, Heidelberg (2004)
10. Mazón, J., Lechtenbörger, J., Trujillo, J.: A Survey on Summarizability Issues in Multidimensional Modeling. DKE, 1452–1469 (2009)
11. Mazón, J.N., Trujillo, J.: An MDA Approach for the Development of Data Warehouses. In: DSS, pp. 41–58 (2008)
12. Muñoz, L., Mazón, J.N., Trujillo, J.: Automatic Generation of ETL Processes from Conceptual Models. In: DOLAP, pp. 33–40 (2009)
13. Romero, O., Abelló, A.: A Framework for Multidimensional Design of Data Warehouses from Ontologies. Data & Knowledge Engineering 69(11), 1138–1157 (2010)
14. Romero, O., Abelló, A.: Automatic Validation of Requirements to Support Multidimensional Design. Data Knowl. Eng. 69(9), 917–942 (2010)
15. Simitsis, A., Wilkinson, K., Castellanos, M., Dayal, U.: QoX-driven ETL design: Reducing the Cost of ETL Consulting Engagements. In: SIGMOD (2009)

16. Simitsis, A., Wilkinson, K., Dayal, U., Castellanos, M.: Optimizing ETL Workflows for Fault-Tolerance. In: ICDE, pp. 385–396 (2010)
17. Skoutas, D., Simitsis, A.: Ontology-Based Conceptual Design of ETL Processes for Both Structured and Semi-Structured Data. IJSWIS, 1–24 (2007)
18. Song, I., Khare, R., Dai, B.: SAMSTAR: A Semi-Automated Lexical Method for Generating STAR Schemas from an ER Diagram. In: DOLAP, pp. 9–16 (2007)
19. TPC: TPC-DS specification (2010), http://www.tpc.org/tpcds/
20. Vassiliadis, P., Simitsis, A., Skiadopoulos, S.: Conceptual modeling for ETL processes. In: DOLAP, pp. 14–21 (2002)
21. Wilkinson, K., Simitsis, A.: Designing Integration Flows Using Hypercubes. In: EDBT (2011)
22. Yu, E.S.K., Mylopoulos, J.: From E-R to "A-R" - Modelling Strategic Actor Relationships for Business Process Reengineering. In: ER, pp. 548–565 (1994)

ETLMR: A Highly Scalable Dimensional ETL Framework Based on MapReduce

Xiufeng Liu, Christian Thomsen, and Torben Bach Pedersen

Dept. of Computer Science, Aalborg University
{xiliu,chr,tbp}@cs.aau.dk

Abstract. Extract-Transform-Load (ETL) flows periodically populate data warehouses (DWs) with data from different source systems. An increasing challenge for ETL flows is processing huge volumes of data quickly. MapReduce is establishing itself as the de-facto standard for large-scale data-intensive processing. However, MapReduce lacks support for high-level ETL specific constructs, resulting in low ETL programmer productivity. This paper presents a scalable dimensional ETL framework, *ETLMR*, based on MapReduce. ETLMR has built-in native support for operations on DW-specific constructs such as star schemas, snowflake schemas and slowly changing dimensions (SCDs). This enables ETL developers to construct scalable MapReduce-based ETL flows with very few code lines. To achieve good performance and load balancing, a number of dimension and fact processing schemes are presented, including techniques for efficiently processing different types of dimensions. The paper describes the integration of ETLMR with a MapReduce framework and evaluates its performance on large realistic data sets. The experimental results show that ETLMR achieves very good scalability and compares favourably with other MapReduce data warehousing tools.

1 Introduction

In data warehousing, ETL flows are responsible for collecting data from different data sources, transformation, and cleansing to comply with user-defined business rules and requirements. Traditional ETL technologies face new challenges as the growth of information explodes nowadays, e.g., it becomes common for an enterprise to collect hundreds of gigabytes of data for processing and analysis each day. The vast amount of data makes ETL extremely time-consuming, but the time window assigned for processing data typically remains short. Moreover, to adapt rapidly changing business environments, users have an increasing demand of getting data as soon as possible. The use of parallelization is the key to achieve better performance and scalability for those challenges. In recent years, a novel "cloud computing" technology, *MapReduce* [6], has been widely used for parallel computing in data-intensive areas. A MapReduce program is written as *map* and *reduce* functions, which process key/value pairs and are executed in many parallel instances.

We see that MapReduce can be a good foundation for the ETL parallelization. In ETL, the data processing exhibits the *composable* property such that the processing of dimensions and facts can be split into smaller computation units and the partial results

A. Cuzzocrea and U. Dayal (Eds.): DaWaK 2011, LNCS 6862, pp. 96–111, 2011.

from these computation units can be merged to constitute the final results in a DW. This complies well with the MapReduce paradigm in term of *map* and *reduce*.

ETL flows are inherently complex, which is due to the plethora of ETL-specific activities such as transformation, cleansing, filtering, aggregating and loading. Programming of highly parallel and distributed systems is also challenging. To implement an ETL program to function in a distributed environment is thus very costly, time-consuming, and error-prone. MapReduce, on the other hand, provides programming flexibility, cost-effective scalability and capacity on commodity machines and a MapReduce framework can provide inter-process communication, fault-tolerance, load balancing and task scheduling to a parallel ETL program out of the box. Further, MapReduce is a very popular framework and is establishing itself as the de-facto standard for large-scale data-intensive processing. It is thus interesting to see how MapReduce can be applied to the field of ETL programming.

MapReduce is, however, a generic programming model. It lacks support for high-level DW/ETL specific constructs such as the dimensional constructs of star schemas, snowflake schemas, and SCDs. This results in low ETL programmer productivity. To implement a parallel ETL program on MapReduce is thus still not easy because of the inherent complexity of ETL-specific activities such as the processing for different schemas and SCDs.

In this paper, we present a parallel dimensional ETL framework based on MapReduce, named *ETLMR*, which directly supports high-level ETL-specific dimensional constructs such as star schemas, snowflake schemas, and SCDs. We believe this to be the first paper to specifically address ETL for *dimensional* schemas on MapReduce. The paper makes several contributions: We leverage the functionality of MapReduce to the ETL parallelization and provide a scalable, fault-tolerant, and very lightweight ETL framework which hides the complexity of MapReduce. We present a number of novel methods which are used to process the dimensions of a star schema, snowflaked dimensions, SCDs and data-intensive dimensions. In addition, we introduce the offline dimension scheme which scales better than the online dimension scheme when handling massive workloads. The evaluations show that ETLMR achieves very good scalability and compares favourably with other MapReduce data warehousing tools.

The running example: To show the use of ETLMR, we use a running example throughout this paper. This example is inspired by a project which applies different tests to web pages. Each test is applied to each page and the test outputs the number of errors detected. The test results are written into a number of tab-separated files, which serve as the data sources. The data is processed to be stored in a DW with the star schema shown in Fig. 1. This schema comprises a fact table and three dimension tables. Note that *pagedim* is a slowly changing dimension. Later, we will consider a partly snowflaked (i.e., normalized) schema.

The remainder of the paper is structured as follows: Section 2 gives an overview of ETLMR. Sections 3 and 4 present dimension processing and fact processing, respectively. Section 5 introduces the implementation of ETLMR in the Disco MapReduce framework, and presents the experimental evaluation. Section 6 reviews related work. Finally, Section 7 concludes the paper and provides ideas for future work.

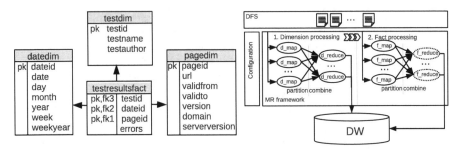

Fig. 1. Star schema of the running example   **Fig. 2.** Data flow on MapReduce

2   Overview

Fig. 2 illustrates the data flow using ETLMR on MapReduce. In ETLMR, the dimension processing is done at first in a MapReduce job, then the fact processing is done in another MapReduce job. A MapReduce job spawns a number of parallel map/reduce tasks[1] for processing dimension or fact data. Each task consists of several steps, including reading data from a distributed file system (DFS), executing the map function, partitioning, combining the map output, executing the reduce function and writing results. In dimension processing, the input data for a dimension table can be processed by different processing methods, e.g., the data can be processed by a single task or by all tasks. In fact processing, the data for a fact table is partitioned into a number of equal-sized data files which then are processed by parallel tasks. This includes looking up dimension keys and bulk loading the processed fact data into the DW. The processing of fact data in the reducers can be omitted (shown by dotted ellipses in Fig. 2) if no aggregation of the fact data is done before it is loaded.

Algorithm 1 shows the details of the whole process of using ETLMR. The operations in lines 2-4 and 6-7 are the MapReduce steps which are responsible for initialization, invoking jobs for processing dimensions and facts, and returning processing information. Line 1 and 5 are the non-MapReduce steps which are used for preparing input data sets and synchronizing dimensions among nodes (if no DFS is installed).

Algorithm 1. The ETL process

1: Partition the input data sets;
2: Read the configuration parameters and initialize;
3: Read the input data and relay the data to the map function in the map readers;
4: Process dimension data and load it into dimension stores;
5: Synchronize the dimensions across the clustered computers, if applicable;
6: Prepare fact processing (connect to and cache dimensions);
7: Read the input data for fact processing and perform transformations in mappers;
8: Bulk load fact data into the DW.

ETLMR defines all the run-time parameters in a configuration file, including declarations of dimension and fact tables, dimension processing methodologies, user-defined-functions (UDFs) for processing data, number of mappers and reducers, and others. A complete example is available at [9].

---

[1] Map/reduce task denotes map tasks and reduce tasks running separately.

3 Dimension Processing

In ETLMR, each dimension table has a corresponding definition in the configuration file. For example, we define the object for the dimension table *testdim* of the running example by *testdim = CachedDimension(name='testdim', key='testid', defaultidvalue =-1, attributes=['testname', 'testauthor'], lookupatts=['testname',])*. It is declared as a cached dimension which means that its data can be temporarily kept in memory. ETLMR also offers other dimension classes for declaring different dimension tables, including *SlowlyChangingDimension* and *SnowflakedDimension*, each of which are configured by means of a number of parameters for specifying the name of the dimension table, the dimension key, the attributes of dimension table, the lookup attributes (which identify a row uniquely), and others. Each class offers a number of functions for dimension operations such as *lookup*, *insert*, *ensure*, etc.

ETLMR employs MapReduce's primitives *map*, *partition*, *combine*, and *reduce* to process data. This is, however, hidden from the user who only specifies transformations applied to the data and declarations of dimension tables and fact tables. A map/reduce task reads data by iterating over lines from a partitioned data set. A line is first processed by *map*, then by *partition* which determines the target reducer, and then by *combine* which groups values having the same key. The data is then written to an intermediate file (there is one file for each reducer). In the reduce step, a reduce reader reads a list of key/values pairs from an intermediate file and invokes *reduce* to process the list. In the following, we present different approaches to process dimension data.

3.1 One Dimension One Task

In this approach, map tasks process data for all dimensions by applying user-defined transformations and by finding the relevant parts of the source data for each dimension. The data for a given dimension is then processed by a single reduce task. We name this method *one dimension one task* (*ODOT* for short).

The data unit moving around within ETLMR is a dictionary mapping attribute names to values. Here, we call it a *row*, e.g., *row*={*'url':'www.dom0.tl0/p0.htm','size':'12553','serverversion':'SomeServer/1.0','downloaddate':'2011-01-31','lastmoddate':'2011-01-01', 'test':'Test001', 'errors':'7'*}. ETLMR reads lines from the input files and passes them on as rows. A mapper does projection on rows to prune unnecessary data for each dimension and makes key/value pairs to be processed by reducers. If we define dim_i for a dimension table and its relevant attributes, $(a_0, a_1..., a_n)$, in the data source schema, the mapper will generate the map output, $(key, value) = (dim_i.name, \prod_{a_0,a_1,...,a_n}(row))$ where $name$ represents the name of dimension table. The MapReduce partitioner partitions map output based on the key, i.e., $dim_i.name$, such that the data of dim_i will go to a single reducer (see Fig. 3). To optimize, the values with identical keys (i.e., dimension table name) are combined in the combiner before they are sent to the reducers such that the network communication cost can be reduced. In a reducer, a row is first processed by UDFs to do data transformations, then the processed row is inserted into the dimension store, i.e., the dimension table in the DW or in an offline dimension store (described later). When ETLMR does this data insertion, it has the following *reduce* functionality: If the row does not exist in the dimension table, the row is inserted. If the row exists and its values are unchanged, nothing is done. If there are changes, the row in the table is updated accordingly. The ETLMR dimension classes provide this functionality in a single function, $dim_i.ensure(row)$. For an SCD, this function adds a new version if needed, and updates the values of the SCD attributes, e.g., the validto and version.

We have now introduced the most fundamental method for dimension processing where only a limited number of reducers can be utilized. Therefore, its drawback is that it is not optimized for the case where some dimensions contain large amounts of data, namely data-intensive dimensions.

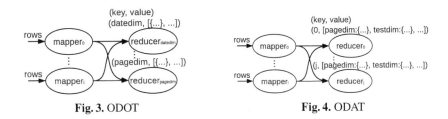

Fig. 3. ODOT   Fig. 4. ODAT

3.2   One Dimension All Tasks

We now describe another approach in which all reduce tasks process data for all dimensions. We name it *one dimension all tasks* (*ODAT* for short). In some cases, the data volume of a dimension is very large, e.g., the *pagedim* dimension in the running example. If we employ ODOT, the task of processing data for this dimension table will determine the overall performance (assume all tasks run on similar machines). We therefore refine the ODOT in two places, the map output partition and the reduce functions. With ODAT, ETLMR partitions the map output by round-robin partitioning such that the reducers receive equally many rows (see Fig. 4). In the reduce function, two issues are considered in order to process the dimension data properly by the parallel tasks:

The first issue is how to keep the uniqueness of dimension key values as the data for a dimension table is processed by all tasks. We propose two approaches. The first one is to use a global ID generator and use *post-fixing* (detailed in Section 3.4) to merge rows having the same values in the dimension *lookup* attributes (but different key values) into one row. The other approach is to use private ID generators and post-fixing. Each task has its own ID generator, and after the data is loaded into the dimension table, post-fixing is employed to fix the resulting duplicated key values. This requires the uniqueness constraint on the dimension key to be disabled before the data processing.

The second issue is how to handle concurrency problem when data manipulation language (DML) SQL such as UPDATE, DELETE, etc. is issued by several tasks. Consider, for example, the type-2 SCD table *pagedim* for which INSERTs and UPDATEs are frequent (the SCD attributes *validfrom* and *validto* are updated). There are at least two ways to tackle this problem. The first one is row-based commit in which a COMMIT is issued after every row has been inserted so that the inserted row will not be locked. However, row-based commit is more expensive than transaction commit, thus, it is not very useful for a data-intensive dimension table. Another and better solution is to delay the UPDATE to the post-fixing which fixes all the problematic data when all the tasks have finished.

In the following section, we propose an alternative approach for processing snow-flaked dimensions without requiring the post-fixing.

3.3 Snowflaked Dimension Processing

In a snowflake schema, dimensions are normalized meaning that there are foreign key references and hierarchies between dimension tables. If we consider the dependencies when processing dimensions, the post-fixing step can be avoided. We therefore propose two methods particularly for snowflaked dimensions: *level-wise processing* and *hierarchy-wise processing*.

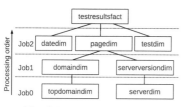

Fig. 5. Level-wise processing

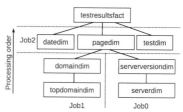

Fig. 6. Hierarchy-wise processing

Level-wise processing. This refers to processing snowflaked dimensions in an order from the leaves towards the root (the dimension table referred by the fact table is the root and a dimension table without a foreign key referencing other dimension tables is a leaf). The dimension tables with dependencies (i.e., with foreign key references) are processed in sequential jobs, e.g., *Job1* depends on *Job0*, and *Job2* depends on *Job1* in Fig. 5. Each job processes independent dimension tables (without direct and indirect foreign key references) by parallel tasks, i.e., one dimension table is processed by one task. Therefore, in the level-wise processing of the running example, *Job0* first processes *topdomaindim* and *serverdim* in parallel, then *Job1* processes *domaindim* and *serverversiondim*, and finally *Job2* processes *pagedim*, *datedim* and *testdim*. It corresponds to the configuration *loadorder = [('topdomaindim','serverdim'), ('domaindim', 'serverversiondim'), ('pagedim','datedim','testdim')]*. With this order, a higher level dimension table (the referencing dimension table) is not processed until the lower level ones (the referenced dimension tables) have been processed and thus, the referential integrity can be ensured.

Hierarchy-wise processing. This refers to processing a snowflaked dimension in a branch-wise fashion (see Fig. 6). The root dimension, *pagedim*, derives two branches, each of which is defined as a separate snowflaked dimension, i.e., *domainsf = SnowflakedDimension([(domaindim, topdomaindim)])*, and *serverversionsf = SnowflakedDimension([(serverversiondim, serverdim)])*. They are processed by two parallel jobs, *Job0* and *Job1*, each of which processes in a sequential manner, i.e., *topdomaindim* followed by *domaindim* in *Job0* and *serverdim* followed by *serverversiondim* in *Job1*. The root dimension, *pagedim*, is not processed until the dimensions on its connected branches have been processed. It, together with *datedim* and *testdim*, is processed by the *Job2*.

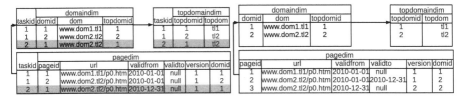

Fig. 7. Before post-fixing   Fig. 8. After post-fixing

3.4   Post-fixing

As discussed in Section 3.2, post-fixing is a remedy to fix problematic data in ODAT when all the tasks of the dimension processing have finished. Four situations require data post-fixing: 1) using a global ID generator which gives rise to duplicated values in the lookup attributes; 2) using private ID generators which produce duplicated key values; 3) processing snowflaked dimensions (and *not* using level-wise or hierarchy.wise processing) which leads to duplicated values in lookup and key attributes; and 4) processing slowly changing dimensions which results in SCD attributes taking improper values.

Example. *Consider two map/reduce tasks, task 1 and task 2, that process the* `page` *dimension which we here assume to be snowflaked. Each task uses a private ID generator. The root dimension,* `pagedim`*, is a type-2 SCD. Rows with the lookup attribute value url='www.dom2.tl2/p0.htm' are processed by both the tasks.*

Figure 7 depicts the resulting data in the dimension tables where the white rows were processed by task 1 and the grey rows were processed by task 2. Each row is labelled with the `taskid` *of the task that processed it. The problems include duplicate IDs in each dimension table and improper values in the SCD attributes,* `validfrom`, `validto`, *and* `version`. *The post-fixing program first fixes the* `topdomaindim` *such that rows with the same value for the lookup attribute (i.e.,* `url`*) are merged into one row with a single ID. Thus, the two rows with* `topdom` = tl2 *are merged into one row. The references to* `topdomaindim` *from* `domaindim` *are also updated to reference the correct (fixed) rows. In the same way,* `pagedim` *is updated to merge the two rows representing www.dom2.tl2. Finally,* `pagedim` *is updated. Here, the post-fixing also has to fix the values for the SCD attributes. The result is shown in Fig. 8.*

The post-fixing invokes a recursive function (see Algorithm 2) to fix the problematic data in the order from the leaf dimension tables to the root dimension table. It comprises four steps: 1) assign new IDs to the rows with duplicate IDs; 2) update the foreign keys on the referencing dimension tables; 3) delete duplicated rows which have identical values in the business key attributes and foreign key attributes; and 4) fix the values in the SCD attributes

---

Algorithm 2. post_fix(*dim*)

---

refdims ← The referenced dimensions of *dim*
for *ref* in *refdims* **do**
    itr ← post_fix(*ref*)
    for ((*taskid, keyvalue*), *newkeyvalue*) in *itr* **do**
        Update *dim* set *dim.key* = *newkeyvalue* where
            dim.taskid=taskid and *dim.key=keyvalue*
ret ← An empty list
Assign *newkeyvalues* to *dim*'s keys and add
    ((*taskid, keyvalue*), *newkeyvalue*) to *ret*
if *dim* is not the root **then**
    Delete the duplicate rows, which have identical values in
    dim's lookup attributes
if *dim* is a type-2 SCD **then**
    Fix the values on SCD attributes, e.g., dates and version
return *ret*

if applicable. In most cases, it is not needed to fix something in each of the steps for a dimension with problematic data. For example, if a global ID generator is employed, all rows will have different IDs (such that step 1 is not needed) but they may have duplicate values in the lookup attributes (such that step 3 is needed). ETLMR's implementation uses an embedded SQLite database for data management during the post-fixing. Thus, the task IDs are not stored in the target DW, but only internally in ETLMR.

3.5   Offline Dimensions

In ODOT and ODAT, the map/reduce tasks interact with the DW's ("*online*") dimensions directly through database connections at run-time and the performance is affected by the outside DW DBMS and the database communication cost. To optimize, the *offline dimension* scheme is proposed, in which the tasks do not interact with the DW directly, but with the distributed offline dimensions residing physically in all nodes. It has several characteristics and advantages. First, a dimension is partitioned into multiple smaller-sized sub-dimension, and small-sized dimensions can benefit dimension *lookup*s, especially for a data-intensive dimension such as *pagedim*. Second, high performance storage systems can be employed to persist dimension data. Dimensions are configured to be fully or partially cached in main memory to speedup the *lookup*s when processing facts. In addition, offline dimensions do not require direct communication with the DW and the overhead (from the network and the DBMS) is greatly reduced. ETLMR has offline dimension implementations for one dimension one task (*ODOT (offline)* for short) and *hybrid*. As the ODOT (offline) is similar to the ODOT we discussed in Section 3.1, we now only describe the latter. Hybrid combines the characteristics of ODOT and ODAT. In this approach, the dimensions are divided into two groups, the most data-intensive dimension and the other dimensions. The input data for the most data-intensive dimension table is partitioned based on the business keys, e.g., on the *url* of *pagedim*, and processed by all the map tasks (this is similar to ODAT), while for the other dimension tables, their data is processed in reducers, a reducer exclusively processing the data for one dimension table (this is similar to ODOT). As the input data for most data-intensive dimension is partitioned based on business keys, the rows with identical business key values are processed within the same mapper such that when we employ a global ID generator to generate the dimension key values, the post-fixing is not needed. This improves the processing performance.

In the offline dimension scheme, the dimensions are expected to reside in the nodes permanently and will not be loaded into the DW until this is explicitly requested.

4   Fact Processing

Fact processing is the second phase in ETLMR, which consists of looking up of dimension keys, doing aggregation on measures (if applicable), and loading the processed facts into the DW. Similarly to the dimension processing, the definitions and settings of fact tables are also declared in the configuration file. ETLMR provides the *BulkFactTable* class which supports bulk loading of facts to DW. For example, the fact table of the running example is defined as *testresultsfact=BulkFactTable(name='testresultsfact', keyrefs=['pageid', 'testid', 'dateid'], measures=['errors'], bulkloader=UDF_pgcopy, bulksize=5000000)*. The parameters are the fact table name, a list of the keys referencing dimension tables, a list of measures, the bulk loader function, and the size of the bulks to load. The bulk loader is a UDF which can be configured to satisfy different types of DBMSs.

Algorithm 3 shows the pseudocode for processing facts.

The function can be used as the map function or as the reduce function. If no aggregations (such as *sum*, *average*, or *count*) are required, the function is configured to be the map function and the reduce step is omitted for better performance. If aggregations are required, the function is configured to be the reduce function since the aggregations must be computed from all the data. This approach is flexible and good for performance. Line 1 retrieves the fact table definitions in the configuration file and they are then processed sequentially in line 2–8. The processing consists of two major operations: 1) look

---
Algorithm 3. *process_fact(row)*

Require: A *row* from the input data and the *config*
1: *facttbls* ← the fact tables defined in *config*
2: **for** *facttbl* in *facttbls* **do**
3:      *dims* ← the dimensions referenced by *facttbl*
4:      **for** *dim* in *dims* **do**
5:          *row[dim.key]* ← *dim*.lookup(*row*)
6:      *rowhandlers* ← *facttbl.rowhandlers*
7:      **for** *handler* in *rowhandlers* **do**
8:          *handler(row)*
9:      *facttbl*.insert(*row*)

---

up the keys from the referenced dimension tables (line 3–5), and 2) process the fact data by the *rowhandlers*, which are user-defined transformation functions used for data type conversions, calculating measures, etc. (line 6–8). Line 9 invokes the insert function to insert the fact data into the DW. The processed fact data is not inserted into the fact table directly, but instead added into a configurably-sized buffer where it is kept temporarily. When a buffer becomes full, its data is loaded into the DW by using the bulk load. Each map/reduce task has a separate buffer and bulk loader such that tasks can do bulk loading in parallel.

5   Implementation and Evaluation

ETLMR uses and extends *pygrametl* [14], a Python code-based programming framework, which enables high programmer productivity in implementing an ETL program. We choose Disco [2] as our MapReduce platform since it has the best support for Python. In the rest of this section, we measure the performance achieved by the proposed methods. We evaluate the system scalability on various sizes of tasks and data sets and compare with other business intelligence tools using MapReduce.

5.1   Experimental Setup

All experiments are conducted on a cluster of 6 nodes connected through a gigabit switch and each having an Intel(R) Xeon(R) CPU X3220 2.4GHz with 4 cores, 4 GB RAM, and a SATA hard disk (350 GB, 3 GB/s, 16 MB Cache and 7200 RPM). All nodes are running the Linux 2.6.32 kernel with Disco 0.2.4, Python 2.6, and ETLMR installed. The GlusterFS DFS is set up for the cluster. PostgreSQL 8.3 is used for the DW DBMS and is installed on one of the nodes. One node serves as the master and the others as the workers. Each worker runs 4 parallel map/reduce tasks, i.e., in total 20 parallel tasks run. The time for bulk loading is not measured as the way data is bulk loaded into a database is an implementation choice which is independent of and outside the control of the ETL framework. To include the time for bulk loading would thus clutter the results. We note that bulk loading can be parallelized using off-the-shelf functionality.

5.2 Test Data

We continue to use the running example. We use a data generator to generate the test data for each experiment. In line with Jean and Ghemawat's assumption that MapReduce usually operates on numerous small files rather than a single, large, merged file [5], the test data sets are partitioned and saved into a set of files. These files provide the input for the dimension and fact processing phases. We generate two data sets, *bigdim* and *smalldim* which differ in the size of the *page* dimension. In particular, 80 GB *bigdim* data results in 10.6 GB fact data (193,961,068 rows) and 6.2 GB *page* dimension data (13,918,502 rows) in the DW while 80 GB *smalldim* data results in 12.2 GB (222,253,124 rows) fact data and 54 MB *page* dimension data (193,460 rows) in the DW. Both data sets produce 32 KB *test* (1,000 rows) and 16 KB *date* dimension data (1,254 rows).

5.3 Scalability of Proposed Processing Methods

In this experiment, we compare the scalability and performance of the different ETLMR processing methods. We use a fixed-size *bigdim* data set (20 GB), scale the number of parallel tasks from 4 to 20, and measure the total elapsed time from start to finish. The results for a snowflake schema and a star schema are shown in Fig. 9 and Fig. 10, respectively. The graphs show the *speedup*, computed by $T_{4,odot,snowflake}/T_n$ where $T_{4,odot,snowflake}$ is the processing time for *ODOT* using 4 tasks in a snowflake schema and T_n is the processing time when using n tasks for the given processing method.

We see that the overall time used for the star schema is less than for the snowflake schema. This is because the snowflake schema has dimension dependencies and hierarchies which require more (level-wise) processing. We also see that the offline hybrid scales the best and achieves almost linear speedup. The ODAT in Fig. 10 behaves similarly. This is because the dimensions and facts in offline hybrid and ODAT are processed by all tasks which results in good balancing and scalability. In comparison, ODOT, offline ODOT, level-wise, and hierarchy-wise do not scale as well as ODAT and hybrid since only a limited number of tasks are utilized to process dimensions (a dimension is only processed in a single task). The offline dimension scheme variants outperform the corresponding online ones, e.g., offline ODOT vs. ODOT. This is caused by 1) using a high performance storage system to save dimensions on all nodes and provide in-memory lookup; 2) The data-intensive dimension, *pagedim*, is partitioned into smaller chunks which also benefits the lookup; 3) Unlike the online dimension scheme, the offline dimension scheme does not communicate directly with the DW and this reduces the communication cost considerably. Finally, the results show the relative efficiency for the optimized methods which are much faster than the baseline ODOT.

5.4 System Scalability

In this experiment, we evaluate the scalability of ETLMR by varying the number of tasks and the size of the data sets. We select the hybrid processing method, use the

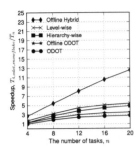 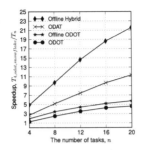 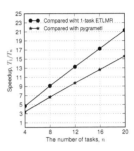

Fig. 9. Parallel ETL for snowflake schema, 20 GB

Fig. 10. Parallel ETL for star schema, 20 GB

Fig. 11. Speedup with increasing tasks, 80 GB

offline dimension scheme, and conduct the testing on a star schema, as this method not only can process data among all the tasks (unlike ODOT in which only a limited number of tasks are used), but also showed the best scalability in the previous experiment. In the dimension processing phase, the mappers are responsible for processing the data-intensive dimension *pagedim* while the reducers are responsible for the other two dimensions, *datedim* and *testdim*, each using only a single reducer. In the fact processing phase, no reducer is used as no aggregation operations are required.

We first do two tests to get comparison baselines by using one task (named *1-task ETLMR*) and (plain, non-MapReduce) *pygrametl*, respectively. Here, pygrametl also employs 2-phase processing, i.e., the dimension processing is done before the fact processing. The tests are done on the same machine with a single CPU (all cores but one are disabled). The tests process 80 GB *bigdim* data. We compute the speedups by using T_1/T_n where T_1 represents the elapsed time for 1-task ETLMR or for pygrametl, and T_n the time for ETLMR using n tasks. Fig. 11 shows that ETLMR achieves a nearly linear speedup in the number of tasks when compared to 1-task ETLMR (the line on the top). When compared to pygrametl, ETLMR has a nearly linear speedup (the lower line) as well, but the speedup is a little lower. This is because the baseline, 1-task ETLMR, has a greater value due to the overhead from the MapReduce framework.

To learn more about the details of the speedup, we break down the execution time of the slowest task by reference to the MapReduce steps when using the two data sets (see Table 1). As the time for dimension processing is very small for *smalldim* data, e.g., 1.5 min for 4 tasks and less than 1 min for the others, only its fact processing time is shown. When the *bigdim* data is used, we can see that partitioning input data, map, partitioning map output (dims), and combination (dims) dominate the execution. More specifically, partitioning input data and map (see the *Part.Input* and *Map func.* columns) achieve a nearly linear speedup in the two phases. In the dimension processing, the map output is partitioned and combined for the two dimensions, *datedim* and *testdim*. Also here, we see a nearly linear speedup (see the *Part.* and *Comb.* columns). As the combined data of each is only processed by a single reducer, the time spent on reducing is proportional to the size of data. However, the time becomes very small since the data has been merged in combiners (see *Red. func.* column). The cost of post-fixing after dimension processing is not listed in the table since it is not required in this case

Table 1. Execution time distribution, 80 GB (min.)

Testing data	Phase	Task Num	Part. Input	Map func.	Part.	Comb.	Red. func.	Others	Total
bigdim data (results in 10.6GB facts)	dims	4	47.43	178.97	8.56	24.57	1.32	0.1	260.95
		8	25.58	90.98	4.84	12.97	1.18	0.1	135.65
		12	17.21	60.86	3.24	8.57	1.41	0.1	91.39
		16	12.65	47.38	2.50	6.54	1.56	0.1	70.73
		20	10.19	36.41	1.99	5.21	1.32	0.1	55.22
	facts	4	47.20	183.24	0.0	0.0	0.0	0.1	230.44
		8	24.32	92.48	0.0	0.0	0.0	0.1	116.80
		12	16.13	65.50	0.0	0.0	0.0	0.1	81.63
		16	12.12	51.40	0.0	0.0	0.0	0.1	63.52
		20	9.74	40.92	0.0	0.0	0.0	0.1	50.66
smalldim data (results in 12.2GB facts)	facts	4	49.85	211.20	0.0	0.0	0.0	0.1	261.15
		8	25.23	106.20	0.0	0.0	0.0	0.1	131.53
		12	17.05	71.21	0.0	0.0	0.0	0.1	88.36
		16	12.70	53.23	0.0	0.0	0.0	0.1	66.03
		20	10.04	42.44	0.0	0.0	0.0	0.1	52.58

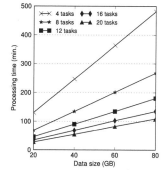

Fig. 12. Proc. time when scaling up bigdim data

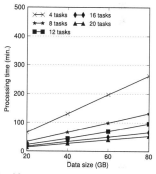

Fig. 13. Proc. time when scaling up smalldim data

where a global key generator is employed to create dimension IDs and the input data is partitioned by the business key of the SCD *pagedim* (see section 3.4).

In the fact processing, the reduce function needs no execution time as there is no reducer. The time for all the other parts, including map and reduce initialization, map output partitioning, writing and reading intermediate files, and network traffic, is relatively small, but it does not necessarily decrease linearly when more tasks are added (*Others* column). To summarize (see *Total* column), ETLMR achieves a nearly linear speedup when the parallelism is scaled up, i.e., the execution time of 8 tasks is nearly half that of 4 tasks, and the execution time of 16 tasks is nearly half that of 8 tasks.

We now proceed to another experiment where we for a given number of tasks size up the data sets from 20 to 80 GB and measure the elapsed processing time. Fig. 12 and Fig. 13 show the results for the *bigdim* and *smalldim* data sets, respectively. It can be seen that ETLMR scales linearly in the size of the data sets.

5.5   Comparison with other Data Warehousing Tools

There are some MapReduce data warehousing tools available, including Hive [15,16], Pig [10] and Pentaho Data Integration (PDI) [3]. Hive and Pig both offer data storage on the Hadoop distributed file system (HDFS) and scripting languages which have some limited ETL abilities. They are both more like a DBMS instead of a full-blown ETL tool. Due to the limited ETL features, they cannot process an SCD which requires UPDATEs, something Hive and Pig do not support. It is possible to process star and snowflake schemas, but it is complex and verbose. To load data into a *simplified* version of our running example (with *no* SCDs) require 23 statements in Pig and 40 statements in Hive. In ETLMR – which in contrast to Pig and Hive is dimensional – only 14 statements are required. ETLMR can also support SCDs with the *same* number of statements, while this would be virtually impossible to do in Pig and Hive. The details of the comparison are available in the full paper [9].

PDI is an ETL tool and provides Hadoop support in its 4.1 GA version. However, there are still many limitations with this version. For example, it only allows to set a limited number of parameters in the job executor, customized combiner and mapper-only jobs are not supported, and the transformation components are not fully supported in Hadoop. We only succeeded in making an ETL flow for the simplest star schema, but still with some compromises. For example, a workaround is employed to load the processed dimension data into the DW as PDI's *table output* component repeatedly opens and closes database connections in Hadoop such that performance suffers.

In the following, we compare how PDI and ETLMR perform when they process the star schema (with *page* as a normal dimension, not an SCD) of the running example. To make the comparison neutral, the time for loading the data into the DW or the HDFS is not measured, and the dimension lookup cache is enabled in PDI to achieve a similar effect of ETLMR using offline dimensions. Hadoop is configured to run 4 parallel task trackers in maximum on each node, and scaled by adding nodes horizontally. The task tracker JVM option is set to be -Xmx256M while the other settings are left to the default. Table 2 shows the time spent on processing 80 GB *smalldim* data when scaling up the number of tasks. As shown, ETLMR is significantly faster than PDI for Hadoop in processing the data. Several reasons are found for the differences. First, compared with ETLMR, the PDI job has one more step (the reducer) in the fact processing as its job executor does not support a mapper-only job. Second, by default the data in Hadoop is split which results in many tasks, i.e., 1192 tasks for the fact data. Thus, longer initialization time is observed. Further, some transformation components are observed to run with low efficiency in Hadoop, e.g., the components to remove duplicate rows and to apply JavaScript.

Table 2. Time for processing star schema (no SCD), 80 GB *smalldim* data set, (min.)

Tasks	4	8	12	16	20
ETLMR	246.7	124.4	83.1	63.8	46.6
PDI	975.2	469.7	317.8	232.5	199.7

6 Related Work

We now compare ETLMR to other parallel data processing systems using MapReduce, and parallel DBMSs. In addition, we study the current status of parallel ETL tools. MapReduce is a framework well suited for large-scale data processing on clustered computers. However, it has been criticized for being too low-level, rigid, hard to maintain and reuse [10,15]. In recent years, an increasing number of parallel data processing systems and languages built on the top of MapReduce have appeared. For example, besides Hive and Pig (discussed in Section 5.5), Chaiken et al. present the SQL-like language SCOPE [4] on top of Microsoft's Cosmos MapReduce and distributed file system. Friedman et al. introduce SQL/MapReduce [7], a user-defined function (UDF) framework for parallel computation of procedural functions on massively-parallel RDBMSs. These systems or languages vary in the implementations and functionalities provided, but overall they give good improvements to MapReduce, such as high-level languages, user interfaces, schemas, and catalogs. They process data by using query languages, or UDFs embedded in the query languages, and execute them on MapReduce. However, they do not offer direct constructs for processing star schemas, snowflaked dimensions, and slowly changing dimensions. In contrast, ETLMR runs separate ETL processes on a MapReduce framework to achieve parallelization and ETLMR directly supports ETL constructs for these schemas.

Another well-known distributed computing system is the parallel DBMS which first appeared two decades ago. Today, there are many parallel DBMSs, e.g., Teradata, DB2, Objectivity/DB, Vertica, etc. The principal difference between parallel DBMSs and MapReduce is that parallel DBMSs run long pipe-lined queries instead of small independent tasks as in MapReduce. The database research community has recently compared the two classes of systems. Pavlo et al. [11], and Stonebraker et al. [13] conduct benchmarks and compare the open source MapReduce implementation Hadoop with two parallel DBMSs (a row-based and a column-based) in large-scale data analysis. The results demonstrate that parallel DBMSs are significantly faster than Hadoop, but they diverge in the effort needed to tune the two classes of systems. Dean et al. [5] argue that there are mistaken assumptions about MapReduce in the comparison papers and claim that MapReduce is highly effective and efficient for large-scale fault-tolerance data analysis. They agree that MapReduce excels at complex data analysis, while parallel DBMSs excel at efficient queries on large data sets [13].

In recent years, ETL technologies have started to support parallel processing. Informatica PowerCenter provides a thread-based architecture to execute parallel ETL sessions. Informatica has also released PowerCenter Cloud Edition (PCE) in 2009 which, however, only runs on a specific platform and DBMS. Oracle Warehouse Builder (OWB) supports pipeline processing and multiple processes running in parallel. Microsoft SQL Server Integration Services (SSIS) achieves parallelization by running multiple threads, multiple tasks, or multiple instances of a SSIS package. IBM InfoSphere DataStage offers a process-based parallel architecture. In the thread-based approach, the threads are derived from a single program, and run on a single (expensive) SMP server, while in the process-based approach, ETL processes are replicated to run on clustered MPP or NUMA servers. ETLMR differs from the above by being open source and based on MapReduce with the inherent advantages of multi-platform support, scalability on commodity clustered computers, light-weight operation, fault tolerance, etc. ETLMR is also unique in being able to scale automatically to more nodes (with no changes to the ETL flow itself, only to a configuration parameter) while at the same time providing automatic data synchronization across nodes even for complex structures like snowflaked dimensions and SCDs. We note that the licenses of the commercial ETL packages prevent us from presenting comparative experimental results.

7   Conclusion and Future Work

As business intelligence deals with continuously increasing amounts of data, there is an increasing need for ever-faster ETL processing. In this paper, we have presented ETLMR which builds on MapReduce to parallelize ETL processes on commodity computers. ETLMR contains a number of novel contributions. It supports high-level ETL-specific dimensional constructs for processing both star schemas and snowflake schemas, SCDs, and data-intensive dimensions. Due to its use of MapReduce, it can automatically scale to more nodes (without modifications to the ETL flow) while it at the same time provides automatic data synchronization across nodes (even for complex dimension structures like snowflakes and SCDs). Apart from scalability, MapReduce also gives ETLMR a high fault-tolerance. Further, ETLMR is open source, light-weight, and easy to use with a single configuration file setting all run-time parameters. The results of extensive experiments show that ETLMR has good scalability and compares favourably with other MapReduce data warehousing tools.

ETLMR comprises two data processing phases, dimension and fact processing. For dimension processing, the paper proposed a number of dimension management schemes and processing methods in order to achieve good performance and load balancing. The online dimension scheme directly interacts with the target DW and employs several dimension specific methods to process data, including *ODOT*, *ODAT*, and *level-wise* and *hierarchy-wise* processing for snowflaked dimensions. The offline dimension scheme employs high-performance storage systems to store dimensions distributedly on each node. The methods, *ODOT* and *hybrid* allow better scalability and performance. In the fact processing phase, bulk-load is used to improve the loading performance.

Currently, we have integrated ETLMR with the MapReduce framework, Disco. In the future, we intend to port ETLMR to Hadoop and explore a wider variety of data storage options. In addition, we intend to implement dynamic partitioning which automatically adjusts the parallel execution in response to additions/removals of nodes from the cluster, and automatic load balancing which dynamically distributes jobs across available nodes based on CPU usage, memory, capacity and job size through automatic node detection and algorithm resource allocation.

References

1. wiki.apache.org/hadoop/PoweredBy (June 06, 2011)
2. http://www.discoproject.org/ (June 06, 2011)
3. http://www.pentaho.com (June 06, 2011)

4. Chaiken, R., Jenkins, B., Larson, P., Ramsey, B., Shakib, D., Weaver, S., Zhou, J.: SCOPE: easy and efficient parallel processing of massive data sets. PVLDB 1(2), 1265–1276 (2008)
5. Dean, J., Ghemawat, S.: MapReduce: A Flexible Data Processing Tool. CACM 53(1), 72–77 (2010)
6. Dean, J., Ghemawat, S.: MapReduce: Simplified Data Processing on Large Clusters. In: Proc. of OSDI, pp. 137–150 (2004)
7. Friedman, E., Pawlowski, P., Cieslewicz, J.: SQL/MapReduce: A Practical Approach to Self-describing, Polymorphic, and Parallelizable User-defined Functions. PVLDB 2(2), 1402–1413 (2009)
8. Kovoor, G., Singer, J., Lujan, M.: Building a Java MapReduce Framework for Multi-core Architectures. In: Proc. of MULTIPROG, pp. 87–98 (2010)
9. Liu, X., Thomsen, C., Pedersen, T.B.: ETLMR: A Highly Scalable Dimensional ETL Framework Based on MapReduce. In: DBTR-29. Aalborg University (2011), www.cs.aau.dk/DBTR
10. Olston, C., Reed, B., Srivastava, U., Kumar, R., Tomkins, A.: Pig Latin: A Not-so-foreign Language for Data Processing. In: Proc. of SIGMOD, pp. 1099–1110 (2008)
11. Pavlo, A., Paulson, E., Rasin, A., Abadi, D., DeWitt, D., Madden, S., Stonebraker, M.: A Comparison of Approaches to Large-scale Data Analysis. In: Proc. of SIGMOD, pp. 165–178 (2009)
12. Ranger, C., Raghuraman, R., Penmetsa, A., Bradski, G., Kozyrakis, C.: Evaluating MapReduce for Multi-core and Multiprocessor Systems. In: Proc. of HPCA, pp. 13–24 (2007)
13. Stonebraker, M., Abadi, D., DeWitt, D., Madden, S., Paulson, E., Pavlo, A., Rasin, A.: MapReduce and Parallel DBMSs: friends or foes? CACM 53(1), 64–71 (2010)
14. Thomsen, C., Pedersen, T.B.: pygrametl: A Powerful Programming Framework for Extract-Transform-Load Programmers. In: Proc. of DOLAP, pp. 49–56 (2009)
15. Thusoo, A., Sarma, J., Jain, N., Shao, Z., Chakka, P., Anthony, S., Liu, H., Wyckoff, P., Murthy, R.: Hive: A Warehousing Solution Over a Map-reduce Framework. PVLDB 2(2), 1626–1629 (2009)
16. Thusoo, A., Sarma, J., Jain, N., Shao, Z., Chakka, P., Zhang, N., Anthony, S., Liu, H., Murthy, R.: Hive – A Petabyte Scale Data Warehouse Using Hadoop. In: Proc. of ICDE, pp. 996–1005 (2010)
17. Yoo, R., Romano, A., Kozyrakis, C.: Phoenix Rebirth: Scalable MapReduce on a Large-scale Shared-memory System. In: Proc. of IISWC, pp. 198–207 (2009)

Complementing Data in the ETL Process

Lívia de S. Ribeiro[1], Ronaldo R. Goldschmidt[2], and Maria Cláudia Cavalcanti[1]

[1] Instituto Militar de Engenharia
Praça General Tiburcio, 80, Praia Vermelha, Urca - 22290-270 - Rio de Janeiro, RJ
[2] Universidade Federal Rural do Rio de Janeiro
Av. Governador Roberto Silveira S/No. Moquetá - 26.020-740, Nova Iguaçu, RJ
{liviaribeiro14,ronaldo.rgold,maryoko}@gmail.com

Abstract. Data quality in a typical Data Warehouse (DW) environment is critical. The process of transferring data from different sources into the DW environment, known as ETL (Extraction, Transformation, and Load), usually takes care of improving the data quality. However, it is not unusual to identify null values in a DW fact table during the ETL process, and this may impact negatively on the accuracy of data analyses results. Data imputation[1] techniques are commonly used for dealing with the missing value problem. Some of them observe table values to generate a new value for the missing one. This paper proposes a new strategy to address the missing data problem on the ETL process. The idea is to enrich the DW fact table with dimension attributes, in order to reach better imputation results. The strategy uses the k-NN algorithm as the imputation approach. Tests performed on an implemented prototype showed promising results with respect to imputation quality.

Keywords: Data Warehouse, Data Imputation, Data Provenance.

1 Introduction

The constant advances in Information Technology have made it possible to produce systems that store and integrate huge amounts of data emerged from different sources. Known as Data Warehouses (DW), such systems have been used in many organizations as important decision support devices. According to Inmon [7], a DW is "*a subject oriented, nonvolatile, integrated, time variant collection of data in support of management's decisions*". Each data in a DW is attached to a timestamp, which enables to observe tendencies using appropriate tools. In general, DW´s environments provide resources for trend detection as well as other data analysis.

A usual practice [8] recommends that data in DW should be organized according to the star schema. The star schema consists of a few fact tables referencing any number of dimension tables. Fact tables hold the main data, while the usually smaller dimension tables describe each value of a dimension and can be joined to fact tables

---

[1] The term *imputation* is largely used in the literature about missing data in the *attribution* sense, i.e., meaning "to give a notional value to goods or services when the real value is unknown".

A. Cuzzocrea and U. Dayal (Eds.): DaWaK 2011, LNCS 6862, pp. 112–123, 2011.

as needed. Generally the fact table contains qualitative attributes (linked to dimension tables) and metric attributes. As the name suggests, qualitative attributes contain categorical data. Metric attributes are quantitative ones. For example, in a typical DW concerning sales of a megastore, supplier, product and date would be qualitative attributes and number of items sold would be a metric attribute.

Corporative data loaded in DW usually come from different and distributed sources. As a consequence, data can present many problems such as: misspelling, illegal values, different domains, missing values and other inconsistencies. These problems can seriously harm data analysis. For example, if missing values are not treated, important facts may not be taken into consideration in the analysis process.

To overcome these problems, data must be submitted into a process called ETL (Extraction, Transformation and Load). The ETL process is generally implemented by a set of software tools properly designed for this task. In the extraction phase, data is captured from multiple sources. Different sources may need different and possibly specific extraction tools. Such tools must periodically capture information from specific environments. Historical information metadata may be collected within data itself. Data's origin and time of extraction are examples of historical metadata. The theory that aggregates historical information to data itself is called data provenance in databases [2]. Hence, every DW naturally deals with data provenance once its data is associated with historical facts.

The transformation phase is the one responsible for data cleaning which consists of detecting and correcting the mentioned problems. In particular, this phase includes data imputation that detects and corrects missing values. Data imputation substitutes missing values by new values inferred from present data. In this scenario, quality of inference is a matter of great importance, once good inference may lead to better and more precise data analysis.

Although there are many preprocessing approaches to perform data imputation, including machine learning based ones [3][5][11][15], none of them use provenance data to improve quality of imputation. In DW, such use becomes possible once fact tables may be enriched with data from dimension tables. Additionally, DW 2.0[2] reveals an increase tendency to integrate data and metadata.

So, the present work has as its main goal to describe the development of a tuple imputation strategy for the fact table in which the metric attributes may have null values. We assume these null values emerge from the cleaning phase of the ETL process, where a set of dimension values combinations that should have been present are said to be missing. Dimension attributes can be seen as provenance attributes, and could be used to enrich the fact table in order to reach better imputation results.

This paper is organized in more six sections. Section 2 provides some background on data provenance and imputation techniques. Related works are described in section 3. Sections 4 and 5 respectively present the proposed approach and the developed prototype. Experiments to confirm the influence of data provenance in the improvement of data imputation are shown in section 6. Section 7 concludes the paper and depicts alternatives of future work.

---

[2] http://www.information-management.com/issues/20060401/1051111-1.html

2 Background Knowledge

Data quality and accuracy are important features in data analysis. Poor quality or imprecise data may lead to bad decisions in any scenario. Historical information about data such as date, author and place of creation are examples of metadata that help validate data. According to Buneman et al. [2], the theory that aggregates historical information to data itself is called data provenance in databases. Data provenance tries to answer the following questions: "How, when, why and where was data created or changed?" and "Who created or changed it?".

Data provenance is represented by metadata [14]. Specifically in DW´s scenarios, data provenance is naturally used once their data is associated with historical facts. It may allow users to identify and correct information failures and errors [12]. Therefore, data provenance may be used to provide data reliability and quality.

Relational database tables of real applications usually present missing data in their attributes/columns. Missing values may occur in only one attribute (univariate problem) or in two or more attributes (multivariate problem) of a table.

Data imputation methods try to fulfill databases by substituting missing values with new data. The new data depend upon the technique used by the imputation method. According to [11], certain imputation methods try to cluster tuples based on data similarity and then use the data cluster (local) to generate the values to replace the missing ones. The k-NN (k-Nearest Neighbors) algorithm is an important and representative local method for data imputation. In spite of its simplicity, this method has been successfully used in many works on machine learning based data imputation [11][5][3]. The algorithm general idea works as follows:

- It receives a new tuple with missing values, possibly in two or more attributes;
- It retrieves from database the k most similar tuples without missing values in the same attributes of the new tuple.
- The method uses the retrieved tuples to fill the gaps.

Some important considerations about the k-NN must be made. (i) Treatment depends on attributes' data type: qualitative or quantitative. (ii) Tuple similarity is calculated by a distance measure. Euclidean distance (eq. 1) is a very popular distance used by data imputation when the database only contains quantitative attributes, while the mixed types distance (eq. 2) is a good alternative when database contains both quantitative and qualitative attributes [5].

$$d(i,j) = \sqrt{(x_{i1} - x_{j1})^2 + (x_{i2} - x_{j2})^2 + ... + (x_{in} - x_{jn})^2} \qquad (1)$$

Where $d(i,j)$ is the distance value, x is the set of attributes of a database, $i = (x_{i1}, x_{i2}, x_{i3}, ..., x_{in})$ and $j = (x_{j1}, x_{j2}, x_{j3}, ..., x_{jn})$ are the tuples to be compared.

$$d(i,j) = \frac{\sum_{f=1}^{p} \delta_{ij}^{(f)} d_{ij}^{(f)}}{\sum_{f=1}^{p} \delta_{ij}^{(f)}} \qquad (2)$$

Where $\delta_{ij}^{(f)} = 0$, if $((x_{if}$ or x_{jf} are missing) or $(x_{if} = x_{jf} = 0))$ and $\delta_{ij}^{(f)} = 1$, otherwise, $d_{ij}^{(f)}$ depends on data type:

(a) Quantitative attributes

$$\frac{\left|x_{if} - x_{jf}\right|}{max_h x_{hf} - min_h x_{hf}} \qquad (3)$$

Where $max_h x_{hf}$ and $min_h x_{hf}$ are maximum and minimum values for attribute f, respectively.

(b) Qualitative attributes

$$d_{ij}^{(f)} = 0 \text{ if } x_{if} = x_{jf} \text{ or } d_{ij}^{(f)} = 1, \text{ otherwise.} \qquad (4)$$

(iii) Average of present values in the **k** tuples is a technique frequently used to calculate the new values to replace the missing ones. It is used when attributes are quantitative. Mode is a statistical measure frequently used when the attribute with missing values is qualitative. Although both average and mode based imputation techniques can introduce biased data, their results have been used in many related works [15][11][5][3], as the baseline to evaluate other data imputation methods.

3 Related Work

As we said before, data quality is a central issue for DW environments. There are works [12] [1] that propose applying data cleaning techniques before loading data into these environments. Most of these works focus on the problem of data duplicities, which means the occurrence of two data items that represent the same real world object. They propose techniques for data deduplication, i.e., the elimination of such data duplicities. Missing data is also a problem in large databases, such as DW databases [9]. However, there are just some works [6] [13] that provide solutions for complementing data in a DW.

In Hong et al. [6], the authors describe the design of a DW database for storing Quick Access Recorder (QAR) data. This database is used for the analysis of aircraft flights of a specific company. They propose a framework to manage the ETL process, which first extracts data from several sources, then identifies absent values in these data, inputs new values, removes duplicated data, and finally, consolidates data. Data imputation occurs before the extracted data is loaded into the fact table, and it is performed according to three approaches. The first one is a manual imputation, usually when the data is already known, but it is missing in the database for some reason. The second one uses a supervised imputation method based on linear regression technique. The third one, also supervised, uses a linear interpolation technique. It is not clear though, when to use each technique. Moreover, besides the fact that this approach was designed for a specific domain (aircraft companies), it does not take into account category or dimension values, focusing only on numeric and continuous values. According to the authors, their approach showed some good results, meaning that data imputation had a positive impact on the quality of the analysis over then QAR data.

Another related work [13] focus on the imputation of semi-continuous values, defined as measure attributes that can often be zero for some combinations of dimensions. The authors propose a two-part model to fill in these values based on the idea of dividing the fact table into smaller cubes (called chunks), and then proceed with the imputation, using techniques such as logistic regression models (to identify which missing positions have zero or non-zero measure values) and loglinear models (to estimate and fulfill missing data) constructed over known values in dataset. They also combine forward variable selection and backward variable elimination algorithms [4] to implement a heuristic strategy to select attributes for logistic model. As imputation occurs after data consolidation, detailed information about the aggregated values cannot be obtained. The authors recommend future investigation in alternatives to fulfill missing values based on data decomposition. Another option would be to impute missing values before data aggregation.

Although many machine learning based data imputation approaches have been developed [3][5][11][15], as far as we could investigate, we found no similar work that could address the missing value problem in the context of the ETL process, taking into account the dimension attributes, as a way of getting better results on data imputation.

4   A Strategy for Data Imputation during the ETL Process

The strategy described in this section is a mechanism for imputation of tuples where there are missing values, taking into account data provenance present in a DW. The proposed mechanism intends to play an important role in the context of the ETL cleaning task. The idea is to apply this mechanism after data integration and some initial cleaning actions (such as treating missing values at the dimension tables), while data load into a fine grained multidimensional schema is already in course, but not yet consolidated. Also, it assumes missing value tuples are already identified, i.e., measure attributes for some dimension combination that should exist according to some business rule. The mechanism uses data provenance to enrich the fact table aiming at a better characterization of tuples, which may lead to a more accurate similarity calculation, and consequently, may provide better imputation results. In the context of this work, provenance data used is obtained in the dimension tables, which naturally refers to the context of each fact. Also, in this proposal, we focus on the imputation of numeric measure attributes of the fact table only.

idProd	idSupp	idClient	idTime	saleqty
1	2	4	2	??
1	3	3	4	50
5	1	5	3	23
5	4	3	1	??
4	1	2	3	30

Fig. 1. Sales Fact Table Example

In order to explain the dynamics of the proposed strategy, we take a DW typical example of a Sales fact table (Figure 1). In this example, the measure attribute saleqty represents the quantity sold for the combination of a product (idProd), a supplier (idSupp), a client (idClient), in a given date (idTime). The idea of the proposed strategy is to depart from a fact table that presents some missing values at a numeric measure attribute, and enrich it with dimension attributes. In the example of Figure 1, the `saleqty` measure attribute presents some missing values (??). Figure 2 presents the enriched fact table, where each tuple contains also values that came from the corresponding dimension tuple, characterizing each fact tuple in the context of dimension categories such as the brand of a product, or the region of a supplier, or even the season of the sale time. Without this information, the imputation would be calculated just according to the dimension foreign key value.

Keys and metrics					Product Dimension Attributes				Supplier Dimension Attributes			
idProd	idSupp	idTime	idClient	saleqty	name	brand	type	size	name	phone	area	region
1	2	4	2	??	Part1	Sun	A	15	Supp2	2222-2222	Area2	Southeast
1	3	3	4	50	Part1	Sun	A	15	Supp3	4545-4545	Area3	North
5	1	5	3	23	Part5	Mars	B	30	Supp1	3333-3333	Area1	Northeast
5	4	3	1	??	Part5	Mars	B	30	Supp4	8675-4333	Area4	South
4	1	2	3	30	Part4	Jupiter	C	10	Supp1	3333-3333	Area1	Northeast

Time Dimension Attributes					Client Dimension Attributes		
day	month	year	season	holiday	name2	region2	segMarketing
1	4	2008	autumn	0	Cli2	Northeast	C
25	12	2009	summer	1	Cli4	North	A
12	10	2009	spring	1	Cli3	Northeast	A
25	12	2009	summer	1	Cli1	South	A
13	4	2009	autumn	0	Cli3	Northeast	A

Fig. 2. Enriched Sales Fact Table

In the example of Figure 2, for the dimension id combination <1,2,4,2>, note that the sale happened in the autumn, similarly to the sale for the combination <4,1,2,3>. If the imputation technique used is based on similar tuples, then these tuples were not supposed to be similar. However, if we analyze the enriched tuples it would be possible to identify a relevant similarity with respect to the season of the year (both sales happened in the autumn season). This means that even though fact tuples may have different key value combinations, they could be evaluated as similar based on the enriched attribute values.

The proposed imputation strategy is performed in four main steps: (i) attribute combination definition, (ii) training set preparation, (iii) performance calculation for combinations, (iv) real imputation. In (i) a manual selection of attributes to be considered for imputation takes place, and then, based on some heuristics, we form an attribute combination set. Each combination is a subset of attributes of the enriched fact table. The training set is prepared based on the enriched fact table. A new training fact table is created, but without the missing value tuples. In this training table, for randomly selected existing tuples, new missing values are created, i.e., we substitute known values of the measure attribute in focus for null values. Once (ii) provides the complete training set, step (iii) initiates. It calculates the imputation and its performance for each attribute combination defined in (i). In step (iv), we analyze the performance results obtained in (iii), identify the best performance attribute combination, and proceed with the real imputation, i.e., the fulfillment of missing values in the original fact table, taking into account the enriched tuple values for the chosen attribute combination. The following subsections describe in more details each step of the proposed strategy.

4.1   Attribute Combination Definition

The first step of the strategy consists in the selection of the best provenance attributes that could be found in the dimension, to enrich the fact table. This selection should be done by a specialized user. In order to help the user on selecting a representative set of attributes, the selectivity estimation of each candidate attribute is calculated. The idea is to identify attributes with a variety of different values (heterogeneity). The more heterogeneous, the more appropriate for an index attribute [2], and in the context of his work, the better it characterizes a set of tuples in the fact table. This calculation is done over a denormalized fact table, which means an extended fact table based on the join of the traditional fact table and its dimensions. The denormalization is a very expensive process, and it would not be viable to do this for each imputation execution. Therefore, we assume that a denormalized fact table is maintained in parallel to the traditional fact table, meaning that the load task is always performed in both tables.

After the user selection of a set of attributes, a set of attribute combinations C is generated. This also depends on a user choice. There are five types of combinations: (i) all user selected attributes; (ii) only user selected numeric attributes; (iii) the user selected attribute (numeric or categorical) with the best selectivity estimation, for each dimension; (iv) the user selected numeric attribute with the best selectivity estimation, for each dimension; (v) substitution of each dimension foreign key with the corresponding user selected dimension attribute(s).

For the best configuration of the proposed strategy, initial tests (described further) were performed in order to select attributes for such combination set. All possible attribute combinations were not tested because of the high processing costs. However, the types of combinations listed above showed promising results.

4.2   Training Set Preparation

Once C is defined, then a training set is prepared in order to define which c_j ($c_j \in C$) is recommended by the strategy, and should then be used for the real imputation. This training set is generated by eliminating, of the denormalized fact table, the tuples which have absent values on the measure attribute in focus (named hereafter, the x attribute). After that, a set of randomly generated absent values are placed in existing tuples, for x, in the same real absence proportion found. The old values are not lost here, as they still exist in the real fact table.

Now we have the complete training set, i.e., the dirty denormalized fact table. It is worth to mention, that for performance reasons, this fact table may not be complete, and include only more recent tuples, for a representative pre-defined period of time (e.g. the last 2 years).

4.3   Performance Calculation for Attribute Combinations

In this step, the imputation is applied over the training set. We calculate the imputation performance for each absent tuple and for each $c_j \in C$. Initially, we identify the absent tuples in the training set. For each f_i absent tuple, $1 <= i <= n$, which contains an absent value for x attribute, the real value x_0^i for x is retrieved from the real fact table and kept for later use. After that, we start an iteration on C elements, i.e., for each $c_j \in C$, $1 <= j <= m$, we apply the k-NN algorithm, to select a set of local similar tuples, in the training set table. The similarity is calculated based only on the attributes of c_j, plus the original fact table attributes, and using the Euclidean distance or the mixed type distance between each tuple pair. Then, the selected set of k similar tuples is used to calculate the new value x_R^i ($f_i[x] = x_R^i$), using the mean of the set of x values for those tuples.

According to the initial tests the best performance k value was 10, which is suggested as a default value. Finally, we calculate the error rate between values x_0^i and x_R^i, based on the *Relative Absolute Derivation* – RAD metric [11], which uses the following formula:

$$RAD = \frac{1}{n} \sum_{i=1}^{n} \frac{|x_0^i - x_R^i|}{x_0^i} \tag{5}$$

where:

- x_0^i is the original value,
- x_R^i is the new calculated value and
- n is the total of absent tuples on x.

There are other formulas for error calculation [13], but RAD was chosen as it has been used successfully in some related works [11]. In the current step, we calculate (and accumulate) each individual imputation error rate for each f_i tuple and for each c_j attribute combination. We generate an array of m error rate values (combination[j]), where each entry is the sum of the error rate values for the n absent tuples. The rest of the RAD formula (division by n) is calculated in the next step.

The following algorithm summarizes this step.

```
While there is a tuple with missing value in desnormal do
   RealValue = corresp. real value obtained from the original table;
   While there is a combination of attributes (combination[j]) do
      NewValue = application of k-NN algorithm for combination[j];
      DiffValue = abs(RealValue - NewValue) / RealValue;
      Add Diffvalue to combination[j];
   End-While
End-While
```

4.4   Real Imputation

In the last step of the proposed strategy we calculate the best combination of attributes by finishing the RAD formula application. The global error rate calculation for each c_j, and the best one is identified c_b. Then, the combination c_b is then used to proceed with the imputation in the original fact table. Initially, we identify the absent tuples in the original fact table. For each f_i tuple, $1 <= i <= n$, which contains an absent value for x attribute, we apply the k-NN algorithm, to select a set of local similar tuples, in the training set table. The similarity is calculated based only on the attributes of c_b, plus the original fact table attributes, and using the Euclidean distance between each tuple pair. Then, the k selected similar tuples are used to calculate the new value, applying the mean of the x values for those tuples.

5   ComplETL

This section describes ComplETL, a computational tool that implements the previously presented provenance based data imputation approach. ComplETL must be used by the end of the transformation phase in ETL process. The target database must be in a traditional star schema with a fact table and its dimensional tables. Once ComplETL has been applied, the target database is ready for the ETL´s loading phase.

ComplETL was developed using packages from Appraisal´s library [3], a workflow management based environment that is used to execute and evaluate missing data imputation processes. ComplETL is able to: (i) implement the proposed data imputation approach as a process; (ii) allow parameter configuration in such approach; (iii) allow access to databases with multiple tables; (iv) deal with big tables, a common situation in data warehouse applications; and (v) treat categorical as well as quantitative data, one of Appraisal´s main limitations.

Like Appraisal, ComplETL was developed in Java, due to its portability and available resources. ComplETL uses Spring Framework[3], JSTL[4] and MySQL[5] DBMS, version 5.1.

The Attribute Combination Definition step was implemented as specified in section 4 and includes some additional configurations: (a) target dataset; (b) k value for the k-NN algorithm; (c) type of attribute combinations; (d) missing value attribute x; (e) fact table denormalization, based on foreign key metadata; (f) foreign key removal; (g) selectivity estimation; (h) user interface for attribute manual selection; and (i) decision whether dimension attribute data should be normalized or not. In order to reduce access to database, ComplETL stores metadata and configuration information in XML documents.

The Performance Calculation step uses the k-NN implementation available in Appraisal´s packages. Simplicity, effectiveness and availability have influenced on this decision.

6   Experiments and Results

Experiments in ComplETL were organized in two groups: initial and evaluation tests. Initial tests aimed at defining which configuration should be used during evaluation tests. All tests were performed in a computational environment with core 2 duo processor, 4 GB RAM, 360 HD GB and Windows 7® operating system.

A customized version of TPC-H[6] benchmark´s database was used for all tests. TPC-H database was transformed, using the Kettle[7] utility, into a traditional DW star schema with a fact table and its dimensional tables. In this database schema, we focused on only one missing value attribute in the fact table (univariate imputation

---

[3] Spring Source, http://www.springsource.org/

[4] JavaServer Pages Standard Tag Library, http://java.sun.com/products/jsp/jstl/

[5] MySQL.com http://www.mysql.com

[6] TPC Benchmark H – Standard Specification Revision 2.8.0.
http://www.tpc.org/tpch/spec/tpch2.8.0.pdf

[7] Pentaho Data Integration. Pentaho. www.pentaho.com

problem). As we did not have real missing values in this dataset, the missing value rate was set to 10% of fact table.

The TPC-H database was populated with DBGEN, a synthetic data generator for TPC-H. Five thousand (5.000) tuples and then 32.000 tuples were generated, configuring 1 and 6 MB databases, for the initial and evaluation tests, respectively.

In order to establish an error threshold for using as a reference in analyzing other tests results, similarly to other related works [3][11][15], we ran a test where we applied an average based data imputation over the complete fact table (taking all tuples into account), and found 1.91 as the error rate threshold. In all tests, the error rate was always below such threshold.

The best k for the k-NN algorithm, found in the initial tests, were $k = 10$ and $k = \sqrt{n_c}$ (where n_c is the total of complete tuples from fact table). Also, when k-NN was configured with the Euclidian distance, it overcame its version with the Mixed Types distance in 69% of the tests.

Linear normalization was employed in TPC-H's dimensions in order to smooth the differences among values from the set of attributes. In the initial tests, the imputation errors calculated over non-normalized database were lower than the ones obtained over the normalized database version.

Initial tests also aimed at the evaluation of the proposed strategy. The following aspects were taken into consideration in the data imputation process:

(a) Influence of dimensional data when used to enrich the fact table. Four groups of attributes were created to represent the following dimensional types: "where", "when", "who", "all".

(b) Attributes' types: (i) only categorical attributes; (ii) only numeric attributes; (iii) both numeric and categorical attributes.

(c) Attributes' selectivity: Experiments were performed in order to vary selectivity level of the attributes.

Table 1 summarizes the main results of initial tests. For these tests 48 imputations were performed, and, in average, error rate with numeric attributes were 40% higher than with categorical data, which means that categorical attributes showed a better performance than numeric ones. Additionally, error rate with $k = 10$ and categorical attributes from all dimensions was the lowest value produced in these tests.

The evaluation tests were performed under the following conditions: (a) Euclidian distance was fixed for the similarity metric; (b) k was set to 10 and √n; (c) non-normalized data. For these tests, three scenarios were configured: (a) only categorical

Table 1. Summary of results (error rate values) of the initial Tests

k	Dimension	Categorical	Numeric	Categorical and Numeric
10	Where	0,817	2,144	2,148
	Who	0,831	2,777	1,645
	When	0,817	1,646	1,655
	All	0,801	1,919	1,565
$\sqrt{n_c}$	Where	0,946	2,180	2,296
	Who	0,951	1,374	1,858
	When	0,947	1,626	1,642
	All	0,952	1,945	1,535

attributes; (b) only numeric attributes; (c) both numeric and categorical attributes. In all scenarios, attributes with highest selectivity were used. Table 2 summarizes the main results obtained with the evaluation tests. Once again, the scenario with categorical attributes and 10 nearest neighbors outperformed the others.

Table 2. Summary of results (error rate values) of the Evaluation Tests

k	Scenario	Error	Combination with lowest error
10	Categorical Attributes	0,831	All attributes
	Numeric Attributes	1,713	All attributes
	Categorical and Numeric Attributes	1,336	All attributes
$\sqrt{n_c}$	Categorical Attributes	0,979	All attributes
	Numeric Attributes	1,668	All attributes
	Categorical and Numeric Attributes	1,549	Numeric attributes with highest selectivity

Test results were promising with respect to the imputation quality. However, a real case study would be necessary to evaluate the impact of such approach on the DW confidence, through the analysis of specific analytical queries (with and without data imputation). Moreover, it is also necessary to prepare a much larger set of tuples, that resembles a real DW, in order to evaluate this approach with respect to performance.

7 Conclusions

This paper proposed a new strategy to address the missing data problem on the ETL process. The idea is to use data provenance (data from dimensional tables) to enrich the fact table aiming at a better characterization of tuples. Our strategy uses some heuristics in order to help final user to identify which provenance attributes can improve imputation quality.

A prototype called ComplETL was implemented in order to evaluate our proposal. Tests were performed over a customized version of TPC-H benchmark's database, which was transformed into a traditional DW star schema with a fact table and its dimensional tables.

Some interesting and promising results could be identified based on the performed experiments: (i) all results achieved with the proposed approach outperformed the ones obtained with average based data imputation, a commonly used technique; (ii) when used to enrich the fact table, categorical attributes showed better imputation results than the numeric ones; (iii) attributes with higher values of selectivity led to the best results; (iv) imputation errors with non-normalized data were lower than with normalized ones.

Future work includes: (i) evaluate other machine learning based imputation algorithms but k-NN; (ii) tests with real and larger databases; (iii) develop a parallel and distributed version of ComplETL; (iv) improve the strategy to take both attribute correlation and ontology resources into account, in the selection of attributes to enrich the fact table.

Acknowledgements. This work was supported in part by CAPES and by CNPq (Proc. 309307/2009-0).

References

1. Boskovitz, A.: Data Editing and Logic: The covering set method from the perspective of logic. Thesis. The Australian National Univ., Research School of Information Sciences and Engineering (2008)
2. Buneman, P., Khanna, S., Tan, W.-C.: Why and where: A characterization of data provenance. In: Van den Bussche, J., Vianu, V. (eds.) ICDT 2001. LNCS, vol. 1973, pp. 316–330. Springer, Heidelberg (2000)
3. Castaneda, R., Ferlin, C., Goldschmidt, R., Soares, J.A., Carvalho, L.A.V., Choren, R.: Aprimorando Processo de Imputação Multivariada de Dados com Workflows. In: XXIII Simp.ósio Brasileiro de Banco de Dados – SBBD, Campinas-SP (2008)
4. Farhangfar, A., Kurgan, L., Pedrycz, W.: A Novel Framework for Imputation of Missing Values in Databases. IEEE Trans. Syst., Man, and Cybern. 37(5), 692–709 (2007)
5. Han, J.Y., Kamber, M.: Data Mining: Concepts and Techiniques, p. 550. Morgan Kaufmann, San Francisco (2001)
6. Hong, W., Xiuxia, H., Hongwei, W.: Research and Implementation of QAR Data Warehouse. In: Proc. of 2nd Int. Symp. on Intelligent Information Technology Application, IITA 2008, pp. 156–162 (2008)
7. Inmon, W.H.: Como Construir o Data Warehouse, p. 388. Rio de Janeiro, Campus (1997)
8. Kimball, R.: The Data Warehouse Toolkit, p. 387. Makron Books, S. Paulo (1998)
9. Rahm, E., Do, H.H.: Data Cleaning: Problems and Current Approaches. IEEE Bulletin Of The Technical Committee On Data Engineering 23(4) (2000)
10. Sarawagi, S., Bhamidipaty, A.: Interactive Deduplication using Active Learning. In: Proc. of the Eighth ACM SIGKDD International Conference on Knowledge Discovery and Data Mining (KDD-2002), Canada (2002)
11. Soares, J.A.: Pré-Processamento em Mineração de Dados: Um Estudo Comparativo em Complementação. Thesis. COPPE-UFRJ, Rio de Janeiro (2007)
12. Woodruff, A., Stonebraker, M.: Supporting Fine-Grained Data Lineage in a Database Visualization. In: Int. Conference on Data Engineering, Birmingham, UK, pp. 91–102 (1997)
13. Wu, X., Barbará, D.: Learning Missing Values from Summary Constraints. ACM SIGKDD Explorations Newsletter 4, 21–30 (2002)
14. Zhao, J., Goble, C., Greenwood, M., Wroe, C., Stevens, R.: Annotating, linking and browsing provenance logs for e-Science. In: Workshop on Semantic Web Technologies for Searching and Retrieving Scientific Data, Florida, pp. 92–106 (2003)
15. Magnani, M., Montesi, D.: A New Reparation Method for Incomplete Data in the Context of Supervised Learning. In: Proc. of the Int. Conf. on Information Technology: Coding and Computing (ITCC 2004), Nevada, pp. 471–475 (2004)

TTL: A Transformation, Transference and Loading Approach for Active Monitoring

Emma Chávez[1,2] and Gavin Finnie[1]

[1] Bond University, Australia
[2] Universidad Católica de la SSMA Concepción, Chile

Abstract. In Data Warehouse (DW) environments, operational processes move data from sources to the warehouse. This includes data export, preparation, and loading usually performed using Extraction, Transformation and Loading (ETL) tools. Past research has treated DW "as collections of materialized views" whose data is regularly refreshed and locally stored [1]. Requirements have changed and real time transactions are required to support on-line operational decision making. Traditional DW systems may impose unacceptable delays due to their batch nature. ETL techniques are difficult to scale up to address the challenge of data loading, performance and low latency to provide real-time decision support. We propose a new approach for designing real-time DW in which traditional ETL does not apply. Data is pre-analysed by agents in each data source before being pushed as needed to the DW. The approach has been evaluated in a simulated environment and some of the results are discussed here.

1 Introduction

In today's information era, organizations must be able to integrate large volumes of data from a variety of sources (i.e operational systems, sensors, other people) in order to support tactical IT plans and strategic decisions. Business Intelligence (BI) seems to be the right paradigm to follow in order to help managers to make timely and effective decisions. BI tools help with information gathering and processing data, building rich and relevant information that is then sent back to decision makers [2].

Most BI architectures use data warehouse technologies as the way to consolidate, analyse and report data. Traditional data warehouses are refreshed in a periodic manner, usually on a daily basis (off-peak hours), where the operational sources and the data warehouse experience low load conditions. There is a cooling-off period between business transactions and their representation in the data warehouse, with the most recent data unavailable for analysis as it is caught in the operational sources [3]. Thus, it is possible to say that traditional data warehouse technologies are "out-of-sync very quickly" which can be an issue in obtaining real time information response [4].

Past research has treated data warehouses "as collections of materialized views" whose data is regularly refreshed and locally stored [5], but today re-

A. Cuzzocrea and U. Dayal (Eds.): DaWaK 2011, LNCS 6862, pp. 124–135, 2011.

quirements have changed and real time transactions are required to support online operational decision making. Active Data Warehousing and real time data warehouse applications are required in which large amounts of heterogeneous information can be updated as frequently as possible [6].

Certainly, no data can be really obtained in real-time, not in a "quantum sense" because by the moment data is seen it is no longer real time [7]. For some researchers real-time means up to time which means that any data change that is taking place in a source system has an immediate and automatic echo in the data warehouse [8]. For others real-time is not about being fast, it is the "utility function" that designates the damage for an organization because of missing a deadline [9]. Therefore, real time is a subjective variable and involves some qualitative and quantitative rules. [10] states that " The critical challenges of decision support in general is how quickly can we make sound decisions? The issue really revolves around time to decision".

This means real time for an organization could be considered as the ability to respond to a decision in a day due to it crossing the overnight-update barrier, or the ability to make data flow without delay (trickle-feed) instead of batch load; or in a practical sense, real time will be defined by the " service level agreement given by the organization deadlines" (e.g. ability to report and fix a problem)[9].

One of the main components of a data warehouse implementation is the process of data integration. Data is integrated into the data warehouse in three steps: Data is extracted first then transformed and loaded into the warehouse. Extraction, Transformation, and Loading processes (ETL)are the key to "bring data from heterogeneous data sources to an homogeneous environment" [11]. These processes tend to take a few hours to complete as they deal with large volumes of data.

Solution techniques vary to provide real time to extract, transform and load data (ETL) [12]. The main approaches are:

- Near real time ETL: e.g. hourly loads.
- Real time solutions:
  - The direct *trickle feed*, in which the data warehouse is continuously fed with new data from the source system.
  - The *Trickle and Flip*, in which the data is continuously fed into staging tables that are in the exact same format as the target tables. It helps with issues such as tables being simultaneously updated.
  - *Real time data cache*, which can be a dedicated database server or another instance of a large database system with the purpose of loading, storing, and processing the real-time data.

Trickle feed applications are mainly in finance where stock prices or currency exchange rates that change during the day are loaded as they change [13]. In general it works under a messaging infrastructure via streaming data. To date, there is little research in the implementation of these technologies as they are mainly treated as a black box by the vendors.

On the other side, the problem with most of the solutions that implement real time date cache is that it is not possible to join reports and co-display alerts to display real-time and historical information together. Therefore, this kind of solution is more efficient when historical information is not needed. Moreover, if complex analytical reports are run on the real-time cache, it is possible for it to start showing the same internal report inconsistencies, database contention, and scalability problems that the warehouse would present [12].

It can be seen that during the last 5 years few studies in the optimization of the ETL process has been conducted. Existing studies focus on a logical optimization of the ETL process such as [5] who proposed a framework to optimize ETL processes by modelling the problem as a state space search problem (in which activities are placed in the flow). Nevertheless concurrency and the real application of this (semantic) was not discussed in the study.

In BI choices of data generation flow solutions vary from batch versus stream, and from push versus pull. Today in most BI architectures all data to be analysed has to be consolidated in the warehouse first, by following a pull approach. Queries are directed to the data sources to extract and integrate all the information [14]. These pull solutions have found federated systems the best way to achieve data freshness in a timely manner. Nevertheless, real time alerting and reporting cannot be done in a query [15]. [16] proposes the idea of an improvement over the traditional batch ETL technologies by considering the idea of ELT where the data is loaded into the warehouse to then continue with the transformation (batch versus streaming). However, no ELT application or research to support the idea of order change in traditional ETL is presented.

[17] offers CTU, a Capture, Transform and Update mechanism to incrementally update the performance of the warehouse in real time. It uses data triggers as the main components to initiate the sequence of actions to push data. However, most of the techniques already in use have to schedule in some way the data extraction to pull or push data in the warehouse, and all of them analyse the data, perform reports and alerts only when all the data extracted has been consolidated in the data warehouse.

By changing the sequence of processes in the traditional ETL approach it may be possible to enable local autonomy at the level of the data sources to push information (transfer data) to the warehouse. Thus, our solution offers an approach that empowers the data sources and moves data analysis to the first level before data integration and data consolidation. Thus, as soon as valuable data arrives at the data source, data is pre-analysed based on previous knowledge (historical information). If there is not enough information to take an action, data is immediately sent to the warehouse. To enable data push, agents can be used as these are defined as entities that enable local intelligence to react in particular environments.

In the following sections the main features of the architecture designed are presented, and the results of the pre-analysis process are discussed. Section 2 describes the main design considerations, section 3 explains the functionalities of agents, and the pre-analysis task results and how this process is implemented. Section 4 presents the main results of some of the tests conducted to then summarize the conclusions and actions for future research in section 5.

2   The TTL Approach

We propose an event driven approach as a way to sense and react in real time to certain environment conditions. Data is filtered, processed and analysed in the sources by enabling learning capabilities in them. Thus, sources of information sense and react by then pushing data into the warehouse only if needed. Real time response will be kept to a minimum latency by eliminating the data availability gap to perform data analysis which will enable organizations to concentrate on accessing and processing valuable data.

To deal with latency issues our architecture empowers the data sources with intelligent capabilities to monitor and pre-analyse valuable data. The pre-analysis is performed by using a Multi Agent System Architecture (MAS). This paradigm has become more and more important in many aspects of computer science by introducing the issues of distributed intelligence and interaction. Agents learn and reveal the data activity patterns through day to day measurements and the data history contained in each source of information. An agent reacts, after the pre-analysis has been done, by sending alarms according to changes in those patterns [18], or transfers data to the warehouse because more actions are needed, or if there is not enough knowledge to perform an action at the source level.

An partial view of the TTL approach can be seen in Fig.1. There are three stages to perform the monitoring process, as in current ETL approaches, nevertheless the modules have been organized in a different way to start pre-analysing data from the very beginning.

- *Data Push*: This module is responsible for monitoring the individual data contained in each source of information. *Source agent (SA)* is subscribed to the ID of the data to monitor in each source of information and through a set of specific rules that it has from the base of knowledge (historical data), it takes the decision to perform an action such as deliver information to the learning repository or to send an alert to data managers.

  Source Agent does not monitor all data available in each source. It monitors only relevant data for that entity that has been declared important to monitor (i.e Particular patient, share or product).Therefore, this is an "individual" specific framework in which local knowledge has been taken from a subset of the original data. The relevant entity to monitor in a source has been called a compound. In our application a particular patient will be a compound.

  Compound normal ranges, and/or valuable data to monitor come from the knowledge obtained in all the historical data available for that compound in the sources of information. It also considers the general base of knowledge that tells us which are the features or factors relevant and necessary to monitor. The General base of knowledge can be the area of interest to monitor. In our application the general base of knowledge comes from the general features to consider for cardiovascular heart disease.

  As soon as valuable data arrives at a source of information a trigger alerts to the *SA* which checks:

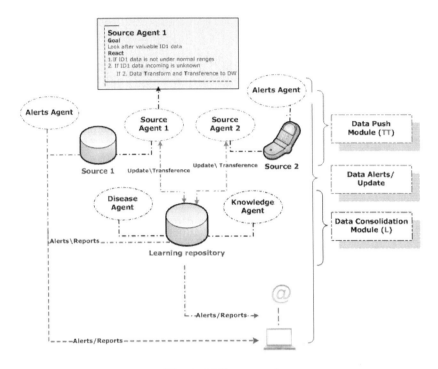

Fig. 1. TTL approach

- IF the data changed (dc) in the source is valuable data THEN check it against normal ranges and data structures (type)
- IF dc=normal THEN go to sleep because no action is needed
- ELSE IF dc!= normal THEN *reacts/alert/transform/transference*

Data is transformed and transferred to the data warehouse when there is not enough knowledge to take an action at the source level and a consolidated view of data is needed.

– *Data consolidation*: To monitor a special compound at the source level and to update the local knowledge of *Source Agent*, a reinforcement learning mechanism was selected. Thus, source agent has a set of rules for which is necessary to provide an alert. Each rule has been built based on the historical information of the compound.

When a set of data is extracted from the sources of information it is compared with the actual rules to decide the possible outcomes. If the set of data does not match any of the rules that *SA* has, the information is then compared with the full base of knowledge of the compound that resides in the *Knowledge Agent(KA)*.

Information is delivered when the data obtained in the source of information is not within normal ranges, does not match any of the cases obtained from the historical information, or there is not enough information to take a decision. Therefore, it represents valuable data to monitor for the compound and may need to be analysed as a whole view in the learning repository.

KA is continuously learning from the data to have the capability of adapting to new environment conditions or requirements, new compound rules or normal data ranges for example.

The data warehouse drives local knowledge updates, consolidates patient valuable data and main rules, and acts as a communication mechanism among agents.

– *Data alerts and updates*: Once data has been analysed, whether this analysis is performed in the central repository or at the agent level, alerts are sent to the decision makers, as risk scenarios might be present. Alerts are also sent to the patient in our application as a sensor device may not be working properly due to the data received in the source being incomplete or not in normal ranges.

We have used real time as follows: *" Any valuable data (key features to monitor at the sources level) that changes will trigger and determine certain reactions (analyse/alert/update/transference) to save time in the decision making process before the deadline is reached. A deadline is reached when clearly the monitoring compound is in a risk scenario".*

By monitoring *key features* only, evaluating, and then responding to them on time the proposed architecture is able to respond and/or alert to risk scenarios in a more effective way than traditional data warehousing strategies have allowed.

3   The Application Domain

The effectiveness of the framework proposed has been assessed by testing it in the area of health informatics. We have proposed a solution to manage cardiac disease patients by designing an architecture that learns and reveals the disease activity patterns through day to day measurements and the clinical history of an individual patient, reacts in real time by sending alarms according to changes in those patterns, and is adaptive to new system conditions and changes in health care requirements.

Cardiac disease monitoring of patients takes place at each step of patient management, from disease detection to disease prognosis and from surgery to recovery. During routine screening, day to day measurements (sensor devices) and patient knowledge can be obtained and risk scenarios can be detected.

Nowadays the "pervasive health care" monitoring environments, in the same way as in business, gather information from a variety of data sources, but they include new challenges because of the use of body and wireless sensors which makes the system more complex to monitor in real time. Here filtering data fusion techniques using data warehouses, context aware and knowledge generation using RFID and data mining techniques to achieve reliability are some of the proposed approaches to achieve real time data monitoring. The use of BI tools are still very limited in healthcare, and the generation of false positive alerts and patient specific data processing in right time is still not achieved [19] [20][21].

3.1 Base of Knowledge

The general knowledge about cardiac disease features (symptoms and combination of symptoms) to consider in heart disease patients was obtained from the list of 24 clinical features of [22]. This list provided us with the main critical diagnostic features of 5 major heart diseases. This includes diagnostic features such as age, dizziness, cyanosis, chest pain, dyspnea, blood pressure and edema of lower limb.

Furthermore, by general expert feedback (four cardiologists) a sub list of 15 symptoms considered important to monitor in ongoing patient assessment, for patients identified with coronary heart disease as well as their relative level of importance was obtained. These can be seen in Table 1.

Table 1. Symptoms

Level of Importance	Symptom
High	ST-T alteration
	Dyspnea
	Hypertension
	Discomfort, heaviness in the chest
	Chest Pain
	Neck venous return or engorgement
Medium	Cyanosis
	Systolic murmur
	Dizziness
	Diastolic murmur
	Blood pressure
Low	Headache
	Second heart sound
	Barrel chest
	Upper respiratory infection

Once the level of importance of a symptom or medical test was found a list of features that triggers alarms for a particular patient (patient's rules) was obtained. Although this list is obviously incomplete, it will be adequate to demonstrate the validity of the approach. An example of patient's case to add knowledge to monitor can be described as follows:

– P1: [ST-T alteration + Chest pain = Cardiac insufficiency]Date

3.2 The Pre-analysis

The sources of information that feed the warehouse have the capability to process local knowledge. A *source agent* resides in each patient data source such as sensors, General Practitioner, and hospital data bases. *Source agents* have the goal to look after valuable data to monitor for an individual patient to control disease prognosis, transform the data received and transfer it (if needed) to the warehouse when local knowledge is not enough to take an action at that level. It also performs on-line alerts according to the data outcomes (certain events) and changes in patient data patterns.

Based on the base of knowledge given by experts in the field (as described in the previous section) and a set of features to be considered in ongoing assessment for patients with heart disease, a simulated environment of patient scenarios disease data and cases was created and deployed. A MySql data base was used which contains patient's data, episodes and cases from the last 10 years for 20 coronary heart disease patients.

Once patient data was simulated, a function was programmed in a query to obtain patient's normal rages. A number of risk scenarios was also simulated given by episodes over a certain period of time for some patients.

By using JADE (Java Agent Development Framework), a software platform to develop distributed applications based in agents [23], a prototype to demonstrate the effectiveness of the local knowledge empowerment in each source was developed. JADE simplifies the development of applications that need coordination and negotiation among various agents. Thus, patient specific information and the general knowledge about heart disease were placed as knowledge rules for *Source Agent*. Thus, values like expected and current for the patient features (compound) allows *SA* to monitor patient's states as soon as new data arrives at any source.

It is important to consider that heart disease normal parameters are well defined in the literature, but each patient might have conditions which do not necessarily fit in the base of knowledge of heart disease. As an example patient normal blood pressure, value/ranges, differs from one patient to another. Thus, *SA* has to contrast for the pre-analysis the general heart disease base of knowledge as well as the patient specific data values for each critical feature relevant to monitor. An example is given in Table.2. According to the features described in Table 1, and the patient individual characteristics (history), patients were classified in high, medium and low risk patients.

Table 2. Sample rules for pre-analysing data at *SA*

SA sample rules
IF blood.pressure is above normal value,
THEN check whether the exception is tolerable
IF blood.pressure is tolerable,
THEN send current blood.pressure record to Knowledge Agent
ELSE IF blood pressure is not tolerable,
THEN check patient classification
IF patient classification equal high risk
THEN *wakeup Alerts Agent* under the message of
feature above normal ranges
for a high risk patient

4   Results of Implementation

The main differences between a traditional clinical data warehouse system and our approach can be seen in Table.3.

Table 3. ETL vs TTL

Processes	ETL	TTL
Data Extraction	1st stage	Does not apply
Data Transformation	2nd stage	1st in conjunction with the pre-analysis
Data loading	3rd stage	3rd stage and only if needed
Data analysis/reporting	After ETL has been completed	Analysis 1st stage Reporting any time if needed

In a system designed to actively monitor data, resources consumption and response time are usually the metrics of interest to evaluate a system. These can be explained from two main aspects. Efficiency as the way to do the task using less resources and Effectiveness by means of doing the task in the right way.

– *Efficiency*

A dedicated machine (Intel core Duo, 3GHz and 3.25GB of RAM) was used. A MySQl data base with 20 heart disease patients, with records from the years 2000 to 2010 was simulated. Data in the database includes, GP patient records (visits,symptoms,outcomes, medication), pathology results (test, ECG results), hospital patient records and sensor monitoring data results). That gave us an environment of around 6000 records for the total of patients.

We used Linux Ksar utility to monitor the system states and resource usage during the tests in order to compare traditional data extraction vs intelligent transference and pre-analysis. The results of these tests can be seen in Table.4.

Table 4. Cpu usage

	Scenario	Duration in sec	Average usage of CPU in %		
			User	System	Idle
Traditional extraction	Simple	1.0027	50.29	19.27	30.44
	Complex	1.0054	51.27	18.29	24.52
Intelligence transference	Simple	0.6378	30.27	21.15	48.58
	Complex	2.0974	44.17	19.31	36.52

Traditional extraction was considered as a simple planned and batched programmed query, that extracts patient's data to be moved to a warehouse in a certain period of time. Intelligent transference is the new approached that we propose instead.

A simple scenario refers to an scenario in which data has changed at the source level but is not relevant to monitor. A complex scenario refers to a new data entry at the source level that is relevant to monitor and an action must be taken.

As can be seen in the table the intelligent transference, (agent pre-analysis) consumes less or almost the same amount of CPU than the traditional data extraction mechanism programmed. Therefore, enabling pre-processing and filtering at the source levels does not stress the sources of information. *Source agent* seems to run to a low priority (given the % CPU idle used) so does not impact programs that run at normal priority in the server.

In the complex scenario *SA* performed pre-analysis and a transference and it did not show mayor differences in relation to traditional transference. These test were planned to move a number of KB only (200 records) which is the best scenario and it does not represent a Very Large Data Base (VLDB) environment. Nevertheless, on a VLDB environment traditional data extraction will use more machine resources and it will be more time consuming [24] [25] while in our case the database size is not relevant as *SA* will keep almost the same average consumption as it will only analyse relevant data only (a small data load) and not all the data that has changed in the source.

In terms of process duration traditional data extraction is affected by the number of rows/bytes to extract while intelligent data transference is affected by the amount of data to analyse. Because in the tests a small data load was programmed, it was not really possible to compare process duration with the two scenarios proposed. Therefore, although these data is included in the table they were not considered enough to be discussed here and more tests to prove this part need to be done in the future.

– *Effectiveness*

We argue that by monitoring key features in each patient, pre-analysing and then if needed transferring them to a central repository the proposed architecture is more effective than traditional ETL and data warehouse architectures.

By having local knowledge and empowering the data sources (using a monitoring agent) we have reduced the numbers of steps to analyse data. Data analysis as been moved to an early stage starting once relevant data to monitor has been changed in a source. That pre-analysis is performed now in the local source and if there is enough knowledge to perform an action, an alert mechanism is activated to either alert the patient because maybe the data that has changed in the source is incomplete (i.e sensor device data) or to the health care staff because the data that has changed is relevant to monitor and implies that the patient might be at risk.

Data inconsistency is detected in an early stage because of the knowledge about data types and data structure that *Source Agent* has in each source of information. Therefore, *SA* knows data structures and types of each source. Thus, data inconsistency is picked up in relevant data as soon as the agent is notified. *Source Agent* checks data structures and value before performing any analysis which help us to inform and not include uncompleted data as part of the analysis.

Therefore, by monitoring only relevant data in a distributed environment and by having local knowledge to check normal patterns it is possible to identify changes in the disease prognosis at an early stage and send an alert as soon as possible to the health care staff in patient risk scenarios.

5 Conclusions

We propose a new approach to active monitoring using data warehouses in which traditional extraction, transformation and loading tools do not apply. The main characteristics of this new approach are that the data warehouse is not programmed for querying the sources for the information, and that there is local knowledge at the sources level which allows data transformation, filtering, and analysis before sending if it needed, to the central repository.

The data analysis to perform data monitoring has been moved to the first stage of the architecture. Therefore, alerts and actions can be taken as soon as relevant data has changed in a source. Through this approach, important time for decision making is saved and a mechanism to support monitoring under patient risk scenarios in real time is proposed. The decision making starts from the owner of information and only patient useful data (data that needs to be monitored in risk scenarios) is sent to a consolidated repository.

Although data security is important, not all the framework has been discussed here with only those areas involved in data management (pre-analysis) being mentioned. A mechanism to consider environmental scenarios needs to be established in the future too. A symptom can be triggered by different factors and scenarios like stress, anxiety and others that may affect the probability of a heart episode to occur. This will affect the alerts module and will eliminate false positives in the monitoring process.

References

1. Sellis, T., Simitsis, A.: ETL workflows: From formal specification to optimization. In: Ioannidis, Y., Novikov, B., Rachev, B. (eds.) ADBIS 2007. LNCS, vol. 4690, pp. 1–11. Springer, Heidelberg (2007)
2. Srinivasan, S., Krishna, V., Holmes, S.: Web-log-driven business activity monitoring. IEEE Computer Society 38(3), 61–68 (2005)
3. Jaorg, T., Dessloch, S.: Near real-time data warehousing using state-of-the-art ETL tools. In: Castellanos, M., Dayal, U., Miller, R.J. (eds.) BIRTE 2009. LNBIP, vol. 41, pp. 100–117. Springer, Heidelberg (2010)
4. Yan, Y., Li, W., Xu, J.: Information value-driven near real-time decision support systems. In: 29th IEEE international conference on Distributed Computing Systems, ICDCS 2009, pp. 571–578 (2009)
5. Simitsis, A., Vassiliadis, P., Sellis, T.: Optimizing etl processes in data warehouses. In: 21st International Conference on Data Engineering, pp. 564–575 (2005)
6. Sutherland, J., Van den Heuvel, W.J.: Clinical process and data integration and evolution. In: 40th Annual Hawaii International Conference on System Sciences in IEEE Database (2007)
7. Raden, N.: Exploring the business imperative of real-time analytics. Hired Brains, Inc. Implementing Business Analytics (2010)
8. Terr, S.: Real-time data warehousing, vol. 101 (2004)
9. Etzion, O.: On real-time, right-time, latency, throughput and other time-oriented measurements (2007)
10. Nelson, G., Wright, J.: Real time decision support: Creating a flexible architecture for real time analytics (2005)

11. Javed, M., Nawaz, A.: Data load distribution by semi real time data warehouse. In: Proceedings of the 2010 Second International Conference on Computer and Network Technology, pp. 556–560 (2010)
12. Langseth, J.: Real-time data warehousing: Challenges and solutions (2004)
13. Taylor, R.: Concurrency in the data warehouse. In: 36th International Conference on Very Large Data Bases, VLDB 2010, pp. 724–727 (2000)
14. Halevy, A., Rajaraman, A., Ordille, J.: Database integration: The teenage years. In: VLDB 2006 Proceedings of the 32nd International Conference on Very Large Databases, pp. 9–16 (2006)
15. Castellanos, M., Casati, F., Shan, M., Dayal, U.: ibom: A platform for intelligent business operation management. In: 21st International Conference on Data Engineering (2005)
16. Dayal, U., Castellanos, M., Simitsis, A., Wilkinson, K.: Data integration flows for business intelligence. In: Proceedings of the 12th International Conference on Extending Database Technology: Advances in Database Technology, pp. 1–11 (2009)
17. Chieu, T., Zneg, L.: Real time perfomance monitoring for an enterprice information managemetn system. In: IEEE International Conference on e-Business Engineering, pp. 429–434 (2008)
18. Chavez, E., Finnie, G.: Empowering data sources to manage clinical data. In: 23rd IEEE International Symposium on Computer-Based Medical Systems, CBMS 2010 (2010)
19. Spil, T., Stegwee, R., Teitink, C.: Business intelligence in healthcare organization. In: 35th Annual Hawaii Internation Conference on System Sciences, p. 142b (2002)
20. Ferdous, S., Fegaras, L., Makedon, F.: Applying data warehousing technique in pervasive assistive environment. In: Proceedings of the 3rd International Conference on PErvasive Technologies Related to Assistive Environments (2010)
21. Lee, H., Park, K., Lee, B., Choi, J., Elmasri, R.: Issues in data fusion for health care monitoring. In: Proceedings of the 1st International Conference on PErvasive Technologies Related to Assistive Environments, vol. 3 (2008)
22. Yang, H., Zheng, J., Jiang, Y., Peng, C., Xiao, S.: Selecting critical clinical features for heart diseases diagnosis with real-coded genetic algorithm. In: Applied Soft. Computing, vol. 8, pp. 1105–1111 (2008)
23. Bellifemine, F., Caire, G., Poggi, A., Rimassa, G.: Jade a white paper. Technical report, Telecom Italia Lab (2003)
24. Yin, Y., Papadias, D.: Just-in-time processing of continuous queries. In: IEEE 24th International Conference on Data Engineering, pp. 1150–1159 (2008)
25. In: Nascimento, M., Zsu, T., Kossmann, D., Miller, R., Blakeley, J., Schiefer, K. (eds.) Proceedings of the 30th International Conference on Very Large Databases. Morgan Kaufmann, San Francisco (2004)

Support for User Involvement in Data Cleaning

Helena Galhardas[1], Antónia Lopes[2], and Emanuel Santos[1]

[1] INESC-ID and Technical University of Lisbon
hig@inesc-id.pt, esantos@ist.utl.pt
[2] Faculty of Sciences, University of Lisbon
mal@di.fc.ul.pt

Abstract. Data cleaning and ETL processes are usually modeled as graphs of data transformations. The involvement of the users responsible for executing these graphs over real data is important to tune data transformations and to manually correct data items that cannot be treated automatically. In this paper, in order to better support the user involvement in data cleaning processes, we equip a data cleaning graph with *data quality constraints* to help users identifying the points of the graph and the records that need their attention and *manual data repairs* for representing the way users can provide the feedback required to manually clean some data items. We provide preliminary experimental results that show the significant gains obtained with the use of data cleaning graphs.

1 Introduction

Data cleaning and ETL processes are commonly modeled as workflows or graphs of data transformations. The logic underlying real-world data cleaning processes is usually quite complex. These processes often involve tens of data transformations that are implemented, for instance, by pre-defined operators of the chosen ETL tool, SQL scripts, or procedural code. Moreover, these processes have to deal with large amounts of input data. Therefore, as pointed out in [14], in general it is not easy to devise a graph of data transformations able to always produce accurate data. This happens for two main reasons. First, individual data transformations that consider all possible data quality problems are difficult to write. Consequently, the underlying logic needs to undergo several revisions, in particular when the cleaning process is executed over a new batch of data. Hence, it is important that users responsible for executing the data cleaning processes have adequate support for tuning data transformations. Second, a fully automated solution that meets the quality requirements is not always attainable. In general, a portion of the cleaning work has to be done manually and, hence, it is important to also support the user involvement in this activity.

When using ETL and data cleaning tools, intermediate results obtained after individual data transformations are typically not available for inspection or eventual manual correction — the output of a data transformation is directly pipelined into the input of the transformation that follows in the graph. The solution we envisage for this problem is to support the specification of the points in

A. Cuzzocrea and U. Dayal (Eds.): DaWaK 2011, LNCS 6862, pp. 136–151, 2011.

the graph of data transformations where intermediate results must be available, together with the *quality constraints* that this data should meet, if the upward data transformations correctly transform all the data records as expected. Because assignment of blame is crucial for identifying where the problem is, the records responsible for the violation of quality constraints are highlighted. This information is useful both for tuning data transformations that do not handle the data as expected and for performing the manual cleaning of records not handled automatically by data transformations.

While the tuning of data transformations requires some knowledge about the logic of the cleaning process, it is useful that manual data repairing actions can also be performed in a black-box manner, namely by the application end-users. As already advocated in the context of Information Extraction [4], in many situations, data consumers have knowledge about how to correctly handle the rejected records and, hence, can provide critical feedback into the data cleaning program. Our proposal is that the developer of the cleaning process has the ability to specify, in the points of the graph of data transformations where intermediate results are available, the way users can provide the feedback required to manually clean certain data items. This may serve two different purposes: for guiding the effort of the user that is executing the cleaning process (even if he/she has some knowledge about the underlying logic) and for supporting the feedback of users that are just data consumers.

In this paper, we put forward a notion of *data cleaning graph* (DCG, for short) that supports the modeling of data cleaning processes that explicitly define where and how user feedback is expected as well as which data should be inspected by the user. The operational semantics of DCGs formally defines the execution of a data cleaning process over source data and past instances of manual data repairs. With this semantics it is possible to interleave the tuning of data transformations with the manual data correction without requiring that the user repeats his feedback actions. We present experimental results that show, for a real-world data cleaning application modeled as a DCG, the gain in terms of the accuracy of the data produced, and the amount of user work involved.

The paper is organized as follows. Section 2 presents the motivation and an overview of the proposed approach. In Section 3, the elements of the approach are presented in detail. In Section 4, we present a case study of a data cleaning process and, in Section 5, we report on the experimental results obtained that show the usefulness of our approach. In Section 6, we discuss the related work and in Section 7 we summarize the conclusions and future work.

2   Motivation

Let us consider that the information required for computing the research performance metrics for a given team is collected into a database with tables Team and Pub as illustrated in Fig.1 (a simplification of the real database used in the CIDS system [6]). The Team table is manually filled with accurate information about the team members. The Pub table stores the information about the citations of team members obtained through queries posed to Google Scholar.

The relationship that exists between the two tables, through the foreign key tld, associates all the publications to a team member. However, this association may be incorrect, namely due to the existence of homonyms. In our example, the first member in Team refers to a colleague of us and the Pub record with pid 4 is not authored by him, but by a homonym. Another problem that affects these tables is the multitude of variants that author names admit. For instance, the records of Pub shown in Fig.1 contain two synonyms of "Carriço, L.".

pId	tId	title	authors	year	event	link	cits	citNS
1	1	Adaptation of digital books	Duarte, C. and Carri{\c{c}}o, L.	2005	International Conference on Human Computer Interaction	scholar?cluster=1749 4767326604985714	12	2
2	1	Ubiquitous Psychotherapy	Sa, M. and Carrico, L. and Antunes, P.	2007	IEEE Pervasive Computing	scholar?cluster=1792	10	1
3	1	Ubiquitous Psychotherapy	de Sa, M. and Carrico, L. and Antunes, P.	2007	IEEE Pervasive Comput			
4	1	Reduction of the 2, 4, 6 radiation	Pereira, C. and Gil, L. and Carrico, L.	2007	Radiation Physics and Che			
5	2	Managing duplicates in a web archive	Santos, A. L. and Silva, M. J.	2006	ACM Symposium on App Computing			

tId	Full Name	tName
1	Luis Carriço	Carriço, L.
2	André Leal Santos	Santos, A. L.
3	André Santos	Santos, A.
4	Antónia Lopes	Lopes, A.
5	Marco Sá	Sá, M.
6	Carlos Teixeira	Teixeira, C.

Fig. 1. Pub and Team tables

The computation of reliable research performance indicators for a team requires a data cleaning process that, among other things, deals with the problems of synonyms and homonyms pointed before. The Team table can be used as reference to identify and correct these problems. State-of-art procedures to solve synonyms are based on the use of approximate string matching [12]. Names as "Carriço, L." in tuple 1 of Team table and "Carrico, L." in tuple 2 of Pub table can easily be found as matches. However, it may also happen that these procedures find several possible correct names for the same author name. For example, "Santos, A." and "Santos, A. L." are the names of two team members and both match the author name "Santos, A. L." encountered in tuple 5 of the Pub table. That is to say, both names in ("Santos, A.","Santos, A. L.") and ("Santos, A. L.", "Santos, A. L.") are similar enough so that both entries of the Team table are considered as potential candidates of team member names for "Santos, A. L.". The problem that remains to be solved is which of the two to choose, or to decide if none of them does in fact correspond to the individual "Santos, A. L.". We believe that this kind of domain knowledge can only be brought by a user that is aware of the team members and their research work. The syntactic similarity value that exists between the two pairs is not enough for automatically taking this decision.

The detection of homonyms in the context of names has been object of active research. For instance, [13] has shown that the detection of homonyms among author names can benefit from the use of knowledge about co-authorship. If this kind of information is available, then a clustering algorithm can be applied with the purpose of putting into the same cluster those author names that share a certain amount of co-authors. In principle, the author names that belong to the same cluster most probably correspond to the same real entity. The problem that remains is how to obtain accurate co-authorship information. Clearly, automatic methods for calculating this information from publications are also subject to the problem of homonyms and, hence, the produced information in general is not accurate. In this case, we believe that the problem of circularity can only be broken by involving the user in the cleaning of the co-authorship information that was automatically obtained.

The example just presented shows the importance of being able to automatically clean data while efficiently employing user's efforts to overcome the problems that were not possible to handle automatically. In this paper, we propose a way of incorporating the user involvement in these processes and present a modeling primitive — the *data cleaning graph*, that supports the description of data cleaning processes that are conceived having user involvement in mind. A DCG encloses a graph of data transformations as used, for instance, in [17,9]. The output of each transformation is explicitly expressed and associated with a *quality constraint*. This constraint expresses the criteria that data produced by the transformation should obey to and its purpose is to call the user attention for quality problems in the data produced by the transformation. Additionally, the DCG encloses the specification of the points where the manual data repairing actions may take place. The aim of this facility is to guide the intervention of the user (end-users included) and, hence, it is important to define which data records can be subject to manual modifications and how. We have only considered actions that can be applied to individual data records for repairing data. Three types of actions were found useful: remove a tuple, insert a tuple, and modify the values of certain attribute of a tuple.

3   Data Cleaning Graphs

In this section we present the concept of *data cleaning graph* — the modeling primitive we propose for describing data cleaning processes. We provide its operational semantics through an algorithm that manipulates sets of tuples.

Terminology. We consider a set $\mathcal{R}$ of relations names and, for every $R \in \mathcal{R}$, a schema $sch(R)$ constituted by an ordered set of attribute names. An *instance* of a relation R is a finite set of $sch(R)$-tuples. We consider a set $\mathcal{T}$ of *data transformations*. Each $T \in \mathcal{T}$ consists of an ordered set $\mathbb{I}_T$ of input relation schemas, an output relation schema $\mathbb{O}_T$ and a total function that maps a sequence of $\mathbb{I}_T$-tuples to $\mathbb{O}_T$-tuples. We use $\mathbb{I}_T^i$ to denote the *i*-ary element of $\mathbb{I}_T$. If G is a *direct acyclic graph* (DAG), we use $^\bullet n$ and $n^\bullet$ to denote, respectively, $\{m : (m, n) \in edges(G)\}$ and $\{m : (n, m) \in edges(G)\}$ and $\leq_G$ to denote the partial order on the nodes of G, i.e., $n \leq_G m$ iff there exists a directed path from n to m in G.

3.1   The Notion of Data Cleaning Graph

The notion of DCG builds on the notion of data transformation graph introduced in [9]. These graphs are tailored to relational data and include data transformations that can range from relational operators and extensions (like the mapper operator formalized in [3]) to procedural code. The partial order $\leq_G$ on $nodes(G)$ partially dictates the order of execution of the data transformations in the process (transformations not comparable can be executed in any order).

A data cleaning graph is a DAG, where nodes correspond to data transformations or relations, and edges connect (input and output) relations to data transformations. In order to support the user involvement in the process of data cleaning, each relation R in a cleaning graph has associated a constraint expressing a *data quality criteria*. If the constraint is violated, it means that there is a set of tuples in the current instance of R that needs to be inspected by the user. Quality constraints can include the traditional constraints developed for schema design, such as functional dependencies and inclusion dependencies, as well as constraints specifically developed for data cleaning, such as conditional functional dependencies [7]. Each relation R in a cleaning graph has also associated a set of *manual data repairs*. These represent the actions that can be performed by the user over the instances of that relation in order to repair some quality problems, typically made apparent by one or more quality constraint labelling that relation or a relation "ahead" of R in the graph. For the convenience of the user, it might be helpful to filter the information available in R and, thus, we have considered that data repair actions are defined over updatable views of R^1. They can range from SQL expressions to relational lenses [2]. The examples of manual data repairs provided in this paper consider an updatable view defined as an SQL expression.

Definition 1. *A* Manual Data Repair *m* over a relation $R(A_1, ..., A_n)$ consists of a pair $\langle view(m), action(m) \rangle$, where $view(m)$ is an updatable view over R and $action(m)$ is one of the actions that can be performed over $view(m)$:

$\quad action ::= $ **delete** | **insert** | **update** A_i

In the case where the action is **update** A_i, we use $attribute(m)$ to refer to A_i.

Definition 2. *A* Data Cleaning Graph $\mathcal{G}$ for a set of input relations R_I and a set of output relations R_O is a labelled directed acyclic graph $\langle G, \langle \mathcal{Q}, \mathcal{M} \rangle \rangle$ s.t.:

- $nodes(G) \subseteq \mathcal{R} \cup \mathcal{T}$. We denote by $rels(G)$ and $trans(G)$ the set of nodes of G that are, respectively, relations and data transformations.
- $R_I \cup R_O \subseteq rels(G)$.
- $n \in R_I$ if and only if $^\bullet n = \emptyset$, and $n \in R_O$ if and only if $n^\bullet = \emptyset$ and $^\bullet n \neq \emptyset$.
- if $(n, m) \in edges(G)$, then either $(n \in \mathcal{R}$ and $m \in \mathcal{T})$ or $(n \in \mathcal{T}$ and $m \in \mathcal{R})$.
- if $T \in trans(G)$ then $\mathbb{I}_T = \{sch(R) : R \in {}^\bullet T\}$ and $\mathbb{O}_T = \{sch(R) : R \in T^\bullet\}$.
- if $R \in rels(G)$ then $^\bullet R$ has at most one element.
- $\mathcal{Q}$ is a function that assigns to every $R \in rels(G)$, a quality constraint over the set of relations behind R in G or in R_I, i.e., $\mathcal{Q}(R) \in \mathcal{L}(R_I \cup \{R' \in rels(G) : R' \leq_G R\})$ such that $\mathcal{Q}(R)$ is monotonic w.r.t. R, i.e., given a set of relation instances that satisfies $\mathcal{Q}(R)$, the removal of an arbitrary number of tuples form the instance of R does not affect the satisfaction of $\mathcal{Q}(R)$.
- $\mathcal{M}$ is a function that assigns to every $R \in rels(G)$, a set of manual data repairs over R.

---

[1] For a definition of an updatable view, see [11], for instance.

The conditions imposed on DCGs ensure that R_I and R_O are input and output relations of the graph; relations are always connected through data transformations; the input and output schemas of a data transformation are those determined by their immediate predecessors and successors nodes in the graph; the instances of a relation in the graph result, at most, from one data transformation; the quality constraints over a relation in the graph can only refer to relations that are either in R_I or behind that node in the graph and must be monotonic w.r.t. to the relation of the node. This last condition is necessary to ensure that quality constraints can be evaluated immediately after the data of the relation is produced, i.e., does not depend on data that will be produced later, by transformations ahead in the graph.

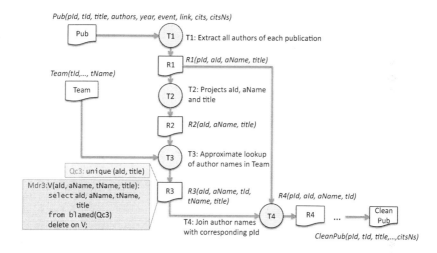

Fig. 2. Excerpt of a data cleaning graph for cleaning Pub table

The example sketched in Fig.2 illustrates an excerpt of the DCG required for cleaning the Pub table introduced in Section 2. It mainly makes use of SQL for expressing constraints and updatable views. The input relations of this DCG are Team and Pub and there is a single output relation, CleanPub that contains only publications authored by a member of Team. In the part of the graph that is shown, we can see that the node R3 is labelled with the quality constraint unique(aId, title). It is not difficult to conclude this is indeed a monotonic constraint over relations $\leq_G R$. The reason for imposing this quality constraint, at this point, is because we want to have at most one matching team member, for each author of a publication in Pub. Since transformation T3 applies a string similarity function to decide if two names (one from Pub and the other from Team) are the same, it might happen that some data produced by T3 violates this constraint. For instance, both Team members "Santos, A." and "Santos, A. L." are found similar to Pub author "Santos, A. L.". The quality constraint will call the attention of the user to the tuples blamed for the violation.

Moreover, the function $\mathcal{M}$ of this DCG assigns to the node R3 a single manual data repair, Mdr3, that consists in the view V defined over R3 that returns only the tuples blamed for the violation of Qc3 (this is formally defined in the next section) and the action **delete**. The view V projects almost all the attributes of the relation but we could use the view to exclude non relevant information and, in this way, limit the amount of information the user has to process in order to decide which are the appropriate manual data repairs to apply.

3.2   Operational Semantics

DCGs specify the quality criteria that the instances of each relation should meet. The records responsible for the violation are identified through the notion of blame assignment for quality constraints.

Definition 3. *Let ϕ be a quality constraint over a set of relations $R_1, ..., R_n$ that is assigned to relation R. Let r and $r_1, ..., r_n$ be instances of these relations s.t. $r, r_1, ..., r_n \nvDash \phi$. The blame of the violation is assigned to the set $blamed(\phi)$, which is defined as the union of all subsets rp of r that satisfy: (1) $r \backslash rp, r_1, ..., r_n \vDash \phi$; (2) rp does not have a proper subset o s.t. $r \backslash o, r_1, ..., r_n \vDash \phi$.*

Each subset rp of r that satisfies the two conditions above represents a way of "repairing" r through the removal of a set of tuples that, all together, cause the violation of ϕ (a particular case of data repairs as introduced in [1]). Hence, all tuples in r that have this type of "incompatibility" share the blame for the violation of ϕ. For instance, suppose that R3 in Fig.2 has the tuples (1, "Santos, A. L.", "Santos, A. L.", 2, "Managing...") and (1, "Santos, A. L.", "Santos, A.", 3, "Managing..."). These tuples are blamed for the violation of the quality constraint Qc3. Notice that this form of blame assignment is only appropriate if constraints are monotonic in R and this is why we limit constraints to be of this type.

Data cleaning of a source of data tends to be the result of numerous iterations, some involving the tuning of data transformations and others involving manual data repairs. Even if the DCG developed for the problem was subject to a strict validation and verification process, it is normal that when it is executed over the real data, small changes in the DCG, confined to specific data transformations, are needed. Because we do not want to force the user to repeat the data repairs previously done that, in principle, are still valid, we define that the execution of a DCG takes as input not only the data that needs to be cleaned but also collections of instances of manual data repairs (mdr, for short). These represent mdr actions enacted at some point in the past. For convenience, we consider that instances of mdrs keep track of their type.

Definition 4. *Let m be a manual data repair. If $action(m)$ is **delete** or **insert**, an $m-$instance ι is a pair $\langle m, tuple(\iota) \rangle$ where $tuple(\iota)$ is a $view(m)$-tuple. If $action(m)$ is **update** A, an $m-$instance ι is a triple $\langle m, tuple(\iota), value(\iota) \rangle$ where $tuple(\iota)$ is a $view(m)$-tuple, $value(\iota)$ is a value in $Dom(A)$.*

For instance, still referring to Fig.2, after analyzing the violation of the quality constraint Qc3 and taking the title into account, the user could conclude that the author "Santos, A. L." does not correspond to the team author "Santos, A." and decide to delete the corresponding tuple from 0R3. This would generate the Mdr3-instance $\langle$mdr3, (1, "Santos, A. L.", "Santos, A.", "Managing...")$\rangle$.

The execution of a DCG is defined over a source of data (instances of the graph input relations) and what we call a *manual data repair state M* — a state capturing the instances of mdrs that have to be taken into account in the cleaning process. Because the order of actions in this context is obviously relevant, this state registers the order by which the instances of mdrs associated to each relation should be executed (what comes in first is handled first).

The execution of a DCG consists in the sequential execution of each data transformation in accordance with the partial order defined by the graph: if $T <_G T'$, then T' is executed after T. The execution of a data transformation T produces an instance of the relation R in $T^\bullet$. This relation is then subject to the mdr instances in $M(R)$. Then, the set of tuples in the resulting relation instance that are blamed for the violation of the quality constraint associated to R, $\mathcal{Q}(R)$ is calculated. Formally, the execution of a DCG can be defined as follows.

Definition 5. *Let $\mathcal{G} = \langle G, \langle \mathcal{Q}, \mathcal{M} \rangle \rangle$ be a data cleaning graph for a set $R_1, ..., R_n$ of input relations. Let $r_1, ..., r_n$ be instances of these relations and M be a manual data repair state for $\mathcal{G}$, i.e., a function that assigns to every relation $R \in rels(\mathcal{G})$, a list of instances of manual data repairs over R. The result of executing $\mathcal{G}$ over $r_1, ..., r_n$ and M is $\{\langle tuples(R), tuples^{bl}(R) \rangle : R \in rels(G)\}$ calculated as follows:*

```
 1: for  i = 1 to n  do                      21: apply_mdr(mdrInstances, vr)
 2:     for each**  ι ∈ M(R_i)  do            22: for each**  ι ∈ mdrInstances  do
 3:         vr ← compute_view(view(ι), tuples(R_i))   23:     if  action(mdr(ι)) = delete  then
 4:         apply_mdr(ι, vr)                  24:         vr ← vr \ {tuple(ι)}
 5:         tuples(R_i) ← propagate(vr)       25:     else if action(mdr(ι)) = insert then
 6:     end for                               26:         vr ← r ∪ {tuple(ι)}
 7: end for                                   27:     else if  action(mdr(ι)) = update  then
 8: for  i = 1 to n  do                       28:         newt ← tuple(ι)
 9:     tuples^{bl}(R_i) ← blamed(tuples(r_i))  29:         newt[attribute(action(mdr(ι)))] ← value(ι)
10: end for                                   30:         vr ← (vr \ {tuple(ι)}) ∪ {newt}
11: for each*  T ∈ trans(G)  do               31:     end if
12:     let {R'_1, ..., R'_k} = •T            32: end for
13:     tuples(T^•) ← T(tuples(R'_1), ..., tuples(R'_k))
14:     for each**  ι ∈ M(T^•)  do
15:         vr ← compute_view(view(ι), tuples(T^•))
16:         apply_mdr(ι, vr)
17:         tuples(T^•) ← propagate(vr)
18:     end for
19:     tuples^{bl}(T^•) ← blamed(tuples(T^•))
20: end for
```

*Assuming that the underlying iteration will traverse the set in ascending element order.
**Assuming that the underlying iteration will traverse the list in proper sequence.

The procedure *compute_view(view,setOfTuples)* encodes the application of the *view* to the base table constituted by the *setOfTuples* whereas *propagate(view)* encodes the propagation of the updates applied to the tuples returned by *view* to the base table. Although this algorithm defines an operational semantics for DCGs, it must not be regarded as a proposal for the implementation of an engine that supports the execution of DCGs. The sole purpose of this algorithm is to formally define what is the result of executing a DCG over a source of data and a manual data repair state.

4 Case Study

We have developed and implemented in full depth the process to clean publication citation data retrieved from the web, introduced in Section 2. The goal of this process is to clean the Pub table and produce a table containing only the publications authored by at least one team member, with duplicate entries for the same real world publication organized in clusters. The process: (i) extracts the author names independently of the publication they are associated to; (ii) matches each of these author names against the names stored in the Team table, and tries to find synonyms (i.e., approximate similar names); (iii) builds the list of co-authors for each author; (iv) removes those publications that are not authored by any team member; and (v) detects and clusters approximate duplicate publication records.

The DCG that models this process is presented in Fig. 3 and in the two tables presented in Fig. 4. It presents slight differences with respect to the excerpt presented in Fig. 2, because therein we made some simplifications (more details can be found in [10]). The condition that an author of each publication can only match one team member is now checked through the quality constraint Qc6 that is imposed after the user gives feedback about the co-authorship tuples (through Mdr5). The data transformation T5 was introduced for gathering the co-authorship information about each author. The co-authorship information, after being validated by the user, can provide additional knowledge that is helpful for automatically deciding whether an author name in a publication refers to a team member.

Based on the matching name pairs produced by T3 and T4, and on the co-authorship tuples produced by T5, the transformation T6 is able to distinguish, among the set of authors for each publication, those who belong to the team from those who do not. The user feedback provided through Mdr6 confirms whether the information automatically produced is true. Finally, T7 discards the publication records whose list of authors does not contain a team member. Besides producing Pub records that concern only team members, the goal of the graph is also to put together Pub records that concern the same real world publication. To this end, the publication records must be compared in order to identify entries that constitute approximate duplicates. For this purpose, transformations T9 and T10 match pairs of publications, and cluster the matched publications.

Other quality constraints were introduced in the graph to call the user's attention for anticipated data problems. Qc0 and Qc8 call the user attention for analyzing and correcting tuples that have the word "others" in its authors attribute value, and tuples that correspond to single-author publications (i.e., by checking if the author attribute value does not contain the conjunction "and", which connects two or more authors names), respectively. Quality constraints Qc3 and Qc9 are imposed on the result of the matching operations encoded in T3 and T9, respectively, that consider the existence of two threshold values. Pairs of records whose computed similarity is below the inferior threshold are considered as non-matches and discarded by the transformations. Pairs of records whose similarity is above the inferior threshold are considered as candidate matches

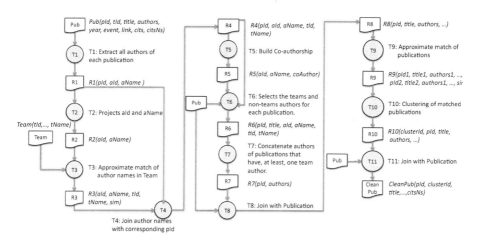

Fig. 3. Data cleaning graph for the case study

Node	Quality Constraint	Mdr	Node	User actions	View
Pub	Qc0: Pub.authors !contains("others")	Mdr0	Pub	delete, update author	**Select** title, authors **From** blamed(Qc0)
R3	QC3: R3.sim ≥ 0.8	Mdr3	R3	update sim	**Select** aName, tname, sim **From** blamed(Qc3)
R6	Qc6: unique(pid,aId)	Mdr5	R5	delete	**Select** aName, coAuthor **From** R5
R8	Qc8: R8.authors !contains("and")	Mdr6	R6	delete	**Select** title, aName **From** blamed(Qc6)
R9	Qc9: R9.sim ≥ 0.8	Mdr8	R8	delete	**Select** title, authors, ... **From** blamed(Qc8)
		Mdr9	R9	update sim	**Select** titel1, ..., title2,.. **From** blamed(Qc9)

Fig. 4. Quality constraints and manual data repairs of the DCG

and returned as a result of the data transformations. Those resulting records whose similarity value (stored in the sim attribute) is inferior to the superior threshold violate the corresponding quality constraints (Qc3 and Qc9). These records do not have a sufficiently high value nor a sufficiently low value of the sim attribute, so the user must analyze them. Then, through Mdr3 and Mdr9, the user may decide whether the corresponding pairs of author names or publications are considered as matches, by modifying the sim value accordingly (1 for matches, and 0 for no matches).

5   Experiments

We performed a set of experiments to evaluate the benefits of involving the user in the data cleaning process described in Section 4. We focused on two different aspects: the data quality obtained at the end of the data cleaning process and the cost of the manual activities that have to be performed by the user.

The experiments were performed with the AJAX data cleaning prototype[8], over a subset of the database of the CIDS[6]. These experiments required to implement two data cleaning programs: P_1 complying with the data transformation graph presented in Fig.3 and P_2 complying with the data transformation graph presented in Fig.3 and capturing, as closest as possible with the means available, the quality constraints presented in the first table presented in Fig.4. Quality constraints in P_2 were encoded inside transformations, making use of exceptions as supported by AJAX. As a result, the tuples available for user inspection are not those blamed for the violation but those that originate a blamed tuple. Moreover, the tuples that raise exceptions are not available as input for the transformations ahead in the graph. However, for the evaluation purpose at hand, these differences were considered to be neglectable.

We performed the following cleaning tasks. $Task_1$: the manual cleaning of the Pub table. $Task_2$: the execution of P_1 and the manual intervention of the user over the produced data in the output CleanPub table so that it contains all publications that are authored by at least one team member with duplicates organized in clusters. $Task_3$: the execution of the P_2 and the manual intervention of the user over the produced data in the CleanPub table guided by the rejected tuples in the different points of the program. $Task_4$: the execution of the data cleaning program and, after receiving user feedback, the re-execution of parts of it — with the user involvement guided by the rejected tuples and the mdrs presented in the second table presented in Fig.4.

The metrics used to evaluate the quality of the CleanPub records produced are recall and precision. *TD Recall* (TD R) is given by the number of CleanPub tuples that are authored by the team (i.e., authored by at least one team member) divided by the number of CleanPub tuples authored by the team that should have been produced. *TD Precision* (TD P) is given by the number of CleanPub tuples that are authored by the team divided by the number of CleanPub tuples that were produced. *DD Recall* (DD R) is given by the number of pairs of CleanPub tuples that were correctly identified as duplicates (i.e., the ones with the same value of the clusterId attribute and that correspond to the same real publication) divided by the total number of pairs of CleanPub tuples that should have been identified as duplicates. *DD Precision* (DD P) is given by the number of pairs of CleanPub tuples that were correctly identified as duplicates divided by the number of pairs of CleanPub tuples that were identified as duplicates.

To evaluate the cost associated to the user feedback, we consider the following metrics that we believe can capture the most relevant aspects of user interaction: the number of characters the user needs to visualize in order to decide which data corrections need to be undertaken; the maximum number of characters that may need to be updated, when attribute values are modified; the maximum number of characters that may need to be deleted or inserted, when tuples are deleted or inserted; and the number of tuples that need to be updated, deleted or inserted. The number of characters is given by the multiplication of the number of tuples by the sum of the sizes of each attribute.

We used an instance of the CIDS database, that contains 509 and 24 tuples in the tables Pub and Team, respectively. It includes all the publication records returned by Google Scholar for five members of the team, chosen beforehand. First, we performed $Task_1$ and obtained the cleaned version of this instance by manually cleaning it. This process was performed by retrieving information from the member's home pages and DBLP. Then, the cleaned Pub table obtained was checked and eventually corrected by each team member. The manually cleaned publication table, named CleanPub$_1$, was used as a reference for computing the quality of the data cleaned automatically and the impact of user feedback.

Data Accuracy. To compute the gain of data quality obtained when incorporating the user feedback, we performed $Task_2$, $Task_3$ and $Task_4$. The resulting publication records obtained in each of these cases were stored in tables named, CleanPub$_2$, CleanPub$_3$, and CleanPub$_4$, respectively. The recall and precision (both TD and DD) of the CleanPub$_3$ and CleanPub$_4$ tables were 100%. We recall that, in both cases, the manual corrections applied by the user are guided by rejected tuples. In the case of CleanPub$_2$, 70% of TD R, 78% of DD R and 100% of precision were obtained. In fact, in $Task_2$, the user only has access to the data produced at the end of the data cleaning process and so there is no way of recovering the data tuples that were not properly handled by some data transformations. Overall, these data accuracy values can be considered as good, but there is a trade-off between data accuracy and the cost of user feedback required.

In the case of $Task_4$, to analyze the effect of the different mdrs in the final result, we measured the values of precision and recall after applying each mdr. We considered that after the mdr instances were applied, the remaining of the DCG was re-executed and the precision and recall of CleanPub$_4$ data was re-computed. The results obtained are summarized in Table 1. We notice that the precision and recall values greatly improved with the user's feedback via mdrs. The non-increasing values of DD P when Mdr8 is applied are justified by the existence of pairs of tuples that correspond to the same single-author publication but whose similarity is inferior to 0.8. These pairs of tuples violated Qc8 and, because we use AJAX exception mechanism for "simulating" quality constraint violation, they were not delivered to transformation T9.

Table 1. Precision and Recall for CleanPub$_4$ table

mdr	TD P	TD R	DD P	DD R
none	0.83	0.70	0.98	0.76
Mdr0	0.83	0.70	0.98	0.76
Mdr3	0.85	0.80	0.98	0.91
Mdr5	1	0.92	0.98	0.91
Mdr6	1	0.92	0.98	0.91
Mdr8	1	1	0.93	0.93
Mdr9	1	1	1	1

Table 2. Cost of user feedback

Cost/Task	$Task_1$	$Task_2$	$Task_3$	$Task_4$
Visualization	200,000	137,000	115,000	32,000
# deleted tuples	164	56	56	134
Deletion	33,500	11,500	11,500	7,500
# updated tuples	121	2	32	21
Updating	2,600	40	800	150
# inserted tuples	0	0	68	0
Insertion	0	0	14,000	0

Cost of User Feedback. We also wanted to find out whether the approach of incorporating the user feedback into the DCG (embodied by $Task_4$) facilitates the work of the user when compared to other approaches. For this purpose, we measured the cost associated to the user actions performed in the four tasks referred above. The results obtained are presented in Table 2. The cost of data visualization, updating, deletion and insertion are approximate values.

In Table 2, we observe that the use of quality constraints and mdrs in $Task_4$ greatly decreases the cost of data visualization with respect to the other tasks. Notice that this result is even true when comparing the cost of data visualization incurred in $Task_2$, which only considers the data produced at the end of the data cleaning process. This result can be explained by the existence of quality constraints that were specified in such a way that only the set of tuples blamed by constraint violations are shown to the user. In other cases, the mdrs define judiciously the data the user needs to analyze in order to decide which action must be applied.

In what concerns the cost of the user feedback incurred in each task, we also observe that the use of mdrs also decreases substantially the number and cost of user actions that must be applied to manually correct data. In comparison to $Task_1$ and $Task_3$, the results obtained by $Task_4$ are significantly improved. Although in $Task_4$ the user deletes a higher number of tuples than in $Task_3$, the cost of delete in $Task_4$ is lower than the corresponding cost in $Task_3$ because the user has to analyse a smaller amount of data in order to apply each delete action. With respect to $Task_2$, the obtained results are slightly better than $Task_4$ because in $Task_2$ the user actions are only applied over data produced at the end of the data cleaning process and, therefore, the rejected tuples are not analyzed, resulting in significantly worst recall values (70% of TD R and a 78% of DD R). Overall, the results show that the use of the new primitives addressing the user feedback ($Task_4$) may significantly improve a data cleaning process.

6   Related Work

Error Handling in ETL and Data Cleaning Tools. In current commercial ETL and data cleaning tools, the developer can specify that input records not handled by some pre-defined operators are written into a *log file* whose contents can be later analyzed by the user. However, no user feedback provided on the data stored in these files can be re-integrated in the flow of data transformations. In some tools (e.g. SQL Server Integration Services), it is possible to partially overcome this limitation, by explicitly specifying an error output flow for some data operators that can be later analyzed by the user or considered as input of further data operators.

Support for error handling in the context of data cleaning was investigated in the context of prototypes AJAX [9] and ARKTOS [18] through the notion of, respectively, *exception* and *rejection*. Both notions correspond to input tuples that are not properly handled by a given data transformation. Rejected tuples and exceptions are stored in a specific table whose schema is the same as the input schema of the transformation (in ARKTOS) or contains the key of the input tuples (in AJAX). The purpose of this information is to call the user's attention for data items not correctly handled in specific points of the graph of data transformations. However, these solutions do not provide the support we believe should be available at the modelling level of data cleaning processes. For instance, AJAX exceptions rely on relational technology to detect the occurrence of integrity constraint violations. As a result, in many situations it is not possible to predict which are the tuples that will be identified as exceptions because it will depend on the order in which tuples of the input tables are processed (typically not under the control of the developer). Other initiatives to encode data quality rules and store the records that violate them have taken place (e.g., [16]).

User Feedback. The incorporation of user feedback has shown to be useful in several automatic tasks. For example, Chai et al [4] propose a solution to incorporate the end-user feedback into Information Extraction programs. An Information Extraction program is composed by a set of declarative rules. The developer writes some of these rules with the purpose of specifying the items of data the users can edit and the user interfaces that can be used. Analogously, we are proposing a way of specifying the exact points in the graph of data transformations where the user can provide feedback to improve the quality of the produced data. Moreover, we are limiting the amount of information the user can visualize and provide some guidance for the manual modification of data. In the context of data cleaning, Potter's Wheel [15] offers a graphical interface through which the developer can specify and quickly debug data cleaning rules that are applied to samples of data.

Data Repairs. In [5], Cong and colleagues propose a framework for data cleaning that supports algorithms for finding repairs for a database and a statistical method to guarantee the accuracy of the repairs found. As noted in Section 3, the notion of blamed tuples introduced in this paper is based on the concept of database repair (considering that repair operations are limited to deletion of tuples). We consider as blamed for the violation of a data quality constraint associated to a relation of a database, those tuples in the relation instance that belong to some repair of the database.

Recently, [19] puts forward a system for guiding data repairing that explicitly involves the user in the process of checking the data repairs automatically produced by the algorithms introduced in [5]. In particular, the authors focused on ranking the repairs in such a way that the user effort spent in analyzing useless information is minimized. In this paper, we aim at reaching the same goal: to minimize the user effort when providing feedback in a data cleaning process. However, in the current version of our research, we do not provide any method for clustering or ranking the tuples that violate constraints. For the moment, we claim that by disclosing a limited set of records to the user, we are able to reduce the amount of data that he/she needs to analyze and eventually modify.

7   Conclusions

In this paper, we address the problem of integrating the user feedback in an automatic data cleaning process. We propose the notion of *data quality constraint* that may be associated to any of the intermediate relations produced by data transformations in a DCG. We also propose that a DCG specifies *manual data repairs*, that to some extend can be regarded as a kind of wizard-based form that limits the amount of data that can be visualized and modified. We have performed preliminary experiments with a real-world data set that show the gain of data quality achieved when the user feedback is incorporated and that the overhead incurred by the user, when providing feedback guided by quality constraints and mdrs, is significantly inferior to the effort involved in cleaning rejected records in an ad-hoc manner.

As future work, we plan to modify the definition of updatable view that is used in the definition of mdrs so that the join of base relations is possible. Special care must be taken so that the view remains updatable in the sense that the updates can always be propagated to the base relations. In addition, the concept of DCG and corresponding operational semantics must be adequately supported by a software platform that should efficiently compute the set of blamed tuples for a given quality constraint violation, enable the automatic re-application of past user actions, and support the incremental execution of data transformations.

References

1. Arenas, M., Bertossi, L.E., Chomicki, J.: Consistent query answers in inconsistent databases. In: PODS, pp. 68–79 (1999)
2. Bohannon, A., Pierce, B.C., Vaughan, J.A.: Relational lenses: a language for updatable views. In: PODS, pp. 338–347. ACM, New York (2006)
3. Carreira, P., Galhardas, H., Lopes, A., Pereira, J.: One-to-many data transformations through data mappers. Data Knowl. Eng. 62(3), 483–503 (2007)
4. Chai, X., Vuong, B.-Q., Doan, A., Naughton, J.F.: Efficiently incorporating user feedback into information extraction and integration programs. In: SIGMOD, pp. 87–100 (2009)
5. Cong, G., Fan, W., Geerts, F., Jia, X., Ma, S.: Improving data quality: Consistency and accuracy. In: VLDB, pp. 315–326 (2007)
6. Couto, F.M., Pesquita, C., Grego, T., Verissimo, P.: Handling self-citations using google scholar. Cybermetrics 13(1) (2009)
7. Fan, W., Geerts, F., Jia, X.: Conditional dependencies: A principled approach to improving data quality. In: Sexton, A.P. (ed.) BNCOD 26. LNCS, vol. 5588, pp. 8–20. Springer, Heidelberg (2009)
8. Galhardas, H., Florescu, D., Shasha, D., Simon, E.: Ajax: An extensible data cleaning tool. In: SIGMOD, p. 590 (2000)
9. Galhardas, H., Florescu, D., Shasha, D., Simon, E., Saita, C.-A.: Declarative data cleaning: Language, model, and algorithms. In: VLDB, pp. 371–380 (2001)
10. Galhardas, H., Lopes, A., Santos, E.: Support for user involvement in data cleaning applications. DI/FCUL TR 2010-03, Faculty of Sciences, University of Lisbon (2010), http://hdl.handle.net/10455/6674
11. Garcia-Molina, H., Ullman, J., Widom, J.: Database Systems: The Complete Book. Prentice-Hall, Englewood Cliffs (2008)
12. Hall, P.A.V., Dowling, G.R.: Approximate string matching. ACM Comput. Surv. 12(4), 381–402 (1980)
13. Kang, I.-S., Na, S.-H., Lee, S., Jung, H., Kim, P., Sung, W.-K., Lee, J.-H.: On co-authorship for author disambiguation. Inf. Process. Manage. 45(1), 84–97 (2009)
14. Rahm, E., Do, H.H.: Data cleaning: Problems and current approaches. IEEE Data Eng. Bull. 23(4), 3–13 (2000)

15. Raman, V., Hellerstein, J.M.: Potter's wheel: An interactive data cleaning system. In: VLDB, pp. 381–390 (2001)
16. Rodic, J., Baranovic, M.: Generating data quality rules and integration into etl process. In: DOLAP, pp. 65–72 (2009)
17. Simitsis, A., Vassiliadis, P., Terrovitis, M., Skiadopoulos, S.: Graph-based modeling of ETL activities with multi-level transformations and updates. In: Tjoa, A.M., Trujillo, J. (eds.) DaWaK 2005. LNCS, vol. 3589, pp. 43–52. Springer, Heidelberg (2005)
18. Vassiliadis, P., Simitsis, A., Georgantas, P., Terrovitis, M., Skiadopoulos, S.: A generic and customizable framework for the design of ETL scenarios. Inf. Syst. 30(7), 492–525 (2005)
19. Yakout, M., Elmagarmid, A.K., Neville, J., Ouzzani, M., Ilyas, I.F.: Guided data repair. PVLDB 4(5), 279–289 (2011)

Efficient Processing of Drill-across Queries over Geographic Data Warehouses

Jaqueline Joice Brito[1], Thiago Luís Lopes Siqueira[2,3], Valéria Cesário Times[4],
Ricardo Rodrigues Ciferri[3], and Cristina Dutra de Ciferri[1]

[1] Department of Computer Science, University of São Paulo at São Carlos, USP
13.560-970, São Carlos, SP, Brazil
[2] São Paulo Federal Institute of Education, Science and Technology, IFSP
São Carlos Campus, 13.565-905, São Carlos, SP, Brazil
[3] Department of Computer Science, Federal University of São Carlos, UFSCar
13.565-905, São Carlos, SP, Brazil
[4] Informatics Center, Federal University of Pernambuco, UFPE
50.670-901, Recife, PE, Brazil
jjbrito@icmc.usp.br, prof.thiago@cefetsp.br, vct@cin.ufpe.br,
ricardo@dc.ufscar.br, cdac@icmc.usp.br

Abstract. Drill-across SOLAP queries (spatial OLAP queries) allow for strategic decision-making through the use of numeric measures from distinct fact tables that share dimensions and by the evaluation of spatial predicates. Despite the importance of these queries in geographic data warehouses (GDWs), there is a lack of research aimed at their study. In this paper, we investigate three challenging aspects related to the efficient processing of drill-across SOLAP queries over GDWs: (i) the design of a GDW schema to enable the performance evaluation of drill-across SOLAP query processing; (ii) the definition of classes of drill-across SOLAP queries to be issued over the proposed GDW schema; and (iii) the analysis of different approaches to process drill-across SOLAP queries, as follows: star-join computation, materialized views and a new proposed approach based on the SB-index, which is named *DrillAcrossSB*. We conclude that the *DrillAcrossSB* approach highly speedups the processing of drill-across SOLAP queries from 39% up to 98%.

Keywords: geographic data warehouse, drill-across SOLAP query, index structure, the SB-index.

1 Introduction

Similar to a conventional data warehouse, a geographic data warehouse (GDW) is a subject-oriented, integrated, historical and non-volatile multidimensional database. Additionally, the GDW holds spatial attributes to store spatial objects that are represented by geometries such as points and polygons [15,5,14]. In relational databases, the GDW multidimensional model is usually implemented as an adapted star schema, which contains a fact table that stores numeric or

A. Cuzzocrea and U. Dayal (Eds.): DaWaK 2011, LNCS 6862, pp. 152–166, 2011.

spatial measures, and several dimension tables that store descriptive or spatial attributes and their hierarchies. While measures are the subject of analysis, the dimensions contextualize these measures. Regarding hierarchies, they impose a partial ordering on conventional or spatial attributes, specifying that one aggregation of higher granularity can be determined using data from another aggregation of lower granularity. In GDW, a predefined spatial hierarchy is a 1:N association among higher and lower granularity spatial attributes that is determined by a spatial predicate [5]. Furthermore, differently from the conventional star schema, spatial attributes are not stored redundantly [13,6].

Example 1. Suppose a GDW schema that represents historical data related to orders and sales of a corporation and that extends the TPC-H benchmark [10] to store spatial attributes about the locations of suppliers and customers (see Figure 1 in Section 4.1). A subset of this GDW schema has *Lineitem* as a fact table that holds numeric measures such as *l_quantity*, *Part* as a conventional dimension table, and *Customer* and *Supplier* as spatial dimension tables. Furthermore, $(region\_geo) \preceq (nation\_geo) \preceq (city\_geo) \preceq (s\_address\_geo)$ is a predefined spatial hierarchy composed of spatial attributes suffixed with *_geo*, which is defined for the dimension table *Supplier*. In this hierarchy, the operator $\preceq$ represents the partial ordering. Also, the spatial relationship is containment, imposing that a given supplier address is inside only one city, a city is inside only one nation, and a nation is inside only one region. Therefore, the quantity sold for a given nation is the sum of the quantities sold in each city inside this nation.   □

GDWs are also characterized by supporting SOLAP (spatial online analytical processing [3]) queries, i.e. analytical operations extended with spatial predicates. Important analytical operations are drill-down, roll-up and drill-across, and spatial predicates frequently used are intersection, containment and enclosure. While spatial drill-down operations analyze data on increasingly higher levels of detail, spatial roll-up operations analyze them on progressively lower levels of detail. Regarding spatial drill-across operations, they use distinct numeric measures whose fact tables are related to each other by at least one shared dimension, strictly taking into account one or more spatial predicates. Correlating fact tables that belong to different star schemas but share dimension tables that have the same semantics and the same hierarchies of attributes originates a fact constellation.

Example 2. Consider the GDW schema introduced in Example 1. In a spatial drill-down operation, a decision-making user may require the *l_quantity* sold by *part* by *nations that intersect a given rectangular window*, and later may require the *l_quantity* sold by *part* by *cities that intersect a smaller rectangular window*. To illustrate a spatial drill-across operation, consider another subset of the GDW schema, which is composed of the fact table *Partsupp* containing numeric measures such as *ps_supplycost*, the conventional dimension table *Part* and the spatial dimension table *Supplier* (see Figure 1). The user may require over the fact constellation the *l_quantity* sold and the *ps_supplycost* of *suppliers* whose *addresses are inside a given rectangular window*.   □

SOLAP queries are more complex and costly than analytical operations involving only conventional attributes. In addition to performing joins and aggregations over huge fact tables and dimension tables, SOLAP queries also require the processing of spatial predicates defined over spatial data. Therefore, improving the performance of SOLAP queries is a core issue in GDW. The challenge is to retrieve data related to ad hoc spatial query windows, avoiding the high cost of joining large fact tables with dimension tables.

In the literature, there are a number of approaches that focus on spatial drill-down and spatial roll-up operations (see Section 2). However, to the best of our knowledge, there is a lack of research aimed at investigating drill-across SOLAP queries. These queries are often used by decision-making users to look across broad perspectives that require the analysis of geographic locations.

In this paper, we focus on the efficient processing of drill-across SOLAP queries over GDWs. We introduce the contributions as described as follows.

- We propose a GDW schema based on predefined spatial hierarchies, which is specifically designed to enable the performance evaluation of drill-across SOLAP query processing.
- We describe novel classes of drill-across SOLAP queries to be issued over the proposed GDW schema, such that these classes also focus on drill-down and roll-up SOLAP queries.
- We investigate different approaches to enhance the query processing performance of drill-across SOLAP queries, as follows. The first approach analyses the star-join computation, and the second approach analyses the use of materialized views. The third approach, which is proposed in this paper and is named *DrillAcrossSB*, investigates the use of the SB-index [13,12].

This paper is organized as follows. Section 2 surveys related work, Section 3 details concepts used as a basis in our work, Section 4 investigates each contribution introduced by our paper, Section 5 discusses the experimental results, and Section 6 concludes the paper.

2   Related Work

In the literature, there are a number of approaches that have been proposed for designing the GDW and improving the performance of OLAP and SOLAP queries, but they differ from our work on their purpose. Regarding the design of the GDW, Malinowski and Zimnyi [5] define the concepts of conventional and spatial facts, dimensions and hierarchies, as well as introduce the use of pictograms for spatial data types, such as *point* and *area* to represent spatial dimensions that contain attributes stored as points and polygons, respectively. Siqueira et al. [13] investigate redundant and non-redundant GDW star schemas. While in the former the dimension tables store both conventional and spatial attributes, in the latter conventional and spatial attributes are stored separately in different dimension tables. Mateus et al. [6] argue that conventional and spatial data should be stored in a single dimension table if there is a 1:1 association between objects from the related conventional and spatial dimensions. Otherwise, these data should be stored separately. Although we base the GDW schema that we propose in this paper in some principles surveyed here, the aforementioned approaches do not focus on drill-across SOLAP queries, which is our main goal. In detail, these approaches do not focus on fact constellations containing spatial dimension tables nor define classes of drill-across SOLAP queries to be issued over the GDW schema.

Regarding improving the performance of OLAP and SOLAP queries, there are several approaches addressing view materialization [15,11], data fragmentation and partitioning [4,1], execution of drill-across queries over fact constellations in conventional data warehouses [2], and also indices [8,9,13,7]. However, despite the importance of drill-across SOLAP queries, there is a lack of research aimed at their study. On the one hand, approaches that improve the performance of drill-across OLAP queries do not focus on GDWs nor consider the processing of spatial predicates. On the other hand, approaches that improve the performance of SOLAP queries do not focus on drill-across SOLAP queries.

3   Theoretical Foundation

SOLAP queries can be processed according to different techniques, such as star-join computation, materialized views and the SB-index. The star-join computation consists in accessing the GDW schema and performing all joins and aggregations required by the SOLAP query, as well as solving all query filter conditions defined over conventional and spatial predicates. Also, spatial indices such as the R-tree can be defined on spatial attributes to improve the spatial predicate processing. Although star-join computation usually refers to conventional star schemas, we adopt this concept throughout this paper to also refer to fact constellation schemas and their derivations in GDW.

Materialized views are an alternative to the star-join computation, as they pre-compute data according to frequent queries and store the result as tables. In detail, these tables are built containing pre-computed data from fact tables that were joined to dimension tables and whose measures were aggregated. As a consequence, the use of materialized views avoids costly join operations among the fact and the dimension tables, as well as simplifies groupings, reduces the number of rows handled and benefits the evaluation of query filter conditions. Although avoiding join operations is straightforward when dealing with conventional data warehouses, GDWs impose that materialized views do not hold redundant spatial data. Therefore, in GDWs, materialized views maintain foreign keys to join spatial dimension tables [13,6].

The Spatial Bitmap Index (SB-index) [13,12] is an index based on the Bitmap [8] and on the minimum bounding rectangle (MBR), which is designed to efficiently index predefined spatial hierarchies over GDWs. It has a sequential structure whose entries maintain a primary key value for the spatial dimension table and a MBR. Also, the i-th entry of the SB-index points to the i-th bit-vector of a star-join Bitmap index. There is exactly one bit-vector associated to each key value, which is used to indicate the tuples of the fact table where the given key value occurs (i.e. bit value 1) and does not occur (i.e. bit value 0). A core aspect of the SB-index's query processing is that it computes the spatial predicate and transforms it into a conventional one, which can be evaluated together with other conventional predicates using the star-join Bitmap index.

4   Efficient Processing of Drill-across SOLAP Queries

In order to investigate the efficient processing of drill-across SOLAP queries over GDWs, we introduce: (i) the design of a GDW schema to enable the performance evaluation of drill-across SOLAP query processing in Section 4.1; (ii) the definition of classes of drill-across SOLAP queries to be issued over the proposed GDW schema in Section 4.2; and (iii) the proposal of an approach based on the SB-index to process drill-across SOLAP queries in Section 4.3.

4.1   The Proposed GDW Schema

In this section, we propose the *SpatialDrillAcross* schema, a GDW schema that faces two challenges. Firstly, it focuses on conventional and spatial dimensions and attributes, as well as hierarchies of conventional attributes and predefined spatial hierarchies. Secondly, it also enables the performance evaluation of drill-across SOLAP query processing.

To develop a GDW schema that addresses these challenges, we propose that this schema is based on the guidelines described as follows.

- The schema must have at least one fact constellation.
- Spatial data should be stored as attributes in dimension tables.
- Dimension tables should maintain descriptive and spatial attributes if and only if there is a 1:1 association between the spatial attribute and the dimension table primary key. Otherwise, the spatial attribute should be stored in a separate spatial dimension table that has its own primary key, which is referenced by the conventional dimension table.
- Spatial hierarchies enable the execution of drill-down and roll-up SOLAP queries together with drill-across SOLAP queries.

Figure 1 depicts the proposed *SpatialDrillAcross* schema. Note that the semantic of the data warehousing application is the same as that introduced by the TPC-H benchmark. However, the *SpatialDrillAcross* schema extends this benchmark to comply with the aforementioned guidelines as explained as follows.

- It contains a fact constellation composed of the fact tables *Lineitem* and *Partsupp*, which share the conventional dimension table *Part* and the spatial dimension table *Supplier*.
- It stores spatial attributes identified by the suffix *_geo* in the spatial dimension tables *Supplier*, *Customer*, *City*, *Nation* and *Region*. Spatial attributes

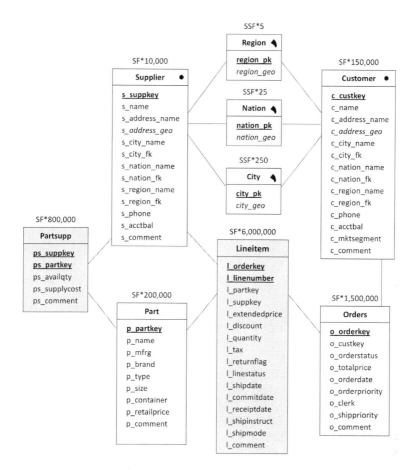

Fig. 1. The proposed *SpatialDrillAcross* schema. SF and SSF refer to the scale factor for conventional and spatial data, respectively.

were introduced in the *SpatialDrillAcross* schema according to their correspondence with conventional data already present in the TPC-H benchmark, except for *City*, which was added to the proposed schema to generate another spatial granularity level. Also, the spatial dimension tables are represented by pictograms for spatial data types described in Section 2, such as point (i.e. *Supplier* and *Customer*) and area/polygon (i.e. *City*, *Nation* and *Region*).

– It stores the addresses of customers and suppliers as spatial attributes in the dimension tables *Customer* and *Supplier*, i.e. in *c_address_geo* and *s_address_geo*, respectively. This design decision was motivated by the fact that there is a 1:1 association between *c_address_geo* and the dimension table *Customer*, as well as a 1:1 association between *s_address_geo* and the dimension table *Supplier*. That is, there is only one address for a customer (or a supplier). Also, customers and suppliers do not share common addresses.

– It has two spatial predefined hierarchies defined by the spatial relationship *containment*: (i) (region_geo) $\preceq$ (nation_geo) $\preceq$ (city_geo) $\preceq$ (c_address_geo) for *Customer*; and (ii) (region_geo) $\preceq$ (nation_geo) $\preceq$ (city_geo) $\preceq$ (s_address_geo) for *Supplier*.

4.2   Classes of Drill-across SOLAP Queries

In this section, we propose three different classes of drill-across SOLAP queries, which focus on the analysis of different spatial data types, different granularities and increasing number of spatial query windows, thus imposing distinct processing costs. The templates of these classes are shown in Figures 2a and 3a. These templates represent drill-across SOLAP queries as they use the numeric measures *ps_supplycost* and *l_quantity* from the distinct fact tables *Lineitem* and *Partsupp*, respectively, and define one or more spatial predicates. In the templates, we highlight in bold both spatial granularity levels and spatial attributes and dimensions that vary according to the spatial granularity level, as well as indicate the need to perform join operations due to the use of the spatial dimensions. We also use two filters defined over conventional attributes: *p_brand = 'Brand#14'* and *extract(year FROM o_orderdate) BETWEEN 1994 AND 1997*. Furthermore, in Figures 2b and 3b, we instantiate the values of spatial granularity levels, spatial attributes, and spatial predicates. Regarding the spatial predicates, we use the WITHIN relationship to represent which points are inside a given query window, and the INTERSECT relationship to represent which polygons intersect a given query window.

Class Q1. Drill-across SOLAP queries of this class include those that define one spatial query window over *supplier*, and that support drill-down and roll-up queries extended with a spatial predicate. Figure 2a depicts the template of queries from class Q1. It compares the average supply cost to the amount sold by part, by supplier, for those parts whose brand are Brand#14 and that were sold between 1994 and 1997, considering suppliers located at a given region. Regarding the spatial predicate, class Q1 applies a spatial query window *QW* to retrieve only those suppliers whose spatial location satisfies the spatial relationship against *QW*.

Example 3. Figure 2b illustrates four queries from class Q1. Q1.1 is defined over the *address* granularity of suppliers, while Q1.2, Q1.3 and Q1.4 are defined over the *city, nation* and *region* granularities of suppliers, respectively. Also, QW_A, QW_C, QW_N and QW_R are the spatial query windows to evaluate the spatial predicate on each granularity. In addition, the consecutive execution of queries starting at Q1.1 and ending at Q1.4 consists of a roll-up SOLAP query, while the inverse order of execution consists of a drill-down SOLAP query.   □

Class Q2. Drill-across SOLAP queries of this class include those that define one spatial query window over *suppliers* and one spatial query window over *customers*, and that support drill-down and roll-up queries extended with a spatial

```
SELECT   granularity_level, p_partkey, total_quantity_sold, average_supplycost
FROM ( SELECT granularity_level, granularity_key, p_partkey, AVG (ps_supplycost) AS average_supplycost
       FROM  Partsupp, Part, Supplier, spatial dimension table
       WHERE ps_partkey = p_partkey AND ps_suppkey = s_suppkey AND p_brand = 'Brand#14 '
             AND spatial_predicate AND join operation due to the use of the spatial dimension
       GROUP BY granularity_level, granularity_key, p_partkey
       ) AS supply_cost,
       ( SELECT  granularity_key, l_partkey, SUM (l_quantity) AS total_quantity_sold
       FROM   Lineitem, Orders, Part, Supplier, spatial dimension table
       WHERE l_orderkey = o_orderkey AND l_suppkey = s_suppkey AND l_partkey = p_partkey
             AND p_brand = 'Brand#14 '  AND extract(year FROM o_orderdate) BETWEEN 1994 AND 1997
             AND spatial_predicate AND join operation due to the use of the spatial dimension
       GROUP BY granularity_key, l_partkey
       ) AS quantity_sold
WHERE    quantity_sold.granularity_key = supply_cost.granularity_key AND p_partkey = l_suppkey
ORDER BY granularity_level, p_partkey DESC;
```

(a) Template of class Q1.

Query	granularity_level	granularity_key	spatial_predicate		
Q1.1	s_address_name	s_suppkey	WITHIN(s_address_geo, QW$_A$)	ROLL-UP	DRILL-DOWN
Q1.2	s_city_name	s_city_fk	INTERSECTS(s_city_geo, QW$_C$)		
Q1.3	s_nation_name	s_nation_fk	INTERSECTS(s_nation_geo, QW$_N$)		
Q1.4	s_region_name	s_region_fk	INTERSECTS(s_region_geo, QW$_R$)		

(b) Values of granularity_level, granularity_key and spatial_predicate for class Q1.

Fig. 2. Drill-across SOLAP queries of class Q1

predicate. Although the spatial query windows are placed on distinct locations, they should be defined over the *same* granularities of *suppliers* and *customers* simultaneously. Figure 3a depicts the template of queries from class Q2. It compares the average supply cost to the amount sold by part, by supplier, for those parts whose brand are Brand#14 and that were sold between 1994 and 1997, considering suppliers located at a given location and customers located at another location. Class Q2 has a query window QW for suppliers and another query window QW' for customers, in order to retrieve only those suppliers and customers whose spatial location satisfies the spatial relationship against QW and QW', respectively. As class Q2 restricts the locations of suppliers and customers, it is more complex and restrictive than class Q1.

Example 4. Figure 3b illustrates four queries from class Q2. Q2.1 is defined over the *address* granularity of suppliers and customers, while Q2.2, Q2.3 and Q2.4 are defined over the *city, nation* and *region* granularities of suppliers and customers, respectively. All the four queries are defined over the same granularities of suppliers and customers simultaneously and evaluate spatial predicates involving attributes that store the same data type, i.e. points for Q2.1 and polygons for the Q2.2, Q2.3 and Q2.4. Also, the consecutive execution of queries starting at Q2.1 and ending at Q2.4 consists of a roll-up SOLAP query, while the inverse order of execution consists of a drill-down SOLAP query.   □

```
SELECT   granularity_level, p_partkey, total_quantity_sold, average_supplycost
FROM ( SELECT granularity_level, granularity_key, p_partkey, AVG (ps_supplycost) AS average_supplycost
        FROM   Partsupp, Part, Supplier, spatial dimension table
        WHERE ps_partkey = p_partkey AND ps_suppkey = s_suppkey AND p_brand = 'Brand#14 '
              AND spatial_predicate_01 AND join operation due to the use of the spatial dimension
        GROUP BY granularity_level, granularity_key, p_partkey
       ) AS supply_cost,
       ( SELECT  granularity_key, l_partkey, SUM (l_quantity) AS total_quantity_sold
         FROM   Lineitem, Orders, Part, Supplier, Customer, spatial dimension tables
         WHERE l_orderkey = o_orderkey AND l_suppkey = s_suppkey AND o_custkey = c_custkey
               AND l_partkey = p_partkey AND p_brand = 'Brand#14 '
               AND extract(year FROM o_orderdate) BETWEEN 1994 AND 1997
               AND spatial_predicate_02 AND join operations due to the use of the spatial dimensions
         GROUP BY granularity_key, l_partkey
       ) AS quantity_sold
WHERE    quantity_sold.granularity_key  = supply_cost.granularity_key AND p_partkey = l_suppkey
ORDER BY granularity_level, p_partkey DESC;
```

(a) Template of classes Q2 and Q3.

Query	granularity_level	granularity_key	spatial_predicate_01	spatial_predicate_02		
Q2.1	s_address_name	s_suppkey	WITHIN(s_address_geo, QW$_A$)	WITHIN(s_address_geo, QW$_A$) AND WITHIN(c_address_geo, QW'$_A$)		
Q2.2	s_city_name	s_city_fk	INTERSECTS(s_city_geo, QW$_C$)	INTERSECTS(s_city_geo, QW$_C$) AND INTERSECTS(c_city_geo, QW'$_C$)	ROLL-UP	DRILL-DOWN
Q2.3	s_nation_name	s_nation_fk	INTERSECTS(s_nation_geo, QW$_N$)	INTERSECTS(s_nation_geo, QW$_N$) AND INTERSECTS(c_nation_geo, QW'$_N$)		
Q2.4	s_region_name	s_region_fk	INTERSECTS(s_region_geo, QW$_R$)	INTERSECTS(s_region_geo, QW$_R$) AND INTERSECTS(c_region_geo, QW'$_R$)		

(b) Values of granularity_level, granularity_key, spatial_predicate01 and spatial_predicate02 for class Q2.

Query	granularity_level	granularity_key	spatial_predicate_01	spatial_predicate_02		
Q3.1	s_city_name	s_city_fk	INTERSECTS(s_city_geo, QW$_C$)	INTERSECTS(s_city_geo, QW$_C$) AND WITHIN(c_address_geo, QW$_A$)		
Q3.2	s_nation_name	s_nation_fk	INTERSECTS(s_nation_geo, QW$_N$)	INTERSECTS(s_nation_geo, QW$_N$) AND WITHIN(c_address_geo, QW$_A$)	ROLL-UP	DRILL-DOWN
Q3.3	s_region_name	s_region_fk	INTERSECTS(s_region_geo, QW$_R$)	INTERSECTS(s_region_geo, QW$_R$) AND WITHIN(c_address_geo, QW$_A$)		

(c) Values of granularity_level, granularity_key, spatial_predicate01 and spatial_predicate02 for class Q3.

Fig. 3. General structure of the proposed drill-across SOLAP queries

Class Q3. Drill-across SOLAP queries of this class include those that define one spatial query window over *supplier* and one spatial query window over *customer*, and that support drill-down and roll-up queries extended with a spatial predicate. The spatial query windows should be defined over *different* granularities of *suppliers* and *customers* simultaneously. Class Q3 is similar to class Q2, except for the fact that the spatial query windows defined over suppliers and customers have different granularities to allow for the processing of different spatial data types and the processing of different cardinalities in the same query.

Example 5. Figure 3c illustrates examples of queries from class Q3. We fixed the granularity of customers as *address* and varied the granularities of suppliers. Therefore, Q3.1, Q3.2 and Q3.3 are defined over the *city, nation* and *region*

granularities of suppliers, respectively. Note that all the queries are defined over spatial attributes with different cardinalities. Also, the spatial data types are different. While the spatial attribute *s_address* is represented by points, the spatial attributes *c_city*, *c_nation* and *c_region* are represented by polygons. □

4.3   The Proposed *DrillAcrossSB* Approach

In this section, we propose *DrillAcrossSB*, an approach to process drill-across SOLAP queries using a spatial index specifically designed to index predefined spatial hierarchies over GDWs. This approach is based on two main tasks. First, each star schema and each spatial dimension table of a fact constellation are separately indexed. Then, each indexed star schema is processed to produce partial results that are merged and ordered to obtain the final answer.

Algorithms 1 and 2 detail the proposed *DrillAcrossSB* approach. Algorithm 1, named **BuildIndices**, generates one star-join Bitmap index for each star schema of the fact constellation (lines 1 and 2), as well as one SB-index for each spatial dimension table present in the fact constellation (lines 3 and 4). This is because the star-join Bitmap index is always applied to a single star schema, while the SB-index defined over shared spatial dimension tables can be used by different star schemas. Regarding Algorithm 2, it is aimed at processing a drill-across SOLAP query Q and calculating Q's answer, using as a basis the indices created by Algorithm 1. The **DrillAcrossProcessing** algorithm first divides Q into several subqueries, so that each subquery is processed over a specific star schema (lines 1 to 4). The answer of Q is obtained by merging the partial results of the subqueries and by ordering the merged results (lines 5 to 7).

Example 6. As an example of input and output produced by the proposed algorithms, consider the *SpatialDrillAcross* schema and query Q1 shown in Figures 1 and 2, respectively. Algorithm 1 generates two star-join Bitmap indices (i.e. SJB_1 for *Lineitem* and SJB_2 for *Partsupp*), and five different SB-index (i.e. SB_1 for *region_geo*, SB_2 for *nation_geo*, SB_3 for *city_geo*, SB_4 for *c_address_geo*, SB_5 for *s_address_geo*). As for Algorithm 2, it: (i) generates two subqueries (i.e. *supply_cost* for the first nested SELECT clause and *quantity_sold* for the second nested SELECT clause), which are processed by the appropriate indices; (ii) merges the partial results according to the conditions *quantity_sold.granularity_key* = *supply_cost.granularity_key* and *p_partkey* = *l_suppkey*; and (iii) orders the final result according to the spatial attribute represented by *granularity_level* and the conventional attribute *p_partkey*.   □

5   Performance Evaluation

5.1   Experimental Setup

In this section, we describe the experimental setup that was used to evaluate and compare the performance of the proposed *DrillAcrossSB* approach with the performance of the star-join computation and materialized views. We used the

---

Algorithm 1. BuildIndices (FC, m, n)

Input : FC {a fact constellation},
$\quad\quad\quad$ m {number of star schemas in FC},
$\quad\quad\quad$ n {number of spatial dimension tables in FC}
Output: $SJB_1, ..., SJB_m$ {a set of star-join Bitmap indices},
$\quad\quad\quad$ $SB_1, ..., SB_n$ {a set of SB-index}
1 **foreach** *star schema* $SC_i \in FC$ **do**
2 $\quad$ create a star-join Bitmap index SJB_i
3 **foreach** *spatial dimension table* $SDT_j \in FC$ **do**
4 $\quad$ create a SB-index SB_j on the spatial attributes of interest

---

Algorithm 2. DrillAcrossProcessing $(Q, FC, SJB_1, ..., SJB_m, SB_1, ..., SB_n)$

Input : Q {the drill-across query},
$\quad\quad\quad$ FC {a fact constelation},
$\quad\quad\quad$ $SJB_1, ..., SJB_m$ {a set of star-join Bitmap indices},
$\quad\quad\quad$ $SB_1, ..., SB_n$ {a set of SB-index}
Output: $FinalResult$ {query answer}
1 **foreach** *star schema* $SC_i \in FC$ **do**
2 $\quad$ create a subquery SQ_i from Q
3 $\quad$ $PartialResult_i \leftarrow$ process the SB-index using SJB_i and
4 $\quad\quad\quad\quad\quad$ the appropriates SB_j over SQ_i
5 $FinalResult \leftarrow$ merge$(PartialResult_1, ..., PartialResult_m)$
6 $\quad\quad\quad\quad\quad$ according to the ORDER BY clause of Q
7 $FinalResult \leftarrow$ sort$(FinalResult)$ according to the WHERE clause of Q

SpatialDrillAcross schema introduced in Section 4.1, which was populated with conventional data generated from the TPC-H benchmark [10] and spatial data generated from the Spadawan benchmark [14]. For this schema, we produced two datasets. The first dataset, named DS_1, required 16.4 GB and was generated with the scale factor of 10 for both conventional and spatial data. The second dataset, named DS_2, required 1.7 GB and was generated with scale factor 1 for conventional data and scale factor 10 for spatial data, thus emphasizing the spatial predicate processing.

The workload was composed of the 4 queries from class Q1, the 4 queries from class Q2 and the 3 queries from class Q3 defined in Figures 2b, 3b and 3c, respectively. For each dataset, we issued each query 5 times, and took the average of the measurements. The system cache was flushed at the end of each execution. Also, aiming at analyzing drill-down and roll-up SOLAP queries together with drill-across SOLAP queries, we defined a set of four spatial query windows, each one associated to a given granularity level (i.e. *address, city, nation* and *region* granularity levels) and of a specific size (i.e. the lower the granularity, the smaller the spatial query window). The query windows were quadratic, correlated with the spatial data and disjoint.

We define in this paper that selectivity is the percentage of the number of tuples that are retrieved by a query. Regarding the templates shown in Figures 2a and 3a, the conventional filter *p_brand = 'Brand#14'* provided a selectivity of 4% and the conventional filter *extract(year FROM o_orderdate) BETWEEN 1994 AND 1997* provided a selectivity of almost 61%. The selectivity provided by each spatial predicate was defined as follows: 0.023% to 0.1% for the *address* granularity level of *suppliers*, 0.025% to 0.05% for the *address* granularity level of *customers*, 0.24% to 0.36% for the *city* granularity level, 1.2% for the *nation* granularity level, and 2% for the *region* granularity level.

The experiments were conducted on a computer with an Intel Core i7 2.67 GHz processor, 12 GB of main memory, 2 SATA 1 TB hard disks, Linux Ubuntu 9.04, PostgreSQL 8.3 and PostGIS 1.3.3. We employed FastBit version 1.2.1 with the WAH compression method as the Bitmap software to implement the star-join Bitmap index and to process the conventional predicates. We implemented the *DrillAcrossSB* approach using the C/C++ language and used the merge-join and the quicksort algorithms to obtain the final result of queries (lines 5 to 7 of Algorithm 2). Also, we used the R-tree to index the spatial attributes handled by the star-join computation and materialized views. We collected the elapsed time in seconds to process the SOLAP queries.

5.2   Performance Results for Dataset DS_1

In this section, we discuss the performance results provided by the star-join computation, materialized views and the *DrillAcrossSB* approach to process drill-across SOLAP queries over the dataset DS_1. This dataset is the most voluminous dataset and has the same scale factor for both conventional and spatial data. For short, we use *star-join*, *views* and *DrillAcrossSB* to refer to the approaches.

Figure 4 shows the performance results for processing queries of class Q1, according to different granularity levels (i.e. Q1.1, Q1.2, Q1.3 and Q1.4 are respectively defined over the *address*, *city*, *nation* and *region* granularity levels). The use of *views* avoids several joins among conventional dimension tables and, therefore, produced a better performance than the *star-join*, which ranged from 65% to 76%. Regarding *DrillAcrossSB*, it produced better results than *views* when compared with the *star-join*, which ranged from 93% to 95%. In fact,

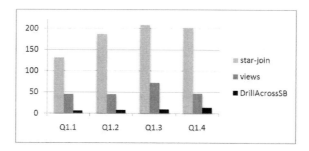

Fig. 4. Performance obtained with the star-join computation, materialized views and the *DrillAcrossSB* approach for queries of class Q1. Elapsed time in seconds.

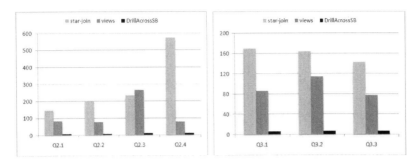

Fig. 5. Performance obtained with the star-join computation, materialized views and the *DrillAcrossSB* approach for queries of classes Q2 and Q3. Elapsed time in seconds.

DrillAcrossSB was at least 70% better than *views*, thus providing a remarkable performance gain. Both *views* and *DrillAcrossSB* required similar storage costs (e.g. for queries of class Q1, *views* required 3.7 GB and *DrillAcrossSB* required 3.5 GB).

The same pattern was observed for queries of classes Q2 and Q3, as shown in Figure 5. *DrillAcrossSB* always produced the better performance results. Furthermore, the drill-down SOLAP queries performed over distinct granularity levels did not impair the performance gains of the proposed approach. *DrillAcrossSB*'s performance gains over the *star-join* computation were at least 94% and over *views* ranged from 87% up to 96%.

5.3   Performance Results for Dataset DS_2

In this section, we discuss the performance results to process drill-across SO-LAP queries over the dataset DS_2. This dataset has a higher scale factor for spatial data (i.e. SSF = 10) than for conventional data (i.e. SF = 1), aiming at impairing the evaluation of spatial predicates. We only present here results for *views* and *DrillAcrossSB*, since *views* outperformed the *star-join*, as shown in Section 5.2.

Figure 6 shows the performance results for processing queries of classes Q1, Q2 and Q3, according to different granularity levels. Regarding queries of class Q1, *DrillAcrossSB* was always faster than views. The performance gain of *DrillAcrossSB* ranged from 39% at the *region* granularity level up to 81% at the address granularity level. Comparing the results presented here with those described in Section 5.2, the performance gain of *DrillAcrossSB* over *views* decreased. This is due to the processing of the spatial predicate for the dataset DS_2, which is more costly than the processing of the conventional predicate. The same pattern was observed for queries of classes Q2 and Q3. *DrillAcrossSB* always produced the better performance results, which ranged from 60% to 98% for queries of class Q2 and from 68% to 90% for queries of class Q3.

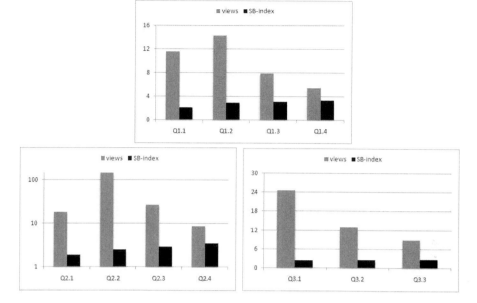

Fig. 6. Performance obtained with materialized views and the *DrillAcrossSB* approach for the dataset DS_2. Elapsed time in seconds. Results for class Q2 are in log scale.

6   Conclusions and Future Work

In this paper, we focused on the efficient processing of drill-across SOLAP queries over GDWs. Our contributions are threefold. We proposed *SpatialDrillAcross*, a GDW schema that is based on the TPC-H benchmark and enables the performance evaluation of drill-across SOLAP query processing. *SpatialDrillAcross* is a fact constellation that contains not only conventional dimensions but also spatial dimensions with spatial attributes and predefined spatial hierarchies, as well as specifies how spatial data should be stored. We also defined a set of classes of drill-across SOLAP queries to be issued over the *SpatialDrillAcross* schema, so that each class imposes distinct costs in query performance. Furthermore, we proposed *DrillAcrossSB*, an approach to process drill-across SOLAP queries using a spatial index, which is characterized by indexing separated star schemas of a fact constellation by using the SB-index and merging the partial results.

The *DrillAcrossSB* approach was validated through performance tests that issued queries from the proposed set of classes over the *SpatialDrillAcross* schema, and that investigated different spatial data types, different granularities and increasing number of spatial query windows. The results demonstrated that *DrillAcrossSB* efficiently answers drill-across SOLAP queries. Comparisons of the *DrillAcrossSB* approach, the star-join computation and materialized views showed that *DrillAcrossSB* highly speedup the processing of drill-across SOLAP queries from 39% to 98%. Furthermore, both materialized views and *DrillAcrossSB* required similar storage costs.

We are currently extending the Spadawan benchmark [14] with the concepts introduced in this paper to also focus on fact constellation schemas and drill-across SOLAP queries. We also plan to investigate other types of spatial objects in our tests, such as lines, polygons with holes, and vague spatial objects.

Acknowledgments. This work has been supported by the following Brazilian research agencies: FAPESP, CNPq, CAPES, INEP and FINEP. The second and the fourth authors also thank the support of the Web-PIDE Project in the context of the Observatory of the Education of the Brazilian Government.

References

1. Bellatreche, L., Woameno, K.: Dimension table driven approach to referential partition relational data warehouses. In: DaWaK, pp. 9–16 (2009)
2. Golfarelli, M., Maniezzo, V., Rizzi, S.: Materialization of fragmented views in multidimensional databases. DKE 49(3), 325–351 (2004)
3. Gómez, L.I., Vaisman, A.A., Zimányi, E.: Physical design and implementation of spatial data warehouses supporting continuous fields. In: Bach Pedersen, T., Mohania, M.K., Tjoa, A.M. (eds.) DAWAK 2010. LNCS, vol. 6263, pp. 25–39. Springer, Heidelberg (2010)
4. Gorawski, M., Gorawski, M.: Balanced spatio-temporal data warehouse with R-MVB, STCAT and BITMAP indexes. In: PARELEC, pp. 43–48 (2006)
5. Malinowski, E., Zimányi, E.: Advanced Data Warehouse Design: From Conventional to Spatial and Temporal Applications (Data-Centric Systems and Applications). Springer, Heidelberg (2008)
6. Mateus, R.C., Siqueira, T.L.L., Times, V.C., Ciferri, R.R., Ciferri, C.D.A.: How does the spatial data redundancy affect query performance in geographic data warehouses? JIDM 1(3), 519–534 (2010)
7. Mohan, P., Wilson, R., Shekhar, S., George, B., Levine, N., Celik, M.: Should SDBMS support a join index?: A case study from CrimeStat. In: ACM GIS, pp. 1–10 (2008)
8. O'Neil, P., Graefe, G.: Multi-table joins through bitmapped join indices. SIGMOD Record 24(3), 8–11 (1995)
9. Papadias, D., Kalnis, P., Zhang, J., Tao, Y.: Efficient OLAP operations in spatial data warehouses. In: Jensen, C.S., Schneider, M., Seeger, B., Tsotras, V.J. (eds.) SSTD 2001. LNCS, vol. 2121, pp. 443–459. Springer, Heidelberg (2001)
10. Poess, M., Floyd, C.: New TPC benchmarks for decision support and web commerce. SIGMOD Record 29(4), 64–71 (2000)
11. Rao, F., Zhang, L., Yu, X., Li, Y., Chen, Y.: Spatial hierarchy and OLAP-favored search in spatial data warehouse. In: DOLAP, pp. 48–55 (2003)
12. Siqueira, T.L.L., Ciferri, C.D.A., Times, V.C., Ciferri, R.R.: The SB-index and the HSB-index: efficient indices for spatial data warehouses. To Appear in Geoinformatica (2011) doi:10.1007/s10707-011-0128-5
13. Siqueira, T.L.L., Ciferri, C.D.A., Times, V.C., Oliveira, A.G., Ciferri, R.R.: The impact of spatial data redundancy on SOLAP query performance. JBCS 15(2), 19–34 (2009)
14. Siqueira, T.L.L., Ciferri, R.R., Times, V.C., Ciferri, C.D.A.: Benchmarking spatial data warehouses. In: Bach Pedersen, T., Mohania, M.K., Tjoa, A.M. (eds.) DAWAK 2010. LNCS, vol. 6263, pp. 40–51. Springer, Heidelberg (2010)
15. Stefanovic, N., Han, J., Koperski, K.: Object-based selective materialization for efficient implementation of spatial data cubes. IEEE TKDE 12(6), 938–958 (2000)

The NOX OLAP Query Model: From Algebra to Execution

Ahmad Taleb, Todd Eavis, and Hiba Tabbara

[1] Najran University, Najran, Saudia Arabia
ahmadtaleb@hotmail.com
[2] Concordia University, Montreal, Canada
eavis@cs.concordia.ca
[3] Concordia University, Montreal, Canada
h_tabarra@encs.concordia.ca

Abstract. Current OLAP servers are typically implemented as either extensions to conventional relational databases or as non-relational array-based storage engines. In the former case, the unique modeling and processing requirements of OLAP systems often make for a relatively awkward fit with RDBM systems. In the latter case, the proprietary nature of the MOLAP implementations has largely prevented the emergence of a standardized query model. In this paper, we discuss an algebra for the specification, optimization, and execution of OLAP-specific queries, including its ability to support a native language query framework. In addition, we ground the conceptual work by incorporating the query optimization and execution facilities into a fully functional OLAP-aware DBMS prototype. Experimental results clearly demonstrate the potential of the new algebra-driven system relative to both the un-optimized prototype and a pair of popular enterprise servers.

1 Introduction

Data warehousing and Online Analytical Processing (OLAP) are two of the most important components of contemporary Decision Support Systems (DSS). Collectively, they allow organizations to make effective decisions regarding both their current and future state. In practice, warehouse databases are implemented via array-based multi-dimensional storage engines (MOLAP) or as extensions to the more familiar relational DBM systems (ROLAP). While the MOLAP tools offer impressive performance, their limited scalability often restricts their use to environments with more modest resource requirements (e.g., departmental data marts). Conversely, enterprise ROLAP systems tend to scale quite well, but offer design and implementation models that are constrained by conceptual and architectural elements intended primarily for transaction processing systems.

Moreover, current warehouse/OLAP systems utilize query mechanisms that were designed decades ago. Specifically, they rely upon a combination of string based query languages such as SQL and MDX, along with various proprietary extensions. These languages (and their APIs) have little in common with the

A. Cuzzocrea and U. Dayal (Eds.): DaWaK 2011, LNCS 6862, pp. 167–183, 2011.
© Springer-Verlag Berlin Heidelberg 2011

safe, flexible Object Oriented languages commonly used in today's development environments. Not only do these languages make client side programming less effective (e.g., no compile time type checking, no semantic verification, no ability to re-factor code, plus the requirement to interleave distinct programming models), but they also make it very difficult for the DBMS server to effectively exploit OLAP-specific constructs at query resolution time. In other words, the requirement to work with existing query languages and APIs largely prevents the backend server from effectively optimizing user queries to take full advantage of either OLAP conceptual structures (e.g., concept hierarchies and aggregation paths) or physical layer extensions (e.g., enhanced indexing or sorting opportunities).

For this reason, we believe that new OLAP query interfaces are required. In an earlier work [13], we discussed an approach that would allow data cube queries to be written in native OOP languages such as Java. In the current paper, we extend that initial research by presenting an expressive multi-dimensional OLAP algebra that can be used to support the language libraries visible to the client side programmer. Moreover, we discuss the integration of the algebra with a robust DBMS backend that not only natively supports the algebraic operators but is able to optimize query plans by applying a series of transformations to the initial parse trees. The fully optimized plan can then be passed to an execution engine that, in turn, exploits indexes and algorithms designed expressly for this purpose. The end result is a framework for an OLAP DBMS that offers the performance of a MOLAP system and the scalability of a ROLAP architecture.

The paper is organized as follows. Section 2 briefly reviews related work. An overview of the Sidera data model and architecture is provided in Section 3, including its application to native language querying. In Section 4, we discuss the formal properties of the current algebra, with Section 5 reviewing some of the server's more important optimization techniques. Key experimental results are then presented in Section 6. Section 7 concludes the paper with a few final observations.

2   Related Work

Over the past decade or so, numerous attempts have been made to simplify, extend, or otherwise improve DBMS query interfaces, languages and data models. One common theme has been the adaptation of APIs to include Object Oriented semantics and syntax. Object Relational Mapping (ORM) frameworks — including JDO (Java Data Objects) [1] and Hibernate [6] — have been used to define *transparent object persistence* for DBMS-backed OOP applications. Still, the query language extensions — including JDOQL (JDO) and HQL (Hibernate) — required to execute joins, complex selections, and sub-queries, produce a development environment that often seems as complex as the model it was meant to replace. More recently, Safe Query Objects (SQO) [10] have been introduced. Rather than explicit mappings, safe queries are defined by a class containing, in its simplest form, a *filter* and *execute* method. The compiler checks the validity of query types, relative to the objects defined in the filter. The *execute* method is then rewritten as a JDO call to the remote database.

Other approaches target the language itself. For example, one can point to language extensions such as those found in Ruby's Active Records [5], HaskellDB [2], and Microsoft's LINQ extensions for its C# and VisualBasic environments [8]. Here, however, one must note that none of these languages are in any way OLAP-aware and, thus, have no native support for concepts such as cubes, dimensions, aggregation hierarchies, granularity levels, and drill down relationships. By contrast, Microsoft's popular MDX query language [22] — while syntactically reminiscent of SQL — provides direct support for both multi-level dimension hierarchies and a crosstab data model. Still, MDX remains an embedded string based language and, as such, cannot provide comprehensive compile-time type checking, a single unified application/DBMS development language, OOP functionality (e.g., inheritance and polymorphism), or efficient source code re-factoring.

In terms of OLAP and BI specific design themes, most contemporary research builds in some way upon the OLAP *data cube* operator [15]. In addition to various algorithms for cube construction, including those with direct support for dimension hierarchies [20], researchers have identified a number of new OLAP *operators* [11], each designed to minimize in some way the relative difficulty of implementing core operations in "raw SQL".

Performance optimization has been another fairly popular target. At various times, researchers have focused on view materialization [17,18], improved indexing [9,12], and parallelization and partitioning [19,16]. In general, all such approaches build on techniques that were developed for OLTP databases. There has also been some interest in the design of supporting algebras [21]. The primary focus of this work has been to define an API that would ultimately lead to transparent, intuitive support for the underlying data cube, and in a more general sense, to the identification of the core elements of the OLAP conceptual data model. OLAP-specific optimization based upon query re-writing has also been proposed. For example, using an OLAP algebra that highlights the visual representation of the data cube, Bellatreche et al. propose a set of rules to re-structure OLAP queries executed against fact and dimension tables (i.e., Star Schema) stored in a standard relational DBMS [7]. Though improved performance is suggested, there is no concrete DBMS implementation (or physical operators) by which to fully quantify or evaluate the proposal.

3   Preliminary Material

Before presenting the algebra, we first review the conceptual and physical model upon which the Sidera DBMS is constructed. To begin, we note that the methods discussed in this paper are part of a larger framework known as NOX (Native language OLAP query eXecution) [13] that is designed to provide native language (e.g., Java) Object Oriented OLAP query facilities. In other words, traditional string-based query languages such as SQL and MDX are not required to access the analytics data. NOX provides the following components:

- **OLAP conceptual model**. NOX allows developers to write code directly at the conceptual level; no knowledge of the physical or even logical schema is required.
- **Client side libraries**. NOX provides a small suite of OOP classes corresponding to the objects of the conceptual model. Collectively, the exposed methods of the libraries form a clean programming API that can be used to instantiate OLAP queries.
- **Augmented compiler**. At its heart, NOX is a query re-writer. During a pre-processing phase, the framework's compilation tools effectively re-write source code to provide transparent model-to-DBMS query translation.
- **Cube result set**. OLAP queries essentially extract a subcube from the original space. The NOX framework exposes the result in a logical, read-only multi-dimensional array.

In short, the developer's view of the OLAP environment consists solely of the API and the Result Set. More to the point, from the developer's perspective, all OLAP data is housed in a series of cube objects housed in local memory. The fact that these repositories are not only remote, but possibly Gigabytes or even Terabytes in size, is largely irrelevant.

3.1   Conceptual Model

As noted in the previous section, NOX allows one to program directly against a conceptual data model. Briefly, we consider analytical environments to consist of one or more *data cubes*. Each cube is composed of a series of d dimensions (sometimes called *feature* attributes) and one or more *measures*. The dimensions can be visualized as delimiting a d-dimensional hyper-cube, with each axis identifying the *members* of the parent dimension (e.g., the days of the year). Cell values, in turn, represent the aggregated measure (e.g., sum) of the associated members. Figure 1(a) provides an illustration of a very simple three dimensional cube. We can see, for example, that 12 units of Product AM54 were sold in the Berkeley location during the month of January (assuming a Count measure).

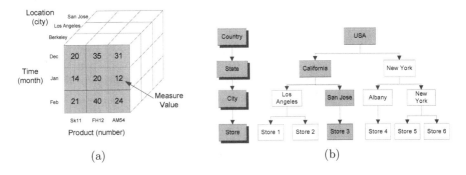

(a)   (b)

Fig. 1. (a) NOX conceptual query model (b) A simple symmetric hierarchy

Beyond the basic cube, however, the conceptual OLAP model relies extensively on aggregation hierarchies provided by the dimensions themselves. In fact,
hierarchy traversal is one of the more common and important elements of analytical queries. In practice, there are many variations on the form of OLAP
hierarchies (e.g., symmetric, ragged, non-strict). NOX supports virtually all of
these, and does so by augmenting the conceptual model with the notion of an
arbitrary graph-based hierarchy that may be used to *decorate* one or more cube
dimensions. Figure 1(b) illustrates a simple geographic hierarchy that an organization might use to identify intuitive customer groupings.

3.2   Native Language Queries

NOX provides a set of client libraries that map directly to the conceptual model
described above. In addition to base classes representing OLAP objects such
as dimensions, hierarchies, cells, and aggregation paths, the framework include
a core OLAPQuery class that exposes methods corresponding to the algebra
described in Section 4. The programmer therefore defines queries not by embed-
ding a non-OOP text string, but by over-riding and extending the OLAPQuery
base class and adding just those constraints relevant to the current query. In
so doing, the NOX environment is able to provide compile time type checking,
semantic verification (as per the client libraries), refactoring facilities, and OOP
functionality (e.g., query inheritance). Figure 4 illustrates an MDX query and
the corresponding NOX query (written in Java). Note that as queries become
larger and more complex, NOX queries tend to maintain their readability much
better than the corresponding MDX queries.

Though the translation and submission of NOX queries is a somewhat complex
process [13], the reader should note the following. The client side query depicted
in Figure 4 is not executed directly. Instead, the NOX processor parses the
source code, identifies the NOX class constructs, and transparently re-writes

```
SELECT
  { [Product].[Type].ALLMEMBERS } ON COLUMNS,
  { [Customer].[Province].ALLMEMBERS } ON ROWS

FROM [Order]

WHERE (
  [Measures].[Quantity_Ordered],
  [Time].[Year].[2007],
  [Time].[Month].[May],
  [Time].[Month].[June],
  [Customer].[Age].[45],[Customer].[Age].[55]
)
```

```
class SimpleQuery extends OlapQuery {
  public boolean select() {
    DateDimension date = new DateDimension();
    Customer customer = new Customer() ;
    OlapProperty dateMonth = new OlapProperty(date.getMonth());
    return (customer.getAge() > 40 && date.getYear() == 2007 &&
        dateMonth.inRange(5, 10));
  }
  public Object[] project() {
    Customer customer = new Customer() ;
    Product product = new Product() ;
    Measure measure = new Measure() ;
    Object[] projections = {product.getType(),
        customer.getProvince(),
        measure.getQuantity_Ordered()};
    return projections;
  }
}
```

(a)   (b)

Fig. 2. (a) A simple MDX query (b) The NOX equivalent

the programmer's source code. In place of the original OLAPQuery definition, the processor inserts a network call to the Sidera DBMS. Within the network packet is a query representation that has already been reduced to its algebraic components. It is this form of the query that is actually optimized and executed by the server at runtime.

3.3   The Sidera Architecture

Sidera is a research DBMS that targets analytics environments. To this end, it provides native, OLAP-specifc support for indexing (bitmaps and R-trees), fault tolerance (network heartbeat), caching (spatial query representation), lightweight graphical interfaces (via the Google Web toolkit) and, of course, query languages (NOX). It is also designed from the ground up as a parallel DBMS that is intended to scale to ROLAP sizes, while giving something close to MOLAP performance. Essentially, Sidera is constructed as a federation of sibling servers that function more or less independently, each accessing and processing a slice of the current query. A Parallel Service Interface (PSI) offers global coordination and merging services as required.

In this section, we discuss those elements of the architecture that support the execution of translated NOX queries. Specifically, we will look at the storage and indexing model with which the query costing and optimization is associated. We begin with the physical representation of the NOX conceptual model described above. Traditionally, relational warehouses use a Star Schema, consisting of a *Fact* table and one or more *Dimension* tables. Process metrics are housed in the Fact table, with dimension tables containing feature information typically used to constrain user queries. A Sidera database is roughly analagous to this design. However, rather than a Fact table, Sidera employs a materialized cube (fully or partially, as space permits) that is constructed as a set of Hilbert packed R-trees, then minimized using a form of tuple differential compression [12]. We then incorporate the (open source) Berkeley DB embedded libraries [3] into the Sidera code base so as to efficiently encode the Fact Structure. Note that we refer to measure data as a Fact Structure, rather than a Fact table, as the storage

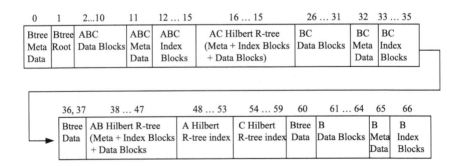

Fig. 3. The physical structure of the indexed cube

format bears little resemblance to a traditional table. Figure 3 illustrates the internal structure of the Sidera/Berkeley cube. Note that the letters A-B-C are simply used as a shorthand for Dimension names such as Product, Date, etc. In short, the cube consists of a packed sequence of meta data, measure data, and index blocks for each aggregated view, as well as a master B-tree that locates the relevant view data, as per the current query specification.

Dimension data is stored independently of the central cube structure, as it requires distinct forms of indexing and representation. Specifically, Sidera is aware of both *hierarchical* and *non-hierarchical* elements. By hierarchical, we mean those values associated with user-defined aggregation pathways (e.g., the common Day-Month-Year Time hierarchy). Sidera uses a structure known as mapGraph to efficiently translate cell values between arbitrary hierarchy levels at run-time [14]. Figure 4(a) shows mapGraph's representation of the meta data associated with a simple symmetric Product-Type-Category hierarchy (Sidera can also support support more complex hierarchies). Note that the integer values in the figure corresponds to ranges of Product ID values (i.e., Product keys) that are encapsulated within the tuple differential values encoded in the Fact Structure. Sidera always stores cell values at the lowest level of granularity so as to permit arbitrary bi-directional translation between hierarchy levels. In effect, the DBMS uses the in-memory mapGraph structure as a join index between the Fact Structure and the hierarchy values.

Non hierarchical attributes such as age, on the the other hand, may be used to constrain user queries but are not associated with identifiable aggregation paths. In this case, dimension attributes are encoded with FastBit [4], an efficient compressed bitmap indexing mechanism. Sidera's Fastbit attribute processing essentially produces contiguous sequences of key values that can be mapped against the Fact Structure. Because the encoded Berkeley R-trees are internally packed level-by-level and processed with a *breadth first* search strategy (rather than the conventional depth first approach), Fastbit key sequence matching can be accomplished with a single pass through the cube index. Figure 4(b) illustrates how the R-tree search algorithm sweeps across levels of the index identifying

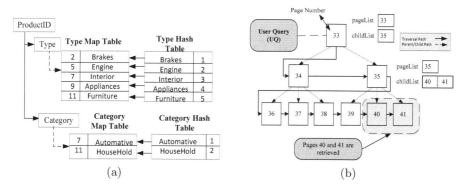

(a)   (b)

Fig. 4. (a) A simple mapGraph translation map (b) Linear Breadth First R-tree search

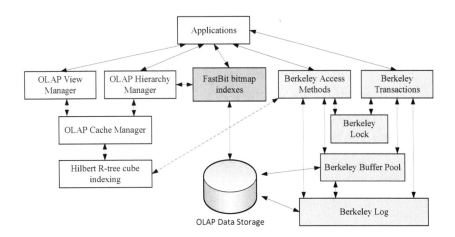

Fig. 5. The architecture of the individual nodes of the cluster DBMS

sequences of pages that correspond to the consecutive key values produced by the bitmap indexes.

As noted previously, Sidera is constructed as a parallel DBMS and runs on commodity Linux clusters (multi-core and GPU extensions are currently being investigated). Figure 5 illustrates the processing model of the individual sibling servers, showing the relationship between the components discussed above.

4   The Sidera Algebra

While the language of OLAP algebras has yet to be standardized, it is nevertheless the case that a core set of operations has been consistently identified in the literature [21]. However, before defining the operators of the Sidera algebra, we will first provide a more formal representation of the conceptual model presented in Section 3.1.

An N-dimensional **cube** C is constructed as $<D, F, M, BasicCube>$ where:

- D is a set of dimension D_i of C, where $D = \{D_1, D_2, ..., D_N\}$, and $1 \leq i \leq N$.
- F is a set of feature attributes F_i of C, $F = \{F_1, F_2, \ldots, F_N\}$, where $1 \leq i \leq N$.
- M is a list of measure attributes M_j of C, $M = \{M_1, M_2, \ldots, M_k\}$, where $j \leq k$.
- $BasicCube$ is a set of cells that describes the *facts* (measure attributes) at the particular level of detail specified by F.

A **dimension** (D_i) is defined by a schema written as $schema(D_i) = <ColumnList, Key, Hierarchy>$ where:

- $ColumnList$ is a set of dimension attributes $D_i.A_j$ of D_i, $ColumnList = \{D_1.A_1, \ldots, D_1.A_n\}$, where n is the number of attributes in dimension D_i.

- *Key* is an attribute $D_i.A_k$ of *ColumnList*, where $D_i.A_k$ is the deepest level of detail for dimension D_i, where $1 \leq k \leq n$.
- *Hierarchy* is a set of hierarchies $D_i.H_j$ of D_i, with *Hierarchy* $=\{D_i.H_1, D_i.H_2,$ ..., $D_i.H_z\}$, where $j \leq z$ and z is the number of hierarchies associated with dimension D_i. Each hierarchy $D_i.H_j$ is of the form $D_i.H_j = \{H_j, D_i.A_r \rightarrow \ldots \rightarrow D_i.A_l\}$, where $D_i.A_r$ is the root hierarchal attribute level, while $D_i.A_l$ is the leaf level in hierarchy H_j of dimension D_i.

A **Feature Attributes** F_i refers to a specific attribute A_j in dimension D_k, where $i,k \subseteq [1,N]$. It is of the form $F_i = \{D_k.A_j\}$, where F_i is an attribute in the *ColumnList* of dimension D_k.

A **BasicCube** is a multidimensional end user representation with a schema of the form schema*(BasicCube)* $= \{F, M\}$. An instance of a *BasicCube* is the set of *cells/facts/records/tuples* that are described by the values of measure attributes M at the level defined by F. Through the remainder of this paper, we will use the terms *cells, facts, records,* and *tuples* interchangeably.

SELECTION. The selection operator identifies one or more cells from within the full d-dimensional search space and its application produces what is commonly referred to as "slicing and dicing". This operator is applied to a data cube and produces a subset of the same data cube. More formally, we can define the SELECTION operator on cube **C** as

$$\sigma_{(D_i.A_j \ OP \ \phi)} C$$

where $D_i.A_j$ is an attribute in dimension D_i, **OP** is a conditional operator such as $\{<, >, =, \ldots,$ etc.$\}$, and ϕ is one or more values in domain$(D_i.A_j)$.

The result of $\sigma_{(D_i.A_j \ OP \ \phi)} C$ is a cube *C1<D, F, M, BasicCube1>*, where sets *D*, *F*, and *M* are equivalent to those in the input cube *C* and schema(*BasicCube1*) = schema(*BasicCube*). From the user's perspective, the query is executed against the physical data cube such that the selection criteria will be iteratively evaluated against each and every cell. If the selection test evaluates to true, the cell is included in the result; if not, then it is ignored.

PROJECTION. Used for the identification of presentation attributes, including both the measure attribute(s) and dimension members, a projection extracts, from a source cube, a new cube composed of only those elements specified with the PROJECTION operator. Formally, the PROJECTION operator can be written as:

$$\pi_{(D_i.A_j, \ y)} C,$$

where $D_i.A_j$ is a list of dimension attributes, and y $\subset$ M. The resulting cube is *C1<D1, F1, M1, BasicCube1>*, where *D1* is a set of dimensions, *F1* = list of dimension attributes $D_i.A_j$, *M1* = y, and Schema(BasicCube1) = F1, M1. Note that the measure value(s) M1 of BasicCube1 are aggregated at the level of the attribute(s) in F1.

CHANGE LEVEL. This operator allows the user to navigate amongst levels of a concept hierarchy, each with a distinct aggregation granularity. We typically refer to these processes as "roll-up" and "drill down." Formally, we denote the change level operator as:

$$\Updownarrow_{(D_i.A_j \rightarrow D_i.A_k)} C,$$

such that $D_i \in D$, $D_i.A_j$ is a feature attribute of cube C and $D_i.A_k$ is a hierarchical attribute level in dimension D_i. The resulting cube is of the form $C1 = <D, F1, M, BasicCube1>$. Note that while the result cube C1 maintains the same dimensions and measure attribute(s), it will have a new feature set($F1 = F - D_i.A_j + D_i.A_k$). The CHANGE BASE operator may also produce multiple level changes as follows: $\Updownarrow_{(D_i.A_j \rightarrow D_i.A_k, D_r.A_s \rightarrow D_r.A_t, ...)} C$, where $i, r = [1 \ldots N]$.

CHANGE BASE. This operator represents the addition or deletion of one or more dimensions from the current result cube **C**. Aggregated cell values must be re-calculated accordingly. CHANGE BASE may be represented as:

$$\pm_{(D_i.A_j \rightarrow Action)} C,$$

where *Action* $\in$ (*Remove* or *Add*). The resulting cube C1 = <D1, F1, M, BasicCube1> has different dimensions, feature attributes and BasicCube relative to that of the source cube **C**.

PIVOT. This is a presentation-specific operation that allows users to reorganize the axes of the cube. No recalculation of cell values is required. Formally, we have:

$$\circlearrowleft_{(D_i.A_j \rightarrow D_k.A_l)} C$$

where $D_i.A_j$ and $D_k.A_l$ are feature attributes in cube C. This operator reorganizes the axes of cube C so that $D_k.A_l$ is viewed instead of $D_i.A_j$, and vice versa. The result cube is equivalent in construction to the source cube.

DRILL ACROSS. Here, we denote the integration of two independent cubes, with each possessing common dimensional axes, so as to compare their measure attributes. In effect, this is a cube "join" (possibly a self join) that changes or extends the subject of analysis. Consider two cubes C1 = <D1, F1, M1, BasicCube1> and C2 = <D1, F1, M2, BasicCube2> having the same set of dimensions and feature attributes but with different sets of measure attributes (M1 and M2). We therefore have:

$$C1(M1) \leftrightarrows C2(M2)$$

The result of this operation is another cube C = <D1, F1, M, BasicCube>, where M is the union of sets M1 and M2 and BasicCube contains the union of BasicCube1 and BasicCube2, with the new measure attributes M.

SET Operations. Set operations may also be applied to data cubes. Given cubes **C1** and **C2**, we have $C1 \cup C2$ (UNION), $C1 \cap C2$ (INTERSECTION), and $C1 - C2$ (DIFFERENCE). In all cases, **C1** and **C2** must be composed of the same feature attribute set (i.e., they must possess the same dimensional axes). For UNION and INTERSECTION, we may aggregate measure values if cells share the same feature attributes.

5 Query Optimization

As noted in Section 3.2, native language client-side queries are decomposed into the associated algebraic operators and passed to the DBMS at runtime. That being said, this initial query form likely does not represent the most efficient execution plan for an OLAP DBMS, as no attempt has been made to either exploit the physical representation of the cube (e.g., indexes, materialized views) or the properties of the algebra itself (e.g., re-ordering logical operations to reduce intermediate cube sizes). In this section, we will discuss optimization principles relevant to OLAP aware servers in general, and to Sidera specifically. We note that due to the length of the paper, it is not possible to present optimization strategies for the full algebra (we intend to do this in a longer version of the paper). Instead, we will focus on SELECTION and PROJECTION strategies, as these two operations typically dominate processing cost.

5.1 Selection

Processing costs in the Sidera DBMS (or any OLAP server) are dominated by Fact Structure access. In a traditional DBMS, OLAP queries would require a join operation between the fact table and one or more dimension tables. Sidera streamlines this process by re-writing the common Fact Structure SELECTION operation as follows:

$$\sigma_{Dim_1(C_1),Dim_2(C_2),...Dim_n(C_n)}C = \sigma_{Dim_1 ID=L_1, Dim_2 ID=L_2...Dim_n ID=L_n}C$$

where $L_1 \ldots L_n$ are lists of Dimension key values associated with rows constrained by conditions $C_1 \ldots C_n$ respectively. In other words, Sidera does not perform traditional relational sort or hash-based joins. Instead, it uses the FastBit indexes to retrieve the relevant dimension keys values, then uses these to directly perform a selection on the Fact Structure. Because the Fact Structure is encoded as a packed R-tree, and is accessed by a linear breadth first search, the "standard" Star Schema query effectively becomes a single pass SELECTION. As a concrete example, a query initially expressed as $\sigma_{Product.Type=BrakesANDEmployee.Age>30}Sales$ — where Product 1 and Product 2 are of Type "brakes", Employee 2 and Employee 3 are older than 30, and the underlying Fact is Sales — would be transformed by Sidera into $\sigma_{ProductID=(1,2)ANDEmployeeID=(2,3)}Sales$.

Pushing transformations, as is the case with any DBMS system, are also important. In other words, we can typically reduce intermediate view sizes by pushing SELECTION operations closer to the data source. The Sidera system

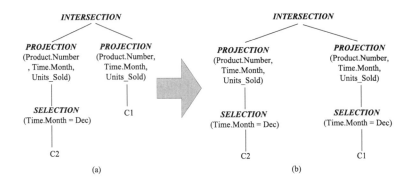

Fig. 6. (a) Initial OLAP expression tree. (b) Improving the initial expression by pulling SELECTION up and then pushing it down the tree.

uses pushing techniques extensively for selections executed in combination will other algebraic operations. We have also found it useful to sometimes combine an initial pull with the push operation. Figure 6, for example, demonstrates that with an INTERSECTION requiring common schemas, a SELECTION operator may be pulled up the left side of the query tree and pushed down the right, thereby reducing the cost of the INTERSECTION operation.

5.2   Projection

Pushing projections down the query tree can also reduce the size of intermediate data sets. Sidera does this as well. However, it is also possible to decompose PROJECTION operations into a <CHANGE LEVEL, PROJECTION> pair in order to take advantage of efficient grouping functionality. In Sidera's case, the mapGraph structure can be used to translate between the base level data (i.e., the most detailed) in the Fact Structure and the hierarchy level listed in the initial query. More formally, we can say:

$$\pi_{(L,M)}C = \Updownarrow_{(L1 \rightarrow L)}(\pi_{(L1,M)}C)$$

Figure 7 illustrates how a projection decomposition would be used in practice. Here, the programmer has specified a query at the level of Product Type. Because the data is physically stored in the Fact Structure at the most granular level, the Sidera optimizer essentially wraps the low level PROJECTION operator (on ProductID) with a CHANGE LEVEL operator that will transform and aggregate the detailed Product data into Product Type groupings at run-time.

6   Experimental Results

Sidera is a relatively sophisticated prototype and, as such, lends itself to meaningful experimental evaluation. We stress that Sidera is a DBMS in the true sense of the word. In other words, it is not simply an interface to a relational or

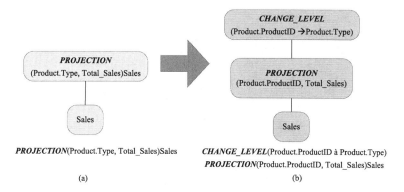

PROJECTION(Product.Type, Total_Sales)Sales

(a)

CHANGE_LEVEL(Product.ProductID à Product.Type)

PROJECTION(Product.ProductID, Total_Sales)Sales

(b)

Fig. 7. (a) Initial OLAP expression tree. (b) Improving the initial expression by decomposing the PROJECTION.

even multidimensional server. Rather, it provides data storage, indexing, query parsing, optimization, and caching services. As such, the experimental results listed below provide a reasonable representation of the potential for this type of OLAP model (i.e., one that uses OLAP-specific indexes, storage and algebraic operations to provide scalable OLAP functionality).

In terms of the environment, tests were conducted on a dual-boot workstation running Windows Vista and a Fedora Linux distribution (2.6.x kernel). (Note that we perform single-node evaluation in this paper rather than utilizing the full cluster architecture). The machine uses 1GB of main memory and houses a standard 160 GB SATA hard drive. The analytics database consists of six dimensions with cardinalities ranging between 300 and one million. Each dimension also has a three or four level hierarchy. Dimension data was generated with an open source data generation tool so as to more accurately represent real (i.e., text) values. In terms of the the Fact Structure, relevant feature attributes (i.e., with matching keys) and measure attributes were produced by a generator designed specifically for Sidera. While the generator has the ability to produce skewed data, the distribution in the current case is essentially uniform as skew is largely irrelevant for the current round of testing. Depending on the test, row counts typically vary from 100,000 records to 10,000,000 records. Once generated, Rtrees and Bitmaps are constructed as required.

Because no true OLAP query benchmark currently exists, we developed a set of "Star Schema queries" representing common OLAP operations (slice and dice, drill down, roll up, etc). In each case, the queries were hand coded in SQL, MDX, and Sidera's XML format as required (Note that in the longer version of the paper, we intend to include the full query suite as an appendix). Unless otherwise indicated, batches of 10-20 such queries are used in a given test, with the average of five runs recorded. Finally, query and OS caches are cleared between runs.

We begin by looking at the performance of the Fact Structure described in Section 3.3. In most environments, indexing demonstrates increasingly poor performance once query selectivity reaches a certain point, typically about 5% of the records in the data set. However, Sidera's Berkeley R-tree storage — with its breadth first traversal pattern that limits access to a single sequential pass — does not degrade in this manner. Figure 8(a) illustrates that for a 12-query batch, with selectivity ranging between 1% and 25%, Sidera's query performance remains 3-4 times faster than that of a sequential scan of the data set. Figure 8(b), on the other hand, demonstrates Sidera's ability to exploit R-tree Fact Structures containing a fully materialized cube (i.e., all aggregation levels included) generated by a Sidera ETL module. Specifically, for data sets of 10 million records, the same query batch completes in one tenth of the time (black bars) if aggregates are available (Note that the query optimizer transparently determines the optimal summary view).

Figure 9 shows query performance — relative to record and dimension counts — on a batch of 16 OLAP queries that have been parsed into the algebraic operations described in the paper and re-written using the join and pushing optimizations described in Section 5. Here, we see performance improve by a factor of 5-15 when optimization steps are undertaken (black bars).

We have also compared Sidera to DBMS systems often used in industrial database environments, namely the open source MySQL server and Microsoft's Analysis Services. In this case, we reproduce the database stored by Sidera and load it into both DBMS platforms in the standard Star Schema format. Queries are re-written in SQL form to match. Figure 10 shows comparative results for both platforms and demonstrates that the MySQL server takes approximately 10-15 times as long to resolve the same queries, while Microsoft's Analysis Service — running in ROLAP mode — is three to six times slower.

Of course, one can argue that MOLAP offers superior performance to ROLAP configurations. So we loaded the same Star Schema data using the MOLAP mode of Microsoft's Analysis Services. Figure 11(a) shows that MOLAP does indeed

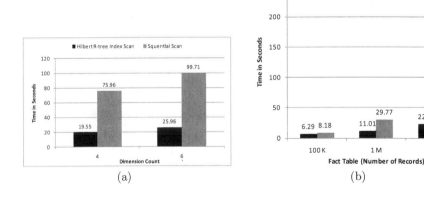

(a)   (b)

Fig. 8. (a) Rtree performance versus sequential scan (10M records) (b) Fact structure performance by record count

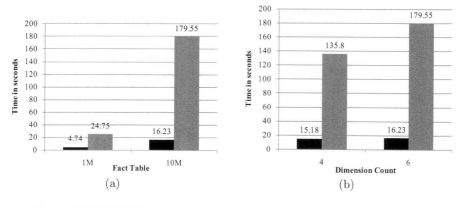

Fig. 9. SELECTION optimization by (a) Record count (b) Dimension count

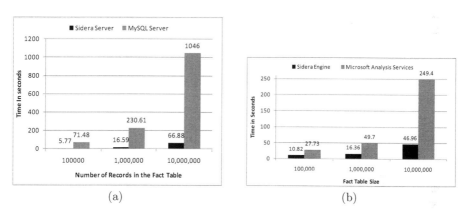

Fig. 10. Sidera versus (a) MySQL (b) MS Analysis Services (ROLAP)

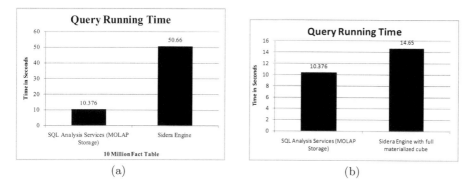

Fig. 11. (a) MOLAP versus non-materialized Sidera (b) MOLAP versus materialized Sidera

outperform the Sidera DBMS by a factor of about 5 to 1. However, we note that in this test, Sidera was not permitted to materialize any additional data; it was essentially just an efficient Star Schema. In Figure 11(b), we see the result once aggregate materialization is added to the R-tree Fact Structure. While Microsoft's MOLAP server still has a slight advantage, we note that (i) the Microsoft DBMS benefits from years of optimization, and (ii) MOLAP is ideally suited to the scale of the current test (i.e., 1-10 million records). Given that the Sidera DBMS framework is not constrained by the limits of array-based storage, these preliminary results suggest that the Sidera DBMS has the potential to provide MOLAP-style performance with ROLAP-style scalability.

7   Conclusions

OLAP servers have traditionally relied either on extensions to DBM systems designed primarily for OLTP environments or on array-based servers that lack a formal query model and tend to provide limited scalability. In this paper, we have discussed the integration of an OLAP-oriented algebra with a DBMS prototype designed specifically for analytical processing. The use of the algebraic operators lends itself to both a clean, native language query interface for end users and a query execution engine that is able to optimize performance by manipulating initial parse trees to more efficiently exploit the available index and storage structures. Initial testing demonstrates that not only does the DBMS provide a contemporary OOP interface for end users, but that it is already competitive in performance to commercial systems optimized for in-memory OLAP. Given that Sidera is ultimately designed as a scalable parallel system, we believe the current work suggests that MOLAP-level performance — at commodity prices — is indeed possible for Terabyte scale analytical environments.

References

1. JSR 243: Java Data Objects 2.0 - An Extension to the JDO specification (2008), http://java.sun.com/products/jdo/
2. HaskellDB (2010), http://www.haskell.org/haskellDB/
3. Berkeleydb (2011),
   http://www.oracle.com/technetwork/database/
   berkeleydb/overview/index.html
4. Fastbit indexing (2011), http://crd.lbl.gov/~kewu/fastbit/index.html
5. Ruby programming language (2011), http://www.ruby-lang.org/en/
6. Bauer, C., King, G.: Java Persistence with Hibernate. Manning Publications Co., Greenwich (2006)
7. Bellatreche, L., Giacometti, A., Laurent, D., Marcel, P., Mouloudi, H.: Olap query optimization: A framework forcombining rule-based and cost-based approaches. In: EDA (2005)
8. Blakeley, J.A., Rao, V., Kunen, I., Prout, A., Henaire, M., Kleinerman, C.: NET database programmability and extensibility in Microsoft SQL Server. In: ACM SIGMOD International Conference on Management of Data, pp. 1087–1098. ACM, New York (2008)

9. Chmiel, J., Morzy, T., Wrembel, R.: Time-hobi: indexing dimension hierarchies by means of hierarchically organized bitmaps. In: Proceedings of the ACM 13th International Workshop on Data Warehousing and OLAP, pp. 69–76. ACM, New York (2010)
10. Cook, W.R., Rai, S.: Safe query objects: statically typed objects as remotely executable queries. In: International Conference on Software Engineering (ICSE), pp. 97–106 (2005)
11. Cunningham, C., Graefe, G., Galindo-Legaria, C.A.: PIVOT and UNPIVOT: Optimization and execution strategies in an RDBMS. In: International Conference on Very Large Data Bases (VLDB), pp. 998–1009 (2004)
12. Eavis, T., Cueva, D.: The lbf r-tree: Efficient multidimensional indexing with graceful degradation. In: Proc. 11th International Database Engineering and Applications Symposium IDEAS 2007, September 6-8, pp. 241–250 (2007)
13. Eavis, T., Tabbara, H., Taleb, A.: The NOX framework: Native language queries for business intelligence applications. In: Bach Pedersen, T., Mohania, M.K., Tjoa, A.M. (eds.) DAWAK 2010. LNCS, vol. 6263, pp. 172–189. Springer, Heidelberg (2010)
14. Eavis, T., Taleb, A.: Mapgraph: efficient methods for complex olap hierarchies. In: Proceedings of the Sixteenth ACM Conference on Information and Knowledge Management, CIKM 2007, pp. 465–474. ACM, New York (2007)
15. Gray, J., Bosworth, A., Layman, A., Pirahesh, H.: Data Cube: A relational aggregation operator generalizing group-by, cross-tab, and sub-total. In: International Conference on Data Engineering (ICDE), pp. 152–159. IEEE Computer Society, Washington, DC, USA (1996)
16. Grund, M., Krüger, J., Plattner, H., Zeier, A., Cudre-Mauroux, P., Madden, S.: Hyrise: a main memory hybrid storage engine. In: Proc. VLDB Endow., vol. 4, pp. 105–116 (November 2010)
17. Hanusse, N., Maabout, S., Tofan, R.: A view selection algorithm with performance guarantee. In: Proceedings of the 12th International Conference on Extending Database Technology: Advances in Database Technology, EDBT 2009, pp. 946–957. ACM, New York (2009)
18. Hose, K., Klan, D., Marx, M., Sattler, K.-U.: When is it time to rethink the aggregate configuration of your olap server? In: Proc. VLDB Endow., vol. 1, pp. 1492–1495 (August 2008)
19. Lauer, T., Datta, A., Khadikov, Z., Anselm, C.: Exploring graphics processing units as parallel coprocessors for online aggregation. In: Proceedings of the ACM 13th International Workshop on Data Warehousing and OLAP, DOLAP 2010, pp. 77–84. ACM, New York (2010)
20. Morfonios, K., Ioannidis, Y.: CURE for cubes: cubing using a ROLAP engine. In: International Conference on Very Large Data Bases (VLDB), pp. 379–390. VLDB Endowment (2006)
21. Romero, O., Abelló, A.: On the need of a reference algebra for OLAP. In: International Conference on Data Warehousing and Knowledge Discovery (DaWak), pp. 99–110 (2007)
22. Whitehorn, M., Zare, R., Pasumansky, M.: Fast Track to MDX. Springer-Verlag New York, Inc., Secaucus (2005)

VarDB: High-Performance Warehouse Processing with Massive Ordering and Binary Search

Pedro Martins[1], João Costa[1], José Cecílio[1], and Pedro Furtado[1]

[1] University of Coimbra
Coimbra Portugal
{pmom,jpcosta,jcecilio,pnf}@dei.uc.pt

Abstract. Current data base management systems (DBMS) compete aggressively for performance. In order to accomplish that, they are adopting new storage schemas, developing better compression algorithms, using faster hardware, optimizing parallel and distributed data processing. Current row-wise systems do not exploit massive ordering redundancy, and current column-wise approaches exploit only partially. An important current research issue concerns replacing optimization and processing complexity by less complex but ultra fast solutions. We propose the varDB approach to optimize performance over data warehouses. The solution minimizes complex operators, by applying a simple scheme and organizing all structures and processing to that end: massive ordering with efficient sorting and log2N searching. Considering data warehouses, with periodic loads and frequent analysis operations, such an approach provides very fast query processing. In our work we show how it is possible to use this massive data ordering/sorting in order to optimize queries for high speed, even without the use of data compression (therefore also avoiding compression/decompression overheads). We dedicate our attention to sort columns of data and correlating them with other replicated and unsorted columns. For querying, we focus on binary-search and the use of mainly offsets. Our tests of loading data, sorting vs. creating indexes and executing very selective operations like data filtering and joining show, using a simple disk based prototype, that we are able to obtain much better performance comparing with optimized row-wise engines, and also improvements when comparing with column-wise optimized engines. Comparing to those we were able to attain at least similar performance for many queries and much better performance for queries with complex joins.

Keywords: data warehousing, query processing, database architectures, efficiency.

1 Introduction

Two paradigms currently stand in the context of databases, row-oriented and column-oriented, both of them exploring memory and/or disk in optimized manners. Over the last decades, the specialization of DBMSs to different niches has increased, each one exploring specific methods and techniques to obtain better performance in the

A. Cuzzocrea and U. Dayal (Eds.): DaWaK 2011, LNCS 6862, pp. 184–195, 2011.
© Springer-Verlag Berlin Heidelberg 2011

respective niche. In order to obtain better scalability and performance, they rely mostly on techniques such as massive indexing, compression algorithms and better hardware such as memories, multi-core CPUs, faster networks, etc. Although DBMS engines have started to target specific niches, giving rise to the statement that the old general-purpose DBMS is dead, they still do not explore to full length the possibilities of different data organization, replication or representation for data to achieve top performance. We explore a kind of RISC-like database architecture. The term RISC was created some decades ago to mean "reduced instruction-set computers", as opposed to CISC processors "complex instruction set computers", and the idea is that it is possible to implement the same processing capabilities with a smaller, "cleaner" and simpler instruction set. For instance, the fact that instructions had fixed size meant that instructions could be processed much faster than in CISC architectures. Likewise, our approach is to focus on the data warehouse engine and explore software techniques that result in a reduced set of simple, fast and uniform processing model. We take into account massive data replication (since disk space is not a limitation nowadays), a few schemes and organizations, and propose a single method to perform fast queries based on disk, data replication and sorts over a column-wise approach.

In order to explore the proposed solutions we developed a DBMS engine, varDB, from scratch, incorporating the proposed mechanisms. VarDB is a column-wise prototype, and the version used for these experiments is based on disk and without compression.

The test results using TPC-H prove that the mass redundancy and ordering approach is able, together with corresponding query techniques, to speedup processing significantly, therefore we adopted the approach for our future varDB architecture and propose the mechanisms in this paper.

The next section presents related work. It is followed by *section 3*, which mentions relevant architectural details of varDB, how data is stored and replicated, and filtering methodologies. *Section 4* presents experimental results, and we conclude in *section 5*, with a conclusion and discussion on future work.

2   Related Work

There have been innumerous efforts by various companies (e.g. Oracle, Vertica, IBM, SUN) to find solutions for data processing on large scale. So emerging approaches have aroused, such as vertical models [2], memory-based databases, the use of optimization strategies such as histograms, indexes and compression mechanisms. Leading to specialization of the DBMSs for processing analytical or transactional tasks with performance optimizations [13][14].

Trends point to three major groups of processing models:

- Row-wise [4], the data is stored in the form of table rows with dynamic characteristics that are good fits for both transactional and analytic loads, although not particularly optimized for any of the contexts (e.g. Oracle, PostgreSQL);
- Column-wise, the data is stored as columns and further compressed [3] (Vertica, Teradata, MonetDB, SadasDB), providing faster processing for analytical workloads;

- Main-memory [8], systems that rely mainly on memory, the disc is only used to ensure ACID properties (e.g. Oracle TimesTen, VoltDB).

Large performance penalties are paid by disk accesses, which are incurred not only for accessing the data that is stored in tables, but also for costly processing of operations such as joins and sorts that may need extra temporary disk space when memory is not enough. Additional disk access costs are also incurred fault-tolerance based on persistent logs or other forms of persistent replication [7]. Column-wise DBMSs [11], such as Vertica, MonetDB or ParAccel, focus partly on decreasing the amount of data that needs to be accessed when compared with row-oriented DBMSs [5][6]. Some column-wise approaches introduced column sorting for additional performance boost. Commercial memory and column-based DBMSs exhibit good performance/price relations for some application contexts when comparing with traditional engines. Some approaches rely on specific hardware, data processing within clusters and main-memory to achieve such performance gains [8][7][1].

There has been a common interest in vertical data partitioning as a means for major performance gains. This technique has been explored by researchers [18] before, some works have the sole objective of minimizing disk I/O [16] such as MonetDB and MonetDB/X100 [15][12], C-Store [9]. Others, like Oracle, increase their systems performance by acquiring companies and integrating their systems based on memory and new hardware with Oracle systems (e.g. Oracle ExaData [1]). Some academic studies point to the creation of hybrid memory based column-wise and row-wise systems such as HyRise [17] and hybrids in-memory/on-disk (HDD and/or SSD) like Vertica. Other solutions based on memory, using a variety of common machines (*share-nothing*), include Oracle Times Ten and VoltDB, oriented solely for performance. MonetDB makes use of large amounts of memory, since it assumes the data to be processed must fit entirely into memory. All these efforts generally focus on hardware, more memory, more CPU for compression, faster disks and networks and in some cases hybrid combinations. Our approach is orthogonal to those ones, since the massive ordering and query processing mechanism proposed here can and will be applied by us together with any of those improvements to yield extremely fast solutions.

3   Relevant Architectural Details

For better support of data sorting and data replication, we chose a column-oriented architecture for varDB. This way we are able to easily sort data columns. The problem is correlating data with other columns. So to overcome that we create offset data maps, which translate current offsets to the offsets in other representations.

In the next sub-sections of this section we will address: generic data processing mechanism; how data is inserted and stored into the columns that are broken into partitions; construction of offset maps, to link columns to each other through the respective offsets; creation of simple histograms to store the data distribution inside partitions and columns; description of the most common filters, group by, join, greater, less and equals operators.

3.1 Introduction to Data Processing Mechanism

VarDB is committed to the following simple principles: fixed-size attributes and sorted columnar partitioned files; cost-based (i.e. selectivity-based) decision on binary-search over which sorted columns; opportunistic sorting (learn-by-use). The desired processing situation happens when binary-search over a sorted version of a very selective column is then followed by sequential range scan of subset over the remaining columns. The exception happens when a column is not sorted as needed for fastest operation, in which case access is either by full-column-scan, or using offsets if those are available from previous processing parts of the query. Cost-based estimation determines whether full-scan is cheaper than ordered offset-based tuples picking. The following flux diagram tries to explain in a simple way that a query is processed based on varDB implemented mechanisms.

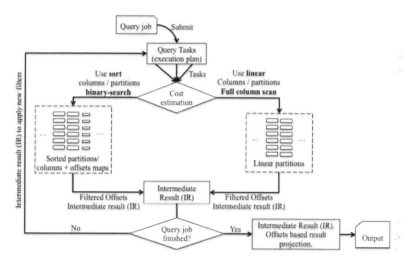

Fig. 1. Query processing simplified flux-diagram

3.2 Storage Architecture

When using common magnetic hard-drives to store data, the most relevant issue is how to minimize I/O and make all accesses - reads and writes - as sequential as possible (since a random access is by far much more expensive than a sequential one). The best way to minimize I/O when inserting is to insert blocks of data sequentially. In varDB we used two main representations, *linear* and *sorted*. In the *linear* representation, data is inserted into partitions of equal size by arrival order.

The figure (*Fig, 2*) represents the conversion process of TPC-H generated information to varDB linear partitions. Concerning *organized/sorted* data representation, it can be created in two ways. On the fly, when *linear* partitions are loaded (with some memory limitations) or on a secondary step using an *external sort merge* [10]. The advantage that varDB explores is the massive *organization/sorting* of data to minimize random disk reads when performing queries. Sorted data

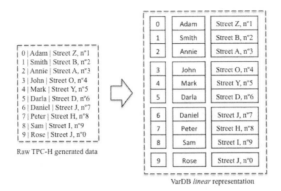

Fig. 2. Conversion of the raw data generated from TPC-H to varDB linear partitioned columns

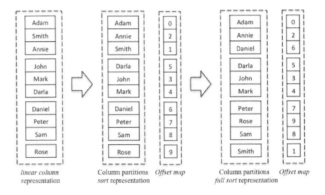

Fig. 3. Creation of the *organized/sorted* representations, respective *offset map* for data linking and replication of other columns following the same order

organizations also make possible to access data using a single *binary-search* plus sequential reads, instead of having to rely on *b-tree* indexes or requiring *full-table-scans*. When *sorting* on the fly, each partition is kept in memory until it is full. When the partition is full, varDB *sorts* it, and stores it on disk. This process is done for each partition. Still, we must be able to correlate by offset the data with the rest of the *unsorted* partitions. So an *offset map* partition is generated to link data between representations.

The *figure 3* represents the partitioned data immediately after insertion and the respective *offset map (middle part, partition sorted column)*. A final optional step is also represented that consists on obtaining the *fully sorted* column (partitions merge). This elementary operation is then applied massively through all columns/tables, with data replication and using the *offset map to* extend the *sort*. Notice that we only sort the data and create the *offset map* according to a single column. Fortunately, hard drive disk space is very cheap and commonly abundant, so no problem results from this massive replication when considering data warehouses.

The process of order replication to other columns is done following strategies of *learn by use*. This means that varDB is capable of self-optimization, sorting the columns needed to execute certain tasks after a few runs. If for instance new-sorted columns are needed for a new task, using the *offset map,* this process is very straightforward by accessing the respective offset in the linear representation.

Other key element of varDB is the *data histograms.* When inserting, data histograms of each column are updated. So, to perform a query, the first operation of the query processor/optimizer is to go to the histogram and choose the most selective column involved to start the data filtering process. When filtering data, after determining the most selective column by access to the histograms, one of two types of search is applied: *full-column-scan* or *binary-search.* If we use a *fully sorted* column representation, we can *binary-search* the entire column, otherwise we may need to do a full scan or partial binary searches if there are sorted and unsorted partitions. As result of each step in processing a *query,* varDB stores only the relevant *offsets* or range of *offsets,* for further exclusion depending on other filters to be applied next. The *offsets* are stored in a hybrid architecture based on memory and disk, so no matter what the size of a task output might be, the engine will always be capable of processing it. VarDB uses this hybrid architecture in all situations where memory is involved to temporarily store intermediate results.

In the next section we describe some of the most relevant operations or filters used during processing and also applied in the experimental tests.

3.3   Some Implemented Filters

VarDB implements most operators as simple "filters", for instance, *between, larger* and *smaller, projections, sums, group by, joins,* and others that combine functionalities. In this section we present a general overview of how some of the filters work.

Between, Larger, Smaller, Projection, Sum
These filters are all very similar, their implementation being straightforward. As already mentioned, two main types of data access methods are available, *full-column-scan* and *binary-search*, from both a column or an intermediate result (IR) generated in a *hybrid* structure (memory and disk). The IRs can be set as input for other filters reuse for final or intermediate processing. Projection involves selecting only a subset of the columns to be read, sum involves adding over expressions on the data being scanned, and range conditions are either processed based on the binary search model or full scan by comparing with the condition.

Group By
Several methods to group data are available [10]. For the proposed work and tests in varDB we will be using only *group by* by *hash* that also operates in a *hybrid* standard. The used method is explained in a simplified form with the help of *fig 4, varDB* creates a *hash* code and assigns to it a unique *id* that points to the data. Each *id* corresponds to a position in a *list* that will contain the *syntax* of the *group* and the data that it contains. All the structures presented are hybrids (disk and memory), meaning that if they overflow a certain size, part of data is swapped into disk.

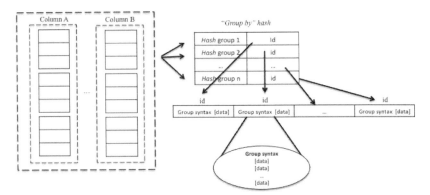

Fig. 4. Simplified description of the hash based *group by* filter

Joins

This filter manages the *join* between two or more tables that may involve several columns. VarDB data *join* method is very simple and based on data *offsets*. *Figure 5*, is a simplified graphical representation of the process. Following the figure we have tree main steps.

1. First, varDB generates the *offset* IR results form the *join* operation involving pairs of tables. According to the image 5, IR1 is created from the *join* of *column A* with *column B,* and the same logic for creating IR2.

2. Secondly, based on the smallest IR (the more selective), varDB will generate an IR3 concerning the *join* of IR1 with IR2 (*join IR1 + IR2*), based on the common column (*column B*).

3. Finally the third step is the result of the *join offsets*, now in order to do the result projection we only need to access the necessary columns, based on the result *offsets*.

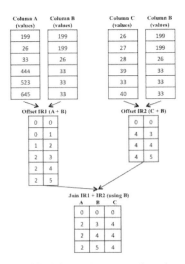

Fig. 5. Simplified data *join* process, based on *offsets*

4 Experimental Results

In this section we show experimental results using varDB and other three engines, two row-wise, and one columns-wise. The engines based on rows are distinct, one is commonly used by large enterprises (RDBMS-X1) and another mainly for web sites (RDBMS-X2). The column-wise engine makes use of large amounts of memory, which led us to use a 64bits OS for all tests (CDBMS-X).

This section is organized as follows: Analysis to *Bulk Load* time for 10GB; Execution of selective queries to test specific functions, without any optimization; Cost of sorting columns in varDB vs. creating indexes in the other DBMSs, for 10GB of data; Execution of selective queries to test specific functions, with indexes, and in varDB with data organization and replication.

4.1 Bulk Load Times

To test the cost of partitioning data through columns and at the same time creating histograms, we compare the load times of all DBMSs with 10GB of data. Notice that RDBMS-X1 supported different types of data loading, so we tested with the standard and the most optimized, which we mention as *direct*.

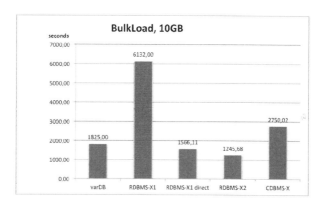

Fig. 6. 10GB data *Bulk Load*

Comparing the results form *figure 6* we manage to obtain very satisfactory results for varDB, specially improving over both CDBMS-X and RDBMS-X1, and only slightly worse than RDBMS-X2. We were glad to see that, all engines scaled well, so all will be apt to the next tests.

4.2 Queries Execution without Indexes

After we had the data loaded, we performed experiments to study how the developed techniques handle queries without optimizations of any kind involved. This means that in this case the data is not indexed in any of the tested database engines and it is not sorted in varDB. These results can then be compared with the results in the following sections, which apply indexes and in the case of varDB apply sorted columns.

We chose a set of TPC-H queries to test specific operations comparing with the other engines from 5GB to 10GB:

- Query 1 (Q1): used to mainly test *group by* tasks;
- Query 14 (Q14): to test *join* operations. We also altered this query (Q14-2j) so it had a more complex *join*, in this case we added, *ps_partkey = p_partkey;*
- Query 6 (Q6): to test basic filtering operations;

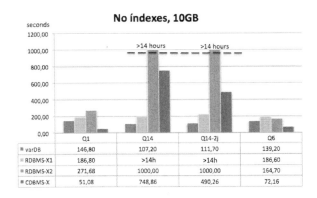

Fig. 7. Query tests for 10GB of TPC-H data without any optimization

First conclusion we may take is that all the engines scale well performing basic filtering operations from 5 to 10GB. Nonetheless, we had to stop processing when using RDBMS-X2, since it was taking too long to complete the task Q14 and Q14-2j involving data *joins*.

In the previous graphics we can conclude that CDBMS-X is generally more efficient than varDB performing data filtering and grouping data. The better performance of CDBMS-X can be explained by the use of large amounts of memory and, above all, data compression. VarDB can still be optimized in those respects, therefore it can match such performance if some form of compression and memory optimizations are added to it. However, when performing *join* operations, varDB was the best of all, since it managed to keep heavy operations as light and in-memory as possible, with low I/O requirements. In contrast, the other engines swap lots of data. We were particularly happy with these results, since the used varDB prototype is still a RISC-style disk-based DBMS lacking compression or other mechanisms of optimization.

4.3 Indexes Creation

In order to test the creation of indexes in each system and to compare with varDB, we decided to create a set of *b-tree* indexes for the engines used as base of comparison. The chosen indexes where made based on the queries used in previous tests.

Analyzing the two graphics bellow (*Fig 8*) we concluded that RDBMS-X1 is very constant while the performance of RDBMS-X2 is degrading as we create more

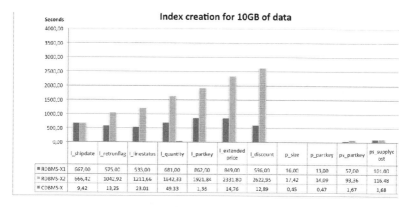

Fig. 8. Index creation times (seconds) for 10GB of TPC-H data

indexes. The CDBMS-X indexes were super fast. To study the impact of indexes on the CDBMS used for comparison, we have ran several queries before and after index creation. We obtained similar performance results with very small differences, leading us to conclude that in fact no indexes were created or were not useful when we specified their creation in the CDBMS.

After these tests, we calculated the average time that each engine took to create the set of indexes, grouping them by the tested queries.

- Q1: *l_sipdate, l_returnflag, l_linestatus.*
- Q14: *l_shipdate, l_partkey, p_size, p_partkey.*
- Q14-2j: *l_shipdate, l_partkey, p_size, p_partkey, ps_partkey, ps_supplycost.*
- Q6: *l_shipdate, l_quantity, l_discount.*

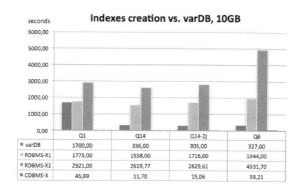

Fig. 9. Index creation times for 10GB of TPC-H data versus varDB

The graphics from *figure 9* show equivalent optimizations in varDB that, when comparing varDB data organization/sort and *replication* with the RDBMSs, it manages to always obtain better performance, leading to the conclusion that in fact data *organization/sort* and replication is not worse than index creation times, in fact it is better.

Since now we have the data loaded and indexes created, in the next section we study the previous queries tested with indexes, comparing with varDB *organization/sort* and *replication*.

4.4 Queries Execution with Indexes

In this section we rerun the tested queries on section *4.1*, but using indexes for the engines used as comparison base, and comparing with varDB, that makes use of data *organization/sort* and *replication*.

The results of our tests (*fig 10*) using data organization and replication in varDB show a large performance gain when compared with the tests without any type of optimization (*fig 7*). Also to notice that, for RDBMS-X2, Q6 with indexes *ps_partkey* and *ps_supplycost* did not bring any advantage.

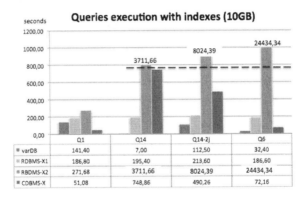

Fig. 10. Query tests for 10GB of TPC-H data using indexes

As before, varDB manages to perform better than all engines when *join* operations were involved, in the other tests varDB and the CDBMS-X are very competitively similar.

5 Conclusion

In this work we have proposed a RISC-like approach to design a DBMS for data warehousing using columnar organization, massive replication and ordering/sorting. We have proven that that the approach manages to obtain superior performance, even when compared with column-wise DBMSs or to row-wise DBMSs with strong markets and fully optimized and tuned. The presented tests are still limited in size and will be extended in the future to include all TPC-H queries. When comparing varDB with two well known RDBMSs and CDBMS, varDB is able to perform the same tasks 3x faster. VarDB still has significant improvement possibilities ahead, which will be part of our future work on the subject. There is still much to enhance and improve, such as methods of optimization of random accesses to disk, data compression, exploring CPU parallelism, optimizing use of available memory and other data representation methods.

References

1. Richard Burns, Senior Consultant. Exadata – the Sequel, Exadata V2 is Still Oracle. Teradata Corporation
2. Stonebraker, M., Abadi, D.J., Batkin, A., Chen, X., Cherniack, M., Ferreira, M., Lau, E., Lin, A., Madden, S., O'Neil, E.J., O'Neil, P.E., Rasin, A., Tran, N., Zdonik, S.B.: C-Store: A column-oriented DBMS. In: VLDB, pp. 553–564 (2005)
3. Stonebraker, M., Hellerstein, J.: What Goes Around Comes Around. In: Readings in Database Systems, 4th edn., pp. 2–41. The MIT Press, Cambridge (2005)
4. Halverson, A., Beckmann, J.L., Naughton, J.F., Dewitt, D.J.: A Comparison of C-Store and Row-Store in a Common Framework. Technical Report TR1570. University of Wisconsin-Madison (2006)
5. Pavlo, A., Rasin, A., Madden, S., Stonebraker, M., DeWitt, D., Paulson, E., Shrinivas, L., Abadi, D.J.: A Comparison of Approaches to Large Scale Data Analysis. In: SIGMOD 2009, June 29-July 2 (2009)
6. Abouzeid, A., Bajda-Pawlikowski, K., Abadi, D., Silberschatz, A., Rasin, A.: HadoopDB: An Architectural Hybrid of Map Reduce and DBMS Technologies for Analytical Workloads. In: VLDB 2009, Lyon, France, August 24-28 (2009)
7. VoltDB Technical Overview White Paper
8. Cole, B.:Hybrid embedded database merges on-disk and in-memory data management. Embedded.com (February 2007)
9. Stonebraker, M., Abadi, D.J., Batkin, A., et al.: C-Store: A Column-oriented DBMS. In: VLDB (2005)
10. Ramakrisnan, R.: Database Management Systems, 3rd edn. University of Wisconsin Madison, Wsiconsin
11. Furtado, P.: A Survey of Parallel and Distributed Data Warehouses. International Journal of Data Warehousing & Mining, 57–77 (April-June 2009) ; University de Coimbra
12. Boncz, P.A., Zukowski, M., Nes, N.: MonetDB/X100: Hyper-Pipelining Query Execution. In: CIDR (2005)
13. Olofson, C.: Worldwide RDBMS 2005 vendor shares. Technical Report 201692, IDC (May 2006)
14. Vesset, D.: Worldwide data warehousing tools 2005 vendor shares. Technical Report 203229, IDC (August 2006)
15. Boncz, P.A., Manegold, S., Kersten, M.L.: Database Architecture Optimized for the New Bottleneck: Memory Access. In: VLDB (1999)
16. Copeland, G.P., Khoshafian, S.: A Decomposition Storage Model. In: SIGMOD (1985)
17. Grund, M., Krueger, J., Plattner, H.: HYRISE—A Main Memory Hybrid Storage Engine. In: VLDB 2010, Singapore, September 13-17 (2010)
18. Titman, P.J.: An Experimental DataBase System Using Binary: Relations. In: IFIP Working Conference Data Base Management (1974)

Vertical Fragmentation of XML Data Warehouses Using Frequent Path Sets

Doulkifli Boukraâ[1], Omar Boussaïd[2], and Fadila Bentayeb[2]

[1] High School of Computer Science, Oued-Smar, Algiers
d_boukraa@esi.dz
[2] Lumière University - Lyon 2, 5 avenue Pierre Mendès-France, 69676 Bron Cedex
{omar.boussaid,fadila.bentayeb}@univ-lyon2.fr

Abstract. Horizontal and vertical fragmentation have been intensively studied for relational and object databases and recently for XML data. However, little work has been done on XML warehouses. In this paper, we address the problem of vertical fragmentation of XML Warehouses. We use Association Rules to partition and cluster frequent path sets into fragments. In addition, at the schema level, we address and solve the problem of reconstructing the original non-fragmented schema to ensure the fragmentation reversibility. At the data level, we propose a data organization within fragments to optimize joint operations. Finally, we present implementation details and show the benefits of our approach over the non-fragmented schema.

Keywords: XML warehouse, vertical fragmentation, frequent path set.

1 Introduction

With the increasingly widespread use of XML in companies, huge amounts of XML data are manipulated. The need to extract valuable knowledge from XML data has naturally emerged and has given rise to XML warehouses [19]. In XML warehouses, performance remains a key issue and performance enhancement techniques, such as indexes and view materialization [13], need to be adapted to cope with XML peculiarities. Among these techniques, we focus on fragmentation. Fragmentation has been intensively studied for relational and object databases and recently for data warehouses and XML data. However, little work has been done on XML warehouses. In relational databases, there are three fragmentation schemes [21]: (i) horizontal fragmentation (HF) where each fragment consists of a subset of the tuples of a relation R, (ii) vertical fragmentation (VF) where each fragment is designed as the projection of a relation on a subset of its attributes and (iii) hybrid fragmentation which is the combination of HF and VF. For a fragmentation to be correct, it has to meet three conditions [21]: (i) *Completeness*, i.e. each tuple in the case of a HF or each attribute in the case of a VF must be assigned to a fragment, (ii) *Disjointness*, i.e. all the fragments are disjoint and (iii) *Reconstruction*, i.e. the original relation can be reconstructed. This last property ensures the fragmentation reversibility. On the other hand,

A. Cuzzocrea and U. Dayal (Eds.): DaWaK 2011, LNCS 6862, pp. 196–207, 2011.

fragmentation is often associated with allocation to allow for parallel processing and load balancing [21]. For relational databases, Ma et al (2006) [16] use a heuristic to derive the fragmentation schema by combining query and site information. Gorla and Wing Yan (2008) [10] adopt association rules to derive candidate fragmentation schemes, then select the best schema. Fragmentation approaches can be driven by a cost model, expressed as an objective function and using different parameters such as cache sizes [11] and query statistics [4]. Ma and Kirchberg (2007) tackle the problem of vertical fragmentation in complex value databases [14]. The authors propose to add internal indexes to solve the problem of fragmentation reversibility. In the context of data warehouses, fragmentation can be logical or physical [13] and may target the basic data [3] or the aggregated data [2]. For instance, Wu and Buchmann (1997) propose to partition the fact table according to its dimensions [22] whereas Golfarelli et al (2000) apply VF to logical aggregated views of data [9]. The fragmentation techniques have been adapted to XML data. Buneman et al (2005) address the problem by totally vectorizing XML and by separating data from structure [8]. In [15], Ma and Schewe (2003) adapt HF and VF to XML. In addition, they define a new XML-specific fragmentation type called *split*, which consists of extracting XML fragments from XML documents, and replacing them by references. Bremer and Getz (2006) [7] define a sub-language of XPath to specify the fragments. They divide a document into two parts: a lower part that contains the fragments and an upper part that acts as a hook to the lower part. In [12], Hartmann et al (2007) developed a cost model for VF. They use, among others, estimations of the intermediate cost of results depending on the type of XML data and on the query operation being performed. As for relational databases, other work on XML fragmentation can be driven by system parameters, such as fragment width, depth and size [5]. For XML Warehouses, to our knowledge, fragmentation has been addressed only in [17] and [20]. In [17], a horizontal fragmentation is proposed using *K-means* to partition and cluster XML fragments based on selection predicates. The approach proposed in [20] deals with multi-version XML data warehouses. Partitioning can be document-based where a fact document is split into sub-documents having the same structure or schema-based where the fact is split into sub-facts having different structures.

To our knowledge, except for [20], VF is still unaddressed for XML warehouses. As for relational databases, VF is more complex than HF. In the case of XML data, the problem is even more complex for many reasons. First, XML queries may target different levels of a same path and some paths can be contained in others, which is contradictory to the disjointness property. Secondly, the reconstruction property becomes an issue when nested XML elements have multiple occurrences. Finally, in the case of XML warehouses, VF adds up to complexity since the number of joins of the warehouse model will explode. In this paper, we address these problems. Our work builds on the assumption that the impact of VF on joins can be reduced if the XML paths that are frequently accessed together are grouped into the same fragments. However, we need to take account of XML specificities to ensure disjointness and reconstruction. The rest

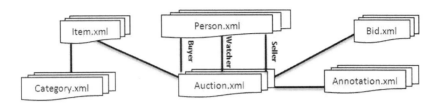

Fig. 1. The XML Warehouse Model

of this paper is organized as follows. In section 2, we present the XML warehouse model and formulate the problem of vertical fragmentation. The fragmentation approach is presented in section 3. In section 4, we present experiments and results. Finally, we conclude and present future work directions.

2   Background

In this section, we outline the necessary background for our approach. We first present the XML warehouse model that we aim to fragment. Then we discuss some XML specificities and we formalize the fragmentation problem.

2.1   XML Warehouse Model

Due to the absence of a standard model for XML warehouses [19], we base our work on the XML warehouse model that we proposed in [6]. In a nutshell, our model is snowflake-like. However, instead of being composed of structured tables, it is composed of XML collections. A collection represents either the fact or a dimension member and contains well-formed XML documents that conform to a same XML schema. In our model, we treat the fact and dimensions equally with regards to fragmentation and we refer to them as *objects*. Figure 1 pictures the XML warehouse model that we will use throughout the paper. The model is adapted from the XMark benchmark project[1] and allows for analyzing **current prices** and **final prices** of **auctions** along the dimensions of **seller, watcher, buyer, item, bid** and **annotation**. Notice the presence of a hierarchy composed of **item** and **category** and that **seller, watcher** and **buyer** are dimension roles related to the same object **person**. Figure 2 zooms into objects **auction, item** and **category** and shows a subset of their structure. A rounded rectangle represents XML Elements, a circle represents XML Attributes and a triangle represents a text node. Particularly, a gray rectangle represents non-terminal XML elements, meaning that the elements are complex-typed and can be further detailed. A black circle represents the identifier of an object to differentiate its instances and a gray circle serves as a linking mechanism between the objects of the model. In what follows, we refer to the black and gray circles respectively as *primary* and *foreign keys*.

---

[1] http://www.xml-benchmark.org/

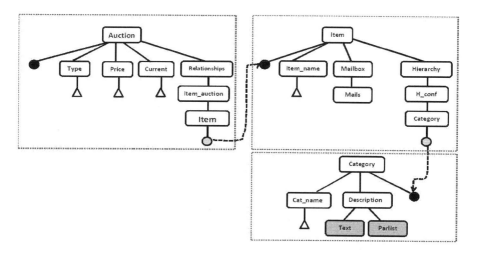

Fig. 2. Examples of object structures

Our model allows to perform OLAP analyzes as in a classical data warehouse model. However, two majors specificities of our model are worth noting. First, the fact and dimension members are not flat but have a hierarchical structure. Thus, a measure or a dimension parameter is accessed via an XML path. For instance, the measure `current` is accessible via `auction/current` whereas the mails concerning items are accessible via `item/mailbox/mails`. Secondly, since XML adds semantics to data, each level in an XML path can be viewed as a descriptive property of the object. Thus, OLAP queries may target different levels of a same path. Further, the properties may be disjointed or contained in each other. For instance, we can describe the object `category` by the paths `item/description`, `item/description/text` and `item/description/parlist`.

2.2   Problem Formulation

In [18], it is stated that vertical partitioning is complex because if a relation has m non-primary key attributes, the number of possible fragments is equal to $B(m)$ which is the mth Bell number. The aforementioned peculiarities of XML add to the complexity of VF. In fact, the path containment between properties of an object is contradictory with the disjointness condition of VF. Furthermore, as data analysis makes intensive use of join operations in a data warehouse, fragmenting each object of the warehouse model will lead to multiplying the number of joins. For instance, if `auction` is fragmented into two fragments, the maximum number of joins jumps from 7 to 13. The problem can be formulated as follows. Given the following

- an XML Warehouse Schema XWS, composed of a set of nb_obj objects, i.e. $XWS = \{Obj_i / i = 1...nb\_obj\}$. For instance, in the auction warehouse model, $XWS = \{auction, person, item, category, bid, annotation\}$.

- the objects in XWS are linked by p links, which is also the maximum number of joins. In our example, there are seven links, six of which link the fact to dimensions and the remaining one links two hierarchy members.
- Each object Obj_i is described as a set of XML rooted paths, i.e. $Obj_i = \{PATH_r^{Obj_i}\}$, that may be overlapping. In our example, the object category is described by the set of paths {category, category/@id, category/description, category/description/text, category/description/parlist}.
- A query load QL composed of m queries, i.e. $QL = \{Q_j/j = 1..m\}$.
- Each query Q_j is abstracted as a set of paths belonging to different objects, i.e. $Q_j = \{PATH_t^{Q_j}\}$.

We then aim at finding a fragmentation schema composed of nb_fg fragments, i.e. $FS = \{FG_i/i = 1...nb\_fg\}$ such as (i) FS is correct with respect to disjointness, completeness and reconstruction and (ii) the total cost of running QL against FS is less than the cost of running it against XWS. That is, $Cost(QL_{/FS}) < Cost(QL_{/XWS})$.

3   Fragmentation Approach

The major drawback of VF is the number of fragments it generates, and thereby the number of necessary joins to put back together the distributed properties. This drawback can be minimized if the properties are grouped based on the frequency of their co-occurrences in the queries. We generalize this principle to the context of data warehouses. The main idea is that although new joins will occur in the fragmented schema, some existing joins may disappear if the properties that originate from different objects are grouped into the same fragments. Nevertheless, in some cases, even grouping is not enough and data need to be further organized to avoid self-joins within objects.

3.1   Fragmentation Process

The input of fragmentation is the XML warehouse schema and data and a set of XML path queries. Its output(s) is a fragmented schema and its data. The process consists of (1) pruning the set of path queries, (2) grouping the paths based on the frequency of their co-occurrences, (3) deriving the fragmentation schemes (FS)s and selecting the best schema and (4) populating the best FS from the XML warehouse.

3.2   Pruning the Set of Path Queries

This step aims at preventing the creation of overlapping fragments, which contrasts with *disjointness*. Pruning the set of queries consists in deleting some paths so that no path is contained in another. For instance, if the set of queries contains the paths category, category/description, category/description/ text and category/ description/parlist, there are three possible sets of non-overlapping paths: {category}, {category/description}, {category/description/ text, category/description/parlist}. XML path pruning them can be automated. For instance, we can keep the most frequent path amongst the overlapping paths with the other non-overlapping paths and delete all the overlapping ones. For example, if category/description/text is the most frequent path, we keep it along with category/description/parlist and we delete category and category/description. It is worth noting that the paths we deal with do not necessarily target text nodes or attributes. For instance, the path category/ description/ parlist, represented in figure 2 by a gray rectangle means that element **parlist** is taken as a whole and will not be subject to VF.

3.3   Grouping the Paths

The second step is to group the paths based on the frequency of their co-occurences. For this purpose, we adopt a similar approach to [10] but we depart from it by using paths instead of relation attributes. We use association rules to discover the frequent path sets, from which we derive the fragmentation schema. To do this, we need to transform the pruned set of queries into a transactional format: each query corresponds to a transaction whereas each XML path corresponds to an item. Then, a frequent itemset corresponds to a group of XML paths, refered to as frequent pathset.

3.4   Deriving the Fragmentation Schema

Once the association rules activity completed, we get the frequent pathsets (FPS). A fragmentation schema is composed of many fragments where each one is the equivalent of a combination of disjoint FPSs. Since the FPSs are not generally disjoint, we need to select only disjoint ones to meet the disjointness property. Yet, there are two kinds of paths we need to be pay attention to: paths targeting primary keys, denoted by PKPs, and those targeting foreign keys, denoted by FKPs. As we saw earlier, vertical fragmentation inevitably induces a duplication of the primary keys and foreign keys in the fragmented schema. Hence, when checking the disjointness of the FPSs, we have to decide whether or not to consider the PKPs and PKPs for the role they play or as normal paths. We can distinguish when analyzing the FPSs. (i) Treat the PKPs and FKPs as normal paths when checking for FPSs disjointness. The idea is that we may obtain fragments that are composed only of PKPs and of FKPs if necessary. Such fragments are beneficial for Rollup/Drill down operations which naturally use primary and foreign keys. Yet, this choice may lead to many fragments in the fragmented schema. (ii) Skip the PKPs and FKPs. The idea is that in a fragmented schema, the disjointness property does not apply to these special attributes. As stated in [18], "as long as the fragments are disjoint except for the key attributes, we can be satisfied and call them disjoint".

Whatever the choice, the subsequent steps remain the same. The process of deriving the partitions is as follows. We sort the FPSs in descending order based on their cardinality. We derive all possible combinations of the disjoint FPSs having cardinality k where k is the maximum cardinality of FPSs. Each combination gives rise to a fragment. Then, we complete each fragment by all possible combinations of k-1 FPS. In this case, we check the disjointness amongst the k-1 FPSs and the current fragment simultaneously. We repeat the process until we reach 1 FPSs. After deriving the fragmentation schema, we complete it by the missing paths from the XML Warehouse schema. There are two kinds of missing paths. (i) Paths belonging to the XML Warehouse schema but that do not appear in any FPS. In this case, we group the missing paths of each object into a new fragment. The creation of these new fragments ensures the *completeness* of fragmentation. (ii) The PKPs and FKPs. The PKPs are added to all fragments if they do not already exist whereas the FKPs are added if they are necessary and do not already exist. For each object of the XML warehouse, its primary key is duplicated in each of its corresponding fragments to ensure the *reversibility* of fragmentation whereas the FKPs are added to preserve all the links between the fact and dimensions or between subsequent hierarchy members. The process of deriving the fragments from the FPSs is expressed with the following algorithm. The algorithm may result in many fragmentation schemes. The best one will be selected using a cost model, which we will not detail here.

Data:
- $SFS := \{\Phi\}$: the set of fragmentation schemes FS
- C : a combination of disjoint FPSs
- SC : the set of path combinations
- K : the cardinality of the biggest FPSs
- $Si - FPS$: the set of FPSs of cardinality i

Result: SFS : the set of fragmentation schemes
for $i := K$ *down to* 1 **do**
    for $FS_j \in SFS$ **do**
        $SC :=$ Derive_Disjoint_Combination $(FS_j, Si - FPS)$ /*deriving all disjoint combinations */;
        for *each* Cm *in* SC **do**
            | $FS_m := FS_j \cup C_m$ /*create a new fragment */;
        end
        ;
        Replace $(FS_j, FS_j, C_m/m = 1, ...)$ /*replace PS_j by the new fragments */;
    end
end

Algorithm 1. Deriving the fragmentation schema from the frequent path sets

3.5   Populating the Fragments

In this section, we provide details on how to organize data in fragments. Data organization depends on the content of the fragment. There are two cases: (i) the fragment is formed by properties that belong to the same object of the original warehouse schema; the fragment is said to be *homogeneous* and (ii) the fragment is made of properties belonging to different objects; the fragment is said to be *mixed*. We treat each case separately.

Homogeneous Fragment.   A homogeneous fragment has as many entries as its corresponding object. Each entry (instance) of the fragment is directly populated from its corresponding entry in the object. However, due to XML peculiarities, the problem of reconstruction occurs again even though we have added primary and foreign keys. To illustrate this problem, let us suppose two paths a/b/c and a/b/d of an object which, after fragmentation, belong to two different fragments, say FG_1 and FG_2. Figure 3 shows the original entries of the object on the left hand and the entries in fragments FG_1 and FG_2. In this case, because element b is multivalued, we lose the link between values of elements c and d, i.e. c1 with d1 and c2 and d2. This problem is similar to vertical fragmentation of complex value databases [14]. To solve this problem, we use a similar approach as [14] which we adapt to XML. Thus, for each path in each fragment, we check the multiplicity of each element node. If the node is multiple-valued, we add an ID-typed XML attribute to the node in the fragment and to the corresponding node in the original schema, unless such attribute already exists. Then, we update the data of the original schema with incremental values for the new added IDs.

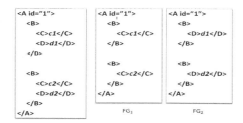

Fig. 3. Example of data organization problem in homogeneous fragments

Mixed Fragment.   In a mixed fragment, the properties originate from different objects. The objects in question may be disjoint in the original schema, such as objects **person** and **category** or they can be directly linked such as **auction** and **person** or **item** and **category**. In case a fragment contains properties from disjoint objects, the number of its entries is the sum of entry numbers of each object. In the second case, we can adopt the same data organisation as in the first case. Even better, since the content of the fragment originates from linked objects, we can further leverage the fragmentation by reorganizing data in the fragment. For instance, let us suppose the properties originate from two joined objects Obj_1 and Obj_2 where a foreign key in Obj_1 references the primary key in Obj_2. The idea is then to embed under each entry of Obj_1 the corresponding entries of Obj_2 using a semi join. The non-corresponding entries of Obj_2 will be kept as separate entries in the fragment. We generalize this principle for any number of joined objects in a fragment. Figure 4 illustrates the case of a mixed fragment made of joint objects `item` and `category`. On the left hand, the figure depicts data organization of two entries of each object in the original schema and to the right hand it shows data organization. Doing so, we avoid joining entries of `item` and `category` to obtain information both on items and categories.

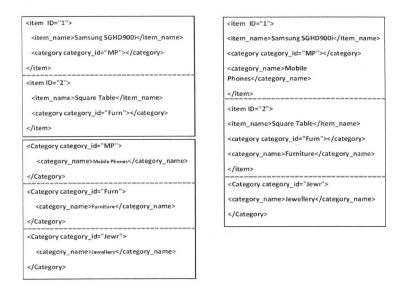

Fig. 4. Example of data organization in mixed fragments

4   Experimentation

We built an XML warehouse by transforming a single XML document, generated from the XMark project through an ETL process. The warehouse model is the same as in figure 1. It describes 192 auctions, 624 bids, 254 persons, 217 items, 98 annotations and 10 categories, stored as XML object tables under Oracle 11g Rel 2. We used *A priori* algorithm [1] as part of Oracle Data Miner 11.1.0.3.0 with a minimum support of 20% and a minimum confidence of 50% [10].

4.1   Workload

The query load is composed of 100 XML-OLAP queries with an average number of 13 XML paths per query and an average number of 2.92 of joins. Also, because

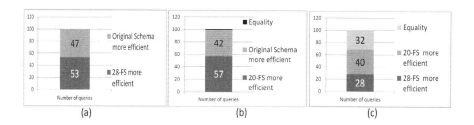

Fig. 5. Query efficiency distribution

the measures `current price` and `final price` are exclusive, each fifty queries target one measure. The transactional form of the query load has 1303 entries. The *A priori* algorithm produced 566 frequent pathsets, distributed as follows: 251 4-FPSs, 202 3-FPSs, 91 2-FPSs and 22 1-FPSs. We derived the fragmentation schemes according to the algorithm of section 3.4. We first treated the PKPs and FKPs as normal paths. The result was one fragmentation schema only, because of the few number of disjoint FPSs. The schema is composed of 28 fragments; we refer to it as 28-FS. The object `person` is the most fragmented object (10 fragments) as it is the most accessed due to its dimension roles. Also, the two exclusive measures `current price` and `final prise` fall into two different fragments, which was expected as they are never queried together. We reapplied the algorithm skipping the PKPs and FKPs. The result was also one fragmentation schema. As expected, the schema has fewer fragments than 28-FS; it is composed of 20 fragments and we refer to it as 20-FS. Then we rewrote the 100 queries against 28-FS and 20-FS.

4.2 Results and Discussion

To assess the benefit of our approach, we first compare each FS to the non-fragmented schema (NFS), then we compare 28-FS to 20-FS. As a measure of comparison, we counted the number of queries for which each schema has a better response time. In figure 5, we report the results. In (a), we compare 28-FS to NFS: 28-FS has better response times for **53%** of the queries against **47%** for NFS. In (b), we compare 20-FS to NFS: 20-FS has better response times for **57%** of the queries against **43%** for NFS. In (c), we compare 28-FS to 20-FS: 20-FS is more efficient for **40%** of the queries against **28%** for 28-FS. For the rest of the queries, the two schemata show equal response times. To summarize, the fragmentation enhances the response time for more than half of the queries on the one hand. On the other hand, treating the PKPs and FPKs as key paths results in a better fragmentation schema. A deep analysis of the nature of queries that make each schema efficient produced the following results. The fragmentation is **less** efficient when the most fragmented object, namely `person`, is queried for few properties or when it is discarded. On the contrary, fragmentation yields **better** results for grouping queries, i.e queries that target small fragments and when these fragments are made up of paths that occur in the grouping clause. Further, although the 20-FG has more efficient queries than 28-FS, the latter one performs better for join queries, since in this schema, many fragments are composed only of PKPs and FKPs, which are the only necessary paths needed for the joins.

5 Conclusion

In this paper, we have proposed a vertical fragmentation approach for XML warehouses using association rules. We addressed some XML specificities with regards to *disjointness* and *reconstruction*. We solved the problem of reconstruction by duplicating the XML paths that represent primary and foreign keys and by adding ID-typed attributes within the multivalued element nodes. We ensured disjointness by pruning the set of paths on the one hand. On the other hand, we proposed an algorithm to derive disjoint fragments from the frequent path-sets. As expected, the fragmentation enhances a portion of the query load. The non-fragmented schema remains better for queries that extract the basic data from the data warehouse. However, since OLAP queries perform many joins and groupings, we believe the fragmentation to be more efficient since the joins are performed on small fragments and grouping usually requires primary and foreign keys only. At this stage of our work, we validated our approach experimentally. For future work, we plan to develop a cost model that takes into account the number of joins and the sizes of fragments and intermediate results. In addition, we intend to combine the cost model with the cost of XML path access, which depends among others on the path length. We also aim at automatizing query rewriting against the fragmented schema. In fact, some queries target disjoint objects only and require performing intermediate joins. The choice of the intermediate fragments to use as *bridges* is not always systematic.

References

1. Agrawal, R., Imielinski, T., Swami, A.N.: Mining association rules between sets of items in large databases. In: SIGMOD Conference, pp. 207–216 (1993)
2. de Aguiar Ciferri, C.D., Ciferri, R.R., Forlani, D.T., Traina, A.J.M., da Fonseca de Souza, F.: Horizontal fragmentation as a technique to improve the performance of drill-down and roll-up queries. In: Proceedings of the 2007 ACM Symposium on Applied Computing (SAC), Seoul, Korea, March 11-15, pp. 494–499. ACM, New York (2007)
3. Almeida, R., Vieira, J., Vieira, M., Madeira, H., Bernardino, J.: Efficient data distribution for DWS. In: Song, I.-Y., Eder, J., Nguyen, T.M. (eds.) DaWaK 2008. LNCS, vol. 5182, pp. 75–86. Springer, Heidelberg (2008)
4. Amossen, R.R.: Vertical partitioning of relational oltp databases using integer programming. In: Workshops Proceedings of the 26th International Conference on Data Engineering, ICDE 2010, March 1-6, pp. 93–98. IEEE, Los Alamitos (2010)
5. Bonifati, A., Cuzzocrea, A.: Efficient fragmentation of large XML documents. In: Wagner, R., Revell, N., Pernul, G. (eds.) DEXA 2007. LNCS, vol. 4653, pp. 539–550. Springer, Heidelberg (2007)

6. Boukraa, D., Messaoud, R.B., Boussaid, O.: Open and novel issues in XML database applications: future directions and advanced technologies. In: Modeling XML Warehouses for Complex Data: The New Issues, pp. 108–135. IGI Global, Information Science Reference, USA/UK (2009)

7. Bremer, J.-M., Gertz, M.: On distributing xml repositories. In: International Workshop on Web and Databases, San Diego, California, June 12-13, pp. 73–78 (2003)

8. Buneman, P., Choi, B., Fan, W., Hutchison, R., Mann, R., Viglas, S.: Vectorizing and querying large xml repositories. In: Proceedings of the 21st International Conference on Data Engineering, ICDE 2005, Tokyo, Japan, April 5-8, pp. 261–272. IEEE Computer Society, Los Alamitos (2005)

9. Golfarelli, M., Maio, D., Rizzi, S.: Applying vertical fragmentation techniques in logical design of multidimensional databases. In: Kambayashi, Y., Mohania, M., Tjoa, A.M. (eds.) DaWaK 2000. LNCS, vol. 1874, pp. 11–23. Springer, Heidelberg (2000)

10. Gorla, N., Yan, B.P.W.: Vertical fragmentation in databases using data-mining technique. International Journal of Data Warehousing and Mining 4(3), 35–53 (2008)

11. Grankov, M.V., Hung, N.T.: New objective function for vertical partitioning in database system. In: Proceedings of the SYRCODIS 2008 Colloquium on Databases and Information Systems, Saint-Petersburg, Russia, May 29-30. CEUR Workshop Proceedings, CEUR-WS.org, vol. 355 (2008)

12. Hartmann, S., Ma, H., Schewe, K.-D.: Cost-based vertical fragmentation for XML. In: Chang, K.C.C., Wang, W., Chen, L., Ellis, C.A., Hsu, C.-H., Tsoi, A.C., Wang, H. (eds.) APWeb/WAIM 2007. LNCS, vol. 4537, pp. 12–24. Springer, Heidelberg (2007)

13. Lin, B., Hong, Y., Lee, Z.H.: Data Warehouse Performance. In: Encyclopedia of Data Warehousing and Mining, 2nd edn., pp. 580–585. IGI Publishing, Hershey (2009)

14. Ma, H., Kirchberg, M.: Cost-based fragmentation for distributed complex value databases. In: Parent, C., Schewe, K.-D., Storey, V.C., Thalheim, B. (eds.) ER 2007. LNCS, vol. 4801, pp. 72–86. Springer, Heidelberg (2007)

15. Ma, H., Schewe, K.D.: Fragmentation of xml documents. In: XVIII Simpósio Brasileiro de Bancos de Dados, 6-8 de Outubro, Manaus, Amazonas, Brasil, Anais/Proceedings, pp. 200–214. UFAM (2003)

16. Ma, H., Schewe, K.D., Kirchberg, M.: A heuristic approach to fragmentation incorporating query information. In: Databases and Information Systems IV - Selected Papers from the Seventh International Baltic Conference, DB & IS 2006, Frontiers in Artificial Intelligence and Applications, Vilnius, Lithuania, July 3-6, vol. 155, pp. 103–116. IOS Press, Amsterdam (2006)

17. Mahboubi, H., Darmont, J.: Data mining-based fragmentation of xml data warehouses. In: Song, I.Y., Abelló, A. (eds.) Proceedings of the ACM 11th International Workshop on Data Warehousing and OLAP, Napa Valley, California, USA, pp. 9–16. ACM, New York (2008)

18. Ozsu, M.T., Valduriez, P.: Principles of Distributed Database Systems, 3rd edn. Springer, Heidelberg (2011)

19. Ravat, F., Teste, O., Tournier, R., Zurfluh, G.: Finding an application-appropriate model for xml data warehouses. Inf. Syst. 35(6), 662–687 (2010)

20. Rusu, L.I., Rahayu, J.W., Taniar, D.: Partitioning methods for multi-version xml data warehouses. Distributed and Parallel Databases 25(1-2), 47–69 (2009)

21. Tan, K.L.: Distributed database design. In: Encyclopedia of Database Systems, pp. 890–894. Springer, US (2009)

22. Wu, M.C., Buchmann, A.P.: Research issues in data warehousing. In: BTW, pp. 61–82 (1997)

Implementing Vertical Splitting for Large Scale Multidimensional Datasets and Its Evaluations

Takayuki Tsuchida, Tatsuo Tsuji, and Ken Higuchi

Graduate School of Engineering, University of Fukui
Fukui 910-8507, Japan
tsuchida@pear.fuis.u-fukui.ac.jp,
{tsuji,higuchi}@u-fukui.ac.jp

Abstract. History-offset encoding we are proposing is a scheme for encoding multidimensional datasets. In general, significant problems in implementing multidimensional databases include the saturation of address space for addressing multidimensional data. One of the solutions against this problem is splitting the dimension attributes of the multidimensional data into more than one group; i.e., vertical splitting. We have implemented the vertical splitting scheme for large scale multidimensional datasets based on the history-offset encoding. In this paper, we describe implementation of the constructed prototype system and experimentally evaluate and compare the system with other systems. These systems include PostgreSQL, which is a relational DBMS conventionally implemented, and UB tree, which is organized in a similar kind of multidimensional approach with our history-offset encoding. The evaluation results prove that our vertical splitting scheme can reduce retrieval I/O cost, while expanding the required logical address space to store large scale multidimensional datasets. Our method far outperforms PostgreSQL and is fairly better than UB tree in retrieval time. The splitting causes increase of storage cost but the cost is not so large compared with those of them.

Keywords: multidimensonal data, address space, vertical splitting, large scale dataset, history-offset encoding.

1 Introduction

Handling multidimensional data efficiently is a key technology for various multidimensional data application areas, such as scientific computations, multidimensional analysis for data mining or image processings. It has been promoting extensive research themes on organization or implementation schemes for multidimensional data structures on computer memory or secondary storage.

Amongst the data structures the fast random accessing capability that is characteristic to multidimensional arrays enables scientific or aggregation computations to be performed efficiently on stored data. Thus, multidimensional arrays have been important data structures for storing large scale multidimensional data, e.g., in scientific computations or.

However, such kind of multidimensional arrays suffer from the problem that each dimension size is fixed in order to be benefited by fast random addressing functions

A. Cuzzocrea and U. Dayal (Eds.): DaWaK 2011, LNCS 6862, pp. 208–223, 2011.

of arrays. A notion of *extendible array* has been proposed in literatures to solve this problem inherent in usual fixed size of multidimensional arrays. An extendible array can extend its size along any dimensions without relocation of any array elements.

History-offset encoding [7] is a scheme for encoding multidimensional datasets based on the notion of extendible arrays. Records in a relational table R can be a multidimensional dataset, and each column of R is mapped to a dimension of the corresponding extendible multidimensional array and each record of R is mapped to its corresponding coordinate in the array. The encoding avoids poor storage utilization, which is common in implementing multidimensional datasets in computer storage using multidimensional arrays. Moreover it enables fast accessing to multidimensional data, while preserving the extendibility along every dimension.

UB tree [8] is another excellent multidimensional data organization and provides fast multidimensional access method. But the method has a critical shortcoming that the parameters of an UB tree (e.g. the range of column value to be inserted) needs to be set before tree construction for address mapping [11]. As we described in section 6, the requirement restricts the usability and performance of UB tree. Such restriction is not shared in our organization scheme based on the history-offset encoding due to the flexible extension capability of an extendible array.

Unfortunately however, significant problems in implementing multidimensional datasets include the saturation of address space for addressing or encoding multidimensional data. We already provided the method to solve this problem by vertically splitting multidimensional data [7]. Various schemes of splitting relational tables have been proposed (e.g., [2][3][9]) aiming the performance improvement of table manipulation. We have implemented the vertical splitting scheme for large scale multidimensional datasets based on the history-offset encoding.

In this paper, we describe implementation of the constructed prototype system and experimentally evaluate and compare the system with other systems. These systems include PostgreSQL, which is a relational DBMS conventionally implemented, and UB tree, which is organized in a similar kind of multidimensional approach with our history-offset encoding. The evaluation results prove that our vertical splitting scheme can reduce retrieval I/O cost, while expanding the required logical address space to store large scale multidimensional datasets. Our method far outperforms PostgreSQL and is fairly better than UB tree in retrieval time. The splitting causes increase of storage cost but the cost is not so large compared with those of them.

2   Employing Extendible Arrays

In this section, the concept of *extendible array* we employ is described. In order to be benefited by the fast random accessing capability of multidimensional arrays, their sizes should be fixed in every dimension; i.e., to store a new dimension value, array size extension along the dimension is necessary and this implies total reorganization of the existing array data according to the modified addressing function. To solve the problem, an extendible array can be employed and the array is extendible in any direction/dimension without any relocation of the data already stored. This advantage makes an extendible array to be applied to wider application area, where necessary array size cannot be predicted. Our extendible array is based on the index array model presented in [5]. An n dimensional extendible array A has a history counter h and three kinds of auxiliary table for each extendible dimension $i(i=1,...,n)$. See Fig.1. These tables are *history table* H_i, *address table* L_i, and *coefficient table* C_i. The history tables memorize extension history. If the size of A is $[s_1, s_2, ... , s_n]$, for an extension of A along dimension i, contiguous memory area that forms an $n-1$ dimensional subarray S of size $[s_1, s_2,...,s_{i-1}, s_{i+1},..., s_{n-1}, s_n]$ is dynamically allocated. Then the current history counter value is incremented by one, and it is memorized on H_i, also the first address of S is held on L_i. Since h increases monotonously, H_i is an ordered set of history values. Note that an extended subarray is one to one corresponding with its history value, so the subarray is uniquely identified by its history value.

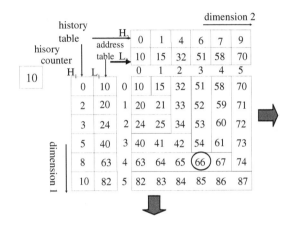

Fig. 1. A two dimensional extendible array

As is well known, element $<i_1, i_2, ..., i_{n-1}>$ in an $n\text{-}1$ dimensional fixed size array of size $[s_1, s_2, ..., s_{n-1}]$ is allocated on memory using addressing function like:

$$f(i_1, ..., i_{n-1})= s_2s_3 ...s_{n-1}i_1+s_3s_4 ...s_{n-1}i_2+ ...+s_{n-1}i_{n-2}+i_{n-1} \qquad (1)$$

We call $(s_2s_3...s_{n-1}, s_3s_4...s_{n-1}, ..., s_{n-1})$ as a *coefficient vector*. Such a coefficient vector is computed at array extension and held in a coefficient table.

To illustrate the element accessing method, for example consider the element $<4,3>$ in Fig.1. Compare the history values $H_1[4]=8$ and $H_2[3]=6$. Since $H_1[4]>H_2[3]$, it can be proved that $<4,3>$ is involved in the subarray S corresponding to the history value $H_1[4]$ in the first dimension and the first address of S is found out in $L_1[4] =63$.

From the first address of S is computed as $63+3 =66$. Note that we can use such a simple computational scheme to access an extendible array element only at the cost of small auxiliary tables. The superiority of this scheme is shown in [5] compared with other schemes such as hashing [4].

3 HOMD Implementation Model

The model that we are going to present is based on the extendible array explained in Section 2. We already described the concept of extendible array. However, any existing extendible array models includes the model in Section 2 are not sufficient to solve the sparse problem, because consecutive storage area including non-effective array elements should be allocated to be benefited by fast random addressing function. Against this problem, data compression technique called *chunk-offset*[1] scheme is widely used, but the technique is applied only to the usual fixed size array .

For a relational table R with n columns, the corresponding logical structure of HOMD (History Offset implementation scheme for Multidimensional Datasets) is the pair (M, A). A is an n dimensional extendible array created for R and M is the set of mappings. Each m_i $(1 \leq i \leq n)$ in M maps the i-th column values of R to subscripts of dimension i of A. A will be often called as a *logical extendible array*. Each element of an n dimensional extendible array can be specified by its n dimensional coordinate. In HOMD model, each element can be specified by using the pair of history value and offset value. Note that since each history value h is unique and one-to-one correspondent with its corresponding subarray S, S is specified uniquely by its history value h. The offset value of each element in S is also unique in the subarray. Hence, an element of A can be referenced by (*history value, offset value*).

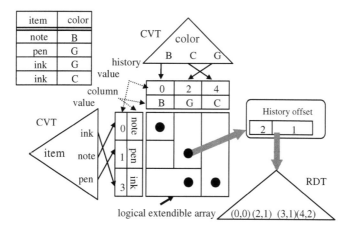

Fig. 2. HOMD physical structure

In the coordinate reference, if the dimensionality becomes higher, the length of the coordinate becomes longer and the storage for referencing records becomes large. On the contrary, in the history and offset reference, the size of the reference is always fixed in short. Moreover, this encoded reference also expresses the record itself, so it greatly saves storage requirements for implementing relational tables by HOMD and makes the internal record handling in DBMS more simple.

Each mapping m_i in M is implemented using a single B$^+$ tree called CVT, and A is implemented using a single B$^+$ tree called RDT and n HOMD tables, each of which is an extension of the three auxiliary tables of an extendible array in Section 2. Fig. 2 shows an example of a two dimensional HOMD data structure.

CVT: CVT_k for the k-th column of R is a B^+ tree with each distinct column value as a key and its associated data is subscript i of the k-th dimension of A. i references to the corresponding entry of the HOMD table.

HT: HT_k(HOMD Table) for the k-th dimension includes the history table and the coefficient table. Note that the address table can be void in our HOMD physical implementation. In addition, *column value* table used for decoding (*history, offset*) into its corresponding record is included.

HT is arranged according to the insertion order. For example, the column value "ink" is mapped to the subscript 2 as the insertion order, though in the sequence set of CVT, the key "ink" is in position 0 due to the property of B^+ tree. At insertion of a record, each column value in it is inserted into the corresponding CVT as a key. If the key doesn't exist, A is extended by one along the dimension.

RDT: The set of (*history, offset*) pairs for all effective elements in A is stored as the keys in RDT. RDT and HT implements A on the physical storage. We assume that a key (*history, offset*) occupies fixed size storage and *history* is arranged in front of *offset*. Hence the keys are arranged in the order of their history values and keys that have the same history value are located consecutively in the sequence set of RDT.

HOMD: For an n columns relational table, its HOMD implementation is the set of n CVTs, n HTs and RDT.

We can see that the two problems in Section 2 are alleviated in the HOMD model.

4   Chunked HOMD

If R has many columns or the column cardinality increases, the *history offset* space would overflow. This problem is very serious for applying our HOMD model to application areas that require large scale multidimensional datasets.

4.1   Chunking

It should be noted that in a subarray whose history value is small, the offset space of the subarray is little used since the subarray size is very small. For example, assume the length of the history and offset values be 32 bits and 64 bits respectively. Let a chunk be an n-dimensional hyper-cube shaped subarray of an n-dimensional extendible array. An extendible array discussed thus far can be partitioned into a set of such chunks. See Fig.3. This chunked extendible array can extend its size by adding not a subarray of elements but a subarray of chunks in arbitrary dimension. A chunk is numbered by the extended order as 0,1,2, …. The location of an element in an extendible array can be specified by the number of the chunk to which it belongs together with its offset in the chunk.

The chunk number is determined using the similar addressing scheme of an extendible array element. We say such an implementation scheme of an extendible array based on chunking as *chunked HOMD* abbreviated as C-HOMD. If we assume that the chunk number occupies 32 bits and an offset in a chunk occupies 64 bits, the maximum chunk size becomes 2^{64}. Hence the address space utilization extremely increases than in usual HOMD.

4.2   Structure of C-HOMD

In C-HOMD, the data structure corresponding to HOMD table is double layered. See Fig.3. This table of C-HOMD will be called a *C-HOMD table*. The lower layer of the table holds *chunk subarray information* and the upper layer holds column value. For a chunk subarray S, its information includes the history value, the first chunk number and the coefficient vector of S. Note that a history value and a coefficient vector are allocated for a chunk subarray not for an element subarray as in usual HOMD, so the storage space for these tables is greatly reduced. As in usual HOMD, key value of a CVT in C-HOMD is a column value, and its associated data value is the subscript of the upper layer of the C-HOMD table. It should be noted that the C-HOMD table is partitioned into the *sections* of chunk dimension size. For each record of a relational table, RDT of the C-HOMD stores the pair of the number of the chunk in which the record is involved and its offset within the chunk.

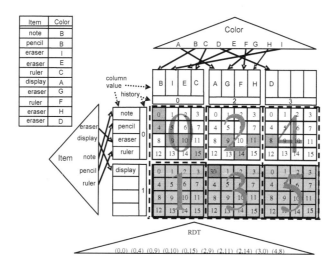

Fig. 3. C-HOMD structure

4.3   Encoding Records into RDT Keys in C-HOMD

Let $r = <v_1, v_2, ..., v_n>$ be a record of a table R. For r the corresponding key (*chunk number, offset*) stored in RDT can be computed as follows. Firstly, searching CVT of each column, the subscript values $<i_1, i_2, \ldots, i_n>$ of r are obtained. Chunk subarray Sc including chunk C containing element $<i_1, i_2, \ldots, i_n>$ is determined. Assume q be the chunk dimension size.

(i) Computing the *chunk number* of C

The subscript values of C in Sc can be computed as $<i_1/q, i_2/q, \ldots, i_n/q>$ (/ denotes the quotient of division). Since the chunks in Sc are arranged in the predefined order of the Sc's dimensions, the required chunk number can be computed by using $<i_1/q, i_2/q, \ldots, i_n/q>$.

(ii) Computing the element *offset* in the chunk

$<i_1\%q, i_2\%q, \ldots, i_n\%q>$ (% denotes the residue of division) are the subscripts of the array element to be accessed in chunk C determined in (i). The element offset in C can be computed by using $<i_1\%q, i_2\%q, \ldots, i_n\%q>$.

The pair (*chunk number, offset*) computed in (i) and (ii) becomes the encoded key in RDT. Conversely given a (*chunk number, offset*), it can be easily decoded to its corresponding subscripts $<i_1, i_2, \ldots, i_n>$. Note that in order to decode quickly, a one dimensional array HA is prepared on main memory. At extension of the extendible chunk array, for the history value h of the allocated chunk subarray, HA[h] memorizes the dimension d to which the chunk subarray belongs and its subscript value i_d/q.

4.4   Retrieval of Records

Let values of some columns in a table be specified in a retrieval query, and the corresponding dimensions be $d_1, d_2, \ldots, d_k$ and their values be $v_{d_1}, \ldots, v_{d_k}$. Let $h_{d_1}, \ldots, h_{d_k}$ be the history values of the chunk subarray that correspond to the subscripts $CVT_{d_1}(v_{d_1}), \ldots, CVT_{d_k}(v_{d_k})$ and the maximum history value be $h_{max} = \max(h_{d_1}, \ldots, h_{d_k})$. The chunk subarray corresponding to h_{max} is called as a *principal chunk subarray*. The first chunk of each chunk subarray is called as the *top chunk*. The top chunk of the principal chunk subarray is the chunk which has the smallest chunk number among those of the retrieval candidate chunks. In the case of retrieval for column value "display" in Fig. 3., top chunk number is 1. Let (*top chunk number, offset*) be a key in the sequence set of RDT.   From (*top chunk number, offset*), the corresponding tuple of the subscripts $<i_1, \ldots, i_n>$ in the extendible chunk array can be uniquely decoded. For (*top chunk number, offset*), by looking HA[h], we can locate the corresponding principal chunk subarray quickly. The subscripts of the dimensions other than d can be simply computed by repeated divisions by the respective coefficient in $HT_d[i_d]$.

The following property is important for retrieval of records in C-HOMD.

Property 1: Among the *known dimensions* only the principal subarray is a candidate for searching. The other candidate subarrays belong to the unknown dimensions and the history values of these subarrays are greater than that of the principal subarray.

This property leads to the *history value dependency* of retrieval time, namely, the smaller the corresponding subscript of the retrieval target column value is, the larger the number of subarrays to be searched is, hence more time consuming.

For the retrieval of RDT, let GTEQ be the flag that returns the smallest key greater than or equal to the specified key and NEXT be the one that returns the next key of the current one in the sequence set. Note that the keys having the same history value are arranged consecutively in the sequence set of RDT. Due to the paper limit, we only outline our retrieval methods. Searching is based on Property 1. It starts working from the root node of RDT with key value (*top chunk number, 0*) by GTEQ. Then sequential search is performed against all the keys in the principal subarray *PS* by NEXT. The keys matching the retrieval condition are included in the retrieval results. After that, the candidate subarrays other than *PS* will be searched and checked out. From Property 1, the history values of these candidate subarrays are greater than h_{max} and do not belong to the known dimensions; note that for the history value h of a subarray, its corresponding dimension can be known from HA[h]. When the searching of a candidate subarray is over, traversing internal nodes of the B$^+$ tree from the root node is performed in order to reach the next candidate chunk subarray. In this way, the key matching continues against the candidate chunk subarrays. In the case of previous example, the gray chunks are retrieval candidate in Fig. 3. Each chunk subarray may not include effective element (i.e. record) in spite of the chunk subarray is a candidate subarray to be searched. The cost of traversing from root node to each chunk subarray is not so small. In order to avoid empty chunk subarray access, we employ *bit array* for checking the condition of each chunk. If and only if the chunk includes effective record, boolean True is stored. Note that boolean true is stored per chunk but chunk subarray. Before the traversing from root node, bit array check is performed and when the corresponding value is true, the chunk subarray is obtained. The bit array is usually loaded in main memory. As an archive, only effective chunk number is stored and the storage cost of bit array is not large as will be presented in Section 6.

4.5   Handling Unique Key Columns

One of the reasons to accelerate the overflow of *chunk number-offset* space is the existence of a unique key column, which has no duplicate values. If a unique key column exists in *R*, whenever a new record is inserted, the logical extendible array is always extended along the key column dimension since its value should not be duplicated. So the corresponding extended subarray will include only a single record. Hence the chunk number and the array size soon become large, and the *chunk number-offset* space soon overflows.

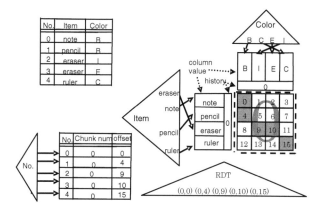

Fig. 4. C-HOMD structure with a unique key

To prevent this situation, they are separately handled from the other columns, and the corresponding extendible array consists of only non-unique columns. This strategy can contribute to delay the *chunk number-offset* space overflow. Fig.4 shows a C-HOMD data structure assuming "No." be a unique key column. The two non-unique columns, "Item" and "Color", constitute the corresponding C-HOMD data structure with a two dimensional extendible array. For the unique key column "No.", a unique key table T is constructed as a relational table implemented by the usual scheme; i.e. records in the table are arranged sequentially on the secondary storage. Each record in T consists of a unique key column value and a (*chunk number, offset*) pair included in RDT that is constructed from the other column values. Note that both the CVT for the unique key column and RDT include the record location in T as data value.

5   Splitting C-HOMD

C-HOMD scheme can provide much larger address space than the non-chunked one. But, it should be noted that the situation becomes harder in higher dimensionality. We can apply the splitting scheme into C-HOMD.

See Fig.5. If the (*chunk number, offset*) key space overflows by inserting a new column value, relational table R would be vertically split and the following reorganization of the original C-HOMD data structure would be triggered. The set of columns of R is divided into two sub-tables. For each of the sub-tables, corresponding new C-HOMD data structure is constructed; for each record of a sub-table its (*chunk number, offset*) key value is recomputed and stored in its corresponding RDT. In this situation, in order to maintain the correct correspondence between the two tables, a unique key table described in Section 4.5 is constructed even if there are no unique keys in R, in which the record number of R is an artificial unique key.

If one of the *chunk number-offset* spaces of the two divided C-HOMD data structures again overflows by succeeding record insertions, it would be further divided and reorganized. Thus each record in the unique key table stores unique key column values and two or more (*chunk number, offset*) pairs. Fig. 5 shows an example of splitting of R and its split HOMD implementation.

Using the above reorganized C-HOMD data structure, if a unique key column value is known, the other column values of the original table can be known without searching the divided RDTs. On the other hand, if a (*chunk number, offset*) key value of one of the RDTs can be known, all the other column values can be known by accessing the corresponding record in the unique key table. Note that even if no unique key columns exist in the original relational table, when overflow occurs by repeated record insertions, a unique key table is created at splitting. But each record of the table contains the pairs of (*chunk number, offset*) key value and the split RDTs contain the record locations in the unique key table as data values; this enables each column value of a record in the original relational table can be obtained by only accessing one of the RDTs.

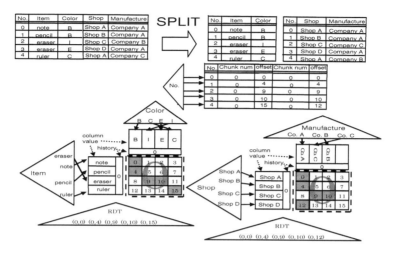

Fig. 5. Split C-HOMD data structure

The time cost of reorganizing C-HOMD data structure when the key space of RDT overflows would be much since all of the components of the C-HOMD data structure such as RDT should be reorganized. Also the space cost would increase due to the splitting of RDT. In order to delay the next possible occurrence of reorganization, we adopt a simple strategy to divide the set of columns into two subsets in order to let the product of the column cardinalities in each subset nearly equal. Note that the column cardinality can be known simply from the corresponding current dimension size of the extendible array.

The above reorganization would be repeatedly triggered by overflow of one of the current split tables, thus the original table would be able to contain its records unlimitedly regardless of the *chunk number-offset* space size.

6   Experimental Evaluations

In this section we compare the four kinds of the implementation model described in the previous sections of relational tables using a constructed prototype system. They are usual HOMD, C-HOMD, split HOMD and split C-HOMD abbreviated as HI, CHI, S-HI, and S-CHI respectively in the following. We also compare our implementation model with UB tree and PostgreSQL that will be abbreviated as Postgres. The experimental evaluation were performed on Sun Fire E4900 server (CPU: 64 bits UltraSparc IV (1050 Mhz), memory size: 48 GB, OS: Solaris 9) and the employed PostgreSQL version is 8.4.2 of 64 bits. We used GiMP[10] as UB tree (column type:float). It is a generalized framework for multidimensional index. Its implementation has been obtained from the author's web page at [14].

The configuration of the employed tables is as follows: total number of records (NR): 1,000,000, number of columns: 5, 6 or 8, column type: 32 bits integer, 32 bytes character string or 32 bits float, cardinality L_i of the i-th column : 1000~25000, duplicate factor $dp_i = NR/L_i$ of the i-th column: 40~1000.

6.1   Retrieval Cost

We have measured the retrieval time when the single column value is specified on a single dimension (range queries in the remaining dimensions). In our methods, due to the *history value dependency* stated in Property 1 in Section 4.4, the retrieval cost depends on the corresponding subscript of the retrieval target column value. For fair comparison, we varied the retrieval target column value and measured the retrieval times in order to average the retrieval time.

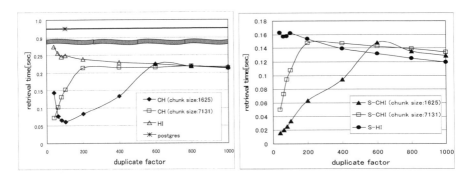

Fig. 6. Retrieval cost in 5 column table (a) CH, HI and postgres (b) S-CHI and S-HI

Fig.6-8 show the retrieval time comparison (time per retrieval) among the six models when a single column value is specified as the retrieval condition for a 5 column table (Fig. 6, Fig. 8) and, 6 or 8 column table (Fig. 7). In the case of Postgres, records would be stored in the input order, and its retrieval cost only depends on the total number of stored records. Therefore, the duplicate factor does not influence the retrieval time. On the contrary, in our schemes (HI, CHI, S-HI, S-CHI), the cost of retrieval depends on the duplicate factor, number of columns and chunk size in the case of CHI or S-CHI. In chunk based method, the chunking can restrict the logical range to be searched and the records stored in the same chunk can be read quickly because the records are placed consecutively on the *sequence set* of RDT. On the other hand, traversing from the root node to reach next chunk subarray takes much time since the disk seek time is dominate in disk I/O time. Thus the average number of records per chunk influences the retrieval performance in our method. Therefore, it is important to adjust chunk size according to the characteristics of the table data, namely, number of distinct column values(i.e., column cardinality) and number of columns(i.e., dimensionality) for efficient retrieval.

See Fig. 6. In the case of large duplicate factor (600~1000), number of distinct column values is smaller than the chunk size, and almost all records are stored in a single chunk. In consequence, there is not so much retrieval time difference among each model. On the other hand, in smaller duplicate factor (40~400), the cost of CHI (chunk size:1625) is low because there are many chunks and the number of records per chunk is appropriate. As a result, its chunk access (from the root) causes small time cost. By vertically splitting the relational table, the sum of chunks can be decreased and it leads to better retrieval cost for S-CHI and S-HI. In the same way, adjustment of chunk size is also effective to improve the retrieval cost for CHI (chunk size:7131). As the total number of chunks is depending on the product of each dimension size, if the number of columns increases, the total number of columns tends to be big. Thus, the retrieval time shown in Fig. 7 is generally bigger than in Fig. 6. In most cases, our method outperforms Postgres because in our methods, every record is encoded to only two values, namely (*chunk number, offset*) pair in RDT. Even the column type is char(32), the size of the pair can be suppressed in small.

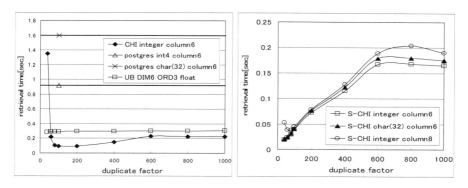

Fig. 7. (a) Retrieval cost in 6 column table (b) Retrieval cost in 6 or 8 column table

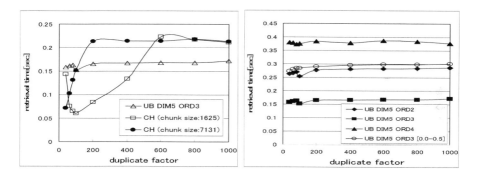

Fig. 8. Retrieval cost in 5 column table (column type:float) (a) CH and UB tree (b) UB tree

As Fig. 7 and Fig. 8 show, our methods outperform UB tree. The UB tree is the tree based on the Z-address [6], and bit-interleaving method [11] is often used for query performance improvement. In the method, several bits from first bit of each column value are combined to generate Z-address. We varied ORD which stands for the bit number to be used in Z-address generation (bit-interleaving). Note that we assume input data are normalized to $[0.0, 1.0]^d$ where d stands for number of columns in comparison between our methods and UB tree. The mapping method of UB tree includes severe shortcoming because the range of column value of input data can be very narrow. Thus, several bits might be the same value regarding all the input data. In case of column value range [0.0-0.5], first decimal place of Z-address source bit strings will be 0, and it means that the concentrated insertions to the restricted area in

UB tree. As Fig. 8 shows, it deteriorates retrieval performance of UB tree. Therefore, UB tree performance depends on the column value range. On the contrary, the range of column values doesn't matter with our methods.

6.2 Storage Cost

The storage costs in each model are shown in Fig. 9-10. In our schemes the required storage consists of the following several kinds of file:

tre file: RDT tree file, *uni file*: unique key table file described in Section 4.5, *save file*: HOMD or C-HOMD tables HTs described in Section 3, *bit array*: bit array descried in Section 4.4.

As the number of distinct column values increases, the size of HTs becomes large. As the result, the save file at dup 40 is five times larger than that at dup 1000. In C-HOMD, the size of HTs is far less than those of HOMD because the table information is stored per chunk (e.g coefficient vector) and not per array element. The costs of S-HI and S-CHI is about three times as large as those of HI and CHI due to the *tre file* for newly created table in the vertical table splitting, and *uni* file to connect split tables. In the case of chunk size 1625, the number of chunks which include effective record become large compared with the case of chunk size 7131. Ditto the size of *bit array* for chunks. According to the decrease of the number of distinct values(duplicate factor 1000), the storage cost of the *save file* decreases. On the contrary, the size of *skl file* includes same record information increases but the total storage size is as much as the case of duplicate 40.

Fig. 9 and Fig. 10 show the comparison between our methods and Postgres in 5 and, 6 or 8 column table respectively. In the case of char(32) C-HOMD table, as *save file* includes distinct column values, its size is bigger than the *integer* C-HOMD table. In non splitting C-HOMD, the size of *bit array* increases because the total number of chunks is larger in 6 or 8 column table than in 5 column table; note that the total number of chunks depends on the product of each dimension size of C-HOMD. In our methods, as all the records are converted into fixed size history-offset value, the increase of the column value size doesn't lead to the increase of storage cost. On the other hand, as Postgres stores a record as a set of column values, its storage cost depends on the sizes of the column values (i.e., record size); the cost is about twice as our method in char(32) table. In UB tree, each column value will be stored as a bit string(Z-address, type long). UB tree also needs to store tree nodes and it takes cost.

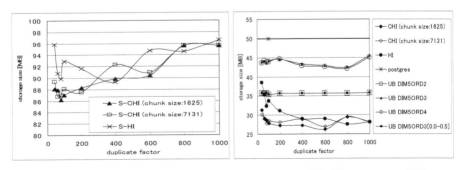

Fig. 9. Storage cost in 5 column table (a) S-CHI and S-HI (b) CHI, HI, postgres and UB tree

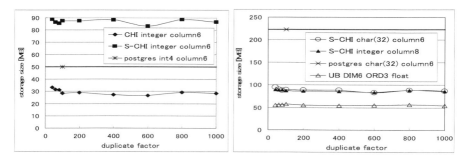

Fig. 10. (a) Storage cost in 6 column table (b) Storage cost in 6 or 8 column table

6.3 Construction Cost

Fig. 11 and Fig. 12 show the construction cost comparison of 5 and 6 column tables respectively. The cost of Postgres depends on the total number of records and the column sizes. Therefore, in terms of the integer table construction cost of Postgres, there is no difference between Fig. 11 and Fig. 12. On the contrary, the cost of the char(32) table is twice as that of the integer table in Postgres. In the case of our methods, all records are encoded into two fixed size values regardless of the record length and the encoded values are inserted into RDT. Thus, there is no difference in the construction time between integer table and char(32) table. HOMD table construction or C-HOMD table construction is also required but the cost is not so big, and disk I/O cost of RDT construction takes time at a grate rate. Regarding split table, two RDTs construction is required and the cost is twice as the single RDT construction. As was stated in Section 6.2, UB tree stores a record as Z-address. The data that have the same Z-address will be stored in the same Z-address list. As the Z-address cardinality decreases, the number of data stored in the same Z-address list increases. It means the increase of the cost to reach the last node of the Z-address list at record insertion (Fig. 11:ORD2 or ORD3[0.0-0.5]). On the other hand, too many Z-address cardinality leads to the decrease of the average number of data stored in the same Z-address list. It also takes time to tree construction because many list nodes are necessary to be read at tree construction (see UB ORD3 in Fig. 12).

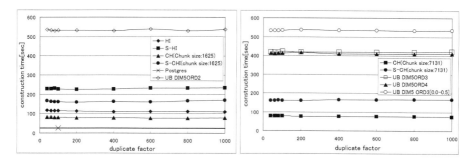

Fig. 11. Construction time in 5 column table (a) HI, S-HI, CHI, S-CHI, postgres and UB tree (ORD2) (b) CHI, S-CHI and UB tree (ORD3-4)

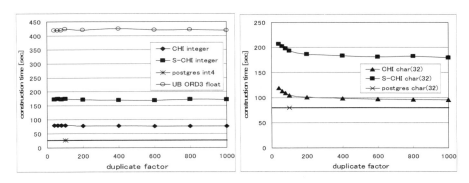

Fig. 12. Construction time in 6 column table (a) integer and float (b) 32 bytes character string

7 Related Work

In addition to indexes and materialized views, partitioning a table is an important aspect of physical design in a relational database system that significantly impact performance [2][9]. [2] presents vertical and horizontal partitioning techniques for designing a scalable solution to the integrated physical design problem that takes both performance and manageability into account. [9] identifies the key parameters for capturing the behavior of an access plan and propose a two-step methodology consisting of a query analysis step to estimate the parameters and a binary partitioning step which can be applied recursively.

In this paper, with the purpose of expanding the logical address space for storing encoded multidimensional data, we designed a vertical splitting scheme for multidimensional dataset encoded by the history-offset scheme. We couldn't find other works that describe splitting scheme for dynamically increasing multidimensional dataset aiming the expansion of the logical address space.

Elements in a fixed size multidimensional array are usually arranged on storage in predetermined dimension order like row-wise or column-wise order. But the arrangement causes *dimension dependency* of retrieval time; retrieval along specific dimension may be very fast, but those along the other dimensions are slow. By chunking multidimensional arrays and placing the elements in a chunk on consecutive memory pages, such dimension dependency can be alleviated since logically adjacent elements along every dimension can be placed on physically near storage locations[1]. As we noted in Section 4.1, such chunking is also another effective scheme for enlarging the logical address space.

Various application area that handle multidimensional datasets can be developed based on the notion of an extendible array or the history-offset encoding scheme described in this paper. [12] describes an incremental maintenance scheme of data cubes based on the notion of extendible arrays. [13] provides a labeling scheme of dynamic XML trees based on history-offset encoding. In these works however, the address space saturation problem makes it difficult to handle large scale multidimensional datasets.

8 Conclusion

We have described an experimental comparison amongst our history-offset based splitting approaches, PostgreSQL and UB tree. In the most conditions, vertical splitting of our method leads to significant reduces of retrieval I/O cost. Our method outperforms PostgreSQL and UB tree in retrieval time. The splitting in our method causes the increase of storage cost but the cost is not so large compared with PostgreSQL and UB tree. The result shows that our method is one of the best methods to handle large scale multidimensional datasets. While keeping the extendibility of multidimensional datasets, our schemes provide faster record accessing capability than conventional implementation irrespective of the size of the dataset.

References

1. Zhao, Y., Deshpande, P. M., Naughton, J. F.: An array based algorithm for simultaneous multidimensional aggregates. In: ACM SIGMOD, 159–170 (1997)
2. Agrawal, S., Narasayya, V., Yang, B.: Integrating Vertical and Horizontal Partitioning into Automated Physical Database Design. ACM SIGMOD, pp. 359–370 (2004)
3. Chakkappen, S., Cruanes, T., Dageville, B., Jiang, L., Shaft, U., Su, H., Zait, M.: Efficient and Scalable Statistics Gathering for Large Database in Oracle 11g. In: ACM SIGMOD, pp. 1053–1063 (2008)
4. Rosenberg, A.L.: Allocating storage for extendible arrays. JACM 21, 652–670 (1974)
5. Otoo, E.J., Merrett, T.H.: A storage scheme for extendible arrays. Computing 31, 1–9 (1983)
6. Orenstein, J.A., Merrett, T.H.: A class of data structures for associative searching. In: SIGACT-SIGMOD Symposium on Principle of Database Systems, pp. 181–190 (1984)
7. Tsuji, T., Kuroda, M., Higuchi, K.: History offset implementation scheme for large scale multidimensional data sets. In: SAC, pp. 1021–1028 (2008)
8. Bayer, R.: The universal B-tree for multidimensional indexing: General concepts. In: World Wide Computing and Its Applications, pp. 198–209 (1997)
9. Navathe, S., Ra, M.: Vertical Partitioning for Database Design: A Graphical Algorithm. In: SIGMOD, pp. 440–450 (1989)
10. Zhang, R., Kalnis, P., Ooi, B.C., Tan, K.L.: Generalized multidimensional data mapping and query processing. ACM Trans. Database Syst. 30(3), 661–697 (2005)
11. Ramsak, F., Markl, V., Fenk, R., Zirkel, M., Elhardt, K., Bayer, R.: Integrating the UB-tree into a database system kernel. In: VLDB, pp. 263–272 (2000)
12. Jin, D., Tsuji, T., Tsuchida, T., Higuchi, K.: An incremental maintenance scheme of data cubes. In: Haritsa, J.R., Kotagiri, R., Pudi, V. (eds.) DASFAA 2008. LNCS, vol. 4947, pp. 172–187. Springer, Heidelberg (2008)
13. Li, B., Kawaguchi, K., Tsuji, T., Higuchi, K.: A Labeling Scheme for Dynamic XML Trees Based on History-offset Encoding. Transactions of Information Processing Soceity of Japan 3(1), 1–17 (2010)
14. http://ww2.cs.mu.oz.au/~rui/code.htm

Describing Analytical Sessions Using a Multidimensional Algebra

Oscar Romero[1], Patrick Marcel[2], Alberto Abelló[1], Verónika Peralta[2], and Ladjel Bellatreche[3]

[1] Universitat Politècnica de Catalunya, BarcelonaTech
Barcelona, Spain
{oromero,aabello}@essi.upc.edu
[2] Université François Rabelais de Tours, Blois, France
{patrick.marcel,veronika.peralta}@univ-tours.fr
[3] ENSMA, Poitiers, France
bellatreche@ensma.fr

Abstract. Recent efforts to support analytical tasks over relational sources have pointed out the necessity to come up with flexible, powerful means for analyzing the issued queries and exploit them in decision-oriented processes (such as query recommendation or physical tuning). Issued queries should be decomposed, stored and manipulated in a dedicated subsystem. With this aim, we present a novel approach for representing SQL analytical queries in terms of a multidimensional algebra, which better characterizes the analytical efforts of the user. In this paper we discuss how an SQL query can be formulated as a *multidimensional algebraic characterization*. Then, we discuss how to *normalize* them in order to *bridge* (i.e., collapse) several SQL queries into a single characterization (representing the analytical session), according to their logical connections.

1 Introduction

Although multidimensional (MD) databases (DBs) and OLAP are mature, there is yet a considerable amount of systems devoted to data analysis based on relational technology. Deploying a MD DB to be exploited by OLAP tools is often a long, tedious, risky and expensive process [8], which remains prohibitive for medium-sized (or even some large) companies that prefer to stand close to the well-known relational model. Furthermore, many data analysts who were constrained to learn SQL in order to conduct their analytical sessions are yet reluctant to change their modus operandi. This trend is rather evident for scientists, who are increasingly using relational databases and SQL for conducting analytical sessions over huge repositories of data [11]. For this reason, novel works have focused on supporting analytical tasks over relational sources [3,4,10,11,14,17]. Specifically, it has already been pointed out the necessity to come up with flexible, powerful means for analyzing the issued queries (the keystone of these systems, usually stored in the DB query log), and decompose, store and handle them

A. Cuzzocrea and U. Dayal (Eds.): DaWaK 2011, LNCS 6862, pp. 224–239, 2011.

Q1	Q2	Q3
select state, sum(cs_quantity) from catalog_sales, date_dim, store_dim where cs_product = '1' and cs_date = date and cs_store = store group by year, state	select month, state, sum(cs_quantity) from catalog_sales, date_dim, store_dim where cs_product = '1' and cs_date = date and cs_store = store group by month, state	select month, state, sum(cs_quantity) from catalog_sales, date_dim, store_dim where cs_product = '1' and region = 'SE' and cs_date = date and cs_store = store group by month, state

Fig. 1. Exemplification of three SQL analytical queries within the same session

in a dedicated subsystem in order to better support any decisional task with the knowledge captured in the analytical queries [10]. As examples of such tasks, the system should be able to support the user when formulating new queries and leverage his / her knowledge with other users (query recommendation) [3,4,11] and, at the same time, database administrators should tune their databases to cope with the evolution of queries issued (physical as well as conceptual design) [14,17].

With this spirit, in this paper we present a novel approach for analyzing the issued analytical queries and storing them in a structured way that facilitates their reuse and exploitation (e.g., understanding their semantics, comparing them, clustering into groups, etc.) in future tasks such as query recommendation or physical and conceptual design. Thus, some kind of smart, *normalized form* is required. In this sense, the relational algebra would be a candidate to characterize the input queries. However, in our approach we move a step further as it has already been discussed that the *whole* relational algebra does not properly suit for analytical queries [12]. We propose, instead, using a *multidimensional algebra*. The correspondence between both models has already been studied in the literature and it has been shown that the MD algebra is a subset of the relational one [15]. Note this is sound with the discussion introduced in [12]: the relational algebra is, simply, too expressive (in the sense it provides functionalities not needed) from an analytical point of view. Thus, the MD algebra is simpler, and we can use it to express the analytical efforts of the user in a more concise, effective way.

The rest of the paper is organized as follows. Section 2 motivates our approach and introduces some basic concepts. Section 3 discusses the related work. Section 4 explains how to characterize an analytical SQL query with the MD algebra, Section 5 presents how to normalize this characterization and Section 6 explains how to exploit it to identify analytical sessions. Section 7 concludes the paper.

2   Motivation and Basic Concepts

In our approach we propose to characterize each issued SQL query (i.e., each query in the query log) by means of the set of *MultiDimensional Algebraic* operators presented in [1] (MDA from here on).

Example 1. Consider the following scenario (inspired by the TPC-DS benchmark [18]), where a relational database is accessed with queries expressed in SQL.

The database schema consists of the following relations (where foreign keys are represented as $attr_1$ ($\rightarrow attr_2$)):

```
catalog_sales (cs_date (→ date), cs_store (→ store), cs_customer (→ customer),
cs_product (→ product), cs_quantity, cs_amount),
date_dim (date, month, quarter, year),
store_dim (store, address, city, state, region),
customer_dim (customer, name, address, city, state, profession, branch),
product_dim (product, description, line)
```

Suppose queries in Fig. 1, extracted from the query log. Q1 asks for the total sales by state and year for a product, Q2 disaggregates sales by month and Q3 focuses on the south-east region. It turns out that these queries can be expressed in MDA, as evidenced in Section 4.

Characterizing an Analytical SQL Query by Means of MDA: We start by characterizing each analytical SQL query by means of MDA (see Section 4). This *Multidimensional Algebraic Characterization* (MAC from now on) forms a *tree* (like in the relational algebra, due to binary operators -such as union or drill-across, see Section 4-). The leafs are tuples *directly* retrieved from the database (i.e., the *materialized data*) and thus, we refer to them as *raw data*. Note that there is a MD schema associated with each operation of this algebraic characterization, in the sense that we know which attributes (either factual or dimensional) are in the output (further details about the MD operators can be found in Section 4). However, this characterization is not intended to be executed but to keep track of the knowledge captured in analytical queries from a MD point of view. Indeed, it is a characterization giving MD sense to the query.

Example 2. The MAC of query Q1 given in the previous example will express the roll-up (to the state and year levels), the projection over the measure (cs_quantity) and the selection (of the product with code '1').

Normalizing the MAC: Once the query has been characterized according to MDA our next step aims at *normalizing* the MAC with the objective of facilitating its comparison. To do so, it is compulsory to store each MAC in a *normalized* form. In our approach we benefit again from the algebraic structure proposed, and we use a set of *equivalence rules* (based on those of the relational algebra) to pull the MD operators up the algebraic structure, and produce a *Normalized MAC* (NMAC from now on).

Identifying Sessions: Finally, this characterization will be exploited in our last step, in which we are interested in discovering and characterizing analytical sessions. Up to now, current methods focus on isolated queries, which are analyzed on their own without considering the logical connection analytical queries from the same session do have. However, it is well-known that analytical sessions are formed of related queries capturing the reasoning flow during the analytical session [8]. Accordingly, we propose to *represent* those queries logically connected by means of a single structure capturing the whole session. We call *bridging* to the process aimed at identifying how similar two NMACs are. We consider that two queries Q1, Q2 could be coalesced in the same session if we only need to add MD operators to obtain Q2's output from Q1's NMAC. In other words, bridging is the process of producing the same result as Q2 by adding operators to Q1's NMAC (thus, we are *bridging* from Q1 to Q2). Based on the length of the bridge found, we can decide whether it makes sense or not to consider both queries in the same session.

Example 3. Consider the scenario introduced in Example 1. Query Q1 can be bridged with query Q2. Indeed, it can be detected that it corresponds to a drill-down from the year level to the month level. Furthermore, Q2 can be in turn bridged with Q3 since it corresponds to adding a selection over region. The three queries thus, should be characterized as a single session.

By iteration, we eventually obtain the whole session. Otherwise, if two queries are not similar enough as to belong to the same session, we restart the process trying to bridge the next query in the log (i.e., identify the start of a new session). We believe that capturing a whole analytical session provides a richer framework than working with isolate queries, as logical connections between queries are otherwise lost. Our contributions can be summarized as follows:

- In order to facilitate query management, we characterize each analytical SQL query as a MD query by means of the MDA, in what we call MAC.
- Next, we aim at normalizing each MAC obtained in order to facilitate its management in future steps, and obtaining its NMAC.
- Then, we bridge consecutive NMACs in order to produce a single structure for each analytical session performed.

This novel approach to describe sessions can be further exploited for diverse decisional tasks such as: (i) recommend queries to the user, (ii) create / tune the logical and physical schema and (iii) produce a MD schema. For example, MAC and bridging will be of particular interest for recommending analytical queries to the user analyzing a database or a data warehouse. To the best of our knowledge, there exists no database query recommendation technique that can construct a recommended query on-the-fly. Using the information extracted by bridging will enable recommending an OLAP operation to be applied to the user's current query (and therefore, potentially recommending queries that never *happened* in the log). Regarding conceptual MD design, this task could also benefit from NMACs. Following the idea in [16], this knowledge can be used to generate *user-oriented* MD schemas from non-MD DBs analytical logs and thus, we may, for example, decide if investing in MD technology is interesting or not for our organization. Indeed, MD DBs can benefit from analytical queries available beforehand in order to find the facts, dimensions and granularity that better suit our needs. The structural part of NMACs corresponds to the data cube the user is interested in. Thus, we could collapse in the same schema those queries whose structural part coincides. This is much more likely to happen after the normalization process, since it guarantees that all operations there are needed to align data and not just for presentation, as discussed in Section 5. Finally, queries are one of the most relevant inputs for physical design / tuning, and knowing them in detail facilitates the resolution of physical design by proposing efficient algorithms. For example, novel approaches exploit similarities between queries to generate optimized query plans. However, instead of using common intermediate results (which can be identified in our approach), common execution plans are used. Furthermore, queries are considered in isolation, although analytical queries are known to have strong logical connections. Our approach allows to tackle this problem at the session level, and inter and intra similarities can be identified between queries of each session, and exploit this information accordingly.

3   Related Work

Management of queries issued on data is rather limited in current DBMS. Most proposals are related to relational databases, which are transaction instead of query-oriented. As stressed in [10], these capabilities are reduced to query-by-example, graphical tools for composing queries, and query logging aimed at physical tuning. More elaborated management was not needed as operational systems mainly issue canned (i.e., known in advance) queries.

To our knowledge, only two works go beyond and propose a framework to manage the knowledge captured in the issued analytical queries (i.e., the DBMS log) to support query recommendation [3,4] or query completion [11] for interactive analysis of relational sources. The first approach follows the idea of recommender systems in the exploration of Web data. In this framework, the queries of a past user can serve as a guide for a new user if both have a similar querying behaviour (thus, they are interested in the same data). To do so, the authors present two approaches. The first one, presented in [4], keeps track of a matrix capturing all the tuples retrieved by each query. Later, by means of a distance function they compute how *similar* two queries are. In their second approach [3], given the time-consuming task of generating these matrixes and compare them, the authors extend their previous work to incorporate two recommendation engines, a tuple-based one that recommends queries that touch similar parts of the database, and a query fragment-based one that recommends structurally similar queries (i.e., a syntactical approach).

Similarly, [11] presents an approach to autocomplete SQL queries while the user writes them. The idea is slightly different but it follows a similar approach. The authors create a directed graph from SQL fragments (i.e., a syntactical approach). Two SQL fragments found in the same query are linked in the built graph. This graph is built in such a way that it guarantees any arbitrary navigation on the graph produces a compilable SQL query.

Finally, although capturing and exploiting this kind of knowledge should be a must for any decisional system, this issue has not been properly addressed for MD DBs and OLAP either. To our knowledge, the only works proposing

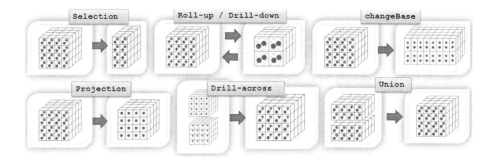

Fig. 2. Conceptual exemplification of the MDA operators

to exploit the issued queries for tackling other processes within the decisional database lifecycle are [6,7]. These works propose an approach for recommending MDX queries for MD DBs. There, the authors keep track of the tuples retrieved by each query and compute a distance function on it, in order to eventually compute their similarity. A possible reason for the lack of efforts on this topic is that we do not benefit from a standard MD language and algebra to query MD DBs. For the same reason, physical tuning depends on the underlying technology used to implement the database.

Our approach in this paper differs from all these as we do not deal with single SQL queries but with characterizations capturing the behaviour of the user all over an analytical session. Also, we take advantage of the well-known MD paradigm to characterize the input SQL queries and facilitate our task.

4   Obtaining the MAC of an SQL Query

In this section, we define a MAC using MDA. First, though, we set a MD notation and terminology. Multidimensionality is based on the **fact** / **dimension** dichotomy. The **fact**, or subject of analysis is placed in the n-dimensional space produced by the analysis dimensions. We consider a **dimension** to contain an aggregation hierarchy of **levels** representing different granularities (or levels of detail) to study data, and a **level** to contain **descriptors** (i.e., level attributes). We differentiate between identifier descriptors (univocally identifying each instance of a level) and non-identifier. In turn, a **fact** contains analysis indicators known as **measures** (which, in turn, can be regarded as fact attributes). A level of detail for each dimension produces a certain data granularity or **data cube**, in which place the measures. Finally, we denote by **base** of the space a minimal set of levels identifying univocally a certain data granularity (this definition is equivalent to *group by set* in [8]).

4.1   The Multidimensional Algebra

MDA was proven to be closed, complete (regarding the cube-query in [12]) and minimal (see [2]), and consists of the following operators (we suggest to check

Figure 2, where dots and triangles represent measures in a cell, for grasping their intuition). All the operators are unary (i.e., apply within a cube) except for drill-across and set operators, which operate over two cubes.

- **Selection** ($\sigma_p cube$): By means of a logic predicate p compound of clauses over descriptors (of the kind *descriptor operator constant*; e.g., *age* $>= 5$), this operator allows to choose the subset of points of interest out of the whole n-dimensional space. As a side note, MDA allows selections over descriptors even if they are not selected to identify the MD space.
- **Roll-up** ($\gamma_{f(measure_1),\dots,f(measure_n)}^{level_i \to level_j} cube$): It groups data instances in the cube based on an aggregation hierarchy. This operator modifies the granularity of data by means of a many-to-one relationship which relates instances of two levels in the same dimension, corresponding to a part-whole relationship. As argued in [9] about drill-down (i.e., the counterpart of roll-up, represented with the same formalization but with a one-to-many relationship between $level_i$ and $level_j$), it can only be applied if we previously performed a roll-up and did not lose the correspondences between instances.
- **Projection** ($\pi_{measure_1,\dots,measure_n} cube$): It selects a subset of measures.
- **ChangeBase** ($\chi_{base_1 \to base_2} cube$): This operator reallocates exactly the same instances of a cube into a new n-dimensional space with exactly the same number of points, by means of a one-to-one relationship. Actually, it allows to replace the current base by one of the alternatives, if more than one set of dimensions identifying the data instances (i.e., alternative bases) exist.
- **Drill-across** ($cube_1 \bowtie cube_2$): This operator fuses the measures in two cubes related by means of a one-to-one relationship. The n-dimensional space remains exactly the same, only the instances placed on it change.
- **Set Operations** ($cube_1 \Theta cube_2$): These operators allow to operate two cubes if both are defined over the same n-dimensional space. We consider union ($\cup$), difference ($\backslash$) and intersection ($\cap$). Nevertheless, from here on we focus on union, since the same considerations can be applied to the others. Also, we assume a perfect data cleaning and ETL phase (if the same cell appears in two different cubes, the values coincide). As a side note, the MDA union allows to unite two different cubes whenever they have the same schema.

The expressive power of this algebra is thoroughly discussed in [2]. Briefly, it fully matches the well-known cube-query pattern presented in [12]. For this reason, it is assumed to be expressive enough for capturing analytical efforts.

4.2 Formulating an SQL Query as a MAC

In [15], we shown how MD operators can be expressed in terms of restricted operators of the relational algebra. We take advantage of this work to identify the MDA operators, given an SQL query. First, we briefly refresh the relationship between both algebras and later, we discuss how to formulate the MAC of an SQL query. Without loss of generality, we denote by raw data (over which apply the MDA operators) the universal relationship of the tables in the FROM.

Reference Operator		"Selection"	"Projection"	"Join"	"Union"	"Group by"	"Aggregation"
Selection		$\checkmark_{Descs}$					
Projection			$\checkmark_{Measures}$				
Roll-up						$\checkmark_{Descs_{id}}$	$\checkmark_{Measures}$
Drill-across			$\checkmark_{Descs_{id}}$	$\checkmark_{Descs_{id}}$			
changeBase	Add Dim.			$\checkmark_{Descs_{id}}$			
	Remove Dim.		$\checkmark_{Descs_{id}}$				
	Alter Base		$\checkmark_{Descs_{id}}$	$\checkmark_{Descs_{id}}$			
Union					$\checkmark$		

Fig. 3. Comparison table between the relational and MD algebras

Table 3 summarizes the mapping between both sets of algebraic operators. Note that we are considering the extended operators of the relational algebra as in [5]. We use the following notation in the table: $\checkmark_{measures}$ if the MD operator is equivalent to the relational one but it can be only applied over measures, $\checkmark_{descs}$ if the MD operator must be applied over descriptors and finally, $\checkmark_{descs_{id}}$ if it can be only applied over level identifiers. Consequently, a $\checkmark$ without restrictions means both operators are equivalent without additional restrictions. If the translation of a MD operator combines more than one relational operator, both appear ticked in the same row.

It is important to state also the constraints of the MD model that affect the usage of these operations:

1. Fact/Dimension dichotomy must be preserved, which is reflected in that descriptors and measures are disjoint.
2. Summarizability necessary conditions (as in [13]) must be preserved, which is reflected in the multiplicities of relationships used in the operations as follows:
   (a) **Roll-up**: $level_i \rightarrow level_j$ must be one-to-many (or many-to-one, if it actually corresponds to a drill-down operation).
   (b) **ChangeBase**: $base_1 \rightarrow base_2$ must be one-to-one.
   (c) **Drill-across**: $cube_1 \rightleftharpoons cube_2$ must be one-to-one.

The first item can be easily validated, whereas testing the cardinalities in the second one is reduced to discover *functional dependencies* among the set of attributes involved in the relationship, by sampling the relational source. Note that we are able to formulate the MAC by directly applying this result (we address the reader to [15] for a detailed justification of this table). In short, The query result is represented as the tree root, the source tables (i.e., raw data) as the leafs and the SQL query is decomposed as a set of MDA operators. If an SQL query cannot be fully formulated in terms of MDA operators it means that, according to MDA, it does not make MD sense and thus, it should be discarded. For example, given an analytical SQL query, any relational selection found in the WHERE clause must be read as a MD selection, and the attribute involved in such selection is known to play a dimensional role in our MAC interpretation. Similarly for the rest of operators described in the table.

Example 4. Consider Q1 from Example 1. The MAC of this query is (where raw data is the universal relation for `catalog_sales` × `store_dim` × `date_dim`, i.e., tables in the FROM):

$$\gamma^{date \rightarrow year}_{sum(cs\_quantity)} (\gamma^{store \rightarrow state}_{sum(cs\_quantity)} (\pi_{cs\_quantity} (\sigma_{cs\_product='1'} (raw\_data))))$$

Example 5. Consider now query Q4, which unites two cubes with the total sales by customer state and month, for year 1999, for the south-east and south-west regions:

```
SELECT d_month_seq as month, state, SUM(cs_quantity) AS sales
FROM catalog_sales, date_dim, customer_dim
WHERE cs_sold_date_sk = d_date_ski AND cs_customer_id = c_customer_id AND d_year = 1999
    AND region = 'SE'
GROUP BY d_month_seq, state
UNION
SELECT d_month_seq as month, state, SUM(cs_quantity) AS sales
FROM catalog_sales, date_dim, customer_dim
WHERE cs_sold_date_sk = d_date_ski AND cs_customer_id = c_customer_id AND d_year = 1999
    AND region = 'SW'
GROUP BY d_month_seq, state;
```

The MAC of this query is:

$$(\sigma_{region='SE'}(\gamma^{date \rightarrow month}_{sum(cs\_quantity)}(\gamma^{customer \rightarrow state}_{sum(cs\_quantity)}(\pi_{cs\_quantity}(\sigma_{year=1999}(raw\_data))))))$$

$$\cup$$

$$(\sigma_{region='SW'}(\gamma^{date \rightarrow month}_{sum(cs\_quantity)}(\gamma^{customer \rightarrow state}_{sum(cs\_quantity)}(\pi_{cs\_quantity}(\sigma_{year=1999}(raw\_data))))))$$

4.3   Interpreting the MAC

A MAC represents the MD counterpart of the analytical SQL statement analyzed. By definition, a MAC is a tree-shaped structure. Like in the relational algebra, this is because of binary operators. The grammar capturing its semantics is as follows (χ, σ, π, γ, $\cup$, $\bowtie$ represent the MDA operators; see Sec. 4.1):

$$\mathcal{MAC} \rightarrow rawData\ \mathcal{NP} \mid (\mathcal{MAC} \cup \mathcal{MAC})\mathcal{NP} \mid (\mathcal{MAC} \bowtie \mathcal{MAC})\mathcal{NP} \qquad \mathcal{Q} \rightarrow \mathcal{CB}\ \mathcal{S}\ \mathcal{R}\ \mathcal{P}$$
$$\mathcal{NP} \rightarrow \mathcal{Q} \mid \mathcal{Q}\ \mathcal{NP} \qquad \mathcal{CB} \rightarrow \emptyset \mid \chi\mathcal{CB} \qquad \mathcal{S} \rightarrow \emptyset \mid \sigma\mathcal{S} \qquad \mathcal{R} \rightarrow \emptyset \mid \gamma\mathcal{R} \qquad \mathcal{P} \rightarrow \emptyset \mid \pi\mathcal{P}$$

From now on, we will talk about the root-side and the leaf-side of the MAC. The tree leafs are raw data (i.e., with no transformations). Furthermore, we call a *navigation path* (NP from here on) to any *partially ordered set of unary operations* consecutive within the tree. These NPs can be thought as data manipulation to produce the desired presentation or alignment (i.e., the data cube MD space -*changeBases*-, slicers -*selections*-, data granularity produced -*roll-ups*- and subset of measures shown -*projections*-), whereas nodes collapsing two *branches* (from here on, we simply refer to the input NPs of binary operators as branches) are generating a new set of tuples (if desired, we may keep manipulating the result with a new NP). Thus, note that a single MAC can contain more than one NP.

Indeed, data might need to be aligned before being able to collapse them. For example, we may need to roll-up to the same granularity level before uniting

Operator	Projection	Roll-up	Selection	ChangeBase
Projection	×	✓	✓	✓
Roll-up	✓	✓	~	~
Selection	✓	✓	✓	~
ChangeBase	✓	~	~	✓
Drill-across	✓	/\	/\	/\
Union	/\	/\	/\	/\

Fig. 4. MDA equivalence rules

or drilling-across data from two different cubes (i.e., align the input branches of binary operators to produce the one-to-one relationship demanded by *union* and *drill-across*).

Example 6. Consider the MAC given in Example 5. It contains two NP, namely:

$$\sigma_{region=' SE'}\left(\gamma^{date\rightarrow month}_{sum(cs\_quantity)}\left(\gamma^{customer\rightarrow state}_{sum(cs\_quantity)}\left(\pi_{cs\_quantity}\left(\sigma_{year=1999}\left(raw\_data\right)\right)\right)\right)\right)$$

and

$$\sigma_{region=' SW'}\left(\gamma^{date\rightarrow month}_{sum(cs\_quantity)}\left(\gamma^{customer\rightarrow state}_{sum(cs\_quantity)}\left(\pi_{cs\_quantity}\left(\sigma_{year=1999}\left(raw\_data\right)\right)\right)\right)\right)$$

Finally, we talk about the *pivotal node* as the tree node dividing the MAC into two well-differentiated layers: the *structural layer* and the *presentation layer* (i.e., the first binary ancestor of the root). In other words, the pivotal node identifies the set of tuples (i.e., the *structural* part) over which we only apply unary operations (i.e., a NP representing how data is *presented* to the user). In Example 5, the pivotal node is the union, because in this case it represents the structural part. We do not have presentation layer in this case, since it is also the root.

5   Normalizing the MAC

Once we have formulated the MAC for a given statement, we aim at normalizing it. In our approach we benefit from the algebraic structure proposed, and we use a set of equivalence rules to pull the MD operators up the algebraic structure. Thus, the MDA equivalence rules (shown in Table 4) are an immediate consequence of considering the MDA operator semantics over the relational algebra equivalence rules (explained in [5]) and considering the constraints introduced in Section 4.2. The meaning of each cell in the table is the following: if the MDA operator in the column *can be pulled up*[1] the operator in the row, the cell is ticked ("✓"). If there is a conflict, the cell is crossed ("×"). Like in the relational algebra equivalence rules, a "~" denotes a partial conflict: the operator can be pulled up whenever the row operator does not remove the attribute needed by the column operator. For example, a selection can only be pulled up a roll-up if the attribute used to select is not rolled-up. Finally, a "/\" refers

---

[1] We recall that a MAC is a tree-shaped structure and consequently, we talk about *pulling up an operator* through the structure.

to binary operators. A unary operator can be pulled up the binary operator if it appears in both branches as explained below. For example, we can only pull up a projection through a union if the same measures are projected in both branches. Note that we assume well-formedness of MAC in the sense that no attribute is used in an operation if it is not present in the output schema of the previous operation(s).

The final aim of normalization is to distinguish between operators producing the set of tuples retrieved by the query (i.e., the structural layer) and operators manipulating these tuples before being presented to the user (i.e., the presentation layer). However, as discussed in Section 4, MACs can contain more than one NP (some of them interleaved in the structural layer for aligning binary operators), although only the root-most NP (i.e., the one amid the pivotal and root nodes) represents the presentation layer. Thus, we *normalize* MACs by *pulling operators in the NPs of the structural part to the presentation layer* (i.e., to the MAC root-side), and we do so by applying Table 4. If an operator remains stuck in the structural part after normalization then, it is needed for retrieving tuples rather than for presentation purposes.

Interestingly, note that, unlike the relational algebra logical optimization that aims at pushing operators as much as possible to the leafs, we aim at pulling MDA unary operators towards the root. Moreover, we find more ticks in Table 4 than we would find if using the relational equivalence rules and, when something needs to be checked, it is much easier, because in MDA we introduce additional constrains that simplify these rules. For example, we know that the relational selection can be pulled up a projection if the attribute involved in the selection is not projected out by the projection. Furthermore, we know that the MDA projection can only be applied to measures, whereas selection only makes sense over descriptors. Consequently, the MDA projection and selection can always be swapped in a MAC, as the set of attributes involved in each operator will always be disjoint (see Section 4 for further details). In the general case, special difficulties arise dealing with the relational group by (basis of roll-up, OLAP key operator). Interestingly, we want to remark the gain when dealing with our restricted group by (i.e., roll-up) instead of the generic one, whose difficulty is discussed in depth in [5] (where it is explicitly said that no law is stated) and specially in [19] (where the whole work is devoted to analyze all possibilities between join and group-by).

The normalization algorithm is just a postorder traversal of the MAC, considering that the nodes to visit are NPs and binary operations (thus, being a postorder algorithm, for each binary operator, it first visits its branches and later the binary operator itself). We then deal with these two kinds of nodes in a different way:

a) For each NP we visit, for each unary operator it contains (from root-side to leafs-side), we pull it up in the direction of the root as much as possible within the NP, following the rules in the white and light gray cells of Table 4.

b) Next, for each binary operator we visit, if both left and right branches are non-empty NPs and some operation coincides in their topmost Qs (see the grammar in Section 4.3), which can be pulled up through its successors in Q according to the light and dark gray cells of Table 4, the unary operator is pulled up from both and added once at the leafs-side of the parent NP of the binary operator. Note that, every binary operator will always have a parent NP (in the trivial case, the one containing the root node). Only exception, according to Table 4, is that it is not necessary that a projection must coincide at both branches of a drill-across to be pulled up.

As a result of this algorithm, we say that a NMAC is a MAC with the following properties:

i) Many NP can appear in a MAC. NPs stuck in the structural part are needed for aligning the inputs of binary operators (and not for presentation purposes).
ii) Many Q may appear at each NP, but the minimum number would be generated, each potentially containing χ, σ and γ, in this order.
iii) π can only appear in the topmost Q of every NP, and following the order imposed by the containment of attributes.

Furthermore, we force a partial order aimed at facilitating the NPs comparison during next step, as follows:

i) γ in Q will be sorted by dimension and then aggregation level.
ii) σ in Q will follow the inverse order the user posed them.
iii) χ in Q will follow the inverse order the user posed them.

Example 7. The MAC in Example 5 is not in normal form, since properties (i) (many operations can be pulled up through the union), (ii) (operations in the NPs are not sorted properly) and (iii) (the projections are not in the topmost position) do not hold. Following an postorder traversal, we would first visit both NPs (case (a)), which would be sorted to result in:

$$\pi_{cs\_quantity}\left(\gamma_{sum(cs\_quantity)}^{customer\to state}\left(\gamma_{sum(cs\_quantity)}^{date\to month}\left(\sigma_{year=1999}\left(\sigma_{region='SE'}\left(raw\_data\right)\right)\right)\right)\right)$$

and

$$\pi_{cs\_quantity}\left(\gamma_{sum(cs\_quantity)}^{customer\to state}\left(\gamma_{sum(cs\_quantity)}^{date\to month}\left(\sigma_{year=1999}\left(\sigma_{region='SW'}\left(raw\_data\right)\right)\right)\right)\right)$$

Afterwards, we would visit their parent (i.e. $\cup$, case (b)), yielding the following:

$$\pi_{cs\_quantity}\left(\gamma_{sum(cs\_quantity)}^{customer\to state}\left(\gamma_{sum(cs\_quantity)}^{date\to month}\left(\sigma_{year=1999}\left(\sigma_{region='SE'}\left(raw\_data\right)\cup\sigma_{region='SW'}\left(raw\_data\right)\right)\right)\right)\right)$$

Finally, we should normalize the presentation layer, but it already is.

6   *Bridging* NMACs

Working with algebraic expressions under normal form makes it easier to detect if, syntactically, two expressions are similar to each other. In our context, similar

NMACs may be considered logically related from an analytical point of view, and if two NMACs are *close enough* to each other, they are considered to belong to the same analytical session. In that case, they are *coalesced* into a session and both NMACs are logically related by *annotating* their *bridging operators*. Formally, given two NMACs n_1, n_2, we say we can bridge them if by means of some MDA operators (the bridging operators), we can transform the output of n_1 into that of n_2.

In our current approach we only analyze those queries whose *structural part* coincide by comparing their *presentation layers* (both concepts have been previously introduced in Section 5). Let P_1 and P_2 be the presentation layer of n_1 and n_2, respectively, and CS_1 and CS_2 their *cube schemas*. A cube schema is a MD interpretation of the output produced by each query. According to the MDA semantics, we can characterize it as follows (see Section 4.3): (i) the set of measures (i.e., data) shown to the user; (ii) the set of dimensional attributes selected to produce the MD space at a certain granularity level and (iii) the set of slicers applied. Now, we take advantage of the MDA minimality (operators cannot be derived by composition) and closeness (their output is a cube) properties. Since MDA is close and every operator has its inverse, by definition, we can transform CS_1 into CS_2 by means of a finite set of MDA operators (in the worst case, it would entail to *undo* all the operators that lead to CS_1 and *redo* those in CS_2). Furthermore, given its minimal property, we know which operators can be applied in order to align each cube schema feature. In other words, we can split the comparison of P_1 and P_2 into smaller comparisons regarding the cube schema part affected by the MDA operators:

i) **Measures:** Let $m1_1, \ldots, m1_n$ and $m2_1, \ldots, m2_t$ the list of measures in CS_1 and CS_2, respectively.
   - If $m1_1, \ldots, m1_n$ and $m2_1, \ldots, m2_t$ coincide nothing has to be done.
   - $\forall\, m1_i \in CS_1$, s.t. $m1_i \notin CS_2$ the corresponding projection disregarding $m1_i$ is annotated in the bridge between n_1 and n_2.
   - $\forall\, m2_i \in CS_2$, s.t. $m2_i \notin CS_1$ the corresponding drill-across is annotated to add $m2_i$ to the output schema.

ii) **MD space:** First, we analyze the relationships between the MD spaces in CS_1 and CS_2.
   - If CS_1 and CS_2 are exactly the same, nothing has to be done.
   - Else, for each one-to-many or many-to-one relationship identified between CS_1 and CS_2 we need to modify the output granularity accordingly (see Section 4). If a one-to-many relationship is identified, a proper drill-down operator is annotated in the bridge. Else, in case of a many-to-one relationship, the corresponding roll-up is added.
   - In any other case, given that the structural part of n_1 and n_2 coincide, a 1-1 relationship, as a whole, should be identified between CS_1 and CS_2. Thus, we need to navigate from the MD space in CS_1 to the alternative space in CS_2 (see Section 4) and the corresponding changeBase is added to the bridge.

iii) **Slicers:** Being p_1 and p_2 the conjunction of predicates in the selections of n_1 and n_2, respectively.

- If $p_1 \equiv p_2$ nothing has to be done.
- Else if $p_1 \sqsubset p_2$, the proper union(s) is (are) added to the bridge.
- Else if $p_1 \sqsupset p_2$, a selection(s) is (are) added.
- Else a union(s) (to undo p_1) and a selection(s) (to carry out p_2) are added.

Again, note that this algorithm is sound thanks to the MDA properties, which allow us to undo and redo complementary operators (i.e., projection Vs. drill-across, union Vs. selection, roll-up Vs. drill-down and changeBase Vs. change-Base) to produce CS_2 from CS_1. The produced bridge is then evaluated to decide whether n_1 and n_2 are similar enough, if so we consider both NMACs to belong to the same session. It is out of our current objectives to provide an empirical function to identify when two NMACs are similar enough as to be coalesced in the same session, as it is an application-dependent task. As result, both NMACs are stored in an ordered structure (i.e., a list of NMACs) representing the session and we annotate their relationship with the bridging operators NP_b (to keep track of their logical connection). Finally, we use the last NMAC to keep looking for other queries in the session, whereas the annotated bridging is kept in order to exploit it in future tasks such as query recommendation.

Example 8. Consider Q2 introduced in Example 1. Its NMAC is:

$$\pi_{cs\_quantity}(\gamma^{date \rightarrow month}_{sum(cs\_quantity)}(\gamma^{store \rightarrow state}_{sum(cs\_quantity)}(\sigma_{cs\_product='1'}(raw\_data))))$$

This query can be bridged with Q1 (whose MAC is given in Example 4, which happens to be already normalized), and, as explained in the motivation example, their cube schemas are exactly the same except for their MD spaces, among which we can identify a many-to-one relationship (from year to month). Thus, a drill-down is annotated as the bridge from Q1 to Q2. In this case, it is clear they are close enough and thus, both NMACs are stored in the same session s. Semantically, the annotated bridge means that Q2's output can be obtained by bridging Q1's NMAC with the annotated drill-down (this is represented in the MAC below, where the drill-down is represented by the left-most operator):

$$\gamma^{year \rightarrow month}_{sum(cs\_quantity)}(\pi_{cs\_quantity}(\gamma^{date \rightarrow year}_{sum(cs\_quantity)}(\gamma^{store \rightarrow state}_{sum(cs\_quantity)}(\sigma_{cs\_product='1'}(raw\_data)))))$$

7 Conclusions

We have presented a novel approach to capture analytical SQL queries in a structured way (i.e., a MAC) based on MD algebra. First, we have shown how to normalize MACs in order to compute the similarity between queries in the log and bridge them to obtain the whole session.

This paper mainly sets a new research line for our next future. Specifically, we aim at exploiting the foundations introduced by producing novel solutions for query recommendation, physical tuning and MD design. Furthermore, this framework can also be useful for testing if the way a relational database is used is compliant with the data warehouse and OLAP practices and thus, to which extent it is worth investing in such technology. We also plan to carry out empirical studies to determine how close two NMACs must be in order to be considered part of the same session. Finally, the implementation of this framework is currently under work.

Acknowledgements. This work has been partly supported by the Ministerio de Ciencia e Innovación under project TIN2008-03863. We also thank Jovan Varga for his insights.

References

1. Abelló, A., Romero, O.: On-Line Analytical Processing. In: Liu, L., Özsu, M.T. (eds.) Encyclopedia of Database Systems, pp. 1949–1954. Springer, Heidelberg (2009)
2. Abelló, A., Samos, J., Saltor, F.: YAM^2 (Yet Another Multidimensional Model): An extension of UML. Information Systems 31(6), 541–567 (2006)
3. Akbarnejad, J., Chatzopoulou, G., Eirinaki, M., Koshy, S., Mittal, S., On, D., Polyzotis, N., Varman, J.S.V.: Sql querie recommendations. PVLDB 3(2), 1597–1600 (2010)
4. Chatzopoulou, G., Eirinaki, M., Polyzotis, N.: Query recommendations for interactive database exploration. In: Winslett, M. (ed.) SSDBM 2009. LNCS, vol. 5566, pp. 3–18. Springer, Heidelberg (2009)
5. Garcia-Molina, H., Ullman, J.D., Widom, J.: Database Systems. Prentice-Hall, Englewood Cliffs (2008)
6. Giacometti, A., Marcel, P., Negre, E.: Recommending multidimensional queries. In: Pedersen, T.B., Mohania, M.K., Tjoa, A.M. (eds.) DaWaK 2009. LNCS, vol. 5691, pp. 453–466. Springer, Heidelberg (2009)
7. Giacometti, A., Marcel, P., Negre, E., Soulet, A.: Query recommendations for olap discovery driven analysis. In: DOLAP, pp. 81–88. ACM, New York (2009)
8. Golfarelli, M., Rizzi, S.: Data Warehouse Design: Modern Principles and Methodologies. McGraw-Hill, New York (2009)
9. Hacid, M.S., Sattler, U.: An Object-Centered Multi-dimensional Data Model with Hierarchically Structured Dimensions. In: Proc. of IEEE Knowledge and Data Engineering Exchange Workshop (KDEX 1997).IEEE, Los Alamitos (1997)
10. Khoussainova, N., Balazinska, M., Gatterbauer, W., Kwon, Y., Suciu, D.: A case for a collaborative query management system. In: CIDR (2009), http://www.crdrdb.org
11. Khoussainova, N., Kwon, Y., Balazinska, M., Suciu, D.: Snipsuggest: Context-aware autocompletion for sql. PVLDB 4(1), 22–33 (2010)
12. Kimball, R., Reeves, L., Thornthwaite, W., Ross, M.: The Data Warehouse Lifecycle Toolkit: Expert Methods for Designing. In: Developing and Deploying Data Warehouses, John Wiley & Sons, Inc., Chichester (1998)
13. Lenz, H.J., Shoshani, A.: Summarizability in OLAP and Statistical Data Bases. In: Ninth Int. Conf. on Scientific and Statistical Database Management (SSDBM), pp. 132–143. IEEE Computer Society Press, Los Alamitos (1997)
14. Platform, S.B.A.: Siebel business analytics server administration guide: Administering the query log, http://download.oracle.com/docs/cd/E12103_/books/admintool/admintool_AdministerQuery14.html

15. Romero, O., Abelló, A.: On the Need of a Reference Algebra for OLAP. In: Song, I.-Y., Eder, J., Nguyen, T.M. (eds.) DaWaK 2007. LNCS, vol. 4654, pp. 99–110. Springer, Heidelberg (2007)
16. Romero, O., Abelló, A.: Automatic validation of requirements to support multidimensional design. Data Knowl. Eng. 69(9), 917–942 (2010)
17. TechNet, M.: Sql server techcenter: Configuring the analysis services query log, http://www.microsoft.com/technet/prodtechnol/sql/2005/technologies/config_ssas_querylog.mspx
18. TPC: TPC-DS specification (2010), http://www.tpc.org/tpcds/
19. Yan, W.P., Larson, P.-Å.: Performing Group-By before Join. In: ICDE, pp. 89–100. IEEE Computer Society, Los Alamitos (1994)

Tagged MapReduce: Efficiently Computing Multi-analytics Using MapReduce

Andreas Williams, Pavlos Mitsoulis-Ntompos, and Damianos Chatziantoniou

Department of Management Science and Technology,
Athens University of Economics and Business (AUEB),
Patission Ave, 104 34 Athens, Greece
{agouil,pmits}@dmst.aueb.gr, damianos@aueb.gr

Abstract. MapReduce is a programming paradigm for effective processing of large datasets in distributed environments, using the *map* and *reduce* functions. The map process creates (key, value) pairs, while the reduce phase aggregates same-key values. In other words, a MapReduce application defines and reduces one set of values for each key, which means that the user only knows *one aspect* of the *key*. Advanced OLAP applications however, require multiple sets to be defined and reduced for the *same* key, not necessarily mutually disjoint. The challenge is to extend MapReduce to support this in a syntactically simple and computationally efficient way. We propose an extension to the classic MapReduce model, called Tagged MapReduce, where data is represented as (key, value, tag) triplets. Users map triplets and reducing takes place for each key *and for each tag*. For example, given a set of pages, one may want to count words' occurrences *per page type*. The page type is represented by the tag. While the classic MapReduce can handle this class of queries, it requires effort and possibly advanced programming skills for efficient implementations. For example, should the tag form a compound object with the key or the value? Our formalism makes it simpler for the programmer to use and easier for the system to identify and apply efficient algorithms.

Keywords: MapReduce, On-Line Analytical Processing, Data Analysis.

1 Introduction

During the last few years, the data analysis community has invested heavily to a new paradigm, called MapReduce. Startups and established companies (Aster Data, Greenplum, Netezza, Oracle, Teradata, [1],[2],[3],[4]) alike developed and marketed data management products incorporating some version of MapReduce, by offering a simple SQL interface and hiding the complexity of the physical cluster, such as in Pig-Latin [5]. The fact that MapReduce is a programming paradigm rather than a new operator within an algebraic framework, created a big controversy within the database community [6],[7]. Parallel database management systems (PDBMS) have good performance on structured data, deployed on a small number of nodes (a few dozen), which have to be homogenous [8]. On the other hand, MapReduce provides a simple model for analyzing data, is flexible, scalable and fault tolerant on unstructured data

A. Cuzzocrea and U. Dayal (Eds.): DaWaK 2011, LNCS 6862, pp. 240–251, 2011.

[9]. In addition, large data-intensive organizations, such as Google, Yahoo and Microsoft, need to analyze large datasets in a rapid, ad hoc way, without deploying complex, expensive PDBMS. Finally, many real world data analysis tasks inherently deal with unstructured data, stored in clusters of servers with different processing capabilities and possibly in different storage systems [9]. As a result, Yahoo (Hadoop, [11]), Google (MapReduce, [10]) and Microsoft (Dryad, [12]) have developed frameworks to support MapReduce.

As pointed out by DeWitt and Stonebraker [6], MapReduce lacks many of the features that have proven invaluable for structured data analysis. Due to that fact many research papers propose MapReduce extensions to allow additional data analysis capabilities, keeping its flexibility, scalability, and fault-tolerance. Pig-Latin [5] is a new language that combines the best of both worlds: high-level declarative querying in the spirit of SQL and low-level, procedural programming of MapReduce. Map-Reduce-Merge [13] joins multiple datasets in a MapReduce fashion. SQL/MapReduce [1] provides an inherently parallel User Defined Function (UDF) that exploits the MapReduce model's parallelism. HadoopDB [8] uses MapReduce as the communication layer above multiple nodes running single-node DBMS instances.

In this paper, we identify a useful and frequent class of analytical queries that require the definition and reduction of multiple value sets for each key. This is roughly the equivalent of defining multiple SQL group-by queries on the same grouping attributes and then joining the results to bring all same-key aggregates to one row. These queries involve many useful examples of data analytics, such as trends, cumulative aggregates, standard pivoting and others. One can approach these queries as multiple MapReduce jobs over the same keys. The reduced sets can or cannot be overlapping, sharing some work. This has recently been identified in MR-Share[14]. One issue in this approach is how to express these queries at a high level language (declarative or semi-declarative), so MR-Share can be exploited. Pig-Latin or ASSET [15] syntax seem sufficient. Another approach is to extend the MapReduce framework so mapping phase produces triplets instead of pairs, adding a "tag" constituent, denoting the set the value belongs to. Since we did not want to change the underlying engine (Hadoop), the tag can become part either of the key or the value during evaluation, based on some reasoning/optimization performed at the high-level language. One can think this approach as producing a multi-column MapReduce in one shot. All these issues are discussed in Section 3.

The primary contribution of our work is to describe Tagged MapReduce and implement it on top of Hadoop. While the proposed implementation may not be the most efficient, it shows a good performance improvement over traditional MapReduce evaluation of our query examples. The goal is to demonstrate that simple, intuitive extensions can allow advanced analysis at minimal cost. Section 2 provides background information and discusses related work. Section 3 motivates this work through a simple web log analysis application. In Section 4, we describe our implementation over Hadoop: users can create triplets (key, value, tag) through an extended map function, which become either ((key, tag), value) or (key, (tag, value)) pairs for standard MapReduce execution – the user can select which way to go. Recall that the user can be the optimizer of a high level language. Section 5 presents some preliminary experimental results. We conclude and discuss future work in Section 6.

2 Background and Related Work

In this section we briefly discuss MapReduce, Hadoop framework, ASSET and Pig Latin syntaxes, which we used for our work.

2.1 MapReduce Overview

MapReduce is a new programming paradigm used by Google in its search engines and other data-intensive applications running on clusters of cheap PCs. The main purpose is to perform simple data analysis on top of large unstructured or semi-structured datasets. The main features of MapReduce are the following: (a) guarantees fault tolerance and automatic failure recovery by restarting the failed tasks [9],[16], (b) provides a simple programming interface, by letting users write two simple functions, *Map* and *Reduce* [9], (c) allows task and data parallelism [9], [16], (d) exhibits excellent performance and scalability, even on top of commodity machines [9], [16], and (e) it is storage independent and can process data without first loading it into a database [9].

2.2 Hadoop Framework

Hadoop consists of two main components: the Hadoop's Distributed File System (HDFS) and the Hadoop MapReduce [11]. The HDFS uses the *namenode* and the *datanodes* in order to manage its data files and the operations that are executed over the files (store, read, write and replicate), while MapReduce uses the other two components of Hadoop's architecture, the *jobtracker* and the *tasktrackers*, in order to schedule and execute the user's applications.

2.3 Pig Latin and ASSET Queries

Pig Latin[5] is a new language that is designed to fit in a sweet spot between the declaration style of SQL, and the low-level, procedural style of MapReduce. However, the MapReduce paradigm leads to a great deal of custom user code that is hard to maintain and reuse. The above reasons, give a great picture of what characteristics of the two worlds have been integrated in Pig Latin. A Pig Latin program is a sequence of steps (operations), much like in a programming language, each of which carries out a single data transformation. At the same time, the transformations carried out in each step are fairly high-level, e.g. filtering, grouping and aggregation, much like in the SQL. The use of relational algebra style primitives, e.g. GROUP, FILTER, allows traditional database optimizations to be carried out. Lastly, Pig Latin is fully implemented by Pig system that uses Hadoop, in order to transform Pig Latin programs to MapReduce jobs.

Associated Sets (ASSET) queries were based on the work of multi-feature queries and grouping variables [17, 18, 19, 20]. Grouping variables can be used to compute multiple features of group-by queries [17], by defining and aggregating *for each group-by value (or key)* multiple, successive and correlated (if necessary) relation subsets in one query block. The definition of subset X_i could involve the key and the aggregates of X_1, X_2, ..., X_{i-1} subsets. Grouping variables can be efficiently evaluated and succinctly represented in relational algebra [21]. This simple concept can represent a wide range of useful and practical analytics. The claim in that framework was similar to Pig-Latin's: looping over groups is important to complex analytics formulation. The work on grouping variables has influenced Oracle's Analytic Functions [22] and the standardization of ANSI SQL (OLAP Amendment). Implementations of it have been studied in the context of telecom applications,medical informatics, finance and others (a survey can be found in [20]).

2.4 Related Work

Our work was motivated, to some degree, by Map-Reduce-Merge [13], in which the user may perform complex analytic tasks by *joining* multiple datasets. At [13], an additional operation (*joining*) is described, which is supported by the DBMS. In this model, a MapReduce job is executed for each dataset creating [key, value] pairs and one merge function to join these pairs creating the final output. Moreover, Map-Reduce-Merge processes only relational data as the merge function expresses basic relational algebra operators (joins) through MapReduce. Our work is also related to MRShare [14], which merges MapReduce jobs coming from different queries in order to save processing time and money. In the MRShare framework a meta-map function merges the similar or identical map functions from the different jobs resulting in less data to be produced after the map phase, and furthermore to multiple query optimization (MPO). Chatziantoniou et. al in [15] mention a plethora of OLAP queries that could benefit from a MapReduce implementation, but cannot be expressed as MapReduce jobs (e.g. pivoting, hierarchical comparisons, complex comparisons, trends, correlated aggregation, etc. [20]). In this paper, we deal with a practical and useful class of data analysis tasks that could be computed via a *single* MapReduce job, if multiple subsets for the same key could be defined and subsequently reduced.

3 Motivation

Let us consider a common web application in which data analysis is applied over a set of log files. Each log file has two columns, the first represents the URL and the second the timestamp. Some common queries that can be applied over a set of these log files are the following:

Q1. For each URL, for each of the twelve months, count the cumulative total for that month, i.e. for month m, we want to count the total hits in months $<= m$. With this query we can identify trends and growth of specific URLs. This is a simple *cumulative* query.

Q2. For each URL, count the hits for each day (or for each month). With this query, one can determine the daily (or monthly) traffic of the URL. This is a simple *pivoting* query.

Let's have a closer look at Query Q1. A straightforward MapReduce implementation would create for each (url, month) source pair, (12-month+1) pairs in the form ((u, i), 1), i=month, month+1, ... , 12 – materializing in effect a join followed by a group by in traditional relational algebra – reducing then by using a simple count. Alternatively, one could create for each (url, month) source pair, (12-month+1) pairs in the form (u, (i, 1)), i=month, month+1, ... , 12, i.e. month is stored with the value this time. This implementation would not change the number of the generated pairs, but it would change the size of the per-key value set (since now the number of the keys is much smaller) and the implementation of the reduce method (a switch statement is necessary and 12 different counters must be maintained.) A more experienced programmer would note that he could avoid the implicit join by utilizing two successive MapReduce jobs: the first one would simply count the hits per (url, month) and the second one would use this input to sum the counts per (url, month) – once again, the second MapReduce invocation would create (12-month+1) pairs for each ((url, month), cnt) input pair. However, a forth, more efficient, implementation exists: create for each (url, month) input pair a (url, (month, 1)) pair and *push* the per month computation to the reduce phase. The performance of these approaches is shown in Figure 1, using Hadoop on a single-node implementation and a data set of 100MB and around 52K distinct URLs. There is almost one order of magnitude performance improvement between the third and the first approach.

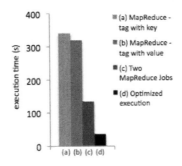

Fig. 1. Different implementations of Query example Q1

In different query examples and/or value distributions over (key, tag) pairs, the first or the second approach may be better, as Section 5 discusses. This suggests that the *tag* constituent should become a first class citizen, as significant as *key* and *value* elements, and not be hidden within map and reduce implementations. Given a high level declarative approach, such as Pig-Latin or ASSET, this analysis can be carried out by the optimizer. In this paper, we propose an extended Map and Reduce interface, called TaggedMap and TaggedReduce, something that could also be utilized by a high level language. In TaggedMap method the user maps triplets instead of pairs (i.e. map(key, tag, value)) and in TaggedReduce method the user reduces a value set *for each key and for each tag*.

Since our implementation is *on top of Hadoop* (future work involves altering Hadoop's engine), we preprocess the specification of these functions to form appropriate and correct specifications of standard map and reduce functions for both alternatives – when the tag value is appended either to the key or the value. The selection is currently hardcoded, however current work tries to embed some reasoning on the preprocessing phase. Under certain syntactic criteria, the preprocessor can identify special cases (similar to "Optimized" case in Figure 1) and do some rewriting on the final map and reduce methods. These cases mainly involve overlapping value sets for each tag, as in Query example Q1. Figure 2 shows the architecture of Tagged MapReduce implementation.

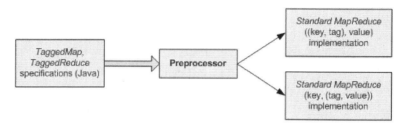

Fig. 2. Tagged MapReduce Implementation

We claim that Tagged MapReduce interface: (a) is simpler and more intuitive for the programmer to use for a practical and useful class of complex analytics, and (b) allows identification of efficient MapReduce implementations.

4   Implementation

This section describes our implementation over Hadoop in order to support the new extended framework. We have used Hadoop's MapReduce framework version 0.20.1. As mentioned in Section 3, we have also created two new interfaces for Map and Reduce, called TaggedMap and TaggedReduce. We describe the extended interface, the preprocessor and the tagging techniques.

4.1   TaggedMap and TaggedReduce

Both TaggedMap and TaggedReduce interfaces are implemented *on top of* Hadoop, and are transformed into standard MapReduce implementations through the *preprocessor*. Similarly to standard Map, in the TaggedMap, the user has to define the key, tag and value parameters for a specific task using the *collect* method, which now takes three arguments instead of two.

In TaggedReduce, similarly to standard Reduce, one iterator over the values is provided. The reduce function is called for each key *and for each tag* and user defined logic is applied to reduce the values. The *collect(key, tag, value)* function, with value being the aggregating result of the input values, is also called to write the reduced triplets to the final output. After defining the TaggedMap and the TaggedReduce functions, the preprocessor chooses whether the tag will be attached to the key or tag as the following section discusses. The number of tags must be known a-priori (an input parameter to the preprocessor.)

4.2 Implementation Alternatives

The two alternatives involve attaching the tag either to the key or the value part to form a compound object. Both of these techniques can be directly implemented in Hadoop's standard MapReduce, however it is not a trivial task for the inexperienced programmer. Keys have to be "writable" and "writableComparable". The "writable" interface is responsible for serialization and deserialization of the keys and "writableComparable" interface is responsible for comparing the keys to each other. When the key part of a (key, value) pair is a composite object, the user has to implement these interfaces each time. In our platform, this is automatically done during the transformation process, if tag is attached to the key.

Once again, when the tag is attached to the value, the user has to create a composite (tag, value) object. The inexperienced programmer may be tempted to use the hashmap data type provided by Hadoop to represent values of different types (i.e. tags) but this comes with a heavy performance penalty as Section 5 shows. We have chosen to implement it as a (tag, value) object, which requires changes to several interfaces. Once again, this is automatically generated during the transformation process.

One can think of an altered Hadoop that provides several alternatives in both cases and the preprocessor chooses the one with the least cost.

4.3 Transformation to Hadoop's MapReduce

The preprocessor is the component that analyzes TaggedMap and TaggedReduce specifications and generates the appropriate rewrites to standard MapReduce, as described in the previous section. Currently, the choice whether to assign the tag to the key or to the value is hardcoded, but the system has been designed in such a way so external information can be read in - such as histogram information on keys and tags, if available.

When the tag is attached to the key to form a compound object, i.e. (key, tag, value) becomes ((key, tag), value) for evaluation, little has to be done: the main body of code in both TaggedMap and TaggedReduce becomes the main body to standard Map and Reduce specifications, using the first implementation, described in Section 4.2.

When the tag is attached to the value to form a compound object, i.e. (key, tag, value) becomes (key, (tag, value)) for evaluation, the main body of TaggedReduce has to be parsed and become a large switch statement based on the tag. All variables have to be replicated with different labels within the switch statement. Tags in our system can only be integers and the number of distinct tags has to be known a-priori (currently is a constant within TaggedReduce method.)

Example 4.1 Let us consider Query Q1. The main body of TaggedMap looks like:

```
for(int i=month; i<=12;i++)
    output.collect(URL, month, 1);
```

while TaggedReduce will be:

```
while(values.hasNext())
  sum += value.next().get();
output.collect(URL, tag.next(), sum);
```

There are 12 tags, 1 to 12.

When the ((key, tag), value) implementation is used, then the main body of standard Map and Reduce methods becomes respectively as below:

```
for(int i=month; i<=12;i++)
  output.collect(new KeyTagWritable(URL, month), 1);
```

and:

```
while(values.hasNext())
  sum += value.next().get();
output.collect(key, sum);
```

When the (key, (tag, value)) implementation is used, then the main body of standard Map and Reduce methods becomes respectively as below:

```
for(int i=month; i<=12;i++)
  output.collect(URL, new TagValueWritable(i,1));
```

and:

```
while(values.hasNext()){
  TagValueWritable value = values.next();
  switch(value.getTag()){
    case 1: sum1 += value.getValue(); break;
    case 2: sum2 += value.getValue(); break;
    . . .
    case 12: sum12 += value.getValue(); break;
  }
}
output.collect(key, new TagValueWritable(1,sum1));
output.collect(key, new TagValueWritable(2,sum2));
. . .
output.collect(key, new TagValueWritable(12,sum12));
```

4.2 Optimizations

In our current work we consider optimization techniques along three axis: choosing between key and value to attach the tag, efficient implementations of Section 4.2 alternatives and efficient rewrites, as those discussed in Motivating Section.

The first question is when the tag should be attached to the key and when to the value part. In Section 5, we argue that this decision depends on query "pattern", the number of distinct keys, tags and the size of the value set. In the presence of system statistics, such as histograms, one could apply heuristics to answer this question.

The second challenge is to have several choices for ((key, tag), value) and (key, (tag, value)) implementation alternatives, as discussed in Section 4.2. Once again, this may depend on the number of distinct keys and tags and the size of the value sets, but also on the type of the tag and the key. For example, instead of having composite key objects like `KeyTagWritable(key, tag)`, one can concatenate key and tag to form a new key and automatically generate the appropriate code to manage this.

Finally, the third challenge has to do with efficient rewrites, such as (c) and (d) for Query Q1 in Figure 1 of Section 3. Such rewrites can lead to orders of magnitude performance improvement, since they avoid the implicit join present in these queries. This can be done easily (more or less) at a high level language such as SQL, but it is not trivial within a procedural language.

5 Experiments

The main goal of our experiments was to validate our argument that different query patterns and value distributions dictate different implementation strategies in terms of tagging. In short, we show that there are cases where tag should be attached to the key part of (key, value) pairs of standard MapReduce and cases where tag should be attached to the value part of (key, value) pairs. In addition, we show that naïve implementations may carry a severe performance penalty.

5.1 Experimental Setting

Both query examples have been tested in small instances of the Amazon EC2 [23] with 1.7GB of memory, 1 virtual core and 32-bit platform. Our dataset was a 20GB log file we created and consists of URLs and timestamps.

We ran query examples Q1 and Q2 in small-sized clusters and benchmarked their execution times as the number of nodes increased from 8 to 16. For each node, a map and a reduce task was invoked, resulting the number of map tasks and the number of reduce tasks to equal the number of nodes. Query example Q1 was applied in a log file of 52.000 distinct URLs. Query example Q2 was applied in two log files with different data distributions; (a) the first log consisted of 52.000 distinct URLs and the analysis was conducted on a "per month" basis, and (b) the second log consisted of only 100 distinct URLs and the analysis was conducted on a "per day" basis.

We have also tested both query examples with the naïve hash-map implementation of Hadoop (in order to attach tag to the value part of (key, value) pairs)) and compared the execution times with our implementation (forming a composite value object). The queries were only tested on a 12-node cluster in this case.

5.2 Results

Figure 3 and Figure 4 illustrate the performance of query examples Q1 and Q2, when Tagged MapReduce implementations are applied. Thus, when executing cumulative tasks an implementation with value being a composite object is more efficient; however, when executing pivoting queries the efficiency of the framework depends on the input data distribution, i.e. the number of distinct keys and tags. So, when the number of tags is relatively small and the number of distinct keys is large (Query Q2 (a)) the implementation with tag attached to the value is better in terms of execution time. But as the number of tags is increasing and the number of distinct keys is decreasing (Query Q2 (b)) the implementation, in which tag is attached to the key proves to be more efficient. The exact execution times for both versions of Query Q2 are demonstrated in Table 1.

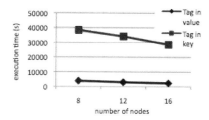

Fig. 3. Different implementations on Query example Q1

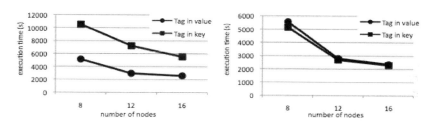

Fig. 4. Different implementations on Query example Q2 with (a) 52.000 distinct URLs and (b) 100 distinct URLs

Table 1. Execution times for different versions of Query example Q2

	Tag in key		Tag in value	
	(a)	(b)	(a)	(b)
8 nodes	10538	5132	5132	5560
12 nodes	7205	2687	2936	2800
16 nodes	5514	2292	2574	2355

Figure 5 demonstrates the normalized execution times when the (key, (tag, value)) approach is implemented through the hashmap data structure, natively supported by Hadoop. This also indicates, that although tag can be relatively easily attached to the value using Hadoop, performance is always an issue.

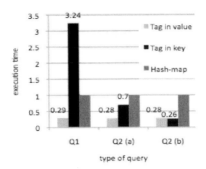

Fig. 5. Tagged MapReduce implementations vs. standard MapReduce hash-map implementation

6   Conclusions and Future Work

In this paper we have proposed an extension of MapReduce, called Tagged MapReduce. We argued that complex data analysis requires multiple aggregates to be computed for a key and this should be supported by a third constituent in the MapReduce framework for usability and efficiency reasons. We described our implementation on top of Hadoop and showed that for different query patterns and (key, tag) value distributions performance may vary significantly on various implementation strategies.

Future work focuses around optimization issues, as those delineated in Section 4.4, especially query rewriting. The set of Multiple-Feature queries [17] is an important subclass of OLAP queries, which had a significant influence on systems, languages and theory. We would like to explore efficient MapReduce implementations on this set.

References

1. Friedman, E., Pawlowski, P., Cieslewicz, J.: SQL/MapReduce: A practical approach to self-describing, polymorphic, and parallelizable user-defined functions. In: VLDB (2009)
2. Hacker, S., Simmons, R., Varming, C.: Netezza meets MapReduce Abstractions for Data Intensive Computing
3. Oracle Corporation: Integrating Hadoop Data with Oracle Parallel Processing. An Oracle white paper (2010)
4. Xu, Y., Kostamaa, P., Gao, L.: Integrating Hadoop and Parallel DBMS. In: SIGMOD (2010)
5. Olston, C., Reed, B., Srivastava, U., Kumar, R., Tomkins, A.: Pig Latin: A Not-So-Foreign Language for Data Processing. In: SIGMOD (2008)
6. DeWitt, D., Stonebraker, M.: MapReduce: A major step backwards. DatabaseColumnBlog, http://www.databasecolumn.com/2008/01/mapreduce-a-major-step-back.html
7. Pavlo, A., Paulson, E., Alexander, R., Abadi, J.D., DeWitt, J.D., Madden, S., Stonebraker, M.: A comparison to Approaches to Large-Scale Data Analysis. In: SIGMOD (2009)
8. Abouzeid, A., Pawlikowski-Bajda, K., Abadi, D., Silberschatz, A., Rasin, A.: HadoopDB: An Architecture Hybrid of MapReduce and DBMS Technologies for Analytical Workloads. In: VLDB (2009)

9. Dean, J., Ghemawat, S.: MapReduce: A Flexible Data Processing Tool. Communications of the ACM 53(1), 72–77 (2010)
10. Dean, J., Ghemawat, S.: MapReduce: Simplified Data Processing on Large Clusters. In: OSDI (2004)
11. Apache Hadoop, `http://hadoop.apache.org`
12. Isard, M., Budiu, M., Yu, Y., Birell, A., Fetterly, D.: Dryad: Distributed data-parallel programs for sequential building blocks. In: Proceedings of EuroSys (2007)
13. Yang, H.-c., Dasdan, A., Hsiao, R.-L., Staf Parker, D..: Parker: Map-Reduce-Merge: Simplified Realtional Data Processing on Large Clusters. In: SIGMOD (2007)
14. Nykiel, T., Potamias, M., Mishra, C., Kollios, G., Koudas, N.: MRShare: Sharing Across Multiple Queries in MapReduce. In: VLDB (2010)
15. Chatziantoniou, D., Tzortzakakis, E.: ASSET Queries: A Declarative Alternative to MapReduce. ACM SIGMOD Record 38(2) (2009)
16. Mackey, G., Sehrish, S., Bent, J., Lopez, J., Habib, S., Wang, J.: Intoducing MapReduce to High End Computing. In: PDSW (2008)
17. Chatziantoniou, D., Ross, K.: Querying Multiple Features of Groups in Relational Databases. In: VLDB (1996)
18. Chatziantoniou, D.: Evaluation of Ad Hoc OLAP: In-Place Computation. In: SSDM (1999)
19. Chatziantoniou, D.: The PanQ Tool and EMF SQL for Complex Data Management. In: KDD, pp. 420–424 (1999)
20. Chatziantoniou, D.: Using grouping variables to express complex decision support queries. DKE Journal 61(1), 114–136 (2007)
21. Chatziantoniou, D., Akinde, M.O., Johnson, T., Kim, S.: The MD-join: An Operator for Complex OLAP. In: ICDE, pp. 524–533 (2001)
22. Oracle: Analytic Functions for Oracle 8i. White Paper, Oracle Corporation (1999)
23. Amazon EC2 cluster, `http://aws.amazon.com/ec2/`

Frequent Pattern Mining from Time-Fading Streams of Uncertain Data

Carson Kai-Sang Leung and Fan Jiang

Department of Computer Science, The University of Manitoba, Canada
`kleung@cs.umanitoba.ca`

Abstract. Nowadays, streams of data can be continuously generated by sensors in various real-life applications such as environment surveillance. Partially due to the inherited limitation of the sensors, data in these streams can be uncertain. To discover useful knowledge in the form of frequent patterns from streams of uncertain data, a few algorithms have been developed. They mostly use the sliding window model for processing and mining data streams. However, for some applications, other stream processing models such as the *time-fading model* are more appropriate. In this paper, we propose mining algorithms that use the time-fading model to discover frequent patterns from streams of uncertain data.

Keywords: Knowledge discovery, data mining techniques, data streams, frequent itemsets, probabilistic data.

1 Introduction

Frequent pattern mining [2] helps discovers implicit, previously unknown, and potentially useful knowledge in the form of frequently occurring sets of items that are embedded in the data. For example, it finds from shopping market basket data those sets of popular merchandise items, which in turn helps reveal shopper behaviour.

Nowadays, the automation of measurements and data collection is producing tremendously huge volumes of data. For instance, the development and increasing use of a large number of sensors (e.g., electromagnetic, mechanical, and thermal sensors) for various real-life applications (e.g., environment surveillance, manufacture systems) have led to *data streams* [5,7,19]. To discover useful knowledge from these streaming data, several mining algorithms [4,6,9] have been proposed. In general, mining frequent patterns from dynamic data streams [11,13] is more challenging than mining from traditional static transaction databases due to the following characteristics of data streams:

1. *Data streams are continuous and unbounded.* As such, we no longer have the luxury to scan the streams multiple times. Once the streams flow through, we lose them. We need some techniques to capture important contents of the streams. For instance, *sliding windows* capture the contents of a fixed number (w) of batches (i.e., w most recent batches) in the streams. Alternatively, *landmark windows* capture contents of all batches after the landmark

A. Cuzzocrea and U. Dayal (Eds.): DaWaK 2011, LNCS 6862, pp. 252–264, 2011.

(i.e., sizes of windows keep increasing with the number of batches). Similarly, *time-fading windows* also capture contents of all the batches but weight recent data heavier than older data (i.e., monotonically decreasing weights from recent to older data).

2. *Data in the streams are not necessarily uniformly distributed.* As such, a currently infrequent pattern may become frequent in the future and vice versa. We have to be careful not to prune infrequent patterns too early; otherwise, we may not be able to get complete information such as frequencies of some patterns (as it is impossible to recall those pruned patterns).

Many existing mining algorithms discover frequent patterns from *precise* data (in either static databases [8,12] or dynamic data streams [10,20]), in which users definitely know whether an item is present in, or absent from, a transaction in the data. However, there are situations in which users are uncertain about the presence or absence of items. For example, due to dynamic errors (e.g., inherited measurement inaccuracies, sampling frequency), streaming data collected by sensors may be uncertain. As such, users may highly suspect but cannot guarantee that an item x is present in a transaction t_i. The uncertainty of such suspicion can be expressed in terms of *existential probability* $P(x, t_i) \in (0, 1]$, which indicates the likelihood of x being present in t_i in probabilistic data. With this notion, every item in t_i in (static databases or dynamic streams of) precise data can be viewed as an item with a 100% likelihood of being present in t_i. A challenge of handling these uncertain data is the huge number of "possible worlds" (e.g., there are two "possible worlds" for an item x in t_i: (i) $x \in t_i$ and (ii) $x \notin t_i$). Given q independent items in all transactions, there are $O(2^q)$ "possible worlds" [14].

In past few years, several mining algorithms have been proposed to discover frequent patterns from uncertain data. However, most of them (e.g., UF-growth [17], UH-Mine [1], U-Eclat [3], UV-Eclat [18]) mine frequent patterns from *static databases*—but *not* dynamic streams—of uncertain data. For the algorithms that mine from data streams (e.g., UF-streaming [15]), they use *sliding windows*. While the use of sliding windows is useful for situations where users are interested in discovering frequent patterns from a fixed-size time window (e.g., frequent patterns observed in the last 24 hours), there are also other situations where users are interested in a variable-size time window capturing all historical data (with or without stronger preference on recent data than older one). In these situations, other window models (e.g., time-fading or landmark model) are needed. Hence, a logical question is: How to discover frequent patterns from dynamic streams of uncertain data when using the time-fading model?

In response to this questions, we conducted a feasibility study [16], which showed that alternatives to sliding windows can be used for mining streams of uncertain data. Hence, *in this DaWaK 2011 paper, we propose algorithms for discovering useful knowledge from streams of uncertain data using the time-fading and landmark models.* Our **key contributions** are (i) the proposal and maintenance of a tree structure in capturing the frequent patterns discovered from batches of transaction in dynamic streams when using the time-fading and landmark models, (ii) the design of tree-based stream mining algorithms that use such a tree structure for discovering and storing frequent patterns—especially the algorithm that does not require the traversal and update of all tree nodes, and (iii) analytical evaluation of these algorithms.

This paper is organized as follows. The next section gives some background information that is relevant to the remainder of this paper. In Section 3, we introduce our mining algorithms that use the time-fading or landmark models to discover frequent patterns from streams of uncertain data. Analytical and experimental results are shown in Sections 4 and 5. Finally, Section 6 presents the conclusions.

2   Background and Related Work

In this section, we provide background information about mining frequent patterns from static databases of uncertain data and using the sliding window model to mine frequent patterns from dynamic streams of uncertain data.

2.1   Mining from Static Databases of Uncertain Data

Among the algorithms that mine frequent patterns from static databases of uncertain data (e.g., UF-growth [17], UH-Mine [1], U-Eclat [3], UV-Eclat [18]), the tree-based *UF-growth* algorithm is used in UF-streaming for stream mining (Section 2.2). To discover frequent patterns, UF-growth constructs a UF-tree to capture contents of uncertain data. Each tree node keeps an item x, its existential probability $P(x, t_i)$, and its occurrence count. The UF-tree is constructed in a similar fashion to that of the FP-tree [12] except that nodes in the UF-tree are merged and shared only if they represent the same x and $P(x, t_i)$. Once the UF-tree is constructed, UF-growth extracts appropriate tree paths to mine frequent patterns using the "possible world" interpretation [14]. A pattern is *frequent* if its expected support $\geq$ user-specified *minsup* threshold. When items within a pattern X are independent, the *expected support* of X in the database DB can be computed by summing (over all transactions $t_1, ..., t_{|DB|}$) the product (of existential probabilities of items within X):

$$expSup(X, DB) = \sum_{i=1}^{|DB|} \left(\prod_{x \in X} P(x, t_i) \right). \tag{1}$$

Note that, while UF-growth discovers frequent patterns from uncertain data, it mines from static databases (instead of dynamic data streams).

2.2   Mining from Uncertain Data Streams with Sliding Windows

Unlike UF-growth [17] (which does not handle data streams) or FP-streaming [10] (which does not handle uncertain data), the *UF-streaming* algorithm [15] mines frequent patterns from uncertain data streams by using a fixed-size sliding window of w recent batches. UF-streaming first calls UF-growth (Section 2.1) to find "frequent" patterns from the current batch of transactions in the streams (using *preMinsup* as the threshold). A pattern is "frequent" (i.e., subfrequent) if its expected support $\geq$ *preMinsup*. Note that, although users are interested in truly frequent patterns (i.e., patterns with expected support $\geq$ *minsup* > *preMinsup*), *preMinsup* is used in attempt to avoid pruning a pattern too early because data in the continuous streams are not necessarily uniformly distributed.

UF-streaming then stores the mined "frequent" patterns and their expected support values in a tree structure, in which each tree node X keeps a list of w support values. When a new batch flows in, the window slides and support values shift so that the "frequent" patterns (and their expected support values) mined from the newest batch are inserted into the window and those representing the oldest batch in the window are deleted. This process is repeated for each batch in the stream. The expected support of any frequent pattern X can be computed by summing all w expected supports of X (one for each batch in the sliding window). Let $expSup(X, B_i)$ denote the expected support of X in Batch B_i. Then, at time T, the expected support of X in the current sliding window containing w batches of uncertain data in Batches $B_{T-w+1}, ..., B_T$ inclusive can be computed as follows:

$$expSup\left(X, \cup_{i=T-w+1}^{T} B_i\right) = \sum_{i=T-w+1}^{T} expSup(X, B_i). \qquad (2)$$

3   Our Proposed Algorithms

In this section, we propose our algorithms—called **TUF-streaming**—that use the *t*ime-fading model in an *u*ncertain data environment to mine "*f*requent" patterns from *streaming* data.

3.1   A Naive Algorithm: TUF-Streaming(Naive)

Among the three commonly used models for processing streams (i.e., sliding window, landmark, and time-fading models), the landmark window keeps all batches after the landmark (i.e., keeps an increasing number of batches). Similarly, the time-fading window also keeps an increasing number of batches, but it weights older data lighter than recent data (i.e., monotonically decreasing weights from current to older data). From that perspective, the landmark window can be considered as a special case of the time-fading window in which all batches have the same weight.

Inspired by UF-streaming (which uses sliding windows), we propose **TUF-streaming(Naive)** that uses *time-fading windows*. The key steps of the algorithm can be described as follows. First, for each batch B_i of uncertain data in the stream, our algorithm applies UF-growth with *preMinsup* to find "frequent" patterns (i.e., patterns with expected support $\geq$ *preMinsup* from a batch). Then, it stores the mined "frequent" patterns and their expected support values in a tree structure called ***UF-stream***, in which each tree node corresponding to a pattern X keeps a list of support values. Note that the time-fading window does not slide. Instead, it grows. This mining process and UF-stream insertion process

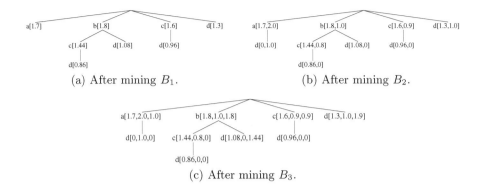

(a) After mining B_1.   (b) After mining B_2.

(c) After mining B_3.

Fig. 1. The UF-stream structures for the TUF-streaming(Naive) algorithm

are repeated for each batch in the stream of uncertain data. Let $expSup(X, B_i)$ denote the expected support of X in B_i. Then, at time T, the expected support of X mined from the time-fading model can be computed by summing over all batches the expected supports of X (weighted by the *time-fading factor* α, where $0 \leq \alpha \leq 1$):

$$expSup\left(X, \cup_{i=1}^{T} B_i\right) = \sum_{i=1}^{T} \left(expSup(X, B_i) \times \alpha^{T-i}\right), \qquad (3)$$

Example 1. Consider the following stream of uncertain data:

Batches	Transactions	Contents
	t_1	$\{a:0.7,\ d:0.1,\ e:0.4\}$
B_1	t_2	$\{a:1.0,\ b:0.9,\ c:0.8,\ d:0.6\}$
	t_3	$\{b:0.9,\ c:0.8,\ d:0.6\}$
	t_4	$\{a:1.0,\ c:0.1,\ d:0.7\}$
B_2	t_5	$\{a:1.0,\ d:0.3,\ e:0.1\}$
	t_6	$\{b:1.0,\ c:0.8\}$
	t_7	$\{a:1.0,\ c:0.9,\ d:0.3\}$
B_3	t_8	$\{b:0.9,\ d:0.8\}$
	t_9	$\{b:0.9,\ d:0.8,\ e:0.7\}$

Here, each transaction contains items and their corresponding existential probabilities, e.g., $P(a, t_1)=0.7$. Let the user-specified *minsup* threshold be 1.0. When using the time-fading model, TUF-streaming(Naive) applies UF-growth to B_1 in the uncertain data stream using $preMinsup < minsup$ (say, $preMinsup=0.8$) and finds "frequent" patterns $\{a\}, \{b\}, \{b, c\}, \{b, c, d\}, \{b, d\}, \{c\}, \{c, d\}$ & $\{d\}$ with their corresponding expected support of 1.7, 1.8, 1.44, 0.86, 1.08, 1.6, 0.96 & 1.3. These patterns and their expected support values are then stored in the UF-stream structure as shown in Fig. 1(a). Each node in UF-stream keeps an item and a *list* of expected support values. So far, each list is of length 1 (e.g., $c:[1.44]$ on the branch $\langle b:[1.8],\ c:[1.44],\ d:[0.86]\rangle$ represents "frequent" pattern $\{b, c\}$ with an expected support of 1.44).

Next, when the second batch B_2 arrives, TUF-streaming(Naive) applies a similar procedure: Call UF-growth to find "frequent" patterns $\{a\}, \{a, d\}, \{b\}, \{b, c\}, \{c\}$ & $\{d\}$

with expected support values of 2.0, 1.0, 1.0, 0.8, 0.9 & 1.0, respectively. Then, the algorithm appends each expected support value to the list of the appropriate tree node in UF-stream. The resulting UF-stream, as shown in Fig. 1(b), consists of nine nodes (due to the addition of the node $d[0,1.0]$ representing the new pattern $\{a, d\}$ having an expected support of 1.0 in B_2 but infrequent in B_1). Note that the list in each node now consists of two expected support values. Expected support of any pattern X can be computed using Equation (3) based on the expected support values stored in the list of X. For instance, let the time-fading factor α be 0.9, then $expSup(\{b, c\}, B_1 \cup B_2)$ $= 1.44\alpha + 0.8 \approx 2.10$.

Similarly, when subsequent batches arrive, TUF-streaming(Naive) applies a similar procedure. Fig. 1(c) shows the resulting UF-stream structure after processing B_3. At that time, $expSup(\{b, c\}, B_1 \cup B_2 \cup B_3) = 1.44\alpha^2 + 0.8\alpha + 0 \approx 1.89$.   □

Note that, when $\alpha=1$, Equation (3) can be simplified to become the following, which computes the expected support of X mined from the *landmark model* by summing all expected supports of X (after the landmark B_1):

$$expSup\left(X, \cup_{i=1}^{T} B_i\right) = \sum_{i=1}^{T} expSup(X, B_i). \tag{4}$$

Example 2. Let us revisit Example 1, but use the *landmark model*. Then, the key difference is that TUF-streaming(Naive) uses a different equation—namely, Equation (4)—for computing expected support. As the contents (e.g., expected support of every pattern for each batch) of UF-stream are the same as those shown in Fig. 1, the expected support values of "frequent" patterns mined from B_1 are the same as those in Example 1. However, the expected support values of "frequent" patterns mined from B_i (for $i \geq 2$) are different. For instance, $expSup(\{b, c\}, B_1 \cup B_2) = 1.44 + 0.8 = 2.24$ (cf. 2.10 in Example 1), and $expSup(\{b, c\}, B_1 \cup B_2 \cup B_3) = 1.44 + 0.8 + 0 = 2.24$ (cf. 1.89).   □

3.2   A Space-Saving Algorithm: TUF-Streaming(Space)

Although TUF-streaming(Naive) finds all "frequent" patterns, it may require a large amount of space. As data streams are continuous and unbounded, storing the expected support value of X for each batch in the streams can be impractical because it could lead to a potentially infinite list for each node. A careful analysis on Equation (3) reveals that the expected support of X is the sum of weighted expected support of X over all batches. Unlike the sliding window model (which requires the deletion of the oldest batch), the fading-time model does not require the deletion of any old batches. Instead, it assigns lighter weights to old batches than recent batches. As a special case, for the landmark model, the algorithm assigns the same weights to all batches (regardless whether they are old or recent). Hence, we propose a space-saving algorithm called **TUF-streaming(Space)**, which does not need to keep track of the details for each batch. We rewrite Equation (3) in a recursive form as follows:

$$expSup\left(X, \cup_{i=1}^{T} B_i\right) = \left[expSup\left(X, \cup_{i=1}^{T-1} B_i\right) \times \alpha\right] + expSup(X, B_T). \tag{5}$$

By doing so, the algorithm keeps only a *single* value—i.e., $expSup(X, \cup_{i=1}^{T} B_i)$—instead of a potentially infinite list of $expSup(X, B_i)$.

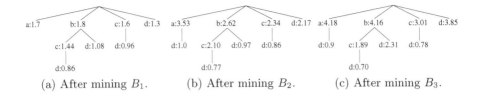

(a) After mining B_1.   (b) After mining B_2.   (c) After mining B_3.

Fig. 2. The UF-stream structures for the TUF-streaming(Space) algorithm

Example 3. Let us revisit Example 1. When using the time-fading model, our TUF-streaming(Space) algorithm uses Equation (5) to compute expected support values. For instance, Fig. 2(a) shows the expected support values stored in UF-stream after mining "frequent" patterns from B_1. They are identical to those shown in Fig. 1(a).

Afterwards (say, after mining B_i for $i \geq 2$), instead of appending the expected support values of "frequent" patterns mined from B_i, the algorithm modified the stored value. For instance, after mining B_2, instead of storing [1.44, 0.8] for $\{b, c\}$ as in Fig. 1(b) for TUF-streaming(Naive), TUF-streaming(Space) stores their sum $1.44\alpha + 0.8 \approx 2.10$ as $expSup(\{b, c\}, B_1 \cup B_2)$ in Fig. 2(b). Similarly, after mining B_3, instead of storing [1.44, 0.8, 0] as in Fig. 1(c) for TUF-streaming(Naive), TUF-streaming(Space) stores their sum $(1.44\alpha + 0.8)\alpha + 0 \approx 1.89$ as $expSup(\{b, c\}, B_1 \cup B_2 \cup B_3)$ in Fig. 2(c).   □

3.3   A Time-Saving Algorithm: TUF-Streaming(Time)

TUF-streaming(Space) greatly reduces the amount of space required from a potentially infinite list of expected support values to a much more realistic and practical requirement of storing only a single expected support value in each node in UF-stream. However, as observed from the recursive formula shown in Equation (5), the expected support of any pattern X up to time T directly depends on the expected support of X up to time $T-1$. As such, TUF-streaming(Space) needs to visit every node in UF-stream after mining each batch (even if the corresponding pattern is not "frequent" in that batch) in order to compute expected support for "frequent" patterns. On the one hand, such a requirement may incur a long runtime. On the other hand, if one were to skip nodes in some batches, then the resulting expected support may not be correct. See Example 4.

Example 4. Let us revisit Example 3. Fig. 2 shows that $\{b, d\}$ is "frequent" with $expSup(\{b, d\}, B_1) = 1.08$. We know that $\{b, d\}$ does not appear in B_2, but it is "frequent" is B_3 with $expSup(\{b, d\}, B_3) = 1.44$. If after mining B_2, we decide to skip the node corresponding to $\{b, d\}$, then the expected support value stored in UF-stream would remain unchanged (i.e., at 1.08). Then, after mining B_3, we decide to visit and update the node for $\{b, d\}$, then the expected support value stored in UF-stream would become $1.08\alpha + 1.44 = 2.52$ (cf. the correct expected support of 2.31). The problem was caused by skipping this node after mining B_2 (even though $\{b, d\}$ is not "frequent"). The skip led to the missing multiplication of α.   □

To solve the above problem, we propose a time-saving algorithm called **TUF-streaming(Time)**, which does not need to visit every node in UF-stream after mining each batch. With this algorithm, the number of nodes visited at each

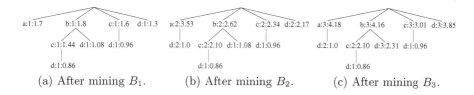

(a) After mining B_1.   (b) After mining B_2.   (c) After mining B_3.

Fig. 3. The UF-stream structures for the TUF-streaming(Time) algorithm

batch is *proportional to* the number of "frequent" patterns mined from that batch. In other words, it visits only those nodes representing patterns that are "frequent" in that batch. It is possible due to our analytical results, which reveal that Equation (5) can be written as follows:

$$expSup\left(X, \cup_{i=1}^{T} B_i\right) = \left[expSup\left(X, \cup_{i=1}^{LV} B_i\right) \times \alpha^{T-LV}\right] + expSup(X, B_T), \quad (6)$$

where LV is an additional field stored in each node of UF-stream to indicate the batch number of last visit of the node.

Example 5. Let us revisit Example 3. When using TUF-streaming(Time), although each node in UF-stream contains an additional "last visit" field (i.e., requires slightly more space), we no longer need to visit every node in UF-stream after mining a batch (i.e., takes less time). This is a space-time tradeoff.

Our TUF-streaming(Time) uses the "last visit" field in Equation (6) for computing expected support values to be stored in UF-stream for the time-fading model. Unlike TUF-streaming(Space) that visits every node, TUF-streaming(Time) visits only "frequent" nodes. After mining B_1, the algorithm visits and stores eight expected support values (i.e., 1.7, 1.8, 1.44, 0.86, 1.08, 1.6, 0.96 & 1.3 for "frequent" patterns $\{a\}, \{b\}, \{b,c\}, \{b,c,d\}, \{b,d\}, \{c\}, \{c,d\}$ & $\{d\}$, respectively) in UF-stream. The "last visit" fields for all these eight nodes are "1", indicating that they were last visited in Batch B_1. For example, the node d:1:0.86 shown in Fig. 3(a) indicates that $\{b,c,d\}$ with expected support of 0.86 was last visited in Batch B_1.

Then, for B_2, only six patterns are "frequent": $\{a\}, \{a,d\}, \{b\}, \{b,c\}, \{c\}$ & $\{d\}$. TUF-streaming(Time) only visits and updates these six nodes. For instance, it visits the node for $\{b,c\}$ and updates its expected support (to 2.10) by multiplying the old $expSup(\{b,c\}, B_1)$=1.44 by α and then adding $expSup(\{b,c\}, B_2)$=0.8 to the product: $1.44\alpha + 0.8 \approx 2.10$. It results in c:2:2.10 as shown in Fig. 3(b). For patterns that are not "frequent" (e.g., $expSup(\{b,d\}, B_2)$=0), the algorithm delays visiting to that node. It explains why the node $\{b,d\}$ is represented as d:1:1.08, which means $\{b,d\}$ with expected support of 1.08 was last visited & updated at Batch B_1.

After mining B_3, TUF-streaming(Time) visits and updates four nodes, including $\{b,d\}$. As shown in Fig. 3(c), the node is represented as d:3:2.31, which indicates that $expSup(\{b,d\}, B_1 \cup B_2 \cup B_3) = 1.08 \times \alpha^{3-1} + expSup(\{b,d\}, B_3) = 1.08\alpha^2 + 1.44 \approx 2.31$. By doing so, TUF-streaming(Time) visits nodes only for "frequent" patterns mined in a batch. It requires less runtime than TUF-streaming(Space), which visits every node in UF-stream. □

3.4   An Enhancement Algorithm for the Landmark Model: TUF-Streaming(Space&Time)

Among the algorithms that we have proposed so far for mining "frequent" patterns from streams of uncertain data with the time-fading model, TUF-streaming(Space) requires less space, but it needs to visit every node in UF-stream. Conversely, TUF-streaming(Time) requires less time, but it needs an additional field for every node in UF-stream. It is a space-time tradeoff. However, when dealing with the special case where $\alpha=1$ (i.e., landmark model), we can get the benefits of both worlds. A careful analysis on Equation (6) reveals that, when $\alpha=1$, we can rewrite the equation to become the following:

$$expSup\left(X, \cup_{i=1}^{T} B_i\right) = expSup\left(X, \cup_{i=1}^{LV} B_i\right) + expSup(X, B_T), \qquad (7)$$

where LV is the batch number in which X was last visited (i.e., when X was "frequent"). Note that, between T and the last visit LV of X, the expected support of X remains changed, i.e., $expSup\left(X, \cup_{i=1}^{LV} B_i\right) = ... = expSup\left(X, \cup_{i=1}^{T-1} B_i\right)$. As such, we propose an enhancement called **TUF-streaming(Space&Time)**. It visits only nodes corresponding to "frequent" patterns mined from each batch, and it does not need to keep track of when they were last visited.

4   Analytical Evaluation

In this paper, we proposed four TUF-streaming algorithms for discovering "frequent" patterns from streams of uncertain data when using the time-fading and landmark models. In this section, let $|FP_i|$ denote the number of "frequent" patterns mined from Batch B_i. When using the time-fading model, the TUF-streaming(Naive) algorithm requires the largest amount of space as it requires $w \times |\cup_i FP_i|$ expected support values to be stored in UF-stream (where w is the number of batches mined so far). In contrast, TUF-streaming(Space) requires the least amount of space because each node only stores a single value (i.e., a total of $|\cup_i FP_i|$ values), whereas TUF-streaming(Time) requires slightly more space than TUF-streaming(Space) because each node needs to keep the "last visit" field in addition to the usual expected support value for each "frequent" pattern (i.e., a total of $|\cup_i 2FP_i|$ values). However, it is bounded (cf. an unbounded or potentially infinite list of expected support values in TUF-streaming(Naive)). Moreover, such a slight increase in space usually pays off as it reduces the runtime. Same comments apply to the landmark model, with an additional observation that TUF-streaming(Space&Time) requires the same amount of space as TUF-streaming(Space).

As for the runtime for the time-fading model, both TUF-streaming(Naive) and TUF-streaming(Space) are required to visit every node in UF-stream regardless whether or not the corresponding pattern is "frequent", i.e., visit $|\cup_i FP_i|$ nodes for each of w batches for a total of $w \times |\cup_i FP_i|$ visits (e.g., visited 26 nodes for Fig. 1 or Fig. 2). In contrast, TUF-streaming(Time) only visits those nodes corresponding to "frequent" patterns, and it requires $\sum_i |FP_i|$ visits (e.g., visited 19 nodes for Fig. 3). Again, same comments apply to the landmark model, except that they require less runtimes than the time-fading model due to simpler calculation. Similar to simplification of Equation (3) to Equation (4), computation of expected support values become simpler when $\alpha=1$ (for the landmark model) because the terms $\left[expSup\left(X, \cup_{i=1}^{T-1} B_i\right) \times \alpha\right]$ and $\left[expSup\left(X, \cup_{i=1}^{LV} B_i\right) \times \alpha^{T-LV}\right]$

in Equations (5) and (6) can be simplified to become $expSup\left(X, \cup_{i=1}^{T-1} B_i\right)$ and $expSup\left(X, \cup_{i=1}^{LV} B_i\right)$, respectively. Moreover, our TUF-streaming(Space&Time) also only visits those nodes corresponding to "frequent" patterns but may require less runtime than TUF-streaming(Time) due to the absence of the "last visit" field.

5   Experimental Evaluation

Different datasets, which included IBM synthetic data and UCI real data, were used for experimental evaluation. For instance, we used an IBM synthetic data with 1M records with an average transaction length of 10 items and a domain of 1,000 items. We assigned an existential probability from the range (0,1] to every item in each transaction. We set each batch to be 5,000 transactions (for a maximum of $w=200$ batches). The reported figures are based on the average of multiple runs in a time-sharing environment using an 800 MHz machine. Runtime includes CPU and I/Os for mining of "frequent" patterns and maintenance of the UF-stream structure. We evaluated different aspects of our four proposed algorithms, which were implemented in C.

First, we evaluated the functionality of our proposed algorithms. When using the time-fading model, TUF-streaming(Naive), TUF-streaming(Space) and TUF-streaming(Time) all gave the same collection of frequent patterns. Similarly, when using the landmark model, these three algorithms gave the same collection of frequent patterns as TUF-streaming(Space&Time). However, their runtimes varied.

In terms of runtime, when the number of batches (w) increased, the runtime increased. See Fig. 4(a) for the time-fading model. Among the three algorithms, TUF-streaming(Naive) and TUF-streaming(Space) took almost the same amount of time. The former appended the expected support values of "frequent" patterns discovered from a new batch whenever the batch was processed and mined, whereas the latter took slightly more time to update the expected support due to multiplication and addition. Both algorithms visited all nodes in UF-stream. In contrast, after mining each batch, TUF-streaming(Time) took less runtime because they visited only nodes corresponding to the patterns discovered from that batch. For example, TUF-streaming(Naive) and TUF-streaming(Space) visited an average of about 22K nodes per batch, whereas TUF-streaming(Time) visited about 35K nodes for the entire mining process. For the landmark model, the trends were very similar. The only difference was that runtimes of the landmark models were slightly shorter as they did not involve the computation of α. Moreover, TUF-streaming(Space&Time) required shorter runtime than TUF-streaming(Time) for the landmark model.

We also varied *minsup* values. Fig. 4(b) shows that, when *minsup* increased, the number of expected support values stored in the UF-stream structure decreased for all algorithms because the number of "frequent" patterns mined from the stream decreased.

Next, we evaluated the memory consumption of our algorithms. Fig. 4(c) shows that, when the number of batches increased, the number of expected

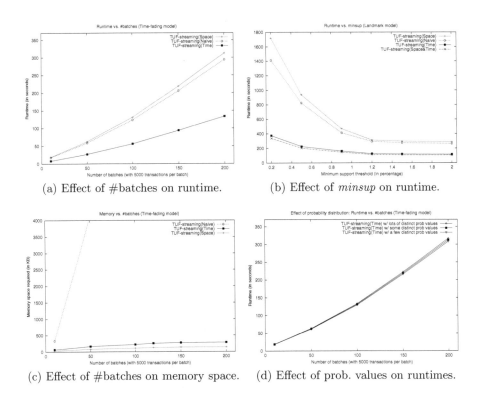

(a) Effect of #batches on runtime.   (b) Effect of *minsup* on runtime.

(c) Effect of #batches on memory space.   (d) Effect of prob. values on runtimes.

Fig. 4. Experimental results of our proposed TUF-streaming algorithms

support values stored in UF-stream increased. For TUF-streaming(Naive) increased almost linearly as the list of expected support values in each node increased proportional to the number of batches. Moreover, as data are not necessarily uniformly distributed, different patterns can be discovered from different batches. These add a few patterns to the collection of patterns to be kept in UF-stream. In contrast, as TUF-streaming(Space) only kept a single value for each node, its memory consumption was independent of the number of batches. TUF-streaming(Time) for time-fading models occupied twice the amount of space as TUF-streaming(Space) due to the extra "last visit" field in each node. When using landmark models, TUF-streaming(Space&Time) required the same amount of space as TUF-streaming(Time).

Furthermore, we also tested the effect of the distribution of item existential probability. When items took on a few distinct existential probability values, UF-trees used in UF-growth became smaller. Regardless of the size of UF-trees, the number of "frequent" patterns returned by UF-growth (i.e., the number of nodes kept in the UF-stream structure) was not different significantly. Hence, as shown in Fig. 4(d), the runtimes for the algorithms were very similar.

6   Conclusions

In this paper, we proposed tree-based mining algorithms that can be used for mining frequent patterns from dynamic streams of uncertain data with both time-fading and landmark models. All algorithms apply UF-growth with *pre-Minsup* to find "frequent" patterns. The mined patterns are then stored in the UF-stream structure together with their expected support values. Then, when the next batch of streaming transactions flows in, the algorithms update the UF-stream structure differently. The naive algorithm keeps a potentially infinite list of expected support values for each node in UF-stream. The space-saving algorithm reduces the memory consumption by keeping only a single value for each node. The time-saving algorithm visits only those nodes corresponding to "frequent" patterns. In addition, we also proposed an enhancement algorithm that reduces both space and time consumption for the landmark model. Analytical and experimental results showed the space and time effectiveness of our TUF-streaming algorithms when using the time-fading and/or landmark models for mining frequent patterns from streams of uncertain data.

Acknowledgements. This project is partially supported by NSERC (Canada).

References

1. Aggarwal, C.C., Li, Y., Wang, J., Wang, J.: Frequent pattern mining with uncertain data. In: ACM KDD, pp. 29–37 (2009)
2. Agrawal, R., Srikant, R.: Fast algorithms for mining association rules. In: VLDB, pp. 487–499. Morgan Kaufmann, San Francisco (1994)
3. Calders, T., Garboni, C., Goethals, B.: Efficient pattern mining of uncertain data with sampling. In: Zaki, M.J., Yu, J.X., Ravindran, B., Pudi, V. (eds.) PAKDD 2010, Part I. LNCS (LNAI), vol. 6118, pp. 480–487. Springer, Heidelberg (2010)
4. Cao, F., Ester, M., Qian, W., Zhou, A.: Density-based clustering over an evolving data stream with noise. In: SDM, pp. 328–339. SIAM, Philadelphia (2006)
5. Castellanos, M., Gupta, C., Wang, S., Dayal, U.: Leveraging web streams for contractual situational awareness in operational BI. In: EDBT/ICDT Workshops, article 7. ACM, New York (2010)
6. Chen, Y., Nascimento, M.A., Ooi, B.C., Tung, A.K.H.: SpADe: on shape-based pattern detection in streaming time series. In: IEEE ICDE, pp. 786–795 (2007)
7. Cuzzocrea, A.: CAMS: OLAPing multidimensional data streams efficiently. In: Pedersen, T.B., Mohania, M.K., Tjoa, A.M. (eds.) DaWaK 2009. LNCS, vol. 5691, pp. 48–62. Springer, Heidelberg (2009)
8. Ezeife, C.I., Zhang, D.: TidFP: Mining frequent patterns in different databases with transaction ID. In: Pedersen, T.B., Mohania, M.K., Tjoa, A.M. (eds.) DaWaK 2009. LNCS, vol. 5691, pp. 125–137. Springer, Heidelberg (2009)
9. Gaber, M.M., Zaslavsky, A.B., Krishnaswamy, S.: Mining data streams: a review. SIGMOD Record 34(2), 18–26 (2005)
10. Giannella, C., Han, J., Pei, J., Yan, X., Yu, P.S.: Mining frequent patterns in data streams at multiple time granularities. In: Data Mining: Next Generation Challenges and Future Directions, pp. 105–124. AAAI/MIT Press (2004)

11. Gupta, A., Bhatnagar, V., Kumar, N.: Mining closed itemsets in data stream using formal concept analysis. In: Pedersen, T.B., Mohania, M.K., Tjoa, A.M. (eds.) DaWaK 2010. LNCS, vol. 6263, pp. 285–296. Springer, Heidelberg (2010)
12. Han, J., Pei, J., Yin, Y.: Mining frequent patterns without candidate generation. In: ACM SIGMOD, pp. 1–12 (2000)
13. Jiang, N., Gruenwald, L.: Research issues in data stream association rule mining. SIGMOD Record 35(1), 14–19 (2006)
14. Leung, C.K.-S.: Mining uncertain data. WIREs Data Mining and Knowledge Discover 1(4), 316–329. John Wiley & Sons, Hoboken, NJ (2011)
15. Leung, C.K.-S., Hao, B.: Mining of frequent itemsets from streams of uncertain data. In: IEEE ICDE, pp. 1663–1670 (2009)
16. Leung, C.K.-S., Jiang, F.: Frequent itemset mining of uncertain data streams using the damped window model. In: ACM SAC, pp. 950–955 (2011)
17. Leung, C.K.-S., Mateo, M.A.F., Brajczuk, D.A.: A tree-based approach for frequent pattern mining from uncertain data. In: Washio, T., Suzuki, E., Ting, K.M., Inokuchi, A. (eds.) PAKDD 2008. LNCS (LNAI), vol. 5012, pp. 653–661. Springer, Heidelberg (2008)
18. Leung, C.K.-S., Sun, L.: Equivalence class transformation based mining of frequent itemsets from uncertain data. In: ACM SAC, pp. 983–984 (2011)
19. Mihaila, G.A., Stanoi, I., Lang, C.A.: Anomaly-free incremental output in stream processing. In: ACM CIKM, pp. 359–368 (2008)
20. Yu, J.X., Chong, X., Lu, H., Zhou, A.: False positive or false negative: mining frequent itemsets from high speed transactional data streams. In: VLDB, pp. 204–215. Morgan Kaufmann, San Francisco (2004)

SPO-Tree: Efficient Single Pass Ordered Incremental Pattern Mining

Yun Sing Koh and Gillian Dobbie

Department of Computer Science, University of Auckland
{ykoh,gill}@cs.auckland.ac.nz

Abstract. Since the introduction of FP-growth using FP-tree there has been a lot of research into extending its usage to data stream or incremental mining. Most incremental mining adapts the Apriori algorithm. However, we believe that using a tree based approach would increase performance as compared to the candidate generation and testing mechanism used in Apriori. Despite this FP-tree still requires two scans through a dataset. In this paper we present a novel tree structure called Single Pass Ordered Tree SPO-Tree that captures information with a single scan for incremental mining. All items in a transaction are inserted/sorted based on their frequency. The tree is reorganized dynamically when necessary. SPO-Tree allows for easy maintenance in an incremental or data stream environment.

Keywords: Incremental Mining, Frequent Pattern Mining, FP-Growth.

1 Introduction

Frequent pattern mining is an important area in data mining and knowledge discovery. Frequent Pattern Tree (FP-Tree) based Frequent Pattern Growth (FP-Growth) mining proposed by Han et al. [1] was an efficient technique to mine frequent patterns based on using a single prefix-tree. Since the introduction of FP-Tree, a large number of research has been carried out to solve the frequent pattern mining problem more efficiently. The main benefit of applying FP-tree was the performance gain due to the compact nature of the data structure. As frequent patterns can be generated by traversing the prefix-tree, this avoids multiple (more than two times) scanning of the dataset. Prefix-tree enables fast computation for the support of all the frequent patterns as well.

With the growing importance of data streams, incremental data mining has become an active area of research with many challenging problems. A data stream is an unbounded sequence of data elements generated at a rapid rate and requires a dynamic environment for collecting data. Some examples of data stream environments include web click streams, network analysis, and sensor network. Incremental data mining algorithms perform knowledge updating incrementally to amend and strengthen what was previously discovered. Incremental data mining algorithms incorporate dataset updates without having to mine the entire dataset again.

A. Cuzzocrea and U. Dayal (Eds.): DaWaK 2011, LNCS 6862, pp. 265–276, 2011.

Examples of some incremental mining techniques include the FUP algorithm [2], the adaptive algorithm [3], and IncSpan [4]. The collective idea in these approaches is that previously mined information should be utilized to reduce maintenance costs. In these approaches, intermediate results, such as frequent patterns, are stored and checked against newly added transactions. This reduces the computation time for maintenance. The algorithms mentioned above are Apriori-based [5] techniques, that depend on a "generate and test" mechanism. Whereas, many of the conventional prefix-tree data mining algorithms cannot handle large and growing data sets, as they require two dataset scans.

The key contribution of this work is proposing and developing a novel tree structure for maintaining frequent patterns in an incremental dataset. We propose a novel tree structure called SPO-Tree (Single Pass Ordered Tree) for incremental mining. The tree captures the content of the transactions dataset in a single pass. The main benefit of this is when a transaction is inserted, deleted or modified, our approach would not require a rescan of the entire dataset.

The rest of the paper is organized as follows. In the next section, we look at previous work in the area. Section 3 introduces our work for SPO-Tree. Our experimental results are presented in Section 4. Finally we summarize our research contributions in Section 5 and outline directions for future work.

2   Related Work

In this section we discuss four existing FP-tree based algorithms that handle stream mining, namely (i) FELINE algorithms with the CATS tree, (ii) the AFPIM algorithm, (iii) CanTree algorithms, and (iv) CP-Tree.

Cheung and Zaiane [6] proposed the Compressed and Arranged Transaction Sequence tree (CATS) for interactive mining. The CATS tree stems from the idea of using FP-tree to improve storage compression. The aim of the work was to build a compact tree representation. This proposed technique requires one pass through the dataset to build the tree. New transactions are added at the root level. At each level, items of the new transaction are compared with children (or descendant) nodes, the transaction is then merged with the node with the highest frequency level. The remainder of the transaction is then added to the merged nodes. This process is repeated recursively until all common items are found. Any remaining items of the transaction are added as a new branch in the last merged node. If the frequency of a node becomes higher than its ancestors, then it has to swap with the ancestors to ensure that its frequency is lower or equal to the frequencies of its ancestors. In CATS we are required to find the right path for each of the new transaction to merge in. It also requires swaps and merges of nodes during the updates, as the nodes in CATS tree are locally sorted.

Example CATS Tree. Consider the dataset in Table 1. Figure 1 shows the resulting CATS tree after each transaction is added. Here we highlight some of the important steps. From the insertion of transactions t_1 to t_2, common items in both transactions $\{a, b, e\}$ are merged into the existing tree. In this step, item e

Table 1. Example of Dataset

TID	Transactions
t_1	{a,b,c,d,e}
t_2	{a,f,b,e}
t_3	{b}
t_4	{d,a,b}
t_5	{a,c,b}
t_6	{c,b,a,e}
t_7	{a,b,d}
t_8	{a,b,d}

is swapped with its ancestors c and d. Since there are no further common items, the remaining item in t_2, f is added as a new branch of e. When t_3 arrives, item b is swapped with item a and moved up. The rest of the transactions are inserted in the same manner.

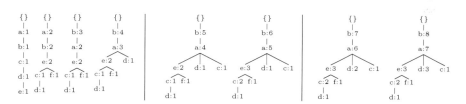

Fig. 1. CATS tree after each transaction is added

Leung et al. [7] proposed the Canonical-Ordered Tree for stream mining. This algorithm is designed so that it only requires one dataset scan. In CanTree, items are arranged in some canonical order, which can be determined by the user prior to the mining process or runtime during the mining process. The items are arranged according to a prefixed tree structure, thus unaffected by the item frequency. CanTree generates compact trees if and only if the majority of the transactions contain a common pattern-base in canonical order. Otherwise, it may generate skewed trees with too many branches and hence with too many nodes. Despite taking less time for tree construction, it requires more memory and more time for extracting frequent patterns from the generated tree.

Example CanTree Tree. Figure 2 shows the resulting CanTree tree after each transaction is added. Like CATS tree this technique keeps track of all items. In this tree, items are inserted in some form of canonical order (lexicographical or arrival). Items in t_1 are sorted in alphabetical order. The subsequent transactions are sorted in the same manner. In this step, item e is swapped with its ancestors c and d. Since there are no further common items the remaining item in t_2 which is item f, is added as a new branch to e. When t_3 arrives, item b is swapped with item a and moved up. The rest of the transactions are inserted in the same manner.

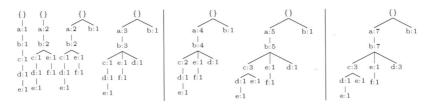

Fig. 2. CanTree in lexicographic order

Tanbeer et al. [8] proposed a tree structure, called CP-tree that constructs a compact prefixed structure. CP-tree has a frequency descending structure by capturing part by part data from the dataset and dynamically restructuring itself. The construction operation consists of two phases: insertion phase and restructuring phase. Insertion phase inserts transaction(s) into CP-tree according to current sorted order of the item list and updates frequency based on the item list. Restructuring phase rearranges the list according to frequency-descending order of items and restructures the tree nodes according to the new ordered item list. The two phases are executed consecutively.

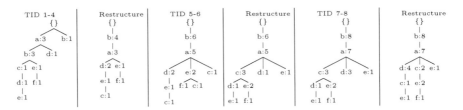

Fig. 3. CP Tree

Example CP Tree. Figure 3 shows the resulting CP-tree after each transaction is added. In this example, we show that restructuring is carried out at the end of every block. In the insertion phase the transactions are inserted in the same way as CanTree following the item-appearance order. In the restructuring phase, at first the items in the tree are rearranged in descending order, which is $I = \{b, a, d, e, c, f\}$ then the tree is restructured to that particular order. In the next insertion phase, items are inserted in the same order as in I. The restructuring phase is carried out as per the previous phases. All subsequent insertion and restructuring phases are carried in a similar fashion. The authors showed that CP-tree outperformed CanTree with a dense dataset. Despite CP-Tree taking a longer tree construction time, it outperformed the CanTree during the mining phase as it produced a more compact tree.

Koh and Shieh [9] developed the Adjusting FP-tree for Incremental Mining (AFPIM) algorithm. This algorithm uses the notion of FP-tree, whereby only the frequent items are kept in the tree. In this algorithm, an item is frequent if its support is no less than a threshold called preMinsup, which is lower than the usual minsup threshold. The frequent items are arranged in descending order of their frequency. Any insertion, deletion, or modification of transactions may affect the frequency of the items, and ordering of the items. As a correction step, the AFPIM algorithm reorders the tree using bubble sort. This may be computationally intensive when applied to all the branches affected by the change in item frequency. Incremental updating of items may also lead to the introduction of new items, which occurs when an infrequent item becomes frequent in the updated dataset. When faced with this scenario, the AFPIM algorithm has to rescan the entire dataset to build a new FP-tree.

Another area of incremental mining is data stream mining [10,11]. We believe that we can transform our work to fit into the data stream framework as well.

3   Single Pass Ordered Tree (SPO-Tree)

The following is a formal definition of association rules. Let $I = \{i_1, i_2, \ldots, i_n\}$, be a set of items. A set $x = \{i_j, \ldots i_k\} \subseteq I$ where $j \leq k$ and $1 \leq j, k \leq n$ is called an itemset. A transaction is $T = (tid, Y)$ where tid is the transaction id and Y is an itemset. If $X \subseteq Y$ is an itemset, then X occurs in T. A transactional dataset D over I is a set of transactions and $|D|$ is the number of transactions in the dataset. The support of an itemset X is the portion of transaction in the dataset that contains X, $supp(X) = \frac{count(X,D)}{|D|}$. An itemset is frequent if its support is no less than a user given support threshold called $minsup$. An association rule is an implication of the form $X \rightarrow Y$, where $X, Y \subset D$, and $X \cap Y = \emptyset$.

In this section we will discuss the preliminaries and the step-by-step construction of our SPO-tree. The SPO-tree has two phases:

Tree Construction Phase: This phase can be broken down into two additional phases, Insertion Phase and Reorganization phase. In the Insertion phase, items in a transaction are inserted into the tree based on a descending order of frequency. The tree is reorganized once the proportion of the edit distance of items in the sorted order changes above a certain threshold as shown in Equation 2.

Tree Mining Phase: The tree mining phase follows the FP-Growth mining technique. Once the SPO-Tree is constructed we use FP-growth to mine patterns with support above a user defined minsup. FP-Growth is used in the mining phase in both the CP-Tree and CanTree approaches.

Figure 4 to 6 is a step-by-step example of the SPO-tree mechanism. Figure 4 shows the resulting tree after transactions t_1 to t_3 are added. The main difference between our technique and previous techniques, is that each transaction is sorted based on the order of frequency (and the order of appearance if the item has the same support) before insertion into the dataset.

In Figure 4, there are 3 tables. In the second and third table, the first two columns so the items sorted according to frequency based on the current inserted transaction, and the last column shows the edit distance, d, between the sorted order based on the current transaction t_n and its previous transaction t_{n-1}. Here t_{n-1} represents the merged result of the previous $n-1$ transactions. In calculating

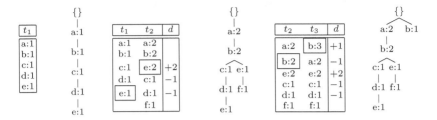

Fig. 4. Insertion of t_1 to t_3

total edit distance / max dist $= \dfrac{6}{24}$

$= 0.25$

In this example, re-sorting of the tree is carried out in the next step as 0.25 is greater or equal to a minimum edited distance proportion set at 0.20.

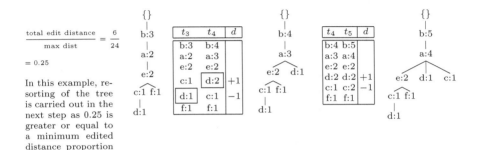

Fig. 5. Insertion of t_4 to t_5 with resorting

the edit distance we consider the shift of the items upwards as positive edit distance and downwards as negative edit distance. In this example in transaction t_1 item e was in the position 5 and in t_2 item e moved up to position 3.

Given the ordering of items should remain fairly stable after the initial set of transactions is inserted. We believe that in some cases this would reduce the overall number of tree branches that need to be sorted as compared to CP-tree.

Figure 5 shows the resorting of a tree after the insertion of t_3. A tree is sorted once the fraction of the total absolute edit distance per total maximum edit distance is above a defined minimum edit distance. In this example this is set to 0.20. The resorting phase is prompted if:

$$\frac{\sum_i^n abs(d)}{\sum_i^n \max(i-1, n-i)} \geq \text{minimum edit distance} \tag{1}$$

Here n is the number of items, and d is the edit distance. In this example the total absolute edit distance is 6 (1+1+2+1+1), and the total maximum distance is 24 (5+4+3+3+4+5).

Table 2 shows how the maximum total edit distance is derived. From the table we notice that if we had 9 items the total maximum edit distance would be 56 and if we had 5 items the total edit distance would be 16. This is equivalent to the calculations of triangular numbers plus quarter squares. We can rewrite the

Table 2. Example of Calculating Total Maximum Edit Distance

Items	1	2	3	4	5	6	7	8	9	10
d_0										9
d_1									8	8
d_2								7	7	7
d_3							6	6	6	6
d_4						5	5	5	5	5
d_6					4	4	4	4	4	5
d_7				3	3	3	3	4	5	6
d_8			2	2	2	3	4	5	6	7
d_9		1	1	2	3	4	5	6	7	8
d_{10}	0	1	2	3	4	5	6	7	8	9
$\sum d$	0	2	5	10	16	24	33	44	56	70

total maximum distance as:

$$\sum_{i}^{n} \max(i-1, n-i) = \frac{i(i-1)}{2} + \text{floor}\left(\frac{i^2}{4}\right) \qquad (2)$$

Following the sorting phase the edit distance, d, for the items are reset to 0. The subsequent transactions $t4$, and t_5 are inserted as usual following the sorted frequency and appearance.

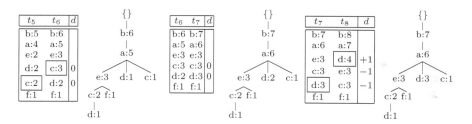

Fig. 6. Insertion of t_6 to t_8

Figure 6 shows the insertion of transactions t_6 to t_8. The reorganizing phase is carried out when required. It does carry out an additional reorganizing phase at the end of each block of transactions.

4   Experimental Results

In the experiments, we tested our program on real-world and synthetic datasets. The programs were written in Microsoft Visual C++, and run on Window 7 operating system on an Intel core 2 Duo machine in a time sharing environment with 4GB of main memory. In all experiments, runtime excludes I/O cost.

4.1   Real-World Datasets

We divided the testing into two sections which includes BMS-POS dataset [12] and several datasets from the UCI repository [13]. Using BMS-POS we carried out an in depth analysis of the performance of SPO-Tree versus CP-Tree. We later ran the SPO-Tree, CP-Tree, and CanTree on several different UCI datasets to examine the efficiency of the algorithms across a range of different datasets.

BMS-POS Dataset. Here we tested our SPO-tree against CP-tree using the BMS-POS dataset. In this experiment we divide the transactions in to the original datasets, and update portion of the dataset. Here we divided BMS-POS into 10 datasets with the initial block of 51,500 and an update of 50,000 subsequent blocks. In the first experiment we compare the tree construction time and the number of nodes produced by SP-Tree as compared to CP-Tree.

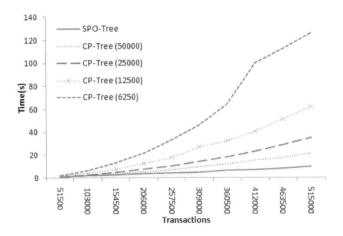

Fig. 7. Execution time for BMS-POS during Tree Construction Phase

Figure 7 shows the time for tree construction BMS-POS using CP-Tree and SPO-Tree. Results shows that the overall restructuring efficiency notably increases as the dataset size increases. For CP-Tree we chose to use a range of the user given fixed slot for restructuring from 6,250 to 50,000. The largest fixed slot was fixed at 50,000 as the incremental blocks used were of size 50,000. We use a minimum edit distance of 0.10 for SPO-Tree.

Table 3 shows the number of nodes in the tree. As the number of nodes increases the time taken to mine will also inadvertently increase. From the table, both SPO-Tree and CP-Tree produces a similar number of nodes. On average SPO-Tree was faster than CP-Tree by 7.4% (minimum 1.1% to maximum 13.3%).

From Table 3 we note the number of nodes generated by the two techniques remains fairly close, but SPO-Tree is constructed more efficiently (as shown in Figure 7). In the last block where BMS-POS dataset has 515,000 transactions,

Table 3. Comparison based on Number of Nodes in BMS-POS

Num Trans	SPO-Tree	CP-Tree			
		50000	25000	12500	6250
51500	208206	208196	208196	208196	208196
103000	381125	381152	381152	381152	381152
154500	545770	545794	545794	545794	545794
206000	698270	698292	698292	698292	698292
257500	811726	811726	811726	811726	811726
309000	924217	924175	924175	924175	924175
360500	1033709	1033639	1033639	1033639	1033694
412000	1204442	1204465	1204465	1204465	1204426
463500	1406072	1406124	1406124	1406124	1406029
515000	1593508	1593516	1593516	1593516	1593520

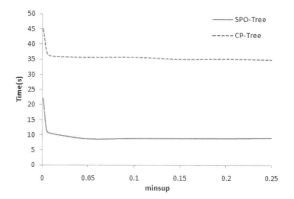

Fig. 8. Execution time by varying minsup

the tree is reorganized seven times, whereas for CP-Tree it is reorganized 10 times for a user-given fixed slot of 50,000 and it is reorganized 62 times for a user given fixed slot of 6,250.

Next we tested how minsup value affects the runtime of the algorithms. Figure 8 shows the runtime for the SPO-Tree versus CP-Tree. We chose to mine CP-tree using a user-given fixed slot of 50,000. We noticed that when minsup decreases the runtime increased but overall the SPO-tree was still more efficient than CP-Tree.

UCI Datasets. We also compared the execution of CP-Tree, CanTree, and SPO-Tree. Table 4 shows the results of execution time for these three algorithms. In these experiments there are on average nine restructuring phases for each of the datasets in CP-Tree. Overall the tree construction time for CanTree is faster than CP-Tree or SPO-Tree. We use a minimum edit distance of 0.10 for SPO-Tree. However both CP-Tree and SPO-tree produce a more compact representation of the tree, thus reducing the tree mining time. From the experiments we can glean that

Table 4. Comparison based on Execution Time(s)

Dataset	CanTree			CP-Tree			SPO-Tree		
	Cons-truction	Mining	Total	Cons-truction	Mining	Total	Cons-truction	Mining	Total
Soybean	0.0	806.0	806.0	0.1	28.6	28.6	0.0	28.1	28.2
Mushroom	0.2	3.6	3.8	0.7	3.1	3.9	0.4	3.2	3.6
Adult	0.6	5.5	6.1	1.2	5.3	6.6	0.7	5.3	6.1
Accidents	3.3	70.4	73.8	16.4	62.5	79.0	5.8	62.9	68.8
Chess	0.2	1624.0	1624.3	0.9	543.0	543.9	0.6	534.6	535.2
Connect-4	2.1	10073.1	10075.3	11.5	669.8	681.3	4.5	657.8	662.4

Table 5. Comparison based on Number of Nodes in Tree

Dataset	CanTree	CP-Tree	SPO-Tree
Mushroom	45704	27165	27021
Adult	71554	56242	56242
Soybean	8336	4405	4390
Accidents	1742760	1393793	1392590
Chess	52074	38609	38610
Connect-4	812529	359969	359292

SPO-tree is faster than CP-Tree. The difference in time becomes more prominent as the density within a datasets increases. From the datasets below Soybean and Mushroom can be considered as the less dense datasets, and Connect-4 can be considered as a denser dataset.

Table 5 shows the number of nodes in each tree. Overall SPO-Tree does produce a more compact tree than CanTree and CP-Tree. As the bottleneck in all these algorithms is the reordering of the tree, we SPO-tree only carries out a reordering when necessary and a quick final resort before mining. It allows us to have a compact representation without incurring a large reordering overhead.

4.2   Synthetic Datasets

We used datasets generated by the program developed at IBM Almaden Research Center. In these experiments, we varied the (a) average length of the transactions and (2) number of unique items in the dataset. In both these experiments the CP-Tree block size was chosen, to replicate the number of organization phases of the SPO-Tree.

In the first experiment, we test the effect of varying the average length of the transactions. Figure 9 shows the total time taken by SPO-Tree and CP-Tree when the average transactions is varied. In this experiment we chose to use the minimum edit distance of 0.10, and the average block size of 2,000 for CP-Tree.

In the second experiment, we test the effect of varying the number of unique items. Figure 10 shows the total time taken by SPO-Tree and CP-Tree when

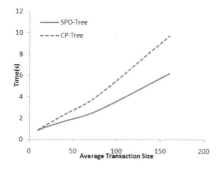

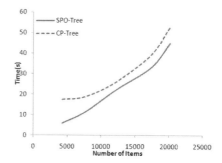

Fig. 9. Varying the average size of the transaction

Fig. 10. Varying the number of Items

the unique item is varied. In this experiment we chose to use the minimum edit distance of 0.10, and the average of block size 500 for CP-Tree.

During the implementation of both SPO-Tree and CP-Tree we cached the result of the comparison, so that sorting uses a faster comparison. When managing the header-list for the tree we kept a pointer to the list node, so that removing and adding elements from/to the list is $O(1)$. A copy of the program can be found at: http://www.cs.auckland.ac.nz/~yunsing/SPO-Tree.html.

5   Conclusions and Future Work

A major contribution of SPO-Tree is that it builds an efficient single pass tree structure for FP-tree based incremental mining. The tree captures the content of the dataset and rearranges it into a more compact representation.

By exploiting the properties in SPO-tree, it can be easily transformed to fit into a data stream environment. In our future work, we will be exploring the possibility of using SPO-Tree in data streams. We will also be adding an additional momentum parameter for each of the items, which will prevent resorting of the branches tree according to the current frequency as every transaction is processed, it will only resort the tree branches according to the current frequency once the momentum inertia threshold is surpassed.

References

1. Han, J., Pei, J., Yin, Y.: Mining frequent patterns without candidate generation. SIGMOD Rec. 29, 1–12 (2000)
2. Cheung, D.W.L., Han, J., Ng, V., Wong, C.Y.: Maintenance of discovered association rules in large databases: An incremental updating technique. In: Proceedings of the Twelfth International Conference on Data Engineering ICDE 1996, pp. 106–114. IEEE, Washington, DC, USA (1996)
3. Sarda, N.L., Srinivas, N.V.: An adaptive algorithm for incremental mining of association rules. In: Proceedings of the 9th International Workshop on Database and Expert Systems Applications, DEXA 1998, p. 240. IEEE Computer Society, Washington, DC, USA (1998)

4. Cheng, H., Yan, X., Han, J.: Incspan: incremental mining of sequential patterns in large database. In: Proceedings of the Tenth ACM SIGKDD International Conference on Knowledge Discovery and Data Mining, KDD 2004, pp. 527–532. ACM, New York (2004)

5. Agrawal, R., Imielinski, T., Swami, A.N.: Mining association rules between sets of items in large databases. In: Buneman, P., Jajodia, S. (eds.) Proceedings of the 1993 ACM SIGMOD International Conference on Management of Data, pp. 207–216 (1993)

6. Cheung, W., Zaiane, O.: Incremental mining of frequent patterns without candidate generation or support constraint. In: Proceedings of Seventh International Database Engineering and Applications Symposium, pp. 111–116 (2003)

7. Leung, C.K.S., Khan, Q.I., Li, Z., Hoque, T.: Cantree: a canonical-order tree for incremental frequent-pattern mining. Knowl. Inf. Syst. 11, 287–311 (2007)

8. Tanbeer, S.K., Ahmed, C.F., Jeong, B.S., Lee, Y.K.: Cp-tree: A tree structure for single-pass frequent pattern mining. In: Washio, T., Suzuki, E., Ting, K.M., Inokuchi, A. (eds.) PAKDD 2008. LNCS (LNAI), vol. 5012, pp. 1022–1027. Springer, Heidelberg (2008)

9. Koh, J.L., Shieh, S.F.: An efficient approach for maintaining association rules based on adjusting FP-tree structures1. In: Lee, Y., Li, J., Whang, K.-Y., Lee, D. (eds.) DASFAA 2004. LNCS, vol. 2973, pp. 417–424. Springer, Heidelberg (2004)

10. Chi, Y., Wang, H., Yu, P., Muntz, R.: Moment: maintaining closed frequent itemsets over a stream sliding window. In: Perner, P. (ed.) ICDM 2004. LNCS (LNAI), vol. 3275, pp. 59–66. Springer, Heidelberg (2004)

11. Chi, Y., Wang, H., Yu, P.S., Muntz, R.R.: Catch the moment: maintaining closed frequent itemsets over a data stream sliding window. Knowl. Inf. Syst. 10, 265–294 (2006)

12. Zheng, Z., Kohavi, R., Mason, L.: Real world performance of association rule algorithms. In: Proceedings of the Seventh ACM SIGKDD International Conference on Knowledge Discovery and Data Mining, KDD 2001, pp. 401–406. ACM, New York (2001)

13. Frank, A., Asuncion, A.: UCI machine learning repository (2010)

RP-Tree: Rare Pattern Tree Mining

Sidney Tsang, Yun Sing Koh, and Gillian Dobbie

The University of Auckland
{stsa027,ykoh,gill}@cs.auckland.ac.nz

Abstract. Most association rule mining techniques concentrate on finding frequent rules. However, rare association rules are in some cases more interesting than frequent association rules since rare rules represent unexpected or unknown associations. All current algorithms for rare association rule mining use an Apriori level-wise approach which has computationally expensive candidate generation and pruning steps. We propose RP-Tree, a method for mining a subset of rare association rules using a tree structure, and an information gain component that helps to identify the more interesting association rules. Empirical evaluation using a range of real world datasets shows that RP-Tree itemset and rule generation is more time efficient than modified versions of FP-Growth and ARIMA, and discovers 92-100% of all the interesting rare association rules.

Keywords: Rare Pattern Mining, FP-Growth, Information Gain.

1 Introduction

Association rule mining techniques are used to extract useful information from databases. The set of association rules that can be extracted from a database can be divided using a support threshold into frequent and rare association rules. Both frequent and rare association rules present different information about the database from which they are found, since frequent rules focus on patterns that occur frequently, while rare rules focus on patterns that occur infrequently. In many domains, events that occur frequently may be less interesting than events that occur rarely, since frequent patterns represent the known and expected while rare patterns may represent unexpected or previously unknown associations, which is useful to domain experts. For example, in the area of medicine, the expected, frequent responses to medications are less interesting than exceptional, rare responses which may indicate adverse reactions or drug interactions.

Algorithms such as Apriori [1] can be used to find both frequent and rare association rules, but the latter requires the minimum support threshold to be set to a low value. However this may cause a combinatorial explosion of itemsets as the number of patterns that meet minimum support becomes insurmountable. Given n items, the number of possible itemsets is $2^n - 1$.

There are three possible types of rare itemsets: first, itemsets which consist of rare items only; second, itemsets which consist of both rare and frequent items; and third, itemsets which consist of only frequent items which fall below the minimum support threshold. We refer to itemsets of the first and second types as *rare-item itemsets*. Rare-item itemsets are generally more interesting than itemsets of the third type, which we

A. Cuzzocrea and U. Dayal (Eds.): DaWaK 2011, LNCS 6862, pp. 277–288, 2011.

call *non-rare-item itemsets*. This is because frequent items occur commonly in the database, and there may be many non-rare-item itemsets that do not represent any interesting connection between items since the items only occurred together by chance. Empricial evidence for the claim that rare-item itemsets are more interesting is given in the results in Section 4. For now, we will illustrate this with the following simple example.

Suppose a database of patient symptoms contains the rare itemsets "1:{elevated heart rate, fever, skin bruises, low blood pressure}" and "2:{muscle pain, tinnitus, sneezing, heartburn}", where all items other than "low blood pressure" are frequent items. Itemset 1 is a rare-item itemset, and itemset 2 is a non-rare-item itemset. Itemset 1 contains a subset of the symptoms of sepsis, will produce a rule such as "{elevated heart rate, fever, skin bruises} → low blood pressure" that highlights the association between the different three former symptoms with low blood pressure, which is a symptom of severe sepsis. However, rules generated from itemset 2, such as "{muscle pain, tinnitus, heartburn} → sneezing" does not give any useful information, since all these symptoms are individually common, and have simply occured together by chance.

The key contribution of the paper is a novel algorithm called RP-Tree that finds rare-item itemsets using a tree structure. Unlike previous level-wise approaches, RP-Tree does not need to generate and test all plausible combinations of rare itemsets, which is more efficient. We empirically show that RP-Tree finds rare itemsets and association rules more effciently than existing algorithms, and identifies 92-100% of rare association rules that meet a confidence and lift threshold. The second contribution of this paper is an extension to RP-Tree that reduces the number of uninteresting association rules generated by excluding items that are poor at predicting the occurrence of rare items. To our knowledge, RP-Tree is the first rare association rule mining algorithm that uses a tree structure.

The paper is organized as follows. In Section 2 we look at previous work in the area of rare association rule mining. In Section 3 we present basic concepts and definitions for rare association rule mining and discuss our novel RP-Tree approach. Section 4 describes the experimental results. Finally, Section 5 concludes the paper.

2   Related Work

Current rare itemset mining approaches are based on level-wise exploration of the search space similar to the Apriori algorithm [1]. In Apriori, k-itemsets (itemsets of cardinality k) are used to generate $k + 1$-itemsets, which are then pruned using the downward closure property. Apriori terminates when there are no new $k + 1$-itemsets remaining after pruning. Rarity, AfRIM, ARIMA and Apriori-Inverse are four algorithms that detect rare itemsets. They all use level-wise exploration similar to Apriori.

Troiano et al. [2] notes that rare itemsets are at the top of the search space, so that bottom-up algorithms must first search through many layers of frequent itemsets. To avoid this, Troiano et al. proposed the Rarity algorithm that begins by identifying the longest transaction within the database and uses them to perform a top-down search for rare itemsets, thereby avoiding the lower layers that only contain frequent itemsets.

In Rarity, potentially rare itemsets (candidates) are pruned in two different ways. Firstly, all k-itemset candidates that are the subset of any of the frequent $k + 1$-itemsets are removed as a candidate, since they must be frequent according to the downward closure property. Secondly, the remaining candidates have their supports calculated, and only those that have a support below the threshold are used to generate the $k - 1$-candidates. The candidates with supports above the threshold are used to prune $k - 1$-candidates in the next iteration.

Adda et al. [3] proposed AfRIM that uses a top-down approach similar to Rarity. Rare itemset search in AfRIM begins with the itemset that contains all items found in the database. Candidate generation occurs by finding common k-itemset subsets between all combinations of rare $k + 1$-itemset pairs in the previous level. Candidates are pruned in a similar way to the Rarity algorithm. Note that AfRIM examines itemsets that have zero support, which may be inefficient.

Szathmary et al. [4] proposed two algorithms that together can mine rare itemsets. As part of those two algorithms, Szathmary et al. defines three types of itemsets: minimal generators (MG), which are itemsets with a lower support than its subsets; minimal rare generators (MRG), which are itemsets with non-zero support and whose subsets are all frequent; and minimal zero generators (MZG), which are itemsets with zero support and whose subsets all have non-zero support. The first algorithm, MRG-Exp, finds all MRG by using MGs for candidate generation in each layer in a bottom up fashion. The MRGs represent a border that separates the frequent and rare itemsets in the search space. All itemsets above this border must be rare according to the antimonotonic property. The second algorithm, ARIMA, uses these MRGs to generate the complete set of rare itemsets. This is done by merging two k-itemsets with $k - 1$ items in common into a $k + 1$-itemset. ARIMA stops the search for non-zero rare itemsets when the MZG border is reached, since above that there are only zero rare itemsets.

Apriori-Inverse [5] proposed by Koh et al. is used to mine perfectly rare itemsets, which are itemsets that only consist of items below a maximum support threshold (maxSup). Apriori-Inverse is similar to Apriori, except that at initialisation, only 1-itemsets that fall below maxSup are used for generating 2-itemsets. Since Apriori-Inverse inverts the downward-closure property of Apriori, all rare itemsets generated must have a support below maxSup. In addition, itemsets must also meet an absolute minimum support, for example 5, in order for them to be used for candidate generation. Since the set of perfectly rare-rules may only be a small subset of rare itemsets, Koh et al. also proposed several modifications that allow Apriori-Inverse to find near-perfect rare itemsets. The methods are based on increasing maxSup during itemset generation, but using the original maxSup during rule generation.

All of the above algorithms use the fundamental Apriori approach, which has potentially expensive candidate generation and pruning steps. In addition, these algorithms attempt to identify all rare itemsets, and as a result spend a significant amount of time searching for non-rare-item itemsets. However, we will show that these non-rare-item itemsets do not tend to give us interesting rare association rules.

The proposed RP-Tree algorithm is an improvement over these existing algorithms in three ways. Firstly, RP-Tree avoids the expensive itemset generation and pruning steps by using a tree data structure, based on FP-Tree, to find rare patterns. Secondly, RP-Tree focusses on rare-item itemsets which generate interesting rules and does not spend time looking for uninteresting non-rare-item itemsets. Thirdly, RP-Tree is based on FP-Growth, which is efficient at finding long patterns, since the task is divided into a series of searches for short patterns. This is especially beneficial since rare patterns tend to be longer than frequent patterns.

3   Rare Pattern Tree Mining

In this section we first discuss basic concepts and the definition of rare-item itemsets. We then describe our proposed RP-Tree algorithm and present a simple example. Finally we describe the modification to RP-Tree using an information gain threshold.

3.1   Basic Concept: Rare Itemsets

Let the set of items $\mathcal{I} = \{i_1, i_2, ...i_m\}$, and the transactional database $\mathcal{D} = \{t_1, t_2, ...t_n\}$ where every $t \subseteq \mathcal{I}$. An association rule is an implication $X \rightarrow Y$ such that $X \cup Y \subseteq \mathcal{I}$ and $X \cap Y = \emptyset$. X is the antecedent and Y is the consequent of the rule. The *support* of $X \rightarrow Y$ in $\mathcal{D}$ is the proportion of transactions in $\mathcal{D}$ that contains $X \cup Y$. The *confidence* of $X \rightarrow Y$ is the proportion of transactions in $\mathcal{D}$ containing X that also contains Y. The *lift* of $X \rightarrow Y$ is confidence($X \rightarrow Y$) / support (Y).

The minRareSup threshold is a noise filter, whereby items that are below this threshold are considered as noise. An itemset is a rare itemset if it has support less than the minimum frequent support threshold (minFreqSup) but above or equal to the minimum rare support threshold (minRareSup). As mentioned in Section 1, rare itemsets can be divided into types: *rare-item itemsets* which refers to itemsets that consist of only rare items and itemsets that consist of both rare and frequent items; and *non-rare-item itemsets* which consist of only frequent items which fall below the minimum support threshold.

For instance, suppose there were 4 items $\{a, b, c, x\}$ with supports $a = 0.80$, $b = 0.30$, $c = 0.50$, and $x = 0.12$, with minFreqSup = 0.15 and minRareSup = 0.05. If the itemset $\{a, b, c\}$ had a support of 0.09, then this itemset would be a non-rare-item itemset ((1) above) since all items are frequent, and its support lies between minFreqSup and minRareSup. The itemset $\{a, x\}$ would be a rare-item itemset ((2) above) assuming that the support of $\{a, x\} > 0.05$, since the itemset includes the rare item x.

Formally, an itemset X is a *rare itemset* iff

$$support(X) < minFreqSup, support(X) \geq minRareSup$$

An itemset X is a *non-rare-item itemset* iff

$$\forall x \in X, support(x) \geq minFreqSup, \; support(X) < minFreqSup$$

An itemset X is a *rare-item itemset* iff

$$\exists x \in X, support(x) < minFreqSup, \; support(X) < minFreqSup$$

3.2   RP-Tree Algorithm

FP-Growth, proposed by Han et al. [6] is a frequent itemset mining algorithm which uses a frequent-pattern tree (FP-Tree) to store a set of database transactions and reduces the required number of database scans to 2. The first scan is used to find the set of items in the database with support over the minimum frequent support threshold; the second is used to construct the initial FP-tree.

The RP-Tree algorithm, shown in Algorithm 1, is a modification of the FP-Growth algorithm. RP-Tree performs one database scan to count item support, similar to FP-Growth. During the second scan, RP-Tree uses only the transactions which include at least one rare item to build the initial tree, and prunes the others, since transactions that only have non-rare items cannot contribute to the support of any rare-item itemset. For example, if $\{x, y, z\}$ was the set of rare items for a given database, minRareSup and minFreqSup, a transaction will have to contain at least one of x, y or z to avoid being pruned.

Note that the ordering of items in each transaction during insertion into the initial tree is according to the item frequency of the original database (and not the database with pruned transactions). This is because rare items in the reduced database may have higher supports than frequent items. If item frequencies of the reduced database were used for transaction item ordering, a frequent item may become the child of a rare item, which invalidates property 1 below.

Using this initial tree, RP-Tree constructs conditional pattern bases and conditional trees for each rare item only. Each conditional tree and the corresponding rare item are then used as arguments for FP-Growth (simplified version shown in Algorithm 2). The threshold used to prune items from the conditional trees is minRareSup. The union of the results from each of these calls to FP-Growth is a set of itemsets that each contain a rare-item, or rare-item itemsets.

The result of RP-Tree is the complete set of rare-item itemsets. This is because:

1. Rare-items will never be the ancestor of a non-rare item in the initial tree due to the tree construction process.
2. All itemsets that involve a particular item a can be found by examining all nodes of a and the nodes of all items that have a lower support than a in the initial tree.

Since RP-Tree examines all rare-item nodes in the initial tree, and all nodes that have a lower support than a rare-item are themselves rare items, RP-Tree must find all rare-item itemsets.

RP-Tree Example. Applying RP-Tree to database $\mathcal{D}$ in Table 1, the support ordered list of all items is $\langle (a{:}7), (i{:}6), (b{:}5), (c{:}4), (l{:}4), (d{:}3), (f{:}3), (e{:}2), (g{:}2), (h{:}1), (j{:}1), (k{:}1), (m{:}1) \rangle$. Using minFreqSup = 4 and minRareSup = 1, only the items $\{d, f, e, g\}$ are rare, and included in $rareItems$.

During construction of the initial RP-Tree, only transactions 1, 3, 4, 5, and 6 are used, since the remaining transactions do not contain any rare items and cannot contribute to any of the result itemsets. In addition, since the support of items h, j, k and m falls below minRareSup, these items are ignored during RP-Tree construction. The initial tree constructed using FP-Growth, which only ignores items that fall below minRareSup, will use all transactions, as shown in Figure 1. This tree has 8 additional

---

Algorithm 1. RP-Tree

1: **Input:** $\mathcal{D}, minRareSup, minFreqSup$;
2: **Output:** $results$;   // Set of rare-item itemsets

3: **Initialisation:**
4: $allItems \leftarrow \{$all unique items in $\mathcal{D}\}$;
5: countSupport($allItems$);   // First scan of database
6: $rareItems \leftarrow \{i \in allItems \mid i.supp \geq minRareSup \wedge i.supp < minFreqSup\}$;
7: $rareItemTrans \leftarrow \{t \in \mathcal{D} \mid \exists r \cdot r \in rareItems \wedge r \in t\}$;
8: $tree \leftarrow$ constructTree($rareItemTrans$);   // Second scan of database

9: **Mining:**
10: $results = \emptyset$;
11: **for** item a in $tree$ **do**
12:     **if** $a \in rareItems$ **then**
13:         construct a's conditional pattern-base and then a's conditional FP-Tree $Tree_a$;
14:         $results \leftarrow results \cup$ FP-Growth($Tree_a, a$);
15:     **end if**
16: **end for**
17: **return** $results$;

Algorithm 2. FP-Growth (without single prefix path optimisation)

1: **Input:** $tree, \alpha$;
2: **Output:** $results$;   // All itemsets generated from $tree$

3: $results \leftarrow \emptyset$;
4: **for** item a in $tree$ do **do**
5:     generate pattern $\beta \leftarrow a \cup \alpha$ with $support = a.support$;
6:     $results \leftarrow results \cup \beta$
7:     construct βs conditional pattern-base and then β's conditional FP-tree $tree_\beta$;
8:     **if** $Tree_\beta \neq \emptyset$ **then**
9:         $results \leftarrow results \cup$ FP-Growth($tree_\beta, \beta$);
10:     **end if**
11: **end for**
12: **return** $results$;

---

nodes compared to the tree built using RP-Tree from the reduced transaction set (shown in Figure 2(a)). The additional nodes are frequent items that correspond to transactions pruned by RP-Tree. To find the rare-item itemsets, the initial RP-Tree is used to build conditional pattern bases and conditional RP-Trees for each rare item $\{d, f, e, g\}$. The conditional tree for item g is shown in Figure 2(b). Each of the conditional RP-Trees and the conditional item are then used as parameters for the FP-Growth algorithm, for example, FP-Growth($Tree_g, g$).

Table 1. Transaction database $\mathcal{D}$

TID	Transactions	TID	Transactions	TID	Transactions
1	{a, b, c, d, f}	5	{a, c, e, f}	9	{i, l, k}
2	{a, c}	6	{a, b, d, g}	10	{i, b, l}
3	{a, c, d, f, g}	7	{i, b, c, l, j}	11	{i, m}
4	{a, b, e, h}	8	{a, i, l}	12	{i}

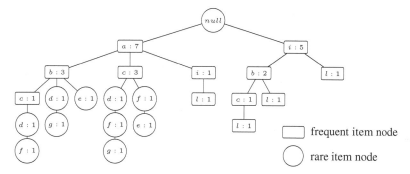

Fig. 1. Pattern tree constructed from database $\mathcal{D}$ using FP-Tree

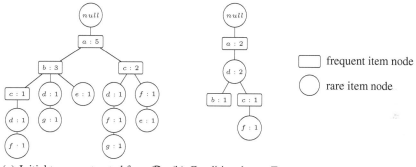

(a) Initial tree constructed from $\mathcal{D}$ (b) Conditional tree, $Tree_g$

Fig. 2. Pattern trees constructed from database $\mathcal{D}$ using RP-Tree

3.3 RP-Tree with Information Gain

Rules that predict the occurrence of rare-items are more interesting than rules that predict the occurrence of frequent items. To identify these rules, RP-Tree has been extended using an information gain component (RP-Tree-IG) to remove frequent items that are not good predictors of rare items. This is done by treating rare items as classifications and each frequent item as a separate attribute. Transactions that contain more than one rare item (and class) are converted into multiple transactions during the information gain calculation so that the transaction contains only 1 rare item. For example, $\{a, b, d, e\}$, where d and e are rare, is split into $\{a, b, d\}$ and $\{a, b, e\}$.

Information gain [7] is calculated as: $IG(X) = \text{Entropy}(Y) - \text{Entropy}(Y \mid X)$ where Y is the set of rare items, and X is a frequent item. Frequent items that do not have an information gain higher than a pre-defined threshold are not used for itemset generation. Specifically, line 11 in Algorithm 1 and line 4 in Algorithm 2 becomes:

$$\text{for item } a \in tree \text{ where } IG(a) \geq minIG$$

where $minIG$ is the minimum information gain threshold an item must meet to be used for generating itemsets. Using the previous example, the classes Y are $\{d, f, e, g\}$, and attributes X are $\{\{a\}, \{b\}, \{c\}\}$. The information gain of c is $IG(c) = 1.971 - 1.842 = 0.129 \, bits$. If, for example, $minIG = 0.1$, then c would be used for generating itemsets.

4   Experimental Results

In our experiments we compared the performance of ARIMA, FP-Growth, and RP-Tree with and without the information gain component. We also generated rules from these itemsets and compared the quality of these rules using the seven interest measures examined in [8]: χ^2, lift, confidence (all and max), coherence, cosine and Kulczynski (abbreviated to kulc). The equations for calculating these measures are shown in Table 2. All algorithms were implemented in Java and executed on an Intel Core 2 Duo 2.33 GHz machine with 4GB of RAM running Windows 7.

In these experiments ARIMA and FP-Growth were modified in order to obtain comparable results within a reasonable time. The ARIMA algorithm was modified in two ways. Firstly, the absolute minimum support (corresponding to minRareSup in RP-Tree) may now be greater than 1. An itemset must meet this support threshold to be included in the result. This is necessary to allow the removal of noisy itemsets, and to allow ARIMA to finish in a reasonable time without setting minFreqSup to an extremely low value. Secondly, candidate support count is done by building a tree structure with candidates from each level, which is more efficient than iterating through each itemset for each transaction. The FP-Growth algorithm was modified to find rare itemsets by generating all itemsets that meet minRareSup, then removing all itemsets that exceed minFreqSup.

Experiments comparing RP-Tree and RP-Tree-IG with Rarity and AfRIM have been omitted since they use a level-wise approach similar to ARIMA, and their performance compared to ARIMA has already been reported in detail in [2] and [3]. It is sufficient to note that AfRIM and Rarity can perform several orders of magnitude faster than ARIMA under specific conditions, such as a low number of rare itemsets, or when there is a small number of items. However, in general, AfRIM performs 2-3 times faster, while Rarity performs about 30 times faster than ARIMA.

Nine datasets from UCI Repository [9] were used in the experiments: Connect-4, Congressional Voting Records (Voting), Primary Tumor (Tumor), Zoo, Teaching Assistant Evaluation (Teaching), Flags, Adult, Dermatology and Soybean Large (Soybean).

4.1   Itemset Generation Performance

In this section we compare the time taken for itemset generation for ARIMA, FP-Growth, RP-Tree and RP-Tree-IG. We use the same minFreqSup and minRareSup threshold across all experiments.

Table 2. Rule Interest Measures [8]

Measure	Definition
χ^2	$\sum \frac{(observed-expected)^2}{expected}$
$Lift(X \rightarrow Y)$	$\frac{sup(X \cup Y)}{sup(X)sup(Y)}$
$AllConf(X \rightarrow Y)$	$\frac{sup(X \cup Y)}{max(sup(X),sup(Y))}$
$MaxConf(X \rightarrow Y)$	$max\{\frac{sup(X \cup Y)}{sup(X)}, \frac{sup(X \cup Y)}{sup(Y)}\}$
$Coherence(X \rightarrow Y)$	$\frac{sup(X \cup Y)}{sup(X)+sup(Y)-sup(X \cup Y)}$
$Cosine(X \rightarrow Y)$	$\frac{sup(X \cup Y)}{\sqrt{sup(X)sup(Y)}}$
$Kulc(X \rightarrow Y)$	$\frac{sup(X \cup Y)}{2}(\frac{1}{sup(X)} + \frac{1}{sup(Y)})$

Table 3. Time taken for itemset generation

Dataset	ARIMA			FP-Growth			RP-Tree			RP-Tree-IG		
	Itemsets	Time (s)	Rel. time	Itemsets	Time (s)	Rel. time	Itemsets	Time (s)	Rel. time	Itemsets	Time (s)	Rel. time
Connect-4	46428	292.53	32.30	46428	9.06	1.00	35494	8.72	0.963	57	2.58	0.285
Voting	1437652	1099.35	230.86	1437652	4.76	1.00	225634	0.87	0.184	16	0.56	0.119
Tumor	1111993	699.12	178.53	1111993	3.92	1.00	309698	0.94	0.239	17	0.15	0.039
Zoo	484139	496.12	194.94	484139	2.55	1.00	117934	0.87	0.343	6	0.05	0.019
Teaching	281	0.38	4.28	281	0.09	1.00	118	0.10	1.067	12	0.05	0.573
Flags	233533	962.66	372.55	233533	2.58	1.00	185	0.33	0.129	8	0.01	0.004
Adult	72658	340.60	47.37	72658	7.19	1.00	57463	6.45	0.898	50	3.65	0.508
Dermatology	-	-	-	4.90E+08	1419.537	1.00	9.12E+07	265.206	0.187	2.37E+06	270.562	0.191
Soybean	-	-	-	1.67E+08	1184.961	1.00	4.34E+06	15.902	0.013	1.40E+05	14.913	0.013

Table 3 shows, for each dataset, the number of itemsets generated, the absolute time taken for each algorithm. The relative time compared to FP-Growth is also given, with relative time for FP-Growth is set to 1.0. The differences in the number of itemsets are due to the types of rare itemsets each algorithm can generate. ARIMA and FP-Growth both generate the complete set of rare itemsets, RP-Tree generates only rare-item itemsets, and RP-Tree-IG generates rare-item itemsets using items that meet an information gain threshold. Note that the results for ARIMA for the Dermatology and Soybean datasets have been excluded since execution did not complete within 2 hours. The runtime for ARIMA is more than 32 times longer than FP-Growth in all datasets except Teaching. This is due to the Teaching dataset being a fairly small dataset, and overhead takes up a large proportion of the time taken. Realistically, most real world datasets would be of a reasonable size and the overhead is negligible. We also see that time taken for RP-Tree-IG is consistently less than that of RP-Tree, which is in turn less than FP-Growth. The time taken for ARIMA is significantly longer than FP-Tree due to the computationally expensive candidate generation and pruning steps. The differences in time taken for RP-Tree and RP-Tree-IG are the result of pruning transactions without any rare items, and pruning itemsets without any rare items above the minIG threshold, respectively. Transaction pruning reduces the size of the initial tree generated, and reduces the amount of computation required and the number of rare itemsets found.

4.2 Changes in Rule Quality

Rules were generated from the itemsets found using ARIMA/FP-Growth (both of which generate the complete set of rare itemsets), RP-Tree and RP-Tree-IG. For all algorithms, parameters are: minFreqSup = 15% and minRareSup = 5. For RP-Tree with information

Table 4. UCI Datasets

	FP-Growth without single prefix path optimisation (removing frequent patterns)											
Dataset	Itemsets	Rules	Time (s)	Support	Conf	χ^2	Lift	AllConf	Coherence	Cosine	Kulc	MaxConf
Connect-4	9.55E+05	243	1317	19.374	0.999	911.416	49.296	0.014	0.014	0.097	0.507	0.999
Voting	2.11E+06	46	425	56.935	0.918	56.094	1.918	0.273	0.267	0.50	0.596	0.918
Tumor	3.40E+06	26858	489	18.099	0.939	12.643	1.686	0.097	0.096	0.281	0.518	0.939
Zoo	6.49E+05	102932	59	11.497	0.951	16.157	2.283	0.272	0.266	0.483	0.611	0.951
Teaching	281	53	<1	6.849	0.992	19.608	3.408	0.170	0.170	0.347	0.581	0.992
Flags	1.50E+08	137133	25394	6.546	0.997	4.064	1.619	0.054	0.054	0.224	0.526	0.997
Adult	1.88E+06	83	1640	1822.120	0.944	2427.051	4.345	0.090	0.088	0.204	0.517	0.944
Dermatology	4.90E+08	29613244	186224	34.352	0.938	10.964	1.375	0.132	0.131	0.343	0.535	0.938
Soybean	1.67E+08	47519598	64834	40.013	1.000	21.678	1.471	0.192	0.192	0.435	0.596	1.000
	RP-Tree											
Dataset	Itemsets	Rules	Time (s)	Support	Conf	χ^2	Lift	AllConf	Coherence	Cosine	Kulc	MaxConf
Connect-4	8.96E+05	243	1270	19.374	0.999	911.416	49.296	0.014	0.014	0.097	0.507	0.999
Voting	3.38E+05	46	46	56.935	0.918	56.094	1.918	0.273	0.267	0.500	0.596	0.918
Tumor	1.41E+05	26858	154	18.099	0.939	12.643	1.686	0.097	0.096	0.281	0.518	0.939
Zoo	1.79E+05	102932	15	11.497	0.951	16.157	2.283	0.272	0.266	0.483	0.611	0.951
Teaching	118	49	<1	6.673	1.000	20.319	3.506	0.172	0.172	0.347	0.586	1.000
Flags	4.69E+07	137048	6517	6.533	0.997	4.061	1.619	0.054	0.054	0.223	0.526	0.997
Adult	1.85E+06	80	1614	1623.950	0.945	2513.977	4.469	0.087	0.085	0.197	0.516	0.945
Dermatology	9.12E+07	29593672	26005	34.340	0.938	10.966	1.376	0.132	0.131	0.343	0.535	0.938
Soybean	4.34E+06	47368525	1150	40.000	1.000	21.704	1.472	0.192	0.192	0.435	0.596	1.000
	RP-Tree with Information Gain (minIG = 0.25)											
Dataset	Itemsets	Rules	Time (s)	Support	Conf	χ^2	Lift	AllConf	Coherence	Cosine	Kulc	MaxConf
Connect-4	10803	0	3	n/a	n/a	n/a	n/a	n/a	n/a	n/a	n/a	n/a
Voting	613987	46	11	56.935	0.918	56.094	1.918	0.273	0.267	0.5	0.596	0.918
Tumor	500	2	<1	9.000	1.000	15.487	2.748	0.071	0.071	0.266	0.536	1.000
Zoo	47364	1140	1	12.039	0.960	24.611	2.808	0.348	0.342	0.551	0.654	0.960
Teaching	51	8	<1	7.125	1.000	58.796	8.138	0.416	0.416	0.591	0.708	1.000
Flags	8167	12	<1	11.750	0.993	41.297	4.245	0.261	0.259	0.49	0.627	0.993
Adult	19397	7	2	1151.286	0.958	1070.297	2.029	0.047	0.047	0.184	0.502	0.958
Dermatology	615585	63869	14	39.003	0.961	13.887	1.336	0.148	0.147	0.37	0.554	0.961
Soybean	292424	257477	8	40.000	1.000	28.510	1.620	0.211	0.211	0.457	0.606	1.000

gain minIG is set to 0.25. Only rules that met the minimum confidence of 0.9 and lift of 1.0 were included for analysis. Table 4 shows the number of rules retained for each dataset and algorithm, the average support and confidence, and the average values for each of the seven measures listed in Table 2.

For the Connect-4 and Adult datasets, FP-Growth and RP-Tree found a very similar number of itemsets. For the remaining seven datasets, RP-Tree generated significantly fewer itemsets compared to FP-Growth, ranging from 42.0% for Adult to 2.60% for Soybean. However, the number of rules that met the confidence and lift thresholds were either identical or very similar. This shows that the set of rare itemsets that are ignored by RP-Tree does not tend to be interesting, since these itemsets do not generate rules that meet both the confidence and lift thresholds. Since fewer itemsets are generated by RP-Tree compared to FP-Growth, the time required for rule generation is also less: for example, time taken for rule generation for RP-Tree for the soybean dataset is reduced to 1.8% of that for FP-Growth, while the number of association rules retained is 99.7% of FP-Growth. Overall the time taken for RP-Tree is lower than FP-Growth.

The Information Gain component for RP-Tree results in far fewer rules than RP-Tree for all datasets except Voting, with no change, and tends to generate rules that are of higher quality. For five datasets (Zoo, Teaching, Flags, Soybean and Dermatology) there are increases in most of the seven interest measures. However, for one dataset (Adult), the measures decreased. There were no rules generated at all for Connect-4. The reduction in the number of rules is due to the minIG threshold reducing the number of items that can participate in itemsets. Overall, the information gain component tends to selectively retain rules that are more interesting according to the seven interest measures.

Case Study. From the Teaching dataset, FP-Growth, RP-Tree and RP-Tree-IG generated 53 rules, 49 rules, and 8 rules respectively. The interest measures of the 4 additional rules generated by FP-Growth from non-rare-item itemsets are shown in Table 5. Rules 1 and 2 have lower than average values for confidence and all interest measures. Rules 3 and 4 have lower values for confidence, lift, kulc and maxConf; and higher values for χ^2, allConf, coherence and cosine. 8 association rules were generated using RP-Tree-IG. Of the 8 rules, 6 had higher than average values for confidence and all 7 interest measures compared to FP-Growth, while the remaining 2 had lower values.

From the Adult dataset, FP-Growth, RP-Tree and RP-Tree-IG generated 83 rules, 80 rules and 7 rules respectively. The 3 additional rules generated by FP-Growth had lower than average values for confidence, χ^2, lift and maxConf; and higher values for allConf, coherence, cosine and kulc, as shown in Table 5 . The 7 rules generated all had several measures that were lower than the average compared to FP-Growth.

The omission of non-rare-item itemsets by RP-Tree only has a small effect on the number and quality of association rules generated compared to FP-Growth, since the additional rules are of average quality and are few in number compared to the overall number of rules generated.

Table 5. Non-rare-item itemsets generated by FP-Growth

Dataset	Rule ID	Confidence	χ^2	Lift	AllConf	Coherence	Cosine	Kulc	MaxConf
Teaching	1	0.900	0.585	1.114	0.074	0.073	0.258	0.487	0.900
	2	0.900	0.227	1.062	0.070	0.070	0.252	0.485	0.900
	3	0.900	21.385	3.315	0.220	0.214	0.444	0.560	0.900
	4	0.900	21.385	3.315	0.220	0.214	0.444	0.560	0.900
Adult	1	0.928	88.662	1.034	0.160	0.158	0.386	0.544	0.928
	2	0.908	208.679	1.062	0.170	0.168	0.393	0.539	0.908
	3	0.915	29.765	1.019	0.164	0.161	0.387	0.539	0.915

5 Conclusions and Future Work

We present a new method for finding rare association rules in large databases. To our knowledge, this is the first algorithm that uses a tree structure to mine rare itemsets. Our algorithm finds a subset of all rare itemsets, which we call rare-item itemsets. We evaluated our method by comparing the quality of association rules generated against those generated using the FP-Growth algorithm from 9 datasets. We found that, in the majority of cases, RP-Tree generated far fewer itemsets for some datasets compared to FP-Growth. This meant that rule generation took much less time for RP-Tree than FP-Growth. However, at the same time, there was very little reduction in the number of rules that met the minimum confidence and lift thresholds. This shows that rare-item itemsets are more interesting since they contribute to almost all the rules that pass the thresholds, and the omission of non-rare-item itemsets by RP-Tree does not reduce rule quality, and in most cases, improves the overall rule quality in the set.

In our future work, we intend to find other ways of focusing on more potentially interesting association rules, such as rules that contain only rare items as the consequent. In addition, we intend to investigate the effect of the minRareSup on the quality of rules generated by RP-Tree, and to find ways of dealing with noise and removing coincidental non-rare-item itemsets.

References

1. Agrawal, R., Srikant, R.: Fast algorithms for mining association rules in large databases. In: Bocca, J.B., Jarke, M., Zaniolo, C. (eds.) Proceedings of the 20th International Conference on Very Large Data Bases, VLDB, Santiago, Chile, pp. 487–499 (1994)
2. Troiano, L., Scibelli, G., Birtolo, C.: A fast algorithm for mining rare itemsets. In: Proceedings of the 2009 Ninth International Conference on Intelligent Systems Design and Applications, pp. 1149–1155. IEEE Computer Society Press, Los Alamitos (2009)
3. Adda, M., Wu, L., Feng, Y.: Rare itemset mining. In: Proceedings of the Sixth International Conference on Machine Learning and Applications, ICMLA 2007, pp. 73–80. IEEE Computer Society Press, Los Alamitos (2007)
4. Szathmary, L., Napoli, A., Valtchev, P.: Towards rare itemset mining. In: Proceedings of the 19th IEEE International Conference on Tools with Artificial Intelligence, ICTAI 2007, vol. 01, pp. 305–312. IEEE Computer Society, Los Alamitos (2007)
5. Koh, Y.S., Rountree, N.: Finding sporadic rules using apriori-inverse. In: Ho, T.-B., Cheung, D., Liu, H. (eds.) PAKDD 2005. LNCS (LNAI), vol. 3518, pp. 97–106. Springer, Heidelberg (2005)
6. Han, J., Pei, J., Yin, Y.: Mining frequent patterns without candidate generation. In: Proceedings of the 2000 ACM SIGMOD International Conference on Management of Data, SIGMOD 2000, pp. 1–12. ACM, New York (2000)
7. Mitchell, T.M.: Machine Learning, pp. 57–60. McGraw-Hill, New York (1997)
8. Wu, T., Chen, Y., Han, J.: Association mining in large databases: A re-examination of its measures. In: Kok, J.N., Koronacki, J., Lopez de Mantaras, R., Matwin, S., Mladenič, D., Skowron, A. (eds.) PKDD 2007. LNCS (LNAI), vol. 4702, pp. 621–628. Springer, Heidelberg (2007)
9. Frank, A., Asuncion, A.: UCI machine learning repository (2010), http://archive.ics.uci.edu/ml

Co-clustering with Augmented Data Matrix

Meng-Lun Wu, Chia-Hui Chang, and Rui-Zhe Liu

Dept. of Computer Science and Information Engineering,
National Central University, Taoyuan, Taiwan

Abstract. Clustering plays an important role in data mining as many applications use it as a preprocessing step for data analysis. Traditional clustering focuses on the grouping of similar objects, while two-way co-clustering can group dyadic data (objects as well as their attributes) simultaneously. Most co-clustering research focuses on single correlation data, but there might be other possible descriptions of dyadic data that could improve co-clustering performance. In this research, we extend ITCC (Information Theoretic Co-Clustering) to the problem of co-clustering with augmented matrix. We proposed CCAM (Co-Clustering with Augmented Data Matrix) to include this augmented data for better co-clustering. We apply CCAM in the analysis of on-line advertising, where both ads and users must be clustered. The key data that connect ads and users are the user-ad link matrix, which identifies the ads that each user has linked; both ads and users also have their feature data, i.e. the augmented data matrix. To evaluate the proposed method, we use two measures: classification accuracy and K-L divergence. The experiment is done using the advertisements and user data from Morgenstern, a financial social website that focuses on the advertisement agency. The experiment results show that CCAM provides better performance than ITCC since it consider the use of augmented data during clustering.

1 Introduction

Co-clustering, the process of clustering dyadic data, has been a hot topic with many concern in the past decade. Co-clustering can be applied to various data mining applications, for example, in text mining to identify similar documents and their interplay with word clusters, in social recommendation systems to create recommendation systems that predict user movie ratings based on the co-clustering relationship between user groups and movie clusters [1], in bioinformatics to find the relationships between genes and data features. However, in addition to the dyadic data, we might also have other descriptions, called augmented data that could be important in clustering. For example, in addition to user-movie click through data in user-movie recommendation systems, we may also have user profiles and movie descriptions; in text mining, documents might have author descriptions and publisher information. In this paper, we consider the problem of co-clustering with augmented data.

This study was motivated by a cooperation with the Umatch website, which runs an online advertising service called Ad$Mart. Similar to Google's AdSense,

A. Cuzzocrea and U. Dayal (Eds.): DaWaK 2011, LNCS 6862, pp. 289–300, 2011.
© Springer-Verlag Berlin Heidelberg 2011

Ad\$Mart share ads profit with users who put links on their webspace. The idea is that an advertiser pays a low cost for its products to be shown on the user's self-portrait (i.e. the member's webspace), while the platform provider shares advertising profits with the registered members who link to the ads on their web space to endorse the product. Note that the profit is shared based on the activity scores of the registered member, not based on CPC (cost per click) of the readers. Since Ad\$Mart services is built on a community entry focused on financial management and monetization, the website also provide risk preference analysis (through Lohas lifestyle survey) to support their members in activities such as financial Olympia, world-wide asset allocation, and other professional competitions. Thus, in addition to user-ad link data, the system also bears two augmented matrices: user profiles and advertisement features. The goal of Ad\$Mart is to create a triple-win commercial platform for the advertisers, registered users and platform provider.

To fully utilize augmented data, we proposed a new method called Co-Clustering with Augmented data Matrix (CCAM). We extent the ITCC (Information Theoretic Co-Clustering) algorithm [5] to consider not only the correlation matrix $p(A, U)$ between ads and users, but also the row (ads) description matrix and column (users) description matrix. We treat these three normalized non-negative matrices as a joint probability distribution $p(A, U)$, $p(A, S)$ and $p(U, L)$, then define a unified information theoretic formulation for this task. The ads descriptions constrain the user clusters, as well as the user descriptions constrain the ads clusters. The objective of ITCC is to minimize the loss function in the mutual information between the two random variables of the three matrices simultaneously.

In addition to formulate the CCAM problem and algorithms, we also propose two evaluation methods for the co-clustering task: the classification-based evaluation and the mutual information based evaluation. The former uses the F-measure of classification models to indicate the performance of a clustering. Since the data does not have manual labels as answers for classification verification, we use clustering result as the target labels for building classification models. The second evaluation method exploits the nature of co-clustering by measuring the mutual information between user groups and ad clusters.

The rest of this paper is organized as follows. In Section 2, we give an overview of related works. The problem will be defined in Section 3. Our algorithm will be stated in Section 4. In Section 5, we present our experiments and evaluations. Section 6 concludes the paper and gives some directions for future research.

2   Related Work

Clustering is a kind of data mining technique that could be used to group the similar objects, and has much application such as user-based web search [15], collaborative filtering [3], and market-basket data analysis. However, the relationship between row and column are not fully considered in the one-way clustering algorithm. For this reason, the two-way co-clustering issue has been arisen to group the dyadic data simultaneously. There are mainly three classes of Co-clustering issues: ITCC (Information Theoretic Co-Clustering), MFCC (Matrix Factorization Co-Clustering) and MOCC (Model-based Overlapping Co-Clustering).

Co-clustering based on information theory has been concerned since 2000. Slonim (2000) et al. [14] start the research on Information Theoretic Co-Clustering (ITCC) where they proposed the concept of document clustering based on word cluster via information theory. Dhillon (2003) et al. [5] proposed the ITCC algorithm by minimizing the difference in mutual information (between document and word) before and after clustering and decomposing the objective function based on the K-L divergence, they design a co-clustering algorithm based on iterative assignment of documents and words to the best cluster. Banerjee et al. [2] extended the ITCC and suggested a generalized maximum entropy co-clustering approach by appealing to the minimum of Bregman information principle.

MFCC (Matrix Factorization Co-Clustering) method has been proposed by Long et al. (2005) [9] where they suggested using the block value decomposition to factorize the correlation matrix into three approximation matrix, and solved the co-clustering problem by optimization method. Ding et al. (2005) [6] gave a similar co-clustering approach based on nonnegative matrix factorization. Later, they add the idea of orthogonal constrain to optimize the nonnegative matrix factorization problem [7], and reach better co-clustering performance.

MOCC (Model-based Overlapping Co-Clustering) [11] solves the co-clustering problem by assuming that topic model to capture the correlation between the dyadic data. Shafiei et al. [12] proposed a generative model for text documents based on a series connection of two Latent Dirichlet Allocation (LDA) models, in which one controls the row cluster generation and the other select the column cluster based on row cluster. The model is able to group both words and documents simultaneously. Shan and Banerjee [13] used a similar architecture and design Bayesian co-clustering method.

In addition to research on co-clustering algorithms, there are also researches on applications of co-clustering. Dai et al. [4] proposed a co-clustering based classification algorithm to classify out-domain data. They assume that in-domain data and out-domain data share the similar distribution and propagate the class structure from in-domain data to out-domain data via transfer learning. Chen et al. [3] extend Ding's MFCC algorithm to help the collaborative filtering to predict ratings in recommendation systems. Li et al. [8] presented a novel cross-domain collaborative filtering method which consider the co-clustering result as the codebook, and transfer knowledge from rating matrix in one domain to remedy the sparsity of the rating matrix in a target domain.

While the goal of this paper is also a form of co-clustering, we have two additional matrices that are different from those appearing in the previous work. In the next section, we will give more detailed descriptions of our problem definition and algorithms.

3   Problem Definition

Let A, U, S, and L be discrete random variables such that A denotes the ads, ranging from $\{a_1, \ldots, a_m\}$, U represents the users, ranging from $\{u_1, \ldots, u_n\}$, S denotes the ad features, which have been discretized and ranged from $\{s_1, \ldots, s_r\}$ and L denotes the possible answers to the user Lohas questionnaire, ranging from $\{t_1, \ldots, t_v\}$. Let $p(A, U)$ denote the joint probability distribution of the ad-user link matrix as an $m \times n$ matrix, $p(A, S)$ represent the joint distribution of the ad feature matrix as an $m \times r$ matrix, and $p(U, L)$ indicate the joint probability distribution of the user Lohas matrix as an $n \times v$ matrix.

We are interested in simultaneously clustering or quantizing A into k disjoint or hard clusters and U into l disjoint or hard clusters. Let the k clusters of A be written as $\{\widehat{a}_1, \ldots, \widehat{a}_k\}$, and the l clusters of U be written as $\{\widehat{u}_1, \ldots, \widehat{u}_l\}$. Our goal is to find C_A and C_U which map each ad a_i / user u_j to some ad cluster $C_A(a_i)$ / user group $C_U(u_j)$, respectively.

$$C_A : \{a_1, \ldots, a_m\} \longrightarrow \{\widehat{a}_1, \ldots, \widehat{a}_k\}$$
$$C_U : \{u_1, \ldots, u_n\} \longrightarrow \{\widehat{u}_1, \ldots, \widehat{u}_l\} \tag{1}$$

For simplicity, we will write $\widehat{A} = C_A(A)$ and $\widehat{U} = C_U(U)$ where $\widehat{A}$ and $\widehat{U}$ are random variables that are deterministic functions of A and U, respectively. To measure the quality of co-clustering, we refer the characteristic of mutual information. Let X and Y be random variable sets with a joint distribution $p(x, y)$ and marginal distribution $p(x)$ and $p(y)$. The mutual information $I(X; Y)$ is defined as

$$I(X; Y) = \sum_x \sum_y p(x, y) \log \frac{p(x, y)}{p(x)p(y)} \tag{2}$$

Mutual information is a measure of the dependency between random variables. It is always non-negative, and it is zero if and only if the variables are statistically independent. The idea is that the higher the mutual information does, the better the clustering result is. Therefore, we can measure the quality of a co-clustering $(\widehat{A}, \widehat{U})$ by maximizing its mutual information $I(\widehat{A}; \widehat{U})$, which is equivalent to minimizing

$$I(A; U) - I(\widehat{A}; \widehat{U}) \tag{3}$$

since $I(A; U)$ is fixed. This form of loss function is the same as that used in [5]. Now to incorporate ad augmented data, we maximize the mutual information $I(\widehat{A}; \widehat{S})$ between ad cluster and ad feature after co-clustering, which is equivalent to minimizing the mutual information loss as follows.

$$I(A; S) - I(\widehat{A}; \widehat{S}) \tag{4}$$

Similarity, we incorporate user augmented data by maximizing the mutual information between user group and their profile data $I(\widehat{U}; L)$, which is equivalent to minimizing the loss in mutual information after co-clustering as

$$I(U; L) - I(\widehat{U}; L) \tag{5}$$

Combining Eq. (3), (4) and (5), the loss function of co-clustering with augmented data matrix can be defined as follow. Due to space limitation, we only show the necessary proof in this paper.

Definition 1. *For a fixed co-clustering $(\widehat{A}, \widehat{U})$, we would like to minimize*

$$f(\widehat{A}, \widehat{U}) = [I(A;U) - I(\widehat{A};\widehat{U})] + \lambda \cdot [I(A;S) - I(\widehat{A};S)] + \varphi \cdot [I(U;L) - I(\widehat{U};L)] \quad (6)$$

subject to constraints on the number of desired row and column clusters, where λ and φ are the trade-off parameter that balances the effect to ad clusters or user groups.

Lemma 1. *For a fixed co-clustering $(\widehat{A}, \widehat{U})$, we can re-write the loss in mutual information as K-L divergence or relative entropy measure as*

$$f(\widehat{A}, \widehat{U}) = D(p(A,U)\|q(A,U)) + \lambda \cdot D(p(A,S)\|q(A,S)) + \varphi \cdot D(p(U,L)\|q(U,L)) \quad (7)$$

where $q(A,U)$, $q(A,S)$ and $q(U,L)$ are the distributions of the form

$$q(a,u) = p(\widehat{a}, \widehat{u})p(a \mid \widehat{a})p(u \mid \widehat{u}), \text{ where } \widehat{a} = C_A(a) \text{ and } \widehat{u} = C_U(u) \quad (8)$$

$$q(a,s) = p(\widehat{a}, s)p(a \mid \widehat{a}), \text{ where } \widehat{a} = C_A(a) \quad (9)$$

$$q(u,l) = p(\widehat{u}, l)p(u \mid \widehat{u}), \text{ where } \widehat{u} = C_U(u) \quad (10)$$

4   Co-clustering with Augmented Data Matrix Algorithm

In this section, we give a description of co-clustering with augmented data, which minimizes the objective function of Eq.(6). The objective function is a multiple function and is hard to optimize. Therefore, our goal is to simplify the optimization. Lemmas 2 represents alternative approaches, which allow us to reduce the divergence values iteratively.

Lemma 2

$$D(p(A,U)\|q(A,U)) = \sum_{\widehat{a}\in\widehat{A}} \sum_{a\in\widehat{a}} p(a)D(p(U|a)\|q(U|\widehat{a}))$$
$$= \sum_{\widehat{u}\in\widehat{U}} \sum_{u\in\widehat{u}} p(u)D(p(A|u)\|q(A|\widehat{u})) \quad (11)$$

$$D(p(A,S)\|q(A,S)) = \sum_{\widehat{a}\in\widehat{A}} \sum_{a\in\widehat{a}} p(a)D(p(S|a)\|q(S|\widehat{a})) \quad (12)$$

$$D(p(U,L)\|q(U,L)) = \sum_{\widehat{u}\in\widehat{U}} \sum_{u\in\widehat{u}} p(u)D(p(L|u)\|q(L|\widehat{u})) \quad (13)$$

Proof. Since Eq. (11) is proved in [5], we focus on the rest two equations.

$$D(p(A,S)\|q(A,S))$$
$$= \sum_{\widehat{a}\in\widehat{A}} \sum_{a\in\widehat{a}} \sum_{s\in S} p(a,s) \log \frac{p(a,s)}{q(a,s)} = \sum_{\widehat{a}\in\widehat{A}} \sum_{a\in\widehat{a}} \sum_{s\in S} p(a,s) \log \frac{p(a,s)}{p(\widehat{a},s)p(a|\widehat{a})}$$
$$= \sum_{\widehat{a}\in\widehat{A}} \sum_{a\in\widehat{a}} \sum_{s\in S} p(a,s) \log \frac{p(a)p(s|a)}{p(s|\widehat{a})p(\widehat{a})\frac{p(a)}{p(\widehat{a})}} = \sum_{\widehat{a}\in\widehat{A}} \sum_{a\in\widehat{a}} \sum_{s\in S} p(a)p(s|a) \log \frac{p(s|a)}{p(s|\widehat{a})} \quad (14)$$
$$= \sum_{\widehat{a}\in\widehat{A}} \sum_{a\in\widehat{a}} p(a) \sum_{s\in S} p(s|a) \log \frac{p(s|a)}{q(s|\widehat{a})} = \sum_{\widehat{a}\in\widehat{A}} \sum_{a\in\widehat{a}} p(a)D(p(S|a)\|q(S|\widehat{a}))$$

Similarly, we could use the same argument to prove Eq.(13).

$$D(p(U,L)\|q(U,L))$$
$$= \sum_{\widehat{u}\in\widehat{U}} \sum_{u\in\widehat{U}} \sum_{l\in L} p(u,l)\log\frac{p(u,l)}{q(u,l)} = \sum_{\widehat{u}\in\widehat{U}} \sum_{u\in\widehat{U}} \sum_{l\in L} p(u,l)\log\frac{p(u,l)}{p(\widehat{u},l)p(u|\widehat{l})}$$
$$= \sum_{\widehat{u}\in\widehat{U}} \sum_{u\in\widehat{u}} \sum_{l\in L} p(u,l)\log\frac{p(u)p(l|u)}{p(l|\widehat{u})p(\widehat{u})\frac{p(u)}{p(u)}} = \sum_{\widehat{u}\in\widehat{U}} \sum_{u\in\widehat{u}} \sum_{l\in L} p(u)p(l|u)\log\frac{p(l|u)}{p(l|\widehat{u})} \quad (15)$$
$$= \sum_{\widehat{u}\in\widehat{U}} \sum_{u\in\widehat{u}} p(y) \sum_{l\in L} p(l|u)\log\frac{p(l|u)}{q(l|\widehat{u})} = \sum_{\widehat{u}\in\widehat{U}} \sum_{u\in\widehat{u}} p(u)D(p(L|u)\|q(L|\widehat{u}))$$

Algorithm 1. Co-Clustering with Augmented data Matrix (CCAM) Algorithm

---

Inputs:
    The joint probability distribution $p(A,U)$, $p(A,S)$,and $p(U,L)$, k is the desired number of row clusters and l is the desired number of column clusters. Initial co-clustering $(C_A^{(0)}, C_U^{(0)})$.
Initialization:
    Set iteration t=0, and compute the joint probability distribution $q^{(t)}(A,U)$, $q^{(t)}(A,S)$, and $q^{(t)}(U,L)$ based on (8), (9) and (10), respectively.
Outputs:
    The partition function $(C_A^{(t)}$ and $C_U^{(t)})$
while $f^{(t)}(\widehat{A},\widehat{U}) - f^{(t+2)}(\widehat{A},\widehat{U})$ is greater than (10^{-3}) **do**
    1. Compute row clusters: For each row a, find its new cluster index by

$$C_A^{(t+1)}(a) = \underset{\widehat{a}}{argmin}\{p(a)D(p(U|a)\|q^{(t)}(U|\widehat{a})) + \lambda\cdot p(a)D(p(S|a)\|q^{(t)}(S|\widehat{a}))\} \quad (16)$$

    2. Update the probability distribution $q^{(t+1)}(A,U)$ and $q^{(t+1)}(A,S)$ based on $C_A^{(t+1)}$ and $C_U^{(t+1)}$, where $C_U^{(t+1)} = C_U^{(t)}$ and $q^{(t+1)}(U,L) = q^{(t)}(U,L)$.
    3. Compute column clusters: For each column u, find its new cluster index by

$$C_U^{(t+2)}(u) = \underset{\widehat{u}}{argmin}\{p(u)D(p(A|u)\|q^{(t)}(A|\widehat{u})) + \varphi\cdot p(u)D(p(L|u)\|q^{(t)}(L|\widehat{u}))\}$$
$$(17)$$

    4. Update the probability distribution $q^{(t+2)}(A,U)$ and $q^{(t+2)}(U,L)$ based on $C_U^{(t+2)}$ and $C_A^{(t+2)}$, where $C_A^{(t+2)} = C_A^{(t+1)}$ and $q^{(t+2)}(A,S) = q^{(t+1)}(A,S)$.
end while

Based on Lemmas 2, the co-clustering with augmented data matrix algorithm is derived. This algorithms starts with an initial co-clustering $(C_A^{(0)}, C_U^{(0)})$ and iteratively refines it to obtain a sequence of co-clustering: $(C_A^{(1)}, C_U^{(1)})$, $(C_A^{(2)}, C_U^{(2)})$, ... $(C_A^{(t)}, C_U^{(t)})$.

As shown in Algorithm 1, the algorithm chooses the best ad cluster for each ad to minimize the multiplication of the marginal probability $p(a)$ with the linear combination of $D(p(U|a)\|q^{(t)}(U|\widehat{a}))$ and $D(p(S|a)\|q^{(t+1)}(S|\widehat{a}))$ in each t+1 iteration. Similarly, the algorithm selects the best user group for each user to minimize the multiplication of the marginal $q(u)$ with the linear combination of $D(p(A|u)\|q^{(t+1)}(A|\widehat{u}))$ and $D(p(L|u)\|q^{(t+1)}(L|\widehat{u}))$ in each t+2 iteration. Both minimizations can reduce the global objective function value. The algorithm keeps iterating Step 1 through 4 until some desired convergence condition is met, which is shown in Theorem 1, guarantees convergence.

Theorem 1 *The CCAM algorithm could monotonically decreases the objective function Eq.(6). Since*

$$f^{(t)}(\widehat{A}, \widehat{U}) \geq f^{(t+1)}(\widehat{A}, \widehat{U}) \tag{18}$$

Proof Let $\Phi = \varphi \cdot D(p(U, L) \| q^{(t+1)}(U, L))$. *For* $t = 1, 3, \cdots, 2T + 1$.

$$f^{(t)}(\widehat{A}, \widehat{U})$$
$$= D(p(A, U) \| q^{(t)}(A, U)) + \lambda \cdot D(p(A, S) \| q^{(t)}(A, S)) + \Phi$$
$$= \sum_{\widehat{a} \in C_A^{(t)}} \sum_{a \in \widehat{a}} \langle p(a) \sum_{\widehat{u} \in C_U^{(t)}} \sum_{u \in \widehat{u}} p(u|a) \cdot \log \frac{p(u|a)}{q^{(t)}(u|\widehat{a})} + \lambda \cdot p(a) \sum_{s \in S} \log \frac{p(s|a)}{q^{(t)}(s|\widehat{a})} \rangle + \Phi$$
$$\geq \sum_{\widehat{a} \in C_A^{(t)}} \sum_{a \in \widehat{a}} \langle p(a) \sum_{\widehat{u} \in C_U^{(t)}} \sum_{u \in \widehat{u}} p(u|a) \cdot \log \frac{p(u|a)}{q^{(t)}(u|C_A^{(t+1)}(a))} + \lambda \cdot p(a) \sum_{s \in S} \log \frac{p(s|a)}{q^{(t)}(s|C_A^{(t+1)}(a))} \rangle$$
$$+ \Phi = D(p(A, U) \| q^{(t+1)}(A, U)) + \lambda \cdot D(p(A, S) \| q^{(t+1)}(A, S)) + \Phi$$
$$= f^{(t+1)}(\widehat{A}, \widehat{U})$$

The inequality follows from Step 1 since $C_A^{t+1}(a)$ *is choosen to minimize the objective function. By using an identical argument, we can prove Eq.(18) for* $t=2,4,\cdots, 2T+2$. *Let* $\Lambda = \lambda \cdot D(p(A, S) \| q^{(t+1)}(A, S))$.

$$f^{(t)}(\widehat{A}, \widehat{U})$$
$$= D(p(A, U) \| q^{(t)}(A, U)) + \varphi \cdot D(p(U, L) \| q^{(t+1)}(U, L)) + \Lambda$$
$$= \sum_{\widehat{u} \in C_U^{(t)}} \sum_{u \in \widehat{u}} \langle p(u) \sum_{\widehat{a} \in C_A^{(t)}} \sum_{a \in \widehat{a}} p(a|u) \cdot \log \frac{p(a|u)}{q^{(t)}(a|\widehat{u})} + \varphi \cdot p(u) \sum_{l \in L} \log \frac{p(l|u)}{q^{(t+1)}(l|\widehat{u})} \rangle + \Lambda$$
$$\geq \sum_{\widehat{u} \in C_U^{(t)}} \sum_{u \in \widehat{u}} \langle p(u) \sum_{\widehat{a} \in C_A^{(t)}} \sum_{a \in \widehat{a}} p(a|u) \cdot \log \frac{p(a|u)}{q^{(t)}(a|C_U^{(t+1)}(u))} + \varphi \cdot p(u) \sum_{l \in L} \log \frac{p(l|u)}{q^{(t)}(l|C_U^{(t+1)}(u))} \rangle$$
$$+ \Lambda = D(p(A, U) \| q^{(t+1)}(A, U)) + \varphi \cdot D(p(U, L) \| q^{(t+1)}(U, L)) + \Lambda$$
$$= f^{(t+1)}(\widehat{A}, \widehat{U})$$

We use the same threshold 10^{-3} in order for comparison between CCAM and ITCC. Regarding to the computational complexity, suppose the total number of ad-user co-occurrences is N. For each iteration, updating C_A takes $O(|A| \cdot N)$ since updating C_U takes $O((|A| + |U|) \cdot N)$. The number of iterations is T, which is based on the convergence of $f^{(t)}(\widehat{A}, \widehat{U}) - f^{(t+2)}(\widehat{A}, \widehat{U})$. Therefore, the total computational complexity is $O((|A| + |U|) \cdot N \cdot T)$.

5   Experiments Result and Evaluation

5.1   Data Description

The data used in our experiment belongs to the category of online contextual advertising. The data comes from Ad$Mart which is an online ad service launched by a finance social web site called Umatch. The goal of Ad$Mart is to create a triple-win commercial platform for advertisers, registered users and platform provider. The idea is similar to AdSense where an advertiser pays a low cost for their products to be shown on the website, while the platform provider shares advertising profits with the registered members who link the ads on their web space to endorse the product. The difference is that AdSense automatically allocates ads for webpages while Ad$Mart requires users to link ads by themselves. Also the ads that are scheduled for display are ranked by their ad amounts (M) one day early for linking.

The Ad$Mart data to be analyzed include three data matrix: the ad-by-user link matrix, the ad feature matrix and the user Lohas matrix. The ad-by-user link data contains the number of ad links for each user during 09/01/2009 to 03/31/2010. Since each ad has its own display schedule (from several days to several weeks), we need discretization steps to categorize the various ad amounts (M), user links (N), and rank orders (O) such that the ad feature matrix represents a joint distribution of the ads and some categories. Here, we use the Sturges rule [10] to discretize M, N and O into 10 intervals.

As for user Lohas matrix, it contains choices of users to 24 survey questions about their preference to life styles. Since each question has discrete (from 2 to 10) possible answers, we can directly use them to represent the categories for the joint distribution. The number of users who are involved in Ad$Mart is 9,866 and the number of users who also played the Lohas game is 2,124 users. Also, there are 530 ads, which have been displayed in the relevant period.

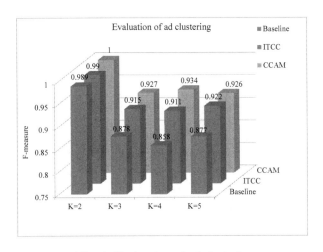

Fig. 1. Evaluation of ad clustering

5.2   Comparison and Evaluation Methods

Cluster evaluation is usually done with classification accuracy based on ground truth. Since there are no predefined categories in our data (both for ads and users), we have to design an alternative way for the evaluation. In this paper, we use the clustering result of the combined ad data (ad-by-user link matrix and ad feature matrix) as the target labels for ad clustering; and similarly, the clustering result of the combined user data (user-by-ad link matrix and user Lohas data) is used as the target labels for user clustering. We then apply classification algorithm on ad data to test the F-measure of 10-fold cross validation as the baseline. Similarly, we will also have the F-measure of the 10-fold cross validation for user classification as baseline.

Now to examine the effectiveness of co-clustering, we reduce the columns of ad-by-user link matrix to a smaller ad-by-user group matrix. The reduced data is then added to our ad data for classification. Likewise, we can reduce the columns of the user-by-ad link matrix to a smaller user-by-ad cluster matrix based on the co-clustering and add it to the user data for classification. If the co-clustering is well produced, we could somehow improve the classification performance both for ad data and user data.

In a way, co-clustering with augmented data is confined by two additional matrixes when maximizing the mutual information between ad clusters and user groups, while single matrix co-clustering like ITCC directly optimizes the mutual information between ad clusters and user groups. Theoretically, ITCC would gain high mutual information than CCAM and baseline from co-clustering. However, in this paper, we will show that CCAM perform closely with ITCC and outperform baseline, but CCAM is better in classification. In this paper, we also implement ITCC as a comparison and evaluate the effectiveness of co-clustering in terms of classification performance and mutual information of the ad clusters and user groups.

5.3   Classification Based Evaluation

In this paper, we apply decision tree to build classification models and conduct 10-fold cross validation to evaluate the F-measure of the new ad data and user data which are generated from co-clustering result as described above. We com-

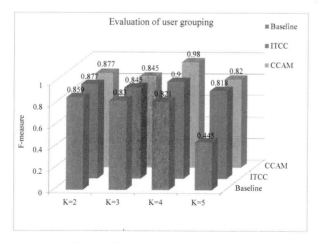

Fig. 2. Evaluation of user grouping

pare CCAM with ITCC as well as the baseline approach which use the original
ad data and user data for classification.

We try different values of K (from K=2 to 5) and examine the performance.
For a given K, We use heuristic method to tune parameter λ and φ based on
classification performance. We first fix λ and try various φ from 0.2 to 1.0. The
average F-measure of ad classification and user classification does not change
with various φ. We suspect the reason to be the null values of many users.
Therefore, we fix $\varphi = 1.0$ and try various λ from 0.2 to 1.0. The best performance
can be achieved when $\lambda = 0.6$ for K=2, 4, $\lambda=0.8$, for K=3, and $\lambda=0.2$, $\varphi=1.0$
for K=5. Fig. 1 reveals that CCAM is better than ITCC and baseline in terms
of ad classification. Similarly, Fig. 2 shows that CCAM outperforms ITCC and
baseline in terms of user classification. By proper tuning of the parameters, we
can obtain better classification result than ITCC.

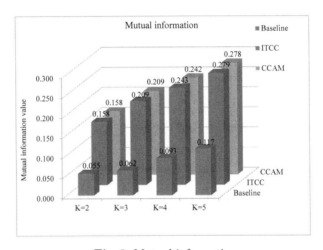

Fig. 3. Mutual information

5.4   Mutual Information Based Evaluation

In order to calculate the mutual information $I(\widehat{A}; \widehat{U})$ of different co-clustering
results, we reduce the number of rows and columns based on the result of ad
cluster $\widehat{A}$ and user group $\widehat{U}$ to generate ad-cluster by user-group joint probability
matrix $p(\widehat{A}, \widehat{U})$.

$$p(\widehat{a}, \widehat{u}) = \sum_{a \in \widehat{a}} \sum_{u \in \widehat{u}} p(a, u) \tag{19}$$

We compare different clustering result from CCAM, ITCC and baseline to con-
struct the corresponding $p(\widehat{A}, \widehat{U})$. After we get $p(\widehat{A}, \widehat{U})$, we can calculate the
mutual information $I(\widehat{A}; \widehat{U})$. For various number of clusters, ITCC performs the
best because ITCC is optimized purely based on the $p(A, U)$ as shown in Fig. 3.
However, CCAM has performance very close to ITCC and outperforms baseline
significantly.

6   Conclusion

Co-clustering issue has been arisen in the past decade. In a way, the problem is to achieve the dual goals of row clustering and column clustering. Although many co-clustering researches have been proposed for two-dimensional data matrix, we sometimes have additional data for the rows and columns. Therefore in this paper, we propose a novel co-clustering algorithm, CCAM to simultaneously co-cluster the dyadic data with two augmented data matrix. We use a linear combination of the mutual information for the three matrixes as the objective function and iteratively update the nearest cluster for each ad and user based on the deduced theorem.

To evaluate the effectiveness of co-clustering with augmented matrix, we present two evaluation methods, classification based evaluation and mutual information based evaluation. In average, CCAM could achieve better performance than ITCC with proper tuning on the parameters. Meanwhile, CCAM also present a comparable performance in the mutual information evaluation.

Acknowledgement. The paper is partially sponsored by national science council, Taiwan under grant NSC98-2622-E-008-023-CC2.

References

1. Agarwal, D., Merugu, S.: Predictive Discrete Latent Factor Models for Large Scale Dyadic Data. In: KDD 2007:Proceedings of the Tenth ACM SIGKDD International Conference on Knowledge Discovery and Data Mining, pp. 26–35. ACM press, San Jose (2007)
2. Banerjee, A., Dhillon, I.-S., Ghosh, J., Merugu, S., Modha, D.-S.: A Generalized Maximum Entropy Approach to Bregman Co-clustering and Matrix Approximation. In: KDD 2004: Proceedings of the Tenth ACM SIGKDD International Conference on Knowledge Discovery and Data Mining, pp. 509–514. ACM Press, Seattle (2004)
3. Chen, G., Wang, F., Zhang, C.: Collaborative filtering using orthogonal nonnegative matrix tri-factorization. In: Information Processing and Management, IPM, pp. 368–379 (2009)
4. Dai, W., Xue, G.-R., Yang, Q., Yu, Y.: Co-clustering based classification for out-of-domain documents. In: Proceedings of the 13th ACM SIGKDD International Conference on Knowledge Discovery And Data Mining, pp. 210–219. ACM Press, New York (2007)
5. Dhillon, I.-S., Mallela, S., Modha, D.-S.: Information Theoretic Co-Clustering. In: KDD 2003: Proceedings of the Ninth ACM SIGKDD International Conference on Knowledge Discovery and Data Mining, pp. 89–98. ACM Press, New York (2003)
6. Ding, C., He, X., Simon, H.-D.: On the equivalence of nonnegative matrix factorization and spectral clustering. In: Proceedings of the 5th SIAM International Conference on Data Mining, Newport Beach, CA, USA, pp. 606–610 (2005)
7. Ding, C., Li, T., Peng, W., Park, H.: Orthogonal nonnegative matrix tri-factorization for clustering. In: Proceedings of the 12th ACM SIGKDD International Conference on Knowledge Discovery and Data Mining, Philadelphia, PA, USA, pp. 126–135 (2006)

8. Li, B., Yang, Q., Xue, X.: Can Movies and Books Collaborate? Cross-Domain Collaborative Filtering for Sparsity Reduction. In: Proc of the 21st Int'l Joint Conf. on Artificial Intelligence (IJCAI 2009), pp. 2052–2057 (2009)

9. Long, B., Zhang, Z., Yu, P.-S.: Co-clustering by Block Value Decomposition. In: KDD 2005: Proceedings of the Eleventh ACM SIGKDD International Conference on Knowledge Discovery in Data Mining, pp. 635–640. ACM press, Chicago (2005)

10. Scott, D.-W.: Sturges' rule. WIREs Computational Statistics 1, 303–306 (2009)

11. Shafiei, M., Milios, E.: Model-based Overlapping Co-Clustering. Supported by grants from the Natural Sciences and Engineering Research Council of Canada. IT Interactive Services Inc., GINIus Inc. (2005)

12. Shafiei, M., Milios, E.: Latent Dirichlet Co-Clustering. In: Perner, P. (ed.) ICDM 2006. LNCS (LNAI), vol. 4065, pp. 542–551. Springer, Heidelberg (2006)

13. Shan, H., Banerjee, A.: Bayesian Co-clustering. In: Perner, P. (ed.) ICDM 2008. LNCS (LNAI), vol. 5077, pp. 530–539. Springer, Heidelberg (2008)

14. Slonim, N., Tishby, N.: Document clustering using word clusters via the information bottleneck method. In: Proceedings of the 23rd Annual International ACM SIGIR Conference on Research and Development in Information Retrieval, Athens, Greece, pp. 208–215 (2000)

15. Sugiyama, K., Hatano, K., Yoshikawa, M.: Adaptive web search based on user profile constructed without any effort from users. In: Proceedings of the 13th International Conference on World Wide Web, New York, NY, USA, pp. 675–684 (2004)

Using Confusion Matrices and Confusion Graphs to Design Ensemble Classification Models from Large Datasets

Patricia E.N. Lutu

Department of Computer Science, University of Pretoria, Pretoria, South Africa
Patricia.Lutu@up.ac.za

Abstract. Classification modeling is one of the methods commonly employed for predictive data mining. Ensemble classification is concerned with the creation of many base models which are combined into one model for purposes of increasing classification performance. This paper reports on a study which was conducted to establish whether the use of information in the confusion matrix of a single classification model could be used as a basis for the design of ensemble base models that provide high predictive performance. Positive-versus-negative (pVn) classification was studied as a method of base model design. Confusion graphs were used as input to an algorithm that determines the classes for each base model. Experiments were conducted to compare the levels of diversity provided by all-classes-at-once (ACA) and pVn base models using a statistical measure of dis-similarity. Experiments were also conducted to compare the performance of pVn ensembles, ACA ensembles, and single *k*-class models using classification trees and multi-layer perceptron artificial neural networks. The experimental results demonstrated that even though ACA base models provide a higher level of diversity than pVn base models, the diversity does result in higher predictive performance. The experimental results also demonstrated that pVn ensemble models can provide predictive performance that is higher than that of single *k*-class models and ACA ensemble models.

Keywords: ensemble classification, pVn classification, confusion matrix, confusion graph, predictive data mining, data mining, artificial neural networks, classification trees.

1 Introduction

Predictive data mining is concerned with the creation of classification and regression models [1]. A classification model predicts the values of a qualitative variable while a regression model predicts the values of a quantitative variable. Ensemble classification [2], also known as model aggregation [3], is the process of constructing several base models which are then combined into one model for prediction. The use of ensemble classification has been studied by many researchers for example [4], [5], [6], [7] who have largely concentrated on modeling from small datasets. Typically a

A. Cuzzocrea and U. Dayal (Eds.): DaWaK 2011, LNCS 6862, pp. 301–315, 2011.

large number of base models (e.g. 30) are used for the ensemble [3] in order to provide a high level of diversity among the base models. Diversity is essential for ensemble base model design since diverse base models do not make correlated errors [5], [7]. The studies reported in this paper were aimed at the design of ensemble base models from large datasets. Information contained in a confusion matrix for a single k-class model was used as a basis for base model design. The base models that are discussed are called positive-versus-negative (pVn) base models [8]. A large dataset of 494022 training and 311029 test instances was pre-processed and used for the experiments. A confusion graph which is derived from a confusion matrix was used as a basis for the design of pVn base models. It is demonstrated in this paper that pVn models of high performance can be obtained for classification tree and artificial neural network models when confusion matrix information is used as a basis for ensemble base model design. It is further demonstrated that, even though ACA base models provided higher levels of diversity, their predictive performance was lower than that of pVn base models for the dataset used for the experiments. The rest of the paper is organised as follows: Section 2 provides background to the studies reported in this paper. Section 3 provides a discussion of the methods used for ensemble model design and implementation. Section 4 provides a discussion of the experimental methods. Section 5 presents the experimental results to compare pVn and ACA ensemble model performance. Section 6 concludes the paper.

2 Background

All the methods employed for ensemble model design aim to achieve diversity and competence for the base models in order to achieve high levels of predictive performance [4], [5], [6], [8], [9], [10], [11]. Base models which make un-correlated errors are said to be diverse. A base model with high predictive performance is highly competent. Dietterich [12] has discussed five general categories of ensemble construction methods. The first category is Bayesian averaging. This involves the creation of all possible models from the training data and then combining the model predictions through Bayesian averaging. Dietterich [12] has observed that the purpose of Bayesian averaging is to reduce the uncertainty in the prediction, especially when the training set size is small. The second category of ensemble construction methods involves the manipulation of the training set instances in order to create many training sets that are then used to create ensemble base models. Bootstrap aggregation [3] is one method in this category. This method involves the creation of many training sets obtained through bootstrap sampling from a small dataset. Each bootstrapped training set is then used to construct one base model for the ensemble. Boosting [13] is a second method that falls in this category. Freund and Schapire [13] have implemented boosted ensemble base models by sequentially selecting instances that are difficult to predict for the current base model and assigning these instances a higher weighting for the next training set that is used in the sequence of base model creation.

The third category involves the manipulation of the input features of the dataset. Here, a different subset of the input features is used for the construction of each base model. Random forests [14] and decision tree forests [10] are examples of this approach. The fourth category involves the injection of randomness in the structure of the base models. Base models of artificial neural network (ANN) ensembles are commonly constructed using a different set of synaptic weights for each base model in order to inject randomness in the ensemble [5], [15]. Kwok and Carter [4] have studied the creation of classification tree base models where the selection of the feature used for splitting a classification tree node is randomised in order to obtain different tree structures across the ensemble. The fifth category of ensemble creation involves the manipulation of the target function. This manipulation is commonly achieved through problem decomposition of a multiclass (k-class) prediction task into many one-class or two-class prediction tasks. Each one-class or two-class task is encoded as an binary classification problem. One-versus-all (OVA) classification [16], [17] involves the creation of k binary classifiers where each binary classifier is trained to predict the jth class in contrast to all the other $k-1$ classes combined. Pairwise (PW) classification [7], [18] involves the creation of $k(k-1)/2$ binary classifiers where each binary classifier is trained to predict the ith class in contrast to the jth class for all possible combinations of i and j, $i \neq j$.

Error correcting output code (ECOC) classification [19] also involves the binarisation of a multiclass prediction task. Binary strings called codewords are assigned to each class and used as a basis for the definition of new functions $b_1,...,b_k$ to be learned by the binary classifiers. Each binary classifier (base model) is trained to learn (how to predict) one of the bit positions in the codewords. Prediction of a new instance involves the generation of a bitstring by the k base models (one bit per model). The class predicted by the ensemble is that class whose codeword is nearest (in Hamming distance) to the codeword generated by the ensemble. Bishop [15] and Jacobs et al. [20] have discussed learning problems for which the target function for classification has a different form in different regions of the instance space. Jacobs et al. [20] have proposed an ensemble modeling approach, called *mixture of experts*, where many ANN models are generated in the training process with each model having expertise in prediction for one region of the instance space.

The method of pVn base model design using a confusion graph derived from a confusion matrix, as presented in this paper, falls in the category of target function manipulation. The method is related to the *mixture of experts* method since base models are created to be experts in predicting a subset of classes that a single k-class model has difficulty in separating. In this respect, the method is also a boosting method [1], [13], since the main objective of base model design is to concentrate on those aspects of the prediction task that are most difficult to model. Bishop [15] has observed that the expert models for the *mixture of experts* method can be identified during the training process as is done by Jacob et al [20], or the expert models may be designed manually if the prediction problem has an obvious decomposition. It is demonstrated in this paper that the information in a confusion matrix of a single k-class model provides an obvious method for the manual decomposition of a k-class prediction task into a set of expert base models.

3   Ensemble Base Model Design from Confusion Matrices

It was stated in section 2 that pVn modeling combines the benefits of the *mixture of experts* model and the boosting approach to modeling, both of which are known to improve predictive performance. This section provides a discussion of how confusion graphs can be used to design pVn ensemble base models, the algorithm used for selecting the classes for the pVn base models, and the method for combining pVn base model predictions.

3.1 Confusion Graphs and pVn Base Models

Positive-versus-negative (pVn) classification is concerned with the design of base models for multiclass prediction tasks for which the number of classes k (categories for the class variable) is more than three. pVn base model design is based on the analysis of the confusion graph of a single k-class ($k > 3$) model in order to determine the classes that should be included in each base model. Consider the confusion matrix of fig. 1 for a simple 4-class classification model. For purposes of simplicity, the leading diagonal cell counts are not shown. The off-diagonal confusion matrix cells with blank entries have zero counts. The graph on the right is called a confusion graph [8]. A confusion graph consists of nodes which represent the classes for the prediction task and arcs (edges) which represent class confusion. An arc (c_i, c_j) represents the fact that in the confusion matrix CM the cell $CM(c_i, c_j)$ has a non-zero count. The absence of an arc between two classes c_i and c_j in a confusion graph may be interpreted to mean that classes c_i and c_j do not share a decision boundary in the instance space [8].

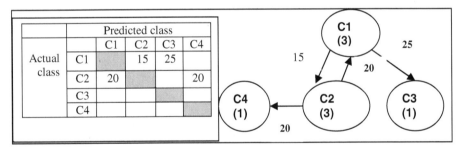

Fig. 1. Confusion matrix and confusion graph for a hypothetical classifier

Boosting [1], [13] is a statistical method used to direct the greatest modeling effort towards those regions of the instance space where correct prediction is most difficult. The boosting technique may be extended to ensemble base model design by creating base models which specialise in predicting only the classes which share decision boundaries (are adjacent) in the instance space, and provide a large amount of training data for those classes in the model. Such base models are called positive-Versus-negative (pVn) base models [8]. In a pVn base model, the classes which are adjacent are the positive classes. Any class which shares a decision boundary with one of the positive classes is called a negative class [8]. As an example, for fig. 1, models M13, M24 and M12 would be used as base models. M13 has class C1 and C3 as positive classes and C2 as the negative class. M24 has classes C2 and C4 as positive classes

---

I. Analyse the confusion graph as follows:
A. Remove all arcs with a very low connectivity value (e.g. connectivity = 1, for one test set)
B. If each node is fully connected to all the other nodes then delete the weakest outgoing link (the outgoing arc with the smallest weight) for each node.
II. Make a copy of the confusion graph
III. Process the confusion graph:
Repeat
    A. Select node with the lowest connectivity. Call it *selnode*. (break ties randomly) and create a set whose elements are all the nodes connected to *selnode*. Add *selnode* to the set. Call the set a *p-set*.
    B: Remove *selnode* from the graph and all arcs that connect *selnode* to each of the nodes in the *p-set* from the graph
Until there are no arcs left in the graph.
    C. For each *p-set* of nodes created in step A, if the *p-set* is a proper subset of another *p-set*, delete the *p-set*.
    D. Assign the classes in each of the remaining *p-sets* as the positive classes for one model.
    E. For each model, create a set of nodes for the negative classes for the model. Call this the *n-set*. For each positive class in the model, add to the *n-set*, all classes that have an arc to the class node, but are not in the *p-set* for the model.

Fig. 2. Algorithm for class selection for pVn base models: adapted from Lutu [8]

and class C1 as the negative class. M12 has classes C1 and C2 as positive classes and classes C3 and C4 as the negative classes. Each base model can predict one of its positive classes or class 'other' when presented with a test or query instance. The design of pVn base models is made possible when the confusion matrix for the single k-class model has off-diagonal cells with zero counts. Lutu [8] has called this the sparse confusion matrix property.

Lutu [8] has proposed an algorithm for determining the pVn base models from a confusion graph. A summarised version the algorithm is given in fig. 2. The essence of the algorithm in fig. 2 is to identify the pVn base models, the positive classes (p-classes), and the negative classes (n-classes) for each pVn base model. The method used to determine the number of training instance for each class that is used in a base model is discussed in section 4.2.

3.2 Combination of Base Model Predictions

In general, a probabilistic classifier outputs predictions for a query instance x_q as a set of probabilistic scores $\{ f_1, f_2, ..., f_k \}$ where f_i is the posterior probability that instance x_q belongs to class c_i [11], [15], [21], [28], [30]. For a stand-alone (single k-class) classifier, the final prediction is typically of the form

$$prediction = (c_i^*, f_i^*) \tag{1}$$

where f_i^* is the largest value in $\{ f_1, f_2, ..., f_k \}$ and c_i^* is the predicted class with the score f_i^*. Several classifier fusion methods for ensemble predictions have been proposed in the literature e.g. [11], [21]. These methods provide different ways of combining the scores $\{ f_1, f_2, ..., f_k \}$ produced by the ensemble base models, in order to determine the prediction by the ensemble. One classifier fusion method called the *max rule* [11], [21] computes the probabilistic score for each class as

$$f_i^{comb} = max\{ f_i^1, f_i^2, ..., f_i^L \} \qquad (2)$$

where f_i^j is the score for class c_i that is assigned by base model j, and L is the number of base models. The *max rule* selects the class with the best score defined as

$$f_{best}^{comb} = max\{ f_1^{comb}, f_2^{comb}, ..., f_k^{comb} \} \qquad (3)$$

The methods adopted for the combination of pVn base model predictions assumes that each base model provides a prediction in the form of equation (1). Recall from section 3.1 that a pVn base model can predict one of the classes it is designed to predict or the class 'other'. The algorithm of fig. 3 was used to select the best prediction for a pVn ensemble. The net effect of applying equation (1) and the algorithm of fig. 3 is equivalent to the application of the *max rule*.

---

1. If all pVn base models predict the class 'other', then the ensemble prediction is 'none'
2. If only one pVn base model predicts a class c_i, and all the other pVn base models predict **other**, then the ensemble prediction is c_i
3. If more than one pVn base model predicts a class c_i, then select the class c_i which is predicted with the largest value of f_i.
4. If there is a tie on f_i between winning classes then break the tie randomly

---

Fig. 3. Algorithm for combining pVn base model predictions

4   Experimental Methods

Experiments were conducted to establish whether ensemble base models designed on the basis of a confusion matrix for a single k-class model provide a high level of predictive performance compared to ACA ensemble models. The dataset, data pre-processing and algorithms used for the experiments are presented in this section. The preliminary experiments to generate the confusion matrices and confusion graphs are discussed. The base model designs for the dataset for each algorithm are presented. The methods for performance evaluation are also presented.

4.1   Datasets and Algorithms for the Experiments

The KDD Cup 1999 dataset available from the UCI KDD Archive [22] was used for the experiments. The KDD Cup 1999 dataset consists of two datasets: a training dataset and a test dataset. The small version of the training dataset with 494,022 instances was used for the experiments. The test dataset consists of 311,029 instances. The training and test datasets have 41 features. The KDD Cup 1999 dataset is a common benchmark for the evaluation of intrusion detection systems (IDS). The training and test dataset consist of a wide variety of computer network intrusions (attack types) simulated for a military environment. The training dataset has 23 classes (attack types) while the test dataset has 40 classes. The test set instances that belong to classes that do not appear in the training dataset were removed for the experiments. The 23 classes were grouped into five categories that were treated as the classes for prediction. The classes are: NORMAL, DOS, PROBE, R2L, and U2R. Shin and Lee [23] have used the same categories as the prediction task classes. Further pre-processing was conducted to balance the distribution of the attack types as recommended by Laskov et al. [24]. The final datasets used for the experiments had 51930 training instances and 70539 test instances [8]. Random samples for training, validation and test data were taken from the datasets using sequential random sampling. Selection of the relevant features for classification was done using the decision rule based method of feature selection proposed by Lutu [8] and Lutu and Engelbrecht [25]. The See5 classification tree algorithm [26], [27] and the SPSS™ Statistics 17.0 multilayer perceptron (MLP) procedure for artificial neural networks [15] were used for the experiments.

4.2 Preliminary Experiments for Confusion Matrix and Confusion Graph Creation

The first step for the experimental studies was to create See5 and MLP ANN single k-class models and generate the corresponding confusion matrices. Both models were created from the same training set of 4000 instances with an equal class distribution. Additionally, a validation set of 2000 instances was used for the MLP ANN model. The single k-class models were then tested on the same five test sets of size 350 instances and the resulting confusion matrices for each model were combined into one matrix. The confusion matrices for the single k-class models are shown in table 1.

Table 1. Confusion matrices for See5 and MLP ANN single 5-class models

Single model	Actual class	Predicted class				
		NORMAL	DOS	PROBE	R2L	U2R
See5	NORMAL		1	30	11	1
	DOS	32		15	10	
	PROBE	4	17			198
	R2L	185		8		20
	U2R	70	10			
MLP ANN		NORMAL	DOS	PROBE	R2L	U2R
	NORMAL		1		1	1
	DOS	9		87	2	
	PROBE	3	42		27	
	R2L	144	6	2		5
	U2R	142	4		56	

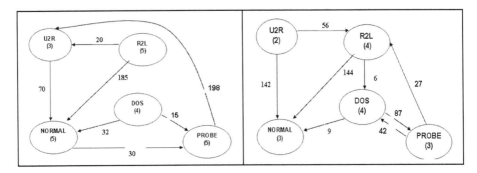

Fig. 4. Confusion graphs for (a) See5 single 5-class model (b) MLP ANN

Both matrices have the sparsity property and are therefore suitable for pVn modeling. The algorithm of fig. 2 was used to process the confusion graphs derived from the confusion matrices of table 1. Fig. 4 shows the confusion graphs after the application of steps I-A and I-B of the algorithm. Application of the steps III-A through III-E of the algorithm to the See5 and MP ANN confusion graphs resulted in the identification of the pVn base models shown in table 2. Each base model is identified by the positive classes it is designed to predict. The training set size for each pVn base model used in the experiments is also shown in table 2. In order to balance the ratio of instances between each positive class and the negative class the instance proportions were set to 80% for all positive instances and 20% for the negative instances. The training set sizes for the MNDP, MNDR and MDPR base models were set to 4000 instances. The training set sizes for the MNRU and MNPU base models were reduced to 1900 instances to avoid excessive bootstrapping of the U2R instances.

The base model design for the ACA ensembles used in the experiments is also given in table 2. The three base models are ACA1, ACA2 and ACA3. The ACA1 for See5 and ACA1 for MLP ANN are also the single k-class models used as a basis for pVn base model design. Each ACA base model was created from a training set of 4000 instances with an equal class distribution.

Table 2. Base model design for See5 and MLP ANN pVn and ACA base models

Base models for:	Base model name	Base model classes		Training set size
		positive classes	negative classes	
See5 pVn ensemble	MNRU	NORMAL, R2L, U2R	DOS, PROBE	1900
	MNDP	NORMAL,DOS, PROBE	R2L, U2R	4000
	MNPU	NORMAL, PROBE, U2R	DOS,R2L	1900
MLP ANN pVn ensemble	MNRU	NORMAL, R2L, U2R	DOS, PROBE	1900
	MNDR	NORMAL, DOS, R2L	PROBE, U2R	4000
	MDPR	DOS, PROBE, R2L	NORMAL, U2R	4000
See5 and MLP ANN ACA ensembles	ACA1	all classes	not applicable	4000
	ACA2	all classes	not applicable	4000
	ACA3	all classes	not applicable	4000

4.3 Methods for Performance Evaluation

It was stated in section 2 that base model diversity and competence are known to result in performance gains for ensemble models. Several measures of diversity have been reported in the literature. Pairwise diversity measures are concerned with measuring the diversity between all possible pairings of base models in an ensemble [7], [11]. The measures are derived from the counts in a 2x2 contingency table which records the performance of a pair of base models on a test set of n instances. The four counts (frequencies) stored in the contingency table are: $n_{rr}, n_{rw}, n_{wr}, n_{ww}$. These counts respectively indicate the number of instances for which both models make the correct prediction (n_{rr}), the number of instances on which only one base model makes the correct prediction (n_{rw} and n_{wr}), and the number of instances on which both models make the wrong prediction (n_{ww}). The disagreement measure between two base models m_i and m_j is defined as [7], [10], [11]

$$Disagr_{i,j} = \frac{n_{rw} + n_{wr}}{n} \qquad (4)$$

This measure, which was used for the experiments on diversity, is related to the Sokal and Michener measure of similarity $SM_{i,j}$ as $Disagr_{i,j} = 1 - SM_{i,j}$ [1].

Fawcett [28], [29] has provided a definition which distinguishes between discrete and probabilistic classifiers. A discrete classifier assigns class labels to test or query instances based on a fixed score value (operating point) for determining class membership. A probabilistic classifier, on the other hand, assigns probabilistic scores for each class c_i and can operate at different operating points. Predictive performance for discrete classification was measured in terms of mean accuracy and mean true positive rate (TPRATE) for each class. Two performance improvement measures namely $Diff_{acc}(A,B) = accuracy_A - accuracy_B$ measuring the difference in accuracy, and $Diff_{tpr}(A,B) = TPRATE_A - TPRATE_B$ measuring the difference in class TPRATE values, were used to compare the predictive performance of the ensemble models.

Receiver Operating Characteristic (ROC) analysis is commonly used to analyse the predictive performance of probabilistic classifiers under different operating conditions [28], [29], [30]. A ROC curve graphically depicts the relationship between the true positive rate (TPRATE) and the miss rate or false positive rate (FPRATE) of a 2-class probabilistic classifier for different operating conditions. Two important statistics used in ROC analysis are the Area Under the Curve (AUC) and the Gini concentration coefficient [21], [28], [29], [30], [31]. The AUC and the Gini concentration coefficient are related statistics and take values in the interval [0.0,1.0]. Hand and Till [30] have identified the following relationship between the AUC and the Gini concentration coefficient: $Gini = 2 \times (AUC - 0.5)$. A probabilistic classifier has practical value if it has an AUC greater than 0.5 and a Gini concentration coefficient greater than 0. Given two classifiers, the classifier with the higher values of the AUC and Gini concentration coefficient provides a higher level of predictive performance. ROC analysis for a k-class (k>2) classifier requires the computation of the Volume Under the Surface (VUS) statistic [28], [29],[30]. The VUS may be estimated by computing the mean AUC of all the one-versus-rest probabilistic classifiers [28], [29]. The pVn ensemble models were compared with single k-class models and ACA ensemble models using one-versus-rest ROC analysis.

5 Experimental Results

The experiments to determine the level predictive performance of pVn ensembles and the performance results are presented in this section. The pVn base model designs of table 2 were used to create See5 and MLP ANN pVn base models which were combined into ensemble models using the algorithm in table 2. The ACA base model designs described in table 2 were used to create base models for the See5 ACA ensemble and MPL ANN ensemble. Each ACA ensemble was made up of three base models: ACA1, ACA2 and ACA3, which were combined using the *max rule*. Experiments were conducted to compare the level of diversity of pVn and ACA base models. Experiments were also conducted to compare the predictive performance of single, pVn ensemble and ACA ensemble models on discrete and probabilistic classification.

5.1 Analysis of Base Model Diversity and Competence

The disagreement measure presented in section 4.3 was used as a basis for measuring base model diversity. Diversity was measured on a class-by-class basis since a pVn base model does not predict all classes. Table 3 provides the disagreement measure results for the pVn and ACA base models using ten test sets. The results indicate that both the See5 and MLP ANN ACA base models provide higher levels of diversity compared to the pVn base models. Base model competence was measured in terms of the true positive rate on the positive classes for the pVn base models in order to facilitate comparison between the pVn and ACA base models. The results of table 4 indicate that for both the See5 and MLP ANN algorithms, two out of three pVn base models have higher TRATE values on the positive classes combined compared to the ACA base models.

Table 3. pVn and ACA base model diversity

Ensemble model (base models)	class	mean $Disagr_{i,j}$ for class	Ensemble model (base models)	class	mean $Disagr_{i,j}$ for class
See5 pVn (MNRU, MNDP, MNPU)	NORMAL	0.05	See5 ACA (ACA1, ACA2, ACA3)	NORMAL	0.07
	PROBE	0.02		PROBE	0.40
	U2R	0.55		U2R	0.00
	DOS	0.00		DOS	0.11
	R2L	0.00		R2L	0.01
MLP ANN pVn (MNRU, MNDR, MDPR)	NORMAL	0.03	MLP ANN ACA (ACA1, ACA2, ACA3)	NORMAL	0.01
	DOS	0.08		DOS	0.11
	R2L	0.08		R2L	0.11
	PROBE	0.00		PROBE	0.14
	U2R	0.00		U2R	0.10

Table 4. pVn and ACA base model competence

Ensemble model	Base model name	p classes for pVn model	Mean TPRATE% on p classes for pVn model	Mean TPRATE% on same classes as pVn, for ACA base model:		
				ACA1 (the single model)	ACA2	ACA3
See5 pVn	MNRU	NORMAL, R2L, U2R	77.4 ± 2.6	67.0 ± 1.6	66.9 ±1.7	69.7 ± 1.5
	MNDP	NORMAL, DOS,PROBE	91.1 ± 1.9	68.1 ± 1.7	86.3 ±1.7	89.9 ± 1.3
	MNPU	NORMAL, PROBE,U2R	74.8 ± 0.4	66.5 ± 1.3	84.9 ±1.2	87.8 ± 0.8
MLP ANN pVn	MNRU	NORMAL, R2L, U2R	62.4 ± 2.1	63.1 ± 2.2	65.6 ±1.7	63.7 ± 1.6
	MNDR	NORMAL, DOS, R2L	81.6 ± 2.1	72.5 ± 3.3	70.6±2.3	75.2 ± 2.3
	MDPR	DOS, PROBE, R2L	79.7 ± 3.4	65.6 ± 5.9	67.5±2.0	72.1 ± 2.2

5.2   Evaluation of Performance for Discrete Classification

The pVn and ACA ensemble models were compared on predictive performance using the accuracy and class true positive rate (TPRATE) measures. Student's paired samples t-test, the $Diff_{acc}(A,B)$ and $Diff_{tpr}(A,B)$ measures were used to establish whether the pVn ensemble models provide significantly higher predictive performance compared to ACA ensembles.

Table 5. Statistical tests to compare See5 ACA and pVn ensemble models

Group name, mean accuracy%, TPRATE% for 10 test sets See5 ensembles		Student's paired t-test (9 df)			Performance improvement $Diff_{acc}(A,B)\%$ or $Diff_{tpr}(A,B)\%$
Group A pVn ensemble	Group B ACA ensemble	95% CI of mean difference	p value (2 tail)	Group A better than Group B?	
All classes-A (79.0 ± 2.1)	All classes-B (77.1± 1.2)	[-0.4, 4.2]	0.092	yes	1.9
NORMAL-A (98.1 ± 0.6)	NORMAL-B (95.1 ± 1.3)	[1.7, 4.3]	0.001	yes	3.0
DOS-A (68.4 ± 6.5)	DOS-S (82.0± 3.8)	[-18.6,-8.6]	0.000	no	-13.6
PROBE-A (97.0 ± 1.0)	PROBE-B (93.6± 1.7)	[1.5, 5.3]	0.003	yes	3.4
R2L-A (54.1 ± 6.9)	R2L-B (37.4 ± 3.5)	[9.6, 23.8]	0.000	yes	16.7
U2R-A (77.1 ± 0.0)	U2R-B (77.1± 0.0)	no variance	no variance	same	0.0

Table 6. Statistical tests to compare MLP ANN ACA and pVn ensemble models

Group name, mean accuracy%, TPRATE% for 10 test sets MLP ANN ensembles		Student's paired t-test (9 df)			Performance improvement
Group A pVn ensemble	Group B ACA ensemble	95% CI of mean difference	p value (2 tail)	Group A better than Group B?	$Diff_{acc}(A,B)\%$ or $Diff_{tpr}(A,B)\%$
All classes-A (75.2 ± 1.2)	All classes-B (69.2 ± 2.1)	[3.2, 8.8]	0.001	yes	6.0
NORMAL-A (98.4 ± 1.0)	NORMAL-B (98.0± 1.2)	[-0.3, 1.0]	0.193	no	0.4
DOS-A (94.7 ± 2.7)	DOS-B (62.5± 5.7)	[24.4, 39.2]	0.000	yes	32.2
PROBE-A (95.3 ± 2.4)	PROBE-B (89.4 ± 1.7)	[3.4, 8.3]	0.000	yes	5.9
R2L-A (52.9 ± 4.5)	R2L-B 52.3 ± 6.0)	[-5.9, 7.1]	0.840	no	0.6
U2R-A (34.6 ± 7.3)	U2R-B (43.5 ± 0.7)	[-17.4,-0.4]	0.042	no	-8.9

Table 5 shows the results of the statistical tests to compare the predictive performance of the See5 models. The results of Student's paired t-tests for the See5 models indicate that the pVn ensemble model performance is slightly higher than that of the ACA ensemble. The $Diff_{tpr}(A,B)$ measure indicates statistically significant increases in the TPRATE for three of the classes range between 3.0% and 16.7%. The $Diff_{acc}(A,B)$ measure indicates a marginal accuracy increase of 1.9%. The test results for the MLP ANN are given in table 6. The results indicate that the pVn ensemble model performance is higher than that of the ACA ensemble model. The $Diff_{tpr}(A,B)$ measure indicates statistically significant increases in the TPRATE for two of the classes are respectively 5.9% and 32.2%. The $Diff_{acc}(A,B)$ measure indicates an accuracy increase of 6.0%.

5.3   Evaluation of Performance for Probabilistic Classification

ROC analysis was conducted to compare one ACA base model (the single 5-class model), the pVn ensemble and the ACA ensemble. Figures 5 and 6 provide a graphic representation of the ROC analysis results based on the Gini concentration coefficient.

The See5 pVn ensemble provides a marked improvement on the R2L class compared to the ACA ensemble. The mean Gini values indicate that both the See5 pVn and ACA ensemble models provide performance improvements compared to a single 5-class model. However, both the See5 pVn and ACA ensemble provide the same level of performance on average. The MLP ANN pVn ensemble provides a large improvement on the DOD class compared to the ACA ensemble. The mean Gini values indicate that both the MLP ANN pVn and ACA ensemble models provide performance improvements compared to a single 5-class model. Additionally, the MLP ANN pVn ensemble provides a higher level of performance compared to the ACA ensemble.

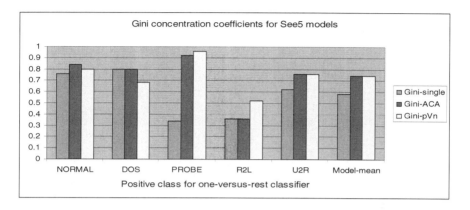

Fig. 5. ROC analysis results for the See5 single and ensemble models

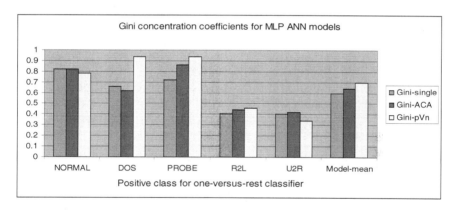

Fig. 6. ROC analysis results for the MLP ANN single and ensemble models

6 Conclusions

The objectives of the research reported in this paper were to establish whether the use of information in the confusion matrix of a single classification model could be used as a basis for the design of ensemble base models that provide high predictive performance. Positive-Versus-negative (pVn) classification was studied as a method of base model design using a large dataset. Confusion graphs derived from confusion matrices were used as input to an algorithm that determines the classes for each base model in an ensemble. Experimental results on the KDD Cup 1999 dataset using the See5 classification tree algorithm and a multilayer perceptron artificial neural network demonstrated firstly, that ACA ensemble base models exhibit higher levels of diversity compared to pVn base models. Secondly, the pVn base models have a higher level of competence (predictive performance). Thirdly, for both discrete and probabilistic classification, pVn ensembles can provide higher levels of predictive performance compared to ACA ensembles.

References

1. Giudici, P.: Applied Data Mining: Statistical Methods for Business and Industry. John Wiley & Sons, Chichester (2003)
2. Hansen, L.K., Salamon, P.: Neural network ensembles. IEEE Transactions on Pattern Analysis and Machine Intelligence 12(10), 993–1001 (1990)
3. Breiman, L.: Bagging predictors. Machine Learning 24, 123–140 (1996)
4. Kwok, S.W., Carter, C.: Multiple decision trees. Uncertainty in Artificial Intelligence 4, 327–335 (1990)
5. Krogh, A., Vedelsby, J.: Neural network ensembles, cross validation and active learning. In: Tesauro, G., Touretzky, D.S., Leen, T.K. (eds.) Advances in Neural Information Processing Systems. MIT Press, Cambridge (1995)
6. Osei-Bryson, K.-M., Kah, M.O., Kah, J.M.L.: Selecting predictive models for inclusion in an ensemble. In: The 18th Triennial Conference of the International Federation of Operational Research Societies (IFORS 2008), Sandton, Johannesburg (July 2008)
7. Kuncheva, L.I., Whitaker, C.J.: Measures of diversity in classifier ensembles and their relationship with ensemble accuracy. Machine Learning 51, 181–207 (2003)
8. Lutu, P.E.N.: Dataset Selection for Aggregate Model Implementation in Predictive Data Mining. PhD thesis, Department of Computer Science. University of Pretoria (2010), http://upetd.up.ac.za/thesis/available/etd-11152010-203041/
9. Ali, K.M., Pazzani, J.: Error reduction through learning multiple descriptions. Machine Learning 24, 173–202 (1996)
10. Ho, T.K.: The random subspace method for constructing decision forests. IEEE Trans. Pattern Analysis and Machine Intelligence 20(8), 832–844 (1998)
11. Kuncheva, L.: Combining Pattern Classifiers: Methods and Algorithms. John Wiley & sons, Hoboken (2004)
12. Dietterich, T.G.: Ensemble methods in machine learning. In: Proc. First International Workshop on Multiple Classifier Systems. Springer, Heidelberg (2000)
13. Freund, Y., Schapire, R.: A decision-theoretic generalization of on-line learning and an application to boosting. Journal of Computer and System Sciences 55(1), 119–139 (1997)
14. Ho, T.K.: Random decision forests. In: Proc. Third International Conference on Document Analysis and Recognition, Montreal, Canada (August 1995)
15. Bishop, C.M.: Neural Network for Pattern Recognition. Clarendon Press, Oxford (1995)
16. Rifkin, R., Klautau, A.: In defense of one-vs-all classification. The Journal of Machine Learning Research 5, 101–141 (2004)
17. Galar, M., Fernández, Z., Barenenchea, E., Bustince, H., Herrara, F.: An overview of ensemble methods for binary classifiers in multi-class problems: Experimental study of one-vs-one and one-vs-all schemes. Pattern Recognition 44, 1761–1776 (2011)
18. Fürnkranz, J.: Pairwise classification as an ensemble technique. In: Elomaa, T., Mannila, H., Toivonen, H. (eds.) ECML 2002. LNCS (LNAI), vol. 2430, pp. 97–110. Springer, Heidelberg (2002)
19. Dietterich, T., Bakiri, G.: Solving multiclass learning problems via error-correcting output codes. Journal of Artificial Intelligence Research 2, 263–286 (1995)

20. Jacobs, R.A., Jordan, M.I., Nowlan, S.J., Hinton, G.E.: Adaptive mixture of local experts. Neural Computation 3(1), 79–87 (1991)
21. Kittler, J.: Combining classifiers: A theoretical framework. Pattern Analysis and Applications 1, 18–27 (1998)
22. Hettich, S., Bay, S.D.: The UCI KDD archive. Department of Information and Computer Science. University of California, Irvine (1999), http://kdd.ics.uci.edu
23. Shin, S.W., Lee, C.H.: Using Attack-Specific Feature Subsets for Network Intrusion Detection. In: Proceedings of the 19th Australian Conference on Artificial Intelligence, Hobart, Australia (2006)
24. Laskov, P., Düssel, P., Schäfer, C., Rieck, K.: Learning intrusion detection: supervised or unsupervised? In: ICAP: International Conference on Image Analysis and Processing, Cagliari, Italy (2005)
25. Lutu, P.E.N., Engelbrecht, A.P.: A decision rule-based method for feature selection in predictive data mining. Expert Systems with Applications 37(1), 602–609 (2010)
26. Quinlan, J.R.: An Informal Tutorial, Rulequest Research (2004), http://www.rulequest.com (accessed October 28, 2005)
27. Quinlan, J.R.: C4.5: Programs for Machine Learning. Morgan Kauffman, San Francisco (1993)
28. Fawcett, T.: ROC graphs: Notes and practical considerations for researchers. HP Laboratories (2004), http://home.comcast.net/~tom.fawcett/public_html/papers/ROC1 01.pdf (Cited March 1, 2010)
29. Fawcett, T.: An introduction to ROC analysis. Pattern Recognition Letters 27, 861–874 (2006)
30. Hand, D.J., Till, R.J.: A simple generalisation of the area under the ROC curve for multiple class classification problems. Machine Learning 45, 171–186 (2001)
31. Breiman, L., Friedman, J.H., Olshen, R.A., Stone, C.J.: Classification and Regression Trees. Wadsworth & Brooks, Pacific Grove (1984)

Pairwise Similarity Calculation of Information Networks

Yuanzhe Cai and Sharma Chakravarthy

CSE Department and Information Technology Laboratory
The University of Texas at Arlington, Arlington, TX 76019, USA
yuanzhe.cai@mavs.uta.edu, sharma@cse.uta.edu

Abstract. We focus on extensions to the pairwise similarity calculation of information networks. By considering both in- and out-link relationships, we propose Additive- and Multiplicative-SimRank to calculate the similarity score. Then we discuss the loop/cycles problem of information networks and propose a method to address this problem. Our extensive experimental results conducted on eight food web data sets show that our approach performs significantly better than earlier approaches.

1 Introduction

In order to study the patterns and processes of information systems, computing pairwise similarity in an information network is a fundamental problem. Food web, a kind of information network, represents the predator-prey relationship between species within an ecosystem. Consider the following example from the food web.

Example 1.(Motivation).*The dodos lived peacefully on Mauritius Island for several hundred years. Because of poaching by the humans and killing by the animals (such as pigs, rats and cats), that have been introduced into the island by sailors, the Dodo bird died off extremely quickly. About 1681, the last Dodo bird died. After about three hundred years, in 1973, Tambalacoque, also called dodo tree, was dying out. There are only about 13 trees left in the island. Scientists found that the dodo tree's seed should pass through the digestive system of dodo before they germinated. Therefore, in order to aid the seed in germination, scientists used turkeys to erode the nutshell of the dodo tree seed. In this case, the humans saved the dodo tree, but the turkey, similar to the cats, rats and pigs, which have been introduced into this island may also spoil the balance of the ecosystem. Some failed examples, such as Austrian Rabbit and Xisha Islands' cat, are also alarming. Therefore, there is an interesting question, "If one species get extinct in an ecosystem and we want to introduce a new species into this ecosystem to keep the balance, what kinds of species should we introduce?"*
  The answer is that we should introduce the species that has "similar food habit" in this ecosystem. In this example, turkey and dodo birds are very similar, because they both eat similar foods, such as the seed of the dodo tree and

A. Cuzzocrea and U. Dayal (Eds.): DaWaK 2011, LNCS 6862, pp. 316–329, 2011.

they both have similar natural enemies. In this example, the prey relationship and is-preyed relationship are used to define the similarity score between two species. Based on this observation, a number of approaches have been proposed to quantify similarity between species in a food web. The most widely used approaches in the former research work [11] [12] [15] are the Jaccardian similarity functions. The intuition behind Jaccardian similarity function is that two species are similar, if they share many similar food web neighbors and the total number of their neighbors is less. The $S_{jaccard}(a, b)$ [11] equation is shown below:

$$S_{jaccard}(a, b) = \left(\frac{|n(a) \cap n(b)|}{|n(a) \cup n(b)|} \right) \tag{1}$$

where $n(a)$ and $n(b)$ is the neighbors of species a and b. $|n(a) \cap n(b)|$ is the total number of prey and predator species that species a and b have in common and $|n(a) \cup n(b)|$ is the total number of prey and predators of species a and b.

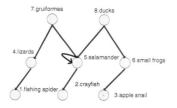

Fig. 1. Segment of CYPWET data set [1]

Table 1. Similarity Score

	Jaccard	SimRank
$S(1,2)$	0	0.36
$S(2,3)$	0	0.36
$S(4,5)$	0.25	0.43
$S(5,6)$	0.25	0.43
$S(7,8)$	0.33	0

However, earlier research only considers the direct relationship in the information network. Considering the example in Figure 1, we want to calculate the similarity between fishing spider and crayfish. However, according to the direct relationship, shown in Table 1, the similarity between these two species is zero, although these two species have some relationship from theirs indirect predator – gruiformes. This example shows that when we consider the similarity between two species in the food web, we also need to consider the indirect relationship between species of other types related to them. This problem is addressed by the *SimRank* algorithm [6] in which the similarity between two objects is recursively defined as the average similarity between two objects. However, this similarity definition only considers the one directional relationship for the information network. In Figure 1, *SimRank* only considers the is-preyed relationship (their predators), but the species' similar prey also contribute to their similarity relationship.

The other major problem is that many real-life information networks contains cycles. Food web, for example, includes many cannibals that create loops and cycles. For example, in figure 1, salamander is a cannibal and they prey the other salamanders for food. These loops in the food web also influence the value of similarity scores.

The main contributions of this are:

- Based on relationship of topical structures in information networks, two similarity algorithms, *Additive-SimRank* and *Multiplicative-SimRank*, are proposed to address this problem. We also prove that the proposed algorithms converge by theoretical analysis.
- We discuss the loops and cycles problem in the information networks and propose a method to handle them.
- Extensive experiments are conducted to evaluate the accuracy of the proposed algorithms. *Additive-SimRank* is shown to have higher accuracy as compared with other methods.

Roadmap: The rest of this paper is organized as follows: We introduce the related work in section 2 and define the graph model in section 3. *SimRank* is overviewed in section 4. Two similarity measures for information network and the cycle problem are discussed in section 5. Our experimental analysis is reported in section 6 and conclusions are in section 7.

2   Related Work

We categorize existing work related to our study into three classes: species aggregation, link-Based similarity calculation, and random walk on graph.

Species Aggregation: Setting a new criterion for searching community food web data, Martineze [11] [12] was the first researcher to systematically analyze the effects of variable species aggregation on the network structure of food webs. There are different indices used to quantify similarity between objects and the Jaccard index is probably the best known and widely used in food web research [11] [12] [15]. Martineze used an *Additive-Jaccard* index to determine the similarity between species in Little Rock Lake and then used the average-linkage-cluster to aggregate taxonomies. However, these methods do not consider the potential relationship between each species.

Link-Based Similarity Calculation: The earliest research work for similarity calculation based on link analysis focuses on the citation patterns of scientific papers. The most common measures are *co-citation* [13] and *co-coupling* [7]. *Co-citation* indicates that if two documents are often cited together by other documents, they may have the same topic. The meaning of *co-coupling* for scientific papers is that if two papers cite many papers in common, they may focus on the same topic. However, all these methods compute similarity only by considering their immediate neighbors. In contrast, *SimRank* [6] considers the entire relationship graph to determine similarity between two nodes. Because of the high time complexity ($O(n^4)$) of this approach, many papers [4] [14] [3] [10] have focused on performance improvement; however a few have focused on the accuracy improvement of *SimRank*. In this paper, our focus is on extending *SimRank* approach by considering bidirectional relationships and cycles to improve the accuracy of the original *SimRank* approach.

Random Walks on Graphs: Theoretical basis of our work uses hit times for two surfers walking randomly on the graph. We mainly refer to research about expected f-meeting distance theory [6]. Other research, such as random walk theory [8] and Markov Model [9] also help understand our research.

3   Graph Model

The food web data can be represented as a directed graph, $G(V, E)$, which consists of a set of nodes V representing species and a set of directed edges E representing the relationships between species. For example, Figure 1 is a relationship graph that describes the predatory relationship in the marshes and sloughs. In this graph, a directed edge $< p, q >$ from species p to species q corresponds to a predator relationship. $I(v)$ denotes the set of predators preying on species v, which is also the in-link neighbors of species v and $O(v)$ denotes the set preyed-by species v, which is also the out-link neighbors of species v.

4   Overview of SimRank

SimRank [6] is a method for measuring link-based similarity between objects in a graph that models the object-to-object relationships in a particular domain. The intuition behind *SimRank* score is that two objects are similar if they link to similar objects. This intuition also indicates that *SimRank* calculation needs to be recursive.

Below, we present the formula to compute SimRank. Given a graph $G(V, E)$ consisting of a set of nodes V and a set of links E, the *SimRank* similarity between objects a and b, denoted as $S(a, b)$, is computed, recursively, as follows:

$$S(a,b) = \begin{cases} 1 & if \ (a = b) \\ \frac{c}{|I(a)||I(b)|} \sum_{i=1}^{|I(a)|} \sum_{j=1}^{|I(b)|} S(I_i(a), I_j(b)) & if \ (a \neq b) \end{cases} \tag{2}$$

where c is a constant decay factor, $0 < c < 1$; $I(a)$ is the set of in-neighbor nodes of a and $I_i(a)$ is the ith in-neighbor node of a. $|I(a)|$ is the number of neighbors of node a. In case that $I(a)$ or $I(b)$ is an empty set, $S(a, b)$ is defined as zero.

A solution to *SimRank* equation (2) can be reached by iteration to a fixed-point. For each iteration k, let $S_k(.,.)$ be an iteration similarity function and

$S_k(a, b)$ be the iterative similarity score of pair (a, b) on iteration k. The iteration process is started with S_0 $(S_0(a, b) = \begin{cases} 0 & if \ (a \neq b) \\ 1 & if \ (a = b) \end{cases})$. To calculate $S_{k+1}(a, b)$ from $S_k(a, b)$, we use the following equation:

$$S_{k+1}(a, b) = \frac{c}{|I(a)||I(b)|} \sum_{i=1}^{|I(a)|} \sum_{j=1}^{|I(b)|} S_k(I_i(a), I_j(b)) \tag{3}$$

In equation (3), $1/|I(a)|$ is a single step probability of walking from node a to a node in $I(a)$. Therefore we can use Backward Transfer Probability Matrix (BT PageRank) to capture the single step probability in a Markov Chain. Thus, SimRank algorithm can be described by matrix calculation. $S_0 = E$, where E is an identity matrix. Equation (3) can be rewritten as:

$$S_k(a, b) = c \sum_{i=1}^{|I(a)|} \sum_{j=1}^{|I(b)|} BT_{aI_i(a)} BT_{bI_j(b)} S_{k-1}(I_i(a), I_j(b)) \tag{4}$$

Although the convergence of iterative SimRank algorithm can be guaranteed in theory, practical computation uses a tolerance factor ε to control the number of iterations such that a finite number of iterations are performed. It is recommend to set $\varepsilon = 0.001$, the same as in PageRank. Specifically, the terminating condition of the iteration is as follows:

$$max(|S_k(a, b) - S_{k-1}(a, b)|/|S_{k-1}(a, b)|) \leq \varepsilon \tag{5}$$

It indicates that the iteration stops if the maximal change rate of similarity value between two iterations for all node pairs is smaller than the threshold ε.

5   Extending the Similarity Measure

In this section, we first describe our analysis of the information network. Then, we describe our topological similarity definition on the network. Finally, we discuss the loops problem on the network.

5.1   Topological Similarity

If we want to compare the similarity between dodo and turkey on the Mauritius Island, we need to answer the following questions:

1. Do dodo bird and turkey eat similar food? If turkey does not eat dodo tree's seed, we do not need to introduce turkey into this ecosystem, because turkey doesn't have the similar role as the dodo bird in this ecosystem.

2. Do dodo bird and turkey have similar natural enemies? If turkey does not have similar natural enemies as the dodo bird or do not have natural enemies, the dodo bird's natural enemies may not find enough food and also become extinct; or turkeys may proliferate and break the biological balance.

Thus, we can identify two intuitions for defining similarity for the food web.

Intuition 1: *Two species are similar, if they are preyed by similar species.*

Intuition 2: *Two species are similar, if they prey similar species.*

Let us look at Table 1 again. Surprisingly, *SimRank* doesn't produce a similarity score for the pair "gruiforms"-"ducks", although these two species have the same classification (avifauna) and prey the same species salamander. The problem for *SimRank* is that *SimRank* only considers is-preyed relationship on the food web, but the other important prey relationship is not considered for similarity calculation.

Considering both relationships for the food web, similarity score should combine the similarity from both relationships. Thus we can add is-preyed relationship similarity score and prey relationship similarity score together and use the parameter γ to adjust the contribution of these two relationships for the total score. We call this the additive method. Thus, we propose the following formula for calculating the similarity score:

$$S(a,b) = \begin{cases} 1 & if \ (a = b) \\ \gamma \frac{c}{|I(a)||I(b)|} \sum_{i=1}^{|I(a)|} \sum_{j=1}^{|I(b)|} S(I_i(a), I_j(b)) \ + \\ (1-\gamma) \frac{c}{|O(a)||O(b)|} \sum_{i=1}^{|O(a)|} \sum_{j=1}^{|O(b)|} S(O_i(a), O_j(b)) & if \ (a \neq b) \end{cases} \quad (6)$$

where c is a constant decay factor, $0 < c < 1$; $I(a)$ is the set of predators of species a and $I_i(a)$ is the ith predators of a. $|I(a)|$ is the number of predator of node a. $O(a)$ is the set of prey of species a and $O_i(a)$ is the ith prey of a. $|O(a)|$ is the number of prey of node a. γ is a constant parameter that use to adjust the different effect of the is-preyed and prey relationships, $0 \leq \gamma \leq 1$.

On the other hand, another way to extend *SimRank* is that we can multiply the is-preyed and prey relationship similarities. This product score can also describe the relationship similarity score. This method is called as the multiplicative method. Then, we have the following formula to calculate the similarity score.

$$S(a,b) = \begin{cases} 1 & if \ (a = b) \\ \frac{c}{|I(a)||I(b)|} \sum_{i=1}^{|I(a)|} \sum_{j=1}^{|I(b)|} S(I_i(a), I_j(b)) \ \times \\ \frac{c}{|O(a)||O(b)|} \sum_{i=1}^{|O(a)|} \sum_{j=1}^{|O(b)|} S(O_i(a), O_j(b)) & if \ (a \neq b) \end{cases} \quad (7)$$

where parameter definitions are the same as that of the *Additive* case.

Algorithm 1 outlines *Additive-SimRank* computation. It takes in 4 arguments. The first two arguments inherit from the original *SimRank* algorithm: the decay

---

Algorithm 1. *Additive-SimRank*

Require:
    Decay Factor, c;
    Tolerance Factor, ϵ;
    Backward Transfer Probability Matrix BT (the backward probability of moving from state i to their j);
    Forward Transfer Probability Matrix FT (the forward probability of moving from state i to state j in one step);
Ensure:
    Similarity Matrix, S_k;
  1: $k \leftarrow 1$;
  2: $S_0 \leftarrow$ identity;
  3: while$(Max(|S_k(a,b) - S_{k-1}(a,b)|/|S_{k-1}(a,b)|) > \varepsilon))$
  4: $k \leftarrow k+1$;
  5: $S_{k-1} \leftarrow S_k$;
  6: for each element $S_k(a,b)$
  7: $S_k(a,b) \leftarrow \gamma c \sum_{i=1}^{|I(a)|} \sum_{j=1}^{|I(b)|} BT_{aI_i(a)} BT_{bI_i(b)} S_{k-1}(I_i(a), I_j(b)) + (1 - \gamma)c \sum_{i=1}^{|I(a)|} \sum_{j=1}^{|I(b)|} FT_{aI_i(a)} FT_{bI_i(b)} S_{k-1}(I_i(a), I_j(b))$;
  8: end for;
  9: end while;
10: **return** S_k;

---

factor c gives the rate of decay as similarity flows across edges in a graph and tolerance factor γ is to control the number of iterations as discussed in section 4. The last parameter is Forward Transfer Probability Matrix FT. As we can see from equation 6, $1/|O(a)|$ is a single step probability of walking from node a to a node in $O(a)$. Thus, we use the Forward Transfer Probability Matrix FT [9] to calculate the similarity score in our algorithm. On the food web, FT matrix is the transfer matrix of prey relationship. The last parameter is Backward Transfer Probability Matrix BT. As we can also see from equation 6, $1/|I(a)|$ is a single step probability of walking from node a to a node in $I(a)$. Thus, we use the Backward Transfer Probability Matrix BT [9] to calculate the similarity score in our algorithm. On the food web, BT matrix is the transfer matrix of is-preyed relationship.

    Additive-SimRank algorithm first initializes variables (lines 1-2). In line 4, the algorithm will stop if the ending condition is equation 5 will satisfied. The algorithm then uses Equation 6 to calculate the similarity score. Although the worst time and space complexity of *Additive-SimRank* is the same as the *SimRank*, its accuracy of *Additive-SimRank* is higher than original *SimRank* as it considers the both relationship of the graph.

    The *Multiplicative-SimRank* algorithm is the same as the previous algorithm except for step 7 where Equation 7 is used. The theoretical foundations of *Additive-SimRank* and *Multiplicative-SimRank* are discussed below.

Forward and Backward Random Walk Model: Since BT and FT in algorithm 1 (and its counterpart for multiplicative-SimRank) can be considered as a single step backward and forward transfer matrix of a Markov Chain, the iteration similarity calculation process of equations 6 and 7 can be explained using *two random surfers walking forward and backward*. Consider two surfers start from two nodes on the graph and they walk from one node to the other nodes step by step. In each step, they will walk one step backward or forward, respectively, and calculate the meeting possibility for these two surfers. The final result of these two methods can be translated into the possibility of two random surfers meeting with each other by considering both forward and backward random walking. For equations 6 and 7, we use different methods to combine these meeting possibilities for each step. In equation 6, we add these meeting possibilities of forward and backward walking and use γ to adjust the proportion of these backward and forward meeting possibilities. In equation 7, we directly multiply the forward and backward meeting score. Since $SimRank$ only considers backward random walk, it is a special case of our method. In equation 6, if γ is set to 1, the equation is the same as the $SimRank$ function.

Theorem 1. *The Additive-simrank and multiplicative-simrank similarity $S(a, b)$ for any node pair (a, b) will converge to a fixed value.*

Proof. See [2] for proof.

5.2   Dealing with Loops in the Network

The other problem of some information networks is that there could be a number of cycles or loops in the network. For example, food web contains frequent cannibalism that induces loops (e.g., salamander in Figure 1). In the dry season, 14% of salamanders' food comes from killing other salamanders. Another example is of steatoda spiders and latrodectus spiders. These two spiders eat each other. Table 2 shows the number of cycles in the real world food web [1]. As we can see, cycles are quite common in the food web.

Fig. 2. Representative graph with a loop/cycle

Table 2. Statistics in Food Web Data sets

Data set	Vertex	Edge	Cycles
CYPWET	68	554	15
CYPDRY	68	545	15
BAYWET	125	1969	21
BAYDRY	125	1938	21
MANGWET	94	1339	8
MANGDRY	94	1340	8
GRAMWET	66	793	10
GRAMDRY	66	793	11

However, these cycles on the food web graph will affect the species' similarity score. Let us look at the similarity score between two species "fishing spider", "salamander" and "fishing spider", "apple snail". Table 3 tabulates these similarity score for figure 1. As we can see S(fishing spider, salamander) is slightly higher than S(fishing spider, apple snail). However, in the biological field, fishing spider and apple snail are classified as macro invertebrates but salamander is classified as herpetofauna. In fact, "fishing spider" and "salamander" are not in the same classification. Similarly, other information networks, such as the web page graphs and paper citation graphs, also has cycles. For example, in the citation graph, the same author can write two papers that are cross-referenced. We can also actually prove the following theorem for the similarity calculation in the presence of loops in a graph.

Table 3. *Additive-SimRank* results for figure 1(with cycles)($\gamma= 0.75$, c = 0.8)

	1	2	3	4	5	6	7	8
1	1	0.09	0.03	0.002	0.03	0.002	0	0
2	0.09	1	0.09	0.065	0.18	0.065	0	0
3	0.03	0.09	1	0.002	0.03	0.002	0	0
4	0.002	0.06	0.002	1	0.21	0.08	0.007	0.007
5	0.03	0.18	0.03	0.21	1	0.21	0.154	0.15
6	0.002	0.06	0.002	0.08	0.21	1	0.007	0.007
7	0	0	0	0.006	0.15	0.007	1	0.157
8	0	0	0	0.006	0.15	0.007	0.157	1

Table 4. A *Additive-SimRank* results for figure 1(no cycles)($\gamma= 0.75$, c = 0.8)

	1	2	3	4	5	6	7	8
1	1	0.09	0.03	0.002	0.03	0.002	0	0
2	0.09	1	0.09	0.065	0.18	0.065	0	0
3	0.03	0.09	1	0.002	0.03	0.002	0	0
4	0.002	0.06	0.002	1	0.21	0.08	0.007	0.007
5	0.03	0.18	0.03	0.21	1	0.21	0.154	0.15
6	0.002	0.06	0.002	0.08	0.21	1	0.007	0.007
7	0	0	0	0.006	0.15	0.007	1	0.157
8	0	0	0	0.006	0.15	0.007	0.157	1

Theorem 2. *Consider one graph G with a cycle l and a line q. Figure 2 shows such a graph as G. Let $l(s_n, s_m)$ denote a sequence of cycle vertices $s_n, s_{i+1}, ..., s_m$. Let $q(s_1, s_n)$ denote a sequence of line vertices $s_1, s_{i+1}, , s_n$. s_n is the crossing point between cycle l and line q. Let $length(p)$ denote the length of path p, and $length(l) = length(q) = k$. Then, $S(s_1, s_n) = c^k$ and $S(s_n, s_m) = 0$.*

Proof. See [2] for proof.

This theorem provides us two insights about *SimRank* scores and why they are not intuitively right for the networks that contain loops. First, s_1 is at the bottom of food web in Figure 2 and in normal cases it is the primary species, such as periphyton, utricularia, and so on. However, s_n is the top consumer, such as bobcat, panther and so forth. However, according to theorem 1, these two species s_1 and s_n has a great similarity between each other. Secondly, s_m is another species in the cycle. In this food web graph, this species is also the top level consumer. However, according to theorem 1, the pair s_1 and s_n have higher similarity score then the pair s_m and s_n. This implies that bobcat and periphyton are more similar than bobcat and panther. That does not match with our intuition. Based on this example, we can address the problem of *SimRank* scores.

In fact, the same problem also exists in *Additive-SimRank* and *Multiplicative-SimRank*. Thus, before we calculate the similarity score on the food web, we will delete all the relationships in the cycle. Table 4 shows the similarity result when cycles are deleted from the food web. The similarity score of the pair "fishing spider" and "salamander" is equal to 0 and in fact those two species are not in the same classification. Clearly, this result matches better with our intuition.

6 Experimental Evaluation

Data Sets: Our experiments use the data sets shown in Table 2. Please refer to [1] for details regarding these data sets. Before we calculate the similarity score, we delete all the cycle in these data sets. These eight data sets come from four areas. CYPWET and CYPDRY data sets are collected from 295,000 hectare wetlands of the big cypress natural preserve in southwest Florida. BAYWET and BAYDRY data sets are collected from a triangular, tropical lagoon/bay. MANGWET and MANGDRY data sets are from the huge mangrove belt along the seaward edge of the Everglades. GRAMWET and GRAMDRY data sets are from the historical Everglades system. In each area, the food web data is collected for different seasons. For example, CYPWET indicates that this data set is collected in wet season and CYPDRY is for the dry season.

Table 5. Classification of for food web data sets

Data Set	C.1	C.2	C.3	C.4	C.5	C.6	C.7	C.8
CYPWET	12	2	16	5	10	3	3	17
CYPDRY	12	2	16	5	10	3	3	17
BAYWET	14	12	2	26	4	48	3	16
BAYDRY	14	12	2	26	4	48	3	16
MANGWET	5	6	12	21	5	22	3	20
MANGDRY	5	6	12	21	5	22	3	20
GRAMWET	4	2	10	8	10	21	3	0
GRAMDRY	4	2	10	8	10	21	3	0

[1]Note: The species in these data sets have been divided into eight classes by their different roles in ecosystem, such as primary producers, micro fauna, mammals, macro invertebrates, herpetofauna, fishes, detritus and avifauna, which are marked from C.1 to C.8.

Table 5 shows that these species data sets are manually divided into eight classes. These classes will be used as the standard/baseline to evaluate the accuracy of our algorithms.

All our experiments are conducted on a PC with a 3.0 GHz Intel Core 2 Duo Processor, 2GB memory, running windows XP Professional. All algorithms are implemented in Java.

6.1 Evaluation Metric

In our food web data sets, there are predefined class labels for these species. For a species on the food web, these algorithms will return a ranked list of relative species. For each species in the list, if this species' label is the same as species s_1, we think these two species are closely related and give a grade 2 (stress the related species); otherwise we associate grade 0. Then, we use the normalized discount cumulative gain (NDCG) [5] to evaluate the performance of this similarity ranking list. While evaluating a similarity ranking list, NDCG follows one principle. The lower ranking position of a species is less valuable for the researcher, because the researchers take great care about species more related to species s_1. According to this principle, the NDCG score of a similarity ranking list at position n is calculated as follows. $N(n) = Z_n \sum_{j=1}^{n} \frac{2^{r(j)} - 1}{log(1+j)}$, where $r(j)$ is the rating of the jth species in the similarity ranked list and the normalization constant Z_n is chosen so that a prefect order gets NDCG value 1. For example, we will calculate the NDCG@10 score for the species "Living sediment" in data set CYPWET because for "living sediment" there is only one species in the micro fauna classification. Thus, Z_n order is 2,0,0,0,0,0,0,0,0,0. We calculate NDCG within 10 related species for each species in each data set and get the average score to evaluate the validity of our experiments.

6.2 Experimental Results

Parameter Study: Two parameters, c and γ affect the accuracy of similarity scores directly. These two parameters are application dependent. We want to study the available parameters for the food web data.

First, we discuss the parameter γ for *Additive-SimRank*. This parameter is used to decide the importance of two relationships: is-preyed and prey for accuracy. In this experiment, we fix the damping factor c to 0.8 and vary γ from 0 to 1. Figure 3 shows that when γ is equal to 0.75, *Additive-SimRank* will receive the highest accuracy. Interestingly, the is-preyed relationship is much more important to decide the species classification.

Second, we determine the damping factor c for these three link-based similarity algorithms. In this experiment, we fix $\gamma = 0.75$ and vary c from 0.05 to 0.95. In

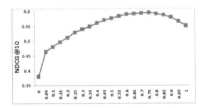

Fig. 3. Parameter γ for Additive-SimRank

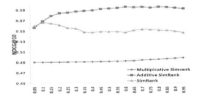

Fig. 4. Parameter c

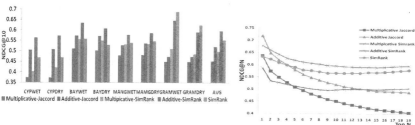

Fig. 5. Segmentation of CYPWET data set [1]

Fig. 6. NDCG@1 to NDCG@19

Table 6. Case study for species "Roots"

Multi.-Jaccard	Additive-Jaccard	Multi.-SimRank	Additive-SimRank	SimRank
Null	Apple Snail	Null	Cypress Wood	Cypress Wood
Null	Crayfish	Null	HW Wood	HW Wood
Null	Prawn	Null	Vine Leaves	Vine Leaves
Null	Aquatic Invertebrates	Null	Cypress Leaves	Cypress Leaves
Null	Vertebrate Det.	Null	Vertebrate Det.	Epiphytes
Null	Ter. Invertebrates	Null	Epiphytes	Vertebrate Det.
Null	Refractory Det.	Null	Float. vegetation	Float. vegetation
Null	Liable Det.	Null	Macrophytes	Macrophytes
Null	Null	Null	Phytoplankton	Living POC
Null	Null	Null	Living POC	Living sediment

fact, the effect of damping factor c is not very obvious. Figure 4 shows that when $c = 0.8$, 0.1 and 0.95, *Additive-SimRank*, *SimRank* and *Multiplicative-SimRank* will receive the highest scores. Thus, for the rest of the experiments, γ is set to 0.75 for *Additive-SimRank* and c is set to 0.8, 0.1 and 0.95 for *Additive-SimRank*, *SimRank* and *Multiplicative-SimRank*, respectively.

Accuracy Analysis: In these experiments, we compare the accuracy among *Multiplicative-Jaccard* [15], *Additive-Jaccard* [15], *Multiplicative -SimRank*, *Additive-SimRank* and *SimRank*. Using the rule of additive and multiplicative methods, it is easy to design *Multiplicative-Jaccard* and *Additive-Jaccard* algorithm. Figure 5 shows the accuracy of these eight methods for food web data sets. We can see *Multiplicative-Jaccard* and *Multiplicative-SimRank* have the lowest accuracy. Because *SimRank* and *Additive-SimRank* consider the potential linkage information, these two algorithms are much better than *Additive-Jaccard* algorithm. Because *Additive-SimRank* considers both is-preyed and prey relationship, it reaches the best accuracy. Figure 6 plots the results of NDCG@1 to NDCG@19 for the each algorithm.

Considering the case study, we analyze the top ten similar species for the species "Roots" in CYPWET food web. We study the is-preyed relationship of species "Roots" and because "Roots" is the primary producer, it does not have prey relationship. The result is shown in table 6. Because multiplicative method is the product of two relationships' similarity score, *Multiplicative-Jaccard* and *Multiplicative-SimRank* can't produce any similar species for "Roots". On the other hand, *Additive-Jaccard* only considers the direct relationship, thus it only searches about eight species for "Roots" but no species are primary producers. The result of *SimRank*, containing seven primary producers, is also very good, but *Additive-SimRank* searches eight primary producers, which is slightly higher than *SimRank*.

7   Conclusions

In this paper, considering both prey (out-link) and is-preyed relationship (in-link) on the food web, we propose *Additive-* and *Multiplicative-SimRank* to calculate the similarity scores. Then, we also discuss the loop problem on the network and propose a method to address this problem. The experimental results conducted on eight food web data sets show that *Additive-SimRank* outperforms the other approaches with γ equal to 0.75 (receives the highest score in the food web). In addition, our methods are also applicable for other information networks that have similar characteristics.

References

1. South florida ecosystems, `http://www.cbl.umces.edu/atlss/ATLSS.html`
2. Cai, Y., Chakarvarthy, S.: Extension to Pairwise Similiarity calculation in Information Networks. Technical Report TR CSE-2010-4, UT arlington. University of Texas, Arlington (May 2010)
3. Cai, Y., Cong, G., Jia, X., Liu, H., He, J., Lu, J., Du, X.: Efficient algorithm for computing link-based similarity in real world networks. In: Proceedings of the 2009 Ninth IEEE International Conference on Data Mining, pp. 734–739 (2009)
4. Fogaras, D., Rcz, B.: Scaling link-based similarity search. In: Proceedings of the 14th International Conference on World Wide Web, pp. 641–650 (2005)
5. Jarvelin, K., Keklinen, J.: Cumulated gain-based evaluation of ir techniques. ACM Transactions on Information Systems 20(4), 422–446 (2002)
6. Jeh, G., Widom, J.: Simrank: a measure of structural-context similarity. In: Proceedings of the Eighth ACM SIGKDD International Conference on Knowledge Discovery and Data Mining, pp. 538–543 (2002)
7. Kessler, M.M.: Bibliographic coupling between scientific papers. American Documentation 14(1), 10–25 (1969)
8. Lovsz, L.: Random walks on graphs: A survey. Bolyai Society Mathematical Studies 2, 1–46 (1991)
9. Langville, A.N., Meyer, C.D.: Deeper inside pagerank. Internet Mathematics 1(3), 335–380 (2004)
10. Lizorkin, D., Velikhov, P., Grinev, M., Turdakov, D.: Accuracy estimate and optimization techniques for simrank computation. The VLDB Journal The International Journal on Very Large Data Bases 19(1), 45–66 (2010)
11. Martinez, N.D.: Artifacts or attributes? effects of resolution on the little rock lake food web. Ecological Monographs 61(4), 367–392 (1991)

12. Martinez, N.D.: Effect of scale on food web structure. Science 260(5105), 242–243 (1993)
13. Small, H.: Co-citation in the scientific literature: A new measure of the relationship between two documents. Journal of the American Society for Information Science 2, 28–31 (1974)
14. Yin, X., Han, J., Yu, P.S.: Linkclus: efficient clustering via heterogeneous semantic links. In: Proceedings of the 32nd International Conference on Very Large Data Bases, pp. 427–438 (2006)
15. Yodzis, P., Winemiller, K.O.: In search of operational trophospecies in a tropical aquatic food web. Oikos 87, 327–340 (1999)

Feature Selection with Mutual Information for Uncertain Data

Gauthier Doquire* and Michel Verleysen

Université catholique de Louvain, Machine Learning Group - ICTEAM
Place du Levant, 3, 1348 Louvain-la-Neuve, Belgium
{gauthier.doquire,michel.verleysen}@uclouvain.be
http://www.ucl.ac.be/mlg

Abstract. In many real-world situations, the data cannot be assumed to be precise. Indeed uncertain data are often encountered, due for example to the imprecision of measurement devices or to continuously moving objects for which the exact position is impossible to obtain. One way to model this uncertainty is to represent each data value as a probability distribution function; recent works show that adequately taking the uncertainty into account generally leads to improved classification performances. Working with such a representation, this paper proposes to achieve feature selection based on mutual information. Experiments on 8 UCI data sets show that the proposed approach is effective to select relevant features.

Keywords: Uncertain data, feature selection, mutual information.

1 Introduction

Nowadays, many machine learning and data mining applications have to cope with data that are inherently uncertain. This uncertainty can be caused by many different factors. As an example, measurement errors from unprecise devices or sensors with a too low resolution typically produce uncertain data. Moreover, in some applications involving continuously moving devices, the exact location of the objects is not always available or is not transmitted precisely due to privacy reasons. Eventually, data quantization or averaging from multiple measurements also lead to uncertainty.

All these reasons explain the recent interest in the development of data mining tools for uncertain data such as classification [1,2,3], clustering [4,5,6,7] or outlier detection [8] to name a few. [9] gives a nice overview on recent developments about uncertain data

A convenient way to model the uncertainty of the data is to represent any value in the data set as an uncertainty region and to define a probability density function (pdf) over it. Using this approach, [1,2] showed that adequately taking the uncertainty into account leads to better classification performances for the

---

* Gauthier Doquire is funded by a Belgian FRIA grant.

A. Cuzzocrea and U. Dayal (Eds.): DaWaK 2011, LNCS 6862, pp. 330–341, 2011.

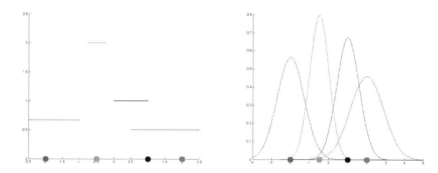

Fig. 1. Examples of modelling of the uncertainty on data with uniform (left) and Gaussian (right) pdf. The curves describe the pdf of the actual values given the observed values (shown by big dots).

decision tree and the Naive Bayes classifiers compared to the case where the values are used directly. In particular, choosing a Gaussian pdf centered in the value and with a well-chosen variance led to very satisfactory results. That is the reason why the same strategy is adopted throughout this paper. However, the proposed methodology can easily be extended to the uniform distribution or to uncertain data described by samples drawn from an underlying unknown distribution. Figure 1 illustrates the modelling of the uncertainty on data with uniform and Gaussian pdf. In this work, the problem of feature selection with uncertain data is considered; it is, to the best of our knowledge, the first time this problem is adressed. Feature selection is a very important preprocessing step for many pattern recognition problems, including classification. Its goal is to determine which (small) subset of features is the most relevant for a given task. Its benefits for classification can be numerous. First, it helps understanding the problem and interpreting the model by determining which factors really influence the output to be predicted. This is of crucial importance for many industrial and medical applications. As an example, in the context of microarray data, feature selection can help discovering a small set of genes linked to a particular disease or pathology. Secondly it generally leads to improved classification performances by removing irrelevant and/or redundant features and by preventing the classification models to suffer from the curse of dimensionality. By decreasing the number of features considered, feature selection also makes the classifiers faster. Eventually, it has also practical advantages in terms of data acquisition and warehousing. Indeed, useless features do not need to be gathered and stored anymore. See [10] for a detailed introduction on feature selection.

The proposed approach is based on the well-known mutual information (MI) criterion [11], which has already been used successfully in many feature selection algorithms. A methodology to estimate MI with uncertain data is proposed and used to rank features according to their dependance to the class labels vector.

The rest of the paper is organized as follows. Section 2 recalls some concepts about MI and its estimation for classical data. Section 3 presents the proposed MI estimator for uncertain data. Section 4 is dedicated to the experimental results and Section 5 concludes the work and gives some future research perspectives.

2   Mutual Information

This section first introduces some basic notions on MI and then shows how it can be estimated since it generally cannot be computed exactly.

2.1   Basic Notions

MI, first introduced by Shannon in 1948 [11], is a quantity describing the amount of information two random variables carry about each other. It is symmetric, i.e. $I(X;Y) = I(Y;X)$ and able to detect non-linear relationships between variables. This last property has made MI a very popular criterion for feature selection [12,13,14,15] since other widely used criteria such as the correlation coefficient can only handle linear dependencies.

Formally, the MI of a pair of random variables X and Y can be defined by means of the pdf of X, Y and the joint variable (X, Y), respectively denoted as f_X, f_Y and $f_{X,Y}$:

$$I(X;Y) = \int \int f_{X,Y}(x, y) \log \frac{f_{X,Y}(x, y)}{f_X(x) f_Y(y)} \, dx \, dy. \tag{1}$$

This definition can also be seen as the Kullback-Leibler divergence between the product of distributions $f_X \times f_Y$ and the joint distribution $f_{X,Y}$. If the variables are independent, then $f_{X,Y} = f_X \times f_Y$ and $I(X;Y) = 0$.

MI can also be expressed in terms of entropy, another information theoretic quantity. The entropy of a random variable is a measure of the uncertainty one has about the values taken by this variable. It is also defined in terms of pdf:

$$h(X) = - \int f_X(x) \log f_X(x) dx. \tag{2}$$

The MI is equal to:

$$I(X;Y) = h(Y) - h(Y|X) \tag{3}$$

where $h(Y|X)$ is the conditional entropy of Y given X, corresponding to the uncertainty about Y when X is known. Following (3), MI can be seen as the reduction of uncertainty about Y brought by the knowledge of X and is thus a natural criterion for feature selection assuming that Y is an output we want to predict from X, a set of possibly multivariate data points. In (3), if X and Y are independent, $h(Y|X) = h(Y)$ and again $I(X;Y) = 0$.

2.2 Estimation

As detailed previously, the MI is entirely determined by the marginal pdf f_X and f_Y and the joint pdf $f_{X,Y}$. However, in practice, these pdf are not known, meaning that the MI has to be estimated from the data set.

Traditionally, the entropy is first estimated by histograms or kernel-based estimators before the MI is computed according for instance to (1). This approach is followed in this paper, where a Parzen-window [16] density estimator is used.

Consider $x_1 \dots x_N$, N i.i.d. samples drawn from the distribution f. The estimated pdf is given by:

$$\hat{f}(x) = \frac{1}{Nb} \sum_{i=1}^{N} k\left(\frac{x - x_i}{b}\right) \tag{4}$$

where k is a kernel and b is called the bandwidth. The most popular choice for k is the Gaussian kernel with zero mean and unit variance:

$$k(x) = \frac{1}{\sqrt{2\pi}} e^{-0.5x^2}. \tag{5}$$

The value of the bandwidth b, which acts as a smoothing parameter, is of crucial importance for the quality of the estimation. In this work, it is chosen according to the popular Silverman rule [17] for one-dimensional data points:

$$b_j = 1.06\sigma_j N \tag{6}$$

where σ_j denotes the standard deviation along the jth dimension of the data set. In the next section, it will be shown how this estimator can be adapted to handle the uncertain data case.

It is worth noting that such density estimators should only be used with low-dimensional data. Indeed, when the dimensionality increases, histograms and kernel based estimators suffer from the curse of dimensionality and from the empty space phenomenon. This phenomenon denotes the fact that the number of points needed to sample a space at a given precision grows exponentially with the dimension of the space [18]. Thus, when working in a high-dimensional space, most of the boxes of an histogram are likely to be empty and the estimated density to be innacurate. Kernel-based estimators are generally smoother but are also dramatically affected by these problems.

One possible way to alleviate the curse of dimensionality is to use nearest-neighbors based MI estimators which do not directly estimate the pdf and are thus expected to be more robust in high-dimensional spaces [19,20].

3   MI Estimation with Uncertain Data

This section shows how the MI can be estimated from uncertain data by using the previously described kernel-based density estimator.

This paper considers classification problems; Given a data set X containing N samples described by d attributes, the goal is to predict the class (a discrete value) of these samples based on previously observed input/output pairs. This means that the MI $I(X;Y)$ has to be estimated between continuous (X) and discrete (Y) random variables, the latter corresponding to the classes we want to predict.

More precisely, we are interested in evaluating $I(X_j;Y)$ for $j = 1 \ldots d$, where X_j denotes the jth attribute or feature of X. The pdf of this j^{th} attribute is denoted by f_{X_j}.

Assume that Y takes k different values $y_1 \ldots y_k$, each y_i being represented by n_i samples $(\sum_i n_i = N)$; Denote by $\hat{p}(y_i)$ the probability that $Y = y_i$, estimated by $\frac{n_i}{N}$. All that is needed to estimate the MI by (3) is:

$$\hat{h}(Y) = -\sum_{i=1}^{k} \hat{p}(y_i) \log \hat{p}(y_i) \tag{7}$$

and

$$\hat{h}(Y|X_j) = -\int_{X_j} \hat{f}_{X_j}(x) \sum_{i=1}^{k} \hat{f}_{Y_i|X_j}(y_i|x) \log \hat{f}_{Y_i|X_j}(y_i|x)dx. \tag{8}$$

Equation (7) is the discrete version of (2) and $\hat{f}_{Y_i|X_j}$ is the estimated density of the ith class conditional to the jth feature. As (7) will be equal for all features, it can be omitted when comparing the individual MI of the features.

According to the Bayes theorem, it is possible the rewrite $\hat{f}_{Y_i|X_j}(y_i|x)$ as:

$$\hat{f}_{Y_i|X_j}(y_i|x) = \frac{\hat{f}_{X_j|Y_i}(x|y_i)\hat{p}(y_i)}{\hat{f}_{X_j}(x)}. \tag{9}$$

We have then:

$$\hat{h}(Y|X_j) = -\int_{X_j} \hat{f}_{X_j}(x) \sum_{i=1}^{k} \frac{\hat{f}_{X_j|Y_i}(x|y_i)\hat{p}(y_i)}{\hat{f}_{X_j}(x)} \log \frac{\hat{f}_{X_j|Y_i}(x|y_i)\hat{p}(y_i)}{\hat{f}_{X_j}(x)}dx. \tag{10}$$

This last equation implies that the MI can be entirely determined by the pdf of the variable X_j, possibly limited to the points with a particular class label y_i. In the following, we show how this pdf can be estimated.

Recall that $X_j = [x_{j1} \ldots x_{jN}]$ is described by Gaussian pdf to model the uncertainty in the data, i.e. $x_{j1} \sim N(\mu_{j1}, \sigma_{j1}) \ldots x_{jN} \sim N(\mu_{jN}, \sigma_{jN})$. μ_{ji} is the observed value for the jth dimension of the ith sample and σ_{ji} is the variance that is determined by the user, following the confidence he has on the precision of the data.

A quite natural approach is to consider the expected value of the kernel k [1]. More precisely, (4) is replaced with

$$\hat{f}(x) = \frac{1}{Nb} \sum_{i=1}^{N} E\left[k\left(\frac{x-x_i}{b}\right)\right].$$ (11)

The following developments then hold:

$$
\hat{f}_{X_j}(x) = \frac{1}{Nb} \sum_{i=1}^{N} \int_{x_{ji}} k\left(\frac{x_{ji}-x}{b}\right) \frac{1}{\sqrt{2\pi}\sigma_{ji}} e^{-0.5\left(\frac{x_{ji}-\mu_{ji}}{\sigma_{ji}}\right)^2} dx_{ji}
$$

$$
= \frac{1}{Nb} \sum_{i=1}^{N} \int_{x_{ji}} \frac{1}{\sqrt{2\pi}} e^{-0.5\left(\frac{x_{ji}-x}{b}\right)^2} \frac{1}{\sqrt{2\pi}\sigma_{ji}} e^{-0.5\left(\frac{x_{ji}-\mu_{ji}}{\sigma_{ji}}\right)^2} dx_{ji} \quad (12)
$$

$$
= \frac{1}{N} \sum_{i=1}^{N} \int_{x_{ji}} \frac{1}{\sqrt{2\pi}b} e^{-0.5\left(\frac{x_{ji}-x}{b}\right)^2} \frac{1}{\sqrt{2\pi}\sigma_{ji}} e^{-0.5\left(\frac{\mu_{ji}-x_{ji}}{\sigma_{ji}}\right)^2} dx_{ji}.
$$

Moreover, it is well-known that the convolution of two Gaussian distributions $f \sim N(\mu_f, \sigma_f)$ and $g \sim N(\mu_g, \sigma_g)$ is another Gaussian distribution $c \sim N(\mu_f + \mu_g, \sqrt{\sigma_f^2 + \sigma_g^2})$. Stated otherwise:

$$
f * g = \int_{\tau} \frac{1}{\sqrt{2\pi}\sigma_f} e^{-0.5\left(\frac{\tau-\mu_f}{\sigma_f}\right)^2} \frac{1}{\sqrt{2\pi}\sigma_g} e^{-0.5\left(\frac{t-\tau-\mu_g}{\sigma_g}\right)^2} d\tau
$$

$$
= \frac{1}{\sqrt{2\pi(\sigma_f^2 + \sigma_g^2)}} e^{-0.5\frac{\left(t-(\mu_f+\mu_g)\right)^2}{\sigma_f^2+\sigma_g^2}}. \quad (13)
$$

By setting $\tau = x_{ji}$, $\sigma_f = b$, $\sigma_g = \sigma_{ji}$, $t = \mu_{ji}$, $\mu_f = x$ and $\mu_g = 0$, the connection between (13) and the last line of (12) is obvious. Combining these two equations, it comes:

$$
\hat{f}_{X_j}(x) = \frac{1}{N} \sum_{i=1}^{N} \frac{1}{\sqrt{2\pi(\sigma_{ji}^2 + b^2)}} e^{-0.5\frac{(x-\mu_{ji})^2}{\sigma_{ji}^2+b^2}}. \quad (14)
$$

With a way to estimate the pdf $\hat{f}_{X_j}(x)$, using (3), (8) and (9), it is now possible to estimate the MI between each feature X_j and the output vector Y. As already stated, evaluating the conditional pdf $f_{X_j|Y_i}$ is done exactly the same way as for f_{X_j}, except that only the samples having the output y_i are included in the computation of (14). The technical details for the numerical integration in (8) are given in the next section.

It is obvious that the developments presented in this section assuming a Gaussian pdf can be adapted to handle other models of uncertainty. For instance, a uniform pdf could be considered instead. This would mean that we believe every observed value has been drawn from a domain of possible values, all having the same probability. In contrast, the Gaussian pdf implies that the observed value is actually the most probable even if some imprecisions are possible. If one wishes to model the uncertainty on x_{ji} by a uniform pdf on the domain $[a; b]$ $(a < b)$, then in (12), $f_{x_{ji}}(x_{ji})$ is equal to the constant $\frac{1}{b-a}$. The estimation of the density then resumes to the integration of a Gaussian function evaluated between a and b. See again Figure 1 for an illustration of the differences between both approaches.

Another way of specifying the uncertainty is to represent each point by numerous samples drawn from its distribution. The expectation in (11) then becomes a sum where each sample contributes to the estimation with an importance weighted by its probability. However, in [1], this approach is shown to be much more time-consuming than the Gaussian pdf based approach, without leading to better classification performances. It is thus not investigated in the present work even if it can be helpful when ones wants to consider a distribution for which (12) has no closed-form solution.

4   Methodology and Experiments

To assess the effectiveness of the proposed feature selection procedure, experiments are carried out on eight data sets from the UCI machine learning repository [21]. They consist of values obtained through measurements, and have been shown to benefit well from taking their uncertainty into account [1,2].

The first part of this section describes exactly how the uncertainty is handled in this paper; technical details about the integration in (8) are also given. Experimental results obtained on the data sets are then presented and commented.

4.1   Methodology

The MI is first evaluated between each feature of the training set and the output vector: the features are then ranked according to this score. The number of selected features should either be set a priori or should be determined by cross-validation procedures on an independent validation set.

The uncertainty on the data set is modelled by a Gaussian pdf with the mean equal to the observed value and the standard deviation defined following [1,2]. If min_j and max_j are respectively the minimum and maximum values taken by the feature X_j, then the standard deviation is $\sigma_j = 0.25\,(max_j - min_j)\,w\,\%$. It is the same for all x_{ji} and w is a parameter representing the level of uncertainty we have about the values of X_j. The rationale behind this choice is thus that the uncertainty about a variable is proportional to the size of the range of values taken by this variable. In other words, the more the observed values for a given variable are close, the more the uncertainty about these values will be considered as small. The values of w chosen in this paper are those already adopted in [1] and/or [2] (except for the Parkinson data set which has not been used in these references). Indeed, even if the two classifiers introduced in these works are very different, both achieve the best performances on the same data sets with very similar values of w.

Table 1. Description of the datasests used in the experiments

Name	Samples	Features	Classes	w
glass	214	9	4	3
iris	150	4	3	20
wine	178	13	3	1
segment	2310	18	7	4
waveform	5000	21	3	3
satellite	6435	36	2	6
pageBlock	5473	10	5	1
parkinson	195	22	2	5

Moreover, the accuracy of these classifiers generally reaches a peak at the optimal value of w, meaning that if this value is slightly increased or decreased, the performances of the classifiers degrade [1,2]. Those observations conjecture the fact that the considered data sets do contain errors and have an intrinsic optimal value of w (at least for the Gaussian pdf). The data sets are described in Table 1 which also gives the corresponding value of w.

The integral in (8) is evaluated numerically using the simple trapeze rule. It consists in interpolating the function piecewise linearly by using its values in a certain number of points. To this end, 1000 equally spaced points are sampled between a_{min} and a_{max}. $a_{min} < min_j$ is the value for which a Gaussian pdf with unit variance and mean min_j equals 10^{-3}. $a_{max} > max_j$ is the value for which a Gaussian pdf with unit variance and mean max_j equals 10^{-3}. It is worth noting that the bandwidth in (14) has to be adapted to each individual feature and to the fact that the density can be conditioned to a class label.

4.2 Experimental Results

Figure 2 shows the classification error rate (the percentage of misclassified samples) as a function of the number of selected features for the Naive Bayes classifier adapted to uncertain data [1] and the first six data sets. For comparison, the error rate is also shown when no uncertainty is taken into account (neither in the feature selection process nor in the classification). Eventually, to show the interest of considering the uncertainty for feature selection, the error rate when uncertainty is only considered in the classification step is also presented.

The reported results are obtained through a 10-fold cross validation procedure. This means that the dataset is first randomly divided into ten disjoint equally sized sets of samples. Then each set is successively used to test the performances of a classifier built on the nine other sets. The ten error rates obtained this way are eventually averaged. In this paper, no additional validation set is needed since there is no parameter to tune.

The interest of the proposed feature selection method is obvious for the considered data sets. Indeed, the first observation is that in each case, it is possible to reduce the classification error by considering only a subset of the original features. In particular for the glass, iris and segment data sets, at least half the

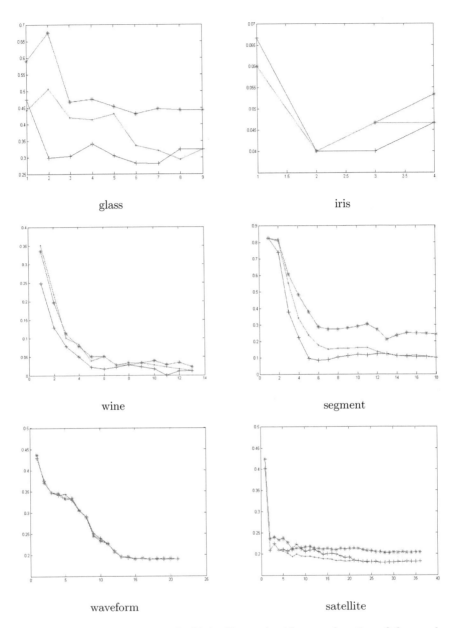

glass

iris

wine

segment

waveform

satellite

Fig. 2. Classification error rate of a Naive Bayes classifier as a function of the number of selected features for six data sets. (+) Uncertainty in the feature selection and the classification; (.) Uncertainty only in the classification; (∗) No uncertainty.

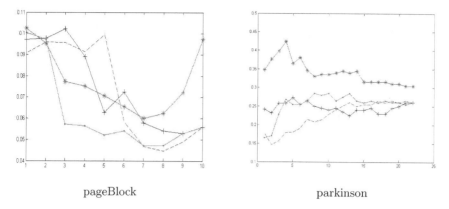

pageBlock   parkinson

Fig. 3. Classification error rate of a Naive Bayes classifier as a function of the number of selected features for two data sets. (+) Uncertainty in the feature selection and the classification; (.) Uncertainty only in the classification; (*) No uncertainty; (−) Same as (+) with normalized data.

features can be discarded without decreasing the original accuracy. In the satellite data set, more than a third of the features can be removed without harming the classifier performances.

Then, it clearly appears that considering the uncertainty allows us to increase the performances of both the feature selection and the classification. For the 6 data sets, lower error rates are obtained with the proposed approach than when no uncertainty at all is considered (except for the satellite data set where equal error rates are achieved). Moreover, taking the uncertainty into account only in the classification step (and not for feature selection) nevers allows to reach better performances than with the suggested methodology.

When applying the same methodology to the parkinson and pageBlock data sets, the results obtained at the first were not so encouraging. The reason is that some features in those data sets have very different ranges of values. The entropy (8) of features with a larger range of values is likely to be higher than for features with a smaller range of values which could bias the MI estimation procedure. As an example, the entropy of a Gaussian variable with variance σ^2 is given by $0.5 \log(2\pi e\sigma^2)$ and thus increases with the dispersion of the data. To circumvent this issue, each feature X_j was normalized by removing its mean and dividing it by its standard deviation σ_{X_j} before the feature selection step. To account for this normalization the parameter w controling the uncertainty for each feature was adapted to $w \times \sigma_{X_j}$.

Figure 3 confirms that the suggested normalization helps improving the feature selection with uncertainty for the two data sets. It is also the case for feature selection without taking the uncertainty into account but the results are not displayed for clarity reasons, since they are inferior to those obtained considering the uncertainty. With the normalization, the best results are again achieved by the proposed methodology. In particular, for the Parkinson data set, the error rate is reduced by more than 10% with only the first two features. When applied to the six first data sets, the normalization leads to very similar results than those presented in Figure 2.

5   Conclusions

This paper is concerned with the important problem of feature selection for classification problems, in the specific context of uncertain data. To this end, it is proposed to rank the features according to their MI with the class labels vector, a widely used criterion for feature selection. The current work is motivated by recent papers showing that properly taking the uncertainty of the data into account generally increases the precision of classifiers.

Following these works, the uncertainty on the data is handled by representing the values in the data set as an uncertainty region and to define a pdf over theses regions. In this work, Gaussian pdf are considered while it is shown how the developments could be easily extended to the uniform distribution or to an arbitrary distribution defined by a collection of samples drawn from it.

A method to evaluate the MI between each uncertain feature and the output is then introduced. It is based on the traditionnal kernel density estimation which is adapted to handle points described as pdf. More precisely, the expected value of the kernel estimator is determined by exploiting the fact that a convolution between Gaussian pdf is still a Gaussian pdf with known mean and variance. A convenient way to numerically evaluate the entropy and thus the corresponding MI is also proposed.

Experimental results on eight UCI databases containing uncertainty show that the proposed approach is effectively able to select relevant features. Indeed, for all data sets, the classification performances can be improved by removing irrelevant features. Moreover, the advantage of considering the inhenrent uncertainty of the data for both feature selection and classification is clearly established. It is also shown how the normalization can help improving the feature selection when some features have large differences in their range value, harming the estimation of the entropy and consequently the estimation of MI.

Future work could be focused on the development of MI estimation algorithms for two uncertain *continuous* vectors. This would be helpful for feature selection in regression problems (problems with a continuous output to predict). It would also allow one to consider the redundancy between features. Indeed, only the relevance (measured by the MI) is considered as a criterion for feature selection in the present work. Taking the redundancy into account could lead to improved performances, especially if one works with highly redundant data such as in near infra-red spectra analysis [14].

References

1. Ren, M., Lee, S.D., Chen, X., Kao, B., Cheng, R., Cheung, D.: Naive Bayes Classification of Uncertain Data. In: 9th IEEE International Conference on Data Mining, ICDM 2009, pp. 944–949 (2009)

2. Tsang, S., Kao, B., Yip, K.Y., Ho, W.-S., Ho, W.-S., Lee, S.: Decision Trees for Uncertain Data. IEEE T. Knwol. Dat. En. 23, 64–78 (2011)
3. Bi, J., Zhang, T.: Support Vector Classification with Input Data Uncertainty. In: Advances in Neural Information Processing Systems, NIPS (2004)
4. Ngai, W.K., Kao, B., Chui, C.K., Cheng, R., Chau, M., Yip, K.Y.: Efficient Clustering of Uncertain Data. In: 6th IEEE International Conference on Data Mining, ICDM 2006, pp. 436–445 (2006)
5. Kriegel, H.-P., Pfeifle, M.: Hierarchical Density-Based Clustering of Uncertain Data. In: 5th IEEE International Conference on Data Mining (ICDM 2005), pp. 689–692 (2005)
6. Kao, B., Lee, D., Cheung, D.W., Ho, W.-S., Chan, K.F.: Clustering Uncertain Data using Voronoi Diagrams. In: 8th IEEE International Conference on Data Mining, ICDM 2008, pp. 333–342 (2008)
7. Cormode, G., McGregor, A.: Approximation Algorithms for Clustering Uncertain Data. In: 27th ACM SIGMOD-SIGACT-SIGART Symposium on Principles of Database Systems (PODS 2008), pp. 191–200 (2008)
8. Aggarwal, C.C., Yu, P.S.: Outlier Detection with Uncertain Data. In: SIAM International Conference on Data Mining (SDM), pp. 483–493 (2008)
9. Aggarwal, C.C., Yu, P.S.: A survey of Uncertain Data Algorithms and Applications. IEEE T. Knwol. Dat. En. 21, 609–623 (2009)
10. Guyon, I., Elisseeff, A.: An Introduction to Variable and Feature Selection. J. Mach. Lear. Res. 3, 1157–1182 (2003)
11. Shannon, C.E.: A mathematical Theory of Communication. Bell Syst. Tech. J. 27, 379–423, 623–656 (1948)
12. Battiti, R.: Using Mutual Information for Selecting Features in Supervised Neural Net Learning. IEEE T. Neural. Networ. 5, 537–550 (1994)
13. Peng, H., Long, F., Ding, C.: Feature Selection Based on Mutual Information: Criteria of Max-Dependency, Max-Relevance, and Min-Redundancy. IEEE T. Pattern. Anal. 27 (2005)
14. Rossi, F., Lendasse, A., François, D., Wertz, V., Verleysen, M.: Mutual Information for the Selection of Relevant Variables in Spectrometric Nonlinear Modelling. Chemometr. Intell. Lab. 80, 215–226 (2006)
15. François, D., Rossi, F., Wertz, V., Verleysen, M.: Resampling Methods for Parameter free and Robust Feature Selection with Mutual Information. Neurocomputing 70, 1276–1288 (2007)
16. Parzen, E.: On Estimation of a Probability Density Function and Mode. Ann. Math. Statist. 33, 1065–1076 (1962)
17. Silverman, B.W.: Density Estimation. Chapman & Hall, London (1986)
18. Verleysen, M.: Learning High-Dimensional Data. In: Limitations and Future Trends in Neural Computation, pp. 141–162 (2003)
19. Kraskov, A., Stögbauer, H., Grassberger, P.: Estimating Mutual Information. Phys. Rev. E 69, 66138 (2004)
20. Gomez-Verdejo, V., Verleysen, M., Fleury, J.: Information-Theoretic Feature Selection for Functional Data Classification. Neurocomputing 72, 3580–3589 (2009)
21. Frank, A., Asuncion, A.: UCI Machine Learning Repository. University of California, School of Information and Computer Science, Irvine (2010), http://archive.ics.uci.edu/ml

Time Aware Index for Link Prediction in Social Networks

Lankeshwara Munasinghe and Ryutaro Ichise

Principles of Informatics Research Division,
National Institute of Informatics, Tokyo, Japan
{lankesh,ichise}@nii.ac.jp

Abstract. Link prediction in social networks such as collaboration networks and friendship networks have recently attracted a great deal of attention. There have been numerous attempts to address this problem through diverse approaches. In the present paper, we focus on the temporal behavior of the link strength, particularly the relationship between the time stamps of interactions or links and the temporal behavior of link strength and how link strength affects future link evolution. Most of the previous studies neglected the impact of time stamps of the interactions and of the links on link evolution. The gap between the current time and the time stamps of the interactions or links is also important to link evolution. In the present paper, we introduced a new time aware index, referred to as *time score*, that captures the important aspects of time stamps of interactions and the temporality of the link strengths. We apply time score to two social network data sets, namely, a coauthorship network data set and a Facebook friendship network data set. The results reveal a significant improvement in predicting future links.

Keywords: Link prediction, Time stamps, Temporal behavior, Social networks.

1   Introduction

Link prediction is introduced in [9] as inferring which new interactions are likely to occur in the near future in a given network. If we are given a snapshot of a network at time t_c, the goal is to predict links that are likely to occur at a future time t_f. The information of the structure of the given network and the features of nodes and edges can be used to predict future links.

Link prediction in social networks has become an important task in network science because of the potential benefit to users of social networking services as well as to various organizations and researchers. Online social networking services can provide their users with more accurate service and more precise recommendations or suggestions. Therefore, users of these services can efficiently find their friends, colleagues, or people whom they wish to meet [10]. Organizations such as security agencies and business organizations will be able to find more accurate information regarding unseen relationships among people or organizations and

A. Cuzzocrea and U. Dayal (Eds.): DaWaK 2011, LNCS 6862, pp. 342–353, 2011.

so may operate more effectively. Researchers can find other individuals in the same research field, experts, and research organizations [15,19,13,7]. However, highly structured massive real-world networks involving heterogeneous entities with complex associations have added new challenges to link prediction research. Supervised and unsupervised learning methods have been used in previous studies with different frameworks for link prediction but machine learning approaches remain an immense challenge [4]. Machine learning methods are difficult to apply because of the complexity and size of the networks as well as the temporal behaviors of the links in the networks.

This temporality can be caused by various factors depending on the nature of the network. The factors that cause the temporal behavior of the links and how these factors can be effectively used for link prediction in networks must be determined. To our knowledge, this scenario has not been discussed sufficiently in the context of link prediction. The links are strong for a certain period of time, but then become weaker and fade. Such link behavior increases the complexity of link prediction because stronger links have a greater influence over link evolution than weaker links. The main contribution of the present study is finding the impact of the relationship between the time stamps of the interactions and the link strength for future links. Therefore, we herein introduce a new index to incorporate the impact of the time stamps of the interactions and the gap between the current time and the time stamps. We use the newly proposed index in conjunction with supervised machine learning methods in order to predict links in network data sets.

The remainder of the present paper is organized as follows. In Section 2, we discuss related studies and discuss the importance of time awareness for link prediction. In Section 3, we introduce a method of link prediction and the newly proposed index. In Section 4, we present experimental results and discuss possible improvements to the proposed index. Section 5 presents conclusions and discusses future research.

2   Related Research

In this section, we review research related to link prediction as well as background information on link prediction. The increasing number of studies related to link prediction in the recent literature reveals the growing interest and importance of link prediction. Diverse approaches, including machine learning approaches and probabilistic approaches, have been proposed to address the problem of link prediction.

Link prediction is a type of link mining, which is a newly emerging research field under data mining, and presents new challenges to machine learning technologies [5]. Feature construction and collective classification using a learned model is a prominent feature of machine learning. A support vector machine (SVM) was used in combination with the structural features of networks introduced in [9] for link prediction in coauthorship networks [13,7]. Later, the introduction of features such as keyword match count for paper topics and abstracts [15,19], in combination with decision trees, provided more accurate link predictions in coauthorship networks. These previous studies have proved the consistency and effectiveness of decision trees and SVM [3] in link prediction task. However, sparse real-world networks have presented additional difficulties in machine learning approaches due to the huge imbalance between possible links and actual links can be observed in these networks. The authors of a previous study [10] interpret the problem of link prediction as a problem in class imbalance between possible links and actual links. They used SMOT [2], which is a widely accepted sampling strategy to overcome imbalance.

Probabilistic approaches basically estimate the likelihoods of the future possible links. Among recent studies, the local probabilistic model was used in [18] to estimate the cooccurrence probability of a node with other nodes within a local proximity of the node. However, possible links with nodes that are not in the defined proximity are still missing. The probabilistic graph created using the structural features introduced in [9] was used in [8] to estimate the probabilities of future links in a network. However, few of the above studies considered the temporal behaviors of the links in the networks. For example, when matching semantic similarities, matching abstract keywords [15], would be more effective if higher weights are assigned to keywords in more recent publications. The random walk [10] would be more effective if the random walker were to choose its path not only according to the path weight but also using the link strength, which varies over time. Recently, the time-aware maximum entropy [16] introduced in order to assign higher weights to more recent collaborations, as compared to older collaborations, in coauthorship networks. Although, the impact of the time stamps on the temporality of the links was discussed, the importance of the gap between the current time and the time stamps of interactions or links has not been discussed sufficiently. These observations inspired us to investigate the temporal behavior of the links. Therefore, we focused on finding a relationship between the time stamps of interactions or links and the temporal behaviors of the links and how this relationship affects future link evolution.

3   Supervised Learning Method for Predicting Links

As discussed above, link prediction deals with predicting future possible links in a given network. Most of the approaches discussed in Section 2 use structural features of networks and the features of the nodes and edges for link prediction. For example, in a coauthorship network, the nodes are authors, and the edges represent the publications by these authors. In online friendship networks such as Facebook, the nodes become users, and the links represent the relationships between them. In both cases, similarities between nodes and structural features of the networks can be used to predict future links. For example, the number of common neighbors of a node pair and Jaccard's coefficient [11] can be computed. Once these features are calculated for a particular node pair, we have a vector of values referred to as a *feature vector*[13], which may be correlated with the future possible link between that node pair.

In a supervised learning approach, we use the feature vectors of each node pair to learn a model that can then be used to predict the appearance of future

Table 1. Feature listing

Feature	Formula	With TS	Without TS
Adamic/Adar	$\sum_{v_k \epsilon \Gamma(v_i) \bigcap \Gamma(v_j)} \frac{1}{log|\Gamma(v_k)|}$	✓	✓
Jaccard's coefficient	$\frac{|\Gamma(v_i) \bigcap \Gamma(v_j)|}{|\Gamma(v_i) \bigcup \Gamma(v_j)|}$	✓	✓
Preferential attachment	$|\Gamma(v_i)|.|\Gamma(v_j)|$	✓	✓
Common neighbors	$|\Gamma(v_i) \bigcap \Gamma(v_j)|$	✓	✓
Time score	$\sum_c \frac{H_m \beta^k}{|t_1 - t_2|+1}$	✓	-

links. In other words, once we compute the feature vectors for each node pair, we obtain a set of feature vectors for node pairs that are already linked and another set of feature vectors for node pairs that are not linked. The goal is to find the feature vectors of unlinked node pairs that are likely to be linked in the future using feature vectors of already linked node pairs. To this end, we train a Weka [6] implementation of a supervised machine learning decision tree algorithm, J48 [14] with default parameters, using the *training set*, which is defined as the set of feature vectors that correspond to linked node pairs, to find feature vectors of unlinked node pairs that are likely to become linked in the future from the *test set*, which is defined as the set of feature vectors of unlinked node pairs.

3.1 Features Used for Link Prediction

We used two different combinations of features in the proposed machine learning approach for link prediction. One set was used as the baseline combination, and the other set includes the new index introduced herein. Table 1 lists the details of the features used in the experiments of the present study. In the formulas, v_i, v_j, and v_k denote nodes, and $\Gamma(v_i)$ and $\Gamma(v_j)$ denote the sets of neighbors of v_i and v_j, respectively. According to the present feature selection, we excluded self links and considered undirected networks. The descriptions of the existing features used in our experiments are shown below, and, in Section 3.2, we discuss the new feature *time score* introduced herein.

Adamic/Adar. [1] This measure indicates that if a node pair has a common neighbor that is not common to several nodes, then the similarity of that particular node pair is higher than that of node pairs having neighbors that are common to several other nodes. This measure assigns higher weights to common neighbors that are not common to several other nodes.

Jaccard's coefficient. [11] Normalized measure of common neighbors.

Common neighbors. Number of common neighbors of a pair of nodes.

Preferential attachment. [12] This measure indicates that new links are more likely to be formed with higher degree nodes, or nodes that are popular in the network.

3.2   New Index for Time Aware Link Prediction

The features discussed in Section 3.1 are based solely on common neighbors, but do not consider the temporal behavior of these common neighbors. The strengths of links with common neighbors vary over time. In the context of social networks, the effectiveness of the common neighbors depends not only on the cooccurrence frequency, or number of common neighbors, but also on how long the neighbors have been in contact. The time stamps of the interactions are useful in finding such information. This information provides a far better view of the importance of common neighbors than considering only the number of common neighbors. Therefore, we introduced a new method to incorporate the effectiveness of common neighbors and their temporality. To this end, we designed a new index based on the following concepts.

1. The strength of a link varies over time. If the nodes at the ends of a link have not interacted with each other for long time with respect to the current time, then the link becomes weaker. Therefore, we represent the weight of a link in terms of its strength over time using damping factor β and k, which is the difference between the current time and the time stamp of the most recent interaction of a common neighbor with its sharing nodes. The term β^k increases as k decreases.

2. If the two nodes have interacted with their common neighbors in closer proximity of time, then the common neighbors are more effective. In other words, if the difference between the time stamps of the most recent interactions of common neighbors having the node pair for which we want to predict linkage is small, then the link is more likely to occur in the future. Taking the most recent time stamps is similar to assuming a Markov property of the interactions. In this case, we assigned higher weights to common neighbors that have interacted recently with their sharing nodes. Hence, we use the term $|t_1 - t_2| + 1$, where t_1 and t_2 are the time stamps of the most recent interactions of the common neighbor with its sharing nodes. This term becomes larger when the difference between t_1 and t_2 becomes larger. Therefore, we use the reciprocal of this term to assign weights to common neighbors. The addition of one in the term is in order to avoid the time score from becoming infinite when the two time stamps are equal.

Combining the above considerations, we introduced a new index to combine time awareness for link prediction. This concept is illustrated in Figure 1. Vertices a and b have common neighbor c. Here, t_1 is the most recent time stamp of the interactions between a and b, and t_2 is the most recent time stamp of the interactions between b and c. Moreover, k is the difference between the current time t_c and the most recent time stamp from t_1 and t_2.

Time Score (definition). For a network $N = (v,e)$ with a set of nodes v and edges e, the time score *(TS)* for a pair of nodes a and b that has n common neighbors is defined as follows:

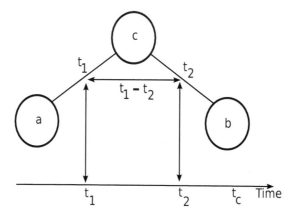

Fig. 1. Vertices a and b have common neighbor c. Here, t_1 is the most recent time stamp of the interactions between a and c, and t_2 is the most recent time stamp of the interactions between b and c. The current time is denoted as t_c.

$$TS = \sum_n \frac{H_m \beta^k}{|t_1 - t_2| + 1} \tag{1}$$

where H_m is the harmonic mean of the cooccurrence frequencies of a and b with a common neighbor that cooccurred at time t_1 with a and t_2 with b.

$$k = current\_time - max(t_1, t_2) \tag{2}$$

$$0 < \beta < 1; \beta \ is \ a \ damping \ factor. \tag{3}$$

In addition, the number of interactions or cooccurrences of a node pair also important in determining link strength. Therefore, we used the harmonic mean of the cooccurrence frequencies of each common neighbor with its sharing nodes. Typically, the harmonic mean is appropriate for situations in which an average of rates is desired. In the present case, we use the cooccurrence frequency, or the number of user interactions, as the rates. Compiling all, the new index *time score* can be used as a feature, which is basically assigned a weight for future possible links. For example, let us assume that two authors, a and b, have common neighbor c. If a and c have published two papers in 2005 and 2006, then b and c have published one paper in 2008. If the current year is assumed to be 2011, then the weight for future possible link ab can be calculated as follows. The harmonic mean $H_m(x_1, ..., x_n)$ of n numbers x_i (*where* $i = 1, ..., n$) is the number H_m defined as follows:

$$\frac{1}{H_m} = \frac{1}{n} \sum_{i=1}^{n} \frac{1}{x_i}. \tag{4}$$

Hence,

$$H_m = \frac{2}{\frac{1}{2} + \frac{1}{1}} = 1.3333. \tag{5}$$

In this case, $k = 2011-2008 = 3$, because the latest time stamp is 2008, and the current year is 2011. The number of common neighbors, n, is 1, and we used $\beta = 0.5$.

$$TS = \left(\frac{0.5^3}{|2008 - 2006| + 1}\right) * 1.3333 \approx 0.05555 \tag{6}$$

4   Experimental Evaluation

In order to test the effectiveness of the proposed method, we performed experiments using two real-world social network data sets, one from the Facebook friendship network and the other from a coauthorship network extracted from condensed matter physics publication data found in *e-print archives* [1]. These real-world networks are very sparse, and so the rate of positive examples is very low. On average, the percentages of positive examples in Facebook data and coauthorship data are 0.05% and 0.08%, respectively. We used the SMOT over-sampling algorithm [2] in these experiments. After oversampling, the percentages of positive examples in Facebook data and coauthorship data are 0.3% and 0.5% respectively. The other important consideration is the unit of time measurement. This unit can be years, days, or hours, depending on the data set. We set β according to the time measurement in order assign higher weights to interactions that occurred more recently. The performance metrics are precision, recall, and F-measure, which are defined as follows:

$$Precision = \frac{|TP|}{|TP| + |FP|}, \tag{7}$$

$$Recall = \frac{|TP|}{|TP| + |FN|}, \tag{8}$$

$$F\text{-}measure = \frac{2 * Precision * Recall}{Precision + Recall}, \tag{9}$$

where $|TP|$, $|FP|$, and $|FN|$ represent True Positives, False Positives, and False Negatives, respectively.

4.1   Experiment Using Facebook Data

We used the Facebook data from [17], which are collected from the regional Facebook network for New Orleans. This data set consists of links between the users and the time stamp of link establishment and the user interactions in terms of wall posts and the time stamps of the wall posts. The wall post data was collected for 60,290 users who are connected by 1,545,686 links. We extracted a snapshot of the data from October 2007 to January 2009.

Supervised machine learning algorithms require data in the form of training and testing data. From the Facebook network data, we constructed training

---

[1] http://arxiv.org/

Table 2. Statistics of the networks

Prediction month	Training data		Test data	
	Nodes	Edges	Nodes	Edges
2009 Jan	28370	106106	31832	123650
2008 Dec	25427	92990	28370	106106
2008 Nov	22732	80848	25427	92990
2008 Oct	20476	71792	22732	80848
2008 Sep	18339	63392	20476	71792
2008 Aug	17268	60718	18339	63392
2008 Jul	16381	58546	17268	60718
2008 Jun	15705	56014	16381	58546
2008 May	14762	50732	15705	56014
2008 Apr	13998	48238	14762	50732
2008 Mar	13732	47986	13998	48238
2008 Feb	13733	50248	13732	47986

data and testing data using four consecutive months. User interactions, i.e., wall postings between users during the first three months are given, and the target is to predict the links in following month. In other words, if we start from time t, the wall postings from t to $t+2$ are given, and the links that appear during $t+3$ is the target of prediction. For example, in order to predict links formed during January 2009, we train the decision tree algorithm using the data from September 2008 to December 2008 and test the data from October 2008 to January 2009. Features are computed using the network data from September 2008 to November 2008, and the links that emerged during December 2008 are considered to be the positive examples for training data. Then, the trained model was tested using the features calculated for the data from October 2008 to December 2008 in order to predict the links that emerged during January 2009. Table 2 shows the statistics of the networks that were created to predict the links during each month. In the Facebook data, the frequency of the wall postings between users is considered as the cooccurrence frequency of each node pair that is already connected. In this data set, the time stamps of the links are created using the Linux time stamp of the wall postings. We converted these time stamps to days. Therefore, the time stamp of a link represents the day of the most recent interaction between two users. Thus, in this experiment, we measured the time in days. We set β to be 0.85.

Results and Discussion: The left-hand side of Figure 2 compares the results obtained with and without the proposed index. In the comparison of Facebook performance shown in Figure 2, the performance metrics show a notable improvement using the new index, as compared to the base methods from June 2008 to January 2009. Based on the wall posts data, and, as mentioned in [17], rapid growth of the wall posts occurs from June 2008 to January 2009. This increment makes the network more active and most of the existing links become stronger. The stronger links have a greater influence on the future link evolution. Therefore, the use of *time score* yields better results than the base methods. This observation further emphasizes that the new index is more sensitive to the temporal behavior of user interactions. However, according to [17], from February

2008 to May 2008, there is no increase or decrease in the wall postings. Thus, the strengths of the links do not exhibit temporal variations in behavior in the network during this period. Therefore, the performance metrics exhibit slightly lower values for the new index than for the base method. In the Facebook friendship network, the friends of a user can see the wall postings of that user if the user chooses share with his/her friends. Thus, users who have that particular user as a common neighbor, while having no other relationship, can become friends through each other's postings. A sudden increase in wall postings indicates that more people interact with each other and become friends. Therefore, recent interactions and interactions happen in closely have a greater influence on link evolution. Furthermore, the results depend on the duration of data collection and the region of the network. In particular, the Facebook network exhibits different patterns depending on the time, the major events that occur during the period of data collection, and the region of the network. Therefore, data collected during different time periods and in different regions of the network must be used during testing. The use of the newly proposed index increased the precision by 6% on average. The improvements in recall and F-measure are indicated by the comparisons of Facebook recall and Facebook F-measure in Figure 2. On average, the recall and F-measure increased by 2% and 5%, respectively.

4.2   Experiment with Coauthorship Data

The undirected coauthorship network was extracted from the available publications in *cond-mat archive*[2]. This data set contains the data of 123,198 publications on condensed matter physics from 1997 to 2010. The data for four consecutive years were used to create the training data and testing data. For example, in order to predict the set of links that emerged in 2010, we used the data of the coauthor network from 2007 to 2009 to calculate the features of the test set. The data for 2009 (considered as the training set) and the features were calculated using the coauthor network from 2006 to 2008. The coauthorship networks created in this manner are very sparse: on average, 0.0015% of the possible links appear in each network. In this data set, the unit of time measurement is years. The time stamp for an interaction between a pair of authors represents the year of publication of the coauthored paper. Hence, the time stamp of a link indicates the year of most recent publication by a pair of authors. A damping factor of $\beta = 0.5$ was used in this experiment.

Results and Discussion: A comparison of the performance metrics of this experiment is shown in the right-hand side of Figure 2. The improvements in precision, recall, and F-measure show the impact of the newly proposed index in link prediction in the coauthorship network that evolves primarily over recent collaborations. In 2003, we observe an exception in the Condmat precision comparison graph, whereas in all other years the results obtained using the newly proposed index are better than the results for the base method. All three performance metrics indicate significant improvements according to a Student t-test

---

[2] http://arxiv.org/archive/cond-mat/

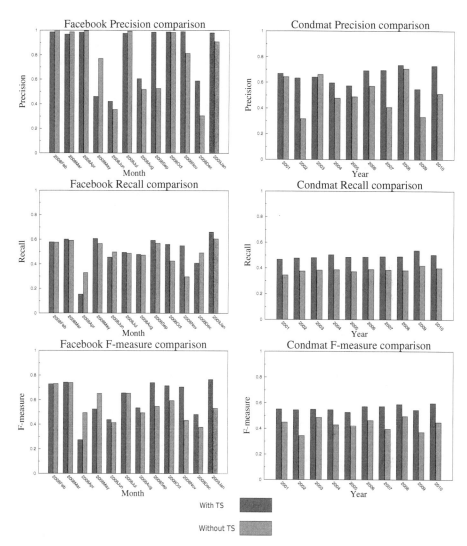

Fig. 2. Comparisons of performance metrics for the Facebook and coauthorship data

with $p = 5\%$. The average improvement in precision is 14%. The results for recall and F-measure indicate consistent improvement in every year; the average
improvements are 11% and 13%, respectively.

The scientific collaborations are time-sensitive. In other words, researchers
prefer to explore evolving topics through new collaborations. To this end, researchers tend to find associates or experts through their most recent collaborations. This increase the temporality of the links among the researchers. On
the other hand, the temporality in coauthorship networks has several causes. For
example, researchers tend to change research fields according to current research
trends and occasionally change institutes or universities. In such situations, the

geographical locations of the researchers and current research trends become important factors in predicting links in coauthorship networks. Therefore, it is necessary to investigate other factors that cause temporal variations in the behaviors of the links.

5   Conclusion and Future Research

In the present paper, we introduced a new time aware index for link prediction in social networks using a supervised machine learning approach. We found that the time stamps of interactions are crucial factors for link evolution. The primary focus of the present study was the impact of the relationship between the temporal behavior of link strength and the time stamps of interactions and links for link evolution, which had not previously been discussed sufficiently. In particular, we focused on the temporal behavior of common neighbors in terms of link strength. We examined the proposed method using two real-world data sets. The improvements in performance metrics indicated by the experimental results verify the effectiveness of the newly proposed index.

In the future, we will extend the proposed method to any node pair in a network. Moreover, we will focus on the development of a method by which to estimate β according to the network and the time measure. We used two different values of β in the experiments of the present study. Exploring other factors of temporal behaviors of networks is one of the primary goals of our future research. Some of these factors are network specific. Therefore, the use of temporal behaviors for link prediction is a challenging task. Furthermore, we intend to demonstrate that the proposed method is applicable to a wide range of algorithms that have been used for link prediction, such as flow-based algorithms and statistical modeling approaches.

References

1. Adamic, L.A., Adar, E.: Friends and neighbors on the web. Social Networks 25, 211–230 (2003)
2. Chawla, N.V., Bowyer, K.W., Hall, L.O., Kegelmeyer, W.P.: Smote: Synthetic minority over-sampling technique. Journal of Artificial Intelligence Research 16, 321–357 (2002)
3. Cortes, C., Vapnik, V.: Support-vector networks. Machine Learning 20, 273–297 (1995)
4. Getoor, L.: Link mining: a new data mining challenge. SIGKDD Explor. 5(1), 84–89 (2003)
5. Getoor, L., Diehl, C.P.: Link mining: a survey. SIGKDD Explor. 7(2), 3–12 (2005)
6. Hall, M., Frank, E., Holmes, G., Pfahringer, B., Reutemann, P., Witten, I.H.: The weka data mining software: an update. SIGKDD Explor. Newsl. 11(1), 10–18 (2009)
7. Hasan, M.A., Chaoji, V., Salem, S., Zaki, M.: Link prediction using supervised learning. In: Proceedings of SDM 2006 Workshop on Link Analysis, Counterterrorism and Security (2006)

8. Leroy, V., Cambazoglu, B.B., Bonchi, F.: Cold start link prediction. In: Proceedings of the 16th ACM SIGKDD International Conference on Knowledge Discovery and Data Mining, pp. 393–402 (2010)

9. Liben-Nowell, D., Kleinberg, J.: The link prediction problem for social networks. In: Proceedings of the 12th International Conference on Information and Knowledge Management, pp. 556–559 (2003)

10. Lichtenwalter, R.N., Lussier, J.T., Chawla, N.V.: New perspectives and methods in link prediction. In: Proceedings of the 16th ACM SIGKDD International Conference on Knowledge Discovery and Data Mining, pp. 243–252 (2010)

11. Manning, C.D., Raghavan, P., Schütze, H.: Introduction to Information Retrieval. Cambridge University Press, Cambridge (2008)

12. Newman, M.E.J.: Clustering and preferential attachment in growing networks. Phys. Rev. E 64(2), 025102 (2001)

13. Pavlov, M., Ichise, R.: Finding experts by link prediction in co-authorship networks. In: Proceedings of the Workshop on Finding Experts on the Web with Semantics (November 2007)

14. Quinlan, J.R.: C4.5: programs for machine learning (1993)

15. Sachan, M., Ichise, R.: Using abstract information and community alignment information for link prediction. In: Proceedings of 2nd International Conference on Machine Learning and Computing (ICMLC), pp. 61–65 (2010)

16. Tylenda, T., Angelova, R., Bedathur, S.: Towards time-aware link prediction in evolving social networks. In: Proceedings of the 3rd Workshop on Social Network Mining and Analysis, pp. 1–10 (2009)

17. Viswanath, B., Mislove, A., Cha, M., Gummadi, K.P.: On the Evolution of User Interaction in Facebook. In: Proceedings of the 2nd ACM SIGCOMM Workshop on Social Networks (August 2009)

18. Wang, C., Satuluri, V., Parthasarathy, S.: Local probabilistic models for link prediction. In: Proceedings of the 7th IEEE International Conference on Data Mining, pp. 322–331 (2007)

19. Wohlfarth, T., Ichise, R.: Semantic and event-based approach for link prediction. In: Yamaguchi, T. (ed.) PAKM 2008. LNCS (LNAI), vol. 5345, pp. 50–61. Springer, Heidelberg (2008)

An Efficient Cacheable Secure Scalar Product Protocol for Privacy-Preserving Data Mining

Duc H. Tran, Wee Keong Ng, Hoon Wei Lim, and Hai-Long Nguyen

Nanyang Technological University, Singapore 639798
{ductran,wkn,hoonwei,longnguyen}@pmail.ntu.edu.sg

Abstract. Computing scalar products amongst private vectors in a secure manner is a frequent operation in privacy-preserving data mining algorithms, especially when data is vertically partitioned on many parties. Existing secure scalar product protocols based on cryptography are costly, particularly when they are performed repeatedly in privacy-preserving data mining algorithms. To address this issue, we propose an efficient cacheable secure scalar product protocol called CSSP that is built upon a homomorphic multiplicative cryptosystem. CSSP allows one to reuse the already cached data and thus, it greatly reduces the running time of any privacy-preserving data mining algorithms that adopt it. We also conduct experiments on real-life datasets to show the efficiency of the protocol.

1 Introduction

With the proliferation of the Internet and the advent of cheap storage devices, data has been collected and stored in many sites. In the last decade, there has been growing interest in privacy-preserving data mining (PPDM). PPDM allows multi-parties to collaborate without disclosing their sensitive data. One of the common approaches is to use cryptographic protocols to pass private data in encrypted form among parties. Although this method demands high computational overheads, it achieves more accurate results than the randomization approach [1].

When data is vertically distributed among multiple parties, many PPDM algorithms require scalar product operations on private data vectors. To date, various secure scalar product (SSP) protocols have been proposed to solve specific data mining algorithms [3,4,7,13,20]. As pointed out by Yang *et al.* [17], high computational overheads have become a major performance bottleneck of SSP protocols. As executing SSP protocols on large datasets incurs high costs, the practicality of PPDM in real applications suffers. Until the efficiency of SSP protocols is substantially improved, PPDM based on cryptographic approach remains a theoretical domain with very limited impact on real-world problems.

We observe that many conventional data mining algorithms execute iterative data computations where intermediate results are produced in one iteration and used in subsequent iterations. Naturally, their privacy-preserving versions also run

A. Cuzzocrea and U. Dayal (Eds.): DaWaK 2011, LNCS 6862, pp. 354–366, 2011.

Table 1. Private datasets of Alice & Bob

A_1	A_2	A_3	B_1	B_2	B_3
1	1	0	0	1	0
1	0	0	1	0	0
0	0	0	0	1	1
1	1	0	1	1	0
1	0	1	1	0	0

Table 2. Apriori Algorithm

Iteration 1		Iteration 2		Iteration 3	
Itemset	Support	Itemset	Support	Itemset	Support
$\{A_1\}$	4	$\{A_1, A_2\}$	2	$\{A_1, A_2, B_2\}$	2
$\{A_2\}$	2	$\{A_1, B_1\}$	3		
$\{A_3\}$	1	$\{A_1, B_2\}$	2		
$\{B_1\}$	3	$\{A_2, B_1\}$	1		
$\{B_2\}$	3	$\{A_2, B_2\}$	2		
$\{B_3\}$	1	$\{B_1, B_2\}$	1		

Highlighted itemsets are eliminated in the next iteration due to low support counts.

iteratively. Privacy-preserving association rule mining (PPARM) algorithm proposed by Vaidya and Clifton [13] is an example. The algorithm is based on the idea of filtering out infrequent dataset iteratively. Similarly, privacy-preserving decision tree induction (PPID3) [14] is another typical iterative PPDM algorithm.

Consider the discovery of frequent itemsets in ARM that involves two parties. As illustrated in Table 1, we assume that Alice holds private attributes A_1, A_2, A_3 and Bob holds B_1, B_2, B_3. We also assume that the *Apriori* algorithm is used with a support threshold of 2. As shown in Table 2, during the second iteration, Alice and Bob exchange data in order to determine the frequency of 2-itemsets $\{A_1, B_1\}$, $\{A_1, B_2\}$, $\{A_2, B_1\}$, and $\{A_2, B_2\}$. Support counts may be securely computed using any SSP protocols. For instance, to jointly and securely determine the support of 2-itemset $\{A_1, B_1\}$, Alice encrypts A_1 using an encryption scheme and sends the ciphertext via a communication network to Bob. Bob then performs some secure computations on the received data and his own data. Together, they both derive the support value of $\{A_1, B_1\}$. In the same way, they determine the support of the remaining 2-itemsets.

This process is repeated in a similar manner in subsequent iterations where frequent 3-itemsets or higher itemsets are discovered. We note that some of Alice's encryption operations are performed on the same data in the next iteration, as in the second iteration. For instance, to determine the support of 3-itemsets $\{A_1, A_2, B_1\}$, Alice needs to encrypt vectors $A_1 \cdot A_2$. We note that vectors A_1 and A_2 have been encrypted individually in the previous iteration. To significantly reduce additional costly cryptographic operations, we seek to derive $\mathsf{Enc_{pk}}(A_1 \cdot A_2)$ directly based on the results computed in the second iteration (*i.e.*, $\mathsf{Enc_{pk}}(A_1)$ and $\mathsf{Enc_{pk}}(A_2)$), where $\mathsf{Enc_{pk}}(X)$ denotes the encrypted value of X using key pk.

To generalize the problem, if one is able to design an SSP protocol such that Alice need not encrypt the same data that has been encrypted before in previous iterations, and simply use the already encrypted data in subsequent iterations, the computation and network communication costs of the protocol can be reduced. The extent of this reduction can be significant, depending on how frequent subsequent iterations require data from earlier iterations. This observation motivates us to design an SSP protocol with the desirable feature of reusing intermediate results. Our contribution in this paper is a new SSP protocol called cacheable secure scalar product (CSSP) that supports intermediate result caching.

The rest of this paper is organized as follows. The background will be discussed in the next section. In Section 3, we use Goethals *et al.*'s popular SSP protocol [7] as an example and examine why intermediate result caching may not be applicable. The CSSP protocol and its security issues are discussed in Section 4. We conduct experiments to evaluate the efficiency of CSSP protocol in Section 5. The last section concludes the paper with a summary.

2   Preliminaries

2.1   Homomorphic Public-key Cryptosystems

For any two plaintexts m_1 and m_2, a public key cryptosystem is said to have the *homomorphic additive* property if it satisfies:

$$\mathsf{Enc}_{\mathsf{pk}}(m_1, r_1) \times \mathsf{Enc}_{\mathsf{pk}}(m_2, r_2) = \mathsf{Enc}_{\mathsf{pk}}(m_1 + m_2, \hat{f}(r_1, r_2)) \qquad (1)$$

where $\mathsf{Enc}_{\mathsf{pk}}(m, r)$ is the encrypted value of plaintext m using public key pk with a random number r, and $\hat{f}$ is a function in polynomial execution time. Based on the *homomorphic additive* property, we are able to simulate encryption by multiplying two plaintexts:

$$\mathsf{Enc}_{\mathsf{pk}}(m \times n, r_1) = (\mathsf{Enc}_{\mathsf{pk}}(m, r_2))^n \qquad (2)$$

This *pseudo multiplication* is the underlying rationale for many existing SSP protocols. Some of the cryptosystems that support this property are those by Paillier [11] and Okamoto-Uchiyama [10].

On the other hand, a cryptosystem is said to have the *homomorphic multiplicative* property if it satisfies:

$$\mathsf{Enc}_{\mathsf{pk}}(m_1, r_1) \times \mathsf{Enc}_{\mathsf{pk}}(m_2, r_2) = \mathsf{Enc}_{\mathsf{pk}}(m_1 \times m_2, \hat{g}(r_1, r_2)) \qquad (3)$$

where $\hat{g}$ is a function in polynomial execution time. RSA [12] and ElGamal [5] cryptosystems have this property.

2.2   Semi-honest Model

In a distributed environment where multiple parties follow and execute secure protocols to perform privacy-preserving data mining, we make assumptions in the way each party abides by the steps of the protocols. A commonly adopted model is the semi-honest one where every party strictly follows and executes the specified protocol and provides the correct input data when executing the protocol. However, after they have completed executing the protocol, every party may attempt to discover as much additional information as possible from the intermediate results received from other parties during protocol execution and its own private data. The semi-honest party model [8] is widely accepted and applied in many PPDM protocols due to its simplicity as generally each party does not wish to collaborate with any malicious parties for risk of compromising data privacy.

2.3   Related Work

We review various work related to multi-party secure scalar product protocols. Du et al. [3,4] applied a *commodity server (CS)* as a computation model in which participants need help from a semi-trusted third party. However, finding such a semi-trusted third party is not easy. Based on the *1-out-of-N Oblivious Transfer* protocol [9], Du and Atallah [2] proposed an SSP protocol as an alternative solution to securely compute scalar product. Vaidya and Clifton [13] proposed another SSP protocol based on matrix operations. However, both are insecure according to Goethals et al. [7]. To address this problem, Goethals et al. [7] proposed an SSP protocol built on a *homomorphic additive* cryptosystem.

Zhan et al. [19] proposed an SSP protocol using homomorphic additive property of a cryptosystem. This protocol does not preserve fairness among parties in general as the final result is held only by the initial party. Furthermore, Zhong [20] also proposed several cryptographic SSP protocols to deal with vertically and horizontally partitioned data. The efficiency of this protocol is relatively low as extra cryptographic computations and vector permute operations are involved. However, none of the above mentioned SSP protocols that fully utilize intermediate results and thus, increase overall system performance.

To address the practical limitations of PPDM systems, Vaidya and Clifton [15] discussed the feasibility of applying the secure set intersection cardinality method to increase the performance of PPARM protocols. However, this method is not applicable to a wide range of protocols other than PPARM. Zhai et al. [18] proposed to improve the performance of several secure protocols such as privacy-preserving k-means, PPARM, PPID3, *etc.*, via a result caching approach. They discussed the caching capability only at the PPDM algorithm level and not at the SSP level. It is also not clear how to apply caching in PPDM. In this paper, we apply result caching at a lower level to further increase system performance on boolean vectors.

3   Caching Analysis of Proposed SSP Protocols

We first review a popular SSP protocol that is dedicated to binary inputs, proposed by Goethals et al. [7] in Section 3.1. We choose this protocol since it is secure and provides fairness between parties [7]. We then attempt to incorporate result caching into the protocol in order to improve its efficiency. Using an illustration involving boolean vectors, we argue in Section 3.2 that the caching concept cannot be successfully applied due to limitations of the adopted cryptosystem. For simplicity, we use $\mathsf{Enc}_{\mathsf{pk}}(m)$ instead of $\mathsf{Enc}_{\mathsf{pk}}(m, r)$ in this section.

3.1   Goethals *et al.*'s SSP Protocol

Protocol 1 illustrates Goethals *et al.*'s protocol [7]. It exploits the *homomorphic additive* property of a suitable cryptosystem (*e.g.*, Paillier cryptosystem [11]) to accomplish operations of data computation in encrypted form; *i.e.*, preserving data privacy. After the initial setup in Step 1, Alice encrypts her vector elements x_i (Step 2) and sends it to Bob (Step 3). In Step 4, Bob incorporates the necessary computations on Alice's encrypted data c_i and his own data y_i in encrypted form by pseudo multiplication (Equation (2)), generating a new vector d as a result. Each element of the vector d is equivalent to the encrypted form of $x_i \cdot y_i$. In Step 7, Bob applies the *homomorphic additive* property of the cryptosystem on the vectors to obtain the encrypted form of the scalar product $\sum_{i=1}^{n}(x_i \cdot y_i)$. Using Steps 8 and 9, each party produces and keeps a portion of the result. Herein, $\mathsf{Dec_{sk}}(C)$ denotes the decrypted value of ciphertext C using decryption key sk.

3.2   Caching Analysis of Goethals *et al.*'s Protocol

In this section, we address how to apply caching to Goethals *et al.*'s protocol. Let us consider the following scenario. Suppose Alice holds two n-dimensional binary vectors $x_a = [x_{a1}, x_{a2}, \ldots x_{an}]$ and $x_b = [x_{b1}, x_{b2}, \ldots x_{bn}]$, and Bob holds two n-dimensional binary vectors $y_a = [y_{a1}, y_{a2}, \ldots y_{an}]$ and $y_b = [y_{b1}, y_{b2}, \ldots y_{bn}]$. While Bob receives ciphertexts from Alice in Step 5 of Protocol 1, he may cache vector c for future use. After they have computed the scalar product of $x_a \cdot y_a$ or $x_b \cdot y_b$ using the protocol, they both hold a share of the final result, as the protocol dictates. During the execution of the protocol, Bob cached encrypted values c_a and c_b where

$$c_a = [\mathsf{Enc_{pk}}(x_{a1}), \mathsf{Enc_{pk}}(x_{a2}), \ldots \mathsf{Enc_{pk}}(x_{an})] \tag{4a}$$

$$c_b = [\mathsf{Enc_{pk}}(x_{b1}), \mathsf{Enc_{pk}}(x_{b2}), \ldots \mathsf{Enc_{pk}}(x_{bn})] \tag{4b}$$

Suppose the data mining algorithm further requires Alice and Bob to securely compute the scalar product of all four vectors $x_a \cdot x_b \cdot y_a \cdot y_b = \sum_{i=1}^{n}(x_{ai} x_{bi} y_{ai} y_{bi})$. In PPARM, the value of $x_a \cdot x_b \cdot y_a \cdot y_b$ corresponds to the support value of itemset $\{X_a, X_b, Y_a, Y_b\}$. In PPID3, this value helps to compute the information gain or entropy.

Steps 6–8 of Protocol 1 make use of the *homomorphic additive* property of the cryptosystem adopted in the protocol. The encryption scheme was earlier used to encrypt x_{ij}, where $i \in \{a, b\}$ and $j \in [1, n]$. From the *homomorphic additive* property, we know that:

$$\mathsf{Enc_{pk}}(x_a \cdot x_b \cdot y_a \cdot y_b) = (((\mathsf{Enc_{pk}}(x_a))^{x_b})^{y_a})^{y_b} \tag{5}$$

From Equation 5, we see that if Bob wants to compute the scalar product of all four vectors, he must receive $(\mathsf{Enc_{pk}}(x_a))^{x_b}$ from Alice. It is clear that Bob cannot make use of cached ciphertexts here.

The implication of this example is that the protocol uses encrypted data repeatedly, and it is known that cryptographic operations can be very costly.

Protocol 1. Goethals *et al.*'s SSP Protocol.

Input: Binary vectors $\boldsymbol{x} = [x_1, x_2, \ldots x_n]$, $\boldsymbol{y} = [y_1, y_2, \ldots y_n]$ held by Alice and Bob respectively.

Output: Alice and Bob get outputs S_A and S_B respectively so that $S_A + S_B \equiv \boldsymbol{x} \cdot \boldsymbol{y}$.

1: Setup phase: Alice generates a *homomorphic additive* public-key cryptosystem with private key sk and public key pk and release pk to Bob.
2: **for** $i = 1$ to n **do**
3:     Alice generates a random number r_i and computes $c_i = \mathsf{Enc}_{\mathsf{pk}}(x_i, r_i)$.
4: **end for**
5: Alice sends vector $\boldsymbol{c} = [c_1, c_2, \ldots c_n]$ to Bob.
6: Bob generates a vector $\boldsymbol{d} = [d_1, d_2, \ldots d_n]$ where $d_i = c_i^{y_i}$ for all $i \in [1, n]$.
7: Bob sets $w = \prod_{i=1}^{n} d_i$.
8: Bob generates a random plaintext S_B and a random nonce r'; and sends $w' = w \cdot \mathsf{Enc}_{\mathsf{pk}}(-S_B, r')$ to Alice.
9: Alice computes $S_A = \mathsf{Dec}_{\mathsf{sk}}(w') = \boldsymbol{x} \cdot \boldsymbol{y} - S_B$.

However, many intermediate results such as $\mathsf{Enc}(\boldsymbol{x_a})$ and $\mathsf{Enc}(\boldsymbol{x_b})$ cannot be reused to further derive $\mathsf{Enc}(\boldsymbol{x_a} \cdot \boldsymbol{x_b})$. Hence, to increase efficiency in subsequent iterations, we propose a new SSP protocol that is applicable to intermediate results caching in the next section.

4   The Cacheable Secure Scalar Product Protocol

In this section, we propose a cacheable secure scalar product (CSSP) protocol that fully supports caching, as illustrated in Protocol 2. The protocol is dedicated to binary vectors as they are widely used in many data mining protocols such as PPARM, PPID3, *etc.* and all categorical data can be converted into binary data.

4.1   The Correctness

Using the *homomorphic multiplicative* property, we have:

$$S_A = \sum_{i=1}^{m+n} h_i = \sum_{i=1}^{m+n} \mathsf{Dec}_{\mathsf{sk}}(g_i) = \sum_{i=1}^{n} \mathsf{Dec}_{\mathsf{sk}}(e_i) + \sum_{i=1}^{m} \mathsf{Dec}_{\mathsf{sk}}(f_i)$$

$$= \sum_{i=1}^{n} (x_i \cdot y_i) + \sum_{i=1}^{m} s_i = \boldsymbol{x} \cdot \boldsymbol{y} + S_B.$$

Thus, the CSSP protocol is correct.

4.2   Caching Analysis

Let consider the example in Section 3.2 again. Alice and Bob want to compute the scalar product of four vectors: $\boldsymbol{x_a}, \boldsymbol{x_b}, \boldsymbol{y_a}, \boldsymbol{y_b}$ in which ciphertexts $\boldsymbol{c_a}$ of $\boldsymbol{x_a}$ and $\boldsymbol{c_b}$ of $\boldsymbol{x_b}$ have been cached on Bob's site. Using *homomorphic multiplicative* property

---

Protocol 2. The Cacheable Secure Scalar Product Protocol.

Input: Alice and Bob have private binary vectors $x = [x_1, x_2, \ldots x_n]$, $y = [y_1, y_2, \ldots y_n]$, respectively. They agree to adopt a *homomorphic multiplicative* public-key cryptosystem. Private key sk is held by Alice; public key pk is known to both parties.

Output: Shares S_A and S_B held by Alice and Bob respectively where $S_A + (-S_B) = x \cdot y$ yields the scalar product value.

1: **for** $i = 1$ to n **do**
2:     Alice generates a random number r_i and encrypts x_i as $c_i = \mathsf{Enc}_{\mathsf{pk}}(x_i, r_i)$.
3:     Bob generates a random number r_i' and encrypts y_i as $d_i = \mathsf{Enc}_{\mathsf{pk}}(y_i, r_i')$.
4: **end for**
5: Alice sends vector $c = [c_1, c_2, \ldots c_n]$ to Bob. **Bob cache c for future uses.**
6: **for** $i = 1$ to n **do**
7:     Bob computes $e_i = c_i \cdot d_i$.
8: **end for**
9: Bob generates a random number m. He then generates a random binary vector $s = [s_1, s_2, \ldots s_m]$ and uses $S_B = \sum_{i=1}^{m} s_i$ as his secret share.
10: **for** $i = 1$ to m **do**
11:     Bob generates a random number $\tilde{r}_i$ and encrypts s_i as: $f_i = \mathsf{Enc}_{\mathsf{pk}}(s_i, \tilde{r}_i)$.
12: **end for**
13: Bob constructs vector $g = [e_1, e_2, \ldots e_n, f_1, f_2, \ldots f_m]$.
14: Bob permutes the elements of vector g to get $g = [g_1, g_2, \ldots g_{m+n}]$.
15: Bob sends g back to Alice.
16: **for** $k = 1$ to $m + n$ **do**
17:     Alice decrypts g_k using sk: $h_k = \mathsf{Dec}_{\mathsf{sk}}(g_k)$.
18: **end for**
19: Alice obtains her secret share $S_A = \sum_{i=1}^{m+n} h_i$.

---

of a cryptosystem, he can compute encrypted vector e in Step 7 of Protocol 2 without any help from Alice: $e = \mathsf{Enc}_{\mathsf{pk}}(x_a) \cdot \mathsf{Enc}_{\mathsf{pk}}(x_b) \cdot \mathsf{Enc}_{\mathsf{pk}}(y_a) \cdot \mathsf{Enc}_{\mathsf{pk}}(y_b) = c_a \cdot c_b \cdot \mathsf{Enc}_{\mathsf{pk}}(y_a) \cdot \mathsf{Enc}_{\mathsf{pk}}(y_b)$. To generalize, we can conclude that CSSP allows Bob to reuse any already cached ciphertext to calculate scalar products.

4.3   Security Analysis

We now analyze the security of our protocol.

Cryptosystem. Throughout the execution of the protocol, only n random ciphertexts are known by Bob in Step 5. It is impossible for Bob to gain any knowledge of Alice's vectors if the adopted cryptosystem is secure. In later iterations, Bob uses the cached vector from previous iterations to perform the computations in the protocol. This requires homomorphic multiplication among several encrypted vectors. During the entire process, Bob is not able to retrieve any valuable information from Alice's inputs. Thus, data privacy of Alice is well preserved. However, permanent reuse of ciphertexts can be a security threat and is against the spirit of probabilistic encryptions. To limit data leakage from reuse of ciphertexts, we suggest that any PPDM algorithm that adopts the CSSP protocol only allows a ciphertext to be reused a random number of times, after which the caching data expires and must be encrypted again from the plaintext. By this way, it is unpredictable how many times a ciphertext is reused, and thus, CSSP is used in a secure manner.

Random Shares. It is possible that after Alice obtains the scalar product by decrypting vector g and summing up all the elements, she may refuse to release the results or deliberately release incorrect values to Bob. To prevent Alice from behaving like this, before sending vector g back to Alice in Step 15, Bob generates a random binary vector s and encrypts it as vector f. He computes his random share S_B in Step 9. Since Bob also holds a share, fairness of the final result between the two parties is achieved. Moreover, the additional vector f serves the purpose of masking the original data passed back to Alice. By appending vector f to vector e, together with the permutation in Step 14, Bob introduces "uncertainty" and "noise" into the original data. Therefore, he is able to prevent any privacy leakage or data pattern revelation to Alice.

Permutation. Re-arranging any elements in a sequence does not change their summation. However, such a randomization process would confuse the other party and makes it difficult to figure out any input data. If Bob chooses a random permutation function properly in Step 14, the resulting vector should contain elements which have been reshuffled randomly. As this protocol focuses on improving the efficiency of PPARM and PPID3 algorithms, the data seen by Alice are limited to binary data only. It is quite impossible to discover any data pattern from Bob's input, especially with a sufficiently large database input. Thus, the permutation process ensures that the private data of Bob is protected.

The dimension m of the appended vector f is highly related to data privacy. Certainly, a greater m value results in a higher level of security. In general, m could be set by the user accordingly. However, in the case when a party has predictable data patterns, a low dimensional vector f may compromise data privacy. For example, if Bob's input vector contains very few 1's, a vector f with a large dimension is preferred. Therefore, we suggest that m value is a large number (*e.g.* $m \geq n$) to avoid any data privacy breaches.

Theorem 1. *Assume that the public-key cryptosystem used in Protocol 2 is semantically secure. The CSSP protocol is secure in the semi-honest model.*

Proof. Bob see only n random ciphertexts received from Alice. Because the cryptosystem is semantically secure, he cannot guess the original plaintexts. Alice's data privacy is thus guaranteed.

Before sending the final result vector back to Alice, Bob generates a random binary vector f, appending to e and permuting vector g. Alice can decrypt vector g, but she is unable to disclose Bob's data. Therefore, Bob's data privacy is also promised. □

4.4   Complexity Analysis

Estimated communication complexity. The drawback of CSSP is the communication cost: Alice sends n ciphertexts to Bob and Bob sends $m + n$ ciphertexts to Alice while Goethals *et al.*'s protocol needs to send only n ciphertexts. However, as stated in [17] and [15], communication overhead is a very small portion compared with computation cost. Moreover, using intermediate caching technique, our protocol significantly reduces the number of ciphertexts to be sent.

Estimated computation complexity. Alice and Bob need n encryption operations in Steps 2–3. It costs Bob more m encryption operations in Steps 10–12. Alice requires $m + n$ decryption operations in Steps 16–18. Hence, the protocol needs $m + n$ encryptions and $m + n$ decryptions. The complexity of the protocol is $O(m + n)$.

Overall complexity. Since the CSSP protocol is not designed to compute a single scalar product, its efficiency surpasses that of Goethals *et al.*'s protocol when both are embedded into iterative PPDM algorithms thanks to its caching capability as theoretically shown in Section 3.2 and will be empirically illustrated in Section 5.

4.5   Extension to Multi-party Environment

Now, we consider a scenario in which multiple parties wish to compute the scalar product of their private vectors. For simplicity, we only present the three-party version of CSSP in Protocol 3. However, the protocol can be easily extended to a multi-party environment. The correctness and security of this protocol can be proven similarly to those of the two-party version.

5   Empirical Evaluations

We conducted our experiments with multi-parties connected via a LAN connection. We used Java on the Windows XP environment and TCP/IP model for communication. Each party has a system with hardware configuration: Intel Core 2 Duo 2.33GHz and 2GB of memory.

To demonstrate efficiency of CSSP over Goethals *et al.*'s protocol, we in turn used two protocols to compute support counts of itemsets in PPARM algorithm proposed by Vaidya and Clifton [13]. We performed experiments on two categorical datasets: "Nursery" and "Adult", both of which are available at the UCI repository [6]. The former has 9 attributes and 12, 960 tuples. The latter consists of 14 attributes and 48, 842 tuples. We first converted all categorical data to strictly binary data to get two datasets of 28 and 91 binary attributes, respectively. "Nursery" dataset is then vertically partitioned for 3 parties with 10, 10, and 8 attributes respectively. "Adult" dataset is vertically partitioned for 5 parties with 18, 18, 18, 18, and 19 attributes respectively.

Protocol 3. The Multi-Party CSSP Protocol.

Input: Alice holds vector $x = [x_1, x_2, \ldots, x_n]$. Bob holds vector $y = [y_1, y_2, \ldots, y_n]$. Carol holds vector $z = [z_1, z_2, \ldots, z_n]$. They agree to adopt a *homomorphic multiplicative* public-key cryptosystem with public key pk, private key sk. Private key sk is held by Alice; pk is known to three parties.

Output: Shares S_A, S_B and S_C held by Alice, Bob and Carol respectively, where $S_A + (-S_B) + (-S_C) = x \cdot y \cdot z$.

1: **for** $i = 1$ to n **do**
2:     Alice generates a random number r_{1i} and encrypts x_i as $c_i = \mathsf{Enc_{pk}}(x_i, r_{1i})$.
3: **end for**
4: Alice sends $c = [c_1, c_2, \ldots, c_n]$ to Bob.
5: Bob generates a new vector $d = [d_1, d_2, \ldots, d_n]$ where $d_i = c_i \cdot \mathsf{Enc_{pk}}(y_i, r_{2i})$, r_{2i} is a random number, for all $i \in [1, n]$ and forwards it to Carol.
6: Carol generates a new vector $e = [e_1, e_2, \ldots, e_n]$ where $e_i = d_i \cdot \mathsf{Enc_{pk}}(z_i, r_{3i})$, r_{3i} is a random number, for all $i \in [1, n]$.
7: Carol generates a random binary vector $u = [u_1, u_2, \ldots, u_p]$, where p is a random number selected by Carol. She uses $S_C = \sum_{i=1}^{p} u_i$ as her secret share.
8: Carol encrypts vector u as vector u':
    $u' = [u'_1, u'_2, \ldots u'_p] = [\mathsf{Enc_{pk}}(u_1, r'_{31}), \mathsf{Enc_{pk}}(u_2, r'_{32}), \ldots, \mathsf{Enc_{pk}}(u_p, r'_{3p})]$ where r'_{3i} is a random number, for all $i \in [1, p]$.
9: Carol constructs vector $f = [e_1, e_2, \ldots e_n, u'_1, u'_2, \ldots u'_p]$.
10: Carol permutes the elements of vector f to get $f = [f_1, f_2, \ldots f_{n+p}]$. She then sends vector f to Bob.
11: Bob generates a random binary vector $v = [v_1, v_2, \ldots, v_q]$, where q is a random number selected by Bob. He uses $S_B = \sum_{i=1}^{q} v_i$ as his secret share.
12: Bob encrypts vector v as vector v':
    $v' = [v'_1, v'_2, \ldots v'_q] = [\mathsf{Enc_{pk}}(v_1, r'_{21}), \mathsf{Enc_{pk}}(v_2, r'_{22}), \ldots, \mathsf{Enc_{pk}}(v_q, r'_{2q})]$ where r'_{2i} is a random number, for all $i \in [1, q]$.
13: Bob constructs vector $g = [f_1, f_2, \ldots f_{n+p}, v'_1, v'_2, \ldots v'_q]$.
14: Bob permutes the elements of vector g to get $g = [g_1, g_2, \ldots g_{n+p+q}]$. She then sends vector g to Alice.
15: **for** $k = 1$ to $n + p + q$ **do**
16:     Alice decrypts g_k using sk: $h_k = \mathsf{Dec_{sk}}(g_k)$.
17: **end for**
18: Alice obtains her secret share $S_A = \sum_{i=1}^{m+n} h_i$.

We used 512 and 1,024 bit keys for both ElGamal cryptosystem in CSSP and Paillier one in Goethals *et al.*'s protocol. We also set value m in CSSP to the number of tuples, *i.e.* $m = n$. The correctness of the results is verified by Weka version 3.5 [16]. The total running time in all experiments includes communication time.

Figure 1 and Figure 2 illustrate the effects of varying the number of input records on the total running time. The records used are selected randomly and uniformly from "Nurse" and "Adult" dataset, respectively. We set the *Minimum Support Threshold (MST)* of the PPARM algorithm to 4% herein. From the figures, we may conclude that as the number of records increases, the CSSP

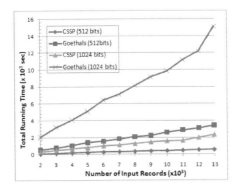

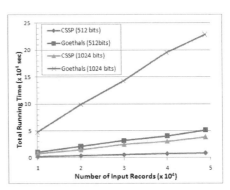

Fig. 1. Number of input records vs. total running time. "Nursery" dataset on 3 vertical parties. $MST = 4\%$.

Fig. 2. Number of input records vs. total running time. "Adult" dataset on 5 vertical parties. $MST = 4\%$.

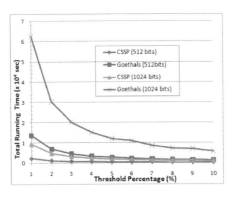

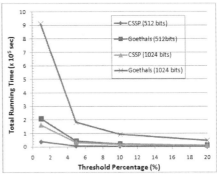

Fig. 3. Threshold percentages vs. total running time. "Nursery" dataset on 3 vertical parties with 12, 960 records.

Fig. 4. Threshold percentages vs. total running time. "Adult" dataset on 5 vertical parties with 48, 842 records.

protocol with caching is much more efficient than Goethals *et al.*'s protocol. The more the number of input records is, the more number of encryption/decryption operations per vector is required. This explains the linear correlation between the total running time and the different number of input records as shown in the figures. As the CSSP protocol is able to fully use the already cached data, the number of cryptographic operations is much lower than that of Goethals *et al.*'s one. Experiments have shown that CSSP's total running time is 5–7 times less than that of Goethals *et al.*'s protocol.

Figure 3 and Figure 4 demonstrate the total running time versus different threshold values. As shown in the figures, the caching efficiency of our protocol is reduced when *MST* increases. When *MST* is high, we are less able to find frequent itemsets satisfying the threshold. Hence, the algorithm may terminate in fewer iterations. As a result, the total processing time is reduced. However, caching still helps to improve the efficiency of the CSSP protocol compared to

Goethals *et al.*'s one. In summary, the efficiency ratio of the CSSP protocol over Goethals *et al.*'s protocol is greatly increased for large input datasets, and the improvements are more effective at low threshold settings.

6   Conclusion

We have presented a new cacheable secure scalar product protocol called CSSP using the *homomorphic multiplicative* property of a public-key cryptosystem. CSSP allows to reuse encrypted data to compute scalar products of vectors. We have shown the correctness and proven the security of the protocol in the semi-honest model. The empirical results showed that when the protocol is properly applied to data mining algorithms, cryptographic computation overheads are much reduced. Since the SSP protocol is a common building block in PPDM, CSSP can be applied to solve many of the associated problems. Moreover, CSSP can be easily extended to multi-party settings.

References

1. Aggarwal, C.C., Yu, P.S.: Privacy-Preserving Data Mining: Models and Algorithms. Advances in Database Systems, vol. 34. Springer, Heidelberg (2008)
2. Du, W., Atallah, M.J.: Privacy-preserving cooperative statistical analysis. In: Proceedings of the 17th Annual Computer Security Applications Conference (2001)
3. Du, W., Han, Y., Chen, S.: Privacy-preserving multivariate statistical analysis: Linear regression and classification. In: Proceedings of the 4th SDM (2004)
4. Du, W., Zhan, Z.: Building decision tree classifier on private data. In: Proceedings of the IEEE International Conference on Privacy, Security and Data Mining (2002)
5. El Gamal, T.: A public key cryptosystem and a signature scheme based on discrete logarithms. In: Blakely, G.R., Chaum, D. (eds.) CRYPTO 1984. LNCS, vol. 196, pp. 10–18. Springer, Heidelberg (1985)
6. Frank, A., Asuncion, A.: UCI machine learning repository (2010)
7. Goethals, B., Laur, S., Lipmaa, H., Mielikäinen, T.: On private scalar product computation for privacy-preserving data mining. In: Park, C.-s., Chee, S. (eds.) ICISC 2004. LNCS, vol. 3506, pp. 104–120. Springer, Heidelberg (2005)
8. Goldreich, O.: Secure multi-party computation (2002) (manuscript)
9. Naor, M., Pinkas, B.: Oblivious transfer and polynomial evaluation. In: Proceedings of the Annual ACM Symposium on Theory of Computing (1999)
10. Okamoto, T., Uchiyama, S.: A new public-key cryptosystem as secure as factoring. In: Nyberg, K. (ed.) EUROCRYPT 1998. LNCS, vol. 1403, pp. 308–318. Springer, Heidelberg (1998)
11. Paillier, P.: Public-key cryptosystems based on composite degree residuosity classes. In: Stern, J. (ed.) EUROCRYPT 1999. LNCS, vol. 1592, pp. 223–238. Springer, Heidelberg (1999)
12. Rivest, R.L., Shamir, A., Adleman, L.: A method for obtaining digital signatures and public-key cryptosystems. Commun. ACM 21(2), 120–126 (1978)
13. Vaidya, J., Clifton, C.: Privacy preserving association rule mining in vertically partitioned data. In: The Eighth ACM SIGKDD, pp. 639–644 (2002)

14. Vaidya, J., Clifton, C.: Privacy-preserving decision trees over vertically partitioned data. In: Jajodia, S., Wijesekera, D. (eds.) Data and Applications Security 2005. LNCS, vol. 3654, pp. 139–152. Springer, Heidelberg (2005)
15. Vaidya, J., Clifton, C.: Secure set intersection cardinality with application to association rule mining. J. Comput. Secur. 13(4), 593–622 (2005)
16. Witten, I., Frank, E., Holmes, G., Mayo, M.: Weka 3 software,
    http://www.cs.waikato.ac.nz/ml/weka/
17. Yang, Z., Wright, R.N., Subramaniam, H.: Experimental analysis of a privacy-preserving scalar product protocol. International Journal of CSSE (2006)
18. Zhai, K., Ng, W.K., Herianto, A.R., Han, S.: Speeding up secure computations via embedded caching. In: 9th SDM (2009)
19. Zhan, J., Matwin, S., Chang, L.: Privacy-preserving collaborative association rule mining. Journal of Network and Computer Applications (2007)
20. Zhong, S.: Privacy-preserving algorithms for distributed mining of frequent itemsets. Information Sciences 177(2), 490–503 (2007)

Learning Actions in Complex Software Systems

Koosha Golmohammadi, Michael Smit, and Osmar R. Zaiane

Department of Computing Science, University of Alberta, Canada
{golmoham,msmit,zaiane}@cs.ualberta.ca

Abstract. Administering service-oriented architecture (SOA) systems could require sophisticated rules to decide for instance whether to add or remove servers and when. Rule construction often necessitates experts to study patterns that contribute to changes or events. This is a time consuming and error-prone process for complex software systems. In this paper we test the feasibility of automating this process by mining historical data such as past service requests (in time series) and server change events that the administrator committed. We propose a new method to relate frequent patterns in a given time series to changes recorded in the event's history. We implemented and tested our method on a simulation system for SOA applications. First, we use Euclidean distance, DTW, and FastDTW to identify frequent patterns in a time series that represents performance metric of a SOA simulation system. Then, we calculate the confidence and support of frequent patterns that contribute to changes to identify a set of rules for automating changes. We tested rules that are generated using the proposed method in a training set on a testing set. The average accuracy of generated rules for the change event "remove" exceeded 80% in our experiments.

Keywords: time series, rule creation, DTW, frequent patterns, data mining.

1 Introduction

Predicting infrastructure changes is an interesting and ubiquitous task in the management of Service-Oriented Architectures (SOAs). These systems are quite complex as they integrate a multitude of services deployed over a large number of servers distributed over a broad network. Their behavior is usually governed by Service-Levels Agreements (SLAs) and the fundamental problem in managing their infrastructure is to meet these SLAs with the minimum possible infrastructure. With that goal, assuming an original satisfying infrastructure has been provisioned, the problem becomes to predict changes in the environment that can lead this infrastructure to fail (either by not meeting the SLAs or by being overly provisioned) and to change the infrastructure to avoid these failures. The management of SOA infrastructure is usually the responsibility of system administrators who, based on their experience, recognize trends in the SOA performance profile that are indicative of infrastructure changes.

In this paper we try to automate this process by mining available historical data of SOA behavioral profiles in order to extract rules for predicting two different types of

A. Cuzzocrea and U. Dayal (Eds.): DaWaK 2011, LNCS 6862, pp. 367–381, 2011.

appropriate changes to the provisioned infrastructure: (a) additions of new servers, in order to avoid imminent SLA failures and (b) removals of servers in order to mitigate over-provisioning. To achieve this goal, we examine different time series analysis methods to identify frequent patterns in the SOA behavioral profile and we try to find correlations between the mined frequent patterns and the expert administrator changes to the SOA infrastructure.

Time series analysis methods have received substantial attention by data-mining research during the last decade. These methods have been applied to different domains such as medicine [2], telemedicine [3], biology [4], and weather prediction [5]. Time series data consists of a set of time-stamped data points where the temporal relationship plays an important role in the dataset [7]. In most cases, traditional data mining methods are not appropriate for time series analysis as the ordering of data points is often ignored with standard methods [8]. Research in time series data mining can be divided in the following general categories: clustering (unsupervised discovery of groups of similar time series based on a distance measure) [19, 36], classification (selecting a class in which a given time series belongs) [20], anomaly detection (finding all subsequences in a given time series that do not match a pre-defined behavior/pattern) [36], summarization (presenting an extremely long time series preserving its "essential features") [1], and indexing (finding similar time series in a database to a given time series based on a distance measure) [17, 18]. An in depth review of time series analysis research is provided in [6].

In this paper we propose a method that automates taking corrective action in complex systems through off-line analysis of historical data. The ultimate goal is to derive a set of rules that can automate the simpler administrative tasks for complex software systems through application of time series analysis methods to available historical data of the system. The main contributions of this paper are as follows:

- We develop a method for identifying the correlation between frequent patterns and events (changes/actions) and finding actionable rules in a SOA application configuration tool.
- We apply different time series analysis methods to find frequent patterns (k^{th}-motifs) through a comprehensive set of experiments.
- We demonstrate through a set of experiments and a case study that the proposed method is an effective solution for classification of changes/actions in a complex software system.

The remainder of this paper is organized into four more sections. Section 2 describes an overview of the related work. Section 3 reviews background, and definitions that are used through out the paper. Section 4 describes our methodology, including both the tool and data generation strategy we use in our evaluation and our approach to identifying frequent patterns. Section 5 presents experimental results and a discussion of the proposed method. Section 6 concludes the paper.

2   Related Work

Sequence mining [28] and episode mining [30] both try to mine iterative patterns – patterns that are repeated a substantial number of times in a sequence. Sequential pattern mining has been applied to different domains such as detecting plan failures

[35], and identifying network alarm patterns [32]. Many sequence mining algorithms are based on ideas proposed for discovery of association rules [33, 34]. A comprehensive survey on association rules can be found in [27].

Sequence mining has also been applied to software engineering problems. Mining history of software execution runs is utilized to detect frequent repetitive series that represent features of a classifier for identifying candidate software specification [29] and capturing software failures [31].

Pradhan and Prabhakaran loosely divided research works in mining predictive rules from time series into supervised, and unsupervised methods [21]. Unsupervised methods aim to extract rules from series, and time series is the only input to the rule mining algorithms in this category. The rules should be informative, representative of data, specific to some extend and interesting for human expert [22]. Many methods in this category count the number of admissible antecedent and consequent in the dataset [23, 24]. Unlike unsupervised methods, the goal in supervised methods is to generate rules for predicting known rule targets (e.g. specific events). These methods use the information about the events that is provided along with the time series to identify rules based on the historical data before events [26]. Our proposed method falls in this category. We identify frequent patterns using time series distance measures and find changes/events that occur after them. We then choose top rules using confidence and support measures.

3 Preliminaries

In this section we give an overview of time series distance measures that we use. We also review the definitions that will be used through out the paper.

3.1 Definitions

Definition 1. A *time series Point* $P=\{v_1, \dots , v_d\}$ is a data point with real values for d dimensions.

Definition 2. A *time series* $T=\{P_1, \dots , P_t\}$ is a collection of time series points (observations) ordered in time t.

Definition 3. A *window* of size m is a sub-sequence of a time series T. A *sliding window* can create a matrix of all possible windows of size m in time series T starting from a given time series point in T where row i represents i^{th} window of size m.

Definition 4. Two time series/windows w_1 and w_2 are similar iff $Dist(w_1, w_2) <$ *maxDist* where *maxDist* is a predefined threshold.

Definition 5. Time series *motifs* are approximate repeat subsequences in a longer time series data [1]. The distance of two time series (or windows of time series) $D(T_i,T_j)$ can be calculated using different distance measures. Identification of motifs is useful in higher-level reasoning and analysis of subject behavior during a short or long period of time. Note there is no point in searching for similar sub-sequences (patterns) in a time series that is not normalized [6]; therefore time series are normalized before finding the similarities.

Definition 6. A kth-*motif* of size m is a motif that appeared k times in a time series T where k is greater than a predefined threshold.

Definition 7. The kth-*motif support of a change* in a time series that includes a set of events/changes in one dimension is the fraction of transactions (a kth-motif followed by a change/event) that contain both the given k^{th}-motif and change.

Definition 8. The kth-*motif confidence of a change* is the fraction of times that the given change appears when the given k^{th}-motif exists over the total number of the given k^{th}-motif.

3.2   Time Series Distance Measures

As we mentioned above, several different distance measures have been proposed for assessing the similarity between two time series.

Euclidean distance is the most common distance measure in time series [6]. Euclidean distance of two time series is defined as the 2-norm distance of the respective points. Euclidean distance is an efficient distance measure. It is often simplified to be the sum of the squared distance of the ith point in each time series. The drawback in using Euclidean distance is its unintuitive and its sensitivity to relatively small changes. For example, the Euclidean distance of two identical time series, where one of them is slightly shifted along the time axis, is misleadingly large.

DTW (Dynamic Time Warping) introduces a more intuitive and flexible distance measure to address this issue [9]. DTW stretches a time series along its time axis to optimally align it with another time series [10]. For two given time series $X = \{X_{P1}, X_{P2}, ..., X_{P|X|}\}$ and $Y = \{Y_{P1}, Y_{P2}, ..., Y_{P|Y|}\}$ with size of $|X|$ and $|Y|$ respectively, DTW constructs a warping matrix (*i.e.* a cost matrix) for W where $W(i, j)$ starts at (X_{P1}, Y_{P1}) and ends at $(X_{P|X|}, Y_{P|Y|})$. The warp is the path taken through the matrix between the start and end points and the optimal warp has the minimum warp distance. The calculation of the DTW measure relies on dynamic programming techniques to find the warp path, as the optimal path from $(1,1)$ to (i,j) in the cost matrix will be minimum (*i.e.* $Dist(i,j) + min [D(i-1,j), D(i,j-1), D(i-1, j-1)]$).

The time and space complexity of DTW is $O(N^2)$ where $N=|X|=|Y|$. This is problematic as the size of time series may be considerable and storing an $|X|$ by $|Y|$ matrix is memory intensive. This information must be stored in order to retrieve the warp path as the warp distance can be calculated only using two previous columns at a time. There are a few approaches to speeding up DTW. One method involves putting a constraint on the number of cells evaluated in the cost matrix such as the Sakoe-Chuba Band [13] or the Itakura Parrallelogram [14]. These constraints prevent pathological warping by imposing global constraints on warp path $W_{warp\_k} = (i,j)_k$ such that $j-r < i < j+r$ where r is range of warping. Data abstraction of the cost matrix and corresponding reduction of its size [15] is another method. The running time remains $O(N^2)$ and the distance of two given time series "becomes increasingly inaccurate" because of ignoring local variations in the full resolution of matrix. Finally, another method involves indexing through application of lower bounding functions to prune the number of times that DTW must be run [16]. These methods speed up DTW applications including finding similar time series, clustering, and classification.

FastDTW exploits two ideas from the above mechanisms for speed-up of DTW, data abstraction and constraints, using an iterative multi-level approach [9]. First, *coarsening*: a reduced size cost matrix is produced using an abstracted representation of the time series by averaging adjacent points. Coarsening is run several times to generate all the resolutions that will be evaluated. Each time coarsening runs it reduces the cost matrix size by a factor of two. Second, *projection*: a warp path is calculated in the lower resolution (smaller) cost matrix to determine cells that are part of the warp path in the next higher resolution matrix. Third, *refinement*: an optimal warp path is refined and evaluated only in the *projected* neighborhood cells. The complexity of FastDTW is O(N), as the size of warp path grows linearly with the size of the given time series.

4 Methodology

The fundamental assumption underlying this work is that SOA administrators make infrastructure provisioning decisions by inspecting trends in the SOA behavioral profiles and by predicting, based on these trends, when the system will start failing its SLAs (in which case they add capacity) or when the system is over-provisioned (in which case, they reduce capacity). If this is indeed the case, then an analysis of a time series of system-behavior observations should reveal k^{th}-*motifs* correlated with infrastructure changes, as the system behavior before the same type of infrastructure changes should be similar. Maintaining SLAs is a complex task that may require monitoring many trends and parameters. Although in this work we only focus on infrastructure management based on the service request time series, this method can be applied to other types of frequent patterns in SOA management.

In this section, we discuss our method for autonomic SOA management based on time series analysis, as implied by the above methodological assumption. Section *4.1.* describes the datasets, which were used to design and test the proposed method. Section *4.2.* describes our method and algorithm.

4.1 Data

Our datasets were created by WSsim – a tool that simulates the run-time behavior of SOAs and presents a dashboard of performance-related data to administrators for managing the simulated SOA infrastructure [11]. Smit *et al.* developed a method and tool that automatically generates code for a simulator based on the WSDL specification of web services and have demonstrated that the simulation behaves quite close to the real system. Through the dashboard, the simulator enables administrators to identify cost-effective configuration of the simulated SOA in order to achieve performance that complies with a SLA without over-provisioning.

They evaluated their simulation-based approach on TAPoRware (Text Analysis Portal for Research) that provides a suite of text-analysis services for researchers and scholars in the digital humanities [12]. The TAPoRware services, including word count, keyword concordance, collocates, summarization and part-of-speech tagging, are CPU-intensive and have substantial performance challenges, making it an appropriate example of an application to be configured and re-configured at run-time.

WSsim was used to create TaporSim, a simulation of TAPoRware. One of its capabilities is creating performance data by generating different types of requests for TAPoRware and recording a variety of metrics. TaporSim also allows real-time tuning and modification of SOA configuration through a set of changes. Such configuration changes are aimed to improve the performance of the SOA application and make efficient use of resources based on the load on system. TaporSim records queue sizes, number of requests, configuration changes, and response time during the simulation. The data is sampled every 5 seconds for all the above parameters and stored in a mySQL database.

We asked an expert developer and user of WSim, not associated in any meaningful way with our project, to generate a dataset. He generated a set of requests with varying arrival rates and sizes that would require configuration changes to handle properly. The changes for this experiment were limited to adding, removing or no change to the number of servers that provide services. Then, a system administrator monitored the parameters as the simulation ran. He added a server if the queue size is increasing to improve system capacity, and removed a server if one or more servers were idle (and thus not making efficient use of resources). We asked the administrator to make changes based on the queue size information to ensure that queue size is the driving parameter that leads to a change in system configuration. We extracted a single-dimensional time series from TaporSim representing queue-size time series to be our training dataset. The queue size time series includes 1439 data points (representing a 7195-second time period). We removed duplicates (i.e. a data point that is repeated in the data set) and checked for missing values to make sure that there is a numerical value for queue size at each time-stamp and no two data points with the same time-stamp. We also generated a change time series that includes changes to the system recorded in the training dataset. The change time series for training dataset includes 16 add actions (represented by 1) and 14 remove actions (represented by -1). Similarly, a testing dataset was generated that includes a queue size time series with 786 data points (representing a 3930-second time period). The testing dataset *change* time series includes 10 adds and 8 removes.

4.2 Design of the Proposed Prediction Method

Our method includes two phases. First, we apply time series analysis techniques to find frequent patterns to already available historical data of a complex system. Next, we investigate the relationship of detected frequent patterns to changes/actions in the system.

Identification of frequent patterns: We normalize the reference time series (queue-size is the reference time series in our experiments) to have mean zero and a standard deviation of one. Then we use a sliding window to identify the similarity of any two time series of window size in the reference time series. In our experiments we used three window sizes of 1 minute (12 data points), 2 minutes (24 data points), and 3 minutes (36 data points).

Algorithm 1. Identifying kth-motifs (frequent patterns)

Input: T = reference time series
Input parameters: maxDist, distanceMeasure, frequencyThreshold
Output: kMotifs list

```
1   for each sliding window w, in T do
2        frequency (w,) =0
3        for each window w, of size w, do
4             if (Dist (w,, w,, distMeasure) < maxDist)
5                  frequency (w,) ++
6             end if
7        end for
8        if(frequency (W,) > frequencyTreshold)
9           add W, to the list of kMotifs
10       end if
11       return kMotifs
12  end for
```

We used all three similarity functions discussed in Section 4.2. to find frequent patterns (k^{th}-motifs): Euclidean, DTW, FastDTW. Clearly, relaxing the lower bound of the requisite similarity between two time series (i.e., increasing maxDist) can result in an increase in the number of kth-motifs and the number of occurrences of these k^{th}-motifs. Application of a lower distance measure can lead to fewer k^{th}-motifs and a smaller number of occurrences for a motif. Application of the same maxDist to different similarity measures is inappropriate because the distance of two given time series using DTW is generally less than their Euclidean distance.

Algorithm 2. Identifying changes after patterns that belong to a change

Input: kMotif_list = list of kMotifs in reference time series
Input: C = change time series that includes set of changes occurred during reference time series period
Input parameters: changeInterval
Output: kMotif_C = kMotif_list with number of respective changes for each motif

```
1   sort kMotif_list by frequency
2   for each motif mi in kMotif_list do
3        for 1 < change(1).size() do
4           mi.change(1) = 0
5        end for
6        for each trend tj in mi do
7             for change(1) in C do
8                  if (tj.getTime - change(1).getTime < changeInterval)
9                       mj.change_1++
10                 end if
11            end for
12       end for
13  end for
14  return kMotif_C
```

Relationship of frequent patterns and changes: We sort the list of kth-motifs by their frequency in the reference time series. These k^{th}-motifs have a frequency higher than a predefined threshold, which, in our experiment, we vary between 5, 10, and 15. A search in change history is performed for every pattern that belongs to a kth-motif to reveal if there has been a change within a predefined time period after a given pattern. This parameter is set based on the data-sampling rate, and an understanding of time interval of changes in the system (we used 85 seconds in our experiments). The number of changes for each kth-motif is calculated by a sum of changes after all patterns that belong to the given k^{th}-motif. This procedure leads to identification of a set of rules with the form X => Y where X is a frequent pattern (k^{th}-motif) and Y is a respective change/event occurred after that. Finally, we evaluate rules by calculating their respective support and confidence. Algorithm 1 describes our approach to identify frequent patterns and Algorithm 2 presents the procedure to identify changes made after k^{th}-motifs.

It is also possible to extract rules by processing only the subsequences before change events. This decreases computation complexity, however evaluating rules becomes an issue as the frequency of kth-motifs would be different because motifs that are not followed by an event are not detected and do not participate in the computations for rules evaluation.

5 Results and Discussion

5.1 Experiment Setup

In the first phase, we find frequent patterns in the queue size time series from the WSsim training dataset (the reference time series in our experiments) using three distance measures: Euclidean distance, DTW, and FastDTW. This process is sensitive to the selection of parameters, so we run a total of 27 scenarios for each distance measure (81 scenarios in total) by using all possible combinations of three different values for three key parameters: window size, maxDist, and minFrequency. maxDist (maximum distance) varies based on the distance measure in use, and determines the threshold for determining if two windows are the same or not (i.e. part of a motif). We define three thresholds for minFrequency, which establishes the minimum number of similar patterns required to be considered a kth-motif. For each scenario, we report the number of kth-motifs found in the time series based on the given parameters in addition to the mean and standard deviation of frequencies of kth-motifs along with the execution time for each scenario. Tables 1 through 3 describe our experimental results for each set of 27 scenarios and distance measures. One of our goals is to identify appropriate parameters for the domain of our experiment, so we include the results in their entirety.

In the second phase, we use the change time series of training dataset to find rules in the form of X => Y where X is a kth-motif and Y is a change derived by counting the number of changes (add/remove) following all patterns that belong to a kth-motif (within 85 seconds). This time interval is based on an expert's opinion that in WSsim no two changes will happen in a time interval less than 110 seconds, and that there is

Table 1. Frequent patterns (k^{th}-motifs) using Euclidean distance measure

window-Size (sec)	maxDist	min-Frequency	Number of Motifs	mean frequency	stdDev of frequency of motifs	time (sec)
		5	24	8.250	5.354	19.223
	0.9	10	5	13.400	1.837	11.446
		15	1	N/A	N/A	10.205
		5	54	11.685	13.955	19.550
90	1.0	10	23	16.783	8.364	19.733
		15	8	25.125	3.403	20.593
		5	74	17.149	20.724	35.804
	1.1	10	61	19.311	17.221	38.701
		15	31	25.419	11.462	32.830
		5	2	6.500	0.277	15.704
	1.3	10	0	N/A	N/A	10.274
		15	0	N/A	N/A	9.122
		5	52	10.750	12.260	25.695
120	1.5	10	17	17.118	5.636	24.147
		15	8	22.250	2.394	26.990
		5	85	17.376	20.237	47.273
	1.7	10	63	21.127	13.200	46.906
		15	48	23.563	10.205	45.908
		5	12	6.250	0.600	14.347
	2.3	10	0	N/A	N/A	9.900
		15	0	N/A	N/A	9.593
		5	45	11.289	6.690	24.705
180	2.6	10	27	13.370	3.692	22.666
		15	4	18.500	1.162	22.079
		5	62	19.758	14.422	44.910
	2.9	10	54	21.537	11.344	44.479
		15	46	22.848	9.866	45.427

a variable time lapse between the ideal time for a change to occur and the time when the change actually occurs. We evaluate these rules by calculating the confidence and support of each rule. Finally we evaluate feasibility of the proposed method by applying rules generated using the training dataset to the testing dataset.

5.2 Frequent Patterns

Euclidean distance is generally an efficient algorithm to calculate the distance between two time series as it relies on only the distance from the nth point in time series A to the nth point in time series B. In our experiments Euclidean distance executes around two times faster than DTW and FastDTW. However, the distances between time series are typically larger since DTW and FastDTW try to find the optimal alignment of two given time series. For this reason we had to use higher maxDist values for experiments using Euclidean distance compared to maxDist values in DTW and FastDTW.

Unlike our expectation FastDTW was slightly slower than DTW in our experiments even though FastDTW is linear to the size of input time series. This happened because of the big constant value involved in FastDTW. Furthermore the execution time reported for each scenario includes other calculations such as IO operations and creating/assigning objects that will be used for confidence/support calculations (these operations are fairly similar for all distance measures). The execution time difference of DTW and FastDTW does not seem substantial in our experiments.

Table 2. Frequent patterns (k^{th}-motifs) using DTW

window-Size (sec)	maxDist	min-Frequency	Number of Motifs	mean frequency	stdDev of frequency of motifs	time (sec)
		5	39	10.846	10.453	41.124
	0.03	10	13	16.846	5.190	45.653
		15	5	23.600	1.610	44.112
		5	61	12.262	16.947	54.156
90	0.034	10	26	18.077	10.284	53.640
		15	8	29.000	4.185	55.292
		5	83	13.530	21.889	65.845
	0.038	10	39	19.923	13.042	65.455
		15	26	23.500	10.031	64.746
		5	13	6.385	0.892	43.567
	0.04	10	0	N/A	N/A	41.193
		15	0	N/A	N/A	42.789
		5	55	8.691	5.951	53.439
120	0.048	10	11	12.545	1.285	54.416
		15	0	N/A	N/A	53.436
		5	89	12.180	15.289	81.247
	0.056	10	48	15.792	9.449	80.772
		15	14	23.143	3.526	80.854
		5	31	9.161	4.991	91.183
	0.08	10	10	12.400	1.892	92.143
		15	1	18.000	0.000	89.622
		5	93	11.409	16.501	114.778
180	0.1	10	44	15.705	9.679	113.015
		15	16	20.313	6.587	115.650
		5	147	13.122	30.854	151.593
	0.12	10	72	19.139	19.472	140.985
		15	39	24.231	14.335	140.465

5.3 Rule Evaluation

Confidence and support is calculated for each kth-motif (frequent pattern) and expected change tuple. Table 4 describes the details of investigating changes after k^{th}-motifs of a scenario (highlighted grey in Table 2) where distanceMeasure = DTW, windowSize = 90 seconds, maxDist = 0.034, and minFrequency = 15. This scenario results in 8 k^{th}-motifs with frequency mean and standard deviation of 29.000 and 4.185 respectively. The results for confidence/support in our dataset are close to zero for *add* actions however the results are promising for remove actions.

The distance of patterns in k^{th}-motifs before changes must be quite high in a dataset to result in values near to 0. We ran a bottom-up experiment to investigate this issue by calculating the actual distance among the time windows immediately before

Table 3. Frequent patterns (k^{th}-motifs) using FastDTW

window-Size (sec)	maxDist	min-Frequency	Number of Motifs	mean frequency	stdDev of frequency of motifs	time (sec)
		5	28	9.750	7.113	85.568
	0.03	10	8	15.125	3.116	76.284
		15	4	18.750	1.438	75.891
		5	50	10.580	12.360	85.609
90	0.034	10	15	17.000	6.287	80.298
		15	5	26.000	1.468	68.668
		5	72	11.903	17.036	74.628
	0.038	10	32	17.031	10.448	74.870
		15	10	26.100	4.901	77.882
		5	4	6.250	0.346	71.001
	0.04	10	0	N/A	N/A	78.423
		15	0	N/A	N/A	70.005
		5	41	7.073	2.280	78.974
120	0.048	10	0	N/A	N/A	81.015
		15	0	N/A	N/A	80.025
		5	68	10.088	9.505	99.894
	0.056	10	24	14.208	3.618	105.649
		15	9	17.444	3.618	98.460
		5	20	7.350	2.623	107.593
	0.08	10	2	11.000	0.000	109.208
		15	0	N/A	N/A	108.354
		5	63	9.238	8.563	128.869
180	0.1	10	19	13.000	4.000	125.953
		15	2	21.500	1.067	127.153
		5	129	10.798	18.632	153.395
	0.12	10	52	15.596	10.156	154.956
		15	18	21.056	5.860	154.897

Table 4. Confidence and support of kth-motifs of a single scenario

k^{th}-motif index	Frequency of kth-motif	ADD		REMOVE	
		confidence	support	confidence	Support
1	39	NA	NA	0.949	0.500
2	35	NA	NA	0.971	0.500
3	34	NA	NA	0.912	0.500
4	33	NA	NA	0.970	0.375
5	33	NA	NA	1.000	0.500
6	24	NA	NA	1.000	0.375
7	18	NA	NA	0.944	0.625
8	16	NA	NA	0.938	0.625

changes (*adds* and *removes*). Since we assume that the windows immediately before a change should be similar, this experiment tests the distance between the various windows. In this experiment we created a list of time series before *adds* (pre-add trends), and a list of time series before *removes* (pre-remove trends) in the training dataset. We then calculated the distance from each trend to all other trends in each list. Figure 1 and 2 describe the mean distance and standard deviation of distance of

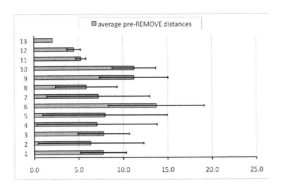

Fig. 1. Euclidean distance of pre-remove trends in training dataset represented

pre-remove trends and pre-add trends respectively. The results show that the distance of pre-add trends are by far higher than distance of pre-remove trends and this confirms confidence/support values near to 0 for pre-add patterns in our experiments. In these cases we haven't found k^{th}-motifs that are followed by the event ADD, hence confidence and support are not defined for these cases (shown as NA in Table 4).

Our experiments show that calculating support and confidence of kth-motif is not effective for *add* actions on the datasets that we have, as trends before *adds* are very distant from each other. We also tried relaxing the maxDist measures, but the difference between the actual distance of pre-add trends and our maxDists is quite high. This means over-relaxing maxDist results in detecting a huge number of kth-motifs and might lead to over-fitting.

We evaluated rules generated for *remove* actions (k^{th}-motifs that belong to *remove* actions) in the training dataset on the testing dataset. We defined accuracy of the proposed method in each scenario as the percentage of *remove* changes that could be predicted using the rules generated in that test scenario. We included all scenarios that generate rules for the change *remove* using DTW on the training dataset (Table 2) if and only if their minFrequency is equal to 10 or higher and their confidence and

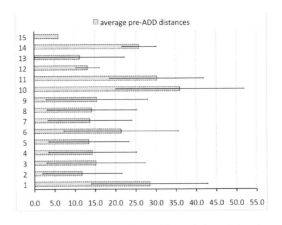

Fig. 2. Euclidean distance of pre-add trends in training dataset

Table 5. Accuracy of remove rules generated using training dataset in testing dataset

window-Size (sec)	maxDist	min-Frequency	Training dataset					Testing dataset
			mean confidence [%]	stdDev of confidence	Mean support [%]	stdDev of support	accuracy [%]	
90	0.03	10	0.915	0.116	0.254	0.111	62.5	
		15	0.948	0.008	0.680	0.048	37.5	
	0.034	10	0.911	0.423	0.138	0.080	100.0	
		15	0.960	0.007	0.500	0.063	100.0	
	0.038	10	0.876	0.822	0.102	0.057	100.0	
		15	0.891	0.464	0.164	0.055	100.0	
120	0.048	10	0.830	0.451	0.405	0.188	75.0	
	0.056	10	0.811	1.346	0.084	0.054	100.0	
		15	0.907	0.085	0.347	0.009	100.0	
	0.08	10	0.947	0.049	0.350	0.365	87.5	
180	0.1	10	0.822	0.669	0.095	0.067	100.0	
		15	0.844	0.126	0.273	0.163	87.5	
	0.12	10	0.784	2.666	0.050	0.063	0.0	
		15	0.818	0.344	0.115	0.041	100.0	

support is higher than 0.8 and 0.1 respectively. Also a scenario in the training set should result in more than 1 frequent pattern (motif) to be considered for evaluation on the testing set. Table 5 describes the accuracy of rules for *remove* action in each scenario in addition to their mean and standard deviation of both confidence and support.

Further investigation of the scenario where windowSize is 180, maxDist is 0.12, and minFrequency is 10 shows that none of the 72 motifs found in this setup have remove support higher than 0.1. Therefore none of the found rules in this scenario qualify for prediction on testing dataset, thus the accuracy of remove rules on testing set is 0 for this scenario. The average accuracy over all scenarios in table 5 is 82.1 percent.

6 Conclusions

We proposed a new method to identify actionable rules to understand the behavior of a system where a frequent pattern (k^{th}-motifs) in a given time series is followed by an action/event. First, we identify k^{th}-motifs using different distance measures: Euclidean distance, DTW, and FastDTW. We then calculate the support and confidence of each kth-motif. We tested rules that are generated using a training dataset on a testing dataset from WSsim - an SOA application configuration tool. Our results on WSsim dataset shows that our method is effective in learning rules for *remove* actions and reaches an average accuracy of over 80%. Although tuning parameters may produce higher accuracies, this may lead to over-fitting. The proposed method can be applied to SOA configuration tools to automate administrative tasks such as resource management or provide configuration recommendation in a decision support system for the administrator.

References

1. Lin, J., Keogh, E., Patel, P., Lonardi, S.: Finding motifs in time series. In: 8th ACM International Conference on Knowledge Discovery and Data Mining, Edmonton, Canada, pp. 53–68 (2002)
2. Arita, D., Yoshimatsu, H., Taniguchi, R.: Frequent motion pattern extraction for motion recognition in real-time human proxy. In: JSAI Workshop on Conversational Informatics, pp. 25–30 (2005)
3. Guyet, T., Garbay, C., Dojat, M.: Knowledge construction from time series data using a collaborative exploration system. Journal of Biomedical Informatics 40, 672–687 (2007)
4. Androulakis, I.P., Wu, J., Vitolo, J., Roth, C.: Selecting maximally informative genes to enable temporal expression profiling analysis. FoSystems Biology in Engineering (2005)
5. McGovern, A., Rosendahl, D., Kruger, A., Beaton, M., Brown, R., Droegemeier, K.: Understanding the formation of tornadoes through data mining. In: 5th Conference on Artificial Intelligence and its Applications to Environmental Sciences at the American Meteorological Society (2007)
6. Keogh, E., Kasetty, S.: On the Need for Time Series Data Mining Benchmarks: A Survey and Empirical Demonstration. In: 8th ACM SIGKDD International Conference on Knowledge Discovery and Data Mining, Edmonton, Canada, pp. 102–111 (2002)
7. Post, A.R., Harrison, J.H.: Temporal Data Mining. Clinics in Laboratory Medicine 28, 83–100 (2008)
8. Morchen, F.: Time Series Knowledge Mining, Dissertation: Philipps-University Marburg, Germany (2006)
9. Salvador, S., Chan, P.: FastDTW: Toward accurate dynamic time warping in linear time and space. In: 3rd Workshop on Mining Temporal and Sequential Data, ACM KDD 2004, Seattle, Washington, USA (2004)
10. Kruskall, J.B., Liberman, M.: The Symmetric Time Warping Problem: From Continuous to Discrete. In: Time Warps, String Edits and Macromolecules: The Theory and Practice of Sequence Comparison, pp. 125–161. Addison-Wesley Publishing Co., Reading (1983)
11. Smit, M., Nisbet, A., Stroulia, E., Iszlai, G., Edgar, A.: Toward a simulation-generated knowledge base of service performance. In: 4th International Workshop on Middleware for Service Oriented Computing, New York, USA, pp. 19–24 (2009)
12. Rockwell, G.: Tapor: Building a portal for text analysis. In: Siemens, R., Moorman, D. (eds.) Mind Technologies, Humanities Computing and the Canadian Academic Community, pp. 285–299. University of Calgary Press, Calgary (2006)
13. Sakoe, H., Chiba, S.: Dynamic programming algorithm optimization for spoken word recognition. IEEE Transactions Acoustics, Speech, and Signal Processing 26 (1978)
14. Itakura, S.: Minimum Prediction Residual Principle Applied to Speech Recognition. IEEE Transactions Acoustics, Speech, and Signal 23, 5–72 (1975)
15. Keogh, E., Pazzani, M.: Scaling up Dynamic Time Warping for Datamining Applications. In: 6th ACM SIGKDD International Conference on Knowledge Discovery and Data Mining, Boston, Massachuseetts, pp. 285–289 (2000)
16. Kim, S., Park, S., Chu, W.: An Index-based Approach for Similarity Search Supporting Time Warping in Large Sequence Databases. In: 17th International Conference on Data Engineering, Heidelberg, Germany, pp. 607–614 (2001)
17. Agrawal, R., Psaila, G., Wimmers, E.L., Zait, M.: Querying Shapes of Histories. In: 21st International Conference on Very Large Databases, Zurich, Switzerland, pp. 502–514 (1995)
18. Keogh, E., Chakrabarti, K., Pazzani, M., Mehrotra, S.: Locally Adaptive Dimensionality Reduction for Indexing Large Time Series Databases. In: Proceedings of ACM SIGMOD Conference on Management of Data, Santa Barbara, CA, USA, pp. 151–162 (2001)

19. Kalpakis, K., Gada, D., Puttagunta, V.: Distance Measures for Effective Clustering of ARIMA Time Series. In: Proceedings of the 2001 IEEE International Conference on Data Mining, San Jose, CA, pp. 273–280 (2001)
20. Fayyad, U., Reina, C., Bradley, P.: Initialization of Iterative Refinement Clustering Algorithms. In: Proceedings of the 4th International Conference on Knowledge Discovery and Data Mining, New York, NY, pp. 194–198 (1998)
21. Hetland, L., Saetrom, P.: Evolutionary rule mining in time series databases. Journal of Machine Learning 58, 107–125 (2005)
22. Freitas, A.: Data Mining and Knowledge Discovery with Evolutionary Algorithms. Springer, Heidelberg (2002)
23. Mannila, H., Toivonen, H., Verkamo, A.I.: Discovery of frequent episodes in event sequences. Journal of Data Mining and Knowledge Discovery 1, 259–289 (1997)
24. Höppner, F., Klawonn, F.: Finding informative rules in interval sequences. In: Hoffmann, F., Adams, N., Fisher, D., Guimarães, G., Hand, D.J. (eds.) IDA 2001. LNCS, vol. 2189, pp. 125–134. Springer, Heidelberg (2001)
25. Weiss, G.M., Hirsh, H.: Learning to predict rare events in event sequences. In: Agrawal, R., Stolorz, P., Piatetsky-Shapiro, G. (eds.) 4th International Conference on Knowledge Discovery and Data Mining (KDD), Menlo Park, USA, pp. 359–363 (1998)
26. Hetland, L., Saetrom, P.: Temporal rule discovery using genetic programming and specialized hardware. In: 4th International Conference on Recent Advances in Soft Computing (RASC), pp. 182–188 (2002)
27. Hipp, J., Guntzer, U., Nakhaeizadeh, G.: Algorithms for association rule mining – a general survey and comparison. SIGKDD Explorations 2, 58–64 (2000)
28. Agrawal, R., Srikant, R.: Mining sequential patterns. In: ICDE, Taiwan (1995)
29. Lo, D., Khoo, S.C., Liu, C.: Efficient mining of iterative patterns for software specification discovery. In: 13th ACM SIGKDD International Conference on Knowledge Discovery and Data Mining (KDD), San Jose, USA, pp. 460–469 (2007)
30. Mannila, H., Toivonen, H., Verkamo, A.I.: Discovery of frequent episodes in event sequences. Journal of Data Mining and Knowledge Discovery (DMKD) 1, 259–289 (1997)
31. Lo, D., Cheng, H., Han, J., Khoo, S.C.: Classification of software behaviors for failure detection: A discriminative pattern mining approach. In: 15th ACM SIGKDD International Conference on Knowledge Discovery and Data Mining, New York, NY, USA, pp. 557–566 (2009)
32. Hatonen, K., Klemettinen, M., Mannila, H., Ronkainen, P., Toivonen, H.: Knowledge discovery from telecomunication network alarm databases. In: 12th International Conference of Data Engineering, ICDE (1996)
33. Agrawal, R., Mannila, H., Srikant, R., Toivonen, H., Verkamo, A.I.: Fast discovery of association rules. In: Fayyad, U.M., Piatetsky-Shapiro, G., Smyth, P., Uthurusamy, R. (eds.) Advances in Knowledge Discovery and Data Mining, pp. 307–328. AAAI Press, MIT Press, Menlo Park, Cambridge (1996)
34. Savasere, Omiecinski, E., Navathe, S.: An efficient algorithm for mining association rules in large databases. In: VLDB Conference, Zurich, Switzerland (1995)
35. Zaki, M.J., Parthasarathy, S., Ogihara, M., Li, W.: New algorithms for fast discovery of association rules. In: Proceedings of 3rd International Conference on Knowledge Discovery and Data Mining (1997)
36. Keogh, E., Lonardi, S., Chiu, W.: Finding Surprising Patterns in a Time Series Database in Linear Time and Space. In: 8th ACM SIGKDD International Conference on Knowledge Discovery and Data Mining, Edmonton, Canada, pp. 550–556 (2002)

An Envelope-Based Approach
to Rotation-Invariant Boundary Image Matching

Sang-Pil Kim, Yang-Sae Moon, and Sun-Kyong Hong

Department of Computer Science, Kangwon National University, Korea
{spkim,ysmoon,hongssam}@kangwon.ac.kr

Abstract. Supporting the rotation invariance is crucial to provide more intuitive matching results in boundary image matching. Computing the rotation-invariant distance, however, is a very time-consuming process since it requires a lot of Euclidean distance computations for all possible rotations. To solve this problem, we propose a novel notion of *envelope-based lower bound*, and using the lower bound we reduce the number of distance computations dramatically. We first present a single envelope approach that constructs a single envelope from a query sequence and obtains a lower bound of the rotation-invariant distance using the envelope. This single envelope approach, however, may cause bad performance since it may incur a smaller lower bound due to considering all possible rotated sequences in a single envelope. To solve this problem, we present a concept of *rotation interval*, and using it we generalize the single envelope lower bound to the *multi-envelope* lower bound. Experimental results show that our envelope-based solutions outperform existing solutions by one to three orders of magnitude.

1   Introduction

Owing to recent advances in computing power and storage devices, similarity search on large time-series databases, called *time-series matching* [3,5,6,9], and its applications have been actively studied. In this paper we focus on the *boundary image matching* for a large image database. Boundary image matching converts (boundary) images to time-series as shown in Figure 1 [8,10], and it identifies similar images using the time-series matching techniques [7,8,10,12].

In boundary image matching, supporting the rotation invariance is crucial to provide more intuitive matching results [7,12].

Definition 1. Given two sequences $Q = \{q_0, \ldots, q_{n-1}\}$ and $S = \{s_0, \ldots, s_{n-1}\}$, their *rotation-invariant distance* $RID(Q, S)$ is defined as Eq. (1).

$$RID(Q, S) = \min_{j=0}^{n-1} D(Q^j, S) = \min_{j=0}^{n-1} \sqrt{\sum_{i=0}^{n-1} \left| q_{(j+i)\%n} - s_i \right|^2}, \tag{1}$$

where $Q^j = \{q_j, q_{j+1}, \ldots, q_{n-1}, q_0, \ldots, q_{j-2}, q_{j-1}\}$, $D(Q, S)$ is the Euclidean distance between Q and S, i.e., $D(Q, S) = \sqrt{\sum_{i=0}^{n-1} |q_i - s_i|^2}$, and % is the modular operator.   □

A. Cuzzocrea and U. Dayal (Eds.): DaWaK 2011, LNCS 6862, pp. 382–393, 2011.
© Springer-Verlag Berlin Heidelberg 2011

In Definition 1, Q^j is obtained from Q by rotating it j times, and we call Q^j the *j-rotation sequence* of Q. For example, 1-rotation sequence of Q is $Q^1 = \{q_1, \ldots, q_{n-1}, q_0\}$, and 5-rotation sequence of Q is $Q^5 = \{q_5, \ldots, q_{n-1}, \ldots, q_4\}$. As shown in Eq. (1), we get the rotation-invariant distance by considering all possible j-rotation sequences.

Definition 2. Given a query sequence Q and the user-specified tolerance ϵ, the *rotation-invariant image matching* is the problem of finding all data sequences whose rotation-invariant distances from Q are less than or equal to ϵ.   □

Definitions 1 and 2 show that, for each data sequence of length n, we need $\Theta(n)$ of Euclidean distance computations (i.e., $\Theta(n^2)$ of time complexity), and which is a very time-consuming process for a large number of data sequences [7,12].

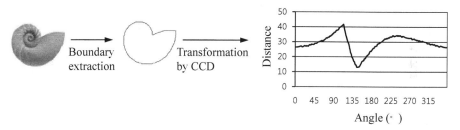

Fig. 1. An example of converting an image to a corresponding time-series by CCD

In this paper we present a novel notion of *envelope-based lower bound*, and using the lower bound we significantly reduce the number of rotation-invariant distance computations that frequently occur in evaluating the rotation-invariant image matching. To this end, we first present a concept of *single envelope* as follows: for a query sequence Q, its single envelope $[L, U]$ is a high-dimensional minimum bounding rectangle that bounds all possible j-rotation sequences of Q, where L (or U) represents a sequence with lowermost (or uppermost) entries of O^j's. We formally prove that the distance between the envelope $[L, U]$ and a data sequence S, $D([L, U], S))$, is a lower bound of the rotation-invariant distance $RID(Q, S)$. Thus, if $D([L, U], S)$ is greater than ϵ, computing $RID(Q, S)$ is no more necessary. We note that computing $D([L, U], S)$ is much simpler than $RID(Q, S)$. We use this pruning property to reduce the number of $RID(Q, S)$ computations and eventually to improve the overall matching performance.

The single envelope-based approach, however, has a problem that its lower bound is not small enough to fully exploit the pruning effect. This is because the envelope $[L, U]$ should bound all possible rotation sequences Q^j's, considering all possible Q^j's produces the larger envelope, and the larger envelope incurs the smaller lower bound. To solve this problem, we present a concept of *rotation interval*, and using it we generalize the single envelope lower bound to the *multi-envelope* lower bound. We obtain rotation intervals by dividing all rotation sequences, Q^j's, into multiple disjoint groups and construct an envelope for each interval by considering its own Q^j's. Since each rotation interval contains only a part of rotation sequences, its corresponding envelope is obviously smaller than a single envelope, and those multiple envelopes eventually produce a tight lower bound, which exploits the large pruning effect. In this paper we formally derive the multi-envelope lower bound; based on it, we propose a multi-envelope matching algorithm. Experimental results show that, compared with existing algorithms, our envelope-based solutions significantly improve the overall performance by one to three orders of magnitude.

2   Related Work and Existing Algorithms

Time-series matching is the problem of finding data sequences similar to the given query sequence [2,3,5,6,9]. Boundary image matching [7,8,12,10] handled in this paper is one of the important applications in these time-series matching solutions. Image matching [4,11], also known as content-based image retrieval (CBIR), identifies data images similar to the given query image by using various features of images. The representative features are colors, textures, and shapes [11,12]. Among these features, we focus on shape features of an image. Main considerations of the shape-based image matching are object boundaries or regions contained in an image [13]. In this paper we use the centroid contour distance (CCD in short) [7,8,12], which is the simplest method that uses boundary features of an image. As shown in Figure 1, CCD maps a boundary image to a time-series of length n [8,10]. Using CCD we can map boundary images to time-series and exploit time-series matching techniques in boundary image matching.

A few recent works were reported in using time-series of boundary images. First, using the rotation-invariant property of DFT magnitudes Vlachos et al. [12] proposed a novel solution to rotation-invariant image matching. Second, Keogh et al. [7] showed that their tight lower bound LB_Keogh [6] could also be used in rotation-invariant image matching and provided a novel solution for the DTW distance as well as the Euclidean distance. Third, our previous work [8,10] proposed efficient solutions for noise control or scaling-invariant boundary image matching. All these solutions, however, focus on reducing the number of candidate data sequences through the filtering process, and computing the rotation/scaling-invariant distances for these filtered candidates is still and inevitably necessary. It means that our solution can be applied to their post-processing part of computing the rotation-invariant distances, and accordingly, our solution is orthogonal to the previous solutions.

Algorithm 1 shows a straightforward solution to rotation-invariant image matching, called RI-Naive. For each data sequence S (Line 2), RI-Naive calculates the rotation-invariant distance from Q and investigates whether $RID(Q,S)$ is less than or equal to ϵ (Lines 3 to 8). We next derive RI-EA by applying the *early abandon* [7] to RI-Naive. The early abandon stops the distance computation if the intermediate distance exceeds the given tolerance, and it is known to reduce a large number of multiplications and summations. That is, in computing $D(Q^j, S)$ of RI-Naive (Line 4), the early abandon immediately stops the further computation if the intermediate square sum is greater than the squared tolerance (i.e., $\sum_{i=0}^{t} |q_{(j+i)\%n} - s_i|^2 > \epsilon^2, t < n$). Except using the early abandon, RI-EA has the same structure of RI-Naive. Existing matching solutions [7,12] use RI-Naive (or RI-EA) for computing the rotation-invariant distance between query and data sequences, and their performance can be improved by replacing RI-EA as our algorithms to be proposed.

Algorithm 1. RI-Naive (query sequence Q, a set $\mathbb{S}$ of data sequences, tolerance ϵ)

1: $\mathbb{R} := \emptyset$;   // $\mathbb{R}$ is the result set.
2: **for each** data sequence $S \in \mathbb{S}$ **do**
3:        **for** $j := 0$ **to** $(n-1)$ **do**   // investigate all j-rotation sequences one by one.
4:            **if** $D(Q^j, S) \leq \epsilon$ **then**   // if Q^j is similar to S,
5:                $\mathbb{R} := \mathbb{R} \cup \{S\}$;   // include S in the result set $\mathbb{R}$.
6:                **break**;
7:            **end-if**
8:        **end-for**
9: **end-for**
10: **return** $\mathbb{R}$; // return the result set containing rotation-invariant similar sequences.

---

3   Single Envelope Lower Bound and Its Matching Algorithm

A big performance problem of RI-Naive and RI-EA is incurring a large number of Euclidean distance computations. In particular, for a large number of data sequences, this higher complexity becomes a critical issue of performance degradation. Thus, in this paper we present an envelope-based lower bound so as to improve the performance of rotation-invariant image matching. We compute the envelope-based lower bound as the distance between the envelope of a query sequence and a data sequence.

Definition 3. Given a query sequence Q, we organize its *envelope* $[L, U] = [\{l_0, \ldots, l_{n-1}\}, \{u_0, \ldots, u_{n-1}\}]$ by Eq. (2) and define the distance between $[L, U]$ and a data sequence S, $D([L, U], S)$, as Eq. (3).

$$l_i = \min_{j=0}^{n-1}(i^{\text{th}} \text{ entry of } Q^j) = \min_{j=0}^{n-1} q_{(i+j)\%n},$$

$$u_i = \max_{j=0}^{n-1}(i^{\text{th}} \text{ entry of } Q^j) = \max_{j=0}^{n-1} q_{(i+j)\%n}, \text{ where } i = 0, \ldots, n-1. \quad (2)$$

$$D([L, U], S) = \sqrt{\sum_{i=0}^{n-1} \begin{cases} |s_i - u_i|^2, & \text{if } s_i > u_i; \\ |s_i - l_i|^2, & \text{if } s_i < l_i; \\ 0, & \text{otherwise.} \end{cases}} \quad (3)$$

Lemma 1 shows the lower bound property of the distance $D([L, U], S)$.

Lemma 1. *Given a query sequence Q and a data sequence S, $D([L,U],S)$ is a lower bound of $RID(Q,S)$. That is, $D([L,U],S) \leq RID(Q,S)$ holds.*

PROOF: The Euclidean distance between Q and S is $\sqrt{\sum_{i=0}^{n-1} |q_i - s_i|^2}$. According to Eq. (2), the lowermost and the uppermost sequences L and U are obtained from the smallest and the largest entries of Q, respectively, and thus, all the entries of Q are resided in between L and U. That is, $l_i \leq q_i \leq u_i$ holds obviously. Here we know that if $s_i > u_i$, $|s_i - q_i| \geq |s_i - u_i|$ holds by $q_i \leq u_i$; if $s_i < l_i$, $|s_i - q_i| \geq |s_i - l_i|$ holds by $l_i \leq q_i$; otherwise (i.e., $l_i \leq s_i \leq u_i$), $|s_i - q_i| \geq 0$ holds obviously. Thus, $D([L,U],S)$ obtained by summing $|s_i - u_i|^2$, $|s_i - l_i|^2$, and 0 should be less than or equal to $RID(Q,S)$ obtained by summing $|s_i - q_i|^2$. Therefore, $D([L,U],S)$ is a lower bound of $RID(Q,S)$.   □

For simplicity, we hereafter denote the lower bound $D([L,U],Q)$ by $LB_{SE}(Q,S)$, where SE stands for Single Envelope. By using $LB_{SE}(Q,S)$, we can discard a large number of data sequences in advance without computing their complex rotation-invariant distances. That is, if $LB_{SE}(Q,S)$ is greater than ϵ, we can conclude that S is not similar to Q without computing their actual rotation-invariant distance $RID(Q,S)$. Thus, by computing $RID(Q,S)$ only for the case of $LB_{SE}(Q,S) \leq \epsilon$, we can reduce actual rotation-invariant distance computations. We now propose Algorithm 2, called RI-SE, as a rotation-invariant matching algorithm that exploits $LB_{SE}(Q,S)$ to prune unnecessary distance computations. Computational complexity of $LB_{SE}(Q,S)$ is merely $\Theta(n)$, which is lower than $\Theta(n^2)$ of $RID(Q,S)$, and thus, RI-SE can improve the overall matching performance if $LB_{SE}(Q,S)$ works well as a lower bound.

RI-SE of Algorithm 2, however, has a problem that, if differences of entries in Q are large, it may not fully exploit the pruning effect due to the large envelope $[L,U]$ (i.e., due to the small $LB_{SE}(Q,S)$).

Example 1. Figure 2 shows sequences of length 360 converted from boundary images. Figure 2(a) shows a query sequence Q, its envelope $[L,U]$, and a data sequence S. The shaded area in Figure 2(b) represents the rotation-invariant distance $RID(Q,S)$, and the shaded area in Figure 2(c) represents its single envelope lower bound $LB_{SE}(Q,S)$, which is actually empty. As shown in

---

Algorithm 2. RI-SE (query sequence Q, a set $\mathbb{S}$ of data sequences, tolerance ϵ)

1: Construct L and U from Q;   // organize an envelope $[L,U]$ from Q.
2: $\mathbb{R} := \emptyset$;   // $\mathbb{R}$ is the result set.
3: **for each** data sequence $S \in \mathbb{S}$ **do**
4:       **if** $LB_{SE}(Q,S) \leq \epsilon$ **then**   // discard S immediately if $LB_{SE}(Q,S) > \epsilon$
5:          **if** $RID(Q,S) \leq \epsilon$ **then**   // compute the actual rotation-invariant distance

6:                   $\mathbb{R} := \mathbb{R} \cup \{S\}$;   // include S in the result
7:             **end-if**
8:       **end-for**
9: **end-for**
10: **return** $\mathbb{R}$;   // return the result set containing rotation-invariant similar sequences.

Figure 2(a), the envelope $[L, U]$ is determined by the *maximum* and the *minimum* among all entries of Q. Thus, $[L, U]$ might be too large, and accordingly, the lower bound $LB_{SE}(Q, S)$ computed from $[L, U]$ might be quite smaller than the actual rotation-invariant distance $RID(Q, S)$. In Figures 2(b) and 2(c), $RID(Q, S)$ is 137.8, but $LB_{SE}(Q, S)$ is merely 0, which means that $LB_{SE}(Q, S)$ does not work as a lower bound of $RID(Q, S)$.   □

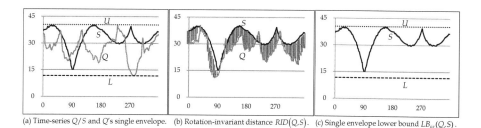

(a) Time-series Q/S and Q's single envelope.   (b) Rotation-invariant distance $RID(Q,S)$.   (c) Single envelope lower bound $LB_{SE}(Q,S)$.

Fig. 2. An example of $RID(Q, S)$ and $LB_{SE}(Q, S)$

4   Multi-envelope Lower Bound and Its Matching Algorithm

RI-SE makes an envelope by bounding all possible rotation sequences Q^j's, and this incurs a smaller lower bound. To overcome this problem, we present a *multi-envelope* approach that divides possible j's into multiple intervals, obtains a local lower bound from each interval, and finally get a global lower bound from those local lower bounds. The intuition behind is that a local lower bound of only a part of Q^j's will be larger than $LB_{SE}(Q, S)$ of all possible Q^j's, and a global lower bound derived from locals will also be larger than $LB_{SE}(Q, S)$. To explain the multi-envelope approach, we first generalize the rotation-invariant distance using a concept of rotation interval.

Definition 4. Let $Q^a, Q^{a+1}, \ldots, Q^b$ be the rotation sequences of a query sequence Q, which are obtained by rotating Q by $a, a + 1, \ldots, b$ times, respectively. Then, the minimum Euclidean distance from $Q^a, Q^{a+1}, \ldots, Q^b$ to a data sequence S is defined as the *rotation-invariant distance over rotation interval* $[a, b]$, and we denote it by $RID(Q^{[a,b]}, S)$. That is, $RID(Q^{[a,b]}, S)$ is computed as Eq. (4).

$$RID(Q^{[a,b]}, S) = \min_{j=a}^{b} D(Q^j, S) = \min_{j=a}^{b} \sqrt{\sum_{i=0}^{n-1} \left| q_{(i+j)\%n} - s_i \right|^2}. \qquad (4)$$

We also call $[a, b]$ the *rotation interval* of $RID(Q^{[a,b]}, S)$.   □

We now present how to construct an envelope for rotation interval $[a, b]$ in Definition 5 and explain its lower bound property in Lemma 2.

Definition 5. Given a query sequence Q and a rotation interval $[a, b]$, we orga-
nize $L^{[a,b]} = \left\{ l_0^{[a,b]}, \ldots, l_{n-1}^{[a,b]} \right\}$ and $U^{[a,b]} = \left\{ u_0^{[a,b]}, \ldots, u_{n-1}^{[a,b]} \right\}$ by Eq. (5) and call
this pair $[L^{[a,b]}, U^{[a,b]}]$ the *envelope of* Q *over* $[a, b]$. We also define the distance
between $[L^{[a,b]}, U^{[a,b]}]$ and a data sequence S as Eq. (6).

$$
l_i^{[a,b]} = \min_{j=a}^{b}(i^{\text{th}} \text{ entry of } Q^j) = \min_{j=a}^{b} q_{(i+j)\%n},
$$

$$
u_i^{[a,b]} = \max_{j=a}^{b}(i^{\text{th}} \text{ entry of } Q^j) = \max_{j=a}^{b} q_{(i+j)\%n}, \quad \text{where } i = 0, \ldots, n-1. \quad (5)
$$

$$
D([L^{[a,b]}, U^{[a,b]}], S) = \sqrt{\sum_{i=0}^{n-1} \begin{cases} \left| s_i - u_i^{[a,b]} \right|^2, & \text{if } s_i > u_i^{[a,b]}; \\ \left| s_i - l_i^{[a,b]} \right|^2, & \text{if } s_i < l_i^{[a,b]}; \\ 0, & \text{otherwise.} \end{cases}} \quad (6)
$$

Intuitively speaking, $[L^{[a,b]}, U^{[a,b]}]$ is an envelope that bounds $Q^a, Q^{a+1}, \ldots, Q^b$
only rather than all possible rotation sequences of $[L, U]$.

Lemma 2. *Given a query sequence Q, a data sequence S, and a rotation interval $[a, b]$, $D([L^{[a,b]}, U^{[a,b]}], S)$ is a lower bound of $RID(Q^{[a,b]}, S)$. That is,
$D([L^{[a,b]}, U^{[a,b]}], S) \leq RID(Q^{[a,b]}, S)$ holds.*
PROOF: We omit the detailed proof since it is the same as Lemma 1. □

Considering a rotation interval ($[a, b]$ in Definition 5) rather than the whole interval ($[0, n-1]$ in Definition 3) has a big advantage of increasing the lower
bound. This is because $[L^{[a,b]}, U^{[a,b]}]$ will be narrower than $[L, U]$, and accordingly, $LB_{[a,b]}(Q, S)$ will be larger than $LB_{SE}(Q, S)$. For simplicity, we hereafter
denote the lower bound $D([L^{[a,b]}, U^{[a,b]}], S)$ by $LB_{[a,b]}(Q, S)$.

Example 2. In Figure 3, query and data sequences Q and S are the same as
those of Figure 2. The envelope in Figures 2(a) and 2(c) bounds all rotation
sequences in the whole interval $[0, 359]$; in contrast, the envelope in Figures 3(a)
and 3(c) bounds only 45 rotation sequences in the rotation interval $[0, 44]$. Figure
3(a) shows a query sequence Q, its envelope over $[0, 44]$, $[L^{[0,44]}, U^{[0,44]}]$, and a
data sequence S. The shaded area in Figure 3(b) represents the rotation-invariant
distance over $[a, b]$, $RID(Q^{[0,44]}, S)$, and the shaded area in Figure 3(c) represents
its lower bound $LB_{[a,b]}(Q, S)$. In Figure 3(a), each entry of $L^{[0,44]}$ (or $U^{[0,44]}$)
is determined by the minimum (or the maximum) among only 45 entries of Q
rather than whole 360 entries. Thus, $[L^{[0,44]}, U^{[0,44]}]$ of Figure 3(a) is narrower
than $[L, U]$ of Figure 2(a), and $LB_{[0,44]}(Q, S)$ is larger than $LB_{SE}(Q, S)$. In this
example, $LB_{[0,44]}(Q, S)$ is 81.7 which is quite larger than 0 of $LB_{SE}(Q, S)$. □

Even though $LB_{[a,b]}(Q, S)$ is tighter than $LB_{SE}(Q, S)$, we cannot use $LB_{[a,b]}$
(Q, S) directly in rotation-invariant image matching since it is a lower bound
of $RID(Q^{[a,b]}, S)$ but not $RID(Q, S)$. That is, in Example 2, $LB_{[0,44]}(Q, S)$ is
larger than $LB_{SE}(Q, S)$ and exploits the pruning effect largely, but we cannot

simply replace $LB_{SE}(Q,S)$ as $LB_{[0,44]}(Q,S)$ because $LB_{[0,44]}(Q,S)$ is a lower bound of $RID(Q^{[0,44]},S)$ but not $RID(Q,S)$. For example, if $RID(Q^{[0,44]},S)$ is larger than $RID(Q^{[45,359]},S)$, $RID(Q,S)$ is determined by $RID(Q^{[45,359]},S)$ rather than $RID(Q^{[0,44]},S)$. To solve this problem, in our multi-envelope approach, we divide the whole rotation interval into multiple disjoint intervals, obtain local lower bounds from those intervals, and use their minimum as a lower bound of the whole interval.

Theorem 1. *For query and data sequences Q and S, if the whole interval $[0, n-1]$ is divided into m disjoint rotation intervals, $[a_0,b_0], [a_1,b_1], \ldots, [a_{m-1},b_{m-1}]$ $(a_0 = 0, a_k = b_{k-1} + 1, b_{m-1} = n - 1, k = 1, \ldots, m - 1)$, the minimum of lower bounds obtained from rotation intervals, $\min_{k=0}^{m-1} LB_{[a_k,b_k]}(Q,S)$, is a lower bound of $RID(Q,S)$.*

PROOF: Let Q^j be the rotation sequence that shows the minimum distance to S, i.e., $D(Q^j,S) = \min_{i=0}^{n-1} D(Q^i,S)$. Then, by Definition 1, $RID(Q,S) = D(Q^j,S)$ holds. Since the whole interval is divided into disjoint intervals, j should be included in a rotation interval, and we let this interval be $[a,b]$, i.e., $j \in [a,b]$. Then, $RID(Q^{[a,b]},S) = D(Q^j,S) = RID(Q,S)$ holds because $RID(Q,S) = D(Q^j,S)$ and $j \in [a,b]$ hold. It means that $LB_{[a,b]}(Q,S)$ is a lower bound of $RID(Q,S)$ as well as $RID(Q^{[a,b]},S)$. Therefore, the minimum of lower bounds of rotation intervals, $\min_{k=0}^{m-1} LB_{[a_k,b_k]}(Q,S)$, is a lower bound of $RID(Q,S)$. □

For simplicity, we hereafter denote the lower bound $\min_{k=0}^{m-1} LB_{[a_k,b_k]}(Q,S)$ by $LB_{ME}(Q,S)$, where ME stands for *Multiple Envelopes*. As we explained in Example 2, a *local* lower bound $LB_{[a,b]}(Q,S)$ is subject to be larger than $LB_{SE}(Q,S)$, and thus, the *global* lower bound $LB_{ME}(Q,S)$ obtained from those local lower bounds is also subject to be larger than $LB_{SE}(Q,S)$. Therefore, if we use $LB_{ME}(Q,S)$ instead of $LB_{SE}(Q,S)$, we can prune more unnecessary $RID(Q,S)$ computations. We thus present Algorithm 3, called RI-ME, as an advanced matching algorithm that exploits $LB_{ME}(Q,S)$. Even though computational complexity of $LB_{ME}(Q,S)$ is also $\Theta(n)$ as that of $LB_{SE}(Q,S)$, computing $LB_{ME}(Q,S)$ is more complex than $LB_{SE}(Q,S)$. Compared to $LB_{SE}(Q,S)$, however, $LB_{ME}(Q,S)$ exploits the better pruning effect and produces the higher performance.

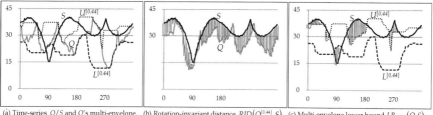

(a) Time-series Q/S and Q's multi-envelope. (b) Rotation-invariant distance $RID(Q^{[0,44]},S)$. (c) Multi-envelope lower bound $LB_{[0,44]}(Q,S)$.

Fig. 3. An example of $RID(Q^{[a,b]},S)$ and its $LB_{[a,b]}(Q,S)$

Algorithm 3. RI-ME (query sequence Q, a set $\mathbb{S}$ of data sequences, tolerance ϵ)

1: Divide the whole interval $[0, n-1]$ to m rotation intervals $[a_0, b_0], \ldots, [a_{m-1}, b_{m-1}]$;

2: Construct $[L^{[a_k, b_k]}, U^{[a_k, b_k]}]$ from Q for each $[a_k, b_k]$ $(k = 0, \ldots, m-1)$;
3: $\mathbb{R} := \emptyset$;   // $\mathbb{R}$ is the result set.
4: **for each** data sequence $S \in \mathbb{S}$ **do**
5:      **if** $LB_{ME}(Q, S) \leq \epsilon$ **then**   // discard S immediately if $LB_{ME}(Q, S) > \epsilon$
6:          **if** $RID(Q, S) \leq \epsilon$ **then**   // compute the actual rotation-invariant distance

7:                  $\mathbb{R} := \mathbb{R} \cup \{S\}$;   // include S in the result
8:          **end-if**
9:      **end-for**
10: **end-for**
11: **return** $\mathbb{R}$;   // return the result set containing rotation-invariant similar sequences.

---

5 Experimental Evaluation

5.1 Experimental Data and Environment

In the experiments we use two datasets. The first one is the SQUID dataset [1] that consists of 1,100 images of marine creatures. This dataset is publicly used for similarity search of images, and we call it *SQUID_DATA*. The second dataset consists of 10,259 images collected from the Web [8,10], and we call it *WEB_DATA*. In the experiments, we first extract boundary images from original images, and then convert them to time-series of length 360.

The hardware platform is a SUN Ultra workstation equipped with Ultra-SPARC IIIi CPU 1.34GHz, 1.0GB RAM, and 80GB hard disk, and its software platform is Solaris 10 operating system. We compare four algorithms: RI-Naive, RI-EA, RI-SE, and RI-ME. As the performance metrics, we measure the number of rotation-invariant distance $(RID(Q, S))$ computations and the actual wall clock time. The former is to show how many (unnecessary) distance computations are pruned by the proposed algorithms; the latter is to show how much performance is improved by the pruning effect. For RI-ME, we divide the whole interval into equal-sized rotation intervals. We need to determine the number m of rotation intervals in RI-ME. In the experiments, we set the number m to 36 since it shows the best performance for all experimental cases. Finding a theoretical optimal number m is another challenging issue since it varies by types of boundary images and lengths of sequences, and we leave it as a further study.

5.2 Experimental Results

Figure 4 shows the experimental result of SQUID_DATA, where we measure the number of $RID(Q, S)$ computations and the actual matching time by varying the tolerance. As shown in Figure 4(a), our RI-SE and RI-ME significantly reduce the number of $RID(Q, S)$ computations compared with RI-Naive and RI-EA. This confirms that our envelope-based approach prunes many unnecessary $RID(Q, S)$ computations. In Figure 4(a), RI-Naive and RI-EA show the same number of $RID(Q, S)$ computations. This is because RI-EA cannot reduce the number itself even though it improves the matching performance through the early abandon (see Figure 4(b)). In Figure 4(a), we note that RI-ME further reduces $RID(Q, S)$ computations compared with RI-SE, which means that $LB_{ME}(Q, S)$ is much tighter than $LB_{SE}(Q, S)$, and the pruning effect of RI-ME is much larger than that of RI-SE.

Figure 4(b) shows that our algorithms significantly reduce the wall clock time compared with the previous ones. (Note that y axis is a log scale.) The reason why our RI-SE and RI-ME outperform RI-Naive and RI-EA is in Figure 4(a), where our algorithms reduce $RID(Q, S)$ computations significantly. Unlike Figure 4(a), RI-EA outperforms RI-Naive since it exploits the early abandon [7] in computing $RID(Q, S)$. In all cases of Figure 4(b), however, our RI-SE and RI-ME outperform

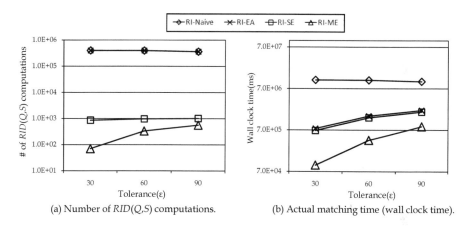

(a) Number of $RID(Q,S)$ computations.   (b) Actual matching time (wall clock time).

Fig. 4. Experimental results of SQUID_DATA

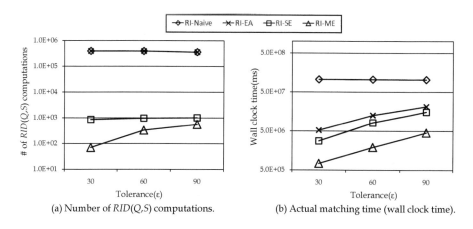

(a) Number of $RID(Q,S)$ computations.   (b) Actual matching time (wall clock time).

Fig. 5. Experimental results of WEB_DATA

RI-EA as well as RI-Naive. In particular, RI-ME show the best performance since it exploits the largest pruning effect. In summary, compared with RI-Naive and RI-EA, our RI-ME reduces the matching time by up to 111.9 and 7.5 times, respectively.

Figure 5 shows the experimental result of WEB_DATA. The overall trend of Figure 5 is very similar to that of Figure 4. The matching performance is ordered by RI-Naive, RI-EA, RI-SE and RI-ME. In Figure 5, RI-ME outperforms RI-Naive and RI-EA by up to 147.7 and 7.4 times, respectively. In summary of Figures 4 and 5, our envelope-based approach improves the performance significantly, regardless of data types and tolerances.

6   Conclusions

In this paper we proposed an envelope-based approach that significantly improved the matching performance in rotation-invariant boundary image matching. We first presented a single envelope lower bound, and using it we proposed an efficient matching algorithm, called RI-SE. We then introduced a multi-envelope lower bound by generalizing a single envelope to multiple envelopes. We explained why the multi-envelope lower bound was tighter than the single envelope lower bound, and using it we proposed another matching algorithm, called RI-ME. Experimental results showed that our envelope-based algorithms significantly outperformed existing algorithms. These results indicate that our envelope-based approach is excellent in handling a large volume of image databases that require frequent computing of rotation-invariant distances.

Acknowledgement. This research was supported by Basic Science Research Program through the National Research Foundation of Korea (NRF) funded by the Ministry of Education, Science and Technology (2010-0002518).

References

1. Abbasi, S., Mokhtarian, F., Kittler, J.: Search for Similar Shapes in the SQUID System: Shape Queries Using Image Databases (2005),
   http://www.ee.surrey.ac.uk/CVSSP/demos/css/demo.html
2. Chan, K.-P., Fu, A.W.-C., Yu, C.T.: Haar Wavelets for Efficient Similarity Search of Time-Series: With and Without Time Warping. IEEE Trans. on Knowledge and Data Engineering 15(3), 686–705 (2003)
3. Faloutsos, C., Ranganathan, M., Manolopoulos, Y.: Fast Subsequence Matching in Time-Series Databases. In: Proc. of Int'l Conf. on Management of Data, ACM SIGMOD, Minneapolis, Minnesota, pp. 419–429 (May 1994)
4. Gonzalez, R.C., Woods, R.E.: Digital Image Processing, 2nd edn. Prentice Hall, New Jersey (2002)
5. Han, W.-S., Lee, J., Moon, Y.-S., Hwang, S.-W., Yu, H.: A New Approach for Processing Ranked Subsequence Matching Based on Ranked Union. In: Proc. of Int'l Conf. on Management of Data, ACM SIGMOD, Athens, Greece (June 2011)

6. Keogh, E.J.: Exact Indexing of Dynamic Time Warping. In: Proc. of the 28th Int'l Conf. on Very Large Data Bases, Hong Kong, pp. 406–417 (August 2002)
7. Keogh, E.J., Wei, L., Xi, X., Vlachos, M., Lee, S.-H., Protopapas, P.: Supporting Exact Indexing of Arbitrarily Rotated Shapes and Periodic Time Series under Euclidean and Warping Distance Measures. The VLDB Journal 18(3), 611–630 (2009)
8. Kim, B.-S., Moon, Y.-S., Kim, J.: Noise Control Boundary Image Matching Using Time-Series Moving Average Transform. In: Proc. of the 19th Int'l Conf. on Database and Expert Systems Applications, Turin, Italy, pp. 362–375 (September 2008)
9. Moon, Y.-S., Whang, K.-Y., Han, W.-S.: General Match: A Subsequence Matching Method in Time-Series Databases Based on Generalized Windows. In: Proc. of Int'l Conf. on Management of Data, ACM SIGMOD, Madison, Wisconsin, pp. 382–393 (June 2002)
10. Moon, Y.-S., Kim, B.-S., Kim, M.S., Whang, K.-Y.: Scaling-Invariant Boundary Image Matching Using Time-Series Matching Techniques. Data & Knowledge Engineering 69(10), 1022–1042 (2010)
11. Pratt, W.K.: Digital Image Processing, 4th edn. Eastman Kodak Company, Rochester (2007)
12. Vlachos, M., Vagena, Z., Yu, P.S., Athitsos, V.: Rotation Invariant Indexing of Shapes and Line Drawings. In: Proc. of ACM Conf. on Information and Knowledge Management, Bremen, Germany, pp. 131–138 (October 2005)
13. Zhang, D.Z., Lu, G.: Review of Shape Representation and Description Techniques. Pattern Recognition 37(1), 1–19 (2003)

Finding Fraud in Health Insurance Data with Two-Layer Outlier Detection Approach

Rob M. Konijn and Wojtek Kowalczyk

Department of Computer Science, VU University Amsterdam
{rmkonijn,wojtek}@few.vu.nl

Abstract. Conventional techniques for detecting outliers address the problem of finding isolated observations that significantly differ from other observations that are stored in a database. For example, in the context of health insurance, one might be interested in finding unusual claims concerning prescribed medicines. Each claim record may contain information on the prescribed drug (its code), volume (e.g., the number of pills and their weight), dosing and the price. Finding outliers in such data can be used for identifying fraud. However, when searching for fraud, it is more important to analyse data not on the level of single records, but on the level of single patients, pharmacies or GP's.

In this paper we present a novel approach for finding outliers in such hierarchical data. Our method uses standard techniques for measuring outlierness of single records and then aggregates these measurements to detect outliers in entities that are higher in the hierarchy. We applied this method to a set of about 40 million records from a health insurance company to identify suspicious pharmacies.

1 Introduction

The inspiration for this paper comes from a real life fraud detection problem in health insurance, in the pharmacy domain. The goal of fraud detection in this context is to identify the most suspicious pharmacies that could possibly be involved in fraudulent activities, rather than identifying single claims that are suspicious. The main reason for not focusing on single outliers is that recovering money from single claims is costly, and that it can harm the relationship between an insurance company and the involved pharmacy, especially in the case of false positives. On the other hand, if the insurance company can detect substantial fraud linked to multiple claims of the same pharmacy, this business relationship is no longer so important and a vigorous money recovery action can follow.

In contrast to typical approaches for finding single outliers, [6], we propose a novel method for finding *groups* of outlying records that belong to the same class. Our method was successfully applied to a large set of health insurance claims, helping to identify several pharmacies involved in fraudulent behaviour.

Our method for detecting group outliers works in two stages. In the first stage we calculate outlier scores of single records. We use here classical methods for outlier detection that are based on distance measures, [2], or density estimation, [5].

Next, we calculate a statistic to measure the *outlierness* of each groups of records, where groups form logical entities. In our case, each entity is formed by all claims

A. Cuzzocrea and U. Dayal (Eds.): DaWaK 2011, LNCS 6862, pp. 394–405, 2011.

related to a pharmacy, or a combination of a pharmacy and a type of medication. We propose four different statistics that are used to define the final outlier score of these entities: (1) a rank-based statistic, (2) a weighted rank-based statistic, (3) a statistic based on the binomial distribution, and (4) a statistic that is based on the mean of the outlier score. These statistics can be applied in different situations to different outlier scores.

The statistics can be computed over different segments of the data to obtain the final score. Extra information about outlying entities can be obtained by constructing, for each entity, a so-called *fraud set*: a set of suspicious claims from a given entity. A fraud set is a minimal set of outlying records that should be removed from the whole set in order to make it "normal" again. Another, very useful instrument for displaying fraud evidence is a *fraud scatter plot*. Each point on such a plot represents a single entity; the x and y coordinates of a point are, respectively, the outlier score of the corresponding fraud set and the total amount of money involved in this fraud set, *fraud amount*. The fraud scatter plot can be used by fraud investigators to decide whether they should investigate the most likely fraud cases, or to focus on cases that are less suspicious, but involve high amounts of money.

Our paper is organized as follows. We start with a brief overview of related work. Then we present two approaches for calculating outlier scores of single records: distance-based and density-based. In Section 4 we explain four methods for aggregating individual scores, a procedure for identifying fraud sets, and a method for visualizing results with help of the fraud scatter plot. Results of our experiments are presented in Section 5, while the last section contains conclusions and some recommendations for further research.

2   Related Work

There is a lot of literature about methods for detecting single outliers in data. They are extensively presented in general survey articles on outlier detection techniques: [7], [1], and [6].

The method described in this paper can be categorised as unsupervised outlier detection. Existing methods for unsupervised outlier detection (a missing label problem) can be split into the following categories: statistical methods and distance-based methods, with the later containing the sub-categories of depth-based methods, density-based methods, and clustering-based methods.

Depth-based methods measure the distance from a point to the center of the data. Points that have the highest distance are considered outliers. There are several definitions of depth, for example the Mahalanobis Depth, which is equal to the distance to the Mahalanobis distance to the mean of the data. Because outliers have a big impact on the location of the mean and the covariance matrix estimate, a robust estimate of these statistics can be used, [12]. The main disadvantage of depth-based methods is their inability of handling clusters in data – these methods assume that the data form a single cluster.

Distance-based methods require a distance measure to determine the distance between two instances. The main idea is that the distance between outlying instances and their neighbors is bigger than the distance between normal instances and their neighbors, [8].

Distance-based methods compare distances with respect to the whole dataset. Outlier score measures that are based on the distances between a specific point and points in its local neighborhood are called density-based methods. Examples are the Local Outlier Factor (LOF), [5], the Connectivity-based Outlier Factor (COF), [13], or the Multi-granularity Deviation Factor (MDEF), [10].

In the statistical community some methods have been investigated to detect multiple outliers at once. Based on a model fitted on the data, outliers are observations that deviate from the model, or that would deviate if the model were fitted without the observation (so-called a *deletion diagnostic*). There are two related issues, called *masking* and *swamping*, that have been investigated in [4]. Masking takes place in a situation when an outlier would not be revealed by calculating a single deletion diagnostic measure for each observation, but it would be detected by a multiple deletion diagnostic. The opposite situation, swamping, occurs when a pair of observations is declared anomalous only because one of the two is extreme: the bigger deviating observation *swamps* the smaller one.

To our best knowledge, the problem of finding a group of outliers that belong to the same entity (such as a pharmacy) has not been addressed yet in the existing literature.

3   Outlier Score for Single Records

In this section we present in more depth two approaches for calculating outlier scores for single records: distance-based and density-based. We start with some definitions and notations. Let D denote a set of n objects (called records or points) and let d denote a distance measure between these objects. The k-*distance* of p, denoted as k-$distance(p)$, is the distance of p to its k-th nearest neighbor. The k-*distance neighborhood* of p contains every object whose distance from p is not greater than the k-$distance(p)$. These objects are called the k-th nearest neighbors of p and are denoted by $S_k(p)$.

Distance-Based Scores. Distance-based methods are based on the proximity of points to each other according to a distance measure. There are several definitions possible that can be used to identify outliers. These definitions are usually based on the concept of the k-nearest neighbor, [11]. An object p is called a (k, n) outlier if no more than n-1 other points in the dataset have a higher value of the k-$distance$ than the point p itself. Note that this is a binary score: the top n points with the highest values of k-$distance$ are declared as an outlier, while all other observations are considered normal. Another definition is given in [8], who defines a $DB(perc, distance)$ outlier as follows: an object p in a dataset D is a $DB(perc, distance)$ outlier if at least fraction $perc$ of the objects in D lies further from p than $distance$. In other words, $distance$ can be seen as a radius around p, and if the percentage of points within this radius is smaller than $(1 - perc)$, p is declared anomalous. A yet another definition, [2], assigns a weight to each point p, which is defined as the sum of the k-$distance$ of all points within the k-$distance neighborhood$ of p. Outliers are those points that have the biggest weight. There are some small differences between the three definitions given above. The first definition by [11] does not provide a ranking of the outliers. For the definition by [8] it may be hard to set the parameters appropriately. The definition of [2] overcomes these problems, but is computationally expensive. We used in our experiments this later definition of the scoring function.

Density-Based Scores. Another scoring function that we used in our experiments is a modification of the well-known LOF score, [5], which is based on the idea of the probabilistic distance that is described in [9].

For the explanation of the LOF Score we first need some definitions. Using the same notation as before, the reachability distance of an object p with respect to an object o is defined as:

$$reachDist_k(p, o) = max(k-distance(p), distance(o, p)) \qquad (1)$$

This distance measure is used to correct for statistical deviations.

The density of each point is called the local reachability density of an object p. It is calculated as follows:

$$lrd_k(p) = (\frac{\sum_{o \in S_k(p)} reachDist_k(p, o)}{|S_k(p)|})^{-1} \qquad (2)$$

In other words, the density of p is the average reachability distance from its k-*distance neighborhood* to the point itself. For sparse regions, the value for lrd will be low, for dense regions it will be high.

Finally, the local outlier factor of an object p is defined as:

$$LOF_k(p) = \frac{\sum_{o \in S_k(p)} \frac{lrd_k(o)}{lrd_k(p)}}{|S_k(p)|} \qquad (3)$$

In other words, for an object p we compare its own density $lrd_k(p)$ with the density of the points in its k-*distance neighborhood*. If the densities are approximately equal, the LOF score will be close to one, if the density of p is relatively low, the LOF score will be high.

In our experiments we used a modified version of the LOF score, because it turned out to work better than other methods in detecting single outliers. We used the probabilistic distance, as defined in [9], to determine the *reachability distance*:

$$probReachDist_k(p, o) = max(pdist_{k,\varphi}(p), distance(o, p)), \qquad (4)$$

where $pdist_{k,\varphi}(p)$ denotes the probabilistic distance of p to its k neighborhood, as measured within the radius φ, i.e., the minimum distance for which φk neighbors of p are covered.

The formulas for calculating the local reachability density and the LOF score remain the same. Note that using the probabilistic distance can also be seen as using two parameters: k_1 to determine a context set S which is used to compare densities, and $k_2 = \varphi k_1$ to calculate the distances between points and eventually their densities.

4 Statistics per Entity

In this section we address our main problem: detection of groups of outliers that belong to the same entity. The proposed approach for this problem involves two steps: (1)

calculation of outlier scores of all records, and (2) calculation of a statistic to measure the outlierness of each entity. In this section we present four different statistics for measuring the entity outlierness.

Each of these statistics is used to quantify the difference between two samples: the set of scores of records belonging to the entity and the set of scores of records that do not belong to the entity. Most outlier measures do not have a direct probabilistic interpretation. Also the range of scores strongly depends on the data set, or even on the scaling of the data set. For some outlier measures only the rank is important, while for others we are mainly interested in relative values. Furthermore, different kinds of fraud are possible. In the case of pharmacies, all fraud can be committed in a single claim or with charges concerning a single patient, but the fraud can also be distributed over many charges, charging just a little more per claim. This is why different statistics are needed. We present four different statistics that can be used under different circumstances: a rank based statistic, a weighted rank based statistic, a statistic based on the binomial distribution, and a statistic that is the standardised residual. The binomial outlier score is different from the other three statistics because of the fact that it does not take the ordering of the outlier scores into account. This statistic works well in combination with single scores that provide a list of top-n outliers, or that provide a binary outlier score. The other three statistics mainly differ in robustness against the outlier score values. The ordering from least robust to most robust is: 1) standardised residual 2) weighted rank outlier score and 3) rank-based outlier score. The positive aspect of using a robust score to aggregate per entity, is that it is not affected by a very high score of one single point thereby declaring the whole entity anomalous. On the other hand, such a single point with a very high score may also be very interesting, which would favor the use of a non-robust score.

Additionally, we describe how to incorporate the monetary value that is related to analysed records in the detection process, and demonstrate how to construct *fraud sets*. Finally, we show how a *fraud scatter plot* can be used to support decisions concerning further investigation of identified suspicious entities.

4.1 Statistics per Entity

In this section we introduce several statistics to calculate the "outlierness" of an entity with respect to all other entities. The common idea behind all these statistics involves measuring the difference between two sets of numbers: a set of scores of all records from one entity and a set of scores of all other records from remaining entities. More precisely, let us suppose that our dataset has n records. For each record, we calculate an outlier score, so we have in total n outlier scores. Let us consider a single entity that we want to compare to other entities. The set of n scores can be split into $X_1, \ldots, X_{n1}$ and $Y_1, \ldots, Y_{n2}$, where $X_1, \ldots, X_{n1}$ are the scores of records from the entity under consideration, and $Y_1, \ldots, Y_{n2}$ are the scores of the remaining records. Now our problem can be formulated as follows: how to measure the difference between X and Y? In our experiments we used the following four methods of comparing X to Y.

Wilcoxon Mann-Whitney test with single outlier score. The first method is based on the popular, non-parametric two-sample test, called the Mann-Whitney-Wilcoxon rank-sum test, [3]. It defines the outlierness score of an entity as the p-value that is returned by the Mann-Whitney-Wilcoxon test when comparing values of sets X and Y to each other.

Weighted rank outlier score. The Mann-Whitney-Wilcoxon test uses only ranks of the scores and not their actual values. However, we can weight the ranks of elements in X and Y by their values: the bigger the outlier the bigger its impact on the final entity score. More precisely, we define:

$$Z_{ij} = \begin{cases} 0 \text{ if } X_i < Y_j \\ \frac{Y_j}{\sum_{k=1}^{n_2} Y_k} \text{ if } X_i > Y_j \end{cases} \tag{5}$$

and

$$U = \sum_{i=1}^{n_1} \sum_{j=1}^{n_2} Z_{ij} \tag{6}$$

For large n we can assume U to be normally distributed and parameters of this distribution can be calculated from the vector of the partial sums of the sorted vector Y. Given these parameters, one can easily find the corresponding p-value.

Binomial outlier score. The calculation of this score starts with calculating the sets of scores X and Y, as described earlier. Then both sets are combined and sorted. The top p percentage of scores are viewed as outliers, where p is a pre-specified parameter. Under this definition of an outlier, the number of outliers that belong to the set X follows a binomial distribution with expected value $n_1 p$ and variance $n_1 p(1 - p)$. The outlier score of X (relative to p) is now defined as $1 - cpdf(binomial(n_1, p), k)$, where k is the number of observed outliers in X, i.e., the mass of the right tail of the binomial distribution with the parameters n_1 and p that starts at k.

The value of parameter p is used to determine the percentage of records that are viewed as outliers. It can be set in different ways. In some cases the value of p is determined by a domain expert. The choice of p can also be based on the probability distribution of the outlier score function. One can approximate this distribution by using a histogram with two bins: one bin for 'low' outlier scores, and another one for 'high' outlier scores. The observations that fall into the bin of 'high' outlier scores are labeled as outliers, so p is the splitting point between the two bins. We estimate p by minimising the Kolmogorov-Smirnov distance, [3], between the distribution of the outlier score and the 'approximate' two-bin distribution. Another possibility is to use a heuristic that is based on the parameter p: for example, take the maximum outlier score per entity for a range of values for p. The disadvantage of this approach is that the final outlier entity score cannot be interpreted as a probability anymore.

Standardized residual of outlier score. This measure of entity outlierness is defined in terms of the average deviation from the mean of the outlier scores that belong to the given entity. The average standardized residual should follow a normal distribution. The corresponding p-value – the mass of the tail on the right from the observed value – is the outlier score.

4.2   Identifying Fraud Sets

Each approach described above uses a statistic U to describe the deviation of an entity. Because U follows a normal distribution, we can easily test the hypothesis that the observed value for U is equal to $E(U)$ with significance level α. This hypothesis will be rejected for the most outlying entities with the highest value of U. Suppose this hypothesis is rejected for an entity with a set of observations X. We define a *fraud set* for an entity X as the minimal set of records that should be removed from X in order to make the null hypothesis that the observed value of $U(X)$ is equal to $E(U(X))$ plausible (i.e., not to be rejected at a given significance level). Because the observations that should be removed are the ones with the highest outlier score, the fraud set is also the set of observations that should be investigated first, when checking if the entity is really outlying.

4.3   The Fraud Scatter Plot

Another very useful instrument for displaying fraud evidence is a *fraud scatter plot*: a graph of fraud amount versus outlier score of all records in the fraud set. Here, the *fraud amount* is defined as the total amount of money that is involved in the observations that are in the fraud set. The fraud scatter plot can be used by fraud investigators to decide whether they should investigate the most likely fraud cases, or to focus on cases that are less suspicious, but involve high amounts of money.

More precisely, for an arbitrary significance level α, the fraud scatter plot contains points, one per entity, with their x-coordinates being the outlierness score of an entity (we use the z-score of the observed value of U), and the y-coordinate being the the fraud amount.

4.4   Aggregation of Scores for Data Segments

In many applications financial transactions can be split into a number of segments. For example, claims can be organized into categories that are determined by the type of medicine involved, and patients allocated to segment per disease type. Each of the four statistics described earlier can be calculated for each segment and the resulting scores aggregated on the level of single entities. For the Wilcoxon-Mann-Whitney test and the statistic based on the binomial distribution, a normal approximation can be obtained (the other two statistics are already normally distributed). Let s_i be the z-score of an entity per segment, and S be $\frac{\sum_{i=1}^{n} s_i}{n}$, where n is the number of segments. The final outlier score of an entity is defined as $\Phi(S)$, where Φ is the cumulative probability density function (cpdf) of the standard normal distribution. This aggregation is not needed if there are no subsegments in the data.

5   Results and Analysis

Now we will describe some results that we obtained when applying our method to a relatively big set of 40 million records related to claims submitted by pharmacies. Each record contained information about the pharmacy (pharmacy ID), the prescribed medicine (type, subtype, product ID), cost, dosage, et cetera. In our research we have focused on three types of deviations: unusual prescriptions, errors that seem to be typos, and unusual number of "expensive" patients.

5.1   Strange Behavior in Prescribing Drugs

A common type of fraud in health insurance is called *unbundling*: a practice of breaking what should be a single charge into many smaller charges. The 'standard' formula for a single claim is $price = c + p * n$, where $price$ is the claim amount, c is a constant charge per claim, n is the number of units, and p is the price per unit. A pharmacy can commit unbundling fraud by splitting the charge into two or more charges, thereby earning the constant amount c twice (or more times). Two other common types of fraud are: delivering more units than stated on the prescription (and thus increasing turnover), and charging money for drugs that have never been delivered.

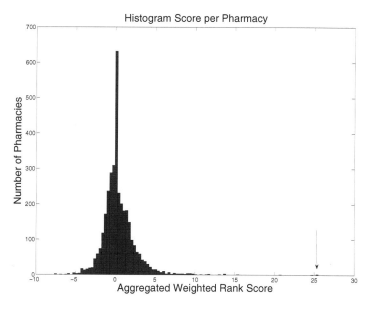

Fig. 1. Histogram of the Weighted Rank Score Statistic. There are two observations with a score higher than 25. We can also see that the distribution of the statistic is not completely normal due to some outliers and due to a peak around zero (these are pharmacies with very few claims).

First we split the data into different segments, one segment per drug type. For each segment we use the following variables for each patient X: X_1: the total number of units (pills) used by a patient within a year, X_2: the total claim amount of a patient within a year, X_3: the number of claims, X_4: $\sum_{i=1}^{n} a_i$, where n is the number of claims, and a_i is 1 if the patient visited his family doctor within two weeks before the claim, and zero otherwise.

An outlier in these dimensions indicates strange or fraudulent claim behavior. We calculate an outlier score for single observations first. For this application we use the modified LOF Score, as described in Section 3.

For each medicine type we calculated the weighted rank score, where each patient is assigned to one or more pharmacies. We aggregated all these scores by summing them up and then standardizing them. The final scores of all pharmacies are shown in Fig. 1.

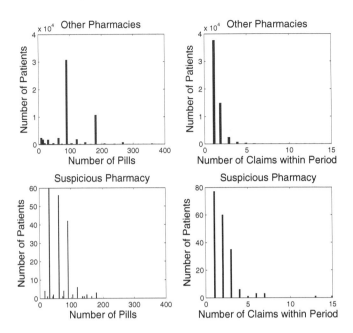

Fig. 2. Histograms of the 'number of pills prescribed' and the 'number of claims' for the drug type Aspirin. The two histograms below show the distribution of patients of the outlying pharmacy. The upper two histograms show the distribution of the other pharmacies. From these graphs it can be concluded that these distributions are different. The number of pills is much lower than expected, while the number of claims is higher: this is a signal for *unbundling* fraud.

We compared data from the two most outlying pharmacies with data from the remaining pharmacies. For the top outlying pharmacy the distributions of variables X_1 (the number of pills) and X_3 for the drug type 'Aspirin' are given in Figure 2.

5.2 Finding Typos

Sometimes pharmacies make mistakes when entering the number of units that is prescribed, thereby 'accidentally' overcharging. We calculated the following z-scores:

- X_1: the standardized claim amount,
- X_2: the claim amount, standardized at the drug type level,
- X_3: the claim amount divided by the total costs of the patient within a year, grouped at the drug type level and then standardized,
- X_4: the claim amount divided by the total costs made by the patient on the same drug, standardized.

Typos will score high within all dimensions, therefore we used as an outlier score for a single record the smallest one: $score = min(X_1, \ldots, X_4)$.

Because this score is really designed for detecting 'top-n' outliers, the binomial statistic to aggregate the outlier scores per pharmacy seems to be the most appropriate.

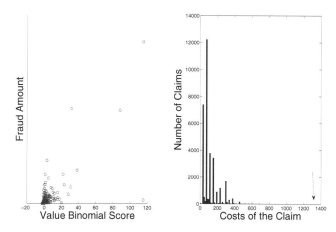

Fig. 3. The graph on the left shows the fraud scatter plot. The score according to the binomial statistic is plotted against the money that is involved in the claims. The most interesting pharmacy is the one in the upper right corner: it has a large deviation and a high fraud amount. The histogram on the right shows an example of an outlier of this pharmacy for the 'Glucose Test strip'. The outlying claim made by this pharmacy is the claim of about 1300 Euros. The pharmacy is outlying because it has many of such claims.

The value of the parameter p can be found after a few trial-and-error attempts followed by a manual inspection of found outliers. The fraud scatter plot and an example outlier are displayed in figure 3.

5.3   Patients with High Claim Costs

Pharmacies may also be delivering more units than stated on the prescription (and thus charging more money). The difference with a typo is that this time the claim amounts are not extremely high, but just a little higher than normal.

To discover this type of outliers we split the data into segments, using one drug type per segment. For each segment we defined the following two variables:

X_1: the claim amount,

X_2: the claim amount divided by the total costs per patient within a year.

We standardized both dimensions. Because we were interested in global outliers we used as an entity outlier score the mean distance to the k nearest neighbors, [2]. Next, we calculated the deviation from the mean statistic per patient per drug type, and aggregated the scores by summing them. Finally, we used the binomial outlier score to aggregate patient scores on the level of pharmacies. We estimated the parameter p by approximating the density of the score per patient by a histogram of two bins, see Figure 4. By inspecting the fraud scatter plot we could conclude that the most interesting outlier is the pharmacy with the highest amount of fraud. For this pharmacy we plotted some of its outlying claims within the drug type 'Erythropoietin' (a.k.a. Epo), see Figure 5. It is evident that those claims of this pharmacy are outliers, because of the high amounts per claim.

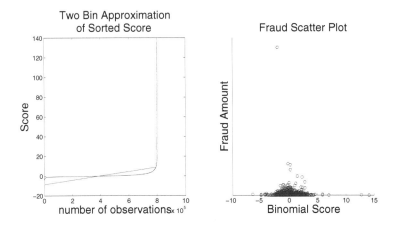

Fig. 4. The graph on the left shows how the cumulative distribution function of the LOF scores is approximated by a histogram of two bins. The bin sizes of this histogram are determined by minimizing the Kolmogorov-Smirnov Distance between the cdf and a function with two linear components. The graph on the right shows the fraud scatter plot. The x-axis shows the deviation from the expected value of the statistic and the y-axis shows the amount of money that is involved within the outlying transactions.

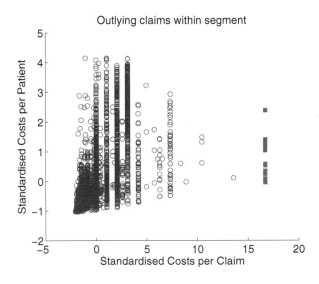

Fig. 5. Scatter plot of some of the outliers of the suspicious pharmacy for the drug 'Erythropoietin' (Epo). The outliers are the red squares on the right. The claims represented by the red squares are all delivered by the same pharmacy.

6   Conclusions and Further Research

We presented a novel approach for finding outlying entities in hierarchical data. Our method uses standard techniques for measuring outlierness of single records and then aggregates these measurements to detect outliers in entities that are higher in the hierarchy. Our approach turned out to work very well in a practical setup, where many fraud cases were detected relatively fast.

Further research will address the issue of adding apriori information about entities (such as pharmacies, hospitals or physicians) into the model. For example, it is well known that some pharmacies (e.g., internet or mail-order pharmacies) exhibit different claim patterns than conventional ones. Discovery and incorporation of this type of information into our method is a challenging research problem.

References

1. Agyemang, A., Barker: A comprehensive survey of numeric and symbolic outlier mining techniques. Intelligent Data Analysis 10(6/2006), 521–538 (2005)
2. Angiulli, F., Pizzuti, C.: Fast outlier detection in high dimensional spaces. In: Elomaa, T., Mannila, H., Toivonen, H. (eds.) PKDD 2002. LNCS (LNAI), vol. 2431, pp. 43–78. Springer, Heidelberg (2002)
3. Bain, Engelhardt: Introduction to Probability and Mathematical Statistics. Duxbury Press, Boston (1992)
4. Barnett, V., Lewis, T.: Outliers in Statistical Data. John Wiley and Sons, Chichester (1994)
5. Breunig, M.M., Kriegel, H.-P., Ng, R.T., Sander, J.: Lof: identifying density-based local outliers. SIGMOD Rec. 29(2), 93–104 (2000)
6. Chandola, V., Banerjee, A., Kumar, V.: Anomaly detection: A survey. ACM Computing Surveys (CSUR) 41, 15:1–15:58 (2009)
7. Hodge, V., Austin, J.: A survey of outlier detection methodologies. Artif. Intell. Rev. 22(2), 85–126 (2004)
8. Knorr, E.M., Ng, R.T.: Algorithms for mining distance-based outliers in large datasets. In: Unknown, pp. 392–403 (1998)
9. Kriegel, H.-P., Kröger, P., Schubert, E., Zimek, A.: Loop: local outlier probabilities. In: Proceeding of the 18th ACM Conference on Information and Knowledge Management, CIKM 2009, pp. 1649–1652. ACM, New York (2009)
10. Papadimitriou, S., Kitagawa, H., Gibbons, P.B., Faloutsos, C.: Loci: Fast outlier detection using the local correlation integral. In: International Conference on Data Engineering, p. 315 (2003)
11. Ramaswamy, S., Rastogi, R., Shim, K.: Efficient algorithms for mining outliers from large data sets. SIGMOD Rec. 29, 427–438 (2000)
12. Rousseeuw, P.J., Driessen, K.V.: A fast algorithm for the minimum covariance determinant estimator. Technometrics 41, 212–223 (1999)
13. Tang, J., Chen, Z., Chee Fu, A.W., Cheung, D.: A robust outlier detection scheme for large data sets. In: 6th Pacific-Asia Conf. on Knowledge Discovery and Data Mining, pp. 6–8 (2001)

Enhancing Activity Recognition in Smart Homes Using Feature Induction

Naveen Nair[1,2,3], Ganesh Ramakrishnan[2,1], and Shonali Krishnaswamy[3,1]

[1] IITB-Monash Research Academy, Old CSE Building, IIT Bombay
[2] Department of Computer Science and Engineering, IIT Bombay
[3] Faculty of Information Technology, Monash University
{naveennair,ganesh}@cse.iitb.ac.in,
Shonali.Krishnaswamy@infotech.monash.edu.au

Abstract. Hidden Markov Models (HMMs) are widely used in activity recognition. Ideally, the current activity should be determined using the vector of all sensor readings; however, this results in an exponentially large space of observations. The current fix to this problem is to assume conditional independence between individual sensors, given an activity, and factorizing the emission distribution in a naive way. In several cases, this leads to accuracy loss. We present an intermediate solution, viz., determining a mapping between each activity and conjunctions over a relevant subset of dependent sensors. The approach discovers features that are conjunctions of sensors and maps them to activities. This does away the assumption of naive factorization while not ruling out the possibility of the vector of all the sensor readings being relevant to activities. We demonstrate through experimental evaluation that our approach prunes potentially irrelevant subsets of sensor readings and results in significant accuracy improvements.

Keywords: Activity recognition, Feature induction, Hidden Markov Model.

1 Introduction

Efficient activity recognition has been a hot topic for researchers since the advent of Artificial Intelligence. An active application area for activity recognition is monitoring elderly activities in homes to ensure their well being. To monitor activities of large number of people living alone in houses and thereby detect unusual patterns of activities, which are indicators of their health condition, automatic activity recognition systems are used [1]. In the following paragraph, we provide a brief overview of a typical activity recognition setting.

A typical minimal intrusive activity recognition setting has on/off sensor devices, which senses user movements or object use, fixed at various locations inside a house. The nodes send binary (sensed) information to a base station/computer. A probabilistic model is trained initially using the information from the sensors and the user annotated information about the activities performed. Later, the

A. Cuzzocrea and U. Dayal (Eds.): DaWaK 2011, LNCS 6862, pp. 406–418, 2011.

model is used for predicting activities performed, based on sensor readings. The Hidden Markov Model (HMM) [5] and the Conditional Random Field (CRF) [6] are two popular probabilistic models used for activity recognition [4]. Kasteren et. al. in [4] reported better class accuracy (average percentage of time a class is predicted correctly) with HMM and better time slice accuracy (fraction of time slices predicted correctly) with CRF. We, in this paper, use HMM as the base line approach and investigate the effectiveness of our approach in HMM. We now give a brief introduction to HMM.

An HMM formulation consists of a hidden variable and an observable/emission variable at each time step. In activity recognition, the activity at each time step t is the label/hidden state y_t. The joint state of the sensors at each time step is the observation x_t. The hidden state y_t at time t is independent of all other variables given the previous hidden state y_{t-1} at time $t-1$ and the observable variable x_t at time t is independent of other variables given y_t. Using these independence assumptions, we can factorize the joint distribution of the sequence of observations (X) and labels (Y) into three factors: the initial state distribution $p(y_1)$, the transition distribution $p(y_t|y_{t-1})$, and the emission distribution $p(x_t|y_t)$ [10][5]. There fore, the joint distribution can be expressed as $p(X,Y) = \prod_{t=1}^{T} p(y_t|y_{t-1})p(x_t|y_t)$, where $p(y_1|y_0)$ is used instead of $p(y_1)$ to simplify notation. Parameters for the distributions are learned by maximizing the joint probability, $p(X,Y)$, of the paired observation and label sequences in the training data. During the inference phase, the parameters are used to determine the sequence of labels that best explains the given sequence of observations. This is efficiently computed using a dynamic programming algorithm called the Viterbi Algorithm [11]. We now discuss the limitations of traditional HMM in the domain of activity recognition.

In a traditional HMM setting for activity recognition, the observation value is a vector of all the sensor readings in the deployment. Thus there are 2^N possible values for the observation variable in a binary sensor deployment with N sensors, which is computationally expensive for learning and inference in real world settings. Typical approaches in activity recognition tend to assume independence between individual sensors given activity to perform naive factorization of the emission distribution [4]. Since the independence assumption is wrong in most of the real world problems, the method suffers from accuracy loss in many cases. More over, the binary sensor values of all the sensors have to be considered for all the activities in every inference step, which is an overhead in large settings. Now we provide a brief introduction to the proposed solutions to these limitations.

Since strong assumptions of dependence or independence among entire set of sensors given activity have their own limitations in activity recognition domain, we identify the need to find a mapping between activities and their relevant subsets of dependent sensors. Manual imposition of such a mapping is neither novel nor feasible in large settings. An efficient feature induction approach that can automatically capture the mapping between activities and conjunctions of sensors can be used. Inductive Logic Programming (ILP), a branch of machine learning, is a learning paradigm capable of learning such mappings or rules.

Given some background knowledge and a set of facts as examples, ILP systems derive hypothesis (structure) that entails all the positive examples and none of the negative examples. It starts with an initial hypothesis and refines it by searching a lattice of clauses (a partially ordered set of clauses or rules) based on a scoring function. Typical structure learning systems that do a Branch and Bound (B&B) search in the lattice of clauses evaluating scores based on positive and negative examples covered, when used to construct features for HMM in activity recognition, suffer from accuracy loss as shown in our experiments. In this paper, we propose and implement a greedy feature induction approach that adapts the structure of HMM using HMM evaluation on the training set as scoring function. Our experimental results suggest a performance improvement over both the traditional HMM and the B&B learning assisted HMM in terms of accuracy. We also show the statistical significance of our proposed approach against the traditional approaches.

The rest of the paper is organized as follows. We discuss some related works in section 2. Section 3 discusses about using feature induction to assist HMM model construction. Experiments and Results are discussed in section 4. We conclude our work in section 5.

2   Related Work

In this section, we look into some of the related works in both the area of activity recognition and feature induction.

Automatic activity recognition has been an active research area in the current era of pervasive systems. Various approaches have been proposed. Wilson experimented with particle filter and context aware recognition for recognizing ADLs at the MIT Laboratory [1]. Gibson et.al. [2] discussed the idea of clustering sensors for recognizing activities and concluded that trivially imposing clusters differs from reality. A relational transformation based tagging system using ILP concepts is proposed in [13]. The approach starts with an initial tag to all the sequences and then improves by learning a list of transformation rules which can re-tag based on context information. The approach is purely logical and not probabilistic. [3] identifies the minimal set of sensors that can jointly predict all activities in the domain. Binsztok et. al. [14] discussed learning HMM structure (number of states and allowed transitions) from data for clustering sequences. An efficient feature induction method for named entity extraction and noun phrase segmentation tasks using CRFs is presented by McCallum [15]. Landwehr et. al., in [7], construct kernel functions from features induced by an ILP approach. The search for features is directed by a Support Vector Machine performance using the current kernel. [9] aims to classifying relational sequences using relevant patterns discovered from labelled training sequences. Here, the whole sequence is labelled and not the individual components of the sequence. Patterns in each dimension of multi dimensional sequences are discovered and a feature vector is constructed. Then an optimal subset of the features is selected using a stochastic local search guided by a naive Bayes classifier. TildeCRF, an extension to CRF, is introduced in [8] to deal with sequences of logical atoms and to model arbitrary dependencies in the input space. The potential functions are represented as weighted sums of relational regression trees.

Many of the learning approaches discussed above suits for general classification. However, in the case of sequential, skewed, and sparse activity recognition data where temporal dependencies dominate over static dependencies, most of the learning approaches that globally normalize the parameters do not fit well. We find a solution to this problem by identifying relevant conjunctions of sensors for each activity as observation for HMM. We then learn conditional probability values for this emission model and combine it with transition distribution. We propose feature induction assisted HMM model construction which we discuss in the following section.

3   Model Construction for Activity Recognition

In this section, we first give a technical explanation to the problem at hand before we discuss the B&B structure learning assisted HMM model construction and the feature induction assisted HMM model construction for activity recognition.

In an HMM set-up, the probability distribution of observation given label, $p(x_t|y_t)$, is represented as an emission matrix. Here the observation vector is $x_t = (x_t^1, x_t^2, ..., x_t^N)^\top$, where x_t^i represents the value of ith sensor at time t and N is the number of sensors. Considering the entire set of sensors results in 2^N values for observation x_t which is computationally feasible only in small settings. Often independence is assumed among sensors, given activity, to simplify the representation and computation of $p(x_t|y_t)$. Conditional probability, when independence is assumed among sensors, is $p(x_t|y_t) = \prod_{i=1}^{N} p(x_t^i|y_t)$. This approach is prone to accuracy loss in many cases where the independence assumption is wrong. To alleviate both the issues, we identify the need to find a mapping between activities and their relevant conjunctions of dependent sensors. Our work underlines the notion that if a few dependent sensors in conjunction with information regarding the previous activity can jointly decide on whether an activity has happened in the current time, then it is better to consider only these conjunctions of sensor readings. That is, we avoid the non relevant x^is and use conjunctions of relevant x^js to improve the prediction accuracy. This also helps to reduce the effect of noise while doing inference.

We propose learning the HMM emission structure that maximizes probabilistic coverage of the training data. In our problem, since there is no ordering among activities, the model learned should allow all inter state transitions. Therefore, we learn the structure of emission distribution while preserving all the $\binom{n}{2}$ transition probabilities. In the next subsection, the B&B structure learning assisted HMM model construction is discussed.

3.1   B&B Structure Learning Assisted HMM for Activity Recognition

In this subsection, we explore the idea of using the B&B structure learning assisted HMM model construction (B&BHMM) for activity recognition.

As discussed above, we are interested in finding a mapping between activities and relevant conjunctions of sensors. The mapping can be expressed as relationships of the form "Activity if a particular set of sensors fired". These type of rules are called definite clause rules and are represented in the form $A \leftarrow B, C, \ldots$ where $A, B, C, \ldots$ are binary predicates. Traditional structure learning systems are capable of discovering rules of the above form. We now analyze the effectiveness of these systems to construct HMM model for activity recognition.

We hypothesize that traditional structure learning systems that do not do HMM evaluation while refining rules learned in each step of rule induction will have reduced impact on the accuracy of prediction. This is because, in traditional systems, the objective is to logically cover all the positive examples. ILP is one of the traditional structure learning paradigms that learn first order relations among entities. For example, Aleph [12] is an ILP system that in each iteration, selects a positive example, builds the most specific clause based on the example, searches for a more general clause that has the best score, and removes examples made redundant by the current clause. Although the current problem does not require learning complex first order structures, we use Aleph as a benchmark system for our experiments.

The scores used by traditional systems such as Aleph are largely based on the number of positive and negative examples covered by the current model. One of the scoring functions is $pos - neg$, where pos and neg are the number of positive and negative examples covered by the clause respectively. Discovery of each of the clauses leads to the removal of positive examples covered.

Since in real world problems, the support for any emission of an activity and the support for inter state transitions are much fewer than that for same state transitions, in learning both the emission and transition dependencies using traditional systems, rules defining transitions within the same state tend to dominate. Such a model tends to predict fewer inter state transitions, and thus affects the accuracy of inference. Hence we focus only on the induction of emission rules and combine them with the set of $\binom{n}{2}$ interstate transitions while learning the parameters of the model. We first study the applicability of the B&B structure learning systems to learn emission rules and identify the limitations.

B&B systems, when used for learning emission rules, evaluate each refinement of clauses using scoring functions based on positive and negative examples. Since the real world data are vulnerable to noisy information, an exact model is hard to get. As the examples covered by a refinement are removed in each step, rules that are learned in subsequent iterations have less confidence than those learned initially, which leads to a less efficient model. Since the objective of traditional systems is to logically cover all positive examples with clauses which is different from the actual objective of building a probabilistic model (HMM), the approach suffers from accuracy loss significantly. We have experimented with this approach using Aleph combined with a customized implementation of HMM. Each rule returned by aleph is a definite rule, which associates a subset of sensors to an activity. A new attribute (feature) is constructed with each such subset. Therefore, the number of attributes equals the number of rules learned. The learned logical model and the training data are passed to a customized implementation of HMM for constructing the probabilistic model. Later, the probabilistic model is used for inference. Our experiments reveal that, HMM with B&B structure learning for feature construction is less efficient than HMM without structure learning, except in a few cases. Although of-the-shelf branch and bound structure learning system assisted HMM gave comparable time slice accuracies in a few experiments, it gave worse class accuracies in all the experiments. The comparison of time slice and average class accuracies are shown in tables 1 and 2 respectively as well as figures 2 and 3 respectively. We now discuss the feature induction assisted HMM model construction for activity recognition.

3.2   Feature Induction Assisted HMM for Activity Recognition

After analyzing the limitations of branch & bound structure learning using $pos-neg$ to assist HMM model construction, we propose a greedy hill climbing feature induction approach wherein we evaluate, in each refinement step, the current model in an HMM setting. That is, the score which has to be maximized is an HMM evaluation on the training data. We call this approach the Feature Induction assisted HMM model construction (FIHMM). The score can be either time slice accuracy or class accuracy of the current model. Time slice accuracy is the fraction of time slices when classes (activities) are predicted correctly and average class accuracy is the average percentage of time a class is classified correctly as given in the expressions reproduced below from [4].

$$TimesliceAccuracy: \frac{\sum_{n=1}^{N}[inferred(n) = true(n)]}{N} . \tag{1}$$

$$ClassAccuracy: \frac{1}{C}\sum_{c=1}^{C}\left\{\frac{\sum_{n=1}^{N_c}[inferred_c(n) = true_c(n)]}{N_c}\right\} . \tag{2}$$

where $[a = b]$ is an indicator giving 1 when true and 0 otherwise, N is the total number of time slices, C is the number of classes and N_c is the number of time slices for the class c.

In data that are skewed towards some activities, predicting a frequent activity for all the time slices gives better time slice accuracy but worse average class accuracy. Therefore, if the data set is skewed and some critical activities have less support, we suggest maximizing the average class accuracy. In all other cases, we suggest maximizing time slice accuracy. This is because the average class accuracy computation does not consider the size of a particular class and its maximization leads to a situation where unimportant classes that occur seldom have more impact on the overall efficiency of the model. We pursued both the cases in different experiments, and the results are given in the experiments section. Trying a combination of both time slice and average class accuracies is a future work direction. Leaving the choice of one of these accuracy values to the user, we now discuss the overall learning algorithm for model construction.

```
1. procedure FIHMM_MODEL_CONSTRUCTION
2.    featureSet ← features representing each sensor
3.    currentModel ← model trained with featureSet
.                                        ▷ Here model is synonymous to HMM model
4.    repeat
5.       previousModel ← currentModel
6.       for each activity i do
7.          for each feature j of activity i do
8.             modelDel(i, j) ← model trained with jᵗʰ feature of iᵗʰ activity dropped
9.             for each feature k of activity i do
10.               modelAdd(i, j, k) ← model trained with features j and k combined
.                                                 to form new feature of activity i
11.            end for
12.         end for
13.      end for
14.      currentModel ← arg max {arg max  modelDel(i, j).accuracy,
                                     i,j
.                                      arg max  modelAdd(i, j, k).accuracy}
                                       i,j,k
15.   until currentModel.accuracy ≤ previousModel.accuracy
16.   return previousModel
17. end procedure
```

$$modelDel(i, j) \leftarrow \text{model trained with } j^{th} \text{ feature of } i^{th} \text{ activity dropped}$$

$$currentModel \leftarrow \arg\max \{ \arg\max_{i,j} modelDel(i, j).accuracy, \arg\max_{i,j,k} modelAdd(i, j, k).accuracy \}$$

Fig. 1. Feature induction assisted HMM model training for activity recognition

During the training phase, we pursue a greedy hill climbing search in the lattice to find a model. The pseudo code for our approach is given in Fig. 1. Initially, the features for each activity are constructed with each of the individual sensors and an initial model is trained. In every iteration, candidate models are constructed by removing features of each activity one at a time as shown in step 8 of the pseudo code. Step 10 constructs new features by combining the features removed in step 8 with other features of the activity and a new candidate model is trained. The best scoring model among all the candidate models, if better than the previous model, is saved. To evaluate a model, an HMM is constructed from the current emission model and the transition distribution. Each of the conjunctions discovered forms a column in the emission probability matrix and the conditional probabilities are learned for these conjunctions given activity. Further, only those columns that are mapped to an activity have to be considered during inference. Each iteration either deletes or adds a feature to the final model based on the HMM evaluation on training data. Unlike in the traditional approaches, no examples are removed during the iterations. In each iteration, the existing logical model is refined, probabilistic parameters are learned and the model is evaluated on the training data. The process is repeated until convergence. In the next section, we describe our experimental set-up and report our results.

4   Experiments and Results

We have implemented all the approaches in java. All our experiments have been performed on an AMD Athlon 64 bit dual core machine (2.90 GHz) with 2.8 GB RAM and running Ubuntu 8.04.

We have carried out our experiments on the data set made available by Kasteren et. al. [4] of the University of Amsterdam. The dataset consists of binary values reported at each time interval by 14 sensors installed at various locations in a house. There are 8 activities annotated. The data is marked for each one minute time slot and there are 40006 instances. In the dataset, some activities occurred more frequently than others and some activities occurred for a longer duration, and hence the data is not balanced. The data is represented in four binary formats: raw, change point, last observation, and a combination of change point and last observation. Interested readers may refer [4] for more details.

We assume the data is complete in our case. Moreover, the use of discrete data enables us to count the number of occurrences of transitions, observations and states [5]. We have performed our experiments in a leave one day out manner in a 28 fold cross validation set-up. The performance is evaluated by the average time slice accuracy and the average class accuracy. We also evaluate the statistical significance of our claims.

We ran four experiments each on raw, change point, last value and change point plus last value data. The First experiment is the traditional HMM as suggested in [4]. The second experiment, B&BHMM, uses Aleph to learn emission rules in the form of definite clauses for each activity. These rules along with the data are passed to a customized implementation of HMM for probabilistic learning and inference. The third and fourth experiments are the proposed FIHMM which inductively learns HMM emission model using HMM evaluation as the score. The emission model is combined with the $\binom{n}{2}$ inter state transitions and the probabilities are learned to obtain the complete HMM model. The third experiment optimizes average class accuracy while the fourth experiment optimizes time slice accuracy. The results are shown in tables 1 and 2. The comparison of time slice accuracies and class accuracies for all the four approaches in all the data formats is shown in Fig. 2 and Fig. 3 respectively.

From the results, it can be noted that the average time slice accuracies of B&BHMM are not better than traditional HMM in any of the data formats except raw data and the average class accuracies (average of the class accuracies obtained from each fold) of B&BHMM are not better than traditional HMM in any of the data formats. This decline in the accuracies is due to the inappropriate evaluation function used by the branch & bound structure learning systems while doing refinement of learned clauses. In contrast, the proposed feature induction assisted HMM model construction approach that uses HMM evaluation as the scoring function performed better than the other two approaches in all the data formats significantly. The average accuracies of the proposed approach on training data in all the data formats are given in Table 3.

In raw data format, maximizing class accuracy yielded better class accuracy but did not yield better time slice accuracy than the B&B learning assisted

Table 1. Average time slice accuracies in percentage for various data representations using traditional HMM, B&B learning assisted HMM and proposed approach. Proposed approach has been used for maximizing class and time slice accuracies.

Data	Traditional HMM	B&BHMM	FIHMM maximizing class accuracy	FIHMM maximizing time slice accuracy
raw	50.49	56.94	54.98	71.59
change point	67.14	44.91	82.93	87.07
last value	86.45	33.69	89.67	93.47
change + last	86.55	64.94	91.15	93.57

Table 2. Average class accuracies in percentage for various data representations using traditional HMM, B&B learning assisted HMM and proposed approach. Proposed approach has been used for maximizing class and time slice accuracies.

Data	Traditional HMM	B&BHMM	FIHMM maximizing class accuracy	FIHMM maximizing time slice accuracy
raw	44.60	27.81	55.11	55.13
change point	61.68	27.21	75.93	68.03
last value	73.47	15.85	74.90	64.44
change + last	76.41	34.87	79.26	76.78

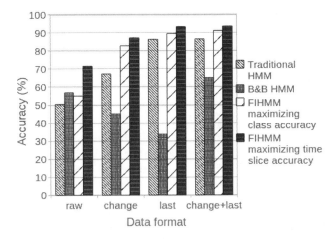

Fig. 2. Comparison of time slice accuracies of traditional HMM, B&BHMM, FIHMM maximizing class accuracy and FIHMM maximizing time slice accuracy on different data representations

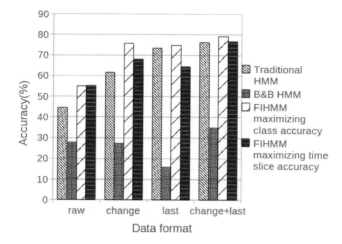

Fig. 3. Comparison of class accuracies of traditional HMM, B&BHMM, FIHMM maximizing class accuracy and FIHMM maximizing time slice accuracy on different data representations

Table 3. Average accuracies of proposed approach on training data in percentage

Data	FIHMM maximizing class accuracy		FIHMM maximizing time slice accuracy	
	Time slice accuracy	Class accuracy	Time slice accuracy	Class accuracy
raw	64.86	71.06	82.02	61.97
change point	87.59	82.88	93.25	69.13
last value	91.09	83.63	95.76	62.43
change + last	93.14	88.01	96.7	83.79

HMM. This is because the objective function maximized was class accuracy and not time slice accuracy. For similar reasons, the average class accuracy of proposed approach maximizing time slice accuracy in last value data is not better than traditional HMM. Therefore choosing appropriate objective function to maximize has an effect on the accuracies. The average confusion matrices got from the proposed approach using class accuracy optimization for each of the data representations are given in tables 4, 5, 6, 7.

The statistical significance of the performances is analyzed using the Wilcoxon signed rank test [16]. This non parametric test finds the probability of the null hypothesis that a pair of algorithms have no significant difference in their median performance. The test uses signed ranks of absolute values of the differences in performance after discarding the ties. The probabilities for the actual signed ranks are determined by exact computation if there are fewer entries or by normal approximation otherwise. In our experiments, we have evaluated two null

Table 4. Confusion matrix of FIHMM for raw data set

	Idle	Leaving	Toileting	Showering	Sleeping	Breakfast	Dinner	Drink
Idle	32	12	7	21	0	4	12	1
Leaving	11	59	4	11	0	0	15	0
Toileting	4	3	64	6	1	4	3	1
Showering	15	3	17	42	0	1	1	0
Sleeping	12	23	1	3	42	0	2	0
Breakfast	14	0	1	0	0	50	3	3
Dinner	9	4	3	0	0	14	9	1
Drink	6	0	0	0	0	12	8	16

Table 5. Confusion matrix of FIHMM for change data set

	Idle	Leaving	Toileting	Showering	Sleeping	Breakfast	Dinner	Drink
Idle	57	3	4	3	10	4	6	3
Leaving	16	84	0	0	0	0	0	0
Toileting	3	2	73	1	1	5	0	1
Showering	10	0	3	66	0	0	0	0
Sleeping	1	9	1	0	71	0	0	0
Breakfast	13	0	1	0	1	43	6	7
Dinner	13	1	1	1	0	14	8	2
Drink	4	1	5	0	0	6	2	24

Table 6. Confusion matrix of FIHMM for last value data set

	Idle	Leaving	Toileting	Showering	Sleeping	Breakfast	Dinner	Drink
Idle	26	7	7	11	7	8	8	16
Leaving	1	97	1	1	0	0	0	0
Toileting	11	2	64	3	3	2	0	1
Showering	5	0	7	67	0	0	0	0
Sleeping	0	0	1	0	81	0	0	0
Breakfast	15	0	0	4	0	49	1	3
Dinner	2	1	0	0	1	10	21	4
Drink	3	0	5	0	0	8	4	24

Table 7. Confusion matrix of FIHMM for change + last data

	Idle	Leaving	Toileting	Showering	Sleeping	Breakfast	Dinner	Drink
Idle	47	5	4	10	5	3	8	7
Leaving	2	96	1	0	0	0	0	0
Toileting	4	1	74	2	1	3	1	1
Showering	1	1	5	72	0	0	0	0
Sleeping	1	0	1	0	80	0	0	0
Breakfast	14	0	1	0	0	40	11	6
Dinner	9	0	1	2	0	8	19	1
Drink	8	1	0	0	0	5	7	22

hypothesis: 1. The prediction accuracies of the B&BHMM and the traditional HMM are not different. 2. The prediction accuracy of FIHMM is not different from traditional HMM and the B&BHMM. The probability values returned, in our experiments, by Wilcoxon test for time slice accuracy comparison and class accuracy comparison are shown in Table 8 and 9 respectively. From the tables, there is little evidence in favour of the null hypothesis for overall results (Tables 8(a),9(a)). From other experiments with different data representations (Tables 8(b−e),9(b−e)), there is enough evidence to reject the null hypothesis. There are two exceptions. First is the probability for the B&BHMM against the traditional HMM in the case of time slice accuracy for raw data and the second is the probability of the proposed approach against the traditional HMM in the case of class accuracy for change+last data. These values are slightly higher than the standard significance levels. The second is because of the inherent sparsity in the data representation. Since the two null hypothesis are rejected, the alternate

Table 8. Probabilities of observing the differences in time slice accuracies for different data sets under the null hypothesis that median accuracies of the pair of approaches being compared are equal. Two tailed probability estimates of the null hypothesis being true are shown.

	Traditional HMM	B&B HMM
a) *Overall*		
B&BHMM	< 0.00006	-
FIHMM	< 0.00006	< 0.00006
b) *Raw Data*		
B&BHMM	0.4849	-
FIHMM	0.00012	0.00156
c) *Change Point*		
B&BHMM	0.0009	-
FIHMM	0.00012	< 0.00006
d) *Last Value*		
B&BHMM	< 0.00006	-
FIHMM	< 0.00006	< 0.00006
e) *Change+Last*		
B&BHMM	< 0.00006	-
FIHMM	< 0.00006	< 0.00006

Table 9. Probabilities of observing the differences in average class accuracies for different data sets under the null hypothesis that median accuracies of the pair of approaches being compared are equal. Two tailed probability estimates of the null hypothesis being true are shown.

	Traditional HMM	B&B HMM
a) *Overall*		
B&BHMM	< 0.00006	-
FIHMM	< 0.00006	< 0.00006
b) *Raw Data*		
B&BHMM	0.0003	-
FIHMM	0.00062	0.00022
c) *Change Point*		
B&BHMM	< 0.00006	-
FIHMM	0.00018	< 0.00006
d) *Last Value*		
B&BHMM	< 0.00006	-
FIHMM	0.0345	< 0.00006
e) *Change+Last*		
B&BHMM	< 0.00006	-
FIHMM	0.09186	< 0.00006

hypothesis are considered proved. There fore, we conclude that the efficiency of the proposed approach of feature induction assisted HMM model construction is statistically significant.

The learning part takes an average of three hours. The inference is faster and converges in fraction of a second. Since the learning is done once and inference being done more often, this relatively long learning time is not considered to be affecting the system performance. Moreover, The relatively longer training time can be justified by the significant accuracy gain and fast inference.

5 Conclusion and Future Work

HMM for activity recognition that has exponential observation space is not feasible in operational settings. Assuming independence among sensors given activity simplifies computation, but at the cost of accuracy. We have proposed to use learning methods to find the mappings between activities and relevant subsets of sensors. We reported the results of using the B&B structure learning system to assist HMM learning and inference and discussed the limitations. As a solution, we have proposed and implemented a feature induction assisted HMM model construction system that maximizes the accuracy of HMM inference on training data. Our experiments show good improvement over traditional HMM and B&B learning assisted HMM.

Applying the approach in other models such as CRF, analysis of actual performance benefit in terms of time and energy savings, parallelizing the learning process to run in multiple cores for speed up are some of the future works.

References

1. Wilson, D.H.: Assistive Intelligent Environments for Automatic Health Monitoring. PhD Thesis, Carnegie Mellon University (2005)
2. Gibson, C.H.S., van Kasteren, T.L.M., Krose, B.J.A.: Monitoring Homes with Wireless Sensor Networks. In: Proceedings of the International Med-e-Tel Conference (2008)
3. Wang, S., Pentney, W., Popescu, A.-M., Choudhury, T., Philipose, M.: Common sense based joint training of human activity recognizers. In: 20th International Joint Conference on Artifical Intelligence (2007)
4. van Kasteren, T., Noulas, A., Englebienne, G., Krose, B.: Accurate activity recognition in a home setting. In: 10th International Conference on Ubiquitous Computing (2008)
5. Rabiner, R.: A tutorial on hidden Markov models and selected applications in speech recognition. Proceedings of the IEEE 77(2), 257–286 (1989)
6. Lafferty, J., McCallum, A., Pereira, F.: Conditional Random Fields: Probabilistic Models for Segmenting and Labeling Sequence Data. In: International Conference on Machine Learning (2001)
7. Landwehr, N., Passerini, A., De Raedt, L., Frasconi, P.: KFOIL: Learning Simple Relational Kernels. In: 21st National Conference on Artificial Intelligence (2006)
8. Gutmann, B., Kersting, K.: TildeCRF: Conditional Random Fields for Logical Sequences. In: 15th European Conference on Machine Learning (2006)
9. Di Mauro, N., Basile, T.M.A., Ferilli, S., Esposito, F.: Feature Construction for Relational Sequence Learning. Technical Report, arXiv:1006.5188 (2010)
10. Getoor, L., Taskar, B.: Statistical Relational Learning. MIT Press, Cambridge (2006)
11. Forney, G.D.: The viterbi algorithm. Proceedings of IEEE 61(3), 268–278 (1973)
12. Srinivasan, A.: The Aleph Manual. Technical Report, University of Oxford (2007)
13. Landwehr, N., Gutmann, B., Thon, I., De Raedt, L., Philipose, M.: Relational Transformation-based Tagging for Activity Recognition. Progress on Multi-Relational Data Mining 89(1), 111–129 (2009)
14. Binsztok, H., Artieres, T., Gallinari, P.: A model-based approach to sequence clustering. In: European Conference on Artificial Intelligence (2004)
15. McCallum, A.: Efficiently Inducing Features of Conditional Random Fields. In: Nineteenth Conference on Uncertainty in Artificial Intelligence (2003)
16. Siegel, S.: Nonparametric statistics for the behavioural sciences. McGraw-Hill, New York (1956)

Mining Approximate Frequent Closed Flows over Packet Streams

Imen Brahmi[1], Sadok Ben Yahia[1], and Pascal Poncelet[2]

[1] Faculty of Sciences of Tunis, Tunisia
sadok.benyahia@fst.rnu.tn
[2] LIRMM UMR CNRS 5506,161 Rue Ada, 34392 Montpellier Cedex 5, France
poncelet@lirmm.fr

Abstract. Due to the varying and dynamic characteristics of network traffic, the analysis of traffic flows is of paramount importance for network security, accounting and traffic engineering. The problem of extracting knowledge from the traffic flows is known as the *heavy-hitter* issue. In this context, the main challenge consists in mining the traffic flows with high accuracy and limited memory consumption. In the aim of improving the accuracy of heavy-hitters identification while having a reasonable memory usage, we introduce a novel algorithm called ACL-STREAM. The latter mines the approximate closed frequent patterns over a stream of packets. Carried out experiments showed that our proposed algorithm presents better performances compared to those of the pioneer known algorithms for heavy-hitters extraction over real network traffic traces.

Keywords: Network Traffic Analysis, Heavy-Hitters, Traffic Flow, Approximate.

1 Introduction

Recently, data streams possess interesting computational characteristics, such as unknown or unbounded length, possibly very fast arrival rate, inability to backtrack over previously arrived items (only one sequential pass over the data is allowed), and a lack of system control over the order in which the data arrive [1]. In this context, the analysis of network traffic has been one of the primary applications of data streams. Generally, the main objectives in network monitoring can be summarized under two aspects as follows: (*i*) understanding traffic features specially the most frequent ones; and (*ii*) detecting outburst network anomalies [11].

For example, given a large-scale campus network or enterprise network, there always exist a huge amount of network flows which have similar traffic features. Flows are usually considered to be sequences of packets with a five-tuple of common values (*i.e.*, protocol, source and destination of IP addresses and port numbers), and ending after a fixed timeout interval when no packets are observed. In this case, many research works considered that the network traffic

A. Cuzzocrea and U. Dayal (Eds.): DaWaK 2011, LNCS 6862, pp. 419–431, 2011.

pattern obey a heavy-tailed distribution [7,14,15], implying a small percentage of flows consuming a large percentage of bandwidth. The flows which are responsible for a huge amount of packets are baptized as *heavy-hitters* [7,15]. The latter have been shown useful for many applications, such as detecting Denial of Service (DoS) attacks, warning heavy network users, monitoring traffic trends and balancing traffic load [15], to cite but a few.

A straightforward approach to detect the heavy-hitters consists of mining the frequent flows with their corresponding frequency count. Nevertheless, this simple approach is not applicable for high-speed traffic streams. In fact, the traffic streams have often a very large number of distinct network packets, which results in overwhelming and unpredictable memory requirements for flow mining. As an example, we consider the case of a small enterprise network and a NetFlow collector that computes the generated traffic flows.The number of flows over a period of a month is close to 100 million, which corresponds to 2.5 GBytes of memory for storing 136-bit flow identifiers and 64-bit counters. Consequently, the large memory requirements hampers the computation of heavy-hitters over packet streams. In addition, the use of a disk to store a subset of the flow identifiers and counters severely impacts performances and is unsuitable when fast processing is required.

In this paper, we investigate another way of computing the heavy-hitters using limited memory resources. Thus, we introduce a single-pass algorithm, called ACL-STREAM (*Approximate CLosed frequent pattern mining over packet Streams*) that provides a condensed representation of heavy-hitters. In this respect, ACL-STREAM allows the incremental maintenance of frequent closed patterns as well as the estimation of their frequency counts over a packet stream. Clearly, it has been shown in [7,14] that, it is unfeasible to find the exact frequency of heavy-hitters using memory resources sub-linear to the number of distinct traffic patterns. Consequently, memory-efficient algorithms approximate the heavy-hitters over a packet stream. Through extensive carried out experiments on a real network traffic traces, we show the effectiveness of our proposal on accuracy, detection ability and memory usage performances.

The remainder of the paper is organized as follows. We scrutinize, in Section 2, the related work. We define the background used to propose our approach in Section 3. In Section 4, we introduce the ACL-STREAM algorithm. We also report the encouraging results of the carried out experiments in Section 5. Finally, we conclude by resuming the strengths of our contribution and sketching future research issues.

2   Related Work

Due to its high practical relevance, the topic of flow mining has grasped a lot of attention in recent years. Generally, within literature, the algorithms, aiming at the identification of heavy-hitters, are the algorithms of frequent pattern extraction over a stream of packets [15]. Indeed, these algorithms can be roughly divided into three categories: sampling-based, hash-based and counter-based algorithms.

Sampling-based algorithms [2,8,9,10] exploit cyclical sampling to reduce memory footprint and processing overhead, but their accuracy is limited by a low sampling rate required to make the sampling operation affordable.

Hash-based algorithms [3,4,5,16] can substantially reduce the storage space for flow recording and accelerate processing speed. However, they need to find a balance between compression ratio and accuracy. Moreover, hash functions need to be carefully chosen in order to avoid collisions.

Counter-based algorithms [6,7,12,14] hold a fixed (or bounded) number of counters for tracking the size of heavy-hitters. In this context, one of the well known examples is the LossyCounting (LC) algorithm [12]. In this respect, it divides the incoming traffic stream into a fixed-size window $w = \lceil 1/\epsilon \rceil$, where ϵ is an error parameter such that $\epsilon \in (0, ms)$ and ms is a user-specified minimum support threshold such that $ms \in [0, 1]$. Querying heavy-hitters consists of mining patterns whose estimated frequencies exceed $(ms - \epsilon)$ over each window. Moreover, LC guarantees that the obtained results does not include false negatives[1]. Although, the smaller value of ϵ is the more accurate approximation is. Thus, it leads to requiring both more memory space and more CPU processing power. In addition, if ϵ approaches ms, then more false positives[2] will be outputted.

Aiming at improving the LC algorithm in computing network traffic heavy-hitters, Dimitropoulos et al. [7] proposed the ProbabilisticLossyCounting (PLC) algorithm. PLC uses a tighter error bound on the estimated sizes of traffic flows. Consequently, it drastically reduces the required memory and improves the accuracy of heavy-hitters identification. However, PLC needs to emulate heavy-tailed distribution at the end of each window, causing a high computational complexity.

Recently, Zhang et al. introduced an algorithm called WeightedLossyCounting (WLC) [15]. WLC is able to identify heavy hitters in a high-speed weighted data stream with constant update time. Moreover, it employs an ordered data structure which is able to provide a fast per-item update speed while keeping the memory cost relatively low.

Due to its usability and importance, reducing the memory space of frequent flows still present a thriving and a compelling issue. In this respect, the main thrust of this paper is to propose a new algorithm, called ACL-Stream, to mine approximate closed frequent patterns from flows, which can be seen as an extension of a concise representation of flows to the heavy-hitters identification search space. The main idea behind our approach comes from the conclusion drawn from the Data Mining community that focused on the closed frequent pattern mining over a data stream. In fact, the extraction of the latter requires less memory. Thus, this fact has been shown to be much suitable for the mining stream, since it presents the best compactness rates.

---

[1] The false negatives are the patterns considered as frequent on the entire traffic data and infrequent in window.

[2] The false positives are the patterns considered as frequent in the window and infrequent on the entire traffic data.

3   Approximate Closed Patterns

One of the most known condensed representation of patterns is based on the concept of closure [13].

Definition 1. *A pattern X is a closed pattern if there exists no pattern X' such that: (i) X' is a proper superset of X; and (ii) every packet in a network traffic[3] containing X also contains X'. The closure of a the maximal superset of X having the same support value as that of X.*

Table 1. A snapshot of network traffic data

Packet_ID	Packets
p_1	src_IP1,protocol
p_2	src_port,dst_port
p_3	src_port,dst_port,src_IP1
p_4	src_port,dst_port,src_IP1
p_5	src_port,src_IP1,protocol

Example 1. Let Table 1 sketching a set of packets. The set of closed patterns with their corresponding frequency counts (*i.e.*, supports) is as follows: { (src_port: 4); (src_IP1: 4); (src_port dst_port: 3); (src_port src_IP1: 3); (src_IP1 protocol: 2); (src_port dst_port src_IP1: 2); (src_port src_IP1 protocol: 1)}.

Due to the dynamically characteristic of traffic stream, a pattern may be infrequent at some point in a stream but becomes frequent later. Since there are exponentially many infrequent patterns at any point in a stream, it is infeasible to keep all infrequent patterns. Suppose we have a pattern X which becomes frequent after time t. Since X is infrequent before t, its support in the stream before t is lost. In this respect, to estimate X's support before t, the counter-based algorithm for heavy-hitters mining [7,12,14,15] uses an error parameter, ϵ. X is maintained in the window as long as its support is at least $\epsilon \times N$, where N is the number of packets within the current window. Thus, if X is kept only after t, then its support before t is at most $\epsilon \times N$. However, the use of small ϵ results in a large number of patterns to be processed and maintained. Consequently, this fact drastically increases the memory consumption and severely degrades the processing efficiency.

   To palliate this drawback, we consider ϵ as *a relaxed minimum support threshold* and propose to progressively increase the value of ϵ for a pattern as it is retained longer in the window.

Definition 2. *The relaxed minimum support threshold is equal to $r \times ms$, where $r(0 \leq r \leq 1)$ is the relaxation rate.*

Since all patterns whose support is lower than $r \times ms$ are discarded, we define the approximate support of a pattern as follows.

---

[3] Network traffic is data in network.

Definition 3. *The approximate support of a pattern X over a time unit t is defined as*

$$\widetilde{SUP(X,t)} = \begin{cases} 0, & \text{if } sup(X,\,t) < r \times ms; \\ sup(X,t), & \text{otherwise.} \end{cases}$$

4 The ACL-Stream Algorithm

To effectively mine the closed frequent patterns within a packet stream environment, we propose a novel algorithm, called ACL-STREAM, for maintaining the frequent closed patterns. The main idea behind their extraction is to ensure an efficient computation of heavy-hitters that reduces the memory requirements.

With the consideration of time and space limitation, the proposed algorithm uses two in-memory data structures which are called CITABLE (*Closed Incremental Table*) and CILIST (*Closed Identifier List*) respectively. In addition, it employs a *hash table*, called $Temp_{New}$, to put the patterns that have to be updated whenever a new packet arrives. In fact, the rationales behind such in-memory data structures are: (*i*) saving storage space; and (*ii*) reducing the cost of the incremental maintenance of patterns.

Table 2. Example of CITABLE

Cid	Clos	Count
0	{0}	0
1	{src_IP1 protocol}	2
2	{src_port dst_port}	3
3	{src_port dst_port src_IP1}	2
4	{src_IP1}	4
5	{src_port src_IP1 protocol}	1
6	{src_port}	4
7	{src_port src_IP1}	3

Table 3. Example of the CILIST

Item	cidset
src_port	{2, 3, 5, 6, 7}
dst_port	{2, 3}
src_IP1	{1, 3, 4, 5, 7}
protocol	{1, 5}

The CITABLE is used to keep track of the evolution of closed patterns. Each record of the CITABLE represents the information of a closed pattern. It consists of three fields: *Cid*, *Clos* and *Count*. Each closed pattern was assigned a unique closed identifier, called Cid. The Cid field is used to identify closed patterns. Given a Cid, the ACL-STREAM algorithm gets corresponding closed patterns in the Clos field. The support counts are stores in the Count field.

Example 2. According to the database shown by Table 1, the CITABLE is sketched by Table 2.

The CILIST is used to maintain the items and their cidsets. It consists of two fields: the Item field and the cidset field. The cidset of an item X, denoted as cidset(X), is a set which contains all cids of X's super closed patterns.

Algorithm 1. The ACL-STREAM algorithm

Input: $\mathcal{T}$, r, ms
Output: Updated CITABLE
1 Begin
2 | $w := [1/r \times ms]$;
3 | **Foreach** $p_{New} \in w$ **do**
4 | | //Phase 1
5 | | $Temp_{New} := (p_{New}, 0)$;
6 | | $SET(\{p_{New}\}) = \text{cidset}(i_1) \cup...\cup \text{cidset}(i_k)$;
7 | | **Foreach** $Cid(i) \in SET(\{p_{New}\})$ **do**
8 | | | $\mathcal{IR} := \text{Null}$;
9 | | | $\mathcal{IR} := p_{New} \cap \text{Clos}[i]$;
10 | | | **If** $\mathcal{IR} \in Temp_{New}$ **then**
11 | | | | **If** $SU\widetilde{P(Clos}[i]) > SU\widetilde{P(Clos}[z])$ **then**
12 | | | | | replace $(\mathcal{IR}, i)$ with $(\mathcal{IR}, z)$ in $Temp_{New}$
13 | | | **Else**
14 | | | | $Temp_{New} := Temp_{New} \cup (\mathcal{IR}, i)$

15 | | //Phase 2
16 | | **Foreach** $(X, c) \in Temp_{New}$ **do**
17 | | | **If** $X == Clos[c]$ **then**
18 | | | | $SU\widetilde{P(Clos}[c]) := SU\widetilde{P(Clos}[c]) + 1$;
19 | | | **Else**
20 | | | | $j := j{+}1$;
21 | | | | CITABLE $:=$ CITABLE $\cup(j, X, SU\widetilde{P(Clos}[c]) + 1)$;
22 | | | | **Foreach** $i \in p_{New}$ **do**
23 | | | | | $\text{cidset}(i) := \text{cidset}(i) \cup j$

24 End

Example 3. According to Table 1 and the CITABLE shown by Table 2, {src_port dst_port} is closed and its Cid is equal to 2. Thus, 2 will be added into cidset(src_port) and cidset(dst_port) respectively. Table 3 illustrates a CILIST. It maintains the items and their corresponding superset cids shown by Table 2.

The pseudo-code of the ACL-STREAM algorithm is shown by Algorithm 1. In this respect, the ACL-STREAM algorithm attempts to mine a concise representation of heavy-hitters that delivers approximate closed frequent flows. Indeed, the algorithm takes on input a network traffic trace $\mathcal{T}$, a minimum support threshold ms and a relaxation rate r. It starts by reading a fixed window of packets, w, such as $w = [1/r \times ms]$ (line 2). The window facilitates the continuous monitoring of changes in the stream. Moreover, it can be used to palliate the drawback of unbounded memory over the packet streams. In addition, whenever a new packet p_{New} arrives, the ACL-STREAM algorithm consists of two phases. During the first one, the algorithm finds all patterns that need to be updated with their closures, and puts them into $Temp_{New}$ (lines 4−13). Within the second phase, the

ACL-STREAM algorithm updates their supports, CITABLE and CILIST (lines 15−22). Consequently, the updated closed patterns can be obtained without multiple scans of whole search spaces, *i.e.*, by scanning the CITABLE once.

4.1   Incremental Maintenance over Packet Streams

We assume that p_{New} denotes a new incoming packet. $\mathcal{T}_{orig}$ the original network traffic, *i.e.*, the network traffic before adding p_{New}. $\mathcal{T}_{up} = \mathcal{T}_{orig} \cup p_{New}$ is the updated network traffic after adding p_{New}. $\text{Clos}_{Torig}(X)$ and $\text{Clos}_{Tup}(X)$ represent the closure of a pattern X within $\mathcal{T}_{orig}$ and $\mathcal{T}_{up}$ respectively.

Property 1. Whenever p_{New} arrives to $\mathcal{T}_{orig}$, then the patterns of $p_{New} \in \text{Clos}_{Torig}$.

Property 2. Whenever p_{New} arrives to $\mathcal{T}_{orig}$, if a pattern Y is not a subset of p_{New}, then the status of Y will not be changed, *i.e.*, $\widetilde{SUP(Y)}$ remains such as it is and $\text{Clos}_{Torig}(Y) = \text{Clos}_{Tup}(Y)$.

Property 3. Suppose a pattern $\mathcal{IR} = p_{New} \cap X$, $X \in \text{Clos}_{Torig}$, $\mathcal{IR} \in \mathcal{T}_{orig}$. If $\mathcal{IR} \neq \emptyset$, then $\mathcal{IR}$ is a closed pattern in $\mathcal{T}_{up}$.

In the following, we thoroughly discuss the two phases of the ACL-STREAM algorithm according to the pseudo-code shown by Algorithm 1.

Phase 1: According to Property 1, whenever a p_{New} arrives it is considered as closed in $\mathcal{T}_{orig}$. The ACL-STREAM algorithm puts p_{New} into $Temp_{New}$. The table $Temp_{New}$ takes the TI field as a key, and the Closure_Id field as value. Initially, ACL-STREAM sets the Closure_Id of p_{New} to 0, since its closure is unknown (line 4). Besides, the ACL-STREAM algorithm intersects p_{New} with its associated closed patterns. The set of cids of associated closed patterns is defined as $\text{SET}(\{p_{New}\}) = \text{cidset}(i_1) \cup...\cup \text{cidset}(i_k)$. Consequently, the algorithm finds the patterns of p_{New} that need to be updated (line 5). According to Property 3, the results of the intersection are closed patterns within the updated network traffic $\mathcal{T}_{up}$. Suppose $\mathcal{IR}$ is the intersection result of p_{New} and a closed pattern C having a Cid $i \in \text{SET}(\{p_{New}\})$ (lines 7−8). If $\mathcal{IR}$ is not in $Temp_{New}$, then ACL-STREAM puts $(\mathcal{IR}, i)$ into $Temp_{New}$ (lines 12−13). Otherwise, if $\mathcal{IR}$ is already in $Temp_{New}$ with its current Closure_Id t, then ACL-STREAM compares $\widetilde{SUP(C)}$ and $\widetilde{SUP(Q)}$ such that Q is an old closed pattern, already in the CITABLE with a Cid z, *i.e.*, $\text{Clos}_{Torig}[z] = Q$ (line 9−10). If $\widetilde{SUP(C)}$ is greater than $\widetilde{SUP(Q)}$, then ACL-STREAM replaces $(\mathcal{IR}, z)$, already in $Temp_{New}$ with $(\mathcal{IR}, i)$ (line 11). The reason is that the closure of $\mathcal{IR}$ has a support greater than any of its superset's support (Properties 2 and 3). The intersections of p_{New} with C iterates till all cids in $\text{SET}(\{p_{New}\})$ are processed (line 6). Consequently, the phase 1 allows the identification of patterns that need to be updated and finds their closure before the new incoming packet arrives.

Phase 2: The ACL-STREAM algorithm gets patterns X with their Closure_Id c from $Temp_{New}$, and checks that whether X is already in the CITABLE. If X is already in the CITABLE with Cid c, then X is originally a closed in $\mathcal{T}_{orig}$.

In this case, ACL-STREAM directly increases $\widetilde{SUP(X)}$ by 1. Otherwise, X is a new closed pattern after the $Temp_{New}$ arrival. In this case, $\widetilde{SUP(X)}$ is equal to the support of its closure increased by 1 (line $16-17$). At the same time, ACL-STREAM assigns to X a new Cid n, puts X into the CITABLE, and updates the CILIST (lines $19-20$). The phase 2 is repeated till all records in $Temp_{New}$ are processed (line 15). Finally, ACL-STREAM comes to end and outputs the updated CITABLE. The obtained CITABLE captures all the information enclosed in a packet stream.

Example 4. According to Table 1, before that p_1 arrives, we have $\mathcal{T}_{orig} = \emptyset$. The first record of the CITABLE is set to $(0, 0, 0)$. Each cidsets in the CILIST is set to $\emptyset$. As $p_1 = \{$src_IP1 protocol$\}$ arrives, $\mathcal{T}_{up} = \mathcal{T}_{orig} \cup p_1$. The ACL-STREAM algorithm puts $\{$src_IP1 protocol$\}$ into $Temp_{New}$ and sets its Closure_Id to 0. Then, ACL-STREAM merges cidset(src_IP1) and cidset(protocol) to get SET($\{$src_IP1 protocol$\}$), *i.e.*, SET($\{$src_IP1 protocol$\}$) = cidset(src_IP1) $\cup$ cidset(protocol) = $\emptyset$. Since SET($\{$src_IP1 protocol$\}$) is empty, p_1 does not need to intersect with any closed patterns. Therefore, the phase 1 was completed. ACL-STREAM goes to phase 2. Within phase 2, ACL-STREAM updates patterns within $Temp_{New}$ by their Closure_Id. Only ($\{$src_IP1 protocol$\}$, 0) in $Temp_{New}$. ACL-STREAM finds a closed pattern whose Cid is 0 from the CITABLE, Clos[0] =$\{0\}$. Since $\{0\}$ is not equal to $\{$src_IP1 protocol$\}$, then $\{$src_IP1 protocol$\}$ is a new closed pattern after the p_1 arrival. Hence, ACL-STREAM assigns $\{$src_IP1 protocol$\}$ a new Cid equal to 1. Then, ACL-STREAM determines $SUP(\{\widetilde{src\_IP1\ protocol}\})$, which is equal to $SU\widetilde{P(Clos}[0])$ increased by 1. Therefore, $SUP(\{\widetilde{src\_IP1\ protocol}\})$ is 1. Finally, ACL-STREAM updates the CITABLE and the CILIST respectively. Thus, it inserts (1, $\{$src_IP1 protocol$\}$, 1) into the CITABLE and inserts 1 into the CILIST. Then, it handles p_2, p_3, p_4 and p_5 in the same manner. After the insertion of the packets shown by Table 1, the obtained CITABLE and CILIST are shown by Table 2 and Table 3, respectively.

Table 4. Example of $Temp_{New}$ whenever p_6 arrives

TI	Closure_id
$\{$src_IP1$\}$	$\{4\}$
$\{$dst_port$\}$	$\{2\}$
$\{$dst_port src_IP1$\}$	$\{3\}$

Assume that a new packet $p_6 = \{$dst_port src_IP1$\}$ arrives, then ACL-STREAM puts $\{$dst_port src_IP1$\}$ into $Temp_{New}$, and sets its Closure_Id to 0. Moreover, SET($\{$dst_port src_IP1$\}$) = cidset(dst_port) $\cap$ cidset(src_IP1) = $\{2, 3\} \cap \{1,$ $3, 4, 5, 7\} = \{1, 2, 3, 4, 5, 7\}$, according to Table 3. Thus, ACL-STREAM intersects p_6 with the closed patterns whose cids belongs to SET($\{$dst_port src_IP1$\}$). Clearly, the first is Clos[1] = $\{$src_IP1 protocol$\}$ and $\{$dst_port src_IP1$\}$ $\cup$ $\{$src_IP1 protocol$\}$ = $\{$src_IP1$\}$. Hence, it puts $\{$src_IP1$\}$ into $Temp_{New}$ and sets its Closure_Id to 1. Then, it deals with 2, Clos[2] = {src_port dst_port} and {dst_port src_IP1} ∪ {src_port dst_port} = {dst_port}. Consequently, ACL-STREAM puts ({dst_port}, 2) into $Temp_{New}$. It deals with Clos[3] = {src_port dst_port src_IP1}, *i.e.*, {dst_port src_IP1} ∪ {src_port dst_port src_IP1}= {dst_port src_IP1}. However, {dst_port src_IP1} is already in $Temp_{New}$ and its current Closure_Id is 0. Additionally, $SUP(\widetilde{Clos}[3])$ is greater than $SUP(\widetilde{Clos}[0])$. Therefore, ACL-STREAM replaces ({dst_port src_IP1}, 0) with ({dst_port src_IP1}, 3). After dealing with the remaining closed patterns with the same processing steps, the result of $Temp_{New}$ is shown by Table 4.

5   Experiments

To evaluate the effectiveness and efficiency of our algorithm ACL-STREAM, we carried out extensive experiments. Indeed, we compare our approach with the pioneering algorithms falling within the detection of heavy-hitters trend, namely, LC [12], PLC [7] and WLC [15]. All experiments were carried out on a PC equipped with a 3GHz Pentium IV and 4GB of main memory running under Linux Fedora Core 6.

During the carried out experiments, we used a real network traffic trace. The latter is collected from the gateway of a campus network with 1500 users in China[4]. Table 5 sketches dataset characteristics used during our experiments.

Table 5. The considered real traffic traces at a glance

Traffic traces	
Source	Campus network
Date	2009-08-24
	16:20-16:35
Packets	49,999,860
Unique flows	4,136,226

During the experiments, we set $r = 0.1$ and vary ms from 0.1 to 1 such that $\epsilon = 0.1 \times ms$ within LC, PLC and WLC.

5.1   Accuracy Assessment

The accuracy of mining results are measured by the use of two metrics, *Precision* and *Recall*.

Since the approximate algorithms, falling within the detection of heavy-hitters trend, possibly return false positives, the precision indicates the number of false positive results [15]. In fact, Figure 1(a) illustrates the precision of ACL-STREAM *vs.* those respectively of LC, PLC and WLC. We remark that the ACL-STREAM algorithm achieves 100% precision. Although, there is no clear difference between

---

[4] We thank Mr. Q. Rong [14] for providing us with the real network traffic trace.

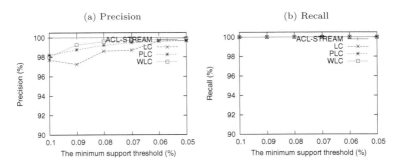

Fig. 1. Precision and Recall of ACL-STREAM *vs.* LC, PLC and WLC

the three algorithms LC, PLC and WLC, such that $\epsilon = 0.1 \times ms$. They attain high precision whenever ms is small. Whereas, their precision drops linearly to be less than 95% as far as ms increases (*i.e.*, the increase in the error parameter ϵ). Thus, the increase of ϵ, associated to ms, results in worsening the precision for the three algorithms. On the contrary, Figure 1(b) shows that whenever ms increases, all algorithms (*i.e.*, ACL-STREAM, LC, PLC and WLC) have 100% recall. This is can be explained by the fact that all algorithms guarantee to retrieval of all frequent patterns over the packet stream.

The experimental results reveal that the estimation mechanism of the LC, PLC and WLC algorithms relies on the error parameter ϵ to control the accuracy. Compared with these three algorithms, ACL-STREAM is much less sensitive to ϵ and is able to significantly achieves high accurate approximation results by increasing ϵ.

5.2   The Detection Ability

Generally, to evaluate the algorithm's ability to detect the heavy-hitters, two interesting metrics are usually of use [14]: the *False Positive Ratio* (FPR) and the *False Negative Ratio* (FPR). Figures 2(a) and 2(b) respectively plot the FPR

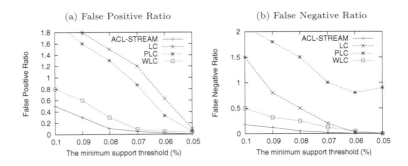

Fig. 2. Detection ability of ACL-STREAM *vs.* LC, PLC and WLC

and FNR against the minimum support threshold ms, for ACL-STREAM, LC, PLC and WLC.

On the one hand, we remark that both PLC and LC generate many false positives along with the decrease of ms. Therefore, they are not suitable for accurate mining of heavy-hitters within high-speed network. For example, if the minimum support threshold is equal to 0.09%, the FPR of LC can reach values as high as 1.8. On the other hand, among the four investigated algorithms, PLC is the most generator of false negatives. Whenever ACL-STREAM, LC and WLC have 0 FNR, PLC has 0.9 FNR. This is due to the probabilistic nature of PLC. Generally, ACL-STREAM exhibits a lower FNR and a lower FPR than the other algorithms. Thus, we conclude that our algorithm is able to correctly detect heavy-hitters with few FPR and FNR.

5.3   Memory Consumption and Throughput

Figure 3(a) shows *the throughput* of ACL-STREAM *vs.* LC, PLC and WLC. The throughput is measured by the number of packets processed per second by the algorithms. Indeed, we remark that the result points out the ability of ACL-STREAM to handle high-speed packet streams as it can process up to 45,000 packets per second. For all minimum support thresholds, the throughput of ACL-STREAM is higher than that of LC, WLC and PLC.

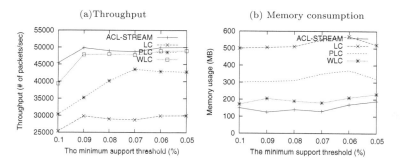

Fig. 3. Throughput and Memory consumption of ACL-STREAM *vs.* LC, PLC and WLC

Moreover, Figure 3(b) shows that ACL-STREAM achieves a roughly constant memory consumption of no more than 150MB. Considering the four algorithms, the memory consumption of ACL-STREAM is considerably lower than that of WLC and substantially lower than that of both LC and PLC.

6   Conclusion

In this paper, we focused on the condensed representation of heavy-hitters algorithms to tackle the mentioned above challenges, *i.e.*, large memory requirement for heavy-hitters computation. Thus, we introduced a novel stream mining algorithm called ACL-STREAM. The carried out experimental results showed the effectiveness of the introduced algorithm and highlighted that the ACL-STREAM presents better performance as well as a good detection ability than the pioneering algorithm in heavy-hitters identification. The approximate but high-quality online results, provided by ACL-STREAM, are well-suited to detect heavy-hitters, where the main goal is to identify generic, interesting or unexpected patterns.

Future issues for the present work mainly concern: (*i*) The consideration of the intrusion detection over on-line packet streams and the mining of closed frequent patterns from flows for network monitoring; (*ii*) Study of the extraction of "generic streaming" association rules based on the ACL-STREAM algorithm for heavy-hitters analysis.

References

1. Aggrawal, C.C.: Data Streams: Models and Algorithms. Springer, Heidelberg (2007)
2. Barakat, C., Iannaccone, G., Diot, C.: Ranking Flows From Sampled Traffic. In: Proceedings of the 2005 ACM Conference on Emerging Network Experiment and Technology, Toulouse, France, pp. 188–199 (2005)
3. Bhattacharyya, S., Madeira, A., Muthukrishnan, S., Ye, T.: How To Scalably and Accurately Skip Past Streams. In: Proceedings of the IEEE 23rd International Conference on Data Engineeringg, Istanbul, Turkey, pp. 654–663 (2007)
4. Bu, T., Cao, J., Chen, A., Lee, P.P.C.: Sequential Hashing: A Flexible Approach for Unveiling Significant Patterns in High Speed Networks. Computer Network 54(18), 3309–3326 (2010)
5. Cormode, G., Muthukrishnan, S.: An Improved Data Stream Summary: The Count-Min Sketch and its Applications. Journal of Algorithms 55(1), 58–75 (2005)
6. Demaine, E.D., López-Ortiz, A., Munro, J.I.: Frequency Estimation of Internet Packet Streams with Limited Space. In: Proceedings of the 10th Annual European Symposium on Algorithms, Rome, Italy, pp. 348–360 (2002)
7. Dimitropoulos, X., Hurley, P., Kind, A.: Probabilistic Lossy Counting: An Efficient Algorithm for Finding Heavy-hitters. ACM SIGCOMM Computer Communications Review 38(1), 5–5 (2008)
8. Duffeld, N., Lund, C., Thorup, M.: Flow Sampling Under Hard Resource Constraints. In: Proceedings of the Joint International Conference on Measurement and Modeling of Computer Systems, pp. 85–96. ACM Press, New York (2004)
9. Kamiyama, N., Mori, T.: Simple and Accurate Identification of High-rate Flows by Packet Sampling. In: Proceedings of the 25th IEEE International Conference on Computer Communications, Barcelona, Spain, pp. 2836–2848 (2006)
10. Kodialam, M., Lakshman, T.V., Monhanty, S.: Runs Based Traffic Estimator (RATE): A Simple, Memory Efficient Scheme for Per-Flow Rate Estimation. In: Proceedings of the 23rd Annual Joint Conference of the IEEE Computer and Communications Societies, Hong Kong, China, pp. 1808–1818 (2004)
11. Li, X., Deng, Z.H.: Mining Frequent Patterns from Network Flows for Monitoring Network. Expert System with Applications 37(12), 8850–8860 (2010)
12. Manku, G.S., Motwani, R.: Approximate Frequency Counts over Data Streams. In: Proceedings of the 28th International Conference on Very Large Data Bases, Hong Kong, China, pp. 346–357 (2002)

13. Pasquier, N., Bastide, Y., Taouil, R., Lakhal, L.: Discovering frequent closed item-sets for association rules. In: Beeri, C., Bruneman, P. (eds.) ICDT 1999. LNCS, vol. 1540, pp. 398–416. Springer, Heidelberg (1998)
14. Rong, Q., Zhang, G., Xie, G., Salamatian, K.: Mnemonic Lossy Counting: An Efficient and Accurate Heavy-hitters Identification Algorithm. In: Proceedings of the 29th IEEE International Performance Computing and Communications Conference, Albuquerque, United States (2010)
15. Zhang, Y., Fang, B.X., Zhang, Y.Z.: Identifying Heavy-hitters in High-speed Network Monitoring. Science 53(3), 659–676 (2010)
16. Zhang, Z., Wang, B., Chen, S., Zhu, K.: Mining Frequent Flows Based on Adaptive Threshold with a Sliding Window over Online Packet Stream. In: Proceedings of the International Conference on Communication Software and Networks, Macau, China, pp. 210–214 (2009)

Knowledge Acquisition from Sensor Data in an Equine Environment[*]

Kenneth Conroy[1], Gregory May[1], Mark Roantree[2], Giles Warrington[1],
Sarah Jane Cullen[3], and Adrian McGoldrick[4]

[1] CLARITY: Centre for Sensor Web Technologies
[2] Interoperable Systems Group, School of Computing
[3] School of Health & Human Performance, Dublin City University, Dublin 9, Ireland
[4] The Turf Club, The Curragh, Co. Kildare, Ireland

Abstract. Recent advances in sensor technology have led to a rapid growth in the availability of accurate, portable and low-cost sensors. In the Sport and Health Science domains, this has been used to deploy multiple sensors in a variety of situations in order to monitor participant and environmental factors of an activity or sport. As these sensors often output their data in a raw, proprietary or unstructured format, it is difficult to identify periods of interest, such as events or actions of interest to the Sport and Exercise Physiologists. In our research, we deploy multiple sensors on horses and jockeys while they engage in horse-racing training exercises. The Exercise Physiologists aim to identify events which contribute most to energy expenditure, and classify both the horse and jockey movement using basic accelerometer sensors. We propose a metadata driven approach to enriching the raw sensor data using a series of Profiles. This data then forms the basis of user defined algorithms to detect events using an Event-Condition-Action approach. We provide an Event Definition interface which is used to construct algorithms based on sensor measurements both before and after integration. The result enables the end user to express high level queries to meet their information needs.

1 Introduction

Given the widespread nature of sensor networks and sensor technology, and the high volumes of data generated on an ongoing basis, it is inevitable that data warehousing and knowledge discovery will be adopted as key technologies for end users and domain experts to improve their abilities in data analysis, decision support, and the automatic extraction of knowledge from data. In many application areas, the volume of data gathered in a single experiment is too great to extract any meaningful knowledge as end users must manually extract data from spreadsheets for simple queries. Where database type solutions may have been used in the past [2], sensor network data management will demand the type of functionality available in data warehouses [6,8]. The continuous refinement of

---

[*] This work is supported by Science Foundation Ireland under grant 07/CE/I1147.

A. Cuzzocrea and U. Dayal (Eds.): DaWaK 2011, LNCS 6862, pp. 432–444, 2011.

query expressions that is taken for granted in data mining is not possible when using the raw data generated by sensors. However, the wide range of sensor devices together with the low level nature of data offers new challenges to data warehouse researchers as they seek to build *generic* solutions to the issues provided by sensor networks. Different domains will bring different requirements and associated issues. In all cases, one feature is common: the significant gap between the abstract queries of domain specialists and the data which they are processing. This paper presents a system to narrow this gap in order that specialist users can fully exploit the data gathered by their sensor networks.

Paper Structure. The paper is structured as follows: in the remainder of this section, we provide the background which motivates this work and provide a statement of our contribution; in §2, we provide a discussion on state of the art; §3 details the profile-based Semantic Enrichment process; in §4, we present our modular approach to complex event detection; in §5 we present our experiments and an evaluation in terms of high level user queries; and finally in §6, we conclude the paper.

1.1   Background and Motivation

A recent collaboration with the Irish Turf Club [16], the regulatory body for horse-racing in Ireland, provided us with an extensive set of data from sensors deployed on multiple horses and jockeys in training. The sensors include multiple accelerometers (Actilife GT3X, Crossbow) mounted on a horse simulator and jockey. These sensors measure: rates of change in direction in uniaxial and triaxial (x,y,z) planes; a Cosmed K4b2 metabolic system [5] measuring a variety of physiological factors from the jockeys breathing; a SenseWear [12] armband, which estimates energy expenditure; and a Garmin GPS system for outdoor trials. Each of these devices has its own format, ranging from plaintext to XML compliant sensor output.

Depending on the distance that the jockey is racing, there are many different factors that can predict competitive performance with predictors that can be physiological, environmental, or equipment specific. By sensing changes in physiological factors, environmental conditions, and equipment and how they affect each other, it is possible to gain a greater understanding of the demands of both racing and training. This could potentially allow for the development of targeted training sessions to investigate aspects of race performance. By capturing race specific data and comparing it to data generated using the horse simulator, it may be possible to see if training addresses the needs of racing and competing. This is not possible without a warehouse-style system that is capable of combining data from each sensor used to monitor the event as well as utilising user defined information on the event and participant, and measuring over a period of time.

The sports physiologists involved in this research have identified key events that must be determined for knowledge acquisition. These events are then incorporated into high level queries that extract the new knowledge and are now described.

- **SimSpeed.** This event classifies the speed at which the horse-simulator moves. It changes the energy demands of jockeys as they try to maintain a race position under great speeds. It has five movement stages, each representing change in gait of the horse; walking, trotting, cantering, fast-cantering and galloping. A combination of GT3X Accelerometer and Activity Profile are used to identify these stages.
- **Energy Expenditure(EE)-Est.** Estimates the amount of energy expended for the amount of time spent in each of the simulator stages. This is a simplified estimation, used when specialist equipment is not available and is based on participant anthropometrics and accelerometer data.
- **Energy Expenditure(EE)-Calc.** Calculates the amount of energy expended during each of the simulator stages based on physiological data captured at the same time using other sensors. Data can be more accurately calculated based on breath-by-breath data from a portable metabolic gas analysis system (Cosmed K4b2 metabolic system). Data can also be calculated from existing algorithms on portable heart-rate monitoring systems (Garmin, Polar, Cardiosport).
- **Whipping.** During the final stages of a race, jockeys use a hand held whip to drive the horse to greater speeds. Although jockeys are predominately one handed they need to be able to do this with both hands under different racing conditions. Sensing these events is based on three GT3X Accelerometers, one on each of the jockeys wrists, and another located on the saddle.
- **Jockey Pushing Out.** Usually occurring towards the end of a race, the jockey is in dynamic imbalance, positioned in a state of forward propulsion, crouching in order to minimise wind resistance, and encourage the horse to maintain speed. This is discovered using information from GT3X Accelerometers located on the chest, and the sacroiliac joint, and by ensuring the corresponding values are also associated with a level 4 Speed - fast canter.

The advances in sensor technology have resulted in significant changes in the ways in which scientists can gather data. In the horseracing domain, the focus is primarily on the health and condition of the horse. However, decreasing the energy expended by the jockey during the early parts of a race may result in gaining a competitive edge when *pushing out* at the end of a race. No standard way of measuring the energy expenditure of jockeys during horse-racing exists, and thus, no specialised systems to understand this data are in place. As a result, the domain experts seek to calculate energy expended and define other horse-related events from a deployment of multiple sensors. Due to a lack of a common standard amongst the sensors deployed, a data management framework for defining events and acquiring knowledge is required.

Contribution. In this paper, we extend the EventSense framework presented in [3] with a new process to extract knowledge from multiple sensor sources. We begin with a metadata driven approach to structural and semantic enrichment using a series of Profiles. We then expand our event detection mechanism to a 3-Tier format: basic event detection; event detection based on results of other defined events; and events definitions based on data integrated from multiple sources and new event definitions. The modular nature of the event definition allows the end user greater control and flexibility in defining events and thus, acquiring different forms of knowledge.

2   Related Research

In [15], the authors present the Semantic Sensor Web (SSW), an approach to annotating sensor data with semantic metadata to improve interoperability and provide contextual information required for knowledge discovery. They leverage Sensor Web Enablement (SWE) [14] and Semantic web standards to do so. Metadata referring to time, space and theme is included as they extend SWE to have more expressive information based on ontological (OWL)[17] representations. Semantics are defined using RDFa [10] with SWRL [11] based rules defined to deduce new ontological *assertations*. The resulting rule-based assertations allow for extended query and reasoning within the sensor domain. While we also use the SOS[13] and O&M[9] components, our approach is more lightweight, with our event definitions not requiring substantial knowledge of programming or complex specification language. In [7], the SSW approach is extended to illustrate the advantages of semantic annotation of SOS services, focusing on a deep analysis of sensor data to discover important environmental events.

The authors of [20] present a framework for sensor data collection, management and exchange conforming to the SWE standard. They have deployed their system for an environmental monitoring purpose, which involves the integration of multiple sensors. Unlike our approach, context applied to the data is limited to location, with additional context requiring the development of applications that access the data. While they support remote access to multiple sensors, it is not designed to be deployed in an environment with legacy sensors transmitting in various formats, or storing information locally. Their approach contains no facility for defining rules for detecting events, other than cross-correlation of multiple sensors measuring similar properties.

In [1], they present an approach to sensor discovery and fusion by semantically annotating sensor services with terms from a defined ontology representing an environmental monitoring setup. Their main goal is to aid in the detection of natural disasters. The sensors used are static and have relationships defined by the ontology. A Geosensor Discovery Ontology (GDO) is defined, specifying a taxonomy of sensor observations, geographic objects and substances. Like our approach, they use a lightweight method to provide added meaning, keeping complexity low in order to maintain usability by end-users from a non-computing background. Information is discovered based on rules defining semantic requirements, location and timepoints. Usability is provided using a GUI. Sensor fusion is performed by a Joint Server Engine (JSE) which takes user input and translates it into SOS requests. The data is then merged, removing duplicates and normalisation is performed during the process. However, the system structure cannot be altered by the creation of interrelated event definitions to define and detect more interesting events, a necessary requirement in our system.

3   Context and Knowledge Representation

In [3], we introduced the EventSense framework with Profiles used to automate the imposition of structural semantics to raw sensor data. Here, we will show how the same concept can be easily extended to the new domain of horse racing. The goal is to demonstrate how basic knowledge is represented and this is fundamental to our mining activities, presented in the next section.

3.1   Context Data

The task of defining the context is split into two constructs, an Activity Profile which is built for each activity (such as horse-racing) and consists of standard information such as the start and end time and the location, and some non-standard activity specific information. The sports physiologists are interested in activity-based effects on energy expended by the jockey. This requirement can involve complex calculations and algorithms to detect these events, as well as the inclusion of some external contextual information. For instance, knowledge of the weather at the time of deployment and the terrain is useful information to determining why performance was not optimal for a certain deployment. While there exist sensors to identify this information, it is often not feasible to do so. As a result, a broad range of manually recorded information is observed by scientists as the deployment of sensors is ongoing. It is this information which is included in an Activity Profile as optional context. A sample Activity Profile for an indoor deployment of a jockey on a simulator is shown in Example 1.

Example 1. Sample Activity Profile: Horse-Racing (Simulator)

```
<HorseRacing-Sim>
    <aid>1</aid>
    <start_time>12:30:00</start_time>
    <end_time>13:30:00</end_time>
    <date>2010-03-10</date>
    <location>indoor</location>
    <jockey>subject1</jockey>
    ...
</HorseRacing-Sim>
```

Further knowledge is encoded in a Participant Profile. This information is primarily anthropometric data measured infrequently by Sport and Exercise Physiologists as they typically do not alter greatly over time. In addition to these standard values, common across all domains, domain specific information is included where necessary, such as a specific multiplier for some algorithm measuring energy expenditure. In Example 2, we show the anthropometric data for 'Participant ID (pid) 1', the EE-Est multiplier figure, and other domain-based information such as jockey class (trainee). As with the Activity Profile, queries can be made on this information following integration, and they can by used as parameters in the formation of event detection rules.

Example 2. Sample Participant Profile: Jockey

```
<Jockey>
    <pid>1</pid>
    <gender>male</gender>
    <height>170.6</height>
    <weight>68</weight>
    <age>22</age>
    <BMI>23.53</BMI>
    <jockey_type>trainee</jockey_type>
    <horse>Sim3</horse>
    <horse_weight></horse_weight>
    <horse_height>15</horse_height>
    ...
</Jockey>
```

3.2   Sensor Representation

A Sensor Profile must be defined for each sensor type, to model the structure of the sensor data. Each sensor is assigned a Profile detailing the fields corresponding to sensor values and instructions to standardise the data format. This includes information relating to which timing protocol is used, and how this is converted to a system standard. For example, some sensors record their timestamps as a fraction of a minute, others in milliseconds. These must be standardised in order to aid in the process of merging multiple data sources.

Example 3. Sample Sensor Profile: GT3X Accelerometer

```
<GT3XAccelerometer>
    <sid>2</sid>
    <time_format>ms</time_format>
    <sample_rate>30</sample_rate>
    <Granularity_min>0.033333</Granularity_min>
    <Granulatity_max>0.033333</Granularity_max>
    <field_formats>int, int, int</field_formats>
    ...
</GT3XAccelerometer>
```

Example 3 shows a sample Sensor Profile for a GT3X Accelerometer. This shows the fields recorded, assigns them tag names, and details the sample rate and timing format used. It provides the basic structure and layout for a sensors output, but in order to make sense of the information, we must use contextual information. We do this by merging the sensor data with the Activity and Participant Profile information, discussed next.

3.3   Imposing Context on Sensor Data

The process of merging static context with dynamic sensor data uses a combination of Java and the XQuery Update Facility [19]. Currently, we perform integration based on the sensor timestamps and granularity constraints and Contextual Profile information, but this research is ongoing. Due to the different sampling rates of devices, there are often many more records for one device over some interval as for another device. For instance, the GT3X Accelerometer monitors the environment at 30Hz, whereas the Heart Rate monitor samples once per second. We take the approach of averaging values where appropriate and leaving blank spaces where averaged values do not correspond to real world conditions. For instance, averaging the following and preceding values of Heart Rate is appropriate in all experiments. However, averages for accelerometers cannot be used. We identify these constraints with the Sensor Profile, where the granularity `min` and `max` ensure the system does not create data outside acceptable limits. Our motivation for this paper was to determine if key events could be accurately detected, and if these events could be used in query expressions. A more holistic integration process will be presented as part of future work.

4   Knowledge Acquisition

Knowledge acquisition in EventSense is based on events defined by the specialist end user events. EventSense provides the ability to build event detection algorithms using sensor data, context profiles, functions and nested events. Events are modular in nature, and we classify them as Tier 1, 2 or 3 depending on their structure. The Tier classification corresponds to the inclusion of pre-condition requirements for some events prior to definition.

- The most basic events are Tier 3, which consist of a single sensor whose values match a specified condition, and may include Activity and Participant Profile knowledge.
- A Tier 2 event can contain other events (ie. their results) within its condition component and therefore, must also explicitly state the pre-condition required to execute the current event detection. This pre-condition is the event definition for detecting the property involved in the condition.
- A Tier 1 event definition can include both the results of previous events and any number of sensor data (i.e. all sensor data available after integration).

The use of a 3-tier system allows us to define a number of relatively basic events which can be combined to form more complex events. To allow Tier 1 and 2 event definitions, it was necessary to extend our original architecture [3]. It is now possible to specify additional operators, standardise the pre-condition element, perform integration of information sources and model how events relate to each other. The remainder of this section details the structure of the basic event detection module (Tier 3), describes the grammar and operators of the system and details how we use the results obtained from these modules to build up more advanced event detection modules (Tier 1 and 2), thus illustrating the power integrated data can provide the user.

4.1   Pre-integration Event Detection

Tier 3 events, which are the building blocks for more advanced events, are generally defined to discover a large amount of single-sensor based events on very large sources of information. For instance, the GT3X Accelerometer accessed in Example 4 has 108,000 data values for each hour of deployment. Pre-processing this information to detect some event (a 'fast-cantering' horse in this case) allows subsequent queries for a fast-canter be executed promptly and ensures additional events (Tier 1 and 2) can be defined using these events. In the example shown, the GT3X Accelerometer located on the saddle is accessed for each entry, and the (x,y,z) values are evaluated accordingly. If the condition is satisfied, this new knowledge is added to the data warehouse, by encoded this value with the `fast-canter` tag.

Example 4. Event Definition: Fast-Cantering Horse

```
<event fast-cantering>
   <condition>
       <GT3XAccelerometer location="saddle">
           <entry>
               <x ge 65222>
               <y ge 65222>
               <z ge 65222>
           </entry>
       </GT3XAccelerometer>
   </condition>
   <action>
       UPDATE <GT3XAccelerometer location="saddle"><entry> WITH <fast-canter>
   </action>
<\event>
```

4.2   Post-integration Event Detection

Example 5. Event Definition: Left-Handed Whip

```
<event Left-Handed-Whip>
   <precondition>
       <event fast-cantering>
   </precondition>
   <condition>
       <GT3XAccelerometer location="LHWrist">
           <entry>
               <x gt 65655>
               <y gt 65655>
               <z gt 65655>
           </entry>
       </GT3XAccelerometer>
       <Logical operator= "AND">
       <GT3XAccelerometer location="saddle">
           <entry><fast-canter></entry>
       </GT3XAccelerometer>
   </condition>
   <action>
       UPDATE <GT3XAccelerometer location="LHWrist"><entry> WITH <LHWhip>
   </action>
</event>
```

To demonstrate Tier 2 events, we introduce the event of *whipping*, as described in the Introduction. This event is defined as: *all three axes of a GT3X Accelerometer located on the left or right wrist reaching their upper threshold at the same time.* Both the left and right wrist values are taken for each jockey as whips are alternated between left and right side towards the end of the race. In addition, whips occur only when the horse is 'fast-cantering', and this constraint is built into the algorithm to improve accuracy.

End users can define this type of knowledge in a step-by-step manner. Firstly, they define the **fast-canter**, as shown in Example 4. Then, they define a whip occurring on either side (a definition for *Left-handed-whip* and *Right-handed-whip*), and finally a generic *whipping* definition which combines the results of left/right whip. Both the left and right whip events involve knowledge previously discovered by prior events. These are the <fast-canter> tags included in updates. It is therefore necessary for the left and right whip event definitions to specify the fast-canter event definition as a pre-condition. This means the **fast-cantering** event definition must be defined and executed prior to executing either the left or right whip event detection. The structure of the left handed whip event is shown in Example 5. Similarly, in the generic *whipping* event definition, shown in Example 6, the left and right whip events are pre-conditions.

Example 6. Event Definition: Whipping

```
<event Whipping>
    <precondition>
        <event Left-Handed-Whip>
        <event Right-Handed-Whip>
    </precondition>
    <condition>
        <GT3XAccelerometer location="LHWrist">
            <entry><LHWhip></entry>
        </GT3XAccelerometer>
        <Logical operator = "OR">
        <GT3XAccelerometer location="RHWrist">
            <entry><RHWhip></entry>
        </GT3XAccelerometer>
    </condition>
    <action>
        UPDATE <GT3XAccelerometer location="saddle"><entry> WITH <whip>
    </action>
</event>
```

The Tier 2 definitions illustrate the combination of event results required to evaluate more complex events. We extend the functionality of our previous system to include the NOT and XOR functions, in addition to the AND and OR previously defined.

Tier 1 events can contain multiple sensor output, each of a different type, and algorithms can contain functions combining values from these sensors to extract more complex knowledge. In Example 7, we show a prototype calculation for energy expenditure (EE-Calc). In this example, data from a Cosmed metabolic system and an accelerometer are used to compute a new measure and update an entry with the computed value. This mining process is ongoing: the team of domain experts are now in a position to refine threshold values as their analytical procedures progress.

Example 7. Event Definition: Energy Expenditure Calculation (Prototype)

```
<event EE-Calc>
    <precondtion>
        <event SimSpeed>
        <event fast-cantering>
    </precondition>
    <condition>
        <GT3XAccelerometer location="saddle">
            <entry><SimSpeed eq 3></entry>
        </GT3XAccelerometer>
        <Logical operator= "AND">
```

```
        <Cosmed><entry><EEm gt 0></entry></Cosmed>
        <Logical operator= "AND">
        <FnCalc-EE>
            <&result gt 0>
        </FnCalc-EE>
    </conditon>
    <action>
        UPDATE <Cosmed><entry><EE-Calc-Sum> WITH <value>&result</value>
    </action>
</event>
```

5 Experiments and Evaluation

Experiments were run on a 2.66GHz Intel Core2 Duo CPU server with 4GB of RAM. The sensors were deployed on a jockey while on a Horse Simulator, as shown in Figure 1. As part of our evaluation, we measure query times for identifying the events pre-defined by the sport scientists. We also measure the time taken to enrich the information both structurally and with the event-definition context.

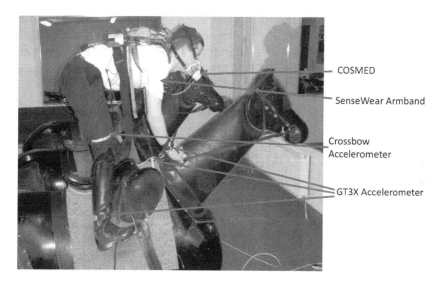

COSMED

SenseWear Armband

Crossbow
Accelerometer

GT3X Accelerometer

Fig. 1. Indoor Simulator Training

Table 1 shows sample event detection times, run following the execution of the event definitions. The instances of *whipping* represent entries matching the criteria given in the event definition. The numbers correspond to entries, which in the case of the GT3X Accelerometer is 0.03333 of a second. After experiments, it was discovered that the average duration of a `whip` is 0.5 seconds (or 15 instances). Analysing a ground-truth for the data concerned (ground truth analysis was performed using video in as many circumstances as possible), confirmed that there were 3 right `whip` events, and 14 left `whip` events, as shown in the query result set.

Table 1. Sample Event Queries and times

	Events	Filename	Size	Values	Query Time	Results
1	Fast-Cantering	GT3Xsaddle.xml	8.12MB	108,009	56ms	13,353
2	Left Whip	leftwrist.xml	7.22MB	108,009	51ms	210
3	Right Whip	rightwrist.xml	7.08MB	108,009	53ms	45
4	Whipping	GT3Xsaddle.xml	8.12MB	108,009	55ms	13,353

Table 2. Sample Enrichment Times

	Event	Filename	Enrichment Time
1	Fast-Cantering	GT3Xsaddle.xml	13,450ms
2	Left Whip	leftwrist.xml	12,221ms
3	Right Whip	rightwrist.xml	11,902ms
4	EE-Est > 90%	Cosmed.xml & HeartRate.xml	1,498ms

A prior experimental run resulted in the (incorrect) discovery of 4 right `whip` events and 20 left `whip` events, a total of seven false positives. It was realised that *other* jockey movements were identifed to be `whip` movements. This event detection evolved to include the use a new `fast-cantering` constraint. Including this constraint and the knowledge that a `whip` can only occur during a `fast-canter`, resulted in removing these false positives (one right hand whip, and six left hand whips). This illustrates how the Sports Physiologists are now in a position to alter their needs using event definition modules to improve accuracy. As the tested jockeys were trainees, they are not allowed to gallop. For any other jockey, this event would be replaced with a `Gallop` event.

For completion, we show a sample of contextual enrichment times in Table 2. The time is the total accumulated from converting raw sensor data to low-level structured information and then to high-level event-rich information. As yet, we have not performed any optimisation on the transformation process, as the motivation was to enable users to define and detect complex requirements from semantically poor information. The main evaluation comes from our collaborators who can now define their requirements in the form of events and extract new knowledge.

6   Conclusions

In this paper, our goal was to reduce the gap between the requirements of our collaborators and the sensors recording movement data on Horse Simulators. We extended the EventSense framework with a new process to extract knowledge from multiple sensor sources. We described our metadata driven approach to structural and semantic enrichment using Sensor and Contextual Profiles. We then introduced our new event detection mechanism in its 3-Tier format: basic event detection; event detection based on results of other defined events;

and events definitions based on data integrated from multiple sources and new event definitions. The modular nature of the event definition allows the end user greater control and flexibility in defining events and thus, acquiring different forms of knowledge. Our experiments have shown how this approach is evaluated and is providing benefit to the end user. Our current work is based on integration, utilising the timing and granularity constraints along with synchronisation techniques and algorithms, to extend the knowledge acquisition capabilities even further.

References

1. Babitski, G., Bergweiler, S., Hoffmann, J., Schon, D., Stasch, C., Walkowski, A.: Ontology-Based Integration of Sensor Web Services in Disaster Management. In: Janowicz, K., Raubal, M., Levashkin, S. (eds.) GeoS 2009. LNCS, vol. 5892, pp. 103–121. Springer, Heidelberg (2009)
2. Bonnet, P., Gehrke, J., Seshadri, P.: Towards Sensor Database Systems. In: Tan, K.-L., Franklin, M.J., Lui, J.C.-S. (eds.) MDM 2001. LNCS, vol. 1987, pp. 3–14. Springer, Heidelberg (2000)
3. Conroy, K., May, G., Roantree, M., Warrington, G.: Expanding Sensor Networks to Automate Knowledge Acquisition. In: To Appear in British National Conference on Databases (BNCOD). LNCS. Springer, Heidelberg (2011)
4. Corrales, J.A., Candelas, F.A., Torres, F.: Sensor data integration for indoor human tracking. Robotics and Autonomous Systems 58(8), 931–939 (2010)
5. Cosmed (2011), http://www.cosmed.it/
6. Da Costa, R.A.G., Cugnasca, A.E.: Use of Data Warehouse to Manage Data from Wireless Sensors Networks That Monitor Pollinators. In: 11th International Conference on Mobile Data Management (MDM), pp. 402–406. IEEE Computer Society, Los Alamitos (2010)
7. Henson, C.A., Pschorr, J.K., Sheth, A.P., Thirunarayan, K.: SemSOS: Semantic sensor Observation Service. In: International Symposium on Collaborative Technologies and Systems (CTS), pp. 44–53 (2009)
8. Marks, G., Roantree, M., Smyth, D.: Optimizing Queries for Web Generated Sensor Data. In: Australasian Database Conference (ADC), pp. 151–159. Australian Computer Society, Inc. (2011)
9. Observations and Measurements (2011), http://www.opengeospatial.org/standards/om
10. Resource Description Framework in attributes (RDFa) (2011), http://www.w3.org/TR/xhtml-rdfa-primer/
11. Semantic Web Rule Language (2011), http://www.w3.org/Submission/SWRL/
12. SenseWear System (BodyMedia) (2011), http://sensewear.bodymedia.com/
13. Sensor Observation Service (2011), http://www.opengeospatial.org/standards/sos
14. Sensor Web Enablement (2011), http://www.opengeospatial.org/projects/groups/sensorweb
15. Sheth, A.P., Henson, C.A., Sahoo, S.S.: Semantic Sensor Web. IEEE Internet Computing 12, 78–83 (2008)

16. The Irish Turf Club (2011), http://www.turfclub.ie/site/
17. Web Ontology Language (2011), http://www.w3.org/TR/owl-features/
18. XQuery (2011), http://www.w3.org/TR/xquery/
19. XQuery Update Facility (2011), http://www.w3.org/TR/xquery-update-10/
20. Yang, J., Zhang, C., Li, X., Huang, Y., Fu, S., Acevedo, M.F.: Integration of wireless sensor networks in environmental monitoring cyber infrastructure. Wireless Networks 16(4), 1091–1108 (2010)

Concurrent Semi-supervised Learning of Data Streams

Hai-Long Nguyen[1], Wee-Keong Ng[1], Yew-Kwong Woon[2], and Duc H. Tran[1]

[1] Nanyang Technological University, Singapore
nguy0105@ntu.edu.sg, wkn@acm.org,ductran@pmail.ntu.edu.sg
[2] EADS Innovation Works Singapore
david.woon@eads.net

Abstract. Conventional stream mining algorithms focus on single and stand-alone mining tasks. Given the single-pass nature of data streams, it makes sense to maximize throughput by performing multiple complementary mining tasks concurrently. We investigate the potential of concurrent semi-supervised learning on data streams and propose an incremental algorithm called CSL-Stream (<u>C</u>oncurrent <u>S</u>emi–supervised <u>L</u>earning of Data <u>Stream</u>s) that performs clustering and classification at the same time. Experiments using common synthetic and real datasets show that CSL-Stream outperforms prominent clustering and classification algorithms (D-Stream and SmSCluster) in terms of accuracy, speed and scalability. The success of CSL-Stream paves the way for a new research direction in understanding latent commonalities among various data mining tasks in order to exploit the power of concurrent stream mining.

1 Introduction

Nowadays, large volumes of data streams are generated from various advanced applications such as informaion/communication networks, real-time surveillance, and online transactions. These data streams are usually characterized as temporally ordered, read-once-only, fast-changing, and possibly infinite, compared to static datasets studied in conventional data mining problems. Although many studies have been conducted to deal with data streams [2,3,7,8,14], most existing data stream algorithms focus on single and stand-alone mining. In many practical applications, it is desirable to concurrently perform multiple types of mining in order to better exploit data streams. For example, website administrators will be interested to use clickstream data to classify users into specific types and cluster webpages of similar topics at the same time in order to enhance the user's experience. In addition, concurrent mining offers a potential synergy: The knowledge gained by one mining task may also be useful to other mining tasks. Unfortunately, there is currently little research on concurrent stream mining.

In order to demonstrate the potential of concurrent stream mining, we propose a stream mining algorithm called CSL-Stream (<u>C</u>oncurrent <u>S</u>emi-supervised <u>L</u>earning of <u>Stream</u> Data) that concurrently performs clustering and classification. We choose to focus on classification and clustering as they share common

A. Cuzzocrea and U. Dayal (Eds.): DaWaK 2011, LNCS 6862, pp. 445–459, 2011.

assumptions that data objects within a cluster (class) are similar and data objects belonging to different clusters (classes) are dissimilar. In addition, it is observed that most data objects in a cluster belong to a dominant class, and a class can be represented by many clusters. Therefore, classifiers can leverage on clustering to improve its accuracy [16]. For example, webpages within a topic are most visited by a specific type of users, and a user can be interested in many topics.

Moreover, CSL-Stream is a semi-supervised algorithm that is applicable to many real applications where only a small portion of data is labeled due to expensive labeling costs. In order to exploit a valuable limited amount of labeled data, CSL-Stream maintains a class profile vector for each node in the synopsis tree of the data stream. The profile vectors play an important role as pivots for the clustering process. The two mining tasks not only run at the same time, but also mutually improve each other. The clustering considers class profile vectors to attain high-purity clustering results. Conversely, the classification benefits clustering models in achieving high accuracy, and even works well with unlabeled data or outliers. Finally, CSL-Stream uses an *incremental learning* approach where the clustering and classification models are continuously improved to handle concept drifts and where mining results can be delivered in a timely manner. By re-using information from historical models, CSL-Stream requires only constant time to update its learning models with acceptable memory bounds.

With its impressive experimental results, we hope that CSL-Stream will inspire a new research direction in understanding latent commonalities among various data mining tasks in order to determine the degree of concurrency possible among them; this requires further research to derive data mining primitives which represent the entire space of data mining tasks.

The rest of this paper is organized as follows: In the next section, we discuss related work in stream clustering, classification and semi-supervised learning. We propose the CSL-Stream algorithm and provide its formal proofs in Section 3. We perform rigorous experiments to evaluate our algorithm with both real and synthetic datasets in Section 4. Finally, we conclude the paper in the last section.

2   Related Work

Various algorithms have been recently proposed for stream data clustering, such as CluStream [2], DenStream [7], and D-Stream [8]. These algorithms adopt an online-offline scheme where raw stream data is processed to produce summary statistics in the online component and clustering is performed in the offline component using summary statistics. Both CluStream and DenStream store summary statistics into a collection of micro-clusters. D-Stream views the entire data space as a finite set of equal-size grids, each of which maintains summary information. The different algorithms vary in their online data processing schemes and offline clustering methods. CluStream applies k-means to perform offline clustering while DenStream and D-Stream perform DBSCAN-like clustering [9]. Both DenStream and D-Stream apply a fading model and a synopsis removal scheme to discard outdated data.

Recent work on data stream classification mainly falls into three categories. The first category extends the decision tree from traditional classification algorithms to the Hoeffding tree, such as CVFDT [10]. The second category uses ensemble classifiers and modify them whenever concept drifts appear [15,18]. The last category is k-NN classification on stream data. An example of k-NN stream classification is On-Demand Classifier [3] that maintains sets of micro-clusters with single-class labels and performs classification on demand.

Semi-supervised learning has been proposed to cope with partially labeled data. Although many semi-supervised learning algorithms have been developed for traditional data [20], there is still insufficient work for data streams.

Recently, Masud et al. proposed a semi-supervised algorithm for data streams, called SmSCluster [12]. The algorithm utilizes a cluster-impurity measurement to construct an ensemble of k-NN classifiers. When a classifier has no knowledge of a certain class, the algorithm copies the knowledge from another classifier with an injection procedure in order to reduce the mis-classification rate. However, SmSCluster suffers from high computational complexity as it performs clustering based on the k-means algorithm [17,5]. The difficulty in choosing the optimal k value is an inherent problem of k-means and this is aggravated by the evolving nature of data streams which inevitably results in more dynamic clusters being formed.

In 2007, Aggrawal et al. proposed a summarization paradigm for the clustering and classification of data streams [1]. This paradigm can be considered as a generalization of CluStream [2] and On-Demand Classification [3]. Unfortunately, the classification and clustering algorithms run separately and there is no mutual relationship between them. The algorithm needs time to process the offline operations and cannot provide timely results. Moreover, the use of a pyramidal time window makes it unstable; the micro-structures become larger and larger over time and this degrades the model's performance [19].

3   Proposed Method

Figure 1 is an overview of our novel concurrent mining approach. CSL-Stream stores a dynamic tree structure to capture the entire multi-dimensional space as well as a statistical synopsis of the data stream. Unlike static grids in D-Stream [8] that use much memory, our dynamic tree structure requires far less storage because unnecessary nodes will be pruned and sibling nodes merged. We apply a fading model to deal with concept drifts; the properties of a tree node will *decrease* according to how long the node has not been updated.

The two mining tasks of CSL-Stream, semi-supervised clustering and semi-supervised classification, are concurrently performed. They leverage on each other in terms of improving accuracy and speed; the clustering process takes into account class labels to produce high-quality clusters; the classification process uses clustering models together with a statistical test to achieve high accuracy and low running time.

CSL-Stream also employs an *incremental learning* approach. The system only needs to update whenever it becomes unstable. To check the system's stability,

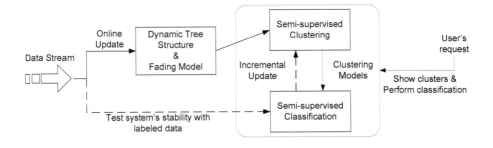

Fig. 1. Overview of CSL-Stream

we select labeled data during each time interval t_p and test them with the classification model. If the accuracy is too low, we will incrementally update the clustering models.

3.1 Dynamic Tree Structure

We assume that the input data stream has d dimensions and forms a hyper-space S. We also assume a discrete time model where the time stamp is labeled by integers $t = 0, 1, 2, \ldots, n$. A record e of the data stream has a coordinate vector $e_x = [x_1, x_2, \ldots, x_d]$, a class label e_l ($0 \le e_l \le L$; $e_l = 0$ if e is unlabeled), and a time stamp e_t.

We construct a dynamic tree structure to capture the entire space S with different levels of granularities as follows. Initially, a tree root at level 0 is created to hold the entire space S. Then for a tree node at level h, we partition each dimension into two equal-sized portions, and the tree node is partitioned into 2^d child nodes at level $h + 1$. We chose 2 as it provides sufficient granularity with reasonable storage requirements. This partitioning process terminates when it reaches a pre-defined maximum tree height H. The tree root contains the overall information of the entire space S. Each tree node at height h stores information of its subspace at granularity h. A tree node is only created if there are some instances belonging to it.

Figure 2 is an example of the tree structure with $d = 2$, $H = 2$. Figure 2(a) is a 2-dimensional data stream whose each dimension has a range [0-1]. Each data instance has a transaction identify, two coordinates $[x_1, x_2]$, a class label (1, 2, or 0 if unlabeled), and a time stamp. The tree root is created at level $h = 0$, then it is divided into four ($2^d = 2^2 = 4$) child nodes at level $h = 1$. Again, a tree node at level 1 is partitioned into four child nodes at level $h = 2$, and the partitioning process stops. Then, a tree node stores information of data instances belonging to its space. For example, in Figure 2(b), the data instance tid_02 with coordinates $[0.6, 0.2]$ is stored in the leaf node B at the bottom level $h = 2$.

Node Storage. Suppose a tree node C receives m data instances $e^1, e^2, \ldots, e^m$. The following information will be stored in the tree node C:

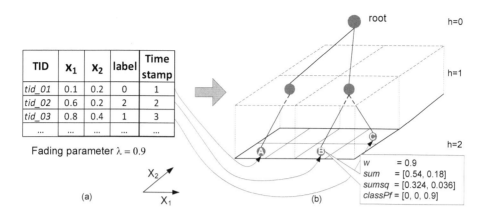

Fig. 2. Synopsis tree for the 2-dimensional data stream with $H = 2$

1. Node weight w is the sum of weights of all data instances, $w = \sum_{i=1}^{m} e_w^i$. The weight of an instance is set to 1 at its arriving time, and then decreased over time to reflect its diminishing effect on the mining processes. Details of the weighting scheme are defined in the next section.
2. A d-dimensional vector sum is the weighted sum of the coordinates of all data instances, $sum = \sum_{i=1}^{m} e_w^i \times e_x^i$.
3. A d-dimensional vector $sumsq$ is the weighted sum of the squared coordinates of all data instances, $sumsq = \sum_{i=1}^{m} e_w^i \times {e_x^i}^2$
4. A $(L+1)$-dimensional vector $classPf$ stores the class profile of the node. The lth element is the sum of weights of all data instances that have label l.

Handling Concept Drift. Concept drift occurs in a data stream when there are changes in the underlying data distribution over time. There are two major approaches to handle concept drifts for data streams: (1) *instance selection*, and (2) *instance weighting*. The instance selection approach uses a sliding window to select recently arrived instances while ignoring older instances [11]. In instance weighting approach, data instances can be weighted according to their age, and their relevance with regard to the current concept, e.g. fading model [8].

In CSL-Stream, we apply a fading model with an exponential function to set the weight of a data instance e: $e_w = f(\Delta t) = \lambda^{\Delta t}$, where $0 < \lambda < 1$, and Δt is the time gap between the current time and the arriving time of the instance e. Figure 2(b) illustrates the fading model. Let us assume that the current time is 3, and the fading parameter λ is 0.9. The instance e with tid_02 that came at time stamp 2 has a weight of $e_w = \lambda^{(3-2)} = 0.9^1 = 0.9$. As the tree node B only receives a data instance tid_02, the node B stores the following information: $w = 0.9$, $sum = 0.9 \times [0.6, 0.2] = [0.54, 0.18]$, $sumsq = 0.9 \times [0.6^2, 0.2^2] = 0.9 \times [0.36, 0.04] = [0.324, 0.036]$, and $classPf = [0, 0, 0.9]$ as the instance tid_02 has 2 as its class label .

Algorithm 1. Online Update

1: initialize tree T
2: **while** data stream is active **do**
3:     read next data point e
4:     $C \leftarrow T.root$
5:     **while** $C.height \leq H$ **do**
6:         $\Delta t \leftarrow t - C.lastUpdateTime$
7:         $C.w \leftarrow C.w \times f(\Delta t) + 1$
8:         $C.sum \leftarrow C.sum \times f(\Delta t) + e_x$
9:         $C.sumsq \leftarrow C.sumsq \times f(\Delta t) + (e_x)^2$
10:        $i \leftarrow e_l;$
11:        $C.classPf[i] \leftarrow C.classPf[i] \times f(\Delta t) + 1$
12:        $C \leftarrow C.getChild(e)$
13:        **if** C is $NULL$ **then**
14:            addSubNode(C)
15:        **end if**
16:    **end while**
17:    **if** $t = t_p$ **then**
18:        Semi-Clustering()
19:    **else if** (t mod $t_p = 0$) **then**
20:        PruneTree()
21:        Incremental_Update()
22:    **else if** ($user\_request$ = true) **then**
23:        Show clustering results
24:        Semi-Classification()
25:    **end if**
26: **end while**

3.2 Online Update

Given an instance e, this online-update process starts from the root and searches through the tree until the maximum height H is reached. At each height h, we update the node C that contains e. Then, we move down to search for the child node of C that contains e and update it. If no such child node exists, we create a new node.

As shown in Algorithm 1, the online-update process consists of two parts:

1. *Top-down updating* of the tree node's information whenever a new instance arrives (lines 6-16): Firstly, the time gap is calculated. All historical information is faded with the exponential function $f(\Delta t)$. The weight and element i-th of class profile are incremented by 1, while the *sum* vector and *sumsq* vector are added by the coordinates and the squares of coordinates respectively.

2. *Periodical pruning* of the tree to conserve memory and accelerate the mining process (line 19): For each time interval $t_p = \lfloor \log_\lambda(\alpha_L/\alpha_H) \rfloor$, which is the minimum time required for a node's density to be changed, CSL-Stream searches through the tree and deletes all sparse nodes (α_L, α_H to be defined in the next section). Next, it searches the tree to find a parent node whose all child nodes are dense. Then, all child nodes are merged and deleted, and the parent node contains the sum of their properties.

3.3 Concurrent Semi-supervised Learning

Semi-supervised Clustering. We use the node weight to define different types of nodes: dense, transitional and sparse nodes. The reachability property of dense nodes is also defined.

Algorithm 2. Semi-Clustering

Input:

A list of labeled dense nodes: *LDSet*

A list of unlabeled dense nodes: *UDSet*

1: Create a cluster for each node in
   LDSet.

2: Extend these clusters sequently with
   neighbor nodes in *UDSet*.

3: Merge any 2 clusters if they have same
   labels.

4: Perform DBSCAN clustering for the
   remaining nodes in *UDSet*

5: Remove clusters whose weights are
   less than ϵ

Node Density: The density of a node is a ratio of its weight to its hyper-volume $V(C)$ (product of d-dimensional lengths). A node at height h is recognized as a dense node if its density is α_H times greater than the average density.

Suppose the volume of the entire data space S is $V(S) = 1$ and the total weight of the synopsis tree is $w_{total} = \frac{1}{1-\lambda}$ according to [8], the average density is $\frac{w_{total}}{V(S)} = \frac{1}{1-\lambda}$. Then, the dense condition for a height-h node with its volume $\frac{1}{2^{dh}}$ and can be written as $w \geq \alpha_H * \frac{1}{2^{dh}(1-\lambda)} = D_H$. Similarly, node g at height h is a sparse node if $w \leq \alpha_L * \frac{1}{2^{dh}(1-\lambda)} = D_L$, where α_L is a parameter to identify a sparse node. A node is a transitional node if the density of the node is between D_H and D_L; i.e., $D_L < w < D_H$.

Node Neighborhood: Two nodes are *neighbors* if their minimum distance or single-link is less than $\frac{\delta}{2^H}$, where δ is a neighbor range parameter. A node C_p is *reachable* from C_q if there exists a chain of nodes $C_1, \ldots, C_k, C_k + 1, \ldots, Cm$, $C_q = C_1$ and $C_p = C_m$ such that each pair of C_i and $C_i + 1$ are neighbors. Moreover, a *cluster* is defined as a set of density nodes where any pair of two grids is reachable.

The semi-supervised clustering of CSL-Stream is performed according to Algorithm 2. Initially, the algorithm traverses the tree to get two sets of dense nodes: a labeled set, *LDSet* and an unlabeled set, *UDSet*. Firstly, we create a cluster for each labeled node (line 1). Next, we extend these clusters step by step with their neighbor nodes. If the neighbor node does not belong to any cluster, we put it into the current cluster (line 2). If the neighbor node belongs to a cluster, we will merge these two clusters if they have the same label (line 3). Then, we continue to build clusters for the remaining nodes in *UDSet*. We perform DBSCAN[9] clustering to find the maximum set of remaining reachable unlabeled dense nodes in the *UDSet* (lines 4). Finally, we remove clusters whose weights are less than a threshold value, ϵ. These clusters are considered as noise.

Semi-supervised Classification. Details of the semi-supervised classification of CSL-Stream are given in Algorithm 3. The input to Algorithm 3 is a list of clusters. Each cluster in the list has a class profile array computed by the sum of class profiles of all its member nodes. For each testing instance, we find the closest cluster and then do a statistical check to decide whether the distance

---

Algorithm 3. Semi-Classification

Input: A test set: *testSet*	6: *dist*←calculateDistance(*e,mean*)
A list of clusters: *listCluster*	7: **if** *dist* < θ ∗ *stDv* **then**
	8: *e*.clusterID ← c̃.getClusterID()
1: **while** *testSet* is not empty **do**	9: *e*.class ← c̃.getDominantClass()
2: *e* ← *testSet*.removeFirst()	10: **else**
3: Select the closet cluster, c̃.	11: Set *e* as noise.
4: *stDv*← c̃.getDeviation()	12: **end if**
5: *mean*← c̃.getMean()	13: **end while**

Algorithm 4. Incremental Update

Input: A list of historical clusters: *listClusters*	5: **end for**
	6: Traverse the tree to get a list β_{dense} of *isolated* dense nodes.
Output: A list of clusters	7: Separate β_{dense} into two sets of labeled and unlabeled nodes, *LDSet* and *UDSet*.
1: **if** *accuracy* ≤ *threshold* **then**	
2: **for all** cluster ĉ in *listCluster* **do**	
3: ĉ.removeSparseNodes()	8: Semi-Clustering(*LDSet,UDSet*);
4: ĉ.checkConsistence()	9: **end if**

---

between the instance and the cluster's center is acceptable. The adequate range is less than θ times of the cluster's standard deviation (line 7). The cluster's center and deviation are computed accordingly $\mu = \frac{sum}{w}$, $\sigma = \sqrt{\frac{sumsq}{w} - \left(\frac{sum}{w}\right)^2}$. If the distance is acceptable, the dominant class of the cluster will be assigned to the testing sample. Else, the instance will be considered as noise.

Incremental Update. CSL-Stream is an incremental algorithm. It can detect and update its learning models incrementally whenever a concept drift occurs.

For each time interval t_p (Algorithm 1, line 21), we select labeled instances and test them with the classification model to check the system's stability. If the accuracy is greater than a predefined threshold value (experiments reveal that 0.9 is an appropriate value); the model remains stable, and we can skip the remaining steps. Else, we need to refine the learning models. CSL-Stream begins to fine-tune the historical clustering model by checking the consistency of each cluster. The algorithm removes sparse nodes, that are dense at the previous learning phase, and splits the cluster if it becomes unconnected or has low purity.

Then, CSL-Stream traverses the tree to get a list of isolated dense nodes β_{dense} (line 6). After separating β_{dense} into two sets of labeled and unlabeled dense nodes, it performs the semi-supervised clustering method to derive new arriving clusters. As the procedure reuses the historical clustering results, the size of β_{dense} is relatively small. Thus, the running time of the clustering process is reduced significantly.

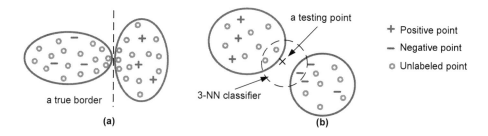

Fig. 3. Examples of the benefits of concurrent semi-learning

Example. Our concurrent approach maximizes computational resources and exploits advantages of the interplay between clustering and classification. CSL-Stream's semi-supervised clustering takes care of data labels by continuously updating the class profile array of each node. It ensures that two clusters are merged only if they have the same dominant class, finds the best borders among clusters. For example, in Figure 3 (a), two clusters with different class labels share the same border. A stand-alone clustering algorithm will probably incorrectly consider them as a single cluster. For example, D-Stream will merge the two clusters as it views the data points at the border as connected due to their proximity to one another [8]. CSL-Stream does not merge them as they have different dominant classes, and thus CSL-Stream correctly considers them as two clusters.

By disregarding unlabeled data, a stand-alone classification may not capture the classes' distribution. Using clustering results with unlabeled data, CSL-Stream can gain knowledge of the classes' distributions and improve its accuracy. For example, in Figure 3 (b), a 3-NN classifier wrongly classifies the testing point because most its neighbors are unlabeled. CSL-Stream selects the label of the nearest cluster, and correctly classifies the testing point as positive.

3.4 Complexity Analysis

Space Complexity

Lemma 1. *If the density threshold to remove sparse node is D_L, then the maximum number of nodes in the synopsis tree is $N_{max-node} \leq \lceil \frac{\log D_L}{\log \lambda} \rceil = O(dH)$*

Proof. In the worst case, we assume that every data point arrives at a different node and no merging is performed. When a node receives a data point, its weight is set to 1. We define t_{max} as the time needed for this node to become sparse with its weight $\leq D_L$, and is removed. After t_{max} time, whenever a data point arrives, a new tree node created, and another one is deleted. This means that t_{max} is the maximum number of tree nodes. We have:
$$\lambda^{t_{max}} = D_L \quad \Rightarrow \quad t_{max} \log \lambda = \log D_L \quad \Rightarrow \quad t_{max} \leq \lceil \tfrac{\log D_L}{\log \lambda} \rceil$$
We also know that: $D_L = \frac{\alpha_L * V(C)}{(1-\lambda)} = \frac{\alpha_L}{(1-\lambda)2^{dH}}$ for a leaf node. Then,
$$\Rightarrow \quad t_{max} \leq \lceil \log_\lambda \alpha_L + \log_\lambda (1-\lambda) - dH \log_\lambda 2 \rceil \quad = O(dH).$$

Table 1. Characteristics of datasets used for evaluation

Name	#Instances	#Attributes	#Classes
RBF	100,000	10	5
HYP	100,000	10	2
LED	100,000	24	3
SHUTTLE	58,000	9	7
KDD'99	494,022	34	5
COVERTYPE	581,012	54	7

Time Complexity. The proposed CSL-Stream has three main operations: up-dating, clustering and classification. The online updating consists of top-down updating and periodical pruning. The top-down updating only requires a con-stant time to update a new data instance and its complexity is $O(nH)$, where n is the number of instances of the data stream. The running time of the prun-ing process depends on the number of tree nodes. In the previous section, we prove that the upper bound of the number of tree nodes is $O(dH)$, so the prun-ing process's complexity is $O(ndH)$. The complexity of the clustering depends on its implementation. If we use R*-trees to implement the synopsis tree, the searching time for neighbor nodes is $O(log(dH))$. And the complexity of cluster-ing operation is $O(dHlog(dH))$. The running time of the classification operation depends on the number of clusters, and this number is usually a multiple of the number of classes. Thus, the classification time can be expected to be $O(nL)$, where L is the number of classes. In summary, the complexity of the algorithm is: $O(nH + ndH + dHlog(dH) + nL) = O(n(dH + L))$

4   Experiments and Analysis

4.1   Experimental Setup

We use both synthetic and real datasets. The three synthetic datasets, Random RBF generator (RBF), Rotating Hyperplane (HYP), and LED dataset (LED), are generated from the MOA framework [6]. Concept drifts are generated by moving 10 centroids at speed 0.001 per instance in the RBF dataset, and chang-ing 10 attributes at speed 0.001 per instance in the HYP dataset. We also use the three largest real datasets in the UCI machine learning repository: SHUT-TLE, KDD'99, and Forest Covertype. Table 1 shows the characteristics of the six datasets.

In order to illustrate the beneficial mutual relationship between clustering and classification, we created two variants of CSL-Stream that do not exploit this relationship as follows.

- *Alone-Clustering:* This variant of CSL-Stream does not consider class labels while clustering.
- *Alone-Classification:* This variant of CSL-Stream finds the nearest tree node to testing instances and classifies them to the dominant class of the tree node.

We compare the performance of CSL-Stream to its stand-alone variants, D-Stream [8], and SmSCluster [12]. The experiments were conducted on a Windows PC with a Pentium D 3GHz Intel processor and 2GB memory.

For D-Stream and SmSCluster, we use the published default parameter configurations. The chunk size *chunk-size* is set to 1000 for all datasets. For CSL-Stream, the dense ratio threshold α_H is set to 3.0, the sparse ratio threshold α_L is set to 0.8, and the fading factor λ is set to 0.998 as recommended in D-Stream [8]. The other parameters of CSL-Stream are set as follows: maximum tree's height $H = 5$, the noise threshold $\epsilon = 1$, and the statistical range factor $\theta = 3$.

To simulate the data stream environment, we divided each dataset into many chunks of size *chunk-size*. These sequential chunks are numbered and their roles are set as follows: the odd chunks are used for training and the even chunks are used for testing. We run the experiments 10 times for each dataset and summarize their running time and performance with their means and standard deviations into Tables 2, 3.

4.2   Clustering Evaluation

There are some constraints to evaluate the performance of a clustering method such as cluster homogeneity constraint, cluster completeness constraint, rag bag constraint, and cluster size vs. quantity constraint. Although many measures have been proposed (for example, purity, inverse purity, entropy, and F-measure), most measures can not satisfy all these constraints.

Given a pair of samples, their correctness is defined as 1 if they are in the same cluster and have the same class label. The BCubed [4] measure computes the average correctness over the dataset. It has been proven to satisfy all the above constraints. Thus, we use BCubed to evaluate clustering results in our experiments. We conducted experiments with the 100%-labeled datasets to assess the clustering results of CSL-Stream, Alone-Clustering and D-Stream. Table 2 shows the running time as well as B-Cubed comparisons among the three clustering methods. We observe that CSL-Stream achieves the lowest running

Table 2. Comparison among CSL-Stream, Alone-Clustering and D-Stream. Time is measured in seconds. For each dataset, the lowest running time is underlined, and the highest B-Cubed value is **boldfaced**.

	CSL-Stream		Alone-Clustering		D-Stream	
	Time	B-Cubed	Time	B-Cubed	Time	B-Cubed
RBF(10,0.001)	$10.64_{\pm1.56}$	$\mathbf{37.67_{\pm4.93}}$	$17.22_{\pm1.72}$	$36.27_{\pm2.32}$	$17.37_{\pm1.36}$	$17.39_{\pm2.41}$
HYP(10,0.001)	$13.37_{\pm1.23}$	$\mathbf{65.24_{\pm10.66}}$	$23.67_{\pm1.66}$	$57.14_{\pm4.01}$	$33.37_{\pm1.46}$	$55.54_{\pm4.66}$
LED	$53.9_{\pm1.68}$	$\mathbf{68.38_{\pm11.74}}$	$205.61_{\pm2.34}$	$19.1_{\pm0.58}$	$203.8_{\pm2.94}$	$19.3_{\pm0.63}$
SHUTTLE	$1.37_{\pm0.16}$	$\mathbf{93.46_{\pm1.04}}$	$1.37_{\pm0.16}$	$89.07_{\pm1.83}$	$1.45_{\pm0.17}$	$88.1_{\pm0.93}$
KDD'99	$39.78_{\pm0.62}$	$\mathbf{76.89_{\pm27.83}}$	$38.68_{\pm0.84}$	$76.88_{\pm27.83}$	$53.79_{\pm1.06}$	$73.5_{\pm31.24}$
COVERTYPE	$130.24_{\pm1.87}$	$26.54_{\pm9.68}$	$212.07_{\pm2.45}$	$\mathbf{35.11_{\pm10.79}}$	$152.46_{\pm2.67}$	$12.55_{\pm5.8}$

time and the highest B-Cubed value for many datasets. Comparing with Alone-Clustering and D-Stream, CSL-Stream takes into account the class labels during clustering and guarantees that no two clusters with the same label are merged. Thus, it achieves better B-Cubed results than Alone-Clustering and D-Stream. Moreover, using the dynamic tree structure, CSL-Stream can adapt quickly to concept drifts. It is also the fastest method because the pruning process helps to remove unnecessary tree nodes. Although CSL-Stream has low B-Cubed values in some datasets, e.g., RBF, HYP, and COVERTYPE as each class has many clusters in these datasets,CSL-Stream still attains high purity in these cases ($> 90\%$). Detailed results of other clustering evaluation measures can be found in our technical report [13].

4.3   Classification Evaluation

We compare the running time and accuracy among CSL-Stream, Alone-Classification, and SmSCluster [12]. The upper part of Table 3 reports the running time and accuracy comparisons among the above classification algorithms when the datasets are fully labeled. It is found that CSL-Stream is the fastest and the most accurate algorithm for many datasets. CSL-Stream is better than Alone-Classification in terms of speed and accuracy because it exploits clustering results for classification. CSL-Stream also takes less time as it only compares the testing instances to a small number of clusters and is resistant to noise. SmSCluster suffers a high time complexity and low accuracy with non-spherical clusters since it is based on the k-Means algorithm.

Furthermore, we measure performances of the above algorithms when unlabeled data is present. We conduct experiments with the Hyperplane and KDD'99 datasets at different proportions of labeled data instances: *50%, 25%* and *10%*.

Table 3. Comparison among CSL-Stream, Alone-Classification and SmSCluster. Time is measured in seconds. For each dataset, the lowest running time is underlined, and the highest accuracy is **boldfaced**.

	CSL-Stream		Alone-Classification		SmSCluster	
	Time	Accuracy	Time	Accuracy	Time	Accuracy
RBF(10,0.001)	$49.29_{\pm2.35}$	$\mathbf{71.57_{\pm6.37}}$	$53.32_{\pm3.24}$	$44.57_{\pm7.18}$	$41.45_{\pm3.35}$	$30.1_{\pm12.38}$
HYP(10,0.001)	$15.78_{\pm1.68}$	$\mathbf{87.88_{\pm1.88}}$	$16.17_{\pm2.03}$	$70.66_{\pm2.09}$	$40.18_{\pm2.65}$	$76.05_{\pm2.61}$
LED	$34.17_{\pm2.16}$	$\mathbf{72.73_{\pm1.82}}$	$98.85_{\pm3.12}$	$10.24_{\pm1}$	$85.69_{\pm3.87}$	$54.70_{\pm3.45}$
SHUTTLE	$2.56_{\pm0.35}$	$\mathbf{98.3_{\pm0.3}}$	$2.64_{\pm0.91}$	$98.28_{\pm0.31}$	$20.35_{\pm2.61}$	$97.50_{\pm0.49}$
KDD'99	$83.06_{\pm2.47}$	$\mathbf{98.06_{\pm8.29}}$	$87.57_{\pm2.13}$	$98.25_{\pm8.24}$	$565.02_{\pm3.87}$	$85.33_{\pm33.39}$
COVERTYPE	$183.75_{\pm3.05}$	$\mathbf{81.63_{\pm10.43}}$	$194.41_{\pm3.46}$	$78.96_{\pm9.39}$	$320.65_{\pm3.02}$	$49.23_{\pm15.42}$
HYP(10,0.001) 50%	$20.08_{\pm1.48}$	$\mathbf{81.6_{\pm3.61}}$	$21.11_{\pm2.16}$	$35.97_{\pm3.02}$	$37.89_{\pm2.14}$	$74.36_{\pm2.68}$
HYP(10,0.001) 25%	$17.34_{\pm1.32}$	$\mathbf{73.88_{\pm4.25}}$	$18.65_{\pm2.09}$	$18.29_{\pm2.1}$	$46.26_{\pm2.09}$	$64.36_{\pm3.11}$
HYP(10,0.001) 10%	$15.97_{\pm1.65}$	$61.18_{\pm7.15}$	$17.47_{\pm2.05}$	$7.57_{\pm1.32}$	$31.56_{\pm1.86}$	$\mathbf{61.41_{\pm4.50}}$
KDD'99 50%	$72.3_{\pm2.65}$	$\mathbf{97.08_{\pm8.71}}$	$77.26_{\pm2.35}$	$95_{\pm12.11}$	$691.25_{\pm2.26}$	$75.33_{\pm14.27}$
KDD'99 25%	$72.56_{\pm2.69}$	$\mathbf{96.49_{\pm9.25}}$	$78.12_{\pm2.48}$	$92.82_{\pm15.47}$	$703.56_{\pm2.53}$	$75.03_{\pm14.65}$
KDD'99 10%	$79.46_{\pm2.13}$	$\mathbf{95.07_{\pm11.7}}$	$85.44_{\pm2.49}$	$90.63_{\pm18.89}$	$821.56_{\pm2.70}$	$75.25_{\pm14.25}$

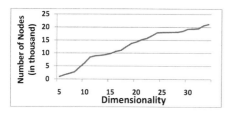

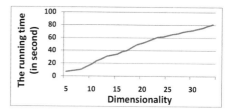

Fig. 4. Number of nodes vs. dimensionality.

Fig. 5. Running time vs. dimensionality.

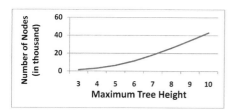

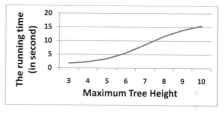

Fig. 6. Number of nodes vs. tree height.

Fig. 7. Running time vs. tree height.

The lower part of Table 3 shows the running time and the accuracy of the above classification algorithms. We observe that CSL-Stream and SmSCluster can work well with partially labeled data. When the percentage of labeled data decreases, the accuracy of Alone-Classification drops quickly while the accuracy of CSL-Stream and SmSCluster remains high. It is obvious too that CSL-Stream outperforms SmSCluster in terms of speed and accuracy. Due to space constraints, we omit classification results of other datasets which are available in our technical report [13]. These results also show that CSL-Stream has the best overall performance.

4.4   Scalability Evaluation

Section 3.4 gives an upper bound for the maximum number of nodes and the running time of CSL-Stream. Here, we have examined the scalability of CSL-Stream in terms of the number of nodes and the running time w.r.t dimensionality and the tree's height.

We conduct experiments with the KDD'99 dataset to assess the scalability w.r.t dimensionality d. We set the maximum tree height to 5, and increase d from 5 to 34 with single steps. With Figures 4 and 5, we can clearly see that the maximum number of nodes and the running time of CSL-Stream increase linearly as the dimensionality increases.

To evaluate the scalability w.r.t the maximum tree height H, we select the first 30K data instances of KDD'99 dataset and set the dimensionality to 34. We increase H from 3 to 10 with single steps. Figures 6 and 7 show that the maximum number of nodes and the running time of CSL-Stream increase linearly as H increases.

4.5   Sensitivity Analysis

In the experiments, we set the neighborhood range $\delta = 2$, the noise threshold $\epsilon = 1$, and the statistical range factor $\theta = 3$. We test the sensitivity of δ, ϵ, and θ with the KDD'99 dataset. We add 10% of random noise with a special label to test the sensitivity of θ. Figure 8 shows the Bcubed values and accuracy of CSL-Stream with different parameters.

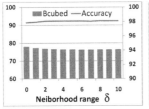 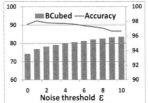 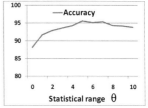

Fig. 8. Sensitivity analysis

5   Conclusions

We have studied the new problem of concurrent mining for data streams and proposed the CSL-Stream as the first attempt to integrate semi-supervised classification and clustering at the same time. We have conducted extensive experiments to show that CSL-Stream outperforms state-of-the-art data stream algorithms. CSL-Stream also overcomes a practical problem with partially labeled data.

With the success of CSL-Stream, we intend to perform an in-depth study on the relationships among basic mining tasks in an attempt to create a framework of mining primitives which will allow us to easily determine the degree of possible concurrency among various tasks.

References

1. Aggarwal, C., Han, J., Wang, J., Yu, P.: On Clustering Massive Data Streams: A Summarization Paradigm. Advances in Database Systems, vol. 31, pp. 9–38. Springer, US (2007)
2. Aggarwal, C.C., Han, J., Wang, J., Yu, P.S.: A framework for clustering evolving data streams. In: VLDB, vol. 29, pp. 81–92. VLDB Endowment (2003)
3. Aggarwal, C.C., Han, J., Wang, J., Yu, P.S.: A framework for on-demand classification of evolving data streams. IEEE TKDE 18(5), 577–589 (2006)
4. Amigo, E., Gonzalo, J., Artiles, J.: A comparison of extrinsic clustering evaluation metrics based on formal constraints. Inf. Retr. 12(4), 461–486 (2009)
5. Basu, S., Bilenko, M., Mooney, R.J.: A probabilistic framework for semi-supervised clustering. In: ACM SIGKDD, pp. 59–68. ACM, New York (2004)

6. Bifet, A., Holmes, G., Kirkby, R.: Moa: Massive online analysis. The Journal of Machine Learning Research 11, 1601–1604 (2010)
7. Cao, F., Ester, M., Qian, W., Zhou, A.: Density-based clustering over an evolving data stream with noise. In: SDM, pp. 328–339 (2006)
8. Chen, Y., Tu, L.: Density-based clustering for real-time stream data. In: ACM SIGKDD, pp. 133–142. ACM, New York (2007)
9. Ester, M., Kriegel, H.-P., Sander, J., Xu, X.: A density-based algorithm for discovering clusters in large spatial databases with noise. In: KDD, pp. 226–231. AAAI Press, Menlo Park (1996)
10. Hulten, G., Spencer, L., Domingos, P.: Mining time-changing data streams. In: ACM SIGKDD, pp. 97–106. ACM, New York (2001)
11. Klinkenberg, R.: Learning drifting concepts: Example selection vs. example weighting. Intell. Data Anal. 8(3), 281–300 (2004)
12. Masud, M.M., Jing, G., Khan, L., Jiawei, H., Thuraisingham, B.: A practical approach to classify evolving data streams: Training with limited amount of labeled data. In: ICDM, pp. 929–934 (2008)
13. Nguyen, H.L.: Concurrent semi-supervised learning of data streams. Technical report, Nanyang Technological Univ., Singapore (2011),
    http://www3.ntu.edu.sg/home2008/nguy0105/concurrent-mining.html
14. Park, N.H., Lee, W.S.: Grid-based subspace clustering over data streams. In: ACM CIKM, pp. 801–810. ACM, New York (2007)
15. Street, W.N., Kim, Y.: A streaming ensemble algorithm for large-scale classification. In: ACM SIGKDD, pp. 377–382. ACM, New York (2001)
16. Vilalta, R., Rish, I.: A decomposition of classes via clustering to explain and improve naive bayes. In: Lavrač, N., Gamberger, D., Todorovski, L., Blockeel, H. (eds.) ECML 2003. LNCS (LNAI), vol. 2837, pp. 444–455. Springer, Heidelberg (2003)
17. Wagstaff, K., Cardie, C., Rogers, S.: Constrained k-means clustering with background knowledge. In: ICML, pp. 577–584. Morgan Kaufmann Inc., San Francisco (2001)
18. Wang, H., Fan, W., Yu, P.S., Han, J.: Mining concept-drifting data streams using ensemble classifiers. In: ACM SIGKDD, pp. 226–235. ACM, New York (2003)
19. Zhou, A., Cao, F., Qian, W., Jin, C.: Tracking clusters in evolving data streams over sliding windows. Knowledge and Information Systems 15(2), 181–214 (2008)
20. Zhu, X., Goldberg, A.B., Brachman, R., Dietterich, T.: Introduction to Semi-Supervised Learning. Morgan and Claypool Publishers, San Francisco (2009)

A Bounded Version of Online Boosting on Open-Ended Data Streams

José Luis Triviño-Rodriguez, Amparo Ruiz-Sepúlveda,
and Rafael Morales-Bueno

Department of Computer Science and Artificial Intelligence
University of Málaga, Málaga, Spain
{trivino,amparo,morales}@lcc.uma.es
http://www.lcc.uma.es

Abstract. In this paper, we propose an incremental learning algorithm for ensemble classifier systems. Ensemble learning algorithms combine the predictions of multiple base models, each of which is learned using a traditional algorithm.

We propose a new method to update weights of classifiers in the weighted majority voting scheme under the one-pass incremental learning situations. This method computes the weights of classifiers and the distribution of training data following an approach based on the computing of prequential error that avoids the overflow of internal values used by the learning algorithm.

Using a prequential approach implies that learned samples are forgotten progressively. Forgetting learned concepts could influence the accuracy of the model. However, in the experiments, we verify that the proposed model can learn incrementally without serious forgetting and that the performance is not seriously influenced by the used re-weighting method in comparison with learning models without forgetting.

Experimental results confirm that the proposed incremental ensemble classifier system yields comparable performance with another learning ensemble classifier system. Moreover, it can be trained with open-ended data streams without data overflow.

Keywords: Boosting, ensemble learning, open-ended data streams, online learning.

1 Introduction

Ensemble methods have been proved to be very effective in improving generalization performance compared to the individual base models. Ensemble learning employs multiple base models, each one using a learning algorithm. The base learner [1] generates weak hypotheses whose outputs are combined to form a final prediction. Theoretical and experimental analysis of boosting [2,3] show that it enhances the generalization performance of ensemble classifier systems.

A. Cuzzocrea and U. Dayal (Eds.): DaWaK 2011, LNCS 6862, pp. 460–470, 2011.

Methods for voting classification algorithms, such as Bagging and Boosting, have been shown to be very successful in improving the accuracy of certain classifiers for artificial and real-world datasets [4,5,6]. Voting algorithms can be divided into those that adaptively change the distribution of the training set based on the performance of previous classifiers, as in boosting methods, and those that do not, as in Bagging.

Boosting was introduced by Schapire [7] in 1990. It is the most widely used ensemble learning method introduced in the last twenty years. It was originally designed for classification problems.

The motivation for boosting is a procedure that combines the output of a succession of models (weak classifiers) trained on a data set. The outputs are combined using voting for classification or averaging for regression creating a final prediction model that often has better accuracy than single classifiers algorithms.

AdaBoost is the most popular boosting paradigm [6]. It was originally developed for two-class problems and it keeps two sets of weights, one on the data, and one on the weak hypotheses. AdaBoost updates the example weights at each training round to form a harder problem for the next round. Specifically, the examples misclassified by a weak learner are given more weight in the training set for the next weak learner. The goal is to force the weak learner to minimize expected error over different input distributions. It has been proved that the boosting enhances the generalization performance of ensemble classifier systems theoretically and experimentally [3].

In recent real-world applications, data flow continuously from a data stream at high speed; producing examples over time, usually one at a time. That is why a learning model is required to have the ability of incremental learning [8]. Originally, the boosting algorithm has been developed mainly in batch mode which requires the entire training set to be available at once and, sometimes, random access to the data. However, in more real-world problems, data flow at high speed continuously and batch models cannot adapt to process data in real time [9].

Online learning algorithms process each training example once by arrival date, without the need for storage and reprocessing, and they maintain a current model that reflects all the training examples seen so far. Such algorithms have advantages over typical batch algorithms in situations with very large data sets on secondary storage, for which the multiple passes through the training set required by most batch algorithms are prohibitively expensive, or when data flow at high speed from an open-ended data stream.

In [10] some desirable properties required in learning systems for efficient, high-volume and open-ended data streams are identified:

- Require small constant time per data entry.
- Use fix amount of main memory, without regard to the total examples that have been seen.
- Built a model using one scan over the examples.
- Produce a model at anytime which is independent from the examples by arrival date.

Taken into account these properties, Friedman et al. showed that boosting is particularly effective when the base models are simple [11]. So, ensemble learning becomes an interesting approach to fast and light ensemble learning on stream data [12].

There has been work related to boosting ensembles on data streams. In 2000, Fern et al. [13] proposed online boosting ensembles, and Street [14] later developed an ensemble algorithm that builds one classifier per data block independently. The type of sequential re-weighting in an online setting, where only one example is kept at any time, was later proposed in different ways by Oza and Russell [15,16]. Other approaches to online boosting have been proposed by [17] and [18].

In this paper, we focus on continuous learning tasks. A new incremental boosting algorithm where newly given training samples are incrementally learned by all the classifiers based on AdaBoost.M1 is implemented. We present an online version of boosting based on previous work by [19,15]. They developed an online version of boosting that requires only one pass through the training data. Our algorithm, like Oza and Russell's algorithm, has a sequential update for the weights of the weak hypotheses.

Two principal questions must be considered before implementing a boosting approach: what incremental learning model should be selected as a classifier, and how to update the weight function of classifiers in a boosting algorithm. A great variety of incremental learning models have been constructed to solve the first question, in neural networks [20,21,22], such as Support Vector Machines [23], decision trees [24], and so forth. As far as the second question is concerned, it is quite hard to solve it if we assume a one-pass incremental learning where training samples are presented only once for a learning purpose and they are discarded after the learning [8].

Oza's online boosting algorithm computes the error of weak classifiers following a frequency count scheme. However, internal values used by this algorithm in order to compute the error of weak classifiers are bounded by the number of training samples seen so far. However, in real environment of open-ended streams, these values are potentially infinite. This implies data overflow problems in the implementation of this algorithm.

In this paper, we propose an alternative approach to compute the error of weak classifiers. It is based on the framework proposed by Gama et al. [25] for assessing predictive stream learning algorithms. They maintain the use of Predictive Sequential methods for error estimate called the prequential error. In these tasks, the prequential error allows us to guide the evolution of the performance of models that evolve over time. Theoretical and experimental results show that the prequential error estimated using fading factors determines reliable estimators. In comparison with sliding windows, fading factors are faster and memory-less; a desirable specification for streaming applications.

This paper is organized as follows. The next section briefly describes two models, AdaBoost.M1 and Oza's boosting learning model, which are the background of the model developed in this paper. In section 3 we propose a new incremental boosting model and we describe the weight function of this model. In section 4 the proposed incremental boosting model is evaluated for several standard datasets. The last section concludes the paper, resuming the main contributions of this work and it gives directions of our future work.

2   Theoretical Background

2.1   AdaBoost.M1

AdaBoost is one of the most known ensemble learning algorithms. In this algorithm, a weak classifier is generated by using a set of training samples weighted by the weight function $D_m(i)$, and the outputs of all classifiers are combined based on the weighted majority voting.

In algorithm 1, the AdaBoost learning algorithm is shown. It is composed of a main loop that computes a set of weak hypothesis $H = \{h_m | 1 \leq t \leq M\}$ and a last statement that computes the final hypothesis by means of equation 1, which is a weighted majority vote of the M weak hypotheses where $\log \frac{1}{\beta_m}$ is the weight assigned to h_m.

Algorithm 1. The AdaBoost.M1 algorithm returning $h_{final} : X \rightarrow Y$

Let:

- A training S set of N samples $S = \{(x_1, y_1), \ldots, (x_N, y_N)\}$ with $x_i \in X = $ {vectors of attribute values} and labels $y_i \in Y$
- A weak learning algorithm $WeakLearner$
- A number of iterations $M \in \mathbb{N}$

1: Let $D_1(i) = 1/N$ for all $1 \leq i \leq N$
2: **for** $m = 1$ to M **do**
3:    Call $WeakLearner$ providing it with the distribution D_m and the set S
4:    Get back a weak hypothesis $h_m : X \rightarrow Y$
5:    Calculate error of h_m: $\epsilon_m = \sum_{i:h_m(x_i) \neq y_i} D_m(i)$. If $\epsilon_m \geq \frac{1}{2}$ then abort this loop
6:    Let $\beta_m = \frac{\epsilon_m}{1-\epsilon_m}$
7:    Update distribution D_m:

$$D_{m+1}(i) = \frac{D_m(i)}{Z_m} * \begin{cases} \beta_m & \text{if } h_m(x_i) = y_i \\ 1 & \text{otherwise} \end{cases}$$

where Z_m is a normalization constant (chosen so that D_{m+1} will be a distribution)
8: **end for**
9: Final hypothesis:

$$h_{final}(x) = \underset{y \in Y}{argmax} \sum_{m:h_t(x)=y} \log \frac{1}{\beta_m} \qquad (1)$$

AdaBoost creates successively *"harder"* filtered distributions $D_t(i)$. In other words, AdaBoost concentrates the probability distribution over the training sample on samples misclassified by weak hypothesis, focusing the learning task more and more on the hard part of the learning problem.Specifically, the examples misclassified by h_{m-1} are given more weight in the training set for h_m so that the weights of all the misclassified samples constitute half of the total weight of the training set.

2.2   Online Boosting

Algorithm 2 shows the pseudocode of Oza's boosting learning model [15]. The online boosting algorithm described by Oza is designed to correspond to the batch boosting algorithm. Just as in AdaBoost, it generates a sequence of base models $h_1, \ldots, h_M$ using weighted training sets so that the training examples misclassifed by model h_{m-1} are given half of the total weight for model h_m, and the correctly classified examples are given the remaining half of the weight. The re-weighting of the samples is carried out by equations 2 and 3 in algorithm 2.

Let us suppose that λ_m^c is the sum of the d_i values for the examples that were classified correctly by the base model at stage m and λ_m^w is the same sum for incorrectly classified examples. For the next stage of boosting, the model needs to scale these two sums to the same value, just as in AdaBoost. Therefore, it needs to find the factors f_m^c and f_m^w that scale λ_m^c and λ_m^w to half the total weight, respectively. The sum of all AdaBoost weights is one; therefore the sum of all the d_i for this online algorithm is N, which is the number of samples seen so far. Consequently, factors f_m^c and f_m^w are computed as follows:

$$\lambda_m^c f_m^c = \frac{N}{2} \implies f_m^c = \frac{N}{2\lambda_m^c}$$
$$\lambda_m^w f_m^w = \frac{N}{2} \implies f_m^w = \frac{N}{2\lambda_m^w}$$

3   Updateable Prequential Boosting

Oza's online boosting algorithm computes the error of the weak classifiers following a frequency count scheme. The error ϵ_m is computed by means of the λ_m^c and λ_m^w values. These values are bounded by N that is the number of training samples seen so far. However, in a real environment of open-ended streams, N is potentially infinite, so λ_m^c and λ_m^w values are unbounded and they could generate overflow errors when the model is trained from an open-ended stream.

In this paper, we propose an alternative approach to compute the error ϵ_m of the weak classifiers. This approach is based on the predictive sequential (prequential) [26] using fading factor as described by Gama [25]. The prequential error estimated using fading factor converges fast to holdout estimate, but it is computed using bound values, so it avoids overflow errors.

Algorithm 3 shows the Updateable Prequential Boosting (UPB) approach proposed in this paper. This algorithm scales the weight d_i of a sample s_i by a value α^t where $0 < \alpha < 1$ is the fading factor and t is the number of samples seen so far since the sample s_i. The sum of the weights of the samples (λ_m^c and λ_m) is multiplies by α with every new sample. Thus, the weight of the last learned sample is scaled by a value α^0 and the first learned sample is scaled by a value

Algorithm 2. The Oza's Online Boosting returning $h_{final} : X \rightarrow Y$

Let:

- A sample $s_i = (x_i, y_i)$ with $x_i \in X = \{$vectors of attribute values$\}$ and label $y_i \in Y$
- A set of weak hypothesis $H = \{h_m | 1 \leq t \leq M\}$
- The sum of weights λ_m^c and λ_m^w of all the samples correctly and incorrectly classified by h_m
- A weak learning algorithm $UpdateWeakLearner$
- The number N of samples used to train h_m

1: Let $d_1 = 1$
2: **for** $m = 1$ to M **do**
3:    Set k according to $Poisson(d_m)$
4:    **for** $i = 1$ to k **do**
5:       Call $UpdateWeakLearner(h_m, s)$ and get back an updated weak hypothesis h_m
6:    **end for**
7:    **if** $h_m(x_i) = y_i$ **then**
8:       Update $\lambda_m^c = \lambda_m^c + d_m$
9:       Let
$$d_{m+1} = d_m \frac{N}{2\lambda_m^c} \qquad (2)$$
10:    **else**
11:       Update $\lambda_m^w = \lambda_m^w + d_m$
12:       Let
$$d_{m+1} = d_m \frac{N}{2\lambda_m^w} \qquad (3)$$
13:    **end if**
14:    Compute the error of h_m: $\epsilon_m = \frac{\lambda_m^c}{\lambda_m^c + \lambda_m^w}$. If $\epsilon_m \geq \frac{1}{2}$ then abort this loop
15:    Let $\beta_m = \frac{\epsilon_m}{1 - \epsilon_m}$
16: **end for**
17: Final hypothesis:
$$h_{final}(x) = \underset{y \in Y}{argmax} \sum_{m : h_m(x) = y} \log \frac{1}{\beta_m} \qquad (4)$$

α^N. The scaling of weights is computed in an online way by equations 5 and 7 in algorithm 3.

For the UPB learning model, the sum of all scaled weights is $\omega = \frac{1 - \alpha^{N+1}}{1 - \alpha}$. Therefore, factors f_m^c and f_m^w are computed as follows:

$$\lambda_m^c f_m^c = \frac{\omega}{2} \implies f_m^c = \frac{\omega}{2\lambda_m^c}$$
$$\lambda_m^w f_m^w = \frac{\omega}{2} \implies f_m^w = \frac{\omega}{2\lambda_m^w}$$

These factors are used to scale the weight of every sample in equations 6 and 8 of algorithm 3. Moreover, the sum of all scaled weights $\omega = \lambda_m^c + \lambda_m^w$ converges to $\frac{1}{1 - \alpha}$ when N approaches infinity. So, λ_m^c and λ_m^w values are bounded.

Algorithm 3. The Updateable Prequential Boosting returning $h_{final} : X \to Y$

Let:

- A sample $s_i = (x_i, y_i)$ with $x_i \in X = \{$vectors of attribute values$\}$ and label $y_i \in Y$
- A set of weak hypothesis $H = \{h_m | 1 \le t \le M\}$
- The sum of weights λ_m^c and λ_m^w of all the samples correctly and incorrectly classified by h_m. They must be initialized to 0 before the first call to this algorithm
- A weak learning algorithm $UpdateWeakLearner$
- The prequential fading factor α
- The value pow that store α^{N+1} where N is the number of samples used to train h_m. It must be initialized to 1.0 before the first call to this algorithm

1: Let $d_1 = 1$
2: **for** $m = 1$ to M **do**
3:     Call $UpdateWeakLearner(h_m, s_i, d_m)$ and get back an updated weak hypothesis h_m
4:     **if** $h_m(x_i) = y_i$ **then**
5:         Update λ_m

$$\begin{aligned} \lambda_m^c &= \lambda_m^c * \alpha + d_m \\ \lambda_m^w &= \lambda_m^w * \alpha \end{aligned} \tag{5}$$

6:         Let

$$\begin{aligned} pow &= pow * \alpha \\ d_{m+1} &= d_m \frac{1-pow}{2(1-\alpha)\lambda_m^c} \end{aligned} \tag{6}$$

7:     **else**
8:         Update λ_m

$$\begin{aligned} \lambda_m^c &= \lambda_m^c * \alpha \\ \lambda_m^w &= \lambda_m^w * \alpha + d_m \end{aligned} \tag{7}$$

9:         Let

$$\begin{aligned} pow &= pow * \alpha \\ d_{m+1} &= d_m \frac{1-pow}{2(1-\alpha)\lambda_m^w} \end{aligned} \tag{8}$$

10:     **end if**
11:     Compute the error of h_m: $\epsilon_m = \frac{\lambda_m^c}{\lambda_m^c + \lambda_m^w}$. If $\epsilon_m \ge \frac{1}{2}$ then abort this loop
12:     Let $\beta_m = \frac{\epsilon_m}{1-\epsilon_m}$
13: **end for**
14: Final hypothesis:

$$h_{final}(x) = \underset{y \in Y}{argmax} \sum_{m:h_m(x)=y} \log \frac{1}{\beta_m} \tag{9}$$

---

4   Empirical Evaluation

In this section, we present an experimental evaluation of our approach. The accuracy of Updateable Prequential Boosting (UPB) is compared with Oza's Online Boosting.

We have used several synthetic datasets from the MOA [27] software. In table 1, the datasets used to compare these methods are shown. It displays the dataset name, the number of attributes including the class attribute and the configuration of the dataset generator. We have taken 20.000 samples for every dataset without concept drift. Since datasets have not concept drift, learning models achieve a stable accuracy after a certain number of samples. So, the difference between the accuracy of the Oza's model and the UPB model does not vary significantly after this point and it is not necessary to use larger datasets to compare both models. Moreover, with larger datasets, the difference between the Oza's model and the UPB model is that the Oza's model crashes when the unbounded variable N is out of the range of the data type of the implementation.

Table 1. Information about MOA synthetic datasets used in the experiments

Dataset	Attributes	Parameters
Agrawal	9	function= 1 ; perturbFraction = 0.05
Hyperplane	10	noisePercentaje = 0
Random RBF	11	numCentroids = 50
Sea concepts	3	function = 1 ; noisePercentaje = 0

In order to implement the Updateable Prequential Boosting (UPB) learning model, a weak learner is needed. The model used as weak learner by UPB must implement a fading factor like the α parameter of the UPB model. An Updateable Decision Stump (UDS) with prequential fading factor has been implemented and integrated into the Weka software package [28]. In the experiments then we will use this UDS and the Updateable Naive Bayes (UNB) model of Weka as a weak learner. Moreover, in order to compare our method with Oza's Boosting, we have implemented and integrated this model into Weka.

Both of the tested learning models have a learning parameter that defines the number of weak learners computed throughout the learning task. We have taken the same number of weak learners for both model (100 weak learners) in order to avoid unfair advantage over UPB.

The α fading factor tunes the memory of the model. The weight of a sample s_i is scaled by α^t where t is the number of samples seen so far since the sample s_i. Hence, the weight of a sample decreased exponentially with t. If α is small then much weight is accumulated in only a few samples from the last of the stream and the model have not much memory. However, if α is near to 1.0, an important portion of the total weight is distributed over a greater number of samples. For example, if $\alpha = 0.99$, then the 80% of the total weight is only in the last 160 samples, but if $\alpha = 0.999$ then the 80% of the total weight is in the last 1600 samples and, if $\alpha = 0.9999$, then the 80% of the total weight is in the last 16000 samples. The optimum value of α depends on the weak learner and the problem. However, in order to avoid unfair advantages over the Oza's algorithm, the fading factor of UPB has not been fully optimized and only the value of 0.9999 has been taken into account.

The accuracy of Oza's Boosting and UPB over the datasets has been computed by means of a *Test-Then-Train* approach. In this approach, each indidual

Table 2. Average accuracies

Dataset	OzaB(UDS)	UPB(UDS)	OzaB(UNB)	UPB(UNB)
Agrawal	0.84	0.82	0.92	0.92
HPlane	0.60	0.57	0.87	0.87
R. RBF	0.78	0.76	0.92	0.92
Sea C.	0.71	0.70	0.94	0.94

sample is used to test the model before it is used for training, and accuracy is incrementally updated. The results of this test and the standard deviation of the accuracy throughout the 20.000 iterations of this test are shown in table 2.

Table 2 shows that UPB has the same accuracy as Oza's Boosting with the Updateable Naive Bayes as weak learner. Furthermore, with the Updateable Decision Stump model as weak learner, UPB achieves significantly the same accuracy as Oza's Boosting with only an average difference of 2% along the data stream. Moreover, the sequence of samples correctly classified and incorrectly classified can be described like a binomial distribution and we can show that they are not statistically significantly different.

Figures 1 show the Oza's Boosting and UPB learning curves for described datasets. Visual inspection confirms that the learning curve of the UPB model is near the learning curve of Oza's Boosting and it reflects the main goal achieved by this paper, since they show that UPB can achieve the same accuracy as Oza's Boosting without unbounded internal values. UPB boosting is under Oza's Boosting learning curve several times, but we must take into account that the fading factor of the UPB model has not been optimized for these curves.

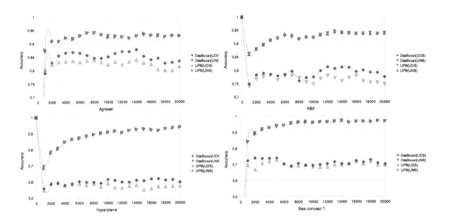

Fig. 1. Learning curves of tested models for described datasets

5   Conclusion

In this paper, we describe an online version of the AdaBoost.M1 boosting algorithm. The described learning model is based in Oza's online boosting model but it avoids the use of internal unbound values.

This modified learning model can be applied to task where huge amount of data come at high speed from a non ended data stream. Examples of these environments are sensor networks, network activity logging, online video surveillance, etc. In these environments, models with unbound variables will crash in a short time.

We have shown, through experiments, that our online version of boosting performs comparably to the model it is based on. This paper compares the accuracy of the UPB model with Oza's boosting model over Decision Stumps and Naive Bayes. This empirical evaluation has shown that the learning curves of both model are closed or even the learning curve of the UPB model improve Oza's model.

Our current empirical work focuses on testing with large, continuously arriving data streams and a wide variety of weak learners such as hoeffding trees or neural networks.

Theoretical tasks include the study of how to compute the prequential error in weak learners.

References

1. Bauer, E., Kohavi, R.: An empirical comparison of voting classification algorithms: Bagging, boosting, and variants. Machine Learning 36(1-2), 105–139 (1999)
2. Schapire, R.E., Freund, Y., Barlett, P., Lee, W.S.: Boosting the margin: A new explanation for the effectiveness of voting methods. In: International Conference on Machine Learning, pp. 322–330. Morgan Kaufmann, San Francisco (1997)
3. Freund, Y., Schapire, R.E.: A decision-theoretic generalization of on-line learning and an application to boosting. Journal of Computer and System Sciences 55(1), 119–139 (1997)
4. Breiman, L.: Bagging predictors. Machine Learning 24(2), 123–140 (1996)
5. Quinlan, J.R.: Bagging, boosting, and c4.5. In: Proceedings of the 13th National Conference on Artificial Intelligence, pp. 725–730. AAAI/MIT Press (1996)
6. Freund, Y., Schapire, R.E.: Experiments with a new boosting algorithm. In: International Conference on Machine Learning, pp. 148–156 (1996)
7. Schapire, R.: The streng of weak learnability. Machine Learning 5(2), 197–227 (1990)
8. Futschik, M.E., Reeve, A., Kasabov, N.: Evolving connectionist systems for knowledge discovery from gene expression data of cancer tissue. Artificial Intelligence in Medicine 28(2), 165–189 (2003)
9. Domingos, P., Hulten, G.: Mining high-speed data streams. In: Proceedings of the 6th ACM SIGKDD International Conference on Knowledge Discovery and Data Mining, pp. 71–80. ACM Press, New York (2000)
10. Domingos, P., Hulten, G.: Catching up with the data: Research issues in mining data streams. In: Workshop on Research Issues in Data Mining and Knowledge Discovery (2001)

11. Friedman, J., Hastie, T., Tibshirani, R.: Additive logistic regression: a statistical view of boosting. Annals of Statistics 28, 2000 (1998)
12. Chu, F., Zaniolo, C.: Fast and light boosting for adaptive mining of data streams. In: Dai, H., Srikant, R., Zhang, C. (eds.) PAKDD 2004. LNCS (LNAI), vol. 3056, pp. 282–292. Springer, Heidelberg (2004)
13. Fern, A., Givan, R.: Online ensemble learning: An empirical study. In: Proceedings of the 17th International Conference on Machine Learning, pp. 279–286. Morgan Kaufmann, San Francisco (2000)
14. Street, W.N., Kim, Y.: A streaming ensemble algorithm (sea) for large-scale classification. In: Proceedings of the 7th ACM SIGKDD International Conference on Knowledge Discovery and Data Mining, pp. 377–382. ACM Press, New York (2001)
15. Oza, N.C., Russell, S.: Online bagging and boosting. In: Artificial Intelligence and Statistics, pp. 105–112. Morgan Kaufmann, San Francisco (2001)
16. Pelossof, R., Jones, M., Vovsha, I., Rudin, C.: Online Coordinate Boosting. ArXiv e-prints (October 2008)
17. Kidera, T., Ozawa, S., Abe, S.: An incremental learning algorithm of ensemble classifier systems. In: International Joint Conference on Neural Networks, pp. 3421–3427 (2006)
18. Ferrer-Troyano, F.J., Aguilar-Ruiz, J.S., Riquelme-Santos, J.C.: Incremental rule learning based on example nearness from numerical data streams. In: Proceedings of the 2005 ACM Symposium on Applied Computing, pp. 568–572 (2005)
19. Oza, N.C., Russell, S.: Experimental comparisons of online and batch versions of bagging and boosting. In: Proceedings of the 7th ACM SIGKDD International Conference on Knowledge Discovery and Data Mining, pp. 359–364. ACM, New York (2001)
20. Yamauchi, K., Yamaguchi, N., Ishii, N.: Incremental learning methods with retrieving of interfered patterns. IEEE Transactions on Neural Networks 10(6), 1351–1365 (1999)
21. Ozawa, S., Toh, S.L., Abe, S., Pang, S., Kasabov, N.: Special issue: Incremental learning of feature space and classifier for face recognition. Neural Networks 18(5-6), 575–584 (2005)
22. Carpenter, G.A., Grossberg, S.: The art of adaptive pattern recognition by a self-organizing neural network. Computer 21(3), 77–88 (1988)
23. Diehl, C.P., Cauwenberghs, G.: Svm incremental learning, adaptation and optimization. In: Proceedings of the 2003 International Joint Conference on Neural Networks, pp. 2685–2690 (2003)
24. Weng, J., Evans, C.H., Hwang, W.S.: An incremental learning method for face recognition under continuous video stream. In: Proceedings of the 4th IEEE International Conference on Automatic Face and Gesture Recognition, p. 251. IEEE Computer Society, Washington, DC, USA (2000)
25. Gama, J., Sebastião, R., Pereira-Rodriguez, P.: Issues in evaluation of stream learning algorithms. In: Proceedings of the 15th ACM SIGKDD International Conference on Knowledge Discovery and Data Mining, pp. 329–338. ACM, New York (2009)
26. Dawid, A.P.: Statistical theory: The prequential approach. Journal of the Royal Statistical Society 147(2), 278–292 (1984)
27. Bifet, A., Holmes, G., Pfahringer, B., Kirkby, R., Gavaldà, R.: New ensemble methods for evolving data streams. In: Proceedings of the 15th ACM SIGKDD International Conference on Knowledge Discovery and Data Mining, pp. 139–148. ACM, New York (2009)
28. Witten, I., Frank, E.: Data Mining: Practical Machine Learning Tools and Techniques, 2nd edn. Morgan Kaufmann, San Francisco (2005)

Moderated VFDT in Stream Mining Using Adaptive Tie Threshold and Incremental Pruning

Hang Yang and Simon Fong

Department of Science and Technology, University of Macau,
Av. Padre Tomás Pereira Taipa, Macau, China
henry.yh@gmail.com, ccfong@umac.mo

Abstract. Very Fast Decision Tree (VFDT) is one of the most popular decision tree algorithms in data stream mining. The tree building process is based on the principle of the Hoeffding bound to decide on splitting nodes with sufficient data statistics at the leaf. The original version of VFDT requires a user-defined tie threshold by which a split will be forced to break to control the tree size. It is an open problem that the tree size grows tremendously with noise as continuous data stream in and the classifier's accuracy drops. In this paper, we propose a Moderated VFDT (M-VFDT), which uses an adaptive tie threshold for node splitting control by incremental computing. The tree building process is as fast as that of the original VFDT. The accuracy of M-VFDT improves significantly even under the presence of noise in the data stream. To solve the explosion of tree size, which is still an inherent problem in VFDT, we propose two lightweight pre-pruning mechanisms for stream mining (post-pruning is not appropriate here because of the streaming operation). Experiments are conducted to verify the merits of our new methods. M-VFDT with a pruning mechanism shows a better performance than the original VFDT at all times. Our contribution is a new model that can efficiently achieve a compact decision tree and good accuracy as an optimal balance in data stream mining.

Keywords: Data Stream Mining, Hoeffding Bound, Incremental Pruning.

1 Introduction

Since the early 2000s, a new generation of data mining called data stream mining (DSM) has received much research attention. DSM requires only one pass on infinite streaming data and the decision model is dynamically trained, while the incoming new data streams are being received in run-time [1]. Very Fast Decision Tree (VFDT) is a well-known decision tree algorithm for DSM [2]. Its underlying principle is a dynamic decision tree building process that uses a Hoeffding bound (HB) to determine the conversion of a tree leaf to a tree node by accumulating sufficient statistics from the new samples. Although VFDT is able to progressively construct a decision tree from the unbounded data stream, VFDT suffers from tree size explosion and the deterioration of prediction accuracy when the data streams are impaired by

A. Cuzzocrea and U. Dayal (Eds.): DaWaK 2011, LNCS 6862, pp. 471–483, 2011.

noise. Such imperfect data often exists in real life, probably because of unreliable communication hardware or temporary data loss due to network traffic fluctuation. Although VFDT and its variants have been extensively studied, many models assume a perfect data stream and have sub-optimal performance under imperfect data streams. In this paper, we devise a new version of VFDT called Moderated VFDT (M-VFDT) that can provide sustainable prediction accuracy and regulate the growth of decision tree size to a reasonable extent, even in the presence of noise. This is achieved by revising the decision tree building process – in particular, the conditional check of whether a leaf should be split as a new tree node is modified. The new checking condition is made adaptive to the distribution of the incoming data samples, which in turn influences the value of the HB that is a key factor in the decision tree construction. It is adaptive in the sense that no human intervention is required during the data stream mining; we let the incoming data decide on how precisely (or how frequently) the tree node splitting should be done, hence the depth of the decision tree. Improved accuracy is achieved by an adaptive tie threshold rather than a user-defined tie threshold, but the tree size is still as big as in VFDT. To solve this problem, incremental pruning methods are proposed to complement the adaptive tie threshold mechanism for controlling the tree size as well as maintaining the accuracy. The result is an optimally compact decision tree that has good prediction accuracy, by M-VFDT. This work is significant because the proposed algorithms (adaptive tie threshold and pruning) are both lightweight and adaptive and this makes M-VFDT favorable in a data stream mining environment.

This paper is structured as follows. Section 2 introduces a research framework that summarizes the background of VFDT, the effect of the tie threshold in tree building and the impact of noise in data stream mining. Section 3 presents details of our proposed model M-VFDT that consists of the adaptive tie threshold and incremental pruning mechanisms. Experimental validation is carried out in the following Section. Both synthetic and real-world stream datasets are used to thoroughly test the performance of M-VFDT compared to VFDT. The experimental results demonstrate that M-VFDT performs better than the original VFDT at all times. The conclusion of this study is given in Section 5.

2   Research Background

2.1 Very Fast Decision Tree (VFDT)

The VFDT system [2] constructs a decision tree by using constant memory and constant time per sample. It is a pioneering predictive technique that utilizes the Hoeffding bound (HB). The tree is built by recursively replacing leaves with decision nodes. Sufficient statistics of attribute values are stored in each leaf. Heuristic evaluation function is used to determine split attributes converting from leaves to nodes. Nodes contain the split attributes and leaves contain only the class labels. The leaf represents a class that the sample labels. When a sample enters, it traverses the tree from root to leaf, evaluating the relevant attribute at every single node. After the sample reaches a leaf the existing statistics are updated. At this time, the system evaluates each possible condition based on attribute values: if the statistics are sufficient to support the one test over the other, a leaf is converted to a decision node. The decision node contains the number of possible values for the chosen attribute of the installed split test. The main elements of VFDT include: firstly, a tree initializing process that only has a single leaf at the beginning; secondly, a tree growing process that contains a splitting check using the heuristic evaluation function $G(.)$ and the HB. VFDT uses information gain as $G(.)$. A flowchart that represents the operation of the VFDT algorithm is shown in Figure 1.

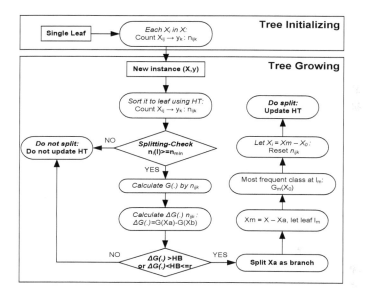

Fig. 1. A workflow representing the VFDT algorithm tree building process

The HB in Equation (1) is used by the necessary number of samples (sample#) to ensure control over error in attribute splitting distribution selection. For n independent observations of a real-valued random variable r whose range is R, the HB illustrates that with confidence level 1-δ, the true mean of r is at least $\bar{r} - \varepsilon$, where $\bar{r}$ is the observed mean of samples. For a probability the range R is 1, and for an information gain the range R is $\log_2$Class#.

$$\varepsilon = \sqrt{\frac{R^2 \ln(1/\delta)}{2n}} .$$

(1)

VFDT makes use of the HB to choose a split attribute as a decision node. Let x_a be the attribute with the highest $G(.)$, x_b be the attribute with the second highest $G(.)$. $\Delta\bar{G} = \bar{G}(x_a) - \bar{G}(x_b)$ is the difference between the two top quality attributes. If

$\Delta \overline{G} > \varepsilon$ with N samples observed in leaf, while the HB states with probability 1-δ that x_a is the attribute with highest value in $G(.)$, then the leaf is converted into a decision node which splits on x_a. However, in some cases the highest and the second highest $G(.)$ do not differ greatly, and so the process gets stuck in a tie condition. Resolving the tie in detail may slow down the VFDT operation. A user pre-defined threshold τ is thus used as an additional splitting condition so that if ΔG is below τ, a split will be enforced and it quickly breaks the tie.

2.2   Effects of Tie Breaking in Hoeffding Trees

When two candidates of nodes competing to become a splitting node are equally good (having almost the same value of information gain), it may take a long time and intensive computation to decide between them. This situation not only drains significant amounts of computational resources, but the tie-breaking result at the end might not always contribute substantially to the overall accuracy of the decision tree model. To alleviate this, the research team [3], introduced a tie breaking parameter τ. This tie threshold is added as an additional splitting condition in VFDT, so that whenever the HB becomes so small that the difference between the best and the second best splitting attributions is not obvious, τ comes in as a quick deceive parameter to resolve the tie. Using less than τ as a comparing condition, with the value of τ arbitrarily chosen and fixed throughout the operation, the candidate node is chosen to be split on the current best attribute, regardless of how close the second best candidate splitting attribute might be. The percentage of the condition being broken is related to the complexity of the problem. It is said that an excessive invocation of tie-breaking significantly reduces VFDT performance on complex and noise data [6], even with the additional condition by the parameter τ.

Their proposed solution [6] to overcome this detrimental effect is an improved tie - breaking mechanism, which not only considers the best and the second best splitting candidates in terms of heuristic function, but also uses the worst candidate. At the same time, an extra parameter is imported, α, which determines how many times smaller the gap should be before it is considered as a tie. The attribute splitting condition becomes: when $\alpha \times (G(X_a) - G(X_b)) < (G(X_b) - G(X_c))$, the attribution X_a shall be split as a node, instead of the original one shown in Figure 1. Obviously, this approach uses two extra parameters, α and X_c, which bring extra computation to the original algorithm. In this paper, we propose an alternative design of a tie threshold parameter that is adaptive and is calculated directly from the mean of the HB, which is found to be proportionally related to the input stream samples.

2.3   Detrimental Effect of Noise in Data Stream

Noise data is considered a type of irrelevant or meaningless data that does not typically reflect the main trends but makes the identification of these trends more difficult. Non-informative variables may be potentially random noise in the data stream. It is an idealized but useful model, in which such noise variables present no information-bearing pattern of regular variation. However, data stream mining cannot eliminate those non-informative candidates in preprocessing before starting classification mining, because concept drift may bring the non-informative noise variables into informative candidates. Our experiment on VFDT reenacts this phenomenon in Figure 2. Evidently, the inclusion of noise data reduces the accuracy of VFDT as well as increasing tree size. This consequence is undesirable in decision tree classification. There has been an attempt to reduce the effect of noise by using supplementary classifiers for predicting missing values in real-time and minimizing noise in the important attributes [7]. Such methods still demand extra resources in computation.

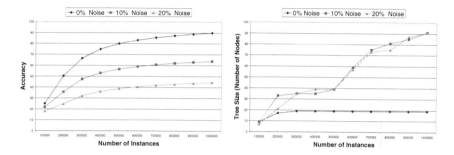

Fig. 2. This experiment demonstrates the detrimental effect of noise data in data stream. Experimental dataset is synthetic one-million samples LED dataset, which contains 24 nominal attributes and one million sample records. VFDT settings – split confidence $\delta = 10^{-7}$, tie threshold $\tau = 0.05$ (small value for smaller tree size), grace period $n_{min} = 200$; the split criterion is information gain.

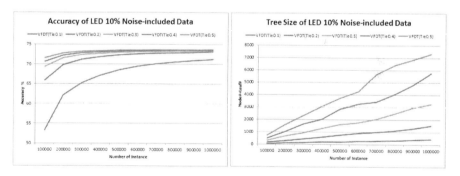

Fig. 3. Influence of tie threshold τ to VFDT. The setup is same as that in Figure 2, except for the selection of τ. The value of τ varies from 0.1 to 0.5.

The experimental results in Figure 3 show the influence of different values of τ to VFDT accuracy and tree size. The high value of τ gives rise to loose (relaxed) attribute splitting conditions, whereby the tree size becomes large. As the tree size grows, more rules are generated and the classification conditions become refined, and a better VFDT accuracy is, therefore, obtained. However, τ is a user predefined value. We are unable to know in advance which value of τ is the best, until all the combinations are tried by means of trial and error. To the best of the authors' knowledge, no in-depth study has yet been conducted on how to find an optimum solution amongst a suitable value of τ, tree size and accuracy in VFDTs. This problem reduces the applicability of VFDT to real-time applications.

3   Moderated Very Fast Decision Tree (M-VFDT)

A new model called Moderated VFDT (M-VFDT) is proposed. It embraces data with noise with two additional techniques called adaptive tie threshold and incremental pruning to control tree size and improve accuracy.

3.1   Observation of Hoeffding Bound Fluctuation

The new technique, namely the Adaptive Tie Threshold, is based on the observation of Hoeffding bound fluctuation. The Hoeffding bound (inequality), or Chernoff bound to use its alternative name, is widely known as an important probabilistic bound for achieving good accuracy of a decision tree in stream mining. In particular, the HB) is used in deciding the attribute on which to split. A splitting attribute appears when tree structure update conditions meet and the corresponding HB is computed according to Equation 1. In terms of the accumulated HB values, the mean and the variance are recorded respectively. Under the noise data stream, it is found that HB values and variances fluctuate within a range of maximum and minimum values. The fluctuation intensifies with the increase of noise. As shown in the group of sub-graphs in Figure 4, the HB values and variances are spread out in groups along the y-axis. Under a noise-free environment, the contrasting HB values and variances differ very little (Fig. 4a).

This phenomenon strongly implies that a steady HB is desirable even though it receives heavy noise data in the construction of a decision tree. In other words, if we can keep a tight hold of the HB fluctuation, the resulting decision tree could be relieved from the ill effects of data noise, at least to certain extent. The mathematical property of HB is defined as a conservative function and has been used classically in Hoeffding tree induction for many years. (HB formulation is simple and works well in stream mining; it depends on the desired confidence and the number of observations.) We were inspired to modify the node splitting function, based on the mean of HB, instead of modifying the HB formulation. Holding on to the mean of HB is equivalent to avoiding the fluctuation of HB values, thereby reducing the noise effects. Table 1 shows the HB changing with different noise percentages. Clearly, a noise-free data stream produces the lowest HB mean and variance during the attribute splitting process. The distributions of the changing HB are represented in Figure 4 in the different settings of noise levels.

Table 1. HB values varying in VFDT (tie0.05) attribute splitting in LED dataset

Noise %	Min. HB	Max. HB	HB Mean	HB Variance
0	0.049713	0.666833	0.084249	0.003667
5	0.049862	0.666833	0.102919	0.005114
10	0.049861	0.666833	0.101125	0.004882
15	0.04986	0.666833	0.108844	0.006011
20	0.049872	0.666833	0.103495	0.005086

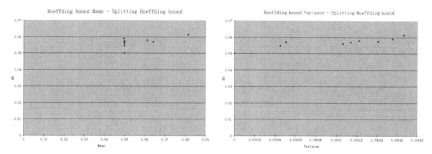

Fig. 4.a. HB distribution in LED dataset NP=0

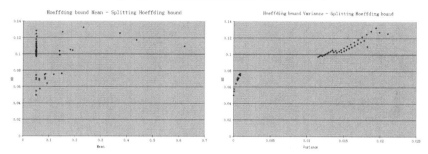

Fig. 4.b. HB distribution in LED dataset NP=5

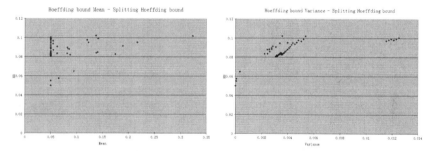

Fig. 4.c. HB distribution in LED dataset NP=10

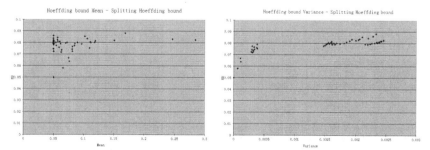

Fig. 4.d. HB distribution in LED dataset NP=15

Fig. 4. Distribution charts of different noise-included datasets in VFDT (tie=0.05), comparing the Hoeffding bound to mean and variance

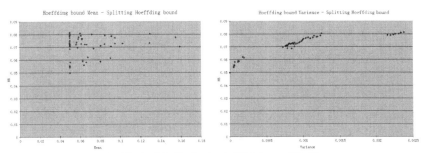

Fig 4.e. HB distribution in LED dataset NP=20

Fig. 4. (*continued*)

3.2 Adaptive Splitting Tie Threshold

As noted in Section 3.1, HB fluctuation intensifies with the increase of noise, which has a detrimental effect on VFDT accuracy. To solve this problem, we modify the attribute splitting process by using a dynamic tie threshold τ that restricts the attribute splitting as a decision node. Traditionally, τ is a user pre-configured parameter with a default value in VFDT. We are not able to know which value of τ is the best until all possibilities in an experiment are tried by brute force. Longitudinal testing on different values in advance is certainly not favorable in real-time applications. Instead, we assign an adaptive tie threshold, equal to the dynamic mean of HB as the splitting tie threshold, which controls the node splitting during the tree building process. Tie breaking that occurs near the HB mean can effectively narrow the variance distribution. The HB mean is calculated dynamically whenever new data arrives and HB is updated. It consumes few extra resources as HB would have to be computed in any case, as shown in Equation 2. When a new splitting method is implemented, τ is updated corresponding to the Hoeffding bound mean value.

$$\tau_k = \frac{\sum_{i=1}^{k} HB_i}{k} \Rightarrow \tau_{k+1} = \frac{(\sum_{i=1}^{k} HB_i) + HB_{k+1}}{k+1} \tag{2}$$

The new τ is updated when HB is computed each time with the incoming data. With this new method in place, M-VFDT has a dynamic τ whose value is no longer fixed by a single default number but adapts to the arrival instances and HB means. The M-VFDT operation with an adaptive τ is presented in Figure 5. The tree initializing process is the same as the original VFDT shown in Figure 1. The main modification is in the tree building process as follows:

- *Count(l)*: sufficient count of splitting-check of examples seen at leaf *l*
- *HBMean(l)*: dynamic mean of HB in splitting of examples seen at leaf *l*
- *HBSum(l)*: incremental statistic sum of HB in splitting of examples seen at leaf *l*
- *Prune*: the pruning mechanism. Default value is Null, which means un-pruning

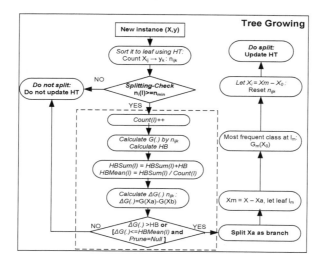

Fig. 5. M-VFDT algorithm. The adaptive tie threshold is computed in the dotted box.

3.3 Pruning Mechanisms

Pruning is an important part of decision tree learning that reduces the tree size by removing sections of the tree which provide little power to classify instances. It helps to reduce the complexity of a tree model. The pruned sections are often the fallout of noisy or erroneous data. By using an adaptive tie threshold for controlling the splitting condition, the accuracy of VFDT has significantly improved, as shown in Section 4. However, high accuracy comes with a large increase in tree size. To rectify the tree size problem, we propose two pruning approaches, the strict pruning mechanism and the loose pruning mechanism, each of which reflects a strong and weak pruning strength, respectively.

VFDT collects sufficient statistics to compute the number of instance counts by filtering the new instance to a leaf by the current tree model. When the splitting condition is satisfied, the attribute splitting approach simply proceeds at various points of the tree construction algorithm, without re-scanning the data stream.

In our pruning mechanisms, a leverage variable is used to identify the observations which have a great effect on the outcome of fitting tree models. The leverage point is set when a new instance is entering into a leaf, according to the current tree building model. It is not absolutely true that all unseen instances can fall into the leaves of the current tree. Suppose the count of unseen instances number falling into an existing leaf is called a *PseudoCount*, and the count of unseen instances number not falling into a current leaf is *RealCount*. We therefore let *Leverage* be the difference of *RealCount* minus *PseudoCount*. *Leverage* can be a negative, zero or positive number. It is calculated by: *Leverage = RealCount – PseudoCount*.

Mechanism 1: Strict Pruning. This pruning mechanism works with dynamic mean splitting condition and it is incremental in nature. It keeps a very small tree size by sacrificing some accuracy. The pruning condition is simply: <u>*Leverage* ≤ 0</u>.

Strict pruning only considers the horizontal comparison of attribute splitting with respect to the current leverage point. It imposes a strict breaking criterion so that the pseudo-count falls beyond the true count during the whole tree building process. In additional to horizontal comparison, we suggest a vertical comparison of current Leverage and the last Leverage estimated at the previous cycle of splitting process. The difference of current Leverage and last Leverage is defined as *DeltaLeverage*, where *DeltaLeverage = Leverage – LastLeverage*.

Mechanism 2: Loose Pruning. This pruning mechanism encompasses strict pruning, adding an optional splitting condition of *DeltaLeveage*. The pruning condition is: *Leverage ≤ 0 OR DeltaLeverage ≤ 0*.

The reasons why these two pruning mechanisms are chosen:

(1) The tree building process of VFDT uses sufficient statistics that count the number of instances filtered to a leaf on the current Hoeffding tree (HT). The splitting is based on these counts. The filtering process can easily compute the number of real counts and pseudo-counts without much extra effort. In strict pruning, if the real count becomes smaller than the pseudo-count, it means the performance of the current HT is not so adaptive to the new arrival instances (noise induced tree branches start building up). It is a strict condition that it shall be pruned during tree building, if the *Leverage* is lower than zero.

(2) In the loose pruning mechanism, *DeltaLeverage* is used as a pre-pruning condition that compares the current Leverage with its previous one. It examines the trend of the built tree's performance in the nearest two splitting processes. If the current Leverage is smaller than its previous one, it means the current HT's performance is declining. In this case, the tree should be pruned by an extra splitting node condition where i is the current step of the HT building process.

4   Experiments

In this section, a variety of large data streams, with nominal and numeric attributes, are used to stress test our proposed model. The M-VFDT with adaptive tie threshold and pruning shows consistently better performance than the VFDT that uses a fixed default tie threshold. The datasets are both synthetic from a stream generator and obtained from live data of real world applications. The characteristics of the experimental datasets are given in Table 2. With the same experiment settings as those in Figure 3, we estimate the best tie threshold value to be used for VFDT as a base comparison to our model by trying different tie threshold values from 0.1 to 0.9.

Table 2. Characteristics of the experimental datasets

Dataset	Description	Type	Attr.#	Class#	Ins#	Best Tie
LedNP10	LED display [4]	Nominal	24	10	1.0×10^6	0.7
LedNP20	LED display [4]	Nominal	24	10	1.0×10^6	0.4
Wave	Waveform [4]	Numeric	22	3	1.0×10^6	0.3
Connect-4	UCI Data [5]	Nominal	42	3	67,557	0.6
Nursery	UCI Data [5]	Nominal	9	5	12,960	0.3

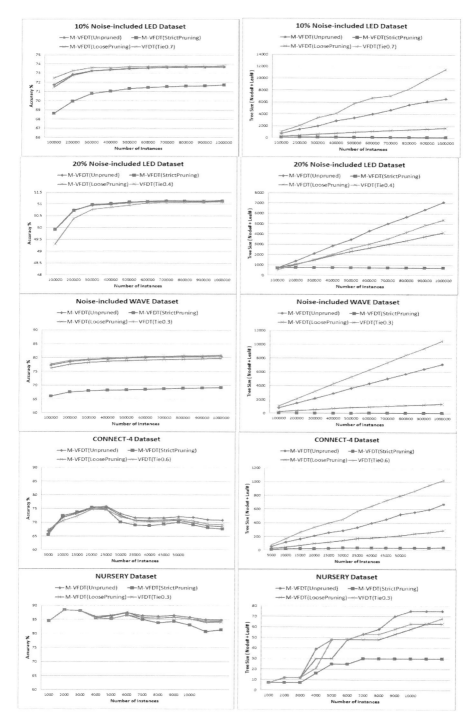

Fig. 6. Accuracy and tree size comparison of M-VFDT and VFDT in different datasets

The results in Figure 6 validate the accuracy and the tree size comparison of these two pruning mechanisms on the same experimental dataset. It compares to the original VFDT with a stationary tie threshold whose value is found to be the best by the brute-force method earlier on. In general, we observe that M-VFDT with strict pruning keeps the tree size smallest, but the accuracy is worse than that of others. The loose pruning method for M-VFDT yields reasonable accuracy that is on par with VFDT, but its tree size is more compact than that of VFDT, although it is still larger than the tree by strict pruning. Both strict and loose pruning methods in M-VFDT make compromises between accuracy and tree size. This can be explained by the fact that a small tree classifies instances coarsely because of the relatively small paths of tree branches, and so accuracy is adversely affected. A classifier that can perform precisely in classification usually requires a bushy tree with many conditional rules.

Our current research focus is on how to choose an optimal between the strict and loose pruning. Strict pruning has its merits in achieving a small tree size, from which concise classification rules can be derived and, generally, they are easily readable. In contrast, the loose pruning mechanism, although resulting in a bigger tree size, achieves much higher accuracy than that of the strict pruning mechanism. A significant contribution of M-VFDT is that loose pruning achieves an almost similar level of accuracy as the VFDT with the best chosen but stationary value of tie-breaking, and M-VFDT results in a much smaller tree size.

5   Conclusion and Future Work

We have proposed an improved decision tree algorithm for data stream mining, which is called Moderated VFDT or simply M-VFDT. M-VFDT embraces an adaptive tie threshold for deciding on splitting nodes whose value is calculated dynamically from the mean of the Hoeffding bound. Tie threshold is an important parameter as advocated by [6] in speeding up the construction of the decision tree in stream mining, however it was assumed to be a stationary default value in most other research works in studying VFDT. With the adaptive tie threshold, the accuracy of M-VFDT has greatly improved in comparison to the original VFDT. The performance improvement by M-VFDT is shown to be more apparent when the data streams are infested by noise. This work is important because noise in input data is already known to cause very adverse effects both on the accuracy degradation and tree size explosion. In addition, we proposed two pre-pruning mechanisms for M-VFDT to reduce the tree size and make the classification model compact. Two types of pruning, namely strict and loose pruning are proposed; they are both incremental in nature (as we know that, in stream mining, post-pruning may not be favorable because the tree is continually being updated as data streams in). All of these extra mechanisms, including incremental pruning and adaptive tie threshold, are lightweight in computation. This makes M-VFDT suitable to a stream mining environment, where speed, accuracy and tree size, as it relates to memory constraint, are of concern.

In the future, we intend to adopt M-VFDT as a core enabling model in different case studies of real-time stream mining applications. We also want to extend the concepts of adaptive tie threshold and incremental pruning to other variants of VFDT.

Furthermore, it will be interesting to find a formula for automatically estimating an optimal balance between tree size and accuracy by using some optimization theories.

References

1. Maron, O., Moore, A.W. Hoeffding races: Accelerating Model Selection Search for Classification and Function Approximation. In: NIPS, pp. 59–66 (1993)
2. Domingos, P., Hulten, G.: Mining high-speed data streams. In: Proceedings of the Sixth ACM SIGKDD International Conference on Knowledge Discovery and Data Mining, pp. 71–80 (2000)
3. Hulten, G., Spencer, L., Domingos, P.: Mining time-changing data streams. In: Proceedings of the Seventh ACM SIGKDD International Conference on Knowledge Discovery and Data Mining. KDD 2001, pp. 97–106. ACM, New York (2001)
4. Breiman, L., Friedman, J.H., Olshen, R.A., Stone, C.J.: Classification and Regression Trees. Wadsworth International Group, Belmont (1984)
5. Frank, A., Asuncion, A.: UCI Machine Learning Repository. University of California, School of Information and Computer Science, Irvine, CA (2010), http://archive.ics.uci.edu/ml
6. Geoffrey, H., Richard, K., Bernhard, P.: Tie Breaking in Hoeffding trees. In: Gama, J., Aguilar-Ruiz, J.S. (eds.) Proceeding Workshop W6: Second International Workshop on Knowledge Discovery in Data Streams, pp. 107–116 (2005)
7. Yang, H., Fong, S.: Aerial Root Classifiers for Predicting Missing Values in Data Stream Decision Tree Classification. In: 2011 SIAM International Conference on Data Mining (SDM 2011), Mesa, Arizona, USA, April 28-30 (2011) (accepted for Publication)

Finding Critical Thresholds for Defining Bursts

Bibudh Lahiri[1,*], Ioannis Akrotirianakis[2], and Fabian Moerchen[2]

[1] Iowa State University, Ames, IA, USA 50011
bibudh@iastate.edu
[2] Siemens Corporate Research, Princeton, NJ, USA 08540
{ioannis.akrotirianakis,fabian.moerchen}@siemens.com

Abstract. A burst, i.e., an unusually high frequency of an event in a time-window, is interesting in monitoring systems as it often indicates abnormality. While the detection of bursts is well addressed, the question of what "critical" thresholds, on the number of events as well as on the window size, make a window "unusually bursty" remains a relevant one. The range of possible values for either threshold can be very large. We formulate finding the combination of critical thresholds as a 2D search problem and design efficient deterministic and randomized divide-and-conquer heuristics. For both, we show that under some weak assumptions, the computational overhead in the worst case is logarithmic in the sizes of the ranges. Our simulations show that on average, the randomized heuristic beats its deterministic counterpart in practice.

Keywords: Analytics for temporal data, Massive data analytics.

1 Introduction

A burst is a window in time when an event shows an unusually high frequency of occurrence, and often indicates a deviation from the norm. E.g., in text streams from news articles or blogs, an important event like the 9/11 attack caused a burst of the keywords like "twin towers" or "terror". A burst in clicks to an online advertisement might indicate a click fraud [8]. Instrusions over the Internet often exhibit a bursty traffic pattern [6]. In astrophysics, a Gamma ray burst might indicate an interesting phenomenon [10,9].

Labelling a window in time as "bursty" calls for at least two thresholds - one on the number of events (k) and the other on the length of the window (t). We call a window (k, t)-*bursty* if at least k events occur in a time window of length at most t. While the problem of identifying (k, t)-bursty windows, given k and t, is interesting in itself, knowing the right thresholds is part of the problem. For a given t, to know what value of k should be termed "unusually high", we first need to know typically how many events to expect in a window of length t. Similarly, for a given k, to know what value of t is "unusually low", we first need to know typically how long it takes to generate k events.

---

* This work was done when this author was an intern at Siemens Corporate Research, Princeton.

A. Cuzzocrea and U. Dayal (Eds.): DaWaK 2011, LNCS 6862, pp. 484–495, 2011.

Before we formally defined the problem of finding the critical thresholds, we had to quantify the notion of "usual" and "unusual". We defined a metric called "coverage": given a threshold pair (k, t), and a sequence of timestamps of n events, the coverage $C_{k,t}$ is the fraction of the n events that were included in *some* (k, t)-bursty window. Note that, a single event can be part of more than one (k, t)-bursty windows. For a given pair (k, t), if we find that $C_{k,t}$ is quite close to 1, then actually we are not interested in such a pair (k, t), because that implies having at least k events in a window of length at most t is not unusual, and hence should hardly be labelled as a burst. On the other hand, a $C_{k,t}$ value quite close to 0 implies having k events in a window of length at most t is not usual, and hence demands attention.

Note that, this definition ensures $C_{k,t} \in [0, 1]$, and makes $C_{k,t}$ monotonically non-increasing in k and non-decreasing in t, properties that we prove and take advantage of in our algorithms.

We focus on identifying *critical* pairs (k^*, t^*) such that C_{k^*, t^*} is abruptly different from values of $C_{k,t}$ for pairs (k, t) which are in the neighborhood of (k^*, t^*) (and $k < k^*$) - this implies having k^* events in a window of length at most t^* is not the norm, yet there are some rare situations when this has happened. Note that, for a given pair (k, t), $C_{k,t}$ can be computed by making a single pass over the data, but if the range of possible values for k and t have sizes K and T respectively, then evaluating $C_{k,t}$ at every point in the two-dimensional space would have a computational overhead of $O(KT)$. Since for most applications, we hardly have any apriori idea what combination of thresholds are critical, each of K and T can be rather large, e.g., t might range from a few minutes to a few hours, depending on the nature of the application, and k might take any value from 2 to a few thousand.

Our contributions can be summarized as follows:

- We formally define the problem of finding critical threshold pairs that should label a subsequence of a time series data as *unusually bursty*. We formulate it as a two-dimesional search problem.
- We prove monotonicity properties of the coverage function rigorously, and exploit them to design deteministic and randomized divide-and-conquer heuristics that explore the search space efficiently. Under some weak assumptions, we show the deterministic heuristic computes $C_{k,t}$ at $O(\log K \log T)$ different points, and, under identical assumptions, the randomized heuristic also computes $C_{k,t}$ at $O(\log K \log T)$ different points on expectation in the worst case. **For lack of space, we only present the claims here - the proofs can be found in the full version [3].**
- We experimentally compared the performance of our deterministic and randomized heuristics with that of a naive algorithm that evaluates $C_{k,t}$ at at most, but typically much less than, KT points. Even with some optimizations of the naive algorithm, the savings made by our heuristics are in the range of 41% to 97%. Note that although our analysis (Section 6) assumes we stop after getting the first (k^*, t^*), in our experiment (Section 7), we continued till we got all possible values of (k^*, t^*).

2   Related Work

Zhu and Shasha [10] addressed "elastic" burst detection, where they kept a different threshold for each among a number of different window sizes and identified windows over the time-series when an aggregate function (sum) computed over the window exceeded the corresponding threshold. Their algorithm builds on the time series a Shifted (binary) Wavelet Tree (SWT) data structure, which was generalized in [9] to a faster data structure called Aggregation Pyramid. [9] and [5] revealed *correlated bursts* among multiple data streams in stock exchange and text data.

Kleinberg [1] investigated how keywords in document streams like emails and news articles show a bursty pattern, and developed a framework in the form of an infinite-state automata to model bursts in a stream. Kumar *et al* [2] extended the ideas of [1] to discover bursts in the hyperlinking among blogs in Blogspace, which occurs when one author publishes an entry on her blog that increases the traffic to her blog and stimulates activities in other blogs that focus on the same topic at the same time. Vlachos *et al* [4] addressed the problem of burst detection for search engine queries to detect periodic (e.g., weekly or monthly) trends. Yuan *et al* [7] worked on trend detection from high-speed short text streams

While all these earlier literature have focused on the *detection* of burts, we focus on finding the thresholds that *define* a burst. A heuristic like ours can be used to learn from historical data what choice of thresholds separates a burst from a non-burst, and can be used later in a real monitoring system for the same application to detect bursts, when some other burst-detection algorithm can also be used.

3   Problem Statement

We have a sequence of events $S' = (e_1, e_2, ...e_n)$. Let t_e be the timepoint at which event e occurs, so the correspoding sequence of timestamps is $S = (t_{e_1}, t_{e_2}, ...t_{e_n})$. Let $N_{k,t}$ be the number of events that are in *some* (k,t)-bursty window. As defined in Section 1, the *coverage* for the pair (k,t), denoted as $C_{k,t}$, is $C_{k,t} = N_{k,t}/n$. Let K_{min} and K_{max} be the minimum and maximum possible values of k, known apriori, and $K = K_{max} - K_{min}$. Similarly, let T_{min} and T_{max} be the minimum and maximum possible values of t, also known apriori, and $T = T_{max} - T_{min}$.

We focus on the following problem:

Problem 1. Given the sequence S, and a user-given parameter $\theta > 1$, find a set $\alpha = \{(k^*, t^*)\}$ such that $\alpha \subset [K_{min} + 1, K_{max}] \times [T_{min}, T_{max}]$, and for any pair $(k^*, t^*) \in \alpha$, $\frac{C_{k^*-1,t^*}}{C_{k^*,t^*}} \geq \theta$.

We first focus on simpler, one-dimensional versions of the problem. Assuming we are dealing with a fixed value of the maximum window length t, this becomes

Problem 2. For a fixed t, and a user-given parameter $\theta > 1$, find a subset $K^* \subset [K_{min} + 1, K_{max}]$ such that for any $k^* \in K^*$, $\frac{C_{k^*-1,t}}{C_{k^*,t}} \geq \theta$.

Alternatively, if we deal with a fixed value of the threshold k on the number of events, this becomes

Problem 3. For a fixed k, and a user-given parameter $\theta > 1$, find a subset $T^* \in [T_{min}, T_{max}]$ such that for any $t^* \in T^*$, $\frac{C_{k-1,t^*}}{C_{k,t^*}} \geq \theta$.

We observed from our experiments that $\frac{C_{k-1,t}}{C_{k,t}}$ remains close to 1 most of the time; however, for very few combinations of k and t, it attains values like 2 or 3 or higher - and these are the combinations we are interested in. Since K and T can be pretty large, searching for the few critical combinations calls for efficient search heuristics.

4   Monotonicity of the Coverage Function

Note that, $C_{k,t}$ is a monotonically *non-increasing* function of k, and a monotonically *non-decreasing* function of t. Intuitively, the reason is that for a fixed t, as k increases, (k, t)-bursty windows become rarer in the data; and for a fixed k, as t increases, it becomes easier to find (k, t)-bursty windows in the same data. The formal proofs can be found in [3].

5   The Divide-and-Conquer Heuristics

5.1   The One-Dimensional Problem

We first discuss the solution for Problem 2 - the solution to Problem 3 is similar. Given the sequence $S = (t_{e_1}, t_{e_2}, ...t_{e_n})$, and a given pair (k, t), $C_{k,t}$ can be computed on S in a single pass by algorithm 1. A naive approach would be to invoke algorithm 1 with the pairs (k, t) $\forall k \in [K_{min} + 1, K_{max}]$, and check when $C_{k-1,t}/C_{k,t}$ exceeds θ. This would take $O(K)$ calls to algorithm 1. To cut down the number of invocations to algorithm 1, we take a simple divide-and-conquer approach, coupled with backtracking, and exploit the monotonicity of the function $C_{k,t}$ discussed in Section 4. We present two variations of the approach - one deterministic and the other randomized. The intuition is as follows:

Intuition: We split the range K of all possible inputs into two sub-intervals. We devise a simple test to decide which of the two sub-intervals this value k^* *may* lie within. The test is based on the observation that if a sub-interval $X = [k_s, k_e]$ contains a k^* where the coverage function shows an abrupt jump (i.e., $C_{k^*-1,t}/C_{k^*,t} \geq \theta$), then the ratio of the coverages evaluated at the two endpoints should also exceed θ (i.e., $C_{k_s-1,t}/C_{k_e,t} \geq \theta$) because of the monotonicity of $C_{k,t}$ in k. Note that, *the reverse is not necessarily true*, as $C_{k_s-1,t}/C_{k_e,t}$ might exceed θ because there was a gradual change (of factor θ or more) from $k_s - 1$ to k_e (if the interval $[k_s, k_e]$ is long enough). Thus, the test may return a positive result on a sub-interval *even if* there is no such value k^* within that sub-interval. However, we repeat this process iteratively, cutting down the length of the interval in each iteration - the factor by which it is cut down varies depending on whether the heuristic is deterministic or randomized. The number of iterations taken to reduce the original interval of width K to a point is $O(\log K)$. Note that, in the case when there is no such point k^*, the intervals might pass the test for first few iterations (because of the gradual change from k_s to k_e), but then, eventually it will be reduced to some interval for which $C_{k_s-1,t}/C_{k_e,t}$ will fall below θ, and hence it will no longer pass the test.

Deterministic vs Randomized Divide-and-Conquer: We always split an interval of width w into two intervals of length $p \cdot w$ and $(1-p) \cdot w$ respectively, where $p \in (0,1)$. For the deterministic heuristic, p is always $\frac{1}{2}$; whereas for the randomized one, p is chosen uniformly at random in $(0,1)$. If both the sub-intervals pass the test, then for the deterministic heuristic, we probe into the sub-intervals serially; whereas for the randomized one, we first process the *smaller* one. The reasons for probing the smaller sub-interval first are the following

1. If it contains a point k^*, then it can be found in fewer iterations.
2. If it does not contain any point k^*, and passed the test of Lemma 1 falsely, then, the algorithm would backtrack after few iterations.

Lemma 1. *For a fixed t, if a sub-interval $X = [k_s, k_e]$ contains a point k^* such that $C_{k^*-1,t}/C_{k^*,t} \geq \theta$, then $C_{k_s-1,t}/C_{k_e,t} \geq \theta$.*

The search for t^* in Problem 3 proceeds similar to the search for k^* as we explained above, the difference being that the test on the sub-intervals is performed using the following lemma. Note the difference: in Lemma 1, the ratio is of coverage at start-point to that at end-point, whereas in Lemma 2, it is the other way round: the difference arises because of the difference in the natures of the monotonicities in k and t.

Lemma 2. *For a fixed k, if a sub-interval $X = [t_s, t_e]$ contains a point t^* such that $C_{k-1,t^*}/C_{k,t^*} \geq \theta$, then $C_{k-1,t_e}/C_{k,t_s} \geq \theta$.*

5.2   The Two-Dimensional Problem

We now advance to the original and more general problem in two dimensions, i.e., Problem 1. Our algorithm for 2D is an extension of the algorithm for the 1D problem discussed in Section 5.1 in the sense that it progressively divides the 2D range of all possible values of k and t, i.e., $[K_{min}+1, K_{max}] \times [T_{min}, T_{max}]$, into four sub-ranges/rectangles. For the 2D problem, the pair(s) (k^*, t^*) for which $C_{k^*-1,t^*}/C_{k^*,t^*}$ exceeds θ will come from one or a few of these four sub-ranges. We devise a test similar to the one in Section 5.1 to identify which of the four sub-ranges *may* include the pair (k^*, t^*); and then probe into that sub-range in the next iteration, cutting down its size again, and so on. If the range of possible values for k and t are of unequal length, i.e., if $K \neq T$, then the length of the range would reduce to unity for the smaller one, and the rest of the search becomes a 1D search on the other dimension, like the ones in Section 5.1.

The test for identifying the correct sub-range in our 2D algorithm is based on the observation in the following lemma.

Lemma 3. *If a sub-range* $X = [k_s, k_e] \times [t_s, t_e]$ *contains a point* (k^*, t^*) *such that* $C_{k^*-1,t}/C_{k^*,t} \geq \theta$, *then* $C_{k_s-1,t_e}/C_{k_e,t_s} \geq \theta$.

Like the algorithms in Section 5.1 for the 1D problems, here also we have two variants: one deterministic and the other randomized. If more than one of the four sub-intervals/rectangles pass the test in Lemma 3, then for the deterministic algorithm, we probe into them serially, and for the randomized one, we probe into the rectangles in increasing orders of their areas.

Algorithm 1 computes the coverage $C_{k,t}$, given a sequence of timestamps $(S = (t_{e_1}, t_{e_2}, \ldots, t_{e_n}))$, a lower bound k on the number of events and an upper bound t on the window length. As we have already pointed out, even if a single timestamp t_{e_i} is included in multiple (k,t)-bursty windows, its contribution to $N_{k,t}$, in the definition of $C_{k,t}$, is only 1. Hence, we maintain a bitmap $(b_1, b_2, \ldots, b_n)$ of length n, one bit for each timestamp in S. We slide a window over S, marking the starting and ending points of the sliding window by s and f respectively all the time. Once all the timepoints in a window are "picked up", we check (in lines 1 and 3) if the number of events in the current window $[s, f]$, i.e., $f - s + 1$, exceeds the threshold k. If it does, then all the bits in the sub-sequence $(b_s, \ldots, b_f)$ of the bitmap are set to 1 (lines 2 and 4) to indicate that the timepoints indexed by these bits are part of *some* bursty window.

Algorithm 2 performs a 1D search over the interval $[k_s, k_e]$, for a fixed t (Problem 2), and is called from Algorithm 3 once the range of t-values reduces to a single point. A 1D search over the interval $[t_s, t_e]$ can be performed similarly, for a fixed k (Problem 3) (we call it "RandomSearcht*"), and is called from Algorithm 3 once the range of k-values reduces to a single point. In algorithm 2 and its counterpart for $[t_s, t_e]$, whenever we need to compute $C_{k,t}$, we first check if it has already been computed, in which case, it should exist in a hashtable with $(k|t)$ being the key; otherwise, we compute it by invoking Algorithm 1, and store it in the hashtable with key $(k|t)$.

Note that, in lines 2 and 3 of Algorithm 2, r might exceed θ because of a divison-by-zero error. In case that happens, we will explore the interval only if $C_{k_s^{small}-1,t} \geq 0$, because $C_{k_s^{small}-1,t} = 0$ implies $C_{k_e^{small},t} = 0$ by the monotonicity, and it is not worth exploring $[k_s^{small}, k_e^{small}]$.

Algorithm 3 performs the search over the 2D interval $[k_s, k_e] \times [t_s, t_e]$ to solve Problem 1. A rectangle is defined as a four-tuple (t_l, t_h, k_l, k_h), i.e., the set of all points in the 2D range $[t_l, t_h] \times [k_l, k_h]$, thus the area being $(t_h - t_l + 1) \cdot (k_h - k_l + 1)$. Since the input rectangle is split into only four rectangles, we use insertion sort in line 2 while sorting them by their areas, which takes $O(1)$ time because the input size is constant.

The deterministic heuristics are very similar to their randomized counterparts (algorithms 2 and 3), with the following differences:

- In line 1 of Algorithm 2 and line 1 of Algorithm 3, k_q and t_q are midpoints ($\lfloor \frac{k_s + k_e}{2} \rfloor$ and $\lfloor \frac{t_s + t_e}{2} \rfloor$) of the intervals $[k_s, k_e]$ and $[t_s, t_e]$ respectively.

- In Algorithm 3, we can do away with the sorting step of line 2, since the four rectangles would be of (almost) equal length.

Algorithm 1. ComputeCoverage $(S = (t_{e_1}, t_{e_2}, \ldots, t_{e_n}), t, k)$

---

output: $C_{k,t}$: the fraction of events that are in some (k, t)-bursty window

$n \leftarrow |S|$;

initialize a bitmap $(b_1, b_2, \ldots, b_n)$ to all zeros;

/* sliding window is $[s, \ldots, f], s \in \{1, \ldots, n\}$, $f \in \{1, \ldots, n\}$ */

$s \leftarrow 0, f \leftarrow 0$;

// Note: t_{e_i} is the ith timepoint in S.

while $(t_{e_f} < t_{e_s} + t) \wedge (f < n)$ **do**
$\quad \lfloor \; f \leftarrow f + 1$;

if $t_{e_f} > t_{e_s} + t$ **then**
$\quad \lfloor \; f \leftarrow f - 1$;

while $f < n$ **do**
$\quad n_w = f - s + 1$;

1 $\quad$ **if** $n_w \geq k$ **then**

2 $\quad \quad \lfloor$ set the bits $(b_s, \ldots, b_f)$ to 1;

$\quad$ /* Move the window, storing pointers to the previous window   */

$\quad s_p = s, f_p = f$;

$\quad$ **while** $(s \geq s_p) \wedge (f \leq f_p)$ **do**
$\quad \quad s \leftarrow s + 1$;

$\quad \quad$ **while** $(t_{e_f} < t_{e_s} + t) \wedge (f < n)$ **do**
$\quad \quad \quad \lfloor \; f \leftarrow f + 1$;

$\quad \quad$ **if** $t_{e_f} > t_{e_s} + t$ **then**
$\quad \quad \quad \lfloor \; f \leftarrow f - 1$;

/* If the last point is within the last window, it will be counted.
   Otherwise, it is an isolated point and hence not interesting.   */

if $f = n$ **then**
$\quad n_w \leftarrow f - s + 1$;

3 $\quad$ **if** $n_w \geq k$ **then**

4 $\quad \quad \lfloor$ set the bits $(b_s, \ldots, b_f)$ to 1;

$C_{k,t} \leftarrow \sum_{j=1}^{n} b_j / n$;

return $C_{k,t}$;

---

6   Complexity Analysis

Let $C(K)$ be the number of calls made to Algorithm 1 from Algorithm 2. We compute $C(K)$ assuming that in Algorithm 2 and its deterministic equivalent, only one of the two sub-intervals passes the test of Lemma 1 between lines 2- 3, so we never probe into the other interval, and we stop as soon as we get the first k^* that satisfies our criterion.

Algorithm 2. RandomSearchk* $(S = (t_{e_1}, t_{e_2}, \ldots, t_{e_n}), t, k_s, k_e, \theta)$

---

if $k_s = k_e$ then

    $r \leftarrow C_{k_s-1,t}/C_{k_s,t}$;

    if $(r \geq \theta) \wedge (C_{k_s,t} > 0)$ then

        output (k_s, t) as a critical threshold pair;

    return;

else

    /* $U([a,b])$ returns a number uniformly at random in $[a,b]$ */

1    $k_q \leftarrow U([k_s, k_e - 1])$;

    between $[k_s, k_q]$ and $[k_q + 1, k_e]$, let $[k_s^{big}, k_e^{big}]$ be the bigger window and $[k_s^{small}, k_e^{small}]$ be the smaller;

    $r_{small} \leftarrow C_{k_s^{small}-1,t}/C_{k_e^{small},t}$;

2   if $(r_{small} \geq \theta) \wedge (C_{k_s^{small}-1,t} \geq 0)$ then

        RandomSearchk*$(S, t, k_s^{small}, k_e^{small}, \theta)$;

    $r_{big} \leftarrow C_{k_s^{big}-1,t}/C_{k_e^{big},t}$;

3   if $(r_{big} \geq \theta) \wedge (C_{k_s^{big}-1,t} \geq 0)$ then

        RandomSearchk*$(S, t, k_s^{big}, k_e^{big}, \theta)$;

Algorithm 3. RandomSearch2D $(S = (t_{e_1}, t_{e_2}, \ldots, t_{e_n}), k_s, k_e, t_s, t_e, \theta)$

---

if $(t_s = t_e) \wedge (k_s = k_e)$ then

    $r \leftarrow C_{k_s-1,t_e}/C_{k_e,t_s}$;

    if $(r \geq \theta) \wedge (C_{k_e,t_s} > 0)$ then

        output (k_s, t_s) as a critical threshold pair;

    return;

else if $t_s = t_e$ then

    RandomSearchk*$(S, t_s, k_s, k_c, \theta)$;

else if $k_s = k_e$ then

    RandomSearcht*(S, k, t_s, t_e, θ);

else

1    $k_q \leftarrow U([k_s, k_e - 1])$; $t_q \leftarrow U([t_s, t_e - 1])$;

    let R be an array of rectangles with $R[1] = (t_s, t_q, k_s, k_q)$, $R[2] = (t_q + 1, t_e, k_s, k_q)$, $R[3] = (t_s, t_q, k_q + 1, k_e)$ and $R[4] = (t_q + 1, t_e, k_q + 1, k_e)$;

2   sort R in increasing order of areas of the rectangles;

    for $p = 1$ to 4 do

        let (t_l, t_h, k_l, k_h) be the 4-tuple for rectangle $R[p]$;

        $r \leftarrow C_{k_l-1,t_h}/C_{k_h,t_l}$;

3   if $(r \geq \theta) \wedge (C_{k_l-1,t_h} \geq 0)$ then

            RandomSearch2D$(S, k_l, k_h, t_l, t_h, \theta)$;

Theorem 1. *For the deterministic counterpart of Algorithm 2, $C(K) = O(\log K)$.*

Let $C(T)$ be the number of calls made to Algorithm 1 for solving Problem 3. Analogous to Theorem 1, we can claim the following:

Theorem 2. *For the deterministic algorithm for solving Problem 3, $C(T) = O(\log T)$.*

For the two-dimensional version, let $C(K,T)$ be the number of calls made to Algorithm 1 for solving Problem 1. For the following theorem, and also for Theorem 6, we assume that in algorithm 3 and its deterministic counterpart, only one of the four rectangles pass the test of Lemma 3 in line 3, and we stop as soon as we get the first (k^*, t^*).

Theorem 3. *For the deterministic counterpart of Algorithm 3, $C(K,T) = O(\log K \log T)$.*

Theorem 4. *For Algorithm 2, the expected complexity in the worst case is $E[C(K)] = O(\ln K)$.*

Analogous to theorem 4, we can claim the following for the complexity $C(T)$ of the randomized algorithm for problem 3.

Theorem 5. *For the randomized algorithm for problem 3, the expected complexity in the worst case is $E[C(T)] = O(\ln T)$.*

Theorem 6. *For Algorithm 3, the expected complexity in the worst case is $E[C(K,T)] = O(\ln K \ln T)$.*

7   Evaluation

Dataset: We implemented both heuristics and compared them with a naive algorithm (which also gave us the ground truth to begin with), by running all 3 on a set of logs collected during the operation of large complex equipment sold by Siemens Healthcare. We chose 32 different types of events that occurred on these equipment, each event identified by a unique code. Each event code occurred on multiple (upto 291 different) machines, so we had to take care of some additional details (which we describe in Section 7 of [3]) while computing $C_{k,t}$ and finding the critical thresholds. The event codes had upto 300,000 distinct time points.

  Experiments: We implemented our heuristics in Java on a Windows desktop machine with 2 GB RAM. We set $T_{min} = 1$ minute, $T_{max} = 100$ minutes, $K_{min} = 2$ and $K_{max} = 100$ for all the event codes. We made the following simple optimizations to the naive algorithm:

1. For each event code e, $C_{k,t}^{(e)}$ for each combination of k and t is computed at most once, stored in a hashtable with the key being $e|k|t$, a concatenation of e, k and t. The stored value of $C_{k,t}^{(e)}$ is used in evaluating both $C_{k-1,t}^{(e)}/C_{k,t}^{(e)}$ and $C_{k,t}^{(e)}/C_{k+1,t}^{(e)}$. We followed the same practice for our heuristics, too.

2. Once $C_{k,t}^{(e)}$ reaches 0 for some k, $C_{k,t}^{(e)}$ is not computed for any larger value of k since it is known that they will be 0 because of the monotonicity property discussed in Section 4.

The ratios $C_{k-1,t}^{(e)}/C_{k,t}^{(e)}$ for all possible combinations of k and t, obtained from the naive algorithm, formed our ground truth. While running our heuristics for each e, we picked the highest value of $C_{k-1,t}^{(e)}/C_{k,t}^{(e)}$, and set θ to that value. We ran the heuristics for an event code only if θ set in this way was at least 1.5. For each event code, we ran the randomized heuristic 10 times, each time with a different seed for the pseudo-random number generator, noted the number of calls to Algorithm 1 for each, and calculated the mean ($\mathcal{N}_R$), the standard deviation (σ) and the coefficient of variation (CV $= \frac{\sigma}{\mathcal{N}_R}$).

Our observations about the number of calls to Algorithm 1 by the naive algorithm ($\mathcal{N}_N$), the deterministic heuristic ($\mathcal{N}_D$) and the mean for the randomized one ($\mathcal{N}_R$) are as follows:

1. For all but one event code, we found $\mathcal{N}_R < \mathcal{N}_D$. The probable reason is, after partitioning the original interval, when the four intervals are unequal, if the smaller interval does not contain (k^*, t^*), then it has less chance of falsely passing the test of Lemma 3 in line 3 of Algorithm 3. Also, as we discussed in Subsection 5.1, even if the smaller interval passes the test falsely, we are more likely to backtrack from it earlier because its sub-intervals have even less chance of falsely passing the test, and so on. Even for the single event code where $\mathcal{N}_D$ beats $\mathcal{N}_R$, the latter makes only 0.4% more function calls than the former. Depending on the event code, $\mathcal{N}_R$ is 4% to 70% less than $\mathcal{N}_D$.

2. We define the "improvement" by the randomized ($\mathcal{I}_R$) and the deterministic ($\mathcal{I}_D$) heuristics as $\mathcal{I}_R = \frac{\mathcal{N}_R}{\mathcal{N}_N}$ and $\mathcal{I}_D = \frac{\mathcal{N}_D}{\mathcal{N}_N}$, which are both plotted in Figure 2. The improvements are more when $\mathcal{N}_N$ is close to or more than a million - the improvement $\mathcal{I}$ in those cases is then 3-11%. In other cases, it is mostly in the range of 40-50%. Hence, the curves for both $\mathcal{I}_R$ and $\mathcal{I}_D$ in Figure 2 show a roughly decreasing pattern as we go from left to right.

3. For 28 out of 32 event codes, the CV ($\frac{\sigma}{\mathcal{N}_R}$) for the randomized heuristic is less than 0.1, which implies a quite stable performance across runs, and hence we would not need multiple runs (and obtain an average) in a real setting, and hence would not ruin the savings obtained by exploiting the monotonicity. In fact, for 22 out of these 28, the CV is less than 0.05. The maximum CV for any event code is 0.18 only.

4. We show the time taken (in minutes) for $10 \cdot \mathcal{N}_R + \mathcal{N}_D$ function calls for each eventcode in Figure 3. The time taken increased as the number of function calls increased, which is quite expected. For 16 out of 32 eventcodes, the time taken for $10 \cdot \mathcal{N}_R + \mathcal{N}_D$ function calls was less than 15 minutes, and for 27 out of 32 eventcodes, this time was less than 2 hours. As an example, an eventcode which took about 19 minutes for $10 \cdot \mathcal{N}_R + \mathcal{N}_D$ function calls had $\mathcal{N}_N = 883,080$, $\mathcal{N}_D = 35,100$ and $\mathcal{N}_R = 24,655$, so the 19 minutes time plotted in Figure 3 is for $10 \cdot 24655 + 35100 = 281650$ function calls, which is less than 32% of $\mathcal{N}_N$.

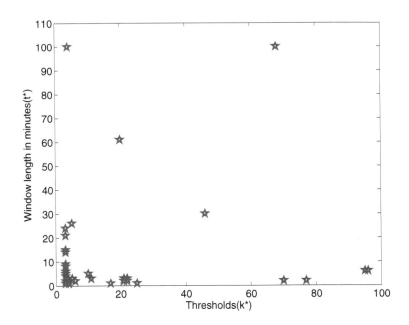

Fig. 1. The critical threshold pairs (k^*, t^*) for all the 32 event codes.

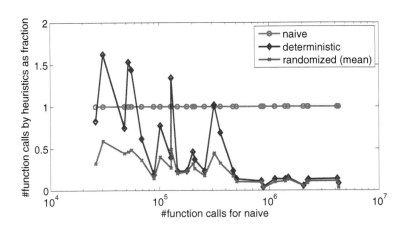

Fig. 2. The improvements by $\mathcal{N}_R$ and $\mathcal{N}_D$ over $\mathcal{N}_N$. On the X-axis we have $\mathcal{N}_N$ (the event codes are sorted by $\mathcal{N}_N$), on the Y-axis we have $\mathcal{I}_R$ and $\mathcal{I}_D$. Note that the savings are in general more for larger valus of $\mathcal{N}_N$, and the randomized heuristic consistently outperforms the deterministic one. The X-axis is logarithmic.

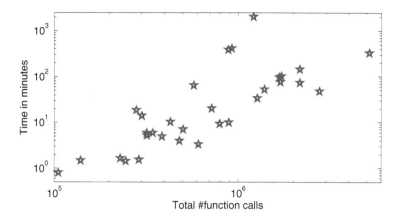

Fig. 3. X-axis shows total number of function calls for 1 run of deterministic and 10 runs of randomized heuristic for each eventcode, i.e., $10 \cdot \mathcal{N}_R + \mathcal{N}_D$, and Y-axis shows total time (in minutes) for all these runs. Both axes are logarithmic.

References

1. Kleinberg, J.M.: Bursty and hierarchical structure in streams. Data Mining and Knowledge Discovery 7(4), 373–397 (2003)
2. Kumar, R., Novak, J., Raghavan, P., Tomkins, A.: On the bursty evolution of blogspace. In: WWW, pp. 568–576 (2003)
3. Lahiri, B., Akrotirianakis, I., Moerchen, F.: Finding critical thresholds for defining bursts in event logs,
   http://home.eng.iastate.edu/~bibudh/techreport/burst_detection.pdf
4. Vlachos, M., Meek, C., Vagena, Z., Gunopulos, D.: Identifying similarities, periodicities and bursts for online search queries. In: SIGMOD Conference, pp. 131–142 (2004)
5. Wang, X., Zhai, C., Hu, X., Sproat, R.: Mining correlated bursty topic patterns from coordinated text streams. In: KDD, pp. 784–793 (2007)
6. Xu, K., Zhang, Z.L., Bhattacharyya, S.: Reducing unwanted traffic in a backbone network. SRUTI (2005)
7. Yuan, Z., Jia, Y., Yang, S.: Online burst detection over high speed short text streams. In: ICCS, pp. 717–725 (2007)
8. Zhang, L., Guan, Y.: Detecting click fraud in pay-per-click streams of online advertising networks. In: ICDCS (2008)
9. Zhang, X., Shasha, D.: Better burst detection. In: ICDE, p. 146 (2006)
10. Zhu, Y., Shasha, D.: Efficient elastic burst detection in data streams. In: KDD, pp. 336–345 (2003)

Author Index

Printed by Publishers' Graphics LLC